Month-By-Month

GARDENING
IN TENNESSEE
& KENTUCKY

Lowe, Judy.
   Month-by-month gardening in Tennessee and Kentucky / Judy Lowe.
      p. cm.
   Includes bibliographical references and index.
   ISBN 1-930604-89-0 (pbk. : alk. paper)
   1. Gardening--Tennessee. 2. Gardening--Kentucky. I. Title.

SB453.2.T2I68 2003
635'.09768--dc21   2003010903

Published by Cool Springs Press, a Division of Thomas Nelson, Inc.,
P.O. Box 141000, Nashville, Tennessee 37214

First printing 2003

Printed in the United States of America
10 9 8 7 6 5 4 3 2 1

Managing Editor: Billie Brownell
Designer: James Duncan Creative
Horticulture Editor: Dr. Willard Witte, Assoc. Prof., University of Tennessee (retired)
Illustrator: Bill Kersey, Kersey Graphics
Production Artist: S.E. Anderson

On the cover: Cosmos, photographed by Thomas Eltzroth

Visit the Thomas Nelson website at www.ThomasNelson.com

Month-By-Month

GARDENING
IN TENNESSEE
& KENTUCKY

JUDY LOWE

COOL
SPRINGS
PRESS

Nashville, Tennessee
A Division of Thomas Nelson, Inc.
www.ThomasNelson.com

Dedication

To my sons, Carlyle and David, for their encouragement and belief that
"someday Mom will write a best seller."

Acknowledgements

A book such as this one isn't the work of just one person. The efforts of
many people make it what it is. I, along with every reader who gains needed information
from this book, owe a debt of gratitude to Billie Brownell, the best and most
conscientious editor anyone can imagine; to Hank McBride, ideas man extraordinaire; to
Dr. Will Witte, whose firm grasp of horticultural names and facts kept us
from unintended goofs; and to Michelle Adkerson, a wonderful copy editor who made
sure that I really said what I intended to say.

Contents

Horticultural Introduction 7
  How Climate Affects
    Garden 7
  Know Your Yard. 8
  Sun and Shade 8
  Soil. 9
  Is Your Soil Acid or
    Alkaline?. 10
  Water 11
  Fertilizer 13
  Terminology 13
  Landscaping 13
  Multiseason Plants 15
  Freeze/Frost Occurences
    Tennessee. 16
    Kentucky. 17
  USDA Cold Hardiness Zone Map
    Tennessee. 18
    Kentucky. 19
  Annual Precipitation
    Tennessee. 20
    Kentucky. 21
  Average First Fall Frosts
    Tennessee. 22
    Kentucky. 23
  Average Last Spring Frosts
    Tennessee. 24
    Kentucky. 25

Chapter 1:
Annuals
  Introduction. 27
  Planting Chart 29
  January. 32
  February 34
  March 36
  April 38
  May. 40
  June 42
  July. 44

August 46
September. 48
October 50
November 52
December 54

Chapter 2:
Bulbs
  Introduction. 55
  Planting Chart 59
  January. 62
  February 64
  March 66
  April 68
  May. 70
  June 72
  July. 74
  August 76
  September. 78
  October 80
  November 82
  December 84

Chapter 3:
Herbs & Vegetables
  Introduction. 85
  Planting Chart 89
  January. 92
  February 94
  March 96
  April 98
  May. 100
  June 102
  July. 104
  August 106
  September. 108
  October 110
  November 112
  December 114

Chapter 4:
Houseplants
  Introduction. 115
  Planting Chart 119
  January. 122
  February 124
  March 126
  April 128
  May. 130
  June 132
  July. 134
  August 136
  September. 138
  October 140
  November 142
  December 144

Chapter 5:
Lawns
  Introduction. 146
  Planting Chart 150
  January. 152
  February 153
  March 154
  April 156
  May. 158
  June 160
  July. 162
  August 164
  September. 166
  October 168
  November 170
  December 172

Chapter 6:
**Perennials &
Ornamental Grasses**
  Introduction. 173
  Planting Chart 175
  January. 178

Contents

February 180
March 182
April 184
May. 186
June 188
July. 190
August 192
September. 194
October 196
November 198
December 200

Chapter 7:
Roses

Introduction. 201
Planting Chart 205
January 206
February 208
March 210
April 212
May. 214
June 216
July. 218
August 220
September. 222
October 224
November 226
December 228

Chapter 8:
Shrubs

Introduction. 229
Planting Chart 232
January 236
February 238
March 240
April 242
May. 244
June 246

July. 248
August 250
September. 252
October 254
November 256
December 258

Chapter 9:
Trees

Introduction. 259
Planting Chart 263
January 264
February 266
March 268
April 270
May. 272
June 274
July. 276
August 278
September. 280
October 282
November 284
December 286

Chapter 10:
Vines & Ground Covers

Introduction. 288
Planting Chart 291
January 294
February 296
March 298
April 300
May. 302
June 304
July. 306
August 308
September. 310
October 312
November 314
December 316

Chapter 11:
Water Gardens

Introduction. 317
Planting Chart 320
January 322
February 324
March 326
April 328
May. 330
June 332
July. 334
August 336
September. 338
October 340
November 342
December 343

Appendix

UT Extension Service
  Offices 344
UK Extension Service
  Offices 348
Color Your Garden With
  Butterflies 354
Composting. 356
Drought Defense 358
Mulch 360
Integrated Pest
  Management 362
Plants for Acid or Alkaline
  Soils 364
Plants for Wet Soils 366
Landscaping for Wildlife . . . 367
Glossary 368
Bibliography 371
Index. 372
Meet Judy Lowe 384

Horticultural Introduction

A wise person once said, "If you do the right thing at the wrong time, it becomes the wrong thing." That holds true in gardening, as well as in life.

No matter how perfectly you prune your **azalea**, if you do it in September or February, it's the wrong thing because those are not the right times of year to prune an **azalea**. And in this case, there's a penalty for pruning at the wrong time of year—the shrub won't bloom in April since the flower buds were cut off in September or February.

But if you're an inexperienced gardener or someone who has moved to Kentucky or Tennessee from another state, you won't necessarily know the best times to plant, prune, fertilize, renovate a lawn, and so forth.

That's when this book comes in handy. We explain things such as why two neighbors living side by side should fertilize their lawns in different months (it has to do with the kind of grass grown). And when houseplants simply don't need fertilizing, so you might as well save your money. At the same time, we also give you all the how-to information you need in order to do the right thing at the right time: how to prune a tree or a rosebush, raise vegetables from seed and construct a water garden.

Our area is a wonderful place to garden. Why?

- We have a long growing season.
- Our winter temperatures are mostly moderate.
- We receive ample rainfall throughout the year.
- Many plants grow here.

So it's easy to be a successful gardener—provided you follow a few basics: paying attention to climate, evaluating the conditions in your yard, choosing the right plant for the right spot, and learning to furnish what plants need to grow and thrive (soil, water, fertilizer, oxygen).

HOW CLIMATE AFFECTS YOUR GARDEN

"What zone does it grow in?" That's a question that all homeowners and budding gardeners learn to ask about plants. For years, the U.S. Department of Agriculture has divided the country into zones based on their average annual minimum temperatures. For Zone 6, it's minus 10 to 0. For Zone 7, it's 0 to 10. For Zone 8, the average low is 10 to 20.

For the past 13 years, gardeners in Tennessee have known they're either in Zone 6 or Zone 7, depending on where they live. All Kentucky counties except two were in Zone 6; the exceptions were Zone 5. All of that has changed this year. Using data collected from 7,000 weather stations from 1986 to 2001, the researchers took the lowest temperature of each year at every weather station and averaged them together.

The result is that your county may be in a new Hardiness Zone now. In Tennessee, six counties adjacent to Kentucky are Zone 6. Chattanooga and the Memphis area have moved into Zone 8. The rest of the state is in Zone 7. Many Kentucky counties are now in Zone 7 too; the remainder are in Zone 6.

Unfortunately, the USDA had not completed its review of the map in time for inclusion in this book. But you can look it up online at the site of the American Horticultural Society (www.ahs.org).

Horticultural Introduction

It's important to realize that these Zones are just a guide, not necessarily the final word on the subject of what plants will or won't live through the winter in your area. For one thing, they're *averages*. Just because your county is now considered to be in Zone 7, that doesn't mean that some winter the temperature will not dip below 0—and kill any plants that can't tolerate such cold.

Low temperatures aren't the only factor that determines which plants grow well in our region. Heat-tolerance has to be considered too. Some plants—those with gray leaves and many needled evergreens, for instance—don't mind our winter temperatures but can't tolerate the heat and humidity. When you're checking the new Hardiness Zones on the AHS's Website, you may also want to take a look at its Heat Zone map. In general, though, knowing particular plants' heat-tolerance is the kind of thing that's learned by experience, by reading local or state-specific garden books and articles, and by asking lots of questions of experienced gardeners, Extension agents, and knowledgeable garden-center personnel.

KNOW YOUR YARD

You may also occasionally find that conditions at your house—or even in various parts of your yard—aren't necessarily what they are at the official weather station in your county or even in your next-door neighbor's yard. They can be wetter, drier, warmer, or colder than the surrounding area. These are called *microclimates*.

There's nothing mysterious about microclimates—you have probably already observed that plants growing next to a building or wall are more protected and often bloom earlier than those in a more exposed spot.

Some other factors that create microclimates include:

- Good-sized bodies of water, such as lakes, moderate temperatures somewhat for adjacent land. Winter temperatures may not be quite as low as they are farther from the water. Spring frosts end earlier, and fall frosts arrive later.
- Cities are warmer than rural areas. Buildings and paved surfaces absorb heat in the day and radiate it into the air at night.

- Cold air flows downward. A valley (or even a dip or the bottom of a hill in your yard) may be as much as 10 degrees Fahrenheit cooler than at the top of the slope. Frosts will penetrate these low-lying areas later in spring and earlier in fall, affecting plants that grow there.

You can see why it's important for gardeners to be aware of not just the weather and climate in their county, but also specific conditions in their yards. This helps you choose the right plants for the right place. Instead of buying a plant and then figuring out where to put it in your yard, it's better to analyze the conditions—soil, sun, shade, and water—in your yard where you want to plant and then select a plant that thrives in those situations.

SUN AND SHADE

Most of us recognize when our yards are in full sun or completely shady. But few portions of our yards are in all sun or all shade all the time. And few of us are able to accurately gauge how sunny or how shady a particular spot is—mostly, we guess. And we set ourselves up for failure when we guess wrong and plant a tree, shrub, or perennial plant that needs either more or less sun than is available. The moral:

Horticultural Introduction

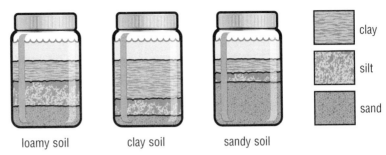

loamy soil   clay soil   sandy soil

Home Soil Test

Take time to watch an area to be sure how many hours it's in the sun and how many in the shade. Full sun is at least eight hours of direct sunshine. Morning sun is mildest and considered best for plants. Afternoon sun is hotter and brighter. You may want to count every hour of afternoon sun as two for the purpose of deciding whether a sun-loving plant will be happy in a particular site. Partial sun is about six hours of direct sunlight; part shade is five or fewer hours of morning sun.

Naturally, you'll find some in-between areas—dappled shade, where dots of sun peek through at certain times of the day, and areas that don't get much direct sun but are actually quite light because those tree limbs start 20 feet up. All these situations call for trial and error. Don't think that you have to depend only on **hostas, ferns, dogwoods**, and **azaleas** in shade. Try some plants that like partial shade or even partial sun and see how they fare. You may be surprised.

Of course, you don't have to live with the current conditions in your yard. If there's too much sun, plant trees or large shrubs, or put up a fence, trellis, or arbor to create some shade. When there's too much shade, consider removing a few trees—especially older ones not in good shape or "weed" trees (**box elder, mimosa**). Or consult an arborist about thinning a tree or removing some of the lower limbs to let light through.

Soil

Soil—dirt, if you must—is often the part of gardening that beginners don't think much about. And that causes many failures that could have been prevented. Soil isn't as "exciting" as plants; it doesn't grow or bloom. But it's the foundation for everything you grow. The condition of the soil is often mirrored in the condition of the plant growing in that soil.

Soil is more complex than it looks to the eye. It's made up of mineral particles, organic material, air, and water. It's also teeming with life—earthworms, tiny insects, and microorganisms that break down organic matter (plant residues that are decomposing).

What do you need to know about soil? Most important are what type of soil is in your yard, its pH, and how quickly it drains. If given a choice, all of us want to have deep, fertile soil that we can dig into with our hands. Unfortunately, few of us have that type of soil naturally.

Soils are classified by their texture—sand, silt, or clay—but most soils are made up of all three. The easiest way to find out what kind of soil is in your yard is to call the Soil Conservation Service office in your county. (Look in the phone book under the government listings.) Most counties have a book listing all the parcels of land in the county, classified by soil type.

Here's a test you can do at home to determine your soil type:

1 Put a trowel of loose soil (remove all rocks and stones) in a glass canning jar.

2 Add 2 cups of water, put the lid on, and shake the jar.

Horticultural Introduction

3 Get a ruler. After one minute, measure the bottom layer, which is the amount of sand. Write that number down.

4 In one hour, measure the layer that's above the sand. That's silt. Make a note of that number.

5 Twenty-four hours after you first shook the jar, measure the top layer, which is clay.

Divide the depth of each layer by the total depth of the settled soil, and then multiply by 100. That gives you the percentage of each particle in your soil.

Sandy soil is fast draining, but doesn't hold water or nutrients. Clay is just the opposite: It drains slowly and holds water and nutrients. It also warms up slowly in spring and is hard to dig.

Fortunately, the solution to sandy or loose, rocky soil (which doesn't hold moisture at the root of plants where they need it) and to clay (which can hold so much water it "drowns" plants) is the same: amending the soil with organic matter.

For clay, the best organic materials are compost (see page 356 for instructions regarding how to make compost), fine bark (such as Nature's Helper™), rotted sawdust, cocoa hulls, rotted leaves, aged mushroom compost, well-rotted manure, and gypsum. Avoid peat moss, which can hold too much moisture. Also avoid sand, unless you can add one-fourth the volume of the soil or more, which (except for small beds) is a huge amount of coarse sand, the recommended kind. Lesser amounts of sand tend to pack in between clay particles, creating a sort of soil cement.

Spread 2 to 3 inches of the organic matter on the surface of clay soil and dig or till into the top 8 inches of the ground.

For sandy or other very loose soils, you can hardly add too much organic matter to the soil. Start with 3 to 4 inches if you can. Good soil amendment for fast-draining soils are compost, humus, spaghnum peat moss (moisten well first), rotted leaves, well-rotted manure, aged mushroom compost, rotted sawdust, cocoa hulls, and seaweed.

Because of our hot climate, amending the soil is an ongoing process. You will need to repeat it at least every few years. Yearly additions are even better in beds that are dug up each spring, such as for vegetables and annual flowers.

You can also grow your own soil amendments. In the vegetable garden and on land not being used, seeds of green manure crops are often sown in the fall and tilled under in the spring. These increase the amount of humus in the soil. **Rye, buckwheat, alfalfa, sweet clover,** and **cowpeas** are good green manure crops.

IS YOUR SOIL ACID OR ALKALINE?

Another aspect of soil that matters to plants—and determines which plants will grow well in your yard—is its pH (the measure of its acidity or alkalinity). The pH scale ranges from 0 to 14, with the lower numbers indicating acidity and the higher numbers alkalinity. Most plants prefer slightly acid to neutral soil, about 6.5 to 7.0, although they may grow in soils 5.5 to 7.3.

How do you know whether your soil is acid or alkaline? Have it tested. Garden centers sell portable kits that give you a quick reading, but a more accurate assessment is available by taking samples of the soil in your yard and sending them to the Extension Service's state lab for analysis. Call your county's Extension Office to get a soil-testing box and instruction sheet. See page 344 for Tennessee or page 348 for Kentucky for addresses and phone numbers.

Horticultural Introduction

What happens if your soil isn't in that "magic" 6.5 to 7.0 range preferred by the majority of plants? Some plants need acid or alkaline soils, and it pays to seek out those plants if you have soil that falls into either range. (See a partial list on pages 364 and 365.)

The problem comes when soil is *extremely* acid or alkaline. This can make some nutrients in the soil unavailable to plants. One solution is to change the pH. It's easy and inexpensive to add dolomitic lime to soil to make it less acid. Fall is the best time of year to do so because it takes several months for the lime to take effect. Addition of sulfur helps acidify alkaline soils. The amounts to use probably came with your soil test results. If not, consult the Extension Service for recommendations.

WATER

Although our area generally receives ample rainfall (see the charts on pages 20 and 21 for the average rainfall in your county), it doesn't necessarily fall right on schedule when your plants need it. That means that homeowners often have to water the plants in their yard.

You need to know a few things about water: when to water, how much, and how to apply it. The rule of thumb is that plants need an inch of rainfall each week. You might think that means you're going to have to pull out the hose and sprinkler every time it doesn't rain that much. But it's not quite that simple. Some plants need watering more often than others; some require less.

Plants that have been set out in the past six months (and especially those planted within the past week or two) are going to need more moisture than that. Many established plants—large trees, for example—may never need supplemental watering except during drought. (See the section on coping with a drought, beginning on page 358.) Plants growing in shade or in clay soil need less-frequent watering than those in full sun or sandy soils. The hotter the weather, the more moisture plants may need.

If you know your plants well, they will give you signs that they need watering—droopy or dull leaves, fewer or smaller flowers or fruits, or leaves that drop off the plant prematurely.

But mostly you have to measure to see how much moisture is in the soil. Carefully insert a thin bamboo stake into the soil near a plant (you don't want it to be so close that it harms the plant's root system) and then pull it out. See whether any part of the probe is damp. That shows how deep the moisture is in the soil. For larger plants, the soil should be moist at least 12 inches deep; water when the soil is dry about 6 inches down. For more shallow-rooted plants, water when the surface of the soil is dry about 4 inches deep—and water enough to wet the soil to about 8 inches deep.

How much water do you have to apply to moisten the soil 8 to 12 inches deep? It depends on how you apply the water and what kind of soil you have. And how long it takes for the water to penetrate depends very much on the type of soil and somewhat on technique.

If you use a sprinkler, put small tuna-sized cans around to measure the amount of water delivered. For other methods, measure the soil twenty-four hours later to see how deeply the water penetrated.

Horticultural Introduction

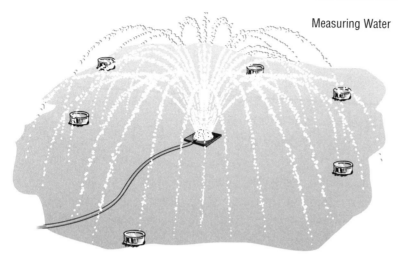
Measuring Water

The most common method of watering is by **HOSE**.

Advantages: It's cheap and easy. The gardener controls where the water is applied, which means less water is wasted because someone is paying attention to how much water is being applied.

Disadvantages: It's easy to use too much force, which can damage plants and cause run-off. Also, it's very easy to underwater when using a hose because it's tiring to stand there holding the hose.

SOAKER HOSES, often made from recycled materials, are generally black and have small holes or pores through which water seeps.

Advantages: Inexpensive and easy to use. They are flexible, so they can be woven in and around plants. Because the water is delivered at a slow rate, there's reduced run-off. The gardener need not stand there while the hose works.

Disadvantages: The pressure of the water decreases as the length of the hose increases. And the hoses don't always last too long.

OSCILLATING SPRINKLERS deliver water in a back-and-forth motion.

Advantages: Allows slow penetration of water into the soil and is useful for large, even areas, such as lawns.

Disadvantages: Water can be blown about by the wind. It's also likely to evaporate more than other methods of watering. Water at the edge of the pattern may run into the street, driveway, or sidewalk.

A FAN SPRINKLER delivers a fine spray of water in a semicircle pattern.

Advantages: The more delicate spray is useful for ground covers and is more accurate than oscillating sprinklers.

Disadvantages: Doesn't cover as much ground as oscillating sprinklers, plus run-off and evaporation may occur.

DRIP IRRIGATION resembles soaker hoses somewhat, but the tubes are smaller and are imbedded with emitters that can be spaced according to where they're needed.

Advantages: Delivers water slowly so there's little run-off or evaporation, and they can be tailored for special plants.

Disadvantages: If the drip irrigation system is under mulch, it's hard to tell whether or not all the emitters are working. And it takes time to install since a pressure-reducer and filters must be attached.

IN-GROUND IRRIGATION SYSTEMS are permanent and costly, but may be just what's required for a large property or for homeowners who are very busy or away a great deal. Collect and read brochures, and then talk to several dealers before you decide.

Horticultural Introduction

FERTILIZER

Plants need at least sixteen nutrients for growth. They obtain three of them from air and water. The rest they obtain from the soil. A soil test tells you which nutrients your soil lacks and the type and amount of fertilizer you need to apply to correct the deficiency.

Every fertilizer container has three numbers listed prominently on it. They may be something like 10-10-10 or 6-12-12. The numbers signifies the percentages by weight of the three major elements:

- The first number: Nitrogen (N), which promotes rapid growth and greening of stem and leaves.
- The second number: Phosphorus (P), which encourages root growth, stimulates flowers, and aids seed formation.
- The third number: Potassium (K), which increases disease- and drought-resistance.

TERMINOLOGY

- A fertilizer that contains one or two of those components—but not all—is called an incomplete fertilizer.
- Sometimes a fertilizer is spoken of as "balanced." That means that all three numbers are the same; the product contains equal amounts of each major element.

- An acid fertilizer (sometimes called azalea-camellia fertilizer or blueberry fertilizer) contains an acidifying ingredient and is used around acid-loving plants, especially if the pH of the soil is higher than desired.
- Water-soluble fertilizers come as powders or crystals that are mixed with water and applied when watering. These may also be applied to the foliage of a plant, for quick absorption. (This technique is called foliar feeding.)
- Slow-release fertilizers provide a long, steady supply of nutrients to plants. This can be beneficial because repeated applications aren't

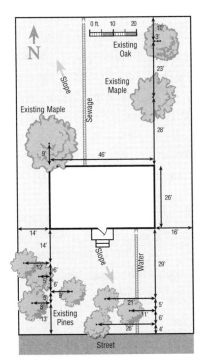

Base Map

necessary and the nutrients are available when the plants need them.

Organic fertilizers are generally slow-release. They are either derived from the remains of once-living organisms or are animal manures. They improve the soil's condition as they feed it. Usually, organic fertilizers contain only small amounts of nitrogen, phosphorus, and potassium; many gardeners see this as an advantage, as it leads to slow but steady growth—which is good for plants. In the past, organic fertilizers weren't always readily available, but that is changing. Common organic fertilizers include cottonseed meal, blood meal, fish emulsion, kelp, and composted manure.

LANDSCAPING

There's more to a yard than simply putting plants about and then taking care of them. A good-looking yard—one that you'll be proud of—is the result of planning. It comes from putting all the basics together in one beautiful picture.

First, look at what you have. Find the property survey that was done when you bought the house. If you can't locate it, sometimes the mortgage company has a copy they'll send you. The alternative is for you to draw an approximate map of your land, noting

Horticultural Introduction

on it any structures (including their measurements), existing trees, shrubs, flower beds, vegetable or water gardens, fences, walls, driveway, walks, playhouses, storage sheds, decks, and patios. It's also a good idea to note drainage ditches (or drainage problems), slopes, and berms. This is called your base map. (You may want to make several copies.)

Be critical at this point. Have the foundation shrubs grown halfway up the living room windows? Does the hedge have bare spots? Are **junipers** blocking your view of the street when you back out of the driveway? Also note plants that you simply don't like.

If a plant has been neglected, it may respond to pruning, fertilizing, and other regular care. If you like the plant where it is, it's worth a try. But some plants are probably best removed and replaced. You can put a big X over those on your landscape plan.

Now, think about what you want your landscape to do for you. I'll bet you never thought of your yard in that way before. Very likely, you've thought mostly about how your yard *looks*, not how it *works*. But just as your home is laid out so it's useful, a landscape should also meet your needs. To help you decide what those are, ask yourself:

- How much outdoor entertaining do we do? What type and how many people at a time?
- Do we need a play area for the children?
- What about dogs?
- Does the yard need more privacy?
- How much time can we devote to maintenance?
- Do we have favorite plants or a favorite style that we want to include?
- Are we interested in growing vegetables or fruits?
- Would we like a water garden?
- Are the driveway and off-street parking adequate?
- Do we need paths?

Dream big when planning a landscape, but don't get carried away. If you have three young preschoolers or your back yard is the impromptu touch-football field for a group of middle-schoolers, an elegant plant-filled landscape may not be in the cards for a few years. But no one says you have to do everything at once. In fact, it's often a good idea to accomplish your landscaping goals over time, not just to ease the budget, but because once we get started, sometimes we change our minds or modify our opinions.

Landscape architects and landscape designers can create a landscape plan for you, if you don't feel comfortable doing it on your own. They can also supervise the installation of the project. Ask for references and check them out.

Whether you'll be working with a professional or doing it yourself, collect photos of yards and plants that you like. You'll also get landscaping ideas by driving through neighborhoods (especially established upscale communities), talking with good gardeners and personnel at top-notch nurseries, and reading *Tennessee Gardener's Guide: Third Edition* or *Kentucky Gardener's Guide*.

In a landscape around a new home, consider first trees, then shrubs. These need to start growing first, and they set the tone for what's to come. When renovating an older property, make a list of priorities: ground covers to replace too much lawn this year, maybe a small water garden next year, and a larger deck two years down the road.

Consider plant textures and color combinations, especially in connection with your house; different shades of brick can clash with red flowers that might be planted against it. Strongly variegated plants, while showy and wonderful, may also have to be carefully positioned to harmonize with their surroundings.

Horticultural Introduction

Begin to draw some of your ideas on a piece of tracing paper placed over your base map. (Or if you have plenty of copies of the base map, do it right on the map.) Then take the map out into the yard and envision what you have drawn. You may even want to go so far as to drag the hose into the shape of a flower bed or pond to see whether the proportions are right.

Multiseason Plants

Your landscape will be more attractive and versatile if you ask one question: How does this plant look in fall or winter? So often, our favorite plants are the ones that are at their peak in spring—**daffodils, redbud trees, creeping phlox**. And there's nothing wrong with that. But you get more impact from multiseason plants, those that look good at several seasons of the year. **Dogwood trees** with flowers, berries, and bright red leaves are a familiar example. But here are some others:

Japanese maple—attractive foliage in spring and summer, fall color, interesting shape in winter

Red maple—red flowers very early in the season, shade in summer, good fall color

Sourwood—tassled flowers in summer, fruits and neon-red fall color.

Yellowwood—white flowers in summer, good fall color, interesting bark in winter.

You'll also be able to find shrubs that shine in several seasons. **Kerria**, for example, flowers in spring and has green stems in winter. **Azaleas** and **rhododendrons** flower in spring and retain their leaves during winter. And many shrubs produce berries, which add an extra dimension to the landscape (and often feed migrating birds).

As you're planning, see what's available at local nurseries. Then decide on one area that you want to focus on first—maybe the entrance to your house or the area beside the deck. When you've finished your first project and you see how much better the area looks (be sure to take before-and-after photos), you'll have a wonderful feeling of accomplishment—and you just may be ready to tackle something bigger.

Don't think of gardening as a chore. Think of it as exercise or as a way of beautifying your surroundings. But it should also be fun and relaxing. As you work through the monthly lists of things to be done in the yard, don't get so busy that you forget to take time to enjoy the pleasures of your landscape—from a tiny **fern** frond unfurling in spring to the majesty of an **oak** that's been providing shade to several generations. Your yard is a living work of art, and you're the artist.

Tennessee

Station Name	Temp Threshold (Degrees F)	50% Probability		
		Fall Freeze	Spring Freeze	Freeze Free Period
Bristol	36	Oct 13	Apr 30	165
	32	Oct 21	Apr 17	186
	28	Nov 01	Mar 03	212
Chattanooga	36	Oct 21	Apr 19	185
	32	Nov 01	Apr 05	209
	28	Nov 08	Mar 21	231
Clarksville	36	Oct 14	Apr 27	169
	32	Oct 22	Apr 12	192
	28	Nov 02	Mar 27	219
Columbia	36	Oct 14	Apr 23	173
	32	Oct 20	Apr 08	194
	28	Nov 05	Mar 28	221
Dyersburg	36	Oct 23	Apr 04	202
	32	Nov 04	Mar 26	222
	28	Nov 13	Mar 12	246
Jackson	36	Oct 18	Apr 11	190
	32	Oct 28	Apr 03	207
	28	Nov 09	Mar 20	233
Knoxville	36	Oct 27	Apr 09	200
	32	Nov 06	Mar 29	221
	28	Nov 15	Mar 14	245
Memphis	36	Oct 31	Apr 03	210
	32	Nov 07	Mar 23	228
	28	Nov 18	Mar 09	253
Nashville	36	Oct 21	Apr 16	187
	32	Oct 29	Apr 05	207
	28	Nov 09	Mar 22	231
Paris	36	Oct 11	Apr 26	167
	32	Oct 22	Apr 11	194
	28	Nov 02	Mar 31	216
Savannah	36	Oct 14	Apr 24	172
	32	Oct 25	Apr 09	198
	28	Nov 04	Mar 28	221
Union City	36	Oct 10	Apr 22	171
	32	Oct 20	Apr 06	196
	28	Nov 04	Mar 27	221

To use this table, locate the recording station nearest you. Using 32 degrees F as an example, and assuming the .5 probability noted in the table (which is a 50/50 chance), this means that five years out of ten, a temperature as cold or colder than 32 degrees is expected to occur later than the date indicated for spring. Conversely, for fall, there is a chance five years out of ten of experiencing temperatures as cold or colder than 32 degrees before the date indicated. This table can be used to determine the chance of the first or last frosts/freezes of the seasons and their relative severity. The period of frost-free days for which the temperature exceeds the specified temperature is also noted. (Source: National Climatic Data Center)

Freeze/Frost Occurrences

Kentucky

Station Name	Temp Threshold (Degrees F)	50% Probability		Freeze Free Period
		Fall Freeze	Spring Freeze	
Ashland	36	Oct 09	May 08	153
	32	Oct 18	Apr 27	173
	28	Oct 28	Apr 12	198
Bowling Green	36	Oct 14	Apr 23	173
	32	Oct 21	Apr 13	191
	28	Nov 04	Mar 31	217
Danville	36	Oct 13	Apr 29	166
	32	Oct 24	Apr 15	192
	28	Nov 04	Apr 04	213
Hopkinsville	36	Oct 15	Apr 22	175
	32	Oct 24	Apr 11	195
	28	Nov 04	Mar 30	219
Leitchfield	36	Oct 12	Apr 29	165
	32	Oct 22	Apr 17	187
	28	Nov 01	Apr 02	212
Lexington	36	Oct 14	Apr 29	167
	32	Oct 25	Apr 17	190
	28	Nov 02	Apr 04	211
Middlesboro	36	Oct 08	May 07	153
	32	Oct 17	Apr 29	170
	28	Oct 29	Apr 12	200
Murray	36	Oct 15	Apr 17	180
	32	Oct 26	Apr 05	203
	28	Nov 07	Mar 28	223
Owensboro	36	Oct 09	Apr 23	169
	32	Oct 21	Apr 10	193
	28	Nov 01	Mar 30	216
Paducah	36	Oct 14	Apr 18	178
	32	Oct 28	Apr 05	205
	28	Nov 07	Mar 22	229
Somerset	36	Oct 06	May 04	154
	32	Oct 16	Apr 22	177
	28	Oct 25	Apr 09	198
Williamstown	36	Oct 10	May 01	162
	32	Oct 22	Apr 20	185
	28	Nov 02	Apr 06	209

To use this table, locate the recording station nearest you. Using 32 degrees F as an example, and assuming the .5 probability noted in the table (which is a 50/50 chance), this means that five years out of ten, a temperature as cold or colder than 32 degrees is expected to occur later than the date indicated for spring. Conversely, for fall, there is a chance five years out of ten of experiencing temperatures as cold or colder than 32 degrees before the date indicated. This table can be used to determine the chance of the first or last frosts/freezes of the seasons and their relative severity. The period of frost-free days for which the temperature exceeds the specified temperature is also noted. (Source: National Climatic Data Center)

Tennessee

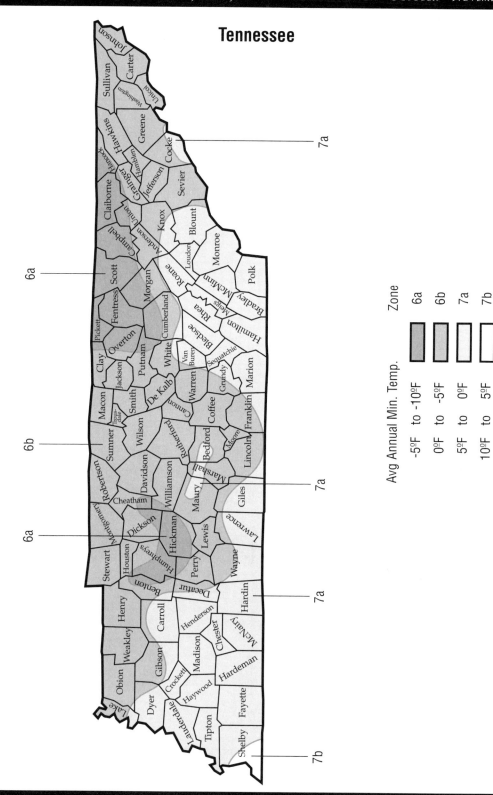

Avg Annual Min. Temp.	Zone
-5ºF to -10ºF	6a
0ºF to -5ºF	6b
5ºF to 0ºF	7a
10ºF to 5ºF	7b

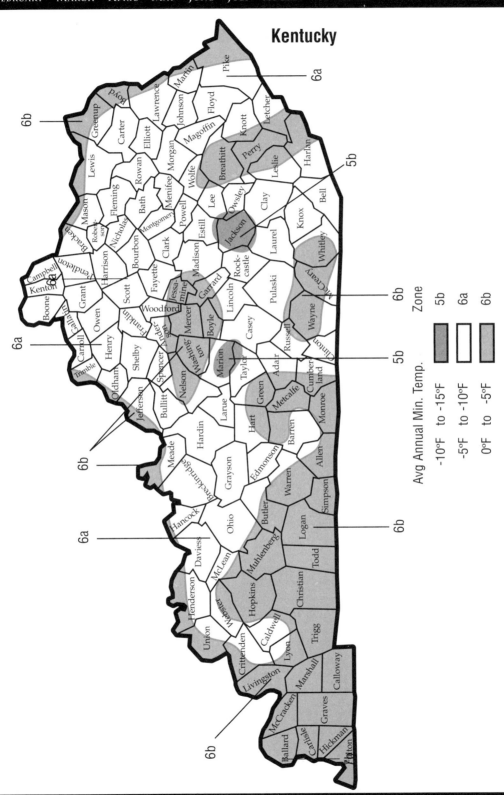

Kentucky

Tennessee

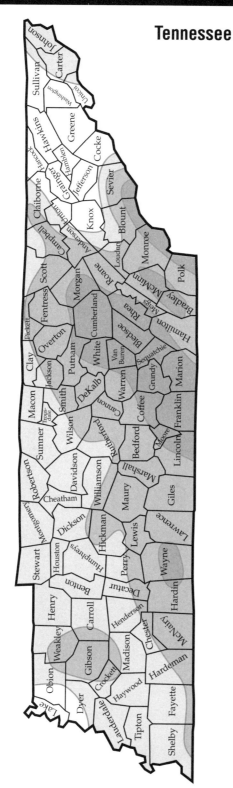

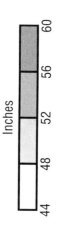

Inches

60
56
52
48
44

Adapted from THE WORLD BOOK ENCYCLOPEDIA. © 2001 World Book, Inc.
By permission of the publisher. www.worldbook.com

Annual Precipitation

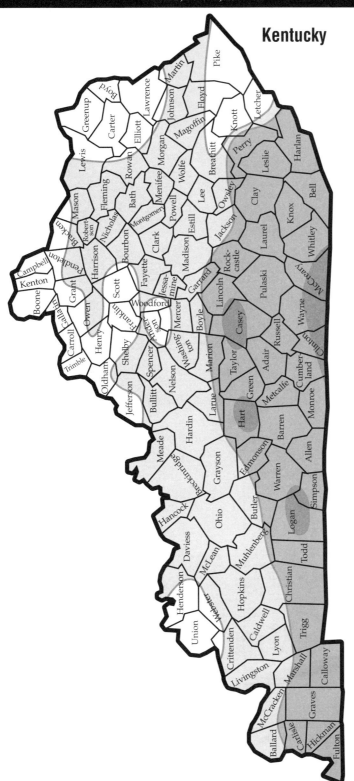

Kentucky

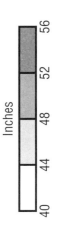

Inches

56
52
48
44
40

Average First Fall Frosts

Tennessee

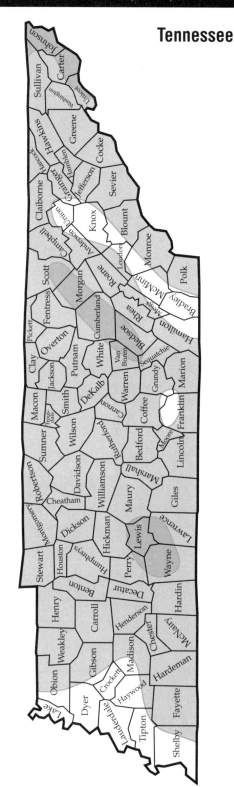

Median Dates
(10% probability of 32° or colder on an earlier date)

Sep. 15 - 30

Oct. 1 - 14

Oct. 15 - 31

Source: National Climate Data Center

Average First Fall Frosts

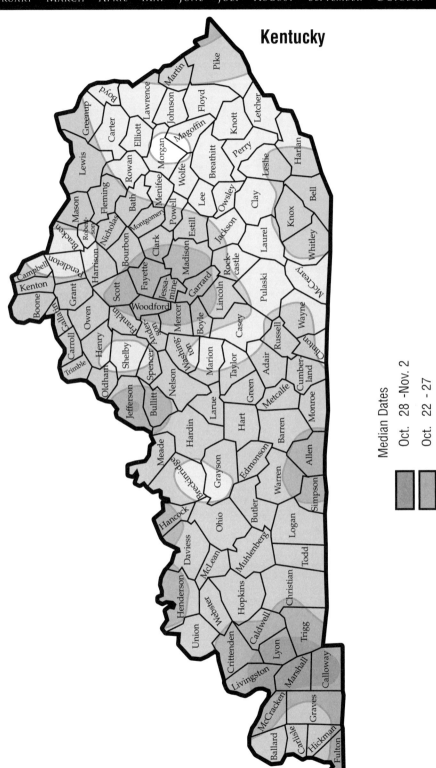

Kentucky

Median Dates

- Oct. 28 - Nov. 2
- Oct. 22 - 27
- Oct. 16 - 21
- Oct. 10 - 15
- Oct. 4 - 9

Source: The Kentucky Climate Center
at Western Kentucky University

Average Last Spring Frosts

JANUARY · FEBRUARY · MARCH · APRIL · MAY · JUNE · JULY · AUGUST · SEPTEMBER · OCTOBER · NOVEMBER · DECEMBER

Tennessee

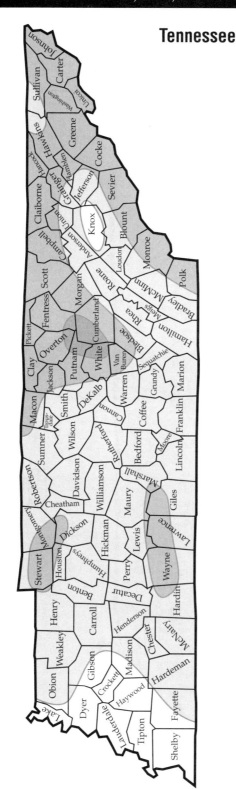

Median Dates
(10% probability of 32° or colder on a later date)

Apr. 1 - 14
Apr. 15 - 30
May 1 - 14
May 15 - 31

Source: National Climate Data Center

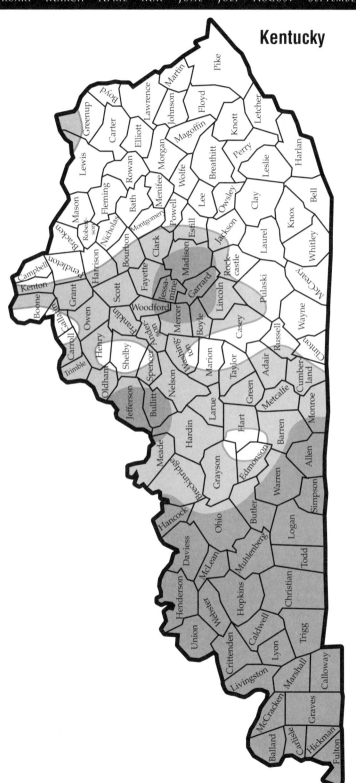

Kentucky

Median Dates

Apr. 1 - 14
Apr. 15 - 22
Apr. 23 - 29

Source: The Kentucky Climate Center at Western Kentucky University

CHAPTER ONE

Annuals

The easiest way to have a great-looking yard is to plant plenty of annuals. They provide instant color, they're simple to grow and require little attention and there's one that will beautify almost any place in your yard. Best of all, even those who consider themselves non-gardeners can be successful with annuals.

Just follow the basics—careful soil preparation, choosing plants that match your light and soil conditions, regular watering, fertilizing, and grooming—and the plants will reward you with bushels of blooms.

Everyone feels comfortable with annuals—they're plants we've known from childhood: **marigolds, petunias,** and **zinnias**. But plant breeders are also tempting advanced gardeners with "new" annuals, sophisticated imports that provide the excitement of something different while still blooming nonstop.

What is an annual, anyway? You may think of an annual as a bedding plant bought in spring that will flower until fall. But the official definition is a plant that lives its whole life in one season. So that includes cool-season annuals such as **pansies**. It also includes some old-fashioned flowers such as **bachelor buttons** and **poppies** that are grown from seed and flower for only a few weeks. And a few perennials—**geraniums** are a good example—sneak into the annuals category because they're perennial only in the warmest regions and are killed by frost everywhere else.

But you don't have to know a thing about this to enjoy annuals. If a plant is listed in the chart on pages 29 to 31, it's a good annual plant.

Planning. Few of us actually plan annual flower beds on paper, as we might a perennial border. It is a good idea, though. Instead of heading to the garden center the first warm weekend of spring, first take time to think about where you would like to plant; what the growing conditions are in those areas; and the flower colors, sizes, and shapes that will fit best into the spots you've chosen. Then you may want to make a quick sketch or two to take along. You'll see a noticeable difference in the results if you make a few decisions ahead of time:

Where will annuals fit into your yard? Annuals are at home in many places: in front of evergreen shrubs or trees; along a wall, fence, path, walkway, or driveway; in island beds; along the house's foundation; beside a vegetable garden; in raised beds; or in containers—hanging baskets, window boxes, and pots, large and small.

Shade or sun? All plants need light; some can tolerate lower levels of light

than others. If you're looking for plants that grow in full shade, full sun, or anywhere in between, check the plant list on pages 29 to 31 for suitable annuals. But if you've had problems in previous years with annuals not being successful in a certain spot, it will pay to take time to measure just how many hours of direct sunlight that area receives. You may be surprised that it isn't as much as you thought.

Colors. Once you know where you want annuals to grow, think of yourself as an artist painting the landscape and start where an artist would—thinking about color. What are your favorites? Do you prefer "cool" pastels or "hot" sunny colors, such as reds and oranges? That's your starting point, of course. But consider also the color of your house and trim, as well as any other structures on your property (fence, storage building, etc.).

• White and very pale colors light up dark places. Whites are especially good beside patios and decks because they will show up at dusk.

• Do you prefer to plant beds of all one color or mix and match various shades? There's no "right" way to do

Annuals

it—you're the final judge of whether it works or not—but massed blocks of color usually make more of an impact than a mixture of colors. If you like to combine colors, make sure they're complementary.

Size and shape. You'll find that annuals of varying heights add interest to the garden. That's true even in containers, where you may want the tallest annuals in the center, those of medium height in the middle row, and low-growing or trailing annuals along the edges of the pots. Good design includes considering flower and even foliage form and size, too. It's more interesting if your annuals are of several flower forms rather than all exhibiting the same shape.

Seeds or plants? Most people buy annuals as bedding plants. Doing so is fast, simple, and almost foolproof. But sometimes you can't find the annuals you want, and other times you'd like to cover a large area with flowers, but find that the cost of enough bedding plants would be prohibitive. In those cases, you may want to investigate growing from seed. It can be done indoors or outside in the garden. See page 32 for directions.

What to look for at the garden center. Strong, healthy plants will be the best performers in your yard.

1 Before buying, check both tops and bottoms of leaves for signs of insects or insect damage.

2 Choose plants with sturdy stems.

3 See if roots are growing out the bottom of the pot. If so, gently remove the plant from the container to see if it's potbound—the roots are circling round and round the soil ball like a web. If so, select another plant.

4 If they are available, select plants that have *not* begun blooming. If a young plant has been devoting most of its energy to growing flowers, the root growth may not have been sufficient—and good root growth makes the difference in the success of your plants during the summer.

Soil preparation. Good soil equals a great-growing garden. Unfortunately, few of us in Tennessee or Kentucky have been blessed by nature with great soil. That means we have to work at building it. To do this:

- **Have your soil tested** through the Agricultural Extension Service. Your local office will provide a box and instructions for taking the sample and sending it off. The results will give you the pH of your soil and tell you what nutrients are lacking. You'll also learn just how much fertilizer you need and what kind.

This may end up saving you quite a bit of money.

- **Check the drainage.** Dig a hole 9 or 10 inches deep and fill it with water. If all the water drains out within twenty-four hours, drainage should be fine for most annuals. If there's still water in the hole after a day, you may need to consider choosing another location.

- **Dig or till the soil** 8 to 10 inches deep, if possible.

- **Amend the soil.** Whether your soil is hard clay or so rocky that water runs right through it, mixing it with amendments makes it a better growing environment for your plants. Good choices are rotted sawdust, finished compost, composted manure, fine bark, old mushroom compost, and composted leaves. For new beds, spread a 3-inch layer on top of the ground and till into the top 6-8 inches of the soil. For previously planted beds, work in about an inch of any of the amendments if you can.

None of those steps is difficult or time-consuming. And they all contribute to making annuals one of the most pleasurable experiences you can have in the garden. That's not much to ask for non-stop color in a dazzling array. If you aren't growing annuals, your yard does not look as spectacular as it might.

Annuals

Common Name (Botanical Name)	Color	Height (Inches)	Spacing (Inches)	Light Level
Ageratum (*Ageratum houstonianum*)	Blue, lavender, pink, white	5 to 30	5 to 12	Sun to partial shade
Cleome (*Cleome hassleriana*)	White, pink, rose, and lavender	12 to 50	12 to 18	Sun
Cockscomb (*Celosia argentea cristata*)	Red, yellow, gold, pink, salmon and other colors	8 to 30	8 to 12	Sun
Coleus (*Solenostemon scutellarioides*)	Red, pink, maroon, yellow, gold, chartreuse, bicolors	6 to 48	8 to 36	Any
Cosmos (*Cosmos bipinnatus*)	Pink, white, rose, fuchsia	24 to 70	12 to 30	Sun
Creeping zinnia (*Sanvitalia procumbens*)	Yellow, gold, orange	4 to 12	6	Sun
Dianthus, Pinks (*Dianthus* x *barbatus*)	Pink, red, white, lavender	4 to 12	10 to 12	Light shade
Dusty miller (*Senecio cineraria*)	Silver	8 to 18	6 to 10	Sun
Flowering tobacco (*Nicotiana* species and hybrids)	White, lime green, red, rose, purple, peach	12 to 60	9 to 24	Sun or light shade
Four-O'Clock (*Mirabilis jalapa*)	Red, pink, yellow, white, striped	24 to 36	12 to 36	Sun
Geranium (*Pelargonium* species and hybrids)	White, red, salmon, pink, lavender	12 to 36	12 to 18	Sun or light shade
Globe amaranth (*Gomphrena globosa*)	White, lavender, red, orangish	10 to 24	12 to 16	Sun

Annuals

Common Name (*Botanical Name*)	Color	Height (Inches)	Spacing (Inches)	Light Level
Impatiens (*Impatiens walleriana*)	White, pink, red, orange, lavender	6 to 36	8 to 24	Shade or partial shade
Madagascar periwinkle (*Catharanthus roseus*)	White, pink, lavender	4 to 24	8 to 18	Sun
Marigold (*Tagetes* species and hybrids)	Yellow, orange, burgundy, cream	6 to 36	10 to 36	Sun
Melampodium (*Melampodium paludosum*)	Yellow	8 to 18	14 to 24	Sun
Moss rose (*Portulaca grandiflora*)	Red, white, pink, yellow, orange, purple	3 to 6	12 to 24	Sun
New Guinea impatiens (*Impatiens hawkeri*)	Pink, red, salmon, white	12 to 20	12 to 15	Sun or partial shade
Ornamental cabbage and kale (*Brassica oleracea*)	Green, white, red, purple	6 to 12	8 to 12	Sun or partial shade
Ornamental pepper (*Capsicum annuum*)	Red, orange, yellow, purple	4 to 36	6 to 24	Sun
Pansy (*Viola* x *wittrockiana*)	Yellow, white, blue, purple, maroon, orange	4 to 8	4 to 5	Partial sun
Pentas (*Pentas lanceolata*)	Red, pink, white	14 to 36	10 to 14	Sun
Petunia (*Petunia* x *hybrida*)	All	6 to 18	12 to 24	Sun or partial sun
Plume celosia (*Celosia argentea plumosa*)	Red, yellow, pink, orange	6 to 36	6 to 12	Sun

Annuals

Common Name (*Botanical Name*)	Color	Height (Inches)	Spacing (Inches)	Light Level
Red salvia (*Salvia* species and hybrids)	Red, pink, cream, purple	10 to 26	12 to 20	Sun
Scaveola (*Scaveola* x 'Blue Wonder')	Blue, violet	4 to 12	18 to 30	Sun
Snapdragon (*Antirrhinum majus*)	All except blue and green	6 to 36	8 to 12	Sun or partial sun
Snow-on-the-mountain (*Euphorbia marginata*)	Green and white	24 to 36	24 to 30	Sun
Sunflower (*Helianthus annuus*)	Yellow, beige, bronze, burgundy, orange	1 to 7 feet	8 to 36	Sun
Swan River daisy (*Brachycome iberidifolia*)	Mauve, violet	12 to 24	24 to 30	Sun
Sweet alyssum (*Lobularia maritima*)	White, pink, purple, salmon	3 to 9	12 to 18	Sun or partial sun
Wax begonia (*Begonia* x *semperflorens-cultorum*)	White, red, pink	6 to 14	6 to 12	Any
Zinnia (*Zinnia elegans*)	Red, pink, orange, purple, yellow, white, green	6 to 48	12 to 24	Sun

JANUARY

 PLANNING

Taking notes. Start the year by reading over the entries in last year's garden notebook. That will jog your memory about what you liked, or didn't like, about the previous season's annuals. Did you write that you wanted to try some new color combinations? That you wanted fewer, or more, flower beds? Did you admire a friend's or neighbor's flowers and want to try something similar this year?

 PLANTING

Growing from seed. Starting bedding plants instead of buying them is fun. Although it seems a long time to spring, seeds of some popular annuals, such as **geraniums, Madagascar periwinkle**, and **wax begonia**, need three to four months to germinate and grow to a good size. So January is the time to start them:

1 **Gather your equipment**.

• Containers can be anything from foam egg cartons to the bottom portions of 2-liter soft-drink bottles or milk jugs. Garden centers sell plastic flats, and six packs, as well as peat pots and pellets for seed starting. If your chosen containers don't have drainage holes, poke some in the bottom.

• A soilless potting mix that's made especially for seed starting is best. Regular potting mix may work too.
• If there isn't enough sun, you may need fluorescent lights.

2 **Consider timing**. Read on the seed packets to see how far they need to be started before the date they're set outdoors. For a typical annual, it's usually six to eight weeks. This group includes **ageratum, celosia, cleome, coleus, dusty miller, flowering tobacco, melampodium, ornamental pepper, red salvia, snow-on-the-mountain**, and **Swan River daisy**. Start **dusty miller, impatiens, petunia**, and **snapdragon** eight to ten weeks ahead. But some annuals—**cosmos, marigold, sunflower**, and **zinnia**—take only a month before they're ready to go outdoors. Count back from the average frost date and make a chart showing when you need to start various types of seeds. Don't start the seeds *before* that date. Seeds that grow indoors too long are likely to be leggy.

3 **Planting.** Moisten the seed-starting mix and pour it into the containers. Level off the top and sow the seeds according to the packet directions. In flats, you'll get more even distribution if you mix small seeds with sand. Do the seeds need to be exposed to light or should they be covered? (See the lists on pages 29 to 31, and check the backs of the seed packages.) Poke larger seeds into the soil at the depth recommended on the seed packet. Lightly water. If seeds need darkness, sprinkle the soil's surface with about 1/4 inch of sand. Label each container with the name of the plant and the date the seeds were sown. Cover the container with plastic or another clear material. Move to a spot where the temperature is between 68 and 75 degrees Fahrenheit. If the only available room is cooler, consider buying a heating cable or mat to place under the containers. If the seeds need light to germinate, place the containers beneath fluorescent light fixtures left on twenty-four hours daily until the seeds sprout.

 CARE

Light. Once seeds have sprouted, place them about 6 inches from light fixtures. Leave the lights on twelve to fourteen hours daily. Unless you have a greenhouse or sunroom, natural light usually isn't sufficient at this point.

 WATERING

Temperature. Water the seedlings with tepid room-temperature water—65 to 70 degrees Fahrenheit.

There's no need to fertilize winter annuals such as pansy or ornamental cabbage and kale this month.

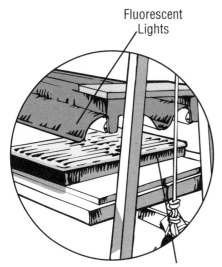

Fluorescent Lights

Seed-Starter Tray in 10x20" Flat Tray

Technique. Until seeds germinate, water from the bottom so as not to dislodge the seeds.

Frequency. Keep the soil consistently moist but not soggy.

FERTILIZING

Indoors. Don't fertilize young plants till they've developed their second set of true leaves. Use a water-soluble plant food mixed at one-fourth to one-half the normal rate.

Outside. There's no need to fertilize winter annuals such as **pansy** or **ornamental cabbage** and **kale** this month.

Timely Tip

Annual seeds that germinate best in light include:

- **Ageratum**
- **Cleome**
- **Cockscomb**
- **Coleus**
- **Creeping zinnia**
- **Dusty miller**
- **Impatiens**

- **Flowering tobacco**
- **Four-o'clocks**
- **Moss rose**
- **Ornamental cabbage**
- **Ornamental kale**

- **Ornamental pepper**
- **Petunia**
- **Red salvia**
- **Snapdragon**
- **Sweet alyssum**
- **Wax begonia**

Annual seeds that need to germinate in darkness include:

- **Celosia**
- **Globe amaranth**

- **Madagascar periwinkle**

- **Melampodium**

Plants that germinate in either light or dark include:

- **Cleome**
- **Cosmos**
- **Dianthus**
- **Geranium**

- **Marigold**
- **Morning glory**
- **Snow-on-the-mountain**

- **Sunflower**
- **Swan River daisy**
- **Zinnia**

GROOMING

Good grooming. Regularly remove yellowing or browned leaves from annuals such as **coleus, impatiens**, and **wax begonias** that are overwintering in the house.

PROBLEMS

Prevent damping off. If young seedlings just keel over, this is usually the result of damping off, a fungal disease. To make sure it doesn't affect your plants:

- Use only new containers or wash old containers with a mixture of 1 part bleach to 9 parts water.
- Use a sterile potting medium.
- Don't smoke when potting up seeds.
- Wash your hands before working with young plants.
- Provide good air circulation.
- Give the seeds adequate water and heat.
- Don't overwater.
- Fertilize only lightly.

FEBRUARY

PLANNING

Are those seeds good? Now's the time to hunt up those seed packets left over from last year. To determine whether you can use them this season or if you should buy new seeds, test them.

1 Wet a paper towel and sprinkle it with ten seeds, evenly spaced.

2 Roll up the towel with the seeds inside, place it in a plastic bag and seal it. Place the bag in a warm spot (on top of a water heater or refrigerator works fine).

3 Begin checking in three days to see whether any seeds have sprouted.

4 The number of seeds that germinate within fifteen days gives you the germination percentage (e.g., eight sprouted seeds equal an 80 percent germination rate). If the rate is 50 to 70 percent, you'll know to sow the seeds more thickly than usual. When germination is less than 50 percent, buy fresh seeds.

Award winners. Consider growing annuals that receive awards (from All-America Selections or state Extension Services, for instance). They are often superior.

Finalizing the list. Use the catalogs you've been collecting to come up with a list of plants you want to grow this year. Stop by your favorite nursery or garden center to see what sorts of seed packets they have and what plants they're expecting to offer in the spring. Some years ago, gardeners considered the seeds sold by local garden centers rather dull. But many now offer seeds from big mail-order nurseries and lines of "gourmet" seeds. You may be pleasantly surprised by what you find.

Getting answers to your questions. It never fails—the first warm weekend in April brings everyone out to garden centers, and the phone rings off the hook at your county's Extension Service office. If you have questions about annual flowers for your yard, *now's* the time to ask. The pros will have more time to talk with you.

How low did it go? Record low temperatures and amounts of any snowfall in your garden notebook.

PLANTING

Start seeds. Start seeds that need about eight weeks before your area's last spring frost to grow and germinate. See page 32 for a list of annuals that usually require eight weeks to reach transplanting size. But double-check your seed packet. Some hybrids may take more or less time.

Take cuttings. If you brought plants or cuttings of some annuals into the house last fall—**coleus, geraniums, impatiens, scaveola**, and **wax begonias**, for instance—this is a good time to take cuttings of them.

• Stems of **begonias, coleus**, and **impatiens** root easily in a glass or jar of water. Keep the water clean, and transplant the cuttings as soon as they've developed a small mass of roots. (If you leave cuttings in water too long, they may rot or have problems adjusting to growing in soil.)

• Or you can root stem cuttings of most annuals in a pot or flat of a sterile medium such as half perlite and half peat moss or equal parts peat moss, sharp sand, and vermiculite. Fill the container to within half an inch of the rim with moistened rooting medium. Take the cuttings and dip the ends in a rooting hormone such as Rootone®. Insert a pencil in the rooting mix to make a hole for the cutting. Once you have all the cuttings in place, place the pot in a clear plastic bag or cover larger containers with plastic. Don't let the cuttings and plastic come into contact with each other. Put the container in a warm spot that receives indirect light. Make sure the soil stays moist, but not wet. If the plastic collects too much moisture, open the bag or vent the plastic to let the cuttings

For the first three weeks after seedlings develop three pairs of true leaves, fertilize them twice a week with a water-soluble fertilizer diluted to half-strength.

dry out a bit. When new growth appears, carefully remove the cuttings from the rooting medium and transplant into small flowerpots.

CARE

Lower the temperature. Although seeds generally need heat to germinate, reducing room temperature to 60 to 65 degrees Fahrenheit after the seeds have sprouted will result in stockier plants. If you keep all the rooms in your house warmer than that, check the temperature in the garage or a below-ground family room to see whether it might work. Or try shutting off the heat in a sunny bedroom during the day.

Bright light. After annual seeds have sprouted, raise the height of fluorescent fixtures so they remain about 6 inches above the tiny plants. If you're keeping your seedlings in natural light, avoid the midday sun.

Check pansies. Watch those **pansies** and **ornamental cabbage** and **kale** growing outdoors. Sometimes a cycle of freezing and thawing pushes them out of the ground. This not only dries out the roots, but it can subject them to freezing temperatures. If you notice that these plants have been heaved out

of the ground, quickly firm soil back around the roots and add extra mulch about the plants.

 WATERING

Not too much or too little. Keep soil moist but not soggy for cuttings that you're rooting indoors and seeds that you've started. It's a fine line that you usually learn by observing results—letting the soil dry out reduces the number of seeds that germinate and puts stress on young plants that have sprouted, but roots will rot in soil that's kept overly wet. So how do you manage to hit this desirable middle ground? Water the soil thoroughly each time, and then let the soil surface dry slightly before watering again. (Test the soil by touching it with your fingertip to see whether it feels wet or dry.)

You may sometimes read that people should water winter annuals growing outdoors this time of year if the weather's dry. But rarely does anyone do it. For one thing, the ground is often frozen. And your hose has been put up for the winter. Then too you'd feel silly out there with a sprinkling can when it's 25 degrees Fahrenheit. So enjoy a rest from watering this month.

FERTILIZING

When to feed. For the first three weeks after seedlings develop three pairs of true leaves, fertilize them twice a week with a water-soluble fertilizer diluted to half-strength. Starting in the fourth week, fertilize about every ten to fourteen days with a full-strength water-soluble plant food such as 15-15-15 or 20-20-20. The same schedule works fine for transplanted cuttings.

GROOMING

If you're not taking cuttings of annuals that you overwintered, keep the plants pinched back so they don't become leggy.

PROBLEMS

If a seedling suddenly begins to wilt, that's a sign of damping-off. Remove the plant from the seed-starting container right away to avoid having the problem spread.

Mites are not usually a problem on tiny seedlings. They might be a problem later if you let the seedlings dry out.

MARCH

Annuals

Annuals

PLANNING

Bedtime. Where are you going to plant annuals this year? Now's the time to plan the locations of any new flower beds or to enlarge existing beds.

- Island beds, in lawns or among trees and shrubs, allow the flowers to be seen from all sides.
- Borders can go beside sidewalks, driveways, paths, walls, the house, or along the street. They create ribbons of color in your landscape.
- Flower beds and borders may be formal (marked by straight lines such as squares and oblongs) or informal (characterized by flowing lines). Informal is more natural looking, but take into account the architecture of your house and the style of your neighborhood when deciding.

Getting a head start. It's fine to dig new flower beds anytime this month if the ground isn't frozen or soggy from lots of rain. See directions on page 28. Cover newly dug beds with an airy mulch such as pine straw so they'll stay in good shape until you're ready to plant. You may want to think about creating a special bed for flowers you can cut and take indoors. (See page 41 for a list of annuals that make good cut flowers.)

Don't buy annual bedding plants before it's warm enough for them in your area.

PLANTING

Setting out new plants. If the plants have been hardened off (been gradually exposed to outdoor temperatures) at the nursery, you may plant **pansies, English daisies, calendula**, and **snapdragons** anytime this month that you find them in garden centers and the ground isn't frozen. All tolerate chilly weather. Mulch them well. If temperatures fall below 20 degrees Fahrenheit, cover the plants with pine straw or several layers of newspapers (anchored with rocks so they won't blow away) to protect them from cold.

Warm areas. If your average date of last frost falls toward the end of March, you may start planting annuals outdoors (see page 38).

Transplanting indoors. Once the cuttings you took have developed roots, and the young seeds have sprouted and have grown two sets of *true* leaves (that is, three total sets of leaves), transplant them into larger containers—either spaced farther apart in new flats or in individual containers. Here are some transplanting tips:

- Use new or carefully cleaned containers and fill them a little more than half full with a packaged potting soil that's been thoroughly moistened.
- Tiny seedlings are very fragile; handle them carefully and never pick them up by the stems.
- Use a plastic spoon or a tongue depressor to lift individual seedlings out of the soil. Disturb the roots as little as possible, and try to keep as much of the growing medium around the roots as you can.
- Place the plant in the new container at the same depth it grew before. (If you're transplanting to another flat, space the little plants 2 to 3 inches apart.) Lightly firm the soil around the stem.
- Water the plants well.
- Give them slightly lower light levels for three or four days, to allow them to adjust.

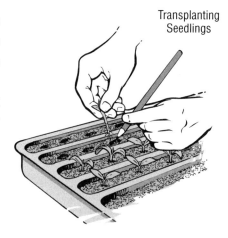
Transplanting Seedlings

If you're growing seedlings in natural sunlight, such as on windowsills, give the containers a quarter to half turn each time you water. This keeps them growing straight.

Sowing seeds. This month, many gardeners in the region can sow seeds of plants that need to be started four to six weeks before the last-frost date. These include **cosmos, marigold**, and **zinnia**. For those in colder areas, see February. See page 32 for seed-starting basics.

Geraniums. Cut back **geraniums** that you brought indoors last fall and repot them if roots are growing out the drainage hole or if the roots are growing around and around the ball of soil. Water well and place in a warm spot that receives bright indirect light. They will start growing soon and be ready to go outdoors when the weather becomes warm.

Cuttings. Take cuttings of **impatiens, scaveola**, and **wax begonias** so they'll be rooted and ready to go outdoors in April.

 CARE

Move this way. If you're growing seedlings in natural sunlight, such as on windowsills, give the containers a quarter to half turn each time you water. This keeps them growing straight.

Follow the bouncing light. In many areas, a south-facing windowsill may become too warm for seedlings. But you may not feel that an east- or west-facing window provides sufficient light. One way to increase light in these situations

is to line the sill and interior edges of the window frame with aluminum foil. That will reflect light onto the plants. If your seedlings are growing lanky, that's a sign they need more light.

 WATERING

Indoors. Remember that seeds need constant moisture to germinate. Once sprouted, young plants shouldn't be allowed to dry out. Check the soil's moisture level daily to be sure.

Outdoors. March can be a very rainy month, but if it should turn out to be dry instead, remember to water **pansies** (and any remaining **ornamental cabbage** and **kale**) every seven to ten days whenever an inch of rain has not fallen and the ground is thawed.

 FERTILIZING

Switcheroo. About six weeks after transplanting seeds or cuttings indoors, change to a fertilizer that's formulated for flowering plants. Super Bloom® is a favorite of mine.

Feed pansies. Whenever the soil is not frozen and **pansies** are blooming, give them a drink of fertilizer-enriched water. No other winter annuals outdoors or overwintering annuals indoors need feeding.

If your young seedlings are growing lanky instead of stocky, pinch out the growing tip to encourage the plants to become bushier.

PROBLEMS

Too many plants. It's difficult to space small seeds evenly when you sow them, so they may sprout in clumps or end up growing much too close to one another. This isn't good for your plants as they're all competing for space, moisture, nutrients, and light. So it isn't cruel to thin your seedlings; it's cruel *not* to.

Thinning how-to. Seedlings can be thinned a couple of ways so that the right number of plants get the space they need. It depends on how closely the plants are growing. The main thing is not to disturb the root systems of the plants you're keeping.

- Gently tug extras out by hand or with tweezers.
- Use cuticle scissors to cut the unwanted plants off at soil level.
- Gently firm any disturbed soil back into place.

APRIL

PLANNING

Take your time. Balmy temperatures and sunshine can be seductive. Even those of us who know our average frost-free date won't arrive for another couple of weeks need to be cautious. We convince ourselves that warm weather has arrived for good at the first string of pretty days. We rush off to the garden center, buy plants, and set them out all across the yard. What frequently happens then is a few nights of temperatures in the 30-degree range. Even if we manage to keep all the plants covered so they aren't harmed by frost, warm-season annuals don't like temperatures that cold—and will sulk. If you want to rush the season, make sure you invest in plenty of protective coverings and that you listen to the local weather forecast each evening, ready to take action if needed.

PLANTING

If the last-frost date has occurred this month in your area, you may begin planting. You can plant annuals over several evenings or weekends, or do it all in one day.

1 If seedlings or bedding plants have been growing in a greenhouse or indoors, they need to be hardened off, or acclimated to outdoor weather, before being planted. Place the plants outdoors during the day in a shady, protected spot, then take the plants indoors—to an unheated area—at night. Gradually move them into a part of the yard where they receive more sun and wind, and leave them out all night. Depending on the temperatures, hardening off can take as little as a week or as long as ten to fourteen days.

2 Prepare the soil, as described in the introduction to this chapter. Water the flower bed the night before planting, if it's dry.

3 If rain has been abundant recently, test the soil to see whether it's too wet for planting. Form a ball of soil in your hand and squeeze it. If it crumbles and falls apart, it's fine to plant. If it remains a lump, wait a few days.

Lady Gardening

4 Choose an overcast day to plant, or do it in early evening.

5 Water the plants thoroughly about twelve hours before you plan to plant.

6 Remove plants from their containers and gently loosen excessive roots that wind around and around the soil.

7 Dig individual holes and place plants in them at the same depth they grew in their pots. Space according to the planting chart in this chapter.

8 Replace the soil around the roots and water.

9 Mulch the flower bed about 1 inch deep. Keep the mulch away from the stems of the plant. For one thing, mulch may overwhelm a tiny seedling. And second, keeping the mulch a few inches from the stem allows the soil to warm up, which is good for the plants.

CARE

Bye-bye blooms. Did you know that one of the best things you can do for all annuals is to pinch off any flowers before you plant seedlings or set out bedding plants? Seems like heresy, doesn't it? But a young plant has only so much energy. If it spends most of it producing flowers, it

The ideal time to water young plants is first thing in the morning. That allows any water that splashed onto the foliage to dry during the day, which cuts the risk of fungus diseases.

doesn't develop as good a root system as it should. But that root system is essential to a strong healthy plant that can tolerate hot, dry weather. So clip off any flowers before planting. You'll reap the rewards later in the season when your plant grows larger and performs better than those whose blooms were left in place.

WATERING

Check often. Young transplants have small root systems that can't absorb a great deal of water at once. For the first few weeks in your garden, they may need to be watered every couple of days (or even daily if the weather is hot). Don't let them wilt, which will stunt their growth.

The ideal time to water young plants is first thing in the morning. That allows any water that splashed onto the foliage to dry during the day, which cuts the risk of fungus diseases.

FERTILIZING

Indoors. Before the weather is warm enough for your seedlings to go outdoors, continue to fertilize them about every ten days with a water-soluble fertilizer made for blooming plants.

Outdoors. Use a transplanting solution when you plant annuals outdoors in a bed or into hanging baskets or containers and then fertilize. Your options include:

- Sprinkle around the plants a balanced timed-release fertilizer (such as Osmocote® 14-14-14) according to package directions. This will feed plants for up to three months. Water after applying.
- Use 10-10-10 granular fertilizer, being careful not to drop any on the plants because it will burn them. Keep a hose handy to wash accidental spills. Water the fertilizer in.
- A third alternative is to use a water-soluble fertilizer on your annuals. But the effects of a water-based fertilizer don't last nearly as long as with granular or timed-release fertilizer. That means you will need to fertilize much more often—which isn't going to be fun when temperatures and humidity levels begin to climb toward the stratosphere.
- Organic gardeners should mix compost liberally with the planting soil and nurture young seedlings with manure tea or compost tea (manure or compost soaked in water until it's the color of weak tea, then strained). Use either of these liquid "teas" in place of the

transplant solution, and then apply it around young plants twice a month.

PROBLEMS

Aphids. Watch out for aphids (tiny, pear-shaped insects) on new growth. If there are only a few, knock them off with a blast of water from the hose. If there are more than a few, spray them with insecticidal soap. Repeat every five days until they're gone.

Cutworms. When plants are cut off at ground level, suspect cutworms. Paper or cardboard collars around the stems can help. So does a sprinkling of Bt.

MAY

Annuals

PLANNING

Go visiting. Visit several garden centers to get an idea of the variety of annuals available—colors, types, and sizes that you may not have expected. Branch out a bit. Try something new to you. You may be delightfully surprised.

Keep records. It's a busy time in the garden, but you'll be happy later that you took time to write down this year's last-frost date. While you have your garden notebook open, why not note the total rainfall for each month?

PLANTING

Hide and seek. As spring-flowering bulbs begin to fade, plant annuals in front of them to hide browning foliage.

Overwintered annuals. If the cuttings you took of overwintered annuals have enough roots, pot them up and move them outdoors, gradually getting them acclimated to the weather outside. (See page 38.) You may want to toss away the original plant. But you also can cut it back and plant in the garden, being sure the roots are loosened from the soil ball and not growing round and round it.

Portable gardens. Sometimes containers filled with flowers supplement a garden's in-ground beds and borders, and sometimes—in the case of condo dwellers—it may be the only way you can grow flowers at all. Choose containers that have drainage holes in the bottom or that you can easily drill holes in. Plastic pots and large containers will require less watering than small containers and clay pots. If you don't have room to bring containers indoors in freezing weather, consider some of the new clay-look pots made from lightweight materials. They aren't harmed by being left outdoors, as terra cotta may be.

To plant your containers:

1 Scrub all previously used pots with soap and water and then rinse with a mixture of 1 part bleach to 9 parts water. Let stand for thirty minutes, and then rinse with clear water.

2 Hose all clay pots with water until they're wet.

3 Put a piece of screening or a coffee filter over the drainage hole to prevent the potting mix from washing out during watering. Do *not* put gravel, rocks, or pieces of broken pots in the bottom. University tests have shown they do not help drainage and can harm plants.

4 Add water to a commercial potting mix so that it's wet all the way through. Mix the soil with a water-holding polymer if it doesn't contain one. Follow directions carefully and don't use more than the instructions indicate. (Although a bit pricey, water-holding polymers will double the normal time between waterings, and most last for about five years.)

5 Fill the container half full of the potting mix. If you're using a very large container, it's all right to use garden soil for the bottom one-fourth. It will give weight to the container and lessen the cost.

6 Mix the rest of the soil (still in its bag or in a wheelbarrow) with timed-release fertilizer such as Osmocote®.

7 Add enough so the planter is about two-thirds full and begin arranging the annuals on top—all one color or several complementary colors. Place taller specimens in the back or center and trailing plants around the edges.

8 Fill in with soil around the plants, making sure they're at the same level that they grew before.

Water until it drains through the bottom, mixing fertilizer with the water if you didn't use timed-release fertilizer pellets.

For successful annuals, pay careful attention to watering in the early part of the growing season. Stick your finger an inch or two into the soil. If you don't feel moisture, water.

 CARE

More mulch. If the weather has warmed up to at least 60 degrees Fahrenheit day and night in your part of the region, begin adding to the mulch in your flower beds. You don't want to apply mulch too soon; that will keep the soil cool. Warm soil encourages annuals to take off. Your eventual goal is 2 to 3 inches of fine bark or 3 inches of pine straw. Don't pile the mulch right up against the stems, but keep it about an inch away.

Inside out. In the warmer parts of our area, it's fine to gradually move the over-wintered tropical plants you grew as annuals back outdoors. **Angel's trumpet** is a good example. Do this over two weeks or so once the weather is reliably warm. Start by moving the plants to the shaded part of the porch, taking them back inside if nighttime temperatures threaten to fall below 50 degrees Fahrenheit. Then gradually move them into more sun.

 WATERING

For successful annuals, pay careful attention to watering in the early part of the growing season. Stick your finger an inch or two into the soil. If you don't feel moisture, water.

If you have spots in your yard that are difficult for you to water, consider planting annuals that can tolerate soil on the dry side once they've gotten established. These include **celosia, cosmos, globe amaranth, melampodium, moss rose, snow-on-the-mountain**, and **sunflower**.

 FERTILIZING

If you used a timed-release fertilizer when you planted, you won't have to worry about fertilizer for some time. If you applied a water-soluble plant food instead, use it again about every three weeks for plants in beds. Exceptions are plantings of **cosmos, globe amaranth**, and **melampodium**, which don't like much fertilizer. Use a water-soluble plant food on all container-grown annuals twice this month.

PROBLEMS

Yellow leaves may be the result of many problems—from too much or too little water to insect damage. But when **Madagascar periwinkle** develops yellow leaves when nighttime temperatures drop below 50 degrees Fahrenheit, it's just telling you that it's cold. The problem will clear up when the weather warms up. But in the meantime, you're stuck with those awful-looking leaves. Don't worry. There's a quick cure. Buy a small bottle of chelated iron at a garden center, mix a tablespoon of it with a gallon of tepid water, and sprinkle over the plants. That will green them up shortly.

JUNE

Annuals

 PLANNING

What to do with the pansies? Up until now, the pansies you planted last fall have probably looked great. But **pansies** generally don't do well in hot weather. Before the end of the month in most of the area, **pansies** will decline. They'll need to be removed and replaced by other annuals. But the gardener is faced with several problems in that scenario: The selection of annuals at garden centers can be small in late June. The only available bedding plants may be in 4-inch pots, which cost more than six-packs. If you can find six packs, the plants in them may have become rootbound. Besides, plants that are set out once hot weather has arrived are going to need quite a bit of watering. The bottom line? Make a note in your garden notebook to remind yourself to replace **pansies** by the end of May next year, even if they look wonderful at that moment.

If you want to plant **zinnia** seed outdoors again next month, don't plant your entire supply.

 PLANTING

It's not too late to plant any and all annual bedding plants, no matter which part of the region you live in. Visit a local nursery and add moss-lined hanging baskets of 'Wave' **petunias** to the porch and a wooden tub of **coleus** by the driveway, or plant a bed of **salvia** out by the mailbox to welcome guests and cheer the spirits of passersby.

Basket favors. Having a backyard barbecue? Buy small wooden baskets, line them with plastic, fill with moist potting soil, and add a **geranium** that's blooming like crazy. When your guests leave at the end of the evening, give them each a basket to take home.

Sowing seeds outdoors. Many annuals can be grown from seeds sown directly in the garden. This doesn't provide instant color, as bedding plants do, but it's inexpensive, it gives you a sense of accomplishment, and it's fun to do with children.

- The easiest annuals to sow outdoors are those with fairly large seeds and quick germination and growth rates. **Marigolds, sunflowers**, and **zinnias** are ideal for your first try.
- Prepare the soil just as you would for setting out bedding plants, but rake the surface so it's relatively smooth. See page 38 for directions.
- You can sow your flowers in rows or you can broadcast them—scatter the seeds about the whole area. When you sow in rows, it's easier to space them correctly and you can tell which are weed seeds that have germinated and which are your annuals. But the look is more formal. When you broadcast seeds, you will have to thin them and it will be easy to confuse flowers and young weeds. Experience is the best teacher in this case. To sow seeds outdoors:
- Read the seed packet for recommended spacing and follow it.
- Cover the seeds with an amount of soil to equal the diameter of the seed. Firm the soil (with a trowel or the back of a hoe) to ensure good contact between seeds and soil.
- Gently water the area.
- Keep the soil moist until most of the seeds germinate.
- Gradually cut back on watering as the plants begin to grow.
- Thin the flower bed—remove plants that are growing too thickly.
- Fertilize with a water-soluble fertilizer after the plants have two sets of true leaves.
- Remove weeds and then apply 2 inches of mulch.

 CARE

In cooler areas of the region, it's now time to move **angel's trumpet** and other tropical plants treated as annuals from the house where they've been overwintering back into the yard. Don't put them in full sun right away.

Because frequent watering washes nutrients out of hanging baskets and pots, feed them twice-monthly with a water-soluble plant food for flowering plants.

 # WATERING

How much? The rule of thumb for watering outdoor plants is to soak the soil whenever rainfall hasn't equaled an inch in the past week. A few annuals can get by with less, though. See the list on page 41. Water at ground level to avoid wetting the leaves when possible.

 # FERTILIZING

Except for plants listed on page 41 (which prefer little feeding), continue regular fertilizing. That works out to about *once a month* (with a granular or water-soluble product) for annuals in flower beds and *once a week* (with a liquid) for container-grown plants. If you used a timed-release fertilizer at planting time, you can skip additional fertilizer for beds and borders. But because frequent watering washes nutrients out of hanging baskets and pots, feed them twice-monthly with a water-soluble plant food for flowering plants.

GROOMING

Deadheading makes a big difference in how your annuals perform. Deadheading is just a gardening term for pinching off

faded flowers. Some plants, such as **Madagascar periwinkle** and **impatiens,** never need deadheading because the plants shed their dead blooms themselves. But many others—from **geraniums** to **petunias** to **marigolds**—must be deadheaded. One reason is that the plants will look better, of course. But removing dead flowers also keeps your plants blooming nonstop. Each time you water, or when you walk by your flowers, take a few moments to snap off old flower heads.

PROBLEMS

Japanese beetles. Do *not* put up traps to attract Japanese beetles. True, the traps may lure these pests away from your **roses** and **crapemyrtles**, but they will attract many more to your yard than would have come otherwise. And while many are caught in the traps, plenty others that aren't lay eggs in your yard, which stay over winter in your lawn or soil as grubs and then hatch the next spring to plague you again. Hand-pick Japanese beetles or spray them with a product that kills them on contact. (Your Extension Service office or favorite garden center can recommend organic as well as chemical controls.)

Powdery mildew is generally not a concern in June for **zinnias** unless it rains all month.

Weeds are no one's favorite subject, but it's easier to remove them when they're young than after they've grown larger and have more extensive root systems. Weeding also goes faster after a soil-soaking rain.

JULY

PLANNING

Say cheese! Get out the camera and fill it with film (or just charge up the battery if you've gone to a digital camera) and take lots of photographs. First of all, shoot your yard and what you planted— even if it doesn't look quite as good as you'd hoped (this step can help you improve next year). But also slip your camera into your pocket or purse so you can record ideas when you visit public gardens or see a commercial landscape that you really like. It's much easier to remember what impressed you if you have a photo to look at.

PLANTING

Continuous bloom. Zinnias are among the easiest flowers to grow from seed, and certain types of **zinnias** make excellent cut flowers to take indoors for arrangements. ('Cut and Come Again' is one variety that's tried and true.) But **zinnias** have a big fault—they mildew easily in times of high humidity or frequent rains. One way to have armloads of inexpensive cut flowers is to set up a little cutting garden for **zinnias** in a raised bed or on the edge of a vegetable garden. Prepare the soil, sow ten to fifteen seeds, and three weeks later, sow more. Cut the flowers soon after they bloom—in about four to six weeks. (That is usually before mildew has taken hold.) At the same time, make another small sowing of **zinnia** seeds. The second sowing should bloom three to four weeks after the first and the third crop a month after that. Not only are you provided with a continuous supply of cut flowers all summer, you generally avoid mildew problems because the plants are cut quickly. Space **zinnias** so there's room for air circulation between the plants and don't let water get on the plants' leaves.

CARE

After-storm care. Sometimes the ubiquitous "scattered thunderstorms" that seem ever-present in our weather forecasts this time of year will flatten an entire bed of taller annuals. Give them a day of sunny weather to see whether they recover on their own, then gently return the plants to an upright position. Some will need to be staked so they'll stay that way. You may want to stake very tall **sunflowers** now.

WATERING

Going on vacation? Ask a green-thumbed neighbor to keep an eye on your yard while you're gone. He or she can check your rain gauge to see whether your garden receives the needed inch of moisture during your absence and, if it doesn't, can then turn on your soaker hoses or drip irrigation. By this time of year, all container plants need to be watered daily. You may want to group them together and pay a neighborhood child to do the job.

FERTILIZING

Time for more. If you applied timed-release fertilizer to your flower beds in mid-April, now's the time for a second application if the product promised that it remained effective for three months. (Some last four to nine months.) Broadcast pellets on top of the soil according to package directions, and water well. Sprinkle with a thin coating of mulch. That should take care of the fertilizing needs of annuals in beds until frost.

Check annuals that don't usually require much fertilizer (see page 41). If they're healthy and growing, there's still no need to feed them. But if they don't look as good as they should, give them a drink of a water-soluble fertilizer such as Super Bloom®.

Containers. Since constant watering washes fertilizer from the soil, pot-grown plants need feeding more often than annuals growing in beds. Weekly fertilizing with a water-soluble food is a good idea from now through the middle of September. You can also reapply timed-release fertilizer pellets now to give your container-grown annuals an extra boost. If you do, you can stop using a liquid plant food for the next month.

Wet the soil first. Spreading granular fertilizer (such as 10-10-10) around parched plants can burn them. To avoid this, make sure you water your plants well before you fertilize.

GROOMING

The benefits of pinching. Your **wax begonias** are blooming well, the plants are looking good—so why would anyone suggest that you pinch off the tips of the stems, maybe removing some of those flowers? It's one of those gardening techniques that isn't well understood. Many annuals—**coleus, geraniums, Madagascar periwinkle**, and **wax begonias** among them—tend to grow leggy (straight up instead of outward) if left to their own devices. Occasionally pinching off the tips of the stems encourages more bushy growth; a

Timely Tips

Be observant. Walk through the yard once a day—early morning and early evening are ideal times—and admire your handiwork. Check also for any problems—holes in leaves that may indicate insects, yellowing foliage, plants that aren't growing as well as they had previously. Most garden problems are resolved more quickly if they're caught early.

Cut flowers. Pick flowers early in the morning. Take a bucket or vase of water into the garden with you and cut the stems on an angle, using sharp pruners. See the list on page 41 for good cut-flower annuals.

fuller, more compact plant; and eventually, more flowers. If you don't believe it, pinch back one plant and don't pinch one of the same type growing next to it. When you assess their appearance at the end of the summer, you'll see a noticeable difference.

PROBLEMS

What is that bug? It's not helpful to you, your plants, or the environment to spray the minute you spy an insect. Take a few minutes to see what the insect is doing. Is it causing a great deal of damage, or has it just munched small holes in a couple of leaves? How many insects do you see? Are there just one or two, or are these insects covering the plants? Many insects are beneficial—they eat the "bad

bugs"—so you don't want to get rid of them. And some bugs eat a leaf or two and then move on. But if the damage is more than minor and the number of pests is increasing, get a description of the insect and the type of damage it's causing and check with the Extension Service or a knowledgeable garden center for advice on controlling them.

Typical pests on annuals include aphids, several kinds of beetles, caterpillars, cutworms, spider mites, slugs and snails, thrips, and whiteflies.

If **zinnia** or any other annual has developed powdery mildew, you have two choices: live with it or pull them up and get them out of the garden.

AUGUST

PLANNING

Relax and enjoy yourself. Buy a hammock, stretch it between two tall trees, and hop in. It's a good time to catch up on those gardening magazines that have been piling up as you worked in the yard all summer. You may want to read with scissors in hand. That way you can clip out articles you'd like to save, putting them in your garden notebook when you return to the house.

PLANTING

On the first day of August ... plant **zinnia** seeds to provide cut flowers during September. You'll need to keep the seeds moist and the plants well watered all month. You may want to choose **zinnias** in fall colors—orange, gold, and yellow—or, as usual, just grow your favorite colors or those that complement the walls and furnishings indoors. It's too late to plant seeds of anything else, except **marigolds**.

Kids bored? Grandchildren visiting? Let them help you plant **marigolds** in foam cups to take home with them if they live some distance away, or in a little flower bed of their own if they live nearby. Seeds sown near the beginning of the month should bloom by the end of September—sooner in warmer parts of the area and if temperatures remain high.

CARE

Check the mulch. Replenish organic mulches, if needed, so they're about 3 inches thick. On slopes, the best choice is pine straw. It won't wash away. On flat ground, use a fine-textured mulch such as pine bark mini-nuggets. They do a better job at holding moisture than mulches that have a coarse texture (large bark chunks, for instance). Avoid piling mulch up against the stems of your annuals—it can lead to rotting.

Out they go. Remove from the garden any annuals that are diseased or dying. Not only will the garden look better, but it may prevent the problem from spreading.

WATERING

Containers. By the time August rolls around, daily or twice-daily watering may be necessary for hanging baskets and other container-grown annuals.

How are you watering? You know that most annuals planted in beds need an inch of water weekly—either from rainfall or supplied by you. But you may not have given much thought to the most efficient way to provide the necessary moisture. The simplest and most common technique—standing over your plants with a hose—is not only time-consuming, but often means that plants may not receive enough water or receive an uneven supply from plant to plant, and that water is wasted because it runs off.

Now may be the time to consider drip irrigation or soaker hoses. The big advantages are that the water stays at the root level, where it's needed, and it doesn't wet the leaves, which can cause diseases.

1 **Soaker hoses** are relatively inexpensive and readily available at home stores, nurseries, and hardware stores. Many are made from recycled materials. They slowly deliver water at the root level, where it's most needed. They save water because it doesn't end up on walks, driveways, or the street. When new, soaker hoses may be a bit difficult to maneuver. But as you put them around your plants, just anchor them in place. Assume that soaker hoses will water the soil about 6 inches on each side of the hose.

2 **Drip irrigation.** Sometimes called "trickle irrigation," this system lets you custom-design water for all your

Remove from the garden any annuals that are diseased or dying. Not only will the garden look better, but it may prevent the problem from spreading.

flower beds. Water flows through flexible tubing and out of emitters. Some tubing already has the emitters installed, which is handy. But the spacing determined at the factory may or may not work well for what you grow, so many gardeners prefer to install their own emitters. It's more work, but it puts the water where you want it. Since emitters can clog up, it's worthwhile installing a filter to catch algae or dirt. Because of time and cost considerations, you may want to start with soaker hoses and see how you like them before investing in drip irrigation.

3 **Slow coverage.** The thing that you'll first notice about these systems is that they water very slowly. That's good because it prevents evaporation loss, but it means the hoses must be left on for at least an hour at a time or often for longer. About twenty-four hours after watering, insert a stick or pole into the soil to see whether the soil is damp at least 9 inches deep. If it is, you've watered the right length of time for annuals. If it isn't, leave the soaker hose or drip irrigation on longer the next time.

What about sprinklers? Use these on your lawn instead of your annuals. While sprinklers provide an even supply of water, and do it relatively quickly, they have two drawbacks in the flower garden. Instead of wetting just the soil, they wet everything they touch. And most flower beds are small or have an irregular shape. A sprinkler is likely to waste water by depositing it on walks, the driveway, or the street.

Water your plants automatically. It's easy with a timer. There are two types. Mechanical timers are inexpensive, easy to find, and can attach to your faucet. Set the timer to turn the water on and off, and the job will be done without any more effort on your part. Electronic timers are more expensive and must connect to your irrigation system but offer more flexibility. You can set an electronic timer to come on or turn off at different times on various days of the week.

FERTILIZING

Apply a water-soluble fertilizer weekly to container plants. Little other fertilizer should be needed if you were faithful about feeding earlier in the summer.

GROOMING

An easy way to keep your annuals looking great and blooming well is to

Timely Tip

Vinegar to the rescue. If drip irrigation emitters get clogged with calcium from hard water, soaking them in vinegar will dissolve it.

deadhead at least weekly and remove damaged leaves whenever you see them.

Cut back **petunias** that aren't blooming well or have grown leggy. They'll be reblooming well in two weeks.

If plants are knocked over by rain and winds, stake them back up. Or as a preventive measure, stake taller annuals that are prone to falling over.

PROBLEMS

Fungus diseases. Mildew—a white, powdery coating on leaves, stems, and sometimes blooms—and leaf spots are signs of fungal problems. It's easier to keep them from occurring than to get rid of them once they're present. Spraying a fungicide after the disease is present doesn't help; these products are only *preventive* measures. You can also sometimes control powdery mildew by cultural practices.

SEPTEMBER

PLANNING

What comes next? When annuals begin to fade, you may not worry about it if they're in out-of-the-way places. But when flower beds are in highly visible spots, you may want them to stay in tip-top shape until frost. Before removing annuals that have seen better days, plan ahead. Would you prefer to replace bedraggled annuals with **chrysanthemums** in full bloom or with **pansies**? You may want to use both—with **mums** in the middle back of the bed and **pansies** up front. Before you head for the garden center, though, decide which colors of **mums** or **pansies** will best complement the shades of the annuals already in the bed.

PLANTING

Pansies and ornamental cabbage. If you want to grow these wonderful cool-season plants over winter, get them into the ground as soon as they become available at nurseries. The more time they have for their roots to grow and become established before frost arrives, the better they'll weather the winter.

Going indoors for winter. If you have a sunroom, a greenhouse, or a sunny windowsill, you may want to save a few annuals to take indoors for winter.

• Good choices are **impatiens, wax begonias**, and **coleus**, all of which do well inside the house if they receive enough light. **Geraniums** often don't look great after a few months, but will survive to provide plants for next year.
• It's easiest to take indoors plants already growing in pots. But if you prefer, you can dig up small clumps of annuals and place them in pots. Do this in the first half of the month so that they become used to their new homes.
• Another method is to take 4-inch cuttings of some annuals around the first of the month, dip the ends in rooting hormone, and then place them in pots filled with packaged potting soil that's been moistened. Keep the soil damp until rooting takes place. Newly rooted cuttings will be small and manageable indoors if you don't have too much room.

Poppies. If you have an empty flower bed, scatter **poppy** seeds on top of the soil. They will germinate in the fall and then bloom in late spring.

CARE

Saving seeds. If your grandparents or great-grandparents were farmers or gardeners, they always collected seeds from their annuals and vegetables at the end of the growing season and saved those seeds from year to year. Today's gardener does it much less frequently because most of the plants we grow are hybrids—they are a cross between two plants of the same species. Seeds of hybrids don't "come true." That is, the plant that grows from a seed saved from a hybrid plant won't produce the same kind of plant. So know which of the plants you're growing are hybrids and don't save their seeds. To save seeds of non-hybrids:

• **Timing.** Start checking seeds a few weeks after the flowers fade. The seeds should feel dry. Watch out for seeds that blow away: Wait a day or two too long, and they'll be gone.
• **Which seeds?** Big seeds are easier to save than little ones.
• **Cleaning.** Separate the seeds from any chaff and spread the seeds over a piece of newspaper, a couple layers of paper towel, or a screen indoors where they'll be protected from the weather and humidity. Small seeds should be dry in seven to ten days.

Larger ones may take two weeks—or longer if they weren't completely dry when harvested.

• **Storage.** Place the seeds in a zipper-type plastic freezer bag or in a glass jar with a screw-on lid. Baby-food and Mason jars are excellent. Close the lids securely. Label the containers with the name of the flower and the date the seeds are being placed into storage. Place the containers in a refrigerator or freezer. You may also store them in an unheated garage, but watch out for fluctuating temperatures, which harm seeds.

# WATERING

Don't stop now. In some years, September is a wet month. Other times, it's dry. And it can be quite warm. So although the season is winding down, don't forget to water your annuals when rainfall has been less than an inch in the previous week, except for those that like to be kept on the dry side. (See page 41.) Container plants still need at least once-daily waterings. When they have plenty of moisture, your plants will reward you with continuous bloom and renewed vigor. Their beauty will be welcome if we have a long fall.

Avoid overhead watering of **zinnias**.

FERTILIZING

Use a transplant solution when setting out **pansies** and **ornamental cabbage** and **kale**. With **cabbage** and **kale**, mix granular fertilizer with the soil at the root level. On newly planted **pansies**, use a water-soluble fertilizer each week until frost. A high-phosphorus fertilizer (usually one that has "bloom" in the name) is best for **pansies**. It will encourage flowering now and bud production for later blooms.

GROOMING

Little things count. Pinch off those yellow, brown, or damaged leaves. Snip off the faded flowers. Your plants will look better and perform better too.

The first of the month, pinch back **ageratum** so it will make a comeback with September's cooler temperatures.

# PROBLEMS

Spider mites. It's easy to mistake these tiny pests for dust on the undersides of leaves. But when leaves begin to look speckled, spotted, and yellowed—and the weather's been dry—suspect spider mites. To be sure, hold a sheet of white paper beneath the foliage and tap a leaf. Mites will fall onto the paper and crawl about a bit. Prevention is best—regular watering during dry weather. But a blast from the hose underneath the leaves each day for a week may clear up the problem. Or try ladybugs and lacewings—both are predators of spider mites. If you turn to chemicals, be sure to buy a miticide. Since spider mites are not insects, general insecticides have no effect on them.

Mites are not plant-specific. They attack anytime the weather is hot and dry. At the end of the season, around the first of September, when plants may be a bit stressed, they're fairly common.

Weeds. The end of the season seems like a good excuse to give up and learn to live with weeds. After all, frost will kill them soon. But frost won't make a difference if the weeds are allowed to go to seed. The old rule holds true: Seeds one year, weeds eight years.

OCTOBER

Annuals

 PLANNING

Find out when the first frost of fall usually occurs in your area. Then make a note each year of the date it occurs in *your yard*. You may also want to write down those spots that freeze sooner or much later than the rest of the yard. And keep a record of which plants withstand a couple of freezes. Sometimes this is because the plant itself withstands the cold, and sometimes it's because the location is protected. It's a handy thing to know. (The maps on pages 22 and 23 gives you an idea of when the date is getting close.)

Watch out for frost. As your area's first frost approaches, listen closely to the local weather forecast each night. Often the first frost is a light one and another may not occur for several weeks afterward. It's a shame to lose your annuals when they can continue blooming for several weeks longer.

• Don't cover plants with plastic. When the sun comes up and hits it the next morning, it will burn the plants beneath the plastic.
• Old bedspreads, mattress pads, and quilts provide good protection and don't have to be removed until the day has warmed up.

• Some gardeners use non-woven landscape fabrics for frost protection. Since they come in rolls, they're handy. But they may not provide more than 2 to 4 degrees of protection. If the temperature falls below 28 degrees Fahrenheit, the plants can be harmed. Consider applying a double thickness in the afternoon to capture the warmth that's already in the soil and around the plant. Also experiment with different brands if you like to protect plants from frost in fall and spring.

 PLANTING

Winter annuals. In our part of the country, **pansies** and **ornamental cabbage** and **kale** have become outdoor decorating "fixtures" in the landscape. Plant as early in the month as possible.

• The **cabbage** and **kale** may not make it all the way through winter, but are unusual enough that they're worth planting even if they last only till January. Place them where you need a bold accent but where they won't be missed if they're removed.
• **Pansies** can grow in sun or partial shade. They look much better over winter when spaced closely—about 4 inches apart. From planting until

frost, fertilize weekly with a liquid fertilizer made for flowering plants.
• Firm soil gently around both kinds of plants so they won't be heaved out of the ground as the soil freezes and then thaws.
• Water thoroughly.
• Mulch with 2 to 3 inches of organic material for protection from the cold.

CARE

Inside or out? If you have pots of annuals that will spend the winter indoors—**geraniums, impatiens, scaveola**, and **wax begonias** will do fine as long as there's enough light—take them in right away. It's harder for the plants to become acclimated when they've been used to temperatures in the 40-degree range and all of a sudden are placed where it's 70 degrees Fahrenheit.

Don't remove **snapdragons** or **annual dianthus (pinks)** from the garden at the end of the season. They will often live through the winters in our region, becoming perennials instead of annuals. Both begin blooming early in spring. Even when **snapdragons** get killed by a bad winter, they often come back from seed.

If some plants had serious fungus problems during the growing season, it may be a good idea to remove the mulch from the bed in which these plants grew and replace it with shredded leaves or other fresh mulch.

You may cut down **sunflowers** now or leave them up for the birds.

 WATERING

Has the rain been sufficient? If October rainfall dips below an inch a week, water **pansies** and **ornamental cabbage** and **kale** deeply so they don't dry out. Do the same for any annuals that continue to grow and bloom until they're cut down by frost.

 FERTILIZING

Rule of thumb. Plants need fertilizer only when they're growing or flowering. So which annuals—indoors or out—fit that criterion this month? Those are the ones you want to fertilize sometime in October. If annuals taken indoors have gotten used to their new surroundings and have begun to grow vigorously, they could use a light feeding, too.

 GROOMING

Do they stay, or do they go? Your yard will usually look nicer if you cut down and remove frost-killed annuals. But you may want to consider leaving a few with large seeds—**sunflowers**, **marigolds**, and **zinnias**, for instance—because they attract birds to the garden in the fall and winter.

Encourage reseeding. Some plants— such as **cleome, cosmos**, and **four-o'clocks**—reseed readily. So don't disturb the soil too much when removing these plants; that way, the seeds will germinate next spring and provide you with free plants.

Discourage fungus diseases. If some plants had serious fungus problems during the growing season, it is a good idea to remove the mulch from the bed in which these plants grew and replace it with shredded leaves or other fresh mulch. Otherwise, the fungus is likely to overwinter in the old mulch and become a problem again next summer.

PROBLEMS

Watch out for bugs. Sometimes insects or their eggs hitchhike into the house in pots of overwintering annuals. Keep an eye out for these intruders, and spray weekly with insecticidal soap until the insects are gone.

PLANNING

Don't wait till next year. Take time now to evaluate what you really liked about your annual garden this past season and what you think could be improved. What did you learn that you don't want to forget? Write all that down in your garden notebook because, while we always think we'll remember, sometimes we don't. If you didn't start a garden notebook earlier in the year, it's not too late. If your garden notebook is getting full, maybe it's time to look for another—or to request one as a gift next month.

Expansion. If you have time, consider a bed of specialty annuals next year—flowers just for cutting, for example, or for drying (such as **cockscomb, globe amaranth**, decorative-type **sunflowers**, and **zinnias**). These could be placed in an out-of-the-way spot where it wouldn't matter how they looked when you harvested the plants. Raised beds are excellent for projects such as this because they require no bending over and they produce few if any weeds.

 PLANTING

Hurry. As long as the ground isn't frozen, it's not too late to plant **pansies** and **ornamental cabbage** and **kale**. Firm the soil around the roots of the plants; you don't want to leave air pockets that can lead to frozen roots. And be sure to mulch well after planting.

 CARE

Empty containers. After annuals fade and are removed from the containers they grew in all summer, what do you do? Much depends on the type of container—particularly the material it's made from—and how much storage space you have.

- **Leave them in place.** This is the easiest solution—provided your pots are *not* clay or terra cotta (which may be harmed by temperatures below freezing) and that no neighborhood cats decide the pots make excellent litter boxes. Unless a clay container is unusual, or large and expensive, you may still decide to leave it outdoors all winter, figuring it's easier to replace it if it cracks, especially if it's several years old.

- **Out goes the soil.** An alternative is to remove the soil and turn the containers upside down. You have several options of what to do with the soil: To reuse for next year, place it in clean garbage cans or in heavy-duty plastic garbage bags. You may also spread it in 8-inch mounds around the bases of rosebushes, to protect them from low temperatures. Or use the soil to fill low places in the yard.

- **Clean up the pots.** Once you've emptied the containers, it's okay to put them in storage after you've let them stay outdoors long enough to dry completely. But that means you'll have to clean the pots next spring before you use them again—and there are so many other things you'll want to be doing in the garden then. You probably have more time on a warmish November day. So fill a tub with soapy water that's been mixed with 1 part household bleach to 9 parts water. Dip or soak pots in it (depending on their size and how dirty they are), then scrub, inside and out, with a stiff brush. Rinse with clear water and let dry. Store out of the weather, and the containers will be ready to replant next spring when you're raring to get going again with annuals.

If you didn't start a garden notebook earlier in the year, it's not too late. If your garden notebook is getting full, maybe it's time to look for another—or to request one as a gift next month.

 # WATERING

How often? Annuals brought into the house for the winter won't need watering as frequently as they did when they were living outdoors. Since you don't want to overwater them, it's best to check the soil. First, look to see whether the surface is damp. If so, wait another day or two. Second, stick your finger into the soil. If you can't feel moisture 1 inch deep into the soil, it's time to water.

Don't forget. If rainfall has been less than usual and the ground isn't frozen, your **pansies** and **ornamental cabbage** and **kale** may need to be watered. Don't let them wilt. Check to see whether seed-sown hardy annuals such as **poppies** have sprouted and need watering.

 # FERTILIZING

Indoors. Annuals that you're overwintering inside the house will need little if any fertilizer from now until spring. That's especially true if light levels aren't equal to six hours of daily sun. But annuals that do receive quite a bit of light may be actively growing. If so, fertilize them lightly with a water-soluble plant food once a month.

Outside. In November, Kentucky and Tennessee typically have periods of weather when the ground freezes and also warmer days. As long as the soil isn't frozen, you may want to give **pansies** a drink of a fertilizer made for blooming plants. Twice during the month is about right. This encourages flower bud production for the next spell of warmer winter weather. It's not necessary to feed **ornamental cabbage** and **kale**.

 # GROOMING

Off with their heads! Dead flower heads, that is. Don't let faded flowers remain on annuals growing indoors. Also pick off damaged or yellowing leaves. On a nice day when you'd like some outdoor exercise, do the same for **pansies** and **ornamental cabbage** and **kale** that you have planted in the yard.

Garden cleanup. It's not too late to remove dead annuals from the garden if you were too busy to do it earlier. This improves the yard's appearance and eliminates places for insects and diseases to overwinter.

 ## Timely Tip

A blanket for your flower beds. If you spread pine straw or several inches of other organic mulch over your annual beds and borders, you'll keep the soil from washing away and help prevent weeds from getting a foothold.

 # PROBLEMS

Too little light. Annuals or cuttings brought indoors for the winter need strong bright light. If they begin to grow leggy—as though they're reaching for the light—they may need to be moved to a sunnier window or even placed under grow lights.

DECEMBER

 PLANNING

Bedtime reading. Life is so hectic in December that you may not have much time to think about gardening—except for making sure that family members know about a few must-have items you're dying to receive as gifts. But a good way to relax is to pile gardening magazines and books by your bedside and read for a little while each evening before you fall asleep. There's something about being transported to warm weather and beautiful surroundings that makes the stress melt away.

 PLANTING

Get ready for next year. If you like to grow annuals from seeds, get your supplies ready. Make sure you have plenty of clean flats or other containers. Also add any equipment that you think will help: grow lights or heavy-duty fluorescent light fixtures and heating cable. If you had problems finding bags of seed-starting mix last winter and had to settle for regular potting mix, check recent catalogs to see whether any is offered. Or put in a call to a garden center; they'll order some for you. Many annuals may be grown from seed. Some take longer to grow than others. The easiest are **marigolds, four-o'clocks, sunflowers**, and **zinnias**.

 CARE

Give your plants a shower. The humidity inside most homes is low. And that sometimes leads to spider mites' attacking annuals that are overwintering indoors. One way to prevent the mites and clean off your plant at the same time is to take small containers to a sink and spray them with water. Larger plants may need to be placed in the shower.

 WATERING

All plants need water. It's up to the gardener to make sure that plants get the right amount of water.

- Outdoors, with **pansies**, it's easy. If the ground isn't frozen and precipitation hasn't equaled an inch in the previous week, soak the soil around the plants until it's moist to a depth of 6 inches.
- For plants growing in pots, feel the soil to find out whether it's wet or dry—and then water accordingly.

 FERTILIZING

A vacation from feeding. Few annuals will need fertilizing in December, but you might give **pansies** a liquid plant food for flowering plants during a warm spell.

 Timely Tip

Save your cooled fireplace ashes in the basement or garage (or outdoors in a container that has a lid). You can use them next spring or summer to deter slugs. Place a ring of wood ashes around annuals; slugs don't like to slither across the ashes.

 GROOMING

Pinching time. When annuals have been indoors a couple of months, they often develop lanky growth because of low light levels. Pinch the tips of the stems back so the plants will develop a more compact shape. Or accomplish two goals at once—pinch off cuttings 4 inches long and root them. Then your current plants are bushier, and you'll have more plants to set outside next spring.

PROBLEMS

Persistent insects. After you've sprayed insects found on overwintering annuals indoors with insecticidal soap, you may find that it's necessary to treat several more times—maybe twice weekly for three weeks.

CHAPTER TWO

Bulbs

Spring simply wouldn't seem like spring without the beauty of bulbs—sunshiny daffodils, jewel-toned tulips, fragrant hyacinths. But as glorious as the show is, it would be a shame to confine it to spring.

Bulbs—and their beautiful kin—make wonderful year-round residents in our yards. Native **crested irises** welcome spring to our woodlands. The giant leaves of **elephant ear** attract attention in the summer garden. **Siberian** and **bearded irises, lilies**, and **dahlias** give us welcome flowers in spring, summer, and fall. **Amaryllis** makes quite a colorful and dramatic statement indoors in the dreary days of winter.

You may be thinking: "I didn't know **irises** or **dahlias** were bulbs." Well, they are—and they aren't. In the gardening world—and in this book— plants that grow from underground storage organs are generally lumped together as "bulbs" although some are really corms, tubers, or rhizomes. We'll help you make sense of the differences, but you may just want to think of them as spring-flowering and summer-flowering. That reminds you when they bloom and therefore when they need to be planted (the season before they flower).

A true bulb is egg-shaped. It is composed primarily of scales, which are storage tissue. Inside the scales—and in the center of the bulb—is a pointed shoot, which contains the preformed leaves and flower stalk. Anchoring all this is the base, from which the roots grow. It's called the basal plate. Most spring-flowering bulbs are enclosed in a dry papery skin known as a tunic, which protects the scales. Because **lilies** lack this protective covering, they dry out more easily and are more easily damaged when out of the ground.

True bulbs include **allium, amaryllis, daffodil, Dutch iris, fritillaria, glory-of-the-snow, grape hyacinth, hyacinth, tulip**, and **wood hyacinth**.

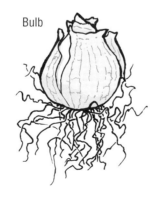
Bulb

A corm appears to be a flattened version of the bulb. It has the same scales (although reduced in size), tunic, or covering, and basal plate from which the roots grow. It has several buds—called eyes—poking up on the top of the corm. **Crocus, crocosmia**, and **gladiolus** are corms.

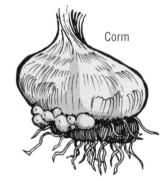
Corm

A rhizome is generally long and oval. It's actually an underground stem and lacks a papery covering. Roots grow from the bottom and shoots from buds on

Rhizome

Bulbs

the top and sides, usually at one end. Examples of rhizomes are **bearded iris, canna, lily-of-the valley** (see the **Perennials** chapter) and **water lily** (discussed in the **Water Gardens** chapter).

A **tuber** is enlarged stem tissue and is either cylindrical and flattened or an odd shape, making it difficult to tell the top from the bottom. You may have to look carefully to find the buds (eyes) from which the shoots grow. **Caladium, dahlia, lotus** (see the **Water Gardens** chapter), and **potatoes** are tubers.

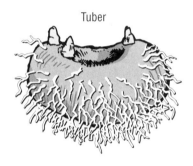

Tuber

BUYING BULBS

- Quality and size count. Big bulbs are worth the extra money you pay for them. The size of the bulb determines the size and number of flowers and the overall vigor of the plants. Bulbs sold individually are generally larger and of higher quality than those sold in mesh bags as a mixture.

- Look for bulbs that show no signs of damage or disease (which cause them to feel soft or look mildewed). Don't worry if the tunic or covering is loose; that doesn't usually matter.

WHEN YOU GET THE BULBS HOME

When you buy summer-flowering bulbs, tubers, or rhizomes, it's usually just before you're going to plant them. But often we purchase spring-flowering bulbs, months before we're ready to plant them or can get around to it. How the bulbs are stored in the interim can make a big difference in how they perform in your garden.

Spring-flowering bulbs require three periods of alternating temperatures in order to bloom—the warmth of summer, the coolness of fall and winter, and finally, the warmth of spring. If they miss ten weeks of chilly temperatures in the fall (twelve or more weeks for **tulips**), they won't bloom well. The best things you can do when you bring your bulbs home are:

- Keep them cool. The ideal storage temperatures are 50 to 60 degrees Fahrenheit. That's not always easy to find early in fall, so put them wherever it's coolest.

- If you know you're going to keep **tulips** for a month or more before planting, place them in a refrigerator. That will give them a head start on the cooling period they need. But keep bulbs—especially **tulips**—away from **apples** and ripening fruit, which give off a gas that harms the bulbs.

WHERE TO PLANT BULBS

"Anywhere you have a spot" is the easy answer.

- Some bulbs bloom nicely in shade (for example, **arum, caladium, crested iris**, and **Spanish bluebell**).
- Some bulbs produce tall plants for the back of the flower border (**canna, elephant ear, giant allium**, and some **dahlias**).
- Some bulbs naturalize well, so they can be planted in the lawn or scattered on the edge of a woodland of deciduous trees (**crocus, daffodil, glory-of-the-snow, grape hyacinth, spring snowflake**, and **windflower**).
- Small bulbs grow well in rock gardens (**crocus, dwarf daffodils, glory-of-the-snow, grape hyacinth**, and **spring snowflake**).

Bulbs

- It's fun to see spring-flowering bulbs poking up through evergreen ground covers.
- Both spring- and summer-flowering bulbs are suitable for containers, but they can be harmed by winter temperatures.

Light

Most summer-flowering bulbs, rhizomes, and tubers—including **bearded iris**, which is a rhizome that flowers in spring—prefer a sunny location. **Caladiums** like partial to full shade. **Blackberry lily, elephant ear,** and **Siberian iris** will grow in light shade.

The majority of spring-flowering bulbs prefer mostly sunny locations, although in our climate they appreciate shade in the middle of the day. Those that do fine in shade are listed on page 56 under where to plant bulbs. But even spring-flowering bulbs that need sun can be planted in the shade of deciduous trees since those spots will be sunny from late fall through mid-spring.

Preparing the Soil

The one thing that bulbs must have is well-drained soil. If they stay too wet, they're likely to rot. With all the clay soil in this region, it's not always easy to find spots that have good drainage.

Often we must improve drainage by mixing the soil with compost, fine bark, or other organic matter. That's why you're likely to be disappointed in the results if you just dig a hole, drop in a bulb, and then replace the original soil on top of the bulb.

The soil's pH also affects bulb success. A soil in the range of 6 to 7 is recommended. Have your soil tested to be sure, or buy a little kit at the garden center and test the pH yourself.

When to Plant

The chart on pages 59 to 61 gives the time of year to plant spring- and summer-flowering bulbs. In fall, don't be too fast to get the bulbs you've bought into the ground. They'll do better if you wait till the temperature of the soil is below 60 degrees Fahrenheit.

How to Plant Spring-Flowering Bulbs

If you're planting just a few bulbs, you'll probably want to dig individual holes with a trowel, a shovel, or—for spring-flowering bulbs only—a sturdy bulb-planting tool. The chart on pages 59 to 61 gives the depth to plant each kind of bulb and also recommends how far apart to space them.

If you plant lots of spring bulbs—and that's how they look their best, in groups of one hundred—you'll find it easier to dig a bed.

1 Make it 8 inches deep or at least 1 inch deeper than the recommended planting depth of the bulbs you're planting. (I always plant **tulips** 12 inches deep. It seems to keep them coming back many more years than they would otherwise.)

2 Place the soil on the driveway or on a tarp.

3 Loosen the soil on the bottom of the bed, and till in some Nature's Helper™ or other fine bark and the amount of Bulb Booster™ fertilizer recommended on the package. (If you can't find Bulb Booster™, use 8-8-8 granular fertilizer.)

4 Space the bulbs in the bed according to the suggestions on pages 59 to 61.

5 Mix the soil removed from the hole with $1/4$ to $1/2$ organic matter and replace half of it over the bulbs.

6 Water thoroughly.

7 Add the remainder of the soil.

8 Water again.

9 Mulch with 2 to 3 inches of shredded leaves, pine straw, or other fine mulch.

Bulbs

Planting summer bulbs. Summer bulbs are usually planted much as perennials are. See directions on page 184 (in the **Perennials** chapter) and also individual instructions for **dahlia, caladium**, and **iris** on pages 66, 68, and 69.

DETERRING WILDLIFE DAMAGE

It's a sad fact of gardening life that deer, chipmunks, and other rodents may treat your bulb beds as banquet tables. You have several options:

- Plant **daffodils**, which aren't bothered by wildlife since the bulbs are poisonous to them. Other bulbs that usually aren't bothered include **crown imperial, grape hyacinths, hyacinths, snowdrops, Spanish bluebells**, and **spring snowflakes**. (Please note the word "usually" in the previous sentence. It often depends both on how hungry the animals are and on location—deer in one part of the area will completely avoid a particular plant that's a favorite of deer in another location.)
- Spray or soak your bulbs with a wildlife repellent before planting. Spray again after leaves appear.
- Use chicken wire around or over the bulbs.

FERTILIZING

Summer-flowering bulbs are fertilized as perennials are—when they're planted and then at intervals throughout the growing season (as noted in the month-by-month listings in this chapter).

Spring-flowering bulbs are fertilized in fall and (depending on what kind of fertilizer you used) possibly again in late winter or very early spring.

If a spring-flowering bulb contains everything it needs inside it to grow and produce a flower, why should you fertilize?

1 It improves the quality of the flowers.

2 It helps the bulbs perennialize, or return for several years.

Timing matters. Do *not* fertilize when the bulbs bloom or shortly afterward. Bulbs need the nutrients that fertilizer supplies only when they're growing—and bulbs begin growing in autumn and stop when they've produced a flower stalk. If you fertilize a bulb in spring, when it has stopped growing, you have wasted your money.

If you use Bulb Booster™ or another slow-release fertilizer (such as an organic fertilizer), mix it into the soil when planting or (for bulbs that were planted in previous years) spread it on top of the soil in early autumn—and that's it. If you spread 8-8-8 in fall, apply it again (1 tablespoon per 100 square feet) when the shoots of the plants are an inch high.

Why not bone meal? Bone meal isn't made the way it was in the past and no longer contains all the nutrients that bulbs need. It may also cause dogs and other animals to dig in the area where it's applied.

Indoor bulbs, too. If you love bulbs outdoors, you'll enjoy them indoors, too. See pages 82 and 83 for directions on growing **crocus, daffodils, hyacinths**, and **tulips** in pots in the house.

Whether they're indoors or outside, bulbs are some of the most rewarding flowers you can grow. And most of them are simple enough for children to grow. But the best reason of all to plant spring-flowering bulbs, in particular, is that their arrival announces that warm weather is truly on its way. After a long winter, it's a welcome message, provided by some of the loveliest flowers imaginable.

Bulbs

Spring-Flowering Bulbs

Common Name (*Botanical Name*)	When to Plant	Planting Depth* (Inches)	Spacing (Inches)	Comments
Allium (*Allium* species)	Fall	5 to 8	3 to 10	*Allium giganteum* has 5-inch purple flowers atop 5-foot stems in June. Very impressive.
Arum (*Arum italicum*)	Early fall	5	12	Silver-veined leaves appear in fall and remain until June. Flower spathes appear in late spring, followed by stalks of reddish-orange berries. Likes moist soil.
Crocus (*Crocus* species and hybrids)	Fall	5	1	Flowers close each night and on cloudy days, and open in sunshine. Will bloom through snow.
Crown imperial (*Fritillaria imperialis*)	Early fall	8	12	Has an unusual bloom that generates much favorable comment. Some people don't like its odor. Prefers poor soil.
Daffodil, Jonquil (*Narcissus* species and hybrids)	Fall	8 (large bulbs); 5 (small bulbs)	3 to 5	If you have deer or vole problems, this is the bulb for you—they are ignored by wildlife. These bulbs return year after year, and most are fragrant.
Dutch iris (*Iris* x *hollandica*)	Fall	5	4	Needs well-drained soil. A wonderful cut flower. Grasslike leaves appear soon after planting and last all winter. May not always be hardy in zone 6.
Glory-of-the-snow (*Chionodoxa* species)	Fall	5	2 to 3	Very early bloomer. Nice for borders.
Grape hyacinth (*Muscari* species and hybrids)	Fall	5	1 to 3	Some have true-blue flowers, a color that's hard to find. Doesn't like wet soil.
Hyacinth (*Hyacinthus orientalis*)	Fall	6	4	Very fragrant. They have a formal appearance. Size of the bulb determines the size of the flowers. Doesn't like heavy soil.
Snowdrop (*Galanthus nivalis*)	Fall	5	2	Very early bloomer. Will perennialize in fertile, moist soil.

Bulbs

Spring-Flowering Bulbs

Common Name (*Botanical Name*)	When to Plant	Planting Depth* (Inches)	Spacing (Inches)	Comments
Spanish bluebell (*Hyacinthoides hispanica*)	Fall	5	3 to 6	Lovely blue flowers. Grows in partially shady spots. Good choice for the woodland garden.
Spring snowflake (*Leucojum vernum*)	Fall	5	3	Flowers will remind you of lily-of-the-valley.
Tulip (*Tulipa* species and hybrids)	Fall	8 to 12	2 to 4	Tulips almost have it all—they are available in numerous colors, sizes, and shapes (parrots and doubles are dramatic). Try early, midseason, and late tulips for a long blooming period. But they're favorites of deer and don't return reliably.
Windflower (*Anemone blanda*)	Fall	5	2	Daisylike flowers in violet, blue, white and shades of pink.

*Planting depth is measured to the **base** of the bulb.

Summer Bulbs, Spring- and Summer-Flowering Rhizomes, and Corms

Common Name (*Botanical Name*)	When to Plant	Planting Depth* (Inches)	Spacing (Inches)	Comments
Blackberry lily (*Belamcanda chinensis*)	Spring	2	9 to 12	Flowers are followed by seedpods that open to show shiny black seeds. Will grow in light shade. Each flower lasts one day.
Caladium (*Caladium bicolor*)	Late spring	2	12 to 16	Grown for their spectacular foliage, caladiums really shine in the shade. But they need hot days and warm nights to grow well.
Canna (*Canna* species and hybrids)	Spring, summer	4 to 6	10 to 30	Cannas add height and boldness to the garden. Look for new cultivars with dramatic foliage—yellow-and-pink striped, for instance.

Bulbs

Summer Bulbs, Spring- and Summer-Flowering Rhizomes, and Corms

Common Name (*Botanical Name*)	When to Plant	Planting Depth* (Inches)	Spacing (Inches)	Comments
Crocosmia (*Crocosmia* x *crocosmiiflora*)	Spring, summer	4 to 10	4 to 6	In Zone 6, plant 8 to 10 inches deep. 'Lucifer' is the hardiest cultivar. Blooms from midsummer on.
Dahlia (*Dahlia* cultivars)	Late spring to early summer	8	8 to 36	If you know how to grow tomatoes, you'll have no problems with dahlias, since they're grown much the same. A constant supply of moisture is necessary during the summer.
Elephant ear (*Colocasia esculenta*)	Late spring	6 to 8	18 to 36	What a statement elephant ear makes in the garden, with leaves up to 2 feet long and at least 18 inches wide. Some have red foliage. Moisture is a must.
Gladiolus (*Gladiolus* species and hybrids)	Spring through summer	4 to 6	3 to 4	You either love them or you don't. If you do, you can't imagine summer without the abundant and colorful blooms of glads.
Iris (*Iris* species and hybrids)	Spring through late August	Bearded and crested iris: Barely covered with soil. All others: 1 inch	4 to 18	There are so many kinds of irises; all are wonderful. Try the ones you haven't grown before.
Lily (*Lilium* species and hybrids)	Spring, fall	Asiatic: 6 to 7; Oriental: 2 to 3	14 to 18	Asiatic lilies bloom first; Oriental lilies flower later in the season.
Lily-of-the-valley (*Convallaria majalis*)	Spring, fall	1½	Pips: 4; Clumps: 12 to 24	Fragrant bell-shaped flowers; shade-loving.
Spider lily, Naked lady (*Lycoris* species)	Mid- to late summer	4 to 6	6 to 12	The leaves die down and then surprise! The flowers pop up as if by magic. Very slow to become established. May take two years from planting till bloom.

*Planting depth is measured to the **base** of the bulb.

JANUARY

 PLANNING

In one way, this is the most enjoyable time of the year for gardening. No, you can't get outside and do much, but you can dream and plan. As garden catalogs arrive, check out the new cultivars of summer flowers that grow from corms, rhizomes, and tubers. Where would you put a couple of **cannas** that are sporting gold-and-maroon-striped foliage? Is this the year you order all those **lilies** you've been admiring? Maybe you want to think about substituting **caladiums** for one of the usual shady beds of **impatiens**. Anything's possible in January. You're limited only by your imagination.

Write down bulb planting ideas in your garden journal. If you don't have a garden notebook, January is the perfect time to buy one. It will keep all your notes together in one place so you can refer to them in future years. Start by recording this month's temperature ups and downs, which can be considerable, and the amount of rainfall. Should **snow-drops** or **crocus** bloom this month—oh joy!—be sure to write down the dates they first flowered. It's interesting to look back and see how that varies from year to year.

 PLANTING

Is it too late? If for one reason or another, you never got around to planting your **tulips, daffodils**, and other spring-flowering bulbs, you can still plant them *as long as the soil isn't frozen*. Check them over to make sure they're still okay (they aren't soft, don't have any damaged spots, and don't have an odd odor), then get them in the ground. (See instructions on page 57.) January-planted bulbs will probably bloom later than those planted last fall or in previous years, but most should flower. **Tulips** that were *not* kept in a refrigerator are the most iffy, since they need three full months of cool temperatures in order to bloom. But even they should bloom next year.

Amaryllis bulbs (*Hippeastrum*), sometimes already potted, are often on sale in January. Pick up a couple in different colors. Choose named varieties if they're available. They'll be of higher quality than those identified only by flower color (red, white, pink, etc.).

- If the bulb is already potted, wet the potting mix thoroughly with tepid water and place the bulb in a warm spot (at least 70 degrees Fahrenheit) that does not receive direct sunlight. Don't water again until you see green shoots emerging from the bulb. Then move the plant into bright light and keep warm. **Amaryllis** prefers moist soil.
- For **amaryllis** bulbs that need to be potted up after you get them home, see page 82 for directions.

Pot up some **paper-white narcissus** for indoor growing, if you can find the bulbs. They really brighten the dreary days typical of January. (See pages 82 and 83 for directions.)

 CARE

Is that a bulb I see? Sometimes the cycle of warm days followed by below-freezing temperatures heaves bulbs out of the ground. If that happens, gently put them back into the hole, being careful to pack the soil around them (so there are no holes in the soil for cold air to get into). Then replace the mulch on top. Mulch moderates soil temperatures to help prevent effects from freezing and thawing. That's one reason mulch is recommended. Also, if a bulb should have been heaved up, it's still under 3 inches of mulch, which is fine protection.

Mulch. Check the mulch over and around your bulbs to make sure it's still 3 inches deep. Discarded Christmas trees make excellent mulch for bulbs—you can prune off limbs and place them over beds or just cut off needles.

Amaryllis. If your **amaryllis** is blooming, give it about four hours of sun daily, but avoid the noonday sun, which can burn the foliage and cause the blooms to wilt prematurely. The plant likes daytime temperatures about 70 degrees Fahrenheit and in the 60s at night. If you have the plant on a windowsill, be sure the straplike leaves don't touch the glass when outdoor temperatures are below freezing.

WATERING

Indoors. Don't let **paper-whites** dry out. Keep the soil around **amaryllis** moist but not soggy. Check bulbs that are being forced to make sure the soil stays moist.

Outdoors. No watering should be necessary outdoors since one of two things are typical for this month in Kentucky and Tennessee—rain or very cold temperatures that have frozen the ground.

FERTILIZING

Indoors. About every six weeks, fertilize **amaryllis** plants that have finished blooming with a regular houseplant fertilizer. Pots of spring-flowering bulbs purchased in bloom *don't* need plant food. Neither do **paper-whites** or bulbs that are being forced.

Outdoors. If you did *not* use a slow-release fertilizer on your spring-flowering bulbs last fall, keep an eye out for the first signs that the bulbs are coming up. When they're an inch above the ground, fertilize with 1 tablespoon of 8-8-8 fertilizer per 100 square feet of bed. If the ground isn't frozen, water the fertilizer in gently.

GROOMING

Remove the entire flower stalk after your **amaryllis** plant finishes blooming. Pinch off spent flowers from **paper-whites** and potted bulbs from the florist.

# PROBLEMS

What happened to my bulbs? The coldest part of winter is usually when mice and other wildlife begin to hunger after your bulbs. Keep an eye out this month and next for any signs that bulbs are being dug up. Temporary steps may help prevent further damage.

- Place chicken wire on top of the ground over bulbs to keep the squirrels or deer from digging into the area.
- If temperatures are above freezing and will remain that way for forty-eight hours and no precipitation is predicted, spray the ground and any shoots with Bulb Guard®, Ro-Pel®, or another wildlife deterrent.

If you've bought pots of **tulips** or other plants at the grocery store or florist and all of a sudden you see tiny insects on the tips of the leaves or on the flowers, they are most likely aphids. Place the pot in the kitchen sink and use the sprayer to dislodge as many as possible. After the plant dries off, spray any remaining aphids with insecticidal soap. You may need to do it several times, a few days apart.

FEBRUARY

Bulbs

PLANNING

Spring will be here before you know it. Are you winnowing down the list of summer-flowering bulbs you want to plant this spring? Or maybe it's growing ever larger before you decide which ones you'll buy this year and which ones will go on the list for future purchases. During the long days of the year's shortest month, it's fun to compile a list of "gotta haves" before the realities of money, space, and time interfere. Before you make the final decision on which ones make the cut this year, talk to a good gardener about his or her experiences with the plants you're considering. While you can find plenty of plant advice on the Internet, first-hand local observation is much more valuable in telling you whether this plant is going to be a winner in Memphis, Louisville, or Knoxville.

The season's first blooms. As the earliest bulbs—**snowdrops, crocus**, and some **miniature daffodils**—open their little flowers, it's a good time to reflect on about how welcome these harbingers of spring are, how happy they make us feel when we see them blooming no matter how cold the weather. But also think about your plantings of early bulbs a bit more critically: Are you happy with the number you have? The color combinations? The location? On the September page in your garden journal, note what improvements you'd like to make. Let that serve as a reminder for your fall bulb purchases.

PLANTING

Indoors. If bulbs are available, pot up **amaryllis** (see page 82), **paper-whites, Chinese sacred lilies**, or **soleil d'or** (page 83). All should bloom in four to six weeks.

Outdoors. If you haven't planted the spring-flowering bulbs you bought last fall, it's probably too late for them to bloom this year (the exception might be **Dutch iris**, which requires only four weeks of cold temperatures in order to flower). But you can still plant them this month if they're in good shape (not shriveled, soft, damaged, or diseased) and the ground isn't frozen. This works best if you plan to put them in an already prepared bed. (Even in February's mild spells, you probably don't want to be digging a hundred holes.) Follow the same instructions (on page 57) as if you'd planted the bulbs in the fall, except do *not* fertilize.

CARE

If **tulips, hyacinths**, and **daffodils** have come up several inches and unusually cold weather threatens, cover them with pine straw.

Check summer-flowering corms and rhizomes stored in the basement, garage, crawl space, or closet. Remove any that are beginning to rot or have rotted and any that appear to be diseased. If the bulbs start to shrivel, sprinkle them very lightly with water. When temperatures plunge outdoors, make sure that the area in which the bulbs are stored isn't allowed to freeze—for most stored bulbs, ideal temperatures should be in the 40-degree Fahrenheit range. One exception is **caladium**, which must have warmth—when winter storage temperatures are much below 65 degrees Fahrenheit, the bulbs probably won't survive.

When **amaryllis** finishes blooming, make sure the plant receives enough light. It should be placed so it's in sun *either* all morning *or* all afternoon (but not at midday). If the leaves aren't a nice medium green, the plant may not be receiving enough light.

If you potted bulbs for forcing in November, the thirteen weeks most of them need to be in darkness should be over sometime this month.

- Begin checking for readiness a couple of weeks earlier—some bulbs are ready to come out of cold storage faster than others.
- How do you judge readiness? Look for a robust root system that has grown through the pot's drainage hole and for shoots that have grown a couple of inches.
- Once those conditions have been met, place the pot on an east-facing windowsill of a room (or the basement) that's kept as cool as possible (60 to 65 degrees Fahrenheit). Keep the soil moist. When the shoots have reached 4 inches tall, move the pot to a warmer room where it can be in full sun.
- When flowers appear, move the pot out of the sun and into bright light. Continue to keep the soil moist.
- Flowers last longer when temperatures are on the cool side, especially at night.
- Snap off flower stalks as the blooms fade.

You may toss the bulbs out after they've bloomed or keep them and plant them outdoors for blooming in coming years; here's the procedure:

- Fertilize the bulbs with a water-soluble fertilizer for blooming plants when shoots are 4 inches high.

- Keep the pot in sunlight even after the flowers have died and the foliage begins to turn yellow. As leaves yellow, cut back on watering.
- Plant the bulbs outdoors after the leaves have turned brown. (See page 57 for bulb-planting directions.)

 # WATERING

Outdoors. The only time you need to water outdoors is if you planted bulbs in January and there's been little or no precipitation since. Even then, don't water unless the ground isn't frozen. Try to empty the hose of water afterward and put the hose back into the basement or garage. A hose will last longer if it isn't subjected to freezing temperatures.

Indoors. Keep the soil of **amaryllis** plants moist, whether the plant is in flower or not. When growing **paper-whites** in trays of water, check the water level daily.

 # FERTILIZING

Indoors. Fertilize **amaryllis** with a water-soluble fertilizer this month if you didn't fertilize in January. The plants need to be fed about every six weeks while they're growing. No fertilizing is necessary for any other indoor bulbs.

Outdoors. If you didn't fertilize **tulips**, **daffodils**, and other spring-flowering bulbs last fall or you did not use a slow-release fertilizer such as Bulb Booster™, fertilize spring-flowering bulbs as soon as you can see 1 inch of green shoot. The recommended rate is 1 tablespoon of 8-8-8 granular fertilizer per 100 square feet of surface.

GROOMING

Remove faded flowers (including the stalks) of **amaryllis** and **paper-white narcissus**. After all **paper-whites** in the pot have finished blooming, toss them out; they can't be forced into bloom another year because they've used up so much energy.

Snap off the flower stalks from **snowdrops** and early **daffodils** as the blooms fade.

 # PROBLEMS

Sometimes forced bulbs rot in the cool, wet environment in which they're growing. If it happens, toss the bulb and soil out. There isn't much you can do about this, except to buy top-quality bulbs, pot them in a commercial potting mix that contains no soil, and use new pots.

MARCH

PLANNING

Start making sketches of new flower beds in which you'd like to put **cannas**, **dahlias**, **glads**, **lilies**, and other summer-flowering bulbs. Often these are placed in perennial beds and borders, but you may decide you want an all-**lily** bed or to add a small section of **crocosmias**, for example, to one edge of an existing bed. Now's the perfect time to figure out where the new bulbs will fit into your landscape.

What about planting a cutting garden of summer-flowering bulbs this year? The best spot is a bit hidden, so it doesn't matter how it looks when you remove the flowers just as they reach their peak. Good choices include a raised bed in an out-of-the-way spot or a section of the vegetable garden that you're not using anymore. All summer-flowering bulbs are excellent for cutting, even **caladium** and **elephant ear**, which are generally used just for their foliage effect.

Why did some **daffodils** bloom one week and others the week before or after? There are many different members of the *Narcissus* family. They vary in size, appearance, and blooming time. If you're used to **daffodils** that are all yellow and have large cups, you may be surprised to find that some are all white, some have small orange cups, some produce a number of flowers on each stem, some have double flowers—the choices are endless. With a little planning, you can have one **daffodil** or another in flower from February until the end of April (or even the first of May in some sections of the region).

PLANTING

If **snowdrops, crocus**, or early **daffodils** need to be divided or moved, do this when their foliage has yellowed but not completely browned. As you replant, space them according to the chart on pages 59 to 61.

March is the time to begin thinking about starting summer-flowering bulbs indoors. Because **caladium** and **elephant ear** need the weather outdoors to be hot when they're transplanted, it's best to let them wait until April.

Dahlia tubers may be started indoors late this month or outdoors anytime between the end of April and the first of July. For indoor growth:

- Buy deep pots or trays for starting **dahlias** indoors since the tubers are a good size.
- Fill with commercial potting mix that has been thoroughly moistened and mixed with a timed-release fertilizer such as Osmocote®.
- If the tuber was divided last fall when it was dug, make sure each piece of tuber has an eye or bud.
- Place the tuber on top of the soil and press it slightly down into the soil. Water again.
- Apply bottom heat, either with a heating mat or by placing the container on top of your home's water heater.
- Shoots should appear in two weeks. Provide bright light.
- If the tuber wasn't divided in the fall, divide it when new growth is 1 inch tall and replant in pots or flats.
- Give the plants sunshine, moist soil, and warm temperatures as they grow.
- Plant outdoors when all chance of frost has past.

CARE

Cut a few early **daffodils** to bring indoors. They have such a cheery presence. If you don't have enough **daffodils** that you feel you can spare any for cutting, make a note in your garden notebook or on your October calendar to buy more. These are perfect bulbs for Kentucky and Tennessee. Not only aren't they bothered by wildlife but, if given the conditions they like, they come back year after year, always increasing.

Although bulbs are tough and can generally tolerate quite a bit of cold weather,

Do not fertilize spring-flowering bulbs that have already bloomed or are ready to bloom. Fall and winter, not spring, are the times to feed these bulbs because that's when they're growing and need nutrients.

extreme cold snaps can make flower stalks fall over if the bulbs have already started blooming. If a warm spell is followed by temperatures in the low 20 degrees Fahrenheit range, you may:

- Accept some minor foliage damage (if there are no flowers yet).
- Mulch with pine straw deep enough to cover the entire plant.
- Pick the flowers the afternoon before the cold weather arrives, so you can continue to enjoy the blooms indoors.

When **dwarf crested iris** (*Iris cristata*) has been in the same place for several years, the center of the rhizome tends to die out. There are two ways of overcoming this. After growth has started this month, dig up the rhizome, remove the unproductive portion, and replant. See directions on page 57. But the easiest way is to cover the underperforming portion of the rhizome with a thin layer of rich compost, which you keep moist. This encourages new shoots and roots.

WATERING

March may be a wet month, so watering is rarely needed outdoors. Indoors, keep the soil moist around your **amaryllis** bulb. Taper off watering your forced

bulbs if they have finished blooming and their leaves are beginning to yellow.

FERTILIZING

Do *not* fertilize spring-flowering bulbs that have already bloomed or are ready to bloom. Fall and winter, not spring, are the times to feed these bulbs because that's when they're growing and need nutrients.

Fertilize **amaryllis** with a water-soluble houseplant fertilizer if you didn't last month.

Fertilize all **irises**.

GROOMING

Remove all faded flowers. If you don't, the bulbs may set seed. Let the energy that would go into forming seeds go instead to the bulb, which is where next year's flowers come from. If you see seedpods, snap them off and toss them away.

When **crocus** and **snowdrop** foliage browns, cut it off and remove it from the garden. If you'll be planting annuals or other plants in the same bed, mark the

location of the early bulbs so they won't be damaged when you add more plants.

Once early **daffodils** have bloomed, let their foliage begin to fade naturally. Do *not* braid it, fold it over, or hold it down with a stone. These methods interfere with photosynthesis, which is how the bulb renews itself for next year.

PROBLEMS

If a **daffodil** doesn't come up, dig down into the soil carefully with your hands to see whether the bulb is still there. If you encounter a bulb, pull it out of the soil. If it feels soft and has a white ring around the base, brown streaks on the side, and an objectionable odor, it is a victim of basal rot. Dig up all the affected bulbs and get rid of them. Then don't plant bulbs in that location for several years. Basal rot can be prevented by making sure that **daffodils** are planted where drainage is good and that summer annuals shade the soil where the bulbs are planted.

APRIL

 PLANNING

Find your camera, buy some film, and take pictures throughout April, usually the prime month for bulb beauty in this area. You'll enjoy these in years to come, but they can also help you with planning your fall bulb purchases. Do you need more **daffodils** around the **kerria** and **forsythia** shrubs? Do the color combinations work well, or do your **tulips** and **azaleas** clash? Don't make all of the photos of your entire front or back yard. If you try to get everything in one shot, you won't be able to spot the details later. Take time for some pictures of just one bed and one border, which record the kind of helpful details that will guide you to making your spring landscape as glorious as you always hoped it could be.

 PLANTING

Easter lily. Wait till all chance of frost has passed to plant your **Easter lily** outdoors in a sunny spot. Do *not* place it in the same bed as other **lilies** because it can transmit a disease to them.

The passing of the average frost-free date is the signal for a flurry of planting. But wait till next month to plant **caladium** and **elephant ears** outdoors—both need very warm weather to root and grow well.

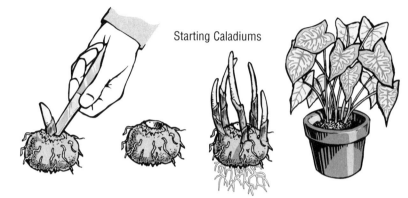

Starting Caladiums

Bearded, dwarf crested, and **Siberian irises** may be planted or replanted while in bloom. Selecting them when they're in bloom allows you to choose favorite colors. But you have other options: **Siberian irises** may be easily transplanted just before and after blooming, and **bearded irises** transplant well about six to eight weeks after they've finished blooming (midsummer). To plant:

• **Bearded iris**, or **German iris**, needs a sunny spot. Well-rotted mushroom compost is a good soil amendment for them. Cut the leaves back in a fan shape about 4 inches high. Dig a hole and make a mound of soil in the center that's slightly lower than the surrounding soil. Place the rhizome on top so that its roots radiate over and down the side of the mound. Cover the roots firmly with soil. The rhizome should be sitting at soil level or no more than $1/4$ to $1/2$ inch below. If a **bearded iris** rhizome is planted too deep, it will rot.
• **Siberian irises** like a spot with moist but well-drained soil and light shade.

Although they tolerate clay soil, it's best to mix rotted leaves, compost, or fine pine bark into the soil before planting. Also incorporate slow-release fertilizer into the soil mixture. Place the rhizome so that the top of it is about 1 inch below the soil surface.
• **Dwarf crested iris** prefers the shade of a woodland, but doesn't want competition from other plants and shouldn't be allowed to dry out. An acid soil rich in humus is ideal. Plant the same as **bearded iris**.

Lilies like soil enriched with organic matter (rotted leaves, compost, fine bark). Dig the soil 8 inches deep, mix in the organic matter and a timed-release fertilizer, and plant the bulbs of **Asiatic lilies** so there's 4 to 5 inches of soil over the tops of them and those of **Oriental lilies** so that they're covered by 1 to 2 inches of soil.

Gladiolus appreciate a spot that's out of the wind. To have a long succession of blooms, plant corms 4 to 6 inches deep in a sunny location with well-drained soil every two weeks until midsummer.

When bulbs are in flower, mark their locations so you'll know where to fertilize in the fall. Some people use short stakes, others golf tees. Or you can draw the bulbs' location on a plan of your yard.

Blackberry lily and crocosmia. Plant at the depth recommended in the chart on pages 59 to 61 in well-drained soil that's been amended with organic matter. **Blackberry lily** grows nicely in light shade. **Crocosmia** needs full sun and doesn't like to be moved.

Caladiums. Although it's best not to plant **caladiums** outdoors until May, you can certainly start them indoors about the first of April. Here's how:

1 Moisten a commercial potting mix, and fill a flat or several plastic pots about three-fourths full.

2 If there's a shoot growing in the center of the tuber, scoop it out with a small pocket knife. This encourages many side shoots to develop, which will produce more foliage.

3 Place the tuber on the soil, with the roots down.

4 Cover the tubers with 1 to 2 inches of soil, and water well.

5 Keep in a warm location. Bottom heat (from a heating mat sold to aid seed germination, or from simply placing a few pots or one flat on top of your water heater or refrigerator) will encourage faster germination and growth.

6 As soon as growth is evident, move the plants into bright light.

 # CARE

When bulbs are in flower, mark their locations so you'll know where to fertilize in the fall. Some people use short stakes, others golf tees. Or you can draw the bulbs' location on a plan of your yard.

As the weather warms up across the region this month, pull back the protective mulch you placed over the **cannas, glads**, and **dahlias** you left in the ground last fall.

After **Siberian irises** finish blooming, divide the clumps if they need it and replant. (See page 74.) Be sure to keep the new divisions watered.

 # WATERING

Should April showers not arrive on schedule, water bulbs if there's been no rainfall in the past two weeks. If bulbs are in bloom, try to keep the water from touching the flowers so they'll last longer.

 # FERTILIZING

Feed **amaryllis** with a water-soluble fertilizer made for houseplants. Spring-flowering bulbs that have bloomed or are in flower do *not* need fertilizer at this time; wait till fall.

Spread a timed-release fertilizer such as Osmocote® (or an organic product such as Milorganite®) around summer-flowering bulbs as they emerge from the soil. These fertilizers slowly release nutrients to the plants over a long period, so you don't have to apply them more than once or twice a season. In contrast, liquids don't persist in the soil and must be reapplied frequently.

 # GROOMING

Continue to remove the faded flowers from bulbs flowering outdoors. It makes the garden look better and prevents seeds from forming. (Seed formation takes energy away from the bulb, which reduces the vigor of the bulb the following year.)

 # PROBLEMS

If any **irises** didn't flower, or if they produced flowers that collapsed, the problem is probably rhizome rot. Dig up the rhizome and remove all soft spots. Before replanting the rhizome, you may want to dust it with sulfur. Preventive measures include shallow planting and removing all dead foliage.

MAY

PLANNING

Many bulb catalogs now arrive in spring, when gardeners are thinking about spring-flowering bulbs because they're in bloom. Often these offer specials for early orders. Sometimes they're a way to obtain bulbs that you haven't found locally. But you have no control over the size or quality of the bulbs that you receive—and those are the biggest influence on bulb success. In a local nursery, you can pick and choose among the bulbs to get the ones you want. Use catalogs to make wish lists and then place small orders, if you like, to compare quality and price.

PLANTING

Any spring-flowering bulbs may be moved when their foliage has yellowed and fallen over or begun to brown. Don't wait too long, or you won't be able to locate the bulbs. Replant immediately.

Once both days and nights are reliably warm, unrooted tubers of **caladiums** and **elephant ears** may be planted outdoors. (**Caladium** plants that have already started growing—either started indoors or bought in pots—may go out early in the month in warmest areas.) Both like rich, moist soil that's been amended liberally with organic matter

(Nature's Helper™, compost, rotted leaves, or aged mushroom compost). Both will also perform nicely in containers. **Caladium** shines in the shade; **elephant ear** will grow in full sun or partial shade. See the chart on pages 59 to 61 for planting depth and spacing requirements. Continue to plant **caladiums** all month, if you like. To encourage the tuber to produce more foliage, use the trick on page 69.

Growing Dahlias From Tubers

1 Plant tubers after all chance of frost has passed. You may continue to plant in June and early July in the warmer parts of the area, for fall flowers.

2 Choose a spot with good soil, full sun, and access to water, the sort of location you'd put a vegetable garden. In fact, a former vegetable garden is an excellent place for tall **dahlias**.

3 Till the soil 8 to 10 inches deep, and incorporate plenty of organic matter into the bed—composted leaves, fine pine bark, compost, etc. Mix in slow-release fertilizer.

4 Dig holes 10 to 12 inches deep and 5 inches wide.

5 Space small **dahlias** 8 to 10 inches apart, medium ones about 18 inches, and large ones 24 to 36 inches from one another.

6 Spread the tuber in a hand shape on the bottom of the hole.

7 Place a stake in the hole now because putting it in place later is likely to damage the tuber.

8 Add 3 inches of soil on top of the tuber, firming it around the stake, so the stake will stand up.

9 As the tuber grows, add more soil, until the hole is filled.

10 If you are growing many **dahlias**, install drip irrigation since they need plenty of water during the steamy days of summer.

11 Top the soil with 2 to 3 inches of mulch.

Bedding plant dahlias. These are small and may be planted just as you would any annual. (See page 38.)

Plant **cannas** in a bed that's in full sun and has moist, rich soil or in containers filled with potting soil mixed with dry bagged manure. See pages 59 to 61 for spacing and depth to plant. Because **cannas** are heavy feeders, incorporate timed-release fertilizer into the soil as you plant, so you won't have to fertilize as frequently throughout the summer.

Continue planting **glads** (see pages 68 and 69) and **lilies**, if bulbs are available.

Plant annuals and perennials in and among bulbs to hide the bulb's ripening foliage. Daylilies and daffodils are an excellent combination. As the daffodils begin to fade, daylily foliage comes on strong.

Because **lily** bulbs lack a protective coating, plant them quickly so they don't dry out.

Plant annuals and perennials in and among bulbs to hide the bulb's ripening foliage. **Daylilies** and **daffodils** are an excellent combination. As the **daffodils** begin to fade, **daylily** foliage comes on strong.

 # CARE

Anytime this month, it's fine to move your potted **amaryllis** outdoors for the summer, if you'd like.

All bulbs—with the exception of **bearded** and **dwarf crested irises**—need some mulch. You may want to wait until the end of May to mulch **caladium** and **elephant ear**, to give the soil time to really warm up around the plants. But check the mulch around everything else and add to it if it's thinner than 3 inches. I prefer pine needles—sold in bales at garden centers as pine straw. It's light and airy, looks natural, and doesn't wash away. And no, it doesn't make your soil acidic.

If you didn't get to it last month, mark bulb plantings in some way so that you'll know where they are when fall fertilizing time arrives.

 # WATERING

Any bulbs, corms, rhizomes, and tubers that were divided, moved, or planted this spring should be watered anytime this month that rainfall is less than 3/4 to 1 inch weekly.

 # FERTILIZING

Fertilize **amaryllis** bulbs outdoors about twice a month since they will need more frequent watering than when they were indoors and that washes the nutrients from the soil. Use a water-soluble fertilizer made for blooming plants.

As you continue to plant summer-flowering bulbs, mix a slow-release fertilizer into the soil. For bulbs such as **dahlias** and **cannas** that were left in the ground over winter, spread the label-recommended amount of Osmocote® over the soil around the plants, if you didn't feed them in April. Place mulch on top, and water. If you used a water-soluble fertilizer on **cannas, glads, dahlias**, or other summer-flowering bulbs last month (instead of a slow-release fertilizer), repeat the application this month.

Fertilize **irises** after they finish blooming.

Don't fertilize any spring-flowering bulbs until fall.

 # GROOMING

Leave the ripening foliage of **tulips, daffodils**, and other spring-flowering bulbs in place until it begins to turn brown, usually about eight to ten weeks after flowering. Don't braid the yellowing foliage; that isn't good for the plant.

Cut back **iris** leaves that have developed spots.

Do *not* remove the seedpods that form on **crown imperials**; they're part of the decoration of these plants.

 # PROBLEMS

Japanese beetles miss spring-flowering bulbs, but do bother some of the summer ones—**cannas** especially. When you know from past experience that Japanese beetles are attracted to certain plants, spray the plants with Neem (which is organic) before the beetles arrive. Sometimes Neem is also effective afterwards, but it varies and depends on how bad the infestation is. You may also pick beetles off by hand and drop them in a can of soapy water. Consult the Extension Service for other controls.

JUNE

 PLANNING

Continue to think about what spring-flowering bulbs you'd like to plant in fall. How did your bulbs perform this spring? Were some so successful that you'd like to add more? Do some of your **tulips** need replacing because they're just about at the end of their life cycle? Are you interested in branching out with some bulbs that you saw in a neighbor's garden? Maybe you'd like to have a longer parade of spring bulbs; if so, look into early, midseason, and late varieties of your favorite bulbs (especially **tulips** and **daffodils**).

 PLANTING

It's not too late to plant **dahlias, caladium**, and **gladiolus**. See pages 66, 68, and 69 for instructions. The **dahlias** and **glads** won't bloom until the end of summer, but that's not necessarily a bad thing since few flowers except annuals are blooming at that time of year. It's nice to have fresh flowers in fall, and both **glads** and **dahlias** make excellent cut flowers to take indoors or to the office with you.

 CARE

As **dahlias** grow, continue to add enough soil to the holes in which **dahlia** tubers were planted so that you barely cover the new growth each time. Do this until the soil reaches the level of the soil around it, then stop. Once the hole is filled with soil, water well and add 2 to 3 inches of mulch on top. See page 70 for more details.

Tie **dahlias** and other tall bulbs such as **lilies** to stakes as they grow taller. Sometimes staking is a chore we tend to postpone, but it's important to go on and get it done. Summer thunderstorms can quickly topple beautiful plants and snap their stems.

The best time to pick flowers is first thing in the morning. They'll stay fresher. With **glads**, wait till the second floret has opened before cutting the stalk.

 WATERING

Daffodil and **tulip** bulbs don't need much water except during spring and fall, so you don't have to worry about watering them during summer. **Irises** that have already bloomed are dormant or going dormant now. They don't need watering.

Caladiums, cannas, dahlias, and **elephant ears** like plenty of water. Make sure the soil they're planted in doesn't dry out.

Don't let **lilies** get stressed from lack of water, but in general **lilies** don't like wet soil. It causes the bulb to rot. In times of drought, when watering is necessary, soak the ground thoroughly to a depth of 8 inches.

Gladiolus and **blackberry lily** like to be watered when rainfall is less than an inch a week. If you don't have a rain gauge so you can be certain of how much rain your yard really received, lift the mulch and stick your index finger several inches into the soil. If you don't feel dampness 2 or 3 inches down, water is probably needed.

Plants in containers need watering much more often than those planted in flower beds. Depending on the size of the pot, and whether you used a water-holding polymer, it may be necessary to water container-grown bulbs every other day or even daily. Check the soil by feeling it. Water in the morning, if possible, so the foliage won't stay wet overnight.

Water **dahlias** at the base of the plants to help prevent mildew and other fungal diseases.

FERTILIZING

Most summer-flowering bulbs prefer a fertilizer that's low in nitrogen and high in potash. If you have a fertilizer made for **tomatoes**, it will work well on all of these plants. Your fertilizer choices are:

- **Slow-release fertilizer.** If you used a slow-release fertilizer such as Osmocote® or Milorganite® in the spring, there's no need to fertilize bulbs growing in the yard during June.
- **Water-soluble fertilizer.** All plants in containers need quite a bit of extra nourishment since frequent waterings flush the nutrients from the soil. Most gardeners who use a watering can (rather than a hose) to water their container-grown plants prefer to use a water-soluble or liquid fertilizer because it's so easy. Apply it at least every other week during June.
- **Granular fertilizer.** If you have many large containers and water them with a hose or drip system, you may want to apply a granular fertilizer on top of the soil every four to five weeks. Keep it off the foliage, and water it in well.

 # GROOMING

Foliage of all spring-flowering bulbs should have died by this month. Remove it and get it out of the garden. If a few yellow leaves haven't turned brown, it's fine to cut them off as long as they've fallen over.

When **bearded iris** foliage begins to look bad, cut it back in a fan shape about 4 to 6 inches high. If you don't get to it, it doesn't make much difference to the plant, but your garden does look neater if you get rid of the damaged tips of the leaves.

When cutting **gladiolus** flowers, leave as much foliage as possible to help the plants grow more corms by fall.

 # PROBLEMS

If **tuberous begonias** aren't flowering as profusely as they did earlier, it's because they don't like heat and humidity. Give them plenty of shade and keep their soil moist. If you can keep them alive all summer, they'll bloom again when cooler weather returns. I generally don't recommend them except in cooler areas. 'Nonstop' is often the best performer.

If newly emerging leaves on **cannas** are distorted or won't unfurl, this is a sign of canna leaf rollers. Cut off the affected foliage, and spray remaining leaves with Bt (*Bacillus thuringiensis*), an organic control. Jot a reminder in your garden notebook to clean up all **canna** foliage from the ground in fall so no leaf roller caterpillars will overwinter to plague the plants again next year.

Aphids are fond of new **gladiolus** foliage. Try to wash them off with a hose. If that doesn't clear up the infestation, spray with insecticidal soap at three-day intervals. Do not spray in the hottest part of the day or when the sun is shining on the plant.

Thrips may be troublesome on **glads**, as well as other summer flowers. They will chew leaves, causing them to wither and die, and deform the blossoms. Pick off affected flowers and remove them from the garden. Ask the Extension Service or your favorite garden center about an insecticide. As a preventive, keep flowers as far from the vegetable garden as possible.

JULY

PLANNING

Are you adding to the list of spring-flowering bulbs you'd like to plant in fall? Even if you plan to buy bulbs from a local nursery, where you can see exactly what you're getting, it's fun to read bulb catalogs. Place your lawn chair in a shady spot on a hot July weekend, and spend some time reading through a couple of bulb catalogs, marking the plants you like. If you've never grown *Arum italicum*, you may want to add it to your list if you have woodlands or a shady spot. It adds interest to the garden during several seasons.

PLANTING

You can still plant **dahlias** the first week of the month, but obviously those planted this late won't produce as many blooms as they would have if planted earlier. Still, growers who are aiming for fall flower shows do plant late. It depends on your perspective.

All through the month, it's fine to continue planting small **dahlias** sold as bedding plants since they will already be in bloom. Since all **dahlias** stand up well to hot weather, they're an excellent choice to add to any flower bed that looks a bit sparse. They also do well in containers.

Caladiums already started into growth at the nursery may be added to beds or containers in shady locations. The same is true for **blackberry lilies** in sunny spots.

Plant **spider lily** (**naked lady, surprise lily**) bulbs when they become available. Remember that they're slow to become established, so don't expect too much the first year.

Mid- to late July is the time to divide **bearded irises**, if they need it (usually every three to five years).

1 Cut the leaves in a fan shape 6 inches high. This helps prevent leaf die-back and also wind damage on newly planted rhizomes that haven't yet developed deep root systems.

2 Lift the clump with a spading fork, and wash the dirt from the tubers with a hose.

3 Remove any part of a rhizome that's diseased, damaged, or soft (the problem area will be dark brown or black).

4 Using a sharp knife, cut the rhizomes into smaller pieces, each with an eye or bud.

5 Cut away and discard older growth, which won't bloom any longer.

6 Because of many fungal problems affecting **irises**, consider soaking the rhizome briefly in a fungicide solution or dusting it with sulfur (don't use sulfur when temperatures are above 89 degrees Fahrenheit). Some gardeners mix 1 part liquid bleach to 9 parts water and quickly dip the rhizome in the solution.

7 Replant the rhizome sections close to the surface of the soil. See page 57 for planting directions. They may need some support to stay upright until new roots and growth have taken place.

8 Water well.

 CARE

Check mulch around all summer-flowering bulbs and replenish if it isn't 3 inches thick. Not only does mulch help conserve moisture in the soil and protect roots from temperature extremes, it also prevents soil from being splashed on plant leaves and stems, which can spread soil-borne diseases. This is especially true for true **lilies**, so be sure they are mulched at all times. But don't mulch **iris** rhizomes; doing so causes them to rot.

Regularly weed flower beds containing summer bulbs. Competition from weeds prevents your good plants from living up to their potential.

If the weather has been hot and dry, spider mites may be troublesome on many summer-flowering bulbs. Look for leaves that first look paler than those nearby and then begin to turn yellowish or look dirty.

 # WATERING

Caladiums like lots of water. Don't let them wilt, because the plants won't grow well afterward. Water early in the morning, and keep the water off the leaves, if possible, since the sun shining on wet **caladium** leaves can burn them.

Also keep soil moist around **cannas, elephant ears**, and **dahlias**. Water all others—except **lilies**—when rainfall doesn't amount to an inch in any week. **Lilies** can usually manage fine without additional water, except in droughts.

Although most **irises** don't need much water in summertime, reblooming **bearded irises** should be watered when rainfall is less than normal.

It's best for the plants if you water enough to wet the soil deeply each time you water, rather than watering frequently and lightly. If only a small amount of water is applied each time, plants may develop shallow roots, which dry out faster in times of drought.

Water **dahlias** at ground level; to avoid powdery mildew or other fungus diseases, don't let water or soil splash up on the leaves.

 # FERTILIZING

All summer-flowering bulbs will need a fertilizer boost this month. A timed-release fertilizer such as Osmocote® will continue to feed plants through the rest of the growing season. A granular fertilizer will be effective for four to six weeks. Water-soluble fertilizers are fast-acting (especially if you spray or pour them over the leaves), but their effects aren't long-lasting. You'll need to apply them again in a few weeks. Cost and convenience may also enter into your decision of which type of fertilizer to use. The initial cost is in reverse ratio to how frequently you use the product—timed-release is most expensive to buy, then granular; water-soluble is the least expensive. Water-soluble fertilizers make good sense for plants that you water by hand—those in containers, for instance. But for plants in beds, granular or timed-release fertilizers are often preferable because they give the gardener a break from having to fertilize frequently.

GROOMING

Cut **lily** flowers when they start to wilt.

Cut off the spathelike flower stalks that develop on **caladiums** so the plant will continue to produce an abundance of colorful leaves.

Pinch **dahlias** back a few inches to encourage branching. When a **dahlia** produces several flower buds next to each other, you have a choice:

- Remove one or more of the buds so you have one (or two) larger blooms This is called "disbudding."
- Leave all the buds to grow and produce more—but smaller—flowers.

If you have the time, you may want to try it both ways and see which you like better.

Remove faded flowers from **cannas** and other summer-flowering bulbs.

Hardy glads bloom in early summer, and their foliage fades in six to eight weeks. As this happens, remove it at ground level. (Leaves of other types of **gladiolus** remain green until frost and are not cut off until then.)

PROBLEMS

If the weather has been hot and dry, spider mites may be troublesome on many summer-flowering bulbs. Look for leaves that first look paler than those nearby and then begin to turn yellowish or look dirty. See page 217 for dealing with spider mites.

AUGUST

PLANNING

Are you running out of space for all the summer-flowering bulbs you'd like to grow? Fall is a good time to prepare new beds and borders since the weather is cooler and homeowners are generally less busy than in springtime. Walk around your yard this month, with pen and notebook in hand, to decide where you might create or renovate flower beds.

PLANTING

Plant **autumn crocus** and **colchicum** if you can find them in local stores. They'll bloom next month. Give them a sunny location, and plant them 4 inches deep (measured from the top of the bulb) and 6 inches apart. Because the foliage (which, in the future, will come up in spring and then die back down before the flowers appear) can be dominating, a shrub border is a good place for **colchicum**.

If your **irises** didn't bloom as well the past year or so as they previously did, and they haven't been divided within four years, you can generally improve their performance by dividing the rhizomes and replanting pieces of them. Mid- to late July is the usual time to do this, but if you didn't get to it then, there's no reason you can't take care of it in August. It's best, however, not to wait any later than this month in order to give the rhizomes a good opportunity to become established before cold weather arrives.

CARE

Make sure that all tall plants—**dahlias, glads, lilies**—have stakes and that you regularly tie new growth to the stakes. Sometimes a plant that's been knocked over by wind can be propped up again— but often the plant is too damaged to recover. You don't want that to happen to your favorites.

WATERING

By the time August rolls around, summer bulbs planted in containers often need daily watering. You may be able to lengthen the time between waterings by repotting plants into larger containers. The smaller the pot, the more often it has to be watered.

When you go on vacation, ask a knowledgeable neighbor to water your **caladiums, cannas**, and **dahlias** deeply once during the week since they need a regular supply of moisture. Have your helper water **blackberry lilies, crocosmia**, and **glads** if there's no rain at all during the week. **Lilies** shouldn't need watering.

FERTILIZING

If you used a granular fertilizer around your summer-flowering bulbs four to six weeks ago, the first of the month is the time for the final application of the season. Those who prefer to apply a water-soluble fertilizer to plants growing in beds should feed once near the first of August and again about the middle of the month.

Fertilize container-grown plants weekly with a water-soluble fertilizer. An exception is **amaryllis**. Do not fertilize it at all. It will soon start going into fall dormancy in preparation for blooming again during the winter, indoors.

Fall is a good time to prepare new beds and borders since the weather is cooler and homeowners are generally less busy than in springtime.

GROOMING

Remove faded flowers from **cannas, dahlias, gladiolus, lilies**, and **crocosmia**. This keeps the plants blooming longer. For a neater appearance, also remove dying leaves from **caladiums** and damaged leaves from **elephant ears**.

In the warmest areas of the region, pinch **dahlias** lightly one last time the first part of the month to encourage growth that produces additional blooms. To encourage dinner-plate-sized flowers, you'll need to remove all but one of the buds in a cluster and leave fewer clusters on the plant. That gives you fewer but bigger flowers. Leaving all the buds to blossom produces many smaller blooms.

As **gladiolus** stalks turn brown, cut them back to the ground. Don't do it before then, though, because the leaves help the bulb gather strength for the next year.

PROBLEMS

Keep an eye out for insects and for signs of disease.

A white powdery coating on leaves is a sign of mildew. **Dahlias** are the most likely summer bulbs to be affected, but it may turn up on other plants, too. It's a fungus and can't be cured, but may be prevented. If only a few leaves are affected, pinch them off. On **dahlias**, where you are expecting the best of the season's performance between now and frost, you may want to spray a fungicide to prevent the disease from spreading. Check with the Extension Service for a recommended product.

Keys to mildew prevention are watering at ground level and not splashing leaves when you water. Air circulation makes a difference, too—planting so that **dahlias** and other summer-flowering bulbs have plenty of room between them.

Remove weeds by hand. If you have mulched your flower beds consistently, you shouldn't have too many weeds. And annual weeds should be easier to pull up through a blanket of mulch. Perennial weeds are the toughest to control—especially those that spread by underground runners since, when you pull up one portion of the weed, the section that's left puts out new roots.

Because of high temperatures, August is not usually a good month to use a weed-killer. Read the product's label to find out its effective temperature range. When you exceed that on the high end, the herbicide may burn good plants nearby.

If you've returned from vacation to find plenty of weeds, go through the garden and snip off all the heads of the weeds, tossing them in a bag or bucket. That prevents them from setting seed. It also buys you a little time to get the weeds out of the garden.

If **glads** aren't looking as good as they should, the problem may be fungal diseases (check the leaves for spots or markings), thrips (which chew the leaves), or aphids (which usually congregate on new growth and can easily be seen). Sometimes it takes a bit of detective work to figure out the cause, which is what dictates the remedy. You may want to cut off a leaf or other affected portion of the plant and take it to a good nursery for a diagnosis and advice on control.

SEPTEMBER

PLANNING

Spring-flowering bulbs will begin appearing in home stores and garden centers across the area this month, but September isn't the best month to plant them. In most areas, you should wait until October or later—when the temperature of the *soil* is 60 degrees Fahrenheit or below.

But just because you're not going to plant right away doesn't mean you shouldn't plan your bulb plantings for next spring and buy many of the bulbs that you'll need. The bulbs available now are fresh and offer the best selection of the season. The main thing to remember when buying bulbs early is to store them correctly. (See page 56.)

Look for bulbs that you haven't grown before, and consider giving one or two new-to-you species a try. There's an interesting world of selections beyond **tulips** and **daffodils**. Many bloom early or late, giving your yard a sparkle of bulb color over a longer period.

If you've become less enthusiastic about planting new bulbs because of damage by deer, chipmunks, and squirrels, buy bulbs that rarely get eaten by wildlife. Among your choices are **crown imperial**, *Crocus tommasinianus*, **grape hyacinths**, **Siberian squill** (*Scilla siberica*), **snowdrops, Spanish bluebells, spring snowflakes, silver bells** (*Ornithogalum nutans*), and **winter aconite** (*Eranthis hyemalis*).

PLANTING

Winter aconite isn't well known, but it's a worthwhile little bulb—a charming late winter/early spring bloomer with single yellow flowers that may remind you of **buttercups**. They often bloom through snow and emit a honeylike fragrance. September is the month to plant **winter aconite**. Soak the bulbs for twenty-four hours in room-temperature water, and plant them 3 inches deep and 4 inches apart in loose, moist soil. Because—in contrast to many of the spring-flowering bulbs—they don't like to dry out over summer, you may want to plant them in a bed of perennials or annuals that you'll be watering regularly. (The **aconite's** foliage will have disappeared long before summer arrives.)

When **lily** bulbs become available in fall, plant them right away. See page 57 for directions.

Although you won't be doing the bulk of your bulb planting till next month, September is a good time to dig new beds. Planting bulbs properly makes all the difference in the world in how they perform and whether or not they return—looking great—year after year. When homeowners complain that their **tulips** didn't look good a second year, it's often because of poor planting practices. The foundation of all good gardens—and therefore good plants—is soil that's been improved with organic matter. Take the time to do it right the first year, and you'll reap the rewards for many seasons to come. See page 57 for directions on how to prepare a bulb bed.

CARE

If you'd like to save your **caladiums** for another year, wait till the leaves begin to die back—but before a frost—to dig them up. Wash the soil off the tubers, and place them in a shaded, well-ventilated area for several days to dry out. Dust with sulfur and pack in a box of dry sphagnum peat moss. Put the box somewhere in the house that the temperature will remain 65 to 70 degrees Fahrenheit. If **caladium** tubers get too cool while in storage, they're likely to rot.

Most winters, **elephant ear** will survive in Zone 7 (and often in Zone 6) if left in the ground and mulched heavily. But if you want to be sure you don't lose them to the cold, dig and store as explained for **caladium**. Otherwise, place an inch or so of extra mulch over them.

Toward the end of the month, begin fertilizing previously planted spring-flowering bulbs. Fall is the time of year that these bulbs begin growing and need the nutrients that fertilizer supplies.

Bring your potted **amaryllis** back into the house the first part of the month. Gradually cut back on watering until the leaves begin to turn yellow, then stop watering altogether. Cut the leaves off close to the top of the bulb. Place the bulb, still in its pot of soil, in a dry, dark spot where temperatures will remain above freezing. The bulb will need to rest at least a month before you start it into growth again. (See page 82.)

 WATERING

If rainfall is less than normal this month, check around your summer-flowering bulbs to see whether the soil is dry, and then water those that need it. Since **dahlias** are in their prime and like plenty of moisture, see that they're watered once or twice a week if rainfall is less than an inch every seven to ten days. Keep the water at ground level to avoid getting the foliage wet and initiating fungal diseases.

 FERTILIZING

Don't feed summer-flowering bulbs any more this year. You want them to slow their growth so they gradually go dormant about the time cold weather arrives.

Toward the end of the month, begin fertilizing previously planted spring-flowering bulbs—everything from **crocus** to **tulips**. Fall is the time of year that these bulbs begin growing and need the nutrients that fertilizer supplies. It really can make a difference in the size and number of the flowers and in whether your bulbs perennialize.

But how do you know where they're located in order to feed them? Ah, that's the difficulty. You have to mark them in some way in the spring:

- Use brightly colored golf tees.
- Place thin bamboo stakes at the corners of bulb beds.
- With bulbs planted near the street, use a squirt of spray paint on the curb.
- Plant **grape hyacinths** or **Dutch iris** in all your bulb beds. Their foliage comes up in fall and marks the areas that need fertilizing.

Bulb Booster™, Bulb Tone™ and Bulb Mate™ are slow-release fertilizers. They will continue to feed all winter. If you'd prefer to use a granular fertilizer that you have on hand, sprinkle 1 teaspoon of 8-8-8 per 100 square feet of bed surface over the bed now or next month. (Then feed again when foliage has grown 1 inch tall. See page 58.)

 GROOMING

Cut **dahlia** flowers in early morning. Take a clean bucket of cool water with you into the garden so the stems of the flowers can be plunged into it immediately. Cut long stems, and make your cut at a 45-degree angle, using a sharp knife or pair of garden shears.

 PROBLEMS

Spider mites, aphids, and thrips may still be active in the garden. Try to wash them off with a squirt of water from a hose. This late in the season, the infestation isn't likely to need a chemical control.

OCTOBER

 PLANNING

If October is a busy month for you, make a date with yourself in November—and mark it on your calendar—to get spring-flowering bulbs planted early next month. Or maybe you'll want to spread the job over a couple of weekends. But if you keep reminding yourself that it needs to be done, you're less likely to end up in December with your bulbs still not planted.

You may be thinking that you'll have to wait till next year before you see any spring-flowering bulbs in bloom. But not so. It's easy to grow some bulbs indoors, either through forcing (see pages 82 and 83) or by growing **paper-white narcissus** and **amaryllis**. With a nice supply of bulbs available in October, this is a good time to make your selections.

Continue to plan for new beds—and buy the bulbs to go in them—all this month. Mesh bags of bulbs may seem to be a bargain, but they're usually smaller bulbs and aren't always cared for in shipping and in stores as carefully as individual bulbs. Remember the rule of thumb: The bigger the bulb, the bigger and more numerous the flowers growing from it.

Get out your garden notebook and write down the names of the bulbs you're planting, their color and height, where you're putting them in the yard, and where you bought them. This record comes in quite handy when you really like a particular **tulip** or other bulb next spring, but can't recall the name of it or even which garden center sold it to you.

While you have your garden journal out, jot down notes about the performance of summer-flowering bulbs, if you haven't already. And be prepared to note the date of the first frost. It's always interesting, and helpful, to look back and see how it varies from year to year.

 PLANTING

Finally, the month you've been waiting for—the time to plant **tulips, daffodils, hyacinths, crocuses**, and a host of other spring-flowering bulbs. The photographs with the bulb bins, or in catalogs and magazines, look so appealing and colorful that you're planting dreams, too. Fortunately for the gardener, unless wildlife interferes, bulbs usually deliver on the dream. See page 57 for bulb-planting instructions and pages 59 to 61 for how deep to plant each type of bulb and how far from each other to space them.

If you plan to use a bulb-digging tool instead of digging up a bed, be sure it's heavy-duty, or it won't last. One handy trick with a bulb planter is not to remove the plug of soil from it. As you step on the crossbar to push the tool down in the ground to dig the second hole, the first plug will be pushed out. It can then be put on top of the previous bulb. Warning: This works only for already-improved soil or light soil. It isn't a recommended technique for clay.

Protect when planting. Remember to use chicken wire or hardware cloth over bulbs if you've had problems with wildlife. Some people make a little basket of chicken wire and put the bulbs inside. Others plant the bulbs, then lay a straight piece of hardware cloth on top, covered by soil. The bulbs will grow through the holes. Or you can soak bulbs in bulb protectant before you plant them. (This is effective only the year of planting, though.) See page 58 for a list of bulbs that aren't usually bothered by wild critters.

 CARE

Digging and storing. Some of the summer-flowering bulbs are always left in the ground over winter—**blackberry lily, crocosmia, iris, lily, lily-of-the-valley**, and **spider lily**—to bloom again the next year. **Caladiums** are tropical plants that will die if exposed to temperatures below freezing, so they're always dug up and stored (see page 78) or treated as annuals.

Dahlias and **cannas** will often survive winter when left in the ground under an extra-thick blanket of mulch, but may not make it through an extra-cold winter. So if you have **dahlias** and **cannas** that are irreplaceable, dig at least some of them for storage. Most growers think **gladiolus** performs best the next year if the corms are dug in the fall and replanted the next spring.

1 Carefully dig up the corms, tubers, or rhizomes, being careful not to damage them.

2 Shake off the soil.

3 Remove small new **gladiolus** corms from the main corm.

4 Trim off any damaged or dead **dahlia** tubers.

5 Place the corms, tubers, or rhizomes in a shady spot that's out of the weather but has good air circulation. Leave them there for about a week to dry out.

6 Brush off any soil that remains.

7 You may want to dust the corms, rhizomes, or tubers with a fungicide such as sulfur to help prevent them from rotting while in storage.

8 Store them in a shallow tray of dry peat moss or vermiculite. (Store **dahlias** upside down.)

9 Place the tray in a spot where you can easily check it several times during the winter. The temperature should stay below 50 degrees Fahrenheit but above freezing.

Fall covering. If you planted new **lily** bulbs last month, add an inch or two more mulch over their soil so they will be protected from the vagaries of winter weather. Do the same for **cannas**, **elephant ears**, and **glads** that you plan to leave in the ground, if you didn't renew their mulch last month.

WATERING

Don't let the soil around newly planted bulbs dry out completely. If October should turn out to be a very dry month, you may need to water the area where they were planted until the first frost. If **dahlias** are still going strong, water them if the rainfall doesn't supply at least an inch of water every five days or so.

FERTILIZING

Fertilize spring-flowering bulbs as you plant, preferably using a slow-release bulb fertilizer. Last month, did you get around to fertilizing the previous year's bulb plantings? If not, do it in October. Follow the directions on the label, watering the fertilizer in after application.

The season has ended for summer-flowering bulbs, so they don't need to be fed.

GROOMING

Remove foliage killed by frost and put it onto the compost pile if it was healthy. If it was diseased or had insects on it, dispose of it away from the garden.

PROBLEMS

If you have had problems with voles, do not put mulch over your **tulip** beds. A covering of mulch gives the voles somewhere warm to spend the winter—eating your bulbs in the meantime.

November

 PLANNING

Naturalizing bulbs is fun—just toss them on the ground and dig holes where they fall. It provides an appealing natural look. **Daffodils** are a good choice for naturalizing since they return reliably each year. Often you see pictures of **daffodils** naturalized in lawns, but there's one problem: Cool-season grasses such as **fescue** and **bluegrass** need mowing long before the **daffodil** foliage has ripened and died. **Crocus** leaves will have ripened sufficiently by the end of March, but they're usually too short to be seen through **tall fescue** or **bluegrass**. Better choices include naturalizing in a wildflower meadow and especially along the edges of the woods. This is a good way to use smaller bulbs, should you find a good end-of-the-planting-season sale. And it's something to keep in mind for next year.

 PLANTING

Continue planting all spring-flowering bulbs in your landscape. Improve the soil first by amending it with organic matter, and always use a bulb fertilizer for best results. Consult the chart on pages 59 to 61 for planting depth and spacing information. Water well, then cover the soil with 3 inches of mulch.

Why not bring the beauty of bulbs indoors? There are several ways of doing this: growing **amaryllis** bulbs in pots of soil, placing **hyacinth** bulbs and **crocus** corms over water in special glasses, and potting up bulbs and giving them a chill in the refrigerator. All are fun. Here's how to do it:

Growing over water. The easiest way to grow bulbs indoors is to buy small crystal "vases" made especially for forcing **crocus** and **hyacinths** into bloom indoors. Fill the container with water and place the bulb in the flared top section. Keep the water at the level of the bottom of the bulb, and the roots will grow into the vase and be visible through the glass. As soon as top growth emerges, move the vase to good light and keep cool.

Amaryllis. If you plan to use your **amaryllis** as a temporary houseplant, tossing it out in spring, the type and size of bulb you buy isn't as important as it is if you plan to keep it for years, bringing it back into bloom each winter. As a long-term investment, buy an **amaryllis** that's as large as you can find (about the size of a **grapefruit**) and a named cultivar (not just red, white, pink, etc.).

- Start with a clean plastic flower pot that's 2 inches wider than the diameter of the bulb.

- Place a coffee filter or piece of screen over the drainage hole.
- Fill the container about halfway with dampened potting soil.
- Position the bulb on top of the soil. One-third to one-half of the bulb should be above the pot's rim.
- Fill in around the bulb with more moist potting soil, firming it gently.
- Water thoroughly.
- Set the pot aside in a warm spot. It doesn't need light and shouldn't be watered again until the bulb starts growing.
- When new growth appears, move the pot into bright light, water enough to keep the soil moist, and fertilize monthly with a houseplant fertilizer.

To bring an **amaryllis** from last year into bloom again, water the soil so that it's wet all the way through. Then follow the final two steps above.

Forcing. The most common bulbs for forcing are **daffodils, tulips, hyacinths**, and **crocus**.

1 Buy bulbs that are marked "for forcing."

2 Buy 6-inch plastic bulbs pots, if available. These are about 2/3 as tall as the regular 6-inch flower pots. (**Hyacinths** can be planted singly in 4-inch pots.) If using old containers,

wash them thoroughly with soapy water, rinse, and soak briefly in a solution of 1 part bleach to 9 parts water.

3 Moisten potting soil and—if you plan to plant the bulbs outdoors after they've been forced—mix in a small amount of Bulb Booster™.

4 Fill the pot about three-fourths full of damp potting soil.

5 Position the bulbs on top of the soil so that they're not touching one another or the container. **Daffodils** and **crocus** should be covered with about 1 inch of soil. The tips of **hyacinths** and **tulips** should be showing above the soil. Place **tulip** bulbs so their flat side faces the outer rim of the pot; then the foliage will gracefully arch over the side.

6 Add more potting soil until it's within ¼ to ½ inch of the rim.

7 Water thoroughly.

8 Write on a plant label the name of the bulb, its color, and the date you planted it. Stick this down into the soil.

9 You may want to place the pots in large clear plastic bags to retain moisture. If so, you'll need to check occasionally to make sure that no mold is developing.

10 Put the pots in the refrigerator.

11 It takes about twelve weeks before most bulbs are ready to be brought into the house to bloom. Check February, page 65, for instructions on what to do then.

 ## CARE

Keep in a cool spot any spring-flowering bulbs that you haven't yet planted. Since it's getting late in the season, it's best to refrigerate **tulips** if you have the space in your fridge. They need a certain amount of chilling before they can bloom. Keep refrigerated bulbs away from apples and other ripening fruit, which give off a gas that may harm them.

If your area got its first killing frost this month, check October for information about digging **dahlias** and other tubers and rhizomes for storing over winter. Most need to be kept somewhere that temperatures remain above freezing, but **caladiums** and **elephant ear** should be stored at a temperature of 55 degrees Fahrenheit or above.

Increase the mulch over **cannas**, **dahlias**, and **glads** as a protection against a possibly colder than usual winter.

 ## WATERING

Once we've had a hard freeze, it's no longer necessary to water outdoors; bulbs can manage on their own unless there's a serious drought.

 ## FERTILIZING

This is the last call to fertilize bulbs that you planted in previous years. You'll see a noticeable difference in your bulbs next spring if you fertilize in the fall.

 ## GROOMING

Clean up frost-killed foliage and remove it from beds, if you haven't gotten to it earlier. You don't want to leave anything that insects or disease spores can overwinter on.

 ## PROBLEMS

Bulbs and poor drainage don't mix. Since winter can be rainy in our region, now is a good time to walk through your yard and note areas that remain wet after a rain. Consult the Extension Service or a landscape architect for advice.

DECEMBER

 PLANNING

On a chilly evening, update your garden journal. It's fun to look back over the year and even more delightful to anticipate the coming season.

 PLANTING

Yes, you can still plant **tulips, daffodils**, and other bulbs outdoors, as long as the ground isn't frozen. Try to get it done by the end of the month; otherwise, blooming may be delayed.

Paper-white narcissus, a bulb with highly fragrant white blooms, and two similar but yellow-flowered relatives— **soleil d'or** and **Chinese sacred lily**— can be quickly forced into bloom this month (or in January, if bulbs are available). There are two ways to do this:

1 Place bulbs in a shallow bowl, and gently pour decorative pebbles around them to the top rim of the bowl. Add water, and place the bowl in a spot with bright, indirect light and cool temperatures. Keep the water level just below the rim.

2 Pot up **paper-whites, soleil d'or**, or **Chinese sacred lilies** as described in November. Leave the tips of the bulbs slightly above the soil.

3 Place **paper-whites** in bright sunlight and **soleil d'or** and **sacred lilies** in darkness. Both prefer nighttime temperatures of 55 degrees Fahrenheit or below.

4 Keep the soil moist.

5 Remove **soleil d'or** and **Chinese sacred lilies** from darkness after ten days, and grow them in sunlight.

6 Fertilize monthly with a houseplant fertilizer.

7 When blooms appear, move the plants out of the sun and into bright indirect light.

 CARE

Are all your bulb beds mulched with about 3 inches of organic material? If not, choose a pretty December day to spread leaves, pine straw, or other mulch.

Shredded leaves make good mulch, and they're readily available this time of year, but don't pile whole leaves onto bulb beds since they're likely to mat down when wet and not let rain through to the soil and bulbs. They could also prevent necessary air from reaching bulb roots.

Keep unplanted bulbs in a cool spot until you can get them in the ground. **Tulips** should be stored at 40 degrees Fahrenheit, if possible.

 WATERING

Watering bulbs outdoors isn't necessary now. Occasionally check pots of forced bulbs to see whether they need watering. Keep **amaryllis** soil moist, but don't let the plants stand in water. If you're going to be out of town over the holidays, ask a friend or neighbor to water the plant.

 FERTILIZING

Fertilize bulbs that you plant outdoors this month. Wood ashes may be used around bulbs, too, especially **daffodils**. Collect the ashes from your fireplace, but let them cool before spreading them on bulb beds. (Avoid ashes near shrubs, such as **azaleas**, which need acid soil.) Fertilize **amaryllis** bulbs once a month with a water-soluble houseplant fertilizer.

 GROOMING

Take a break from grooming this month.

 PROBLEMS

If you were too busy to clean up the garden right after frost, it's not too late to do so now—remove all dead foliage from summer-flowering bulbs so insects or diseases don't overwinter on it.

CHAPTER THREE

Herbs & Vegetables

There's something special about the flavor of a just-picked tomato on a summer day or the taste of pesto made from basil grown in your own garden. They simply aren't the same if they're bought. Fortunately, as generations know, growing vegetables and herbs is easy in our climate.

If we make the effort, those in the warmest areas can often fill our salads with fresh **lettuce** and **radishes** beginning around the middle of March and harvest that first ripe red **tomato** by July 4.

The ideal spot for a garden:

- faces south
- is in an open area—far away from the invasive roots of trees
- receives full sun—or at least six hours of direct sunlight
- is near a source of water
- has well-drained soil (Poor soil can be remedied by adding amendments, growing in raised beds, or planting in containers.)
- can be fenced if deer or other wildlife are a problem in your area
- is *not* in a low-lying frost pocket

But don't think you're out of luck if you don't have room for a traditional garden. Both herbs and some vegetables may also be grown in containers as well as in and among ornamental plantings in the yard, provided the soil is fertile and well drained.

Planning is important for a vegetable or herb garden—to use the space wisely and to get the most from what you grow. The size will probably be determined by what you want to grow in it. If you haven't grown edibles before, start small. Everyone is enthusiastic in April, at planting time, but not nearly so motivated at the end of June when the weeds try to take over. You can always increase the size in the fall or next spring if it wasn't big enough, but if you get discouraged by your experience with a too-large garden, you may not try again.

Choose what you will grow by four criteria:

1 **Space.** Some vegetables, such as **corn, melons**, and **pumpkins**, take up a great deal of room.

2 Your **favorite vegetables** and those of family members. There's no point in growing **eggplant** if no one in your household eats it.

3 **Cost and availability** of store-bought produce. **Yellow squash, cabbage**, and **zucchini** are readily available at any supermarket. "Burpless" **cucumbers** aren't. It costs very little to grow **mesclun** (young mixed **lettuces**) and colored **bell peppers**, but it's expensive to buy them. Most culinary herbs, except **chives**, are fairly costly at the grocery store and may or may not be available when you need them. For some reason, **English peas** and **sugar snaps** are difficult to find in supermarkets. If you want to enjoy their fresh, crisp taste, you have to grow them yourself.

4 **Taste.** Some home-grown vegetables—such as **tomatoes**—have far superior flavor to anything you can buy, even at a farmers' market.

Once you've decided on the vegetables you want to grow, investigate the best varieties of each. Get recommendations from other local gardeners, the Extension Service, *The Tennessee Fruit and Vegetable Book,* or *The Kentucky Fruit and Vegetable Book.* The most important quality to look for is disease resistance. **Tomatoes** should have VFN after the variety name, which indicates their resistance to two kinds of plant-killing wilts and nematodes (microscopic soil insects that adversely affect the roots and growth of **tomatoes** and some other plants).

Herbs & Vegetables

As you plan your vegetable garden on paper, keep in mind:

• Tall-growing crops (**tomatoes, pole beans, corn, okra**) need to be planted where they won't shade shorter vegetables.

• Crops should be rotated from year to year so that plants in the same family (and which therefore attract the same kinds of insects and diseases) move from place to place in the garden. (See page 95.)

• Some vegetables are heat lovers and should be planted only after the weather has really, truly warmed up. Cool-season vegetables must be planted early in spring, since they won't bear well once summer temperatures arrive. (See the chart on pages 89 to 90.)

• Vegetables may be divided into two other groups: those that mature in a relatively short time (**lettuce, radishes, spinach, summer squash, beets, bush beans, turnips,** and **Swiss chard**) and those that take up space in the garden much—if not most—of the summer (**peppers, tomatoes, eggplant, corn, melons, sweet potato, winter squash**, and most herbs).

As soon as a short-season crop is harvested, plan to remove it from the garden and plant something else in its place. This is called *succession planting* and allows you to grow more vegetables in less space.

In our region, vegetable gardening isn't just a summer pastime. Some years, in some parts of the area, gardeners may be planting seeds of **Alaska peas** on Valentine's Day, pulling **carrots** for the Thanksgiving table, and cutting **collards** in December or January—all from the same plot of ground.

Have your soil tested as early in the year as possible—or even in the fall before planting, in case you need to work in lime (lime doesn't affect pH for several months). The soil test results also give fertilizer recommendations.

An easy way to kill grass and weeds, as well as some pathogens in the soil, is to *solarize* (sterilize) the new vegetable garden area during summer the year *before* digging and planting.

1 Keep in mind that **hot weather is essential** to the process.

2 Wet the soil thoroughly, cover with a sheet of clear plastic, and anchor the edges with rocks or soil.

3 Leave the plastic on for at least four weeks—until the grass has been killed. If you prefer, leave the plastic on all winter. Or you can remove it when the grass is dead and cover the area with leaves,

Soil Solarization

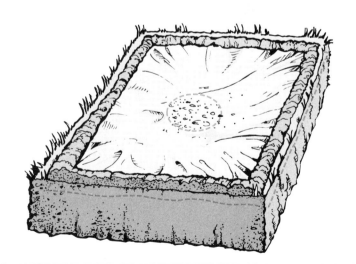

Herbs & Vegetables

which will be tilled into the soil in the spring.

Place several inches of organic matter—compost, rotted leaves or manure, aged sawdust, old mushroom compost—on top of the soil and till it in 8 to 12 inches deep.

Because the soil can be too wet to work in early spring (see page 38), many gardeners like to till at least part of the vegetable garden in the fall, leaving some rows in furrows or mounds. These will warm up sooner than surrounding flat ground and be ready to plant with seeds or plants of cool-season vegetables at the proper time.

Then you're ready to plant—when the time comes. (See more about timing on page 89.) Inspect the plants carefully when you buy them—you want the strongest and healthiest plants you can find; your harvest depends on it. Use a starter solution when planting, because its high-phosphorous content encourages good root growth. For organic gardeners, an excellent substitute is one cup of *manure tea* (manure steeped in water for twenty-four to forty-eight hours, then strained and the liquid mixed with an equal amount of plain water).

The discussion of preventing insect damage and disease on pages 362 to 363 applies particularly to growing vegetables. Numerous insects and diseases theoretically could attack your crops, but many can be deterred by a few simple precautions.

SPECIAL NOTES ON HERBS

Most of the information about growing vegetables also applies to herbs. But there are a few differences:

- Some herbs can grow nicely in partial shade. (See page 91 for a list.)
- Many herbs must be planted in soil that's very well drained (page 100).
- Herbs generally don't require as much fertilizer as vegetables and don't need to be fertilized several times during the growing season (unless you're using a liquid fertilizer).
- Some herbs are perennials (see page 91) and are left in place from year to year, so they may need winter protection. They may also be propagated to increase your supply.

- Different parts of herbs (leaves, stems, flowers, roots, seeds) are harvested at various times during the season for a wide variety of uses—salads to soups and vinegars, crafts, potpourri, and as beauty aids.
- Some herbs can be grown indoors on a sunny windowsill.
- Although herbs may be placed in the vegetable garden or among flowers, a separate herb garden is an attractive option.
- Herbs are versatile. They can be used for edging, as a ground cover, between steppingstones, peeking out from the crevices of a wall, and in many types of containers.

The most important thing that beginning herb gardeners should know is that gray- or silver-leaved herbs usually don't like heat and humidity. Many of them can be problematic in our climate, "melting out" in the middle of the summer. If your area has an herb society, ask for advice. Otherwise, try one or two varieties of the species you're interested in, give them excellent drainage, and don't let the leaves get wet when you water.

Herbs & Vegetables

HERB GARDEN DESIGN

The design of an herb garden can be informal—much like a cottage garden or just a junior version of a vegetable plot—or formal, such as a knot garden. Because herbs have been grown for centuries, there are many traditional designs and a number of variations on these themes: medieval gardens with paths, Williamsburg gardens, a fragrance garden, a Shakespeare garden (herbs mentioned in Shakespeare's writings), a tea garden (with plants used to make herbal teas), herbs with **old garden roses**. To find ideas for your yard, visit your public library and look through books that feature designs or photographs of herb gardens.

Do you want a small garden of culinary herbs that you can use in the kitchen? If so, place it near the back door. If you don't, you'll always regret it.

Herbs and vegetables fall into the category of "useful plants." But that doesn't mean they are dull. Just ask a child who pulls his first **radish** from the still-cool spring soil or the home cook who snips a few leaves of **lemon balm** to give a distinctive tang to a pitcher of iced tea. Vegetables and herbs can be as attractive as any other plants in the landscape, and they give the grower a big sense of satisfaction—and a colorful array of edibles—for many months of the year.

Summer Garden

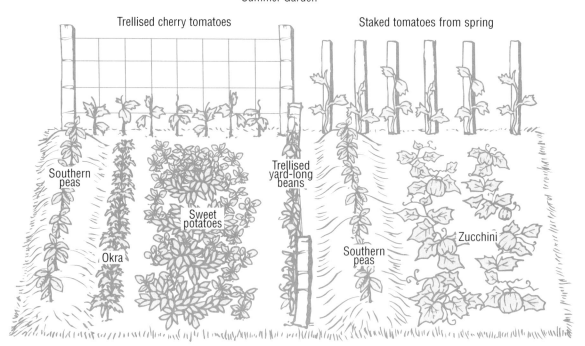

Trellised cherry tomatoes

Staked tomatoes from spring

Southern peas

Trellised yard-long beans

Sweet potatoes

Okra

Southern peas

Zucchini

Vegetables

Vegetable	Can Be Started from Seed Indoors	When to Plant Outdoors (Air temperature range in degree F.)	Days to Harvest
Asparagus	Yes	55 to 70*	360 to 720
Bean, bush	No	65 to 80	50 to 59
Bean, pole	No	65 to 80	63 to 65
Bean, lima	No	80+	68 to 72
Beet	No	55 to 70*	50 to 60
Broccoli	Yes	55 to 70*	48 to 70
Brussels sprouts	Yes	55 to 70*	90 to 92
Cabbage	Yes	55 to 70*	64 to 76
Cantaloupe	Yes***	70 to 80+	75 to 96
Carrot	No	58 to 70**	58 to 72
Cauliflower	Yes	58 to 70**	50 to 70
Collards	Yes	55 to 70*	60 to 80
Corn	No	65 to 80	65 to 92
Cucumber	Yes***	65 to 80	52 to 65
Eggplant	Yes	80+	64 to 80
Kale	Yes	55 to 70*	50 to 70
Kohlrabi	No	55 to 70*	50 to 60
Lettuce, leaf	Yes	55 to 70*	45 to 50
Okra	Yes	80+	52 to 60
Onion	Yes	55 to 70*	70 to 110 (sets)
Parsnip	No	55 to 70*	100-120
Peas, English	No	55 to 70*	60 to 70
Peas, 'Sugar Snap'	No	55 to 70*	58 to 72
Peas, edible-podded	No	55 to 70*	50 to 68
Peas, field (Southern peas)	No	80+	55 to 89
Pepper	Yes	65 to 80	60 to 86
Potato, Irish	No	55 to 70**	80 to 130
Potato, sweet	No	80+	90 to 135
Pumpkin	Yes***	65 to 80	95 to 120
Radish	No	5 to 70*	22 to 30
Spinach	Yes	55 to 70*	39 to 46
Squash, summer	Yes***	65 to 80	46 to 50
Tomato	Yes	65 to 80	56 to 79
Turnip greens	No	55 to 70*	28 to 30
Turnip	No	55 to 70*	58 to 60
Watermelon	Yes***	80+	72 to 90
Zucchini	Yes***	65 to 80	48 to 55

*Can tolerate some frost. **Can tolerate cold, but not freezing. ***Doesn't like roots disturbed when transplanted into the garden. Start in individual peat pots.

Vegetables

Vegetable	Space Between Plants (Inches)	Space Between Rows (Inches)
Asparagus	12 to 18	36 to 48
Bean, bush	3	24
Bean, lima	3	24
Bean, pole	36	30
Beet	3	12 to 18
Broccoli	16 to 24	30
Brussels sprouts	16 to 24	30
Cabbage	15 to 18	24
Cantaloupe	3 seeds per hill	Hills 3 feet apart; rows 4 to 6 feet apart
Carrot	1 to 3	12 to 18
Cauliflower	16 to 24	30
Collards	16 to 24	30
Corn	8 to 10	36
Cucumber	6 to 8	48
Eggplant	24	24
Kale	6 to 12	24
Kohlrabi	5 to 6	24
Lettuce, leaf	8 to 10	18
Okra	12	36
Onion	3	12 to 15
Parsnip	2 to 3	18 to 24
Peas, English	1	12 to 18
Peas, edible-podded	1	12 to 18
Peas, field (Southern peas)	4 to 6	36
Pepper	12 to 18	18 to 24
Potato, Irish	10 to 15	24 to 36
Potato, sweet	12	36 (48 for mounds)
Pumpkin, bush	36	36
Pumpkin, vining	3 seeds per hill	Hills 10 feet apart
Radish	1/2 to 1	8 to 10
Spinach	6 to 8	12 to 18
Squash, summer	36	36
Squash, winter	36	36
Tomato	36 to 42	42
Turnip greens	1	12
Turnip	4 to 6	12 to 18
Watermelon, bush	36	48
Watermelon, vining	3 seeds per hill	Hills 10 feet apart
Zucchini	36	36

Herbs

Common Name (*Botanical Name*)	Type	Light Level	Height (Inches)	Spacing (Inches)
Basil (*Ocimum basilicum*)	Annual	Sun	10 to 24	12 to 18
Chives (*Allium schoenoprasum*)	Perennial	Sun to partial shade	12	6 to 12
Cilantro/Coriander (*Coriandrum sativum*)	Annual	Sun to partial shade	24	6 to 18
Dill (*Anethum graveolens*)	Annual	Sun	36 to 60	6 to 12
Fennel (*Foeniculum vulgare*)	Perennial	Sun	48 to 60	6 to 12
French tarragon (*Artemisia dracunculus*)	Perennial	Sun	24	12 to 18
Lavender (*Lavandula* species and hybrids)	Perennial	Sun to partial sun	18 to 36	18
Lemon Balm (*Melissa officinalis*)	Perennial	Sun to partial sun	24	12 to 18
Oregano, Greek (*Origanum heracleoticum*)	Perennial	Sun	24	9 to 12
Parsley (*Petroselinum crispum*)	Biennial	Sun to partial shade	6	6 to 8
Rosemary (*Rosmarinus officinalis*)	Tender perennial (May be overwintered indoors.)	Sun	18 to 30	18
Sage (*Salvia officinalis*)	Perennial	Sun	18	12 to 18
Summer savory (*Satureja hortensis*)	Annual	Sun	18	12 to 18
Sweet bay (*Laurus nobilis*)	Tender perennial (May be overwintered indoors.)	Partial shade	4 to 12 feet	12 feet
Sweet marjoram (*Origanum majorana*)	Perennial	Sun	8	6 to 12
Thyme (*Thymus vulgaris*)	Perennial	Sun	4 to 8	6 to 12

JANUARY

Herbs & Vegetables

PLANNING

Let's put first things first this year: Have you had your garden's soil tested within the past three years? Have you added large quantities of wood ashes or other amendments to the garden since the soil was last tested? If you answered no to the first question or yes to the second, it's time to take samples of the soil and send them off for testing. The Agricultural Extension Service office in your county (pages 344 to 353) will have all the details.

If you don't have a garden notebook, January is the ideal time to start one. Once you've formed the habit of writing down the day-to-day details of the garden—the plants, the challenges, what you hope to accomplish in the future—and adding an article about a plant you'd love to own—you'll wonder how you ever managed to do without it.

What does a gardener with hard clay soil or poor drainage if he or she wants to enjoy homegrown **tomatoes** and **basil**? The easy answer is *raised beds*. Use long-lasting wood to build a frame at least 2 feet high (be sure to attach the corners securely). Fill it with high-quality, weed-free topsoil, and you are ready to plant. These can be put together on nice days between now and March so that you can plant when the mood strikes and

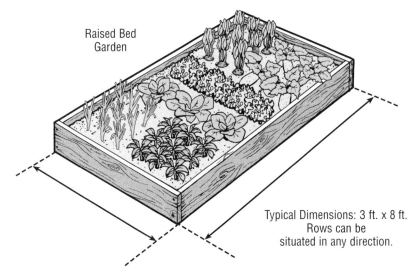

Raised Bed Garden

Typical Dimensions: 3 ft. x 8 ft.
Rows can be
situated in any direction.

the weather cooperates. You may also want to use these dreary winter days to track down a good source of topsoil for your raised beds.

Many vegetables and herbs are easily grown from seed—most outdoors, but many indoors, too. If this appeals to you, page 89 has a list of vegetables that may be started from seed indoors. Herbs that are easily seed-grown—indoors and out—include **basil, chervil, cilantro, dill, fennel, hyssop, lovage, marjoram, parsley, sage, summer savory**, and **thyme**. Order seeds now. With a few exceptions (see **Planting**), most should be started in February or March, but you'll want to take time now to round up the equipment you'll need—containers, commercial potting mix, maybe even grow lights.

January and February are the months to plan your vegetable garden—what you

want to change and the new varieties you want to try. The January issue of many garden magazines often reports on new vegetables and other plants, and how they perform. Spend some chilly evenings carefully reading garden catalogs. Even when you buy mostly locally—always a good idea—you can learn a great deal from catalogs. They include charts and general growing information, as well as descriptions and length of time to harvest. Planting so that you spread out the dates to maturity is important for at least two reasons—most gardeners want to begin harvesting as soon as possible, and they want to keep the harvest going for as long as possible.

PLANTING

Sow seeds of **parsley** indoors this month. The seeds are hard, so to speed up germination, soak them in warm water for twenty-four hours before planting or nick them (or do both).

Several cool-season vegetables may also be started indoors during January: **broccoli** and **cauliflower** (which need a five- to seven-week headstart before going outdoors), **cabbage** (which takes four to six weeks to reach transplant size), **Brussels sprouts** (which receives eight weeks), and onion (which goes outdoors in February). See the **Annuals** chapter, page 42, for directions on sowing seeds.

CARE

Once seeds grown indoors have germinated, be sure they are given ample light. Fluorescent shop lights are an inexpensive way to supplement January's sometimes-missing sunshine.

Warmth is needed for seeds to germinate, but once the plants are up and growing, the room where they are can be cooler (65 to 68 degrees Fahrenheit in the daytime; down to 60 degrees at night).

WATERING

Use tepid water on flats of seeds or seedlings indoors. Cold water straight from the tap can shock the plants. The

Timely Tip

If you're new to vegetable gardening, these are the easiest veggies to grow. Because all are grown from seeds, they are also inexpensive.

- Beans
- Beets
- Cucumber
- English peas
- Leaf lettuce
- Radish
- Summer squash
- Spinach

best method is to fill a clean milk jug with water and let it stand at room temperature at least overnight before using it.

Keep seeds moist but not wet till they germinate. Once seeds have bcome young plants, let the soil's surface dry slightly before watering. Soggy soil—especially if the temperature is chilly—can cause seeds or young plants to rot.

FERTILIZING

Apply a water-soluble fertilizer to young seedlings after they have developed their first set or two of true leaves.

PRUNING

If you're growing herbs on sunny windowsills over the winter, pinch them back regularly to keep them from getting leggy. Use the cuttings of culinary herbs to add some zip to winter salads.

PROBLEMS

When young seedlings wilt and there's plenty of moisture in the soil, the cause is usually damping off, a fungal disease. It can often be prevented by:

- Using only sterilized or commercial soilless potting mixes.
- Adding some sand to the potting mix to make it fast draining.
- Not sowing seeds too thickly (or thinning crowded plants quickly).
- Increasing air circulation near the young plants with a fan. (Don't let the fan blow directly on the seedlings; just circulate the air near them.)
- Not overwatering.

If just one or two seedlings are affected by damping off, remove them promptly. Then increase air circulation. If the soil is too wet, sprinkle it lightly with charcoal. After the soil has dried out a little, water from below the next few times, instead of from above.

FEBRUARY

PLANNING

About the only way we can consistently grow iceberg or other head **lettuce** is to plant it in a cold frame in February. You can either start the seeds indoors and transplant them into the cold frame early in the month or sow them directly in six-packs or in a bed of rich soil in the bottom of the cold frame.

Cold frames are available in many garden catalogs and from some garden centers. Gardeners also make their own from old storm windows and scrap lumber. Unless you're home all day, it's good to buy an automatic opening device that will crack the lid when temperatures inside reach a certain level. Otherwise, on sunny days, plants can get much too warm. Cold frames are also useful for hardening off **cabbage, broccoli**, and **Brussels sprouts** seedlings before placing them in the garden.

Gardeners new to herbs are sometimes surprised at the eventual size of the herbs they've chosen, especially when some—such as **scented geraniums**— may sprawl more than expected. Read

Cold Frame

up on sizes as you plan your herb garden. Here is a general guide:

- Large or tall herbs: **anise, bay, dill, fennel, hyssop**, and **lemon verbena**
- Medium: **artemisia, basil, lavender**, and **sage**
- Small: **Lamb's ear, santolina**, and **thyme**

As you plan the layout of your vegetable garden, remember to rotate crops. This is the practice of planting vegetables that are members of the same family in different parts of the garden each year. This can minimize diseases and insects.

PLANTING

If you plan to start seeds indoors instead of buying transplants, this is the time of year that you need to check the seed packets for the recommended length of time between sowing and setting the plants outdoors. Use that figure to count back from your area's average last-frost date (see pages 24 and 25 for an approximation), and you'll know when to sow the seeds. There's little point in starting too soon—the plants will grow leggy while waiting to go outdoors.

Herbs that need to be started six to eight weeks before setting them outdoors include: **chervil, cilantro, dill, hyssop, lovage,**

marjoram, sage, and **thyme**. You may also plant **parsley** seeds, if you didn't last month. (See **January**.)

Tomato and **pepper** seeds also take six to eight weeks to reach transplanting size and so may be sown indoors this month or next.

Outdoors, some gardeners like to plant **onion** sets and **English peas** (especially 'Alaska'). In zones 6, 7, and 8, mid- to late February is the time for a first sowing of **spinach** and **Irish potatoes**, if the soil isn't too wet to work (or if it was prepared in the fall). It's fine to wait till early March, though. Sometimes too-cold and too-wet soil causes seeds planted early to rot. See page 90 for spacing recommendations. Work about 1 to 1½ pounds of 6-12-12 or 10-10-10 fertilizer into 100 square feet of soil before planting. You may want to buy row-cover fabric to keep handy to toss over plants if temperatures threaten to go much below freezing.

If you started **onion** seeds indoors in January, plant them outdoors when they're about four weeks old. Space them about 3 inches apart in rows a foot apart. Harden them off by first letting them spend the days outdoors in a protected spot and then gradually giving them more exposure to the weather. When seedlings in flats develop two to three sets of true leaves, you may transplant them into individual pots.

CARE

See that plants being grown indoors from seed receive enough light. If necessary, supplement sun with artificial light.

At the end of the month, pull the mulch back from part of your **asparagus** bed. That portion will warm up and bear soonest, extending the harvest.

WATERING

Outdoors, if you are growing **garlic** in raised beds and no rain has fallen for the past several weeks, check to see whether the **garlic** is in completely dry soil. If so, water, as long as the soil isn't frozen.

Indoors, keep seeds moist but not soggy until they germinate; then, when seedlings have sprouted, water after the soil's surface has become barely dry. When soil is always wet, fungal problems are likely. But seedlings must be kept moist enough that they don't wilt.

FERTILIZING

Every other week, fertilize seedlings being grown indoors. A water-soluble plant food for vegetables is fine for this or a balanced houseplant fertilizer such as 20-20-20. If the numbers that indicate the nutrient content are in the single digits (5-4-5), use the fertilizer at the recommended strength. If the numbers are in the double digits, apply half the recommended amount.

PRUNING

Continue to pinch back windowsill herbs to keep the plants compact.

Timely Tip

Vegetable and Herb Families

CARROT
Anise
Carrot
Celery
Chervil
Cilantro
Dill
Fennel
Lovage
Parsley
Parsnip

CUCURBITS
Cantaloupe
Pumpkin
Squash
Watermelon

GOOSEFOOT
Beet
Chard
Spinach

LEGUMES
English peas
Lima beans
Peanuts
Snap beans
Southern peas

MUSTARD
Broccoli
Brussels sprouts
Cabbage
Cauliflower
Collards
Horseradish
Kale
Radish
Rutabaga
Turnip
Watercress

NIGHTSHADE
Eggplant
Irish potato
Peppers
Tomato

ONION
Garlic
Leek
Onion
Shallot

SUNFLOWER
Artichoke
Jerusalem artichoke
Lettuce
Sunflower
Tarragon

PROBLEMS

Watch out for early-season weeds, especially if there's been plenty of rain and a few mild spells. When the soil is still cool, pull weeds by hand instead of using mulch to suppress their germination.

With seeds started indoors, keep an eye out for insects. Aphids and whiteflies (see page 101) are the most common.

MARCH
Herbs & Vegetables

PLANNING

If you want to grow vegetables or herbs in containers, begin shopping for pots now. Clay and terra cotta are often the most attractive, but they don't hold moisture in as well as plastic pots do—and you need a place indoors to store them over winter (they can crack in below-freezing temperatures). Wood can be attractive but is heavy and therefore difficult to move. Check out the newer containers that mimic the look of terra cotta, but are lightweight and impervious to the weather. Whichever type you choose, be sure the pots are large enough and have ample drainage holes in the bottom.

PLANTING

Prepare the soil anytime this month that the soil isn't too wet (see page 38). Then you may plant seeds of **carrots, peas (English** or **sugar snap), radish, spinach**, and **turnips**. (See the **Annuals** chapter, page 38.) To know which depth to plant which seeds, consult the chart on page 99. If your garden is large, you may want to plant in rows, spacing according to the chart on page 90. But alternatives include broadcasting vegetable seeds in wide rows (16 to 20 inches apart) or in squares (typically 1 to 2 feet square, depending on the size of

the plant—**squash**, for instance, requires more room). These techniques produce more vegetables in the same amount of space than in evenly spaced rows. But they require the gardener to know the difference between a weed and a veggie, and they preclude the use of a tiller or even a hoe for weeding.

Once soil has been prepared, set out transplants of **broccoli, cabbage, cauliflower**, and **onions** (also **onion** sets) anytime this month.

Plant two-year-old **asparagus** roots by digging a hole 8 to 12 inches deep and 18 inches wide. In the bottom of the hole, make a mound of soil that's been mixed with compost and other organic matter. Drape the roots of the **asparagus** plant over the mound, leaving the crown (top) about 3 inches below the soil level. Fill the hole with amended soil, firming it around the roots. Water well. Space the plants about a foot apart.

Four to six weeks before your county's average last frost date, start seeds of **basil** and **fennel** indoors. You may also sow seeds of other herbs inside, if you haven't already (see **February**).

Sow seeds of **borage, caraway, cilantro, leaf lettuce**, and **mustard** in the garden two to three weeks before your area's last frost. That may mean March or April, depending on where you live.

Many perennial herbs (and **parsley**) don't mind chilly weather, so if you find them growing outdoors at nurseries, ask if they're left out at night or taken indoors. If they've been left outside at night, it's fine to plant them in your garden. If they've been taken inside, harden them off or acclimate them to outdoor conditions gradually over a week to ten days before placing them in their permanent homes in the garden. (Annual herbs such as **basil** are planted after the frost-free date because they don't like cold weather.)

Start seeds of **Swiss chard** and **eggplant** indoors. You may still start seeds of **tomatoes** to be set out in May. (See page 32 for tips on seed starting.)

Divide **chives** if necessary. Replant about 8 inches apart in good soil. Or plant some of the **chives** in containers. They are excellent container plants and, with their purple blooms, look nice among ornamentals.

CARE

Near the beginning of March, improve the soil by tilling under any cover crops planted last fall.

Wait until at least May before mulching the vegetable garden so the soil stays as warm as possible. Warm soil results in better germination and growth.

WATERING

Don't let the soil around young vegetables and herbs planted outdoors dry out. Because their root systems are still small, they may need watering if rainfall is below average. Check every few days to be sure.

Indoors, continue to water young seedlings whenever the soil's surface has dried. Let the soil of transplants in individual pots dry out about half an inch down before watering. As the weather warms up and the plants grow, the soil may dry out increasingly faster, so it's smart to check each day.

FERTILIZING

Typically, unless your soil test has a different recommendation, 1 to 1½ pounds of 6-12-12 or 10-10-10 fertilizer is mixed into a 10-foot by 10-foot portion of the garden when planting vegetables. But some vegetables need more fertilizer than others. (See Timely Tip above.)

Herbs usually need very little additional fertilizer beyond what they get from soil amended with organic matter. They may appreciate a drink of manure or compost tea (dried manure or compost soaked in water, then strained and mixed with enough additional water to make the liquid the color of tea).

Timely Tip

Vegetable Fertilizer Needs

Heavy

Cabbage	Lettuce	Sweet potatoes
Celery	Onions	Tomatoes
Irish potatoes		

Medium

Asparagus	Edible-podded peas	Peppers
Beans	Eggplant	Pumpkin
Beets	English peas	Radish
Carrots	Greens	Squash
Corn	Melons	Swiss chard
Cucumber	Okra	

Light

Southern peas

Heavy = 6 cups of 6-12-12 or 10-10-10 per 100 square feet; Medium = 3 cups of 6-12-12 or 10-10-10 per 100 square feet; Light = 2 cups of 6-12-12 or 10-10-10 per 100 square feet.

PRUNING

Trim back **artemisia** to prevent it from becoming leggy. If the plants haven't been cut back in some time, you may trim them to about 6 inches high.

About the middle of the month, prune back perennial herbs such as **rue, sage**, and **thyme** to fresh green wood. This removes dead stem tips, helps shape the plants, and encourages new growth.

PROBLEMS

Watch out for cabbage loopers this month. They can be prevented by covering **cabbage** and other cole crops with row covers when they're planted, or you can dust or spray the loopers with Bt, an organic control.

APRIL

 PLANNING

The next time you're at a garden center, look at all the different kinds of **radishes** in the seed rack. While you may want to stick with your old favorite for your main crop, it's fun to experiment with various types.

 PLANTING

When the frost-free date for your area has passed, you can plant just about any vegetable or herb in the garden except those that are true heat lovers. Wait till May or later for **melons, okra, eggplant, Southern peas, pumpkins**, and **sweet potatoes**. Don't plant **basil** till you're sure that there's no frost in the forecast—it's very sensitive to cold.

Harden off transplants grown indoors before moving them to their final homes in the garden. (See page 38.)

After chance of frost has passed, sow seeds of these herbs where they are to grow: **basil, caraway, chervil, dill, hyssop, lovage, marjoram, summer savory, thyme,** and **fennel**. You may also plant **parsley** seeds, but soak them in water twenty-four to thirty-six hours first or nick the hard seed covering with a knife.

The first week of the month, continue sowing seeds or setting out plants of **cabbage, spinach, broccoli**, English and edible-podded **peas, potatoes, onions, mustard, turnips**, and **beets**. After that, it will be too hot when the plants mature.

For best pollination, sow **corn** in blocks rather than one or two straight rows.

Continue sowing seeds of **radishes** and different kinds of **leaf lettuce**. To extend the harvest and not end up with too much one week and not enough later in the month, sow a small amount of both every ten days during April.

Scientific research has shown that the best way to plant a **tomato** is the way you plant a **pepper**—at the same depth it grew before. Don't lay it on its side, don't bury it up to its top leaves in an extra-deep hole, don't remove all the top leaves. None of those techniques produce results as good as regular planting.

When you plant, install supports—trellises for **cucumbers**, poles for **beans**, and cages for **tomatoes**. In fact, it's best to install **bean** poles and **cucumber** trellises first, then plant the seeds at the base. **Tomato** cages should be at least 5 feet tall and 2 feet in diameter and anchored well at the base.

Chives, bee balm, lemon balm, mint, and **tansy** may all be divided this month,

if needed. Slice through the center of the plant with a sharp shovel, or dig up the plant and divide it with two spading forks. Replant the divisions at the same depth they grew before, and water well with a transplanting solution.

 CARE

Thin **radishes, beets, carrots, Swiss chard**, and other seed-sown vegetables. See page 90 for correct spacing. Thinning is tough work—it's hard to pull up and throw away a perfectly good vegetable. But think of it as something you're doing to help the plants that are left. They'll have more room to grow to their full potential.

Even if **asparagus** puts up stalks the first year, don't harvest them. Wait till the second year and then cut them only when they reach 8 inches high. Once the new stalks are about the size of a pencil, stop picking and wait till next year. Being patient helps the plant renew itself and ensures a larger harvest in the future.

Harvest **beets** when the roots reach 2 to 3 inches in diameter. Pull **carrots** when the tops or shoulders are $1/2$ to $3/4$ inch across. If you want to pull some **green onions** to use in spring salads, do so whenever they reach the size you like. Cut **rhubarb** stalks when they reach 8 to 15 inches.

WATERING

Seeds must be kept moist, but not soggy, until they germinate. If rainfall is irregular, water the seeds you've sown so they come up.

The usual rule of an inch of water per week holds true for vegetables although there are times when that water is essential and others times when the plant may be able to slide by a few extra days, if necessary. (See page 100.) But remember that if plants are stressed from lack of water, they aren't going to produce well and they're more likely to be attacked by insects.

FERTILIZING

Mix in fertilizer when preparing the vegetable garden for planting. (See page 97.) Herbs generally need little fertilizer if they're grown in soil that's been enriched with organic matter.

Side-dress **asparagus, broccoli, cabbage**, and **cauliflower** when they've been planted about a month. Also **Irish potatoes** after they have sprouted. *Side dressing* is the practice of applying a band of fertilizer about 3 inches away from plants. Use half the amount recommended on page 97.

(See page 100.) ... (See page 97.) ... recommended on page 97.

Timely Tip

Planting Depths for Vegetable Seeds

Beans	1 to 1½ inches	**Okra**	1 inch
Cantaloupe	1 inch	**Peas**	1 to 2 inches
Carrot	¼ inch	**Radish**	½ inch
Collards	½ inch	**Southern peas**	1 to 2 inches
Corn	1 to 1½ inches	**Spinach**	½ to ¾ inch
Cucumber	½ to ¾ inch	**Summer squash**	1 to 2 inches
Kale	½ inch	**Turnip**	½ inch
Lettuce	⅛ inch	**Watermelon**	1 to 2 inches
Mustard	½ inch	**Winter squash**	1 to 2 inches

Side Dressing

PRUNING

When planting, remove any damaged leaves. Also pick yellowing or brown leaves from plants when you see them in the garden. The garden will look better and is more likely to remain insect- and disease-free when you practice good sanitation.

PROBLEMS

Lemon verbena is one of the last herbs to leaf out. After cold winters, it may not return, but it could be next month before you know for sure.

Each time you visit the garden in April, take a hoe with you and chop down a few weeds. It's easier to control weeds when they're young.

If young seedlings are cut off at ground level, that's the work of cutworms. Paper collars around the stems of transplants are the best preventive.

MAY

 ## PLANNING

Some herbs—**lavender, artemisia**, and **santolina**, for instance—require well-drained soil. If you haven't been able to grow these herbs but you really want to, consider planting them in containers. They look especially nice grouped together, so look for containers that match but are different sizes.

 ## PLANTING

Once the temperature is consistently 80 degrees Fahrenheit or above, plant the crops that need heat—**eggplant, melons, okra, pumpkins, Southern peas**, and **sweet potatoes**.

Plant **sweet potato** slips so that the top two leaves are above soil level. Space them about a foot apart in rows that are 3 feet apart or in hills or mounds 4 feet from one another. Avoid wet spots and don't mix fertilizer in the soil when planting.

Continue planting all herbs and all warm-season vegetables—**beans, corn, cucumbers, pepper, summer squash, tomato**, and **zucchini**.

You may also plant more **leaf lettuce** in May, but sow the seeds in a spot that will be shaded some in the afternoon. Also, choose a heat-tolerant cultivar of **lettuce**.

The nice thing about container gardening is that it's never too late to plant. If you don't have enough space—or enough sun—in the yard for a garden, try a few herbs and vegetables in pots near the back door. Mix a water-holding polymer such as Moisture Mizer™ and a slow-release pelleted fertilizer into the potting mix before moistening it and planting.

If you have a sunny place in the garden where you'd like to plant herbs, but it isn't close enough to stretch a hose there easily, these herbs like dry soil, once they're established: **Dill, hyssop, lamb's ear, rosemary, sage**, and **santolina**.

University research has shown that **tomatoes** planted in cages bear more fruits than those that are staked, but they do begin bearing slightly later. If you're trying for the earliest **tomato** harvest in your neighborhood, you may want to stake a couple of 'Early Girl' plants and put the main-season **tomatoes** in cages.

 ## CARE

To have the **"baby lettuces"** that are so popular—and so pricey—start snipping **leaf lettuce** when the plants reach about 6 inches high. Cut them with sharp scissors and leave about 1 inch at the base of the leaf on the plant so it will resprout. You will get several cuttings from each plant.

Depending on when you planted **cauliflower**, it may need blanching the first of the month. When small heads form, pull the outer leaves over the head and fasten them with string or a rubber band. This keeps the **cauliflower** white.

If the soil is warm, it's fine to mulch vegetable and herb plants with 2 to 4 inches of organic matter—straw, hay, shredded leaves, etc. Those in the cooler parts of the area may want to wait till June 1 to mulch warm-season crops since soil slows down their growth.

Pick **peas** when the pods are deep green and the peas are small- to medium-sized. Cut **cabbage** when the heads are good-sized but still firm and the leaves are tight around the head.

 ## WATERING

All vegetables need an inch of rain weekly. When rain doesn't total that much in any week, it's up to the gardener to supply the shortfall. Vegetables that need water, especially when buds and fruits are being formed, include **cucumber, melons, peas**, and **squash**. Vegetables that need an even supply of water throughout their growing season are **beets, carrots, eggplant, greens, peppers, radishes**, and **tomatoes**.

Be aware that many insecticides are toxic to bees. Read the label of the product you're planning to use; if it isn't safe around bees, apply it at dusk when bees are no longer active in the garden.

Take the time to water the soil thoroughly to make sure it soaks in deeply. That does your plants the most good. Water herbs only when the soil is dry 2 inches deep. After the entire vegetable garden is planted for the season, consider installing drip irrigation or laying soaker hoses at the base of the plants. This is the easy way to supply the moisture that your plants will need in the coming months.

 # FERTILIZING

Fertilize vegetables at planting time, mixing granular 6-12-12 or 10-10-10 with the soil. Side-dress **corn** with 6-12-12 or 10-10-10 when it reaches 6 inches high. (See page 97.)

 # PRUNING

Cut back the woody centers that develop on older **thyme** plants.

 # PROBLEMS

Aphids and whiteflies are common problems in the yard this time of year. If they turn up in the vegetable or herb garden, try hosing them off with water. Then, if necessary, spray with insecticidal soap. If whiteflies are a persistent problem, buy yellow sticky traps at the garden

Timely Tip

It's fun to grow vegetables in containers, but it isn't always easy to know exactly what size container to use and how many seeds or plants to put in it. Here's a handy guide for regular-sized plants. You may be able to fit more in if you use dwarf varieties:

Beans	2 plants per 8-inch pot
Beets	4 plants per 8-inch pot
Broccoli	1 plant per 12-inch pot
Brussels sprouts	1 plant per 12-inch pot
Cabbages	1 plant per 10-inch pot
Carrots	1 plant per inch of diameter (the pot must be deep)
Cauliflower	1 plant per 12-inch pot
Cucumbers	1 plant per 8-inch pot (must have trellis or support)
Eggplant	1 plant per 12-inch pot
Lettuces	1 plant per 8-inch pot
Onions	1 plant for each 3 inches of diameter
Peas	1 plant per 6-inch pot (must have trellis or support)
Peppers	1 plant per 8-inch pot
Radishes	1 plant per inch of diameter
Spinach	2 plants per 8-inch pot
Squash	1 plant per 12-inch pot
Swiss chard	1 plant per 12-inch pot
Tomatoes	1 plant per 12- to 18-inch pot (must have support)

center and put them next to susceptible plants. The insects are attracted by the yellow color and get stuck in the goo. The first **tomato** blossoms may not become pollinated, but you can do the job yourself by gently tapping the flower as soon as it is completely open.

Mexican bean beetles may become a problem on all types of **beans**, turning the leaves into clear skeletons. They can be controlled by insecticides or picked off by hand.

Don't be concerned when the first few **squash** blossoms fall off without producing any fruit. The early blossoms are usually male, and it's the female blossoms that produce the **squash**.

Be aware that many insecticides are toxic to bees. Read the label of the product you're planning to use; if it isn't safe around bees, apply it at dusk when bees are no longer active in the garden.

JUNE
Herbs & Vegetables

 PLANNING

If you enjoy having hummingbirds in your garden, look for a **pineapple sage** plant (*Salvia rutilans*). Its red blossoms attract the tiny hummers, and the scent of the leaves is enticing to gardeners. To get the most of the fragrance, grow the plant in a container and place it in front of a fan on the deck or patio. That really circulates the pineapple aroma.

 PLANTING

To grow **lettuce** in the summertime, you must do three things:

1 Choose a heat-resistant variety of **leaf lettuce**.

2 Sow the seeds in a partially shady spot early in the month. If you don't have a shady spot, rig up a row cover over the **lettuce** bed. If temperatures are 90 degrees Fahrenheit or above, **lettuce** seed won't germinate, so you may have to start it indoors and transplant it into the garden.

3 Sow only what you can eat in two to three weeks, and harvest it regularly. The longer **lettuce** has been in the garden, the more likely it is to bolt (go to seed).

It's not too late to set out **eggplant, pepper**, or **tomato** plants, or sow seeds of

beans, **cucumber, melons, okra, Southern peas, summer squash**, and any herb plants.

You may also sow seeds of annual herbs such as **basil, caraway, chervil**, and **dill** where you want them to grow.

This is a good month to take cuttings of herbs. The herbs that are most easily propagated by cuttings are **artemisia, bay, French tarragon, lavender, lemon balm, rosemary, rue, santolina, scented geraniums**, and **winter savory**. Cut off 3 to 5 inches of new growth, strip off all but the top leaves and dip the end of the cutting in a rooting hormone such as Rootone®. Plant the cuttings in a flat or pot of moist potting mix. Place in the shade and keep the soil moist until the cuttings have rooted (three to four weeks, usually). Remove the rooted cuttings and pot them individually or plant them in the herb garden.

Plant **sweet potato** slips the first of the month if you haven't earlier. (See page 100.) To avoid disease problems, don't plant them where they grew last year. They take about four months to reach maturity.

Continue planting **beans, cucumbers, eggplant, melons, okra, pepper plants, pumpkins, Southern peas, summer squash, tomato** plants, and **zucchini**.

 CARE

Pick **peas** and harvest **broccoli, cabbage, carrots**, and other cool-season crops regularly. Once hot weather is here to stay, they will rapidly deteriorate. Harvest **garlic** when the majority of the leaves have turned yellow.

Mulch all garden plants with 2 to 4 inches of organic material—anything from pine straw or cocoa hulls in the herb garden to weed-free straw in the vegetable plot. Remove weeds, and water the soil deeply before mulching. One trick to get more moisture-retention from your mulch is to water the soil, lay two or three sheets of newspaper on top, water the paper, and then spread your usual mulch on top. Regularly tie **tomatoes** to stakes or other supports.

WATERING

An old-fashioned way to water the vegetable garden is still effective. Wash plastic milk jugs and then, using a nail, poke holes in the sides of them. Bury the jugs up to their necks next to plants (this works best for individual plants, such as **tomatoes**, rather than row crops such as **beans**). Fill the jugs with water, or water mixed with a soluble fertilizer, and replace the lid. The water drains out slowly near the plants' roots.

When using this technique, dig into the soil and see when it needs watering again, but if there's no rainfall during the summer months, a rule of thumb would be 1½ gallons of water per week for each plant of **cucumber, eggplant, melons, peppers**, and **squash**. Give **tomato** plants about 2½ gallons. Start with these figures and adjust according to your soil, the amount of rainfall, the temperature, and the size of the plants. You may find that some plants need two or three times these amounts in the hottest part of summer, others only half when they're small.

FERTILIZING

Side-dress **corn** when it's about 6 inches high and **sweet potatoes** a month after planting. (see page 99.) **Sweet potatoes** don't like fertilizer with a high nitrogen content, so stick with 6-12-12 or a fertilizer with a high potash content (such as kelp).

Lightly fertilize **eggplant, peppers**, and **tomatoes** after they set their first fruits.

PRUNING

Cut back **rue** so it doesn't become woody. Pinch **scented geraniums** to keep the plants compact.

Timely Tip

Harvesting Herbs

The best time to harvest herbs is just before they bloom because their essential oils are strongest then.

- Cut herbs by midmorning (when there's no dew on the leaves). Don't cut more than one-fourth or one-third of the plant, especially in very hot weather. Avoid harvesting herbs in rainy weather.
- Rinse briefly in cold water, if needed, and let them air dry. Place in a plastic bag and refrigerate until dinnertime.

There are several methods of freezing herbs:
- Rinse them briefly and pat dry. Strip the leaves from the stems. Chop the leaves in a food processor, mix with stock or water, and freeze in ice cube trays. Add to soups or stews in place of other liquid.
- Rinse briefly, pat dry, and strip leaves from stems. Chop the leaves in a food processor, gradually adding about ½ cup oil for each 2 cups of herbs. Spoon into small containers and freeze. Use as the oil portion of a salad dressing or marinade, or use to sauté meat.
- Rinse and dry herbs; remove the leaves from the stems and place them in a small plastic container with a lid. Fill the container as full as possible, and place it in the freezer.

See page 105 for tips on drying herbs.

When growing **tomatoes** on stakes, pinch out the suckers that develop between the main stem and branches since they grow into branches on their own and make the plant too heavy. These suckers can be used to start a fall crop of **tomatoes**. Root them as explained under **Planting**. (It's fine to leave the suckers in place if your **tomatoes** are caged, rather than staked.)

PROBLEMS

A leathery patch on the end of **tomatoes** is a symptom of blossom-end rot. It occurs after too much rain followed by a dry spell. Remove the affected fruit and toss it away. Try to provide a more even moisture supply in the future. Next spring, two months before planting **tomatoes**, apply lime where **tomatoes** will grow. That helps prevent blossom-end rot. So does using 6-12-12 instead of 10-10-10.

JULY

PLANNING

If you want to grow a fall vegetable garden, begin planning now.

1 Think about varieties—some grow better in the spring and some in the fall. Consider how long it takes a particular variety to reach maturity (this information is available on seed packets and in catalogs; also see page 89). Because fall days may be cool, add ten days to that number.

2 See pages 22 or 23 for the average first frost in your area (or check with your local Extension Service if you live at a higher elevation than most of your county). All warm-season vegetables (**beans, cucumbers**) will need to reach maturity at least two weeks before frost. Crops that don't mind some cold weather (**broccoli, carrots, cabbage, cauliflower, collards, kale, kohlrabi, mustard, spinach, turnip greens**) can mature about two weeks after the average first frost date.

3 To determine the last possible planting date for warm-season vegetables, subtract the number of days to maturity (don't forget to add ten days) from the date of two weeks before the first frost. For cool-season vegetables, subtract the number of days to maturity (plus ten) to the date two weeks after the average first frost.

PLANTING

As one vegetable crop finishes bearing, pull it up and plant another—some **pattypan squash** where **beans** have finished bearing or **cucumbers** where **English peas** grew. This lets you grow more vegetables on less land and gives you a harvest that's more evenly spread out through the summer.

The first of July isn't too late to plant seeds of **black-eyed peas** or other **Southern peas** that mature in sixty days or fewer. No fertilizer is needed.

Indoors, you may want to start seeds of **cabbage, cauliflower**, and **broccoli**. See page 32 for tips on starting seeds.

CARE

To encourage the plants to continue producing, pick **cucumbers** and **squash** when they're small. The skin of **summer squash** and **zucchini** should be soft enough to pierce with a fingernail.

Check the garden daily, and harvest when vegetables have reached the optimum size. **Corn** is ripe when the silk turns brown and the kernels are plump and filled with "milk." **Eggplant** skin should be glossy and spring back when poked. **Onion** tops turn yellow and fall over. The tops of **Irish potatoes** begin to die back. Pick **okra** when the pods are 2 to 3 inches long. **Bell peppers** can be harvested when they're green, or they may be left on the plant until they turn red, if you prefer.

WATERING

The higher the temperature, the more moisture vegetables will need if rainfall isn't at least an inch per week. Herbs typically require less watering than vegetables but you shouldn't let them wilt.

FERTILIZING

When temperatures are high, avoid fertilizing except for water-soluble fertilizers applied weekly to plants growing in containers.

When you pull up a spent crop, work some compost or rotted manure into the soil if you plan to plant the area again soon. This will improve the soil's texture and provide a mild fertilizing effect.

PRUNING

Pinch back **scented geraniums, basil, mint**, and **oregano** as needed to keep the plants compact.

When temperatures are high, avoid fertilizing except for water-soluble fertilizers applied weekly to plants growing in containers.

Continue to remove suckers on staked **tomato** plants.

Remove diseased, damaged, or yellow leaves from vegetable or herb plants. These often attract insects if left in the garden.

 PROBLEMS

Sometime this month, pull back the mulch in various places about the garden and see whether drip irrigation is leaving an unbroken line of moisture along the length of the tubes. If you notice a dry spot, it probably means that one or more of the emitters is clogged and needs to be cleared.

Caterpillars on **parsley, dill**, and **fennel** are likely to be black swallowtail butterflies. Try to keep the caterpillars confined to one or two plants. This will contribute to the development of the butterflies while not sacrificing your entire crop of herbs.

If **mints** develop rust spots (usually orange, but occasionally black or purple) on their leaves, cut the plants back to 1 inch high and remove the affected foliage from the garden. The new growth should be clear of the problem. Try to avoid overhead watering, and increase air circulation where possible.

You've tried to contain **mint** and it just hasn't worked—the plant has escaped and is taking over. A barrier must extend about a foot below soil level, but even then you have to watch and see that **mint** doesn't grow over the top of the barrier or over the rim of the container in which it is planted. Regularly pull up any plants that have rooted where you don't want them to grow. Also watch out for **oregano**, which spreads by underground runners.

If you see black or brown insects on **squash, gourds**, or **pumpkins**, they will likely be squash bugs. They suck plant juices. A mild infestation can often be controlled with insecticidal soap, but it's important to spray the undersides as well as the tops of the leaves. Also inspect the leaves and stems carefully, removing any egg masses by hand.

Timely Tip

Tips on Drying Herbs

1 Rinse herbs briefly and pat dry.

2 The best way to dry herbs is on a screen. With very small herbs or seedheads, cover the screen with paper towels. (Leave **basil** leaves whole, and place them between paper towels.) Place the screen indoors in a well-ventilated place. (Never dry herbs outdoors in the sun.) Stir the herbs with your hands three or four times daily so they'll dry more evenly. Complete drying takes from three days to a week.

3 If drying herbs in a microwave, use the lowest power setting. Place herbs on a paper towel or paper plate and cover with a paper towel. Start with one minute and see what results you get. Increase or decrease time by a few seconds as needed for the next batch. If herbs turn brown, they've been dried too long. **Parsley** and **chives** often dry well in the microwave.

4 Herbs for craft use are often air dried by tying them into bunches and hanging them upside down in a warm, dry spot for one to two weeks. (This isn't recommended for herbs you plan to use for cooking; they can get dusty, and it's often difficult to separate the leaves and stems.)

5 A really easy trick, if you have a frost-free refrigerator, is to place herbs in a single layer on a paper towel in the fridge. They'll dry in 24 hours.

AUGUST

PLANNING

If you've done a good job in the garden, you should have an abundance of produce this month. What will you do with all of it? Eat it, of course, and share with friends and neighbors. But don't overlook the opportunity to do a good deed with your produce. Soup kitchens, nursing homes, and the food bank in your area would be delighted to receive your excess vegetables and herbs to distribute to the less fortunate. It will give you a good feeling to share your bounty and know that it will be put to good use. In fact, you may want to consider planting a bit extra next year just for this purpose. The Garden Writers Association has a program called Plant-a-Row that encourages gardeners to do just that. For more information, e-mail PAR@gwaa.org or call toll-free (877) 492-2727.

The dog days of August offer the opportunity to catch up on writing in your garden journal. Which vegetables and herbs have been spectacular successes, and which didn't perform up to expectations? Which varieties would you try again? What pests have you had to contend with? Write it all down so that when you're planning next year's garden, you'll remember exactly what happened this year—and you can profit from the experience.

PLANTING

If you're a big fan of **cucumbers** or want to put up one more batch of pickles, plant seeds no later than August 1.

For fall gardens, these vegetables should be planted no later than the middle of the month: seeds of **bush beans, carrots**, and **summer squash**, and plants of **broccoli, cabbage**, and **cauliflower**.

You may also sow seeds of **kale, mustard**, and **turnip greens** this month. Plant a smaller amount than usual, and follow with another planting in two weeks and a final sowing two weeks after that.

CARE

Pay attention when the greenish skin of **cantaloupes** begins to lighten. That's a sign they're reaching maturity. These **melons** are ready to be eaten when you tug the stem and it separates from the fruit. You should also be able to detect the fragrance of the fresh fruit. On **watermelons**, the top will become dull and the area of the skin that's closest to the ground will turn from light to bright yellow. The stem should also begin to turn brown.

If you're picking **tomatoes** before they're completely red because birds are pecking on them don't place the **tomatoes** on a sunny windowsill to finish ripening. Put them on the kitchen counter instead. They'll ripen just as soon but be of higher quality.

Harvest **Southern peas** when the seeds are fully developed and the pods are still soft.

Remove damaged or overripe vegetables from plants and toss them on the compost pile (if you keep a "hot" pile that will kill the seeds) or in the trash. Leaving them on the plants attracts insects, which may winter over and cause you problems next year.

Onions are ready to be dug when at least three fourths of the tops have fallen over.

WATERING

One of the big drawbacks of a fall garden is that it usually needs more frequent watering than a spring garden, because temperatures are higher and average rainfall is typically less. The soil in which any seeds have been sown must be kept moist until the seeds germinate, and then, if rainfall is lacking, the young seedlings may need frequent watering while they're small.

When there's no rain within a week, water deeply any vegetables that are bearing fruit. Often the plants will keep producing far into fall if given adequate moisture during late-summer dry spells.

Don't let perennial herbs go completely dry. To survive winter, they need to go into cold weather in good shape.

FERTILIZING

Lightly fertilize fall crops as you plant, or wait until they are about 4 inches tall and side-dress with 10-10-10 granular fertilizer (see page 97 for amounts).

About twice a week, apply a water-soluble fertilizer as you water container-grown vegetables. Feed containerized herbs only if they aren't growing well.

PRUNING

By the middle of the month, stop pinching or harvesting perennial herbs. This gives them plenty of time to harden off and prepare for cold.

Timely Tips

Make herb vinegars (great for gift giving) by adding 1 part washed herbs—leaves, whole stems, or flowers—to 4 parts white vinegar. Leave the herbs in the vinegar for three to six weeks, then strain. If you like, add a few sprigs of fresh herbs to the bottle before pouring the vinegar back in.

You may freeze **dill, parsley, oregano, sage, tarragon**, and **thyme**. Rinse the herbs gently, if needed, and pat dry. Place the herbs—one type to a container—in a plastic bowl or other freezer container with a tight-fitting lid. Be sure to use them within four months.

Once herbs have flowered, they're not as potent for using fresh or for preserving, but you can still get use from the plant: Cut off the flowers and use them in salads or cooking. Try **basil** blossoms with **tomato** dishes.

PROBLEMS

Tiny holes in the leaves of **eggplants** are usually the result of flea beetles. Spraying the leaves and also the ground around plants with water can help. So can an application or two of insecticidal soap.

When leaves of **tomato** plants are gobbled up, suspect the tomato hornworm, which will also munch hungrily on the **tomato** fruit, too. This large green caterpillar is easily picked off by hand, but it's hard to spot because it blends into its surroundings so perfectly. A spraying or dusting of Bt will kill small hornworms,

but larger ones may need a chemical control. Check with the Extension Service for recommendations.

When temperatures top 90 degrees Fahrenheit, blossoms of **tomatoes** and **peppers** fail to pollinate and fall off. There's nothing wrong with your plants; they will return to normal when temperatures moderate somewhat. There are varieties of **tomatoes** that do continue producing new fruit even in high temperatures. Read up on them; you might want to try one or two plants next year.

SEPTEMBER

PLANNING

With cold weather on the horizon, what are you going to do about your potted herbs? By the end of the month, decide whether to bring some or all indoors over the winter, take cuttings so you can bring smaller plants inside, or just let them succumb to frost.

If you've waited too late to sow a cover crop (see **Planting**), you may want to write a note to yourself in your garden journal or notebook about buying the seed next spring so you'll be ready to plant a soil-improving green manure on vacant areas throughout the growing season—or at least at the end of summer.

PLANTING

By the first of September, you should have planted **collards, kale, kohlrabi,** and **mustard** in the fall garden. By the middle of the month, plant **leaf lettuce, radishes, spinach**, and **turnip greens**. See page 90 for spacing and page 99 for the depth to plant. Mix 10-10-10 granular fertilizer with the soil before sowing the seeds. Water thoroughly, and keep the soil moist until seeds sprout.

If you have them, seeds of annual herbs or **parsley** may be started in individual pots to grow indoors in a sunny spot over winter. Depending on the weather, you may start them outdoors and move them inside after they've germinated and begun growing or you can just keep the pots of seeds indoors where you want them to grow. See page 32 in the **Annuals** chapter for tips on growing plants from seeds.

Because frost will soon be upon us, September is a good month to take cuttings of herbs that you'd like to over-winter. See page 102 for a list of herbs that propagate well by cuttings. If you haven't rooted cuttings before, see page 102 for help. All herbs growing indoors need as much sun as possible.

Using a sharp trowel, insert it in the soil straight down in a clump of **chives** to remove a small portion to pot and keep indoors. **Chives** are one of the most easy-going and useful herbs. They're handy to have in a pot in a sunny windowsill in cold weather.

To improve the soil in your vegetable plot, plant a green manure crop—also called a *cover crop*—in areas where the vegetables have already been harvested. These are grasses or grains that protect bare soil over winter and then are tilled under in early spring to produce valuable organic matter and add nutrients to the soil. **Alfalfa, buckwheat, soybeans**, and **Southern peas** are usually sown in August, but will still improve the soil if sown in early September. **Crimson clover, annual rye**, and **vetch** may be sown anytime this month. Don't wait too late—plant seeds about a month before your average last frost day.

CARE

Annual herbs are going to get killed by the first frost, so harvest as much as you can use this month. See page 105 to learn about drying herbs and page 103 for advice on freezing them. If you want to harvest more than usual at one time (because a rainy spell is forecast, for instance), don't refrigerate them. (Annual herbs don't like low temperatures.) Instead, use or preserve them right away or fill a glass with water, put the cuttings in it, and keep them at room temperature for a day or two.

WATERING

Keep perennial herbs watered during September dry spells so they'll go into winter in good shape. This gives them a better chance of survival.

All seeds sown this month—indoors or out—must be kept moist until they're sprouted. Then, because the root systems of the young plants are still small and can't absorb too much moisture at one time, continue to water whenever the soil surface dries slightly—provided a rainfall doesn't do the job for you.

Tomatoes and other long-season vegetables can often be kept bearing until the first frost and, if protected then, even beyond. But that requires you to care for the plants as if they were new—and that means seeing that they receive plenty of water if rainfall amounts are low this month.

 FERTILIZING

Fall vegetable crops need some fertilizer—especially nitrogen, which is no longer in the soil from your spring or early summer fertilizing. Often the fertilizer mixed with the soil at planting time is sufficient, especially if your soil is well amended with organic matter, but keep an eye on the new plants as they sprout and grow. If they aren't growing as quickly as normal in fall, or if they aren't as green as they should be, sprinkle a handful of granular fertilizer around each plant or side-dress with 10-10-10.

Apply a water-soluble fertilizer for houseplants to the herbs in pots that you have taken indoors.

Timely Tip

How to Make Potpourri

Take the herbs that are left in the garden—even those that have flowered—and make sweet-smelling potpourri.

- Harvest 4 cups of fragrant herb leaves (**scented geraniums** and **lemon balm**, for instance). Dry them according to the directions on page 105. It's important that all ingredients be completely dry, or they may mildew.

- Pick 4 cups of flowers (fragrant ones such as **roses** are nice, but any may be used). Dry them completely.

- Buy 1 ounce of fixative (usually orris root or vetiver) and some essential oil at a craft or herbal shop.

- Place the herbs and flowers in a large plastic bowl with a lid. Add the fixative and 9 drops of essential oil, and mix well.

- Put the lid on the bowl, and place the bowl in a cool dark spot.

- Shake the bowl once a week.

- The potpourri should be ready to use in forty to sixty days.

Do not fertilize perennial herbs. Their growth needs to slow down so there's no excessive new growth to get killed by frost.

 PRUNING

If you have **melons, gourds**, or **pumpkins** actively growing in the garden this month, pinch the tips of the vines. That will cause the plants to direct their energies into ripening the fruits already on the vines instead of putting on more

green growth or developing tiny fruits that will never mature.

 PROBLEMS

Just because the vegetable growing season is coming to an end, don't let insects or disease get a foothold. Many such problems in the garden persist from year to year because they overwinter. It's smarter to handle the problem now so that it doesn't come back to affect you in the future.

OCTOBER

Herbs & Vegetables

PLANNING

It can take years to get some garden soils to the point where you feel they're just right, and even then, organic matter added to soils decays rapidly in our climate. What's a gardener to do? Keep improving the soil with a new batch of organic matter each year. That can get expensive if you buy soil amendments, but if you make your own compost, it's free. With leaves falling this month and vegetable plants being killed by frost, fall is a good time to get serious about composting. The general directions are on page 356. You can go the fast route— making a layered compost pile as you would lasagna, keeping it moist and turning it regularly. Or if time doesn't matter, you can just pile everything into a bin and let it eventually rot. In the latter case, though, you have to be careful not to toss anything with seeds into the pile (from weeds to rotten **tomatoes**), any diseased or insect-covered plant part, or any plant that has been treated with a chemical. Even if you choose the let-it-rot method, as most people do, you can speed the process some by cutting up in small pieces everything you add to the pile. What about newspapers as compost? A few—shredded or torn to bits—are okay, but mostly they're better as mulch. If you don't have a compost bin, consider building or buying one in October.

PLANTING

Plant **garlic** this month. Separate a bulb into individual cloves and plant each clove 2 inches deep and 4 inches apart in a part of the garden that has well-drained soil. (**Garlic** stays small if grown in unamended clay.) Since the **garlic** will stay in place until about June, place it where it won't be in the way as you till the garden in the fall or spring.

If you have a sunny place indoors where you can grow pots of herbs, start them from seed anytime this month. (See page 32.)

CARE

Consider protecting some of your herbs and vegetables that are in excellent shape and still bearing well. Often the first frost of fall is followed by a spell of mild weather, so if you keep plants from being killed by an early frost, they continue bearing for some weeks longer. Quick overnight protection can be as simple as tossing an old quilt or mattress pad over a desirable plant and anchoring it so it won't blow or fall off. Row covers (available at garden centers) can be set up over larger spaces and kept in place all the time. Be careful about using clear plastic, however. The sun shining through plastic can burn the leaves and fruits.

Pick green **tomatoes** if a frost threatens and you don't plan to protect them. Wash them carefully, and place them in a single layer in a dark spot. Check them weekly, and toss out any that have rotted. Don't place them on a sunny windowsill.

Harvest **winter squash** before frost. The skins should be hard enough that a fingernail can't pierce them. **Pumpkins** should be an even color. Cut the stem from the vine, and let the **squash** or **pumpkin** dry in the garden for a week or two. Then store in as cool a spot as is available (50 to 55 degrees Fahrenheit is excellent).

All herbs that are going to overwinter indoors should be in the house by the first of the month. This is especially true for **bay trees** and **rosemary**. The cooler the temperatures they're exposed to outdoors, the harder it is for the plants to become acclimated to conditions indoors.

Harvest vegetables regularly. This is especially important for warm-season crops that will soon be killed by frost. Besides, plants continue to produce more vegetables if they're picked regularly.

Keep an eye on cool-season vegetables such as **kale, collards**, and **cauliflower**; harvest them as they begin to mature this month.

Remove **asparagus** ferns after they've been killed by frost. Mulch the plants with 2 to 4 inches of organic matter.

During a dry spell, dig **sweet potatoes** when the roots are about 2 to 3 inches in diameter and soil temperature is above 55 degrees Fahrenheit. Dig carefully since the skins are thin and easily damaged. Place the **sweet potatoes**—unwashed—in a warm, dry spot (in a heated part of the house if temperatures outside or in the garage have gotten chilly). Avoid sun. They will need to cure for ten to fourteen days. Then store them in a single layer in a dark, cool place (but with temperatures above 50 degrees Fahrenheit—don't refrigerate). Check **sweet potatoes** weekly to make sure they haven't begun to rot. Remove any that have deteriorated.

WATERING

Water potted herbs growing indoors when the soil's surface has dried.

Water perennial herbs if rainfall is below normal.

All container vegetables and herbs that are still growing should be watered daily if there's no rain.

In the garden, water vegetables and herbs that are still in good shape just as carefully at the end of the season as you do earlier in the year. As long as they're producing, take good care of them.

Check fall vegetables during dry spells to make sure they don't dry out, which will reduce your harvest.

FERTILIZING

No more fertilizing is required outdoors in the vegetable or herb garden.

If potted herbs indoors are in full sun and growing actively, they may be fertilized with a water-soluble plant food once a month until growth slows. Use a balanced formula, such as 5-5-5 or 20-20-20, or use a high-nitrogen fertilizer (10-5-5) since you want to encourage leaf growth.

PRUNING

As plants are killed by frost, remove them from the garden. If they suffered no disease or insect problems, break them into small sections and toss them onto the compost pile with the leaves you're probably adding weekly.

PROBLEMS

Cabbage loopers may still be a problem in the fall, before frost, on all cole crops (**broccoli, Brussels sprouts, cauliflower**, and **cabbage**). They may also eat holes in **lettuce** and in **beet** leaves. Hand picking works fine if the infestation is small and you can reach the caterpillars, but you may also spray or dust with Bt, an organic control.

NOVEMBER

 ## PLANNING

This is the time of year when the thoughts of a dedicated vegetable grower turn to greenhouses. It's always so difficult to give up fresh-grown produce and have to return to the pallid stuff sold at the supermarket. Could this be the year that you break down and buy or build a greenhouse? Many growers who start plants from seed find them ideal for that purpose, as well as perfect for extending the season to almost year-round growing (depending on whether and how much you plan to heat the structure). Greenhouses come in a wide range of configurations—from plastic-covered "hoop houses" to elegant glass-walled additions to the house. Size and materials determine the cost; there's usually one for every budget and circumstance.

 ## PLANTING

Garlic and **Egyptian (multiplier) onions** may still be planted outdoors if the ground isn't frozen (see page 110).

Start seeds of **leaf lettuce** and **spinach** in a cold frame. (Or the seeds may be sown indoors and the plants moved out into the cold frame.)

The only other planting that continues in November is indoors and in greenhouses. Sow seeds of annual herbs and **parsley** in pots if you have a sunny windowsill. **Leaf lettuce** is grown easily under grow lights.

 ## CARE

Some cultivars of **rosemary** may live through mild winters in parts of the region, but after a heavy frost or two, be sure to mulch plants heavily—use about 4 inches of shredded leaves. But if the area where the **rosemary** is planted isn't well drained, it may be best to dig up the plant and take it indoors. You may also take cuttings, before frost, and root them indoors.

Lightly mulch all perennial and biennial herbs (see page 91 if you don't know which are annuals and which perennials). Several herbs also appreciate wind protection during winter. These include **chamomile, lavender, sage**, and **tarragon**. Use row-cover material to build a little three-sided box to block wind, or cover the plants with evergreen boughs.

If you didn't last month, mulch the **asparagus** bed during November. Remove the tops of the plants first, and toss them onto the compost pile.

Mulch vegetables that are staying in the ground over winter—use a 6-inch-thick blanket of straw over **carrots** and 2 to 3 inches of hay, straw, or shredded leaves at the base of **collards**.

Remove all plant supports—**tomato** cages, **bean** poles, **cucumber** trellises—from the garden. Clean and store them in a shed or garage if possible. They will last longer if not exposed to winter weather.

November is garden clean-up time if you haven't kept up with this earlier in the fall. Pull up all plants and compost them or till them under.

Drain all hoses, including soaker hoses, and store than in the garage or basement for the winter. Do the same with drip or trickle irrigation systems in the vegetable garden, since you'll have to till the area soon or in the spring. Store all parts of the system together indoors.

Many vegetable gardeners who like to plant crops early in the spring till the garden now, turning under all mulch and old plants. This improves the soil, helps kill overwintering insects, and readies the garden for the new planting season. Leave a few rows in furrows or in mounds 6 to 8 inches high. These will warm up and dry out first and be ready to plant sooner than the rest of the garden.

To protect the garden from erosion over winter, cover regular rows with fresh shredded leaves. Don't cover hilled-up rows since the mulch will keep the soil cool in spring.

Another way to use fall's abundance of leaves to good advantage in the garden is to pile them in the paths between rows. That prevents your feet from getting muddy when you walk in the garden, and it improves the soil when you till in the leaves next fall. Some gardeners alternate rows and paths—that is, this year's leaf-filled paths become next year's garden rows.

On a warm day, pour soil from containers into a black plastic garbage bag and wash the pots using soapy water. Scrub off dirt and fertilizer salts with a wire brush. Then rinse the pots well and let them soak for a few minutes in a tub of 9 parts water mixed with 1 part liquid bleach. After the containers dry, store them in a shed, the garage, or the basement—clay or terra cotta pots should be kept somewhere that the temperature doesn't fall below freezing during winter. Save the soil for future use.

 # WATERING

Little watering should be needed this month, except indoors. Herbs growing in clay pots need water more frequently than those in plastic containers. Those in the most sun require the most water.

If you've started seeds, keep them moist but not wet until they sprout.

 # FERTILIZING

Plants use fertilizer only when they're growing; since plants have stopped growing this time of year (except indoors or in greenhouses and cold frames), there's no need to feed them.

Store all fertilizer in a dry place during winter.

 # PRUNING

No pruning is necessary this month.

 # PROBLEMS

When herbs taken indoors lose some leaves, it's usually due to lower light levels and the process of becoming acclimated to less-than-ideal conditions. If possible, give them more light. But it's natural for **lemon verbena** to lose all its foliage—it's a deciduous plant.

If November is rainy, walk around the herb and vegetable gardens after a rain to see whether there's standing water anywhere. Puddled water can kill perennial herbs, and its presence tells you that you may need to work on drainage in the vegetable garden next spring.

DECEMBER

 ## PLANNING

If you've been hankering after a cold frame or raised bed, now's the time to plan them. They're inexpensive and easy to build, and they make vegetable growing much easier. Check with the Extension Service (see pages 344 to 353 for the one in your county) or on the Internet to find plans.

As garden catalogs begin to fill mailboxes this time of year, set them aside in one spot if you can't get to them right away. When you're ready to dream of summer and warm ripe **tomatoes**, it helps to have the catalogs—and a yellow legal pad or your garden notebook—all in the same place for easy reference and comparison.

Were you pleased with the performance of your vegetable or herb garden this year? If not, is there something you can do to change the situation next year? Cold winter nights are excellent for planning. Even during hectic holiday times, you may find an hour spent thinking about next year's garden will alleviate some of the stress and sense of hurry. Use your garden journal or notebook as an aid in planning. Look back through it for notes of things you want to try and ideas that you picked up here and there but haven't tried yet.

 ## PLANTING

If the ground isn't frozen, you could plant **garlic**, since it needs a long growing season, beginning in winter. See page 110.

Indoors, you can start annual herbs from seed if you have a sunny spot in which to grow them.

 ## CARE

Is all the garden debris cleaned up and removed from the area or tilled under? Are supports out of the weather? Have hoses been moved to the garage? If any of these chores are still undone, take care of them on a mild day this month. In March, you will be happy that you did.

 ## WATERING

Water herbs indoors when the soil's surface dries. As weather gets cooler, the plants may not need water as often as before. Don't water just because it's Tuesday and that's when you usually water. Always check the soil to see whether it needs moisture. If it's still damp, wait a day or two before watering. Use room-temperature water that has stood overnight, and don't let water remain in the saucers.

 ## FERTILIZING

The only plants that are likely to need fertilizing this time of year are herbs actively growing indoors in a sunny spot. Use a balanced houseplant fertilizer (10-10-10) once every four to six weeks. If herbs aren't growing, don't fertilize them.

 ## PRUNING

Keep brown or yellowing leaves removed from potted herbs that are overwintering indoors.

The best way to keep herb plants from getting leggy is to pinch them occasionally. With culinary herbs, you're probably doing this regularly. But you may need to think about occasionally pruning herbs that you're growing more for scent or decoration.

 ## PROBLEMS

You shouldn't have any problems to worry about in December.

CHAPTER FOUR

Houseplants

Anyone can grow houseplants successfully. Honest. Still, millions of people believe otherwise. They usually shake their heads when the subject of houseplants comes up and say, "I always kill them. I must have a purple [brown, or black] thumb."

Plants know nothing of the color of your thumb. If they could talk, they'd probably tell you what makes them happy and healthy—how much light they need (probably more than you'd guess) and when they should be watered.

The path to failure usually begins by selecting a houseplant on the spur of the moment. It looks great, and you have the perfect spot for it on an end table in the family room. So you take it home. But maybe that plant needs a half day of sunlight and the end table it's destined for is in a dark corner. Or the plant's soil dries out about every other day and you just don't think about watering it more than once a week since you lead a busy life.

The moral is this: Do your homework before buying a houseplant. Match the conditions that the plant requires to those in your home. When you see a plant you like in the supermarket or garden center, read the label. It should give the name of the plant and its likes as far as light, temperature, and watering. If it doesn't tell you those things, don't buy the plant right then. Jot down the name and look for it on the list of easy-to-grow houseplants on page 137.

LIGHT

So you've looked up **arrowhead plant**, which says *Light: high to low*. And you wonder what in the world that means. It means the plant prefers bright light, but will grow in medium or low light. In other words, it's a versatile plant that will make itself at home in a number of different places around your house.

But how do you determine whether the various places around your house where you might like to grow houseplants have high, medium, or low light levels? Here's an easy test for any location: On a sunny day, place a sheet of white paper where you want to put a houseplant. Hold your open hand about 12 inches above the paper.

1 If you can't see a shadow, the natural light is too low unless supplemented by artificial light.

2 A fuzzy shadow that isn't recognizable as a hand indicates low light. (Refer to the list of plants on this page that will tolerate low light levels.)

3 A shadow that is a bit fuzzy but can be discerned as a hand indicates medium light.

4 A clear shadow means the area receives a high level of light.

Also keep in mind these general rules for houseplant lighting:

- The light is always going to be brighter near a window than it is 10 feet or more away.
- The sun shines in some windows more than others because of obstructions—a fence, roof overhang, nearby building, etc.
- Larger windows let in more light than smaller ones, and clean windows more than dirty ones.
- Light levels are higher in summer and lower in winter.

Plants for Low Light

No plant *prefers* low light, but some tolerate it nicely. These include:

- **Arrowhead plant**
- **Cast iron plant**
- **Chinese evergreen**
- **Corn plant**
- **Peace lily**
- **Peperomia**
- **Philodendron** (heart-leaf type)
- **Pothos**
- **Snake plant**

Houseplants

Plants for Medium Light

- **Aluminum plant**
- **Asparagus fern**
- **Boston fern**
- **Bromeliads**
- **Dieffenbachia**
- **Grape ivy**
- **Lady-slipper orchid**
- **Moth orchid**
- **Parlor palm**
- **Polka-dot plant**
- **Prayer plant**
- **Rubber plant**
- **Schefflera**
- **Spider plant**
- **Swedish ivy**

Start With Healthy Plants. That sounds pretty obvious, doesn't it? Who would do anything else? But so often people complain that a houseplant has died within two or three weeks of their buying it. Unless you didn't water at all during that time, or watered every day, there's no reason a healthy plant should die that quickly. People are so quick to blame themselves—"I'm just no good with houseplants"—when the problem obviously existed before the plant was purchased.

Avoid plants that:

- Look stressed or wilted.
- Have brown leaves or brown tips on leaves.
- Have several yellowing leaves (one at the bottom of the plant is okay).
- Have leaf spots.
- Lean to one side.
- Exhibit signs of insects (look under the leaves and where the leaves and stem intersect).
- Have no signs of new growth.
- Have soil that's bone dry.
- Have soil that smells odd (a sign of potential rotting).
- Are leggy.
- Have been exposed to freezing temperatures.

WATERING

Where most of the less-than-successful indoor gardeners go wrong is in watering. They either water too much—killing a plant with "kindness"—or they forget to water except at irregular intervals. Do either of those descriptions sound like you? Well, you don't have to keep making the same mistakes.

Solutions to Underwatering:

1 Buy plants that need very little water, such as **cactuses, snake plant**, and the bromeliad known as **silver vase** (*Aechmea fasciata*).

2 Make a weekly "watering date" with your houseplants and mark it on your calendar or in your PDA. If weekly isn't the right frequency, do it twice a week or every other week.

3 Use self-watering pots.

Solutions to Overwatering:

1 Grow only plants that need lots of water, such as **African violet, aluminum plant, croton** (*Codiaeum variegatum pictum*), **polka-dot plant**, and **wandering Jew** (*Zebrina pendula*).

2 Always test the soil before you water. (See below.)

3 Buy a moisture meter.

4 Never use pots without drainage holes.

5 Don't let excess water collect in saucers, cachepots, or decorative foil wrappings on plants from the florist.

General Rules for Watering

- Plants that need "average" watering (see list on pages 119 to 121) should be watered until the excess runs out of the drainage hole in the bottom of the pot. Empty the water from the saucer or decorative pot. Then don't water again until the soil is dry an inch below the surface.

- Water plants that want constantly moist soil just as you do those with average watering needs—but don't let the soil dry out between waterings. As soon as the soil's surface dries, water again.

How to Tell If a Plant Needs Watering

1 Pick up the pot. Does it feel very light? Then the plant generally needs watering.

2 Stick your index finger a couple of inches into the soil of a small- or medium-sized houseplant. Is it wet when you pull it out? If so, wait a few days before checking again. If it's dry, water.

3 Stick a wooden chopstick into the soil of a plant in a large pot to see whether it looks damp when you retrieve it. If it's not damp, water the plant.

4 Use a moisture meter. (These can give incorrect readings because of excess minerals in the soil of older plants, but are generally a boon to gardeners who aren't sure whether it's time to water or not.)

Help! My Houseplant Needs Watering Every Day!

It could be because it's very small and doesn't have much soil from which to draw water. Or the plant is potbound and needs repotting (see page 128). But the most common cause is that the soil has been allowed to completely dry out on some occasion and now the water runs right through; it isn't absorbed. There are two ways of overcoming this:

1 Place a small- or medium-sized plant in a bucket or sink of tepid water that's deeper than the container is tall. Hold the pot under the water until the bubbling stops.

2 For a large plant, add two drops of a mild dishwashing liquid (such as Ivory) to a gallon of tepid water. Pour the water slowly over the soil, trying to stay away from the edge where the soil has pulled away from the pot (otherwise the water will go directly to the saucer). Do the same thing the next two or three times the plant needs watering. (The dishwashing liquid helps the soil absorb the water.)

Once the soil has been thoroughly moistened, don't let it dry out completely again.

Fertilizer

Just like people, plants need nutrients to help them grow well. These are supplied by the soil, air, water—and the gardener in the form of fertilizer. A balanced fertilizer—14-14-14 or 20-20-20—is an excellent choice for indoor foliage plants. It also works fine for flowering plants, but if you like, a phosphorus-rich fertilizer (19-30-15, for example) is good to encourage bud formation and blooming.

A houseplant fertilizer can be a water-soluble formula (that is, you mix it with water) or the same slow-release kind you use outdoors in the garden (Osmocote®, for instance). The difference is how often you use them—typically once a month during the growing season for water-soluble brands and once a season for slow-release.

Most people fertilize too much or at the wrong times of year. A few fertilizer cautions:

- Fertilize only when the soil is moist.
- Fertilize only when a plant is growing or flowering. For most plants, this means do *not* fertilize in winter.
- Don't fertilize a sick plant. The plant simply can't cope with the food until it's on the road to recovery.
- Don't fertilize plants kept where room temperatures are 60 degrees Fahrenheit or below. Although few people keep the temperature this low, plants can't absorb the nutrients. Also, time-release fertilizers and such organic fertilizers as fish emulsion aren't effective at low temperatures.
- Don't use more fertilizer than the label recommends. In fact, many gardeners use just half the suggested amount.
- Plants growing in low light conditions need less plant food than those growing in high light.

Houseplants

HUMIDITY

Most houseplants don't like dry air, especially in winter. Symptoms of too-dry air include brown leaf tips, flower buds dropping off before they open, soil drying out prematurely, and leaves that turn brown and fall off. You can increase the humidity levels for your houseplants by doing the following:

1 Group houseplants together.

2 Line a waterproof tray with decorative stones or pebbles, add water to just below the top of the rocks, and then place plants (with their saucers) in the tray. Each time you water the plants, add water to the tray.

3 Use a humidifier.

4 Keep a kettle of water on wood stoves.

What about misting? Unfortunately, its effects don't last long enough to do much good.

See page 143 for a list of plants that don't mind low humidity.

SOIL

Does it matter which brand of potting soil you use? Yes and no. For a few plants it does—**cactuses** need soil that drains quickly and doesn't hold too much moisture. **Orchids** demand special mixes. And if you grow dozens of **African violets**, you may want to try a mix made especially for these flowering beauties. But for the majority of foliage houseplants, it's better to choose one mix that you like and stick with it. Ingredients vary depending on the mix, and not all soil mixes perform the same. When you use only one, you know its characteristics: what it looks like when the soil surface is dry, the average time it takes to dry out, and whether the mix contains a water-holding polymer or fertilizer.

CONTAINERS

Mostly you can choose pots by appearance. But here are a few other considerations:

- Unless you tend to overwater, plastic pots generally work best for most indoor plants because they hold moisture longer than clay.
- Clay is an excellent choice for **cactuses** and **orchids**, however.
- A houseplant pot should *always* have a drainage hole.
- When choosing a new container for repotting a houseplant, pick one that's no more than one size larger. That is, if the plant is now growing in a 4-inch pot, move it into a 6-inch container, *not* into an 8-inch one. (In overly large pots, the soil can stay wet too long, which will cause the roots to rot.)

Just as with any other type of gardening, knowing the needs of the plants—and supplying them—are the simple keys to success with houseplants. There's no hocus-pocus and no inside knowledge that only those with green thumbs understand. All It takes is putting the plant where it receives the right amount of light and watering it enough but not too much. Add a bit of fertilizer occasionally, and repot when the plant has outgrown its container. Soon you'll have an indoor garden that enhances your dècor and soothes the spirit. What a balm over winter or anytime of the year.

Houseplants

Foliage Houseplants

Common Name (Botanical Name)	Light	Watering Needs	Culture
Aluminum plant (*Pilea cadierei*)	High to medium	Average	Crinkled, silver-veined leaves are attractive. Pinch back monthly so plant keeps its shape. Yearly, take cuttings and start over, tossing out old plant.
Arrowhead plant (*Syngonium podophyllum*)	High to low	Average	Arrowhead-shaped leaves may be all green, have silver veins, or touches of cream or pink.
Asparagus fern (*Asparagus densiflorus* 'Sprengeri')	High to medium	Average	Grows best in high light. Occasionally produces red berries. If water runs right through the soil of larger plants, change your watering method: Immerse the pot in a bucket or sink of tepid water until bubbling stops.
Boston fern (*Nephrolepis exaltata* 'Bostoniensis')	High to medium	Keep moist	Indoors, keep the plant groomed by removing yellowing or brown fronds. During winter, increase humidity around the plant, if possible.
Cast iron plant (*Aspidistra elatior*)	High to low	Average	A Victorian charmer. Some plants have variegated leaves, but they're likely to revert to all green if grown in low light.
Chinese evergreen (*Aglaonema* hybrids)	High to low	Average	Leaves marbled in silver or white. Slow grower. Survives nicely in very low light.
Corn plant (*Dracaena fragrans*)	High to low	Average	Treelike plant with green or yellow-variegated leaves. May eventually produce fragrant flowers.
Dieffenbachia (*Dieffenbachia*)	High to medium	Average	Tall, but slow-growing plant with marbled foliage.
English ivy (*Hedera helix*)	High to low	Average	Spider mites are the biggest problem when growing English ivy indoors. It's a particular problem on topiaries. To help prevent spider mites, keep humidity levels high.
Grape ivy (*Cissus rhombifolia*)	High to low	Keep moderately moist	Good choice for a hanging basket.
Norfolk Island pine (*Araucaria heterophylla*)	High to low	Keep moderately moist	Will drop its lower limbs in low light. Never prune the top of the plant; new growth will be horizontal instead of vertical, ruining the look of the plant.
Parlor palm (*Chamaedorea elegans* 'Bella')	High to medium	Keep moderately moist	Very slow-growing. Prefers warm temperatures. Watch out for spider mites.
Peperomia (*Peperomia* species and hybrids)	High to medium	Average	One species has thick leaves like a miniature rubber plant. Another has puckered foliage, which on some cultivars is variegated.

Houseplants

Foliage Houseplants

Common Name (*Botanical Name*)	Light	Watering Needs	Culture
Philodendron (*Philodendron* species and hybrids)	High to low	Average	Heart-leaf philodendron is one of the easiest houseplants to grow. Let it trail or train it as a vine. Tree philodendron may eventually need staking.
Polka-dot plant (*Hypoestes phyllostachya*)	High to medium	Keep moderately moist	Colorful leaves dotted in white, red or pink. For best appearance, start new plants from cuttings each year and toss out tired old plant.
Pothos (*Epipremnum aureum*)	High to low	Average	Tolerates low light, but doesn't thrive in it. Foliage resembles heart-shaped leaves of philodendron, but are variegated.
Prayer plant (*Maranta leuconeura*)	High to medium	Keep moderately moist	Deep-green leaves with veins of other colors. The name comes from the plant's habit of folding its leaves at night.
Purple passion plant (*Gynura aurantiaca* 'Purple Passion')	High to medium	Average	Velvety purple leaves definitely make this plant the center of attention. If not grown as a vine, it needs frequent pinching to keep the plant from looking lanky.
Rubber plant (*Ficus elastica*)	High to medium	Average	Grow plants with variegated foliage in high light. The white sap that comes out when the plant is pruned or a leaf removed can be stopped by spraying the area with water. (The sap was once used to make rubber.)
Schefflera (*Schefflera* species and hybrids)	High to medium	Average	Dwarf versions of schefflera—often called arboricola—aren't any shorter than the regular schefflera, but do have smaller leaves and can tolerate low light levels.
Snake plant (*Sansevieria trifasciata*)	Any	Average	This plant is almost impossible to kill; a good choice for "black thumbs." Variegated types must be reproduced by division (new plants that grow from leaf cuttings will be all green).
Spider plant (*Chlorophytum comosum*)	High to medium	Keep moderately moist	Usually grown in a hanging basket. If babies (offsets) aren't produced, raise the light level.
Swedish ivy (*Plectranthus australis*)	High to low	Average	Actually a native of Australia, not Sweden. Can be allowed to trail (as in a hanging basket) or trained to climb.

Houseplants

Flowering Houseplants

Common Name (*Botanical Name*)	Light	Watering Levels	Comments
African violet (*Saintpaulia ionantha*)	High to medium	Keep moderately moist	Flowers all year if given enough light. Look for miniature African violets and cultivars with variegated foliage. Blossoms in many colors and forms (including double).
Angelwing begonia (*Begonia* 'Lucerna')	High to medium	Average	Leaves, which are red underneath, have an interesting shape and are often dotted with white spots. Blooms are usually pink, red or white.
Bromeliads (Many genera, species, and hybrids)	High to medium	Average	A very unusual-looking group of houseplants. The flowers may be small, but they're usually surrounded by extremely colorful bracts and colorful foliage.
Christmas cactus (*Schlumbergera* x *buckleyi*)	Medium	Average	There are several plants sold under this name, or as Thanksgiving cactus. All are easy to grow. Flowers may be red, white, fuchsia, or gold.
Clivia (*Clivia miniata*)	High	Average	Orange (or yellow) bell-shaped flowers. Young plants bloom once yearly. Older ones, several times. Doesn't like to be repotted.
Lipstick plant (*Aeschynanthus lobbianus*)	High to medium	Keep moderately moist	May bloom in spring or fall or several times during the year. Grow in a hanging basket.
Orchid (Many genera, species, and hybrids)	High to medium	Average	The best orchids for growing as houseplants are moth orchids (*Phalaenopsis*) and lady's slipper orchids (*Paphiopedilum*). Moth orchids produce numerous flowers—white, pink, red, purple, or yellow—on an arching stem. Lady's slipper orchids resemble the wildflower lady slipper, except the blossoms are waxier and quite colorful.
Peace lily (*Spathiphyllum wallisii*)	High to low	Keep moist	This plant tolerates very low light levels, but won't bloom unless grown in at least medium light. It's the easiest flowering plant you can grow.

JANUARY

Houseplants

 PLANNING

Now that the holidays are past, you may want to evaluate where you might place new houseplants to liven up the indoors. Make a list of spots where a plant would be welcome—near an east-facing window, in the master bathroom, the family room, or the kitchen. Note the light in each spot (using the test on page 115). Also see whether there are potential problems that would limit a plant in this particular spot—cold air blowing on it each time an outside door is opened or heat from a vent or fireplace. Take your list to the store where you usually buy houseplants. Look first for plants that match the light conditions in your home, then opt for color—plants with variegated leaves, flowering plants (all the plants on page 121 are simple to grow, but **bromeliads** and **peace lilies** are the easiest).

 PLANTING

Unless a houseplant needs repotting (see directions on pages 124 and 128), there isn't much to plant this time of year. But what about starting an **avocado** from seed? It's fun, and you get a free houseplant for your efforts. Florida **avocados** (with dark, rough skin) germinate faster and grow more quickly than

those from California (smooth skins). Here's how:

1 Carefully remove the pit from the **avocado**, rinse it off in tepid water, and dry it with a paper towel.

2 Place it somewhere warm for twenty-four hours.

3 Peel the parchment-like coating from the big seed.

4 If the seed has already sprouted when you remove it, skip the first three steps and go directly to Step 5.

5 Fill a 6-inch flower pot three-quarters full of dampened potting mix.

6 Place the pit on the soil with the base—the flatter, larger, indented end—down.

7 Add more soil, but make sure the tip is exposed.

8 Water.

9 Put the pot in a spot that has warmth and good light.

10 Keep the soil moist until the pit germinates (usually within a month, but sometimes as long as three months).

11 Once new growth is 4 to 5 inches high, cover the pit with soil.

12 **Avocados** like bright light and moist soil.

13 Begin pinching them back when they reach 6 to 8 inches tall, to cause them to branch.

You may also germinate an **avocado** seed over water, but eventually you'll have to pot it in soil. Wash the pit and pat it dry with a paper towel. Insert three toothpicks around the middle of the pit and suspend it over a glass of water so that the rounded end is partially submerged in the water. Put in a warm spot with bright light, but no sun. Replace the water twice a week so it stays fresh and the pit remains wet. Pot the plant in soil when you think the **avocado** has developed enough leaves to live on its own.

 CARE

When you bring a new houseplant home, isolate it from other plants for about a month. That way, if it has some hidden insect or disease problem that wasn't noticed at the time of purchase, it won't spread to your other plants.

If you acquired an **ivy** topiary over the holidays, it's important to keep the humidity high around it. Spider mites may severely damage **ivy** if the air is too dry. (You'll first notice their presence when leaves begin to look dull and less green.) See page 118 for tips on increasing humidity.

When you bring a new houseplant home, isolate it from other plants for about a month. That way, if it has some hidden insect or disease problem that wasn't noticed at the time of purchase, it won't spread to your other plants.

WATERING

Because of lower temperatures and less light, indoor plants need watering less frequently in winter. Always check the soil (see page 117) before watering. Overwatering, combined with cool temperatures, can lead to root rot.

The chart on pages 119 to 121 tells you which plants need moist soil and which should be allowed to dry out between waterings. **Lady-slipper orchids** should be kept moist.

If you're growing an **amaryllis**, see page 65 for after-bloom watering instructions.

FERTILIZING

The only houseplants that need feeding in January are those that are actively growing or blooming. Feed those monthly with a water-soluble fertilizer, using the amount listed on the label. You can use a balanced fertilizer such as 20-20-20 on both types of plants, but if you have a number of flowering plants, you may want to buy a fertilizer for **African violets** or flowering plants—and use it when buds are forming and flowers blooming. Some gardeners like to alternate using all-purpose and flowering formulas.

Don't fertilize **cactuses** or nongrowing foliage plants this month or next. They're resting.

Check page 144 for information about caring for holiday gift plants such as **poinsettia, cyclamen,** and **kalanchoe.**

GROOMING

Each time you water your houseplants, groom them by cutting off yellowing leaves and removing dead or dying foliage. Are the leaves dusty? Dust prevents plants from absorbing as much light as they should. Move plants with smooth foliage to a sink or shower (depending on their size) and gently shower them clean. See page 125 to learn how to clean plants with hairy leaves.

PROBLEMS

Too little light? It's a big problem in January. Symptoms include:

- Leaves cupping upward
- Plant growing toward the light
- New leaves that are smaller than old leaves and pale green
- No flowers
- Leaves falling off the plant

What to do about it?

1 If plants are growing on a windowsill, move them to the next brightest window until mid-March. That is, if a plant is growing on a north-facing sill, move it to an east-facing one. If it's growing on a sill with an eastern exposure, move it to one that faces west.

2 Move plants that are not on windowsills or in front of windows closer to the light.

3 Give plants extra hours of light from ordinary lamps or from a portable lamp or spotlight. If a houseplant shares an end table with a lamp, turn the lamp on in the evening as soon as natural light has gone and leave it on till you go to bed. Those extra hours can make quite a bit of difference. Consider doing the same with a portable light clipped to the edge of the pot of a large plant.

There's cotton on my plant. No, it's mealybugs. Dip a cotton swab in rubbing alcohol and lightly rub the cottony masses. Be sure to check under leaves and where stems and leaves join. After 24 hours, pick off as many of the masses as you can. Then spray with insecticidal soap twice a week until the problem seems to abate. Often the mealybugs return and must be treated again.

FEBRUARY

PLANNING

Because of their heart-shaped leaves and red flowers (other colors are available, too), **anthuriums** are widely available in February. They're a good choice to brighten up the house, so look for them as you shop this month. They need warm temperatures (60 degrees Fahrenheit is the minimum), bright light but no sun, and evenly moist soil while they're in bloom. Feed them twice a month as long as they are in flower.

Stores also offer **miniature roses** in February. Don't fall for them unless you have a spot in full sun and are willing to give them a fair amount of attention until you can place them outdoors. (See the **Roses** chapter, page 207.) Or since they're inexpensive, you can treat them as temporary plants, tossing them out as you would cut flowers when they begin to fade. In either case, give them sun and moist soil. If you plan to keep the plant, fertilize twice monthly as long as it's in flower. Watch out for spider mites (see page 217).

PLANTING

If one houseplant requires watering more frequently than others and roots are beginning to grow through the drainage hole, it's probably potbound and needs repotting. Gently lift the dry soil ball from the container and see whether roots are growing around and around. If they are, buy a bigger container, make sure you have enough potting soil, and move the plant into its new pot. (See page 128 for complete directions.)

If an **orchid** is overgrown, repot it after it has bloomed. Some nurseries, especially those that specialize in **orchids**, will do the repotting for you. If not, it isn't difficult to do at home.

1 Buy a prepared **orchid** mix at a nursery or home store.

2 Choose a pot that's 2 inches wider in diameter than the current container. Clay is the best choice unless you know you won't overwater.

3 Remove the **orchid** from its pot.

4 Tease the bark chips and other material from the roots, or wash them away.

5 Trim back any black or mushy roots.

6 Moisten the potting mix.

7 Add a layer of potting mix to the pot.

8 Place the **orchid** on the mix at the same depth it grew before.

9 Add more mix, pushing the bark pieces through the roots.

10 Water thoroughly.

11 Return to bright light. New growth should start in spring, if not sooner.

CARE

A cautionary tale. February often has a few sunny and warm days, so many gardeners take their houseplants outdoors for the day to enjoy the sun. Bad idea. What feels, to a person, like a warm day in winter is often much too chilly for a tropical plant. Also, after months of living in low light, plants are suddenly being asked to cope with six hours of sun. That means the same thing for plants as it does for people—possible sunburn. So resist the temptation to take your houseplants outside until May, and even then, move them into sun gradually.

Give all plants a one-quarter turn each time you water so that they grow evenly. If the foliage of variegated plants is becoming all green, light levels are too low. Move the plants so they will receive more light.

At night, move *Cattleya, Paphiopedilum*, and *Phalaenopsis* **orchids** to a cooler part of the house. These **orchids** should be kept about 10 degrees Fahrenheit cooler at night than during the daytime.

When an **orchid** is developing flower buds, keep the plant away from drafts.

WATERING

Check **cactuses** that are being kept cool and dry (see page 140). If you notice the beginning of shriveling, mist the plant with tepid water. If there's no improvement, water very lightly.

When temperatures and sunlight levels are low, it's easy to overwater houseplants, causing them to rot. Be sure you don't water until plants need it and that you never let plants stand in water.

Most good gardeners run tap water into a clean gallon milk jug at least twenty-four hours before they water their houseplants. (Don't put the lid on.) This allows the water to come to room temperature, which is a good thing. Very cold tap water can damage tropical plants. Letting the water sit for a day before using it also lets chlorine evaporate.

If a houseplant wilts, revive it by:

1 Moving it out of bright light.

2 Watering it thoroughly.

3 Misting it several hours later if it has recovered some but not completely.

If further first aid is needed, stick several thin wooden stakes into the pot, then cover the pot and plant with a large plastic bag. Breathe into the bag and seal the top with a twister tie. Make sure the bag doesn't touch the leaves. Once the plant has perked up, remove the bag.

Water holiday gift plants according to recommendations on page 144.

FERTILIZING

Feed **African violets, amaryllis, bromeliads, poinsettias**, and **orchids** monthly. Wait until next month to fertilize all other indoor plants.

GROOMING

Regularly remove fading flowers from **African violets**.

If an occasional leaf turns yellow, cut it off since yellow attracts some insects.

How do you clean the leaves of plants such as **gloxinia** and **African violet**, which are hairy instead of smooth? Experienced gardeners sometimes spray them gently and lightly with tepid water, just as they might a plant with smooth foliage. The trick is to spray first thing in the morning and to never put the plant where sun can hit the leaves while they're wet. Inexperienced gardeners are probably better off dusting the leaves with the softest brush they can find.

PROBLEMS

If leaves of **wandering Jew** roll up, the plant isn't getting enough humidity.

It's easy to recognize whiteflies—they are small white flying insects. They suck sap from leaves, which causes the foliage to turn yellow. They may also leave the foliage—especially the undersides of the leaves—sticky. Treat the plant in the evening when the whiteflies are less likely to fly away:

1 Vacuum as many as possible using a portable hand vac. (Enclose the vac in a large plastic bag, seal, and open outdoors—away from plants—the next day.)

2 Then spray with insecticidal soap, making sure you treat the undersides of the leaves.

3 Get a yellow sticky trap at the garden center and insert it in the pot. Whiteflies are attracted to the color and then get stuck in the glue.

You may need to repeat steps 1 and 2. Remove the sticky trap from the pot when you spray and then put it back afterwards. When half of the trap's surface is covered by whiteflies, replace it.

MARCH

PLANNING

If a number of your houseplants will need repotting in the next few months, begin looking for containers now. Measure the current pots (the size is the number of inches at the widest part of the top rim), and carry that list with you as you shop. Look for new containers that are one size (2 inches) larger than the ones the plants are now growing in.

PLANTING

If you're growing other plants, such as annuals or vegetables, from seed this time of year, you may enjoy trying a few houseplants, too, if you can find seeds in catalogs or at garden centers. The easiest ones are **asparagus fern, flowering maple** (*Abutilon* x *hybridum*), and **polka-dot plant**.

1 Fill 2¹/₂- to 3-inch pots with moistened potting soil to within ¹/₂ to ³/₄ inch of the rim.

2 Sow three seeds of the same plant in each pot, spacing them evenly.

3 Barely cover seeds with soil. It's not necessary to cover dustlike seeds; just sow them on top of the soil.

4 Write the plant name and the date on a label and insert it into the soil.

5 Place the pot in a plastic bag and seal it.

6 Put the pot in a warm spot that receives bright light, but no direct sun.

7 When seeds have germinated, remove the plastic bag.

8 Water enough to keep the soil moist.

9 If all the seeds germinate, cut the weakest off at soil level to allow the remaining plant to reach its full potential.

If you have a variegated **snake plant** and want some more, you should divide the plant. Don't take cuttings, since they will yield all-green plants, not variegated plants. Division is simple:

1 Remove the plant from the pot.

2 Carefully wash most of the soil from the roots.

3 Using a sharp knife, cut the plant into sections, each with an ample amount of roots.

4 Repot.

5 Water thoroughly.

6 On tall plants, you may need to provide a stake or light support for a few weeks until root growth takes hold.

7 Place the pot in medium light for two weeks, then move to the preferred type of light for that plant.

Other plants that can be divided include **aloe, anthurium, asparagus fern, Boston fern, bromeliads, cast iron plant, Chinese evergreen, lipstick plant** (*Aeschynanthus lobbianus*), **mother of thousands** (*Tolmiea menziesii*), **orchids, peace lily, polka-dot plant, prayer plant**, and **spider plant.**

CARE

About the middle to end of March, bring **cactus plants** back into light and warmth. Those that are mature enough may begin to bloom within weeks after a winter regimen of coolness and dry soil.

WATERING

When **cactuses** have returned to their usual places in the house, begin watering them again. The wrong way to water a **cactus** (or any other houseplant) is to give it a tiny drink of water occasionally. Instead, water the plant thoroughly—until the excess drains out the hole in the bottom of the pot—and then don't water again until the soil dries out.

If you're growing a **bromeliad** keep water in the plant's cup at all times.

Chemically softened water isn't recommended for houseplants, but may be used occasionally if it sits overnight first.

The wrong way to water a cactus (or any houseplant) is to give it a tiny drink of water occasionally. Instead, water the plant thoroughly—until the excess drains out the hole in the bottom of the pot—and then don't water again until the soil dries out.

Toward the end of the month, light gets brighter, temperatures become warmer, and houseplants may need to be watered more frequently. If you have a regular schedule for watering, begin checking plants to see whether they should be watered at least a day earlier than usual.

 FERTILIZING

Begin fertilizing houseplants again about the middle of the month, if you like. Some gardeners prefer to mix a soluble fertilizer in water and apply it monthly during the growing season. Others like to use one-fourth the recommended fertilizer when they water each week. Either way works fine.

Or you can use the same 14-14-14 or 20-20-20 timed-release fertilizer that you do outdoors. You might think that since the most important feature of a houseplant is its leaves, it might prefer a high-nitrogen fertilizer. Not so. One too high in nitrogen can cause too much growth too fast, which means the plant often succumbs to insects and diseases.

 GROOMING

March is a good time to pinch back plants that have grown a bit lanky or that need to be shaped. Those may include aluminum plant, arrowhead, English ivy, grape ivy, peperomia, heart-leaf philodendron, pothos, purple passion, and Swedish ivy.

Have you ever wondered about the plant-shine products sold to make leaves of houseplants glisten? Or maybe a friend has done the same thing using mayonnaise or a light coating of salad oil. None of these is recommended because they can stop up the plants' stomata, which cuts off respiration. Some homemade plant polishes can also cause excessive dust collection, lessening the absorption of needed sunlight.

 PROBLEMS

Leaf spots can be the result of several different problems. They may just be caused by sun shining on wet leaves, or they may be telling you the plant has been affected by a fungal disease. The first thing to do is remove the spotted leaf or leaves from the plant and dispose of them. In the future, make sure you keep the leaves dry. It may also help to water slightly less often. Unless it's a plant that needs its soil constantly moist, let the soil dry out between waterings.

If you're going to use an insecticide on a houseplant—even if it's insecticidal soap—water the plant deeply the night

Timely Tip

Insecticides (even organic products) tend to lose their effectiveness over time. To be certain the product you're using does the job it's supposed to, use a permanent marking pen to write the date on an insecticide container when you buy it. Then check the dates yearly, disposing of those you've had longer than two years. (Check with your local government for the recommended way to dispose of insecticides.)

before. Otherwise, the product may burn the plant's leaves.

A wilting plant may be the result of too little water. (See page 116 for solutions.) But sometimes wilting is caused by too much water. If the soil is damp around a wilted plant, the problem may be overwatering. If you catch it in time, you may be able to save the plant by removing it from its current container and potting it in another container, which has been filled with moistened (but not wet) potting mix. Don't water the plant again until the soil has dried. If it's still wilted, it was probably too far gone to save.

APRIL

 PLANNING

When you're at the garden center or nursery picking up bedding plants for the garden, take time to pick up several good-sized bags of your favorite houseplant potting soil, some water-soluble fertilizer (if you're getting low), and new pots for your houseplants. Stores usually have an excellent selection in spring, so you may want to purchase a few extra containers, or cachepots, to have on hand if you see some you fall in love with.

Temperatures this month can bounce back and forth between warm and downright chilly. On the warm days, you'll be tempted to take your houseplants out to their summer home in your yard. But since many houseplants are from tropical climates, nighttime temperatures in the 40- or even 50-degree Fahrenheit range can harm them. It's best to be patient and wait till next month, when you know the weather is much more likely to be consistently warm.

PLANTING

Many houseplants have grown enough since last fall that they need to be placed in new containers. Also, since repotting is a messy job, it's best to do it outdoors whenever possible—and that means when temperatures are warm enough.

April is the ideal month to repot houseplants. Here's how:

1 Water the plant the day before repotting it.

2 Moisten the potting soil.

3 If using a clay or terra cotta container, wet it thoroughly a few hours beforehand.

4 Cover the drainage hole with a small piece of screening. (Forget putting pebbles in the bottom of the pot—university tests have shown that's detrimental rather than helpful.)

5 Remove the plant from its pot.

6 Gently tease loose roots that have tightly encircled the root ball.

7 Pour a few inches of potting mix into the new pot.

8 Place the old pot into the center of the new one, and put more soil around its edges.

9 Firm the soil against the sides of the old container, and then carefully pull the pot out. That gives you the perfect hole for inserting the new plant.

10 Place the plant in the container, making sure it's at the same level it grew before. Add more soil to fill. Firm the soil with your fingers.

11 Water till the excess runs from the drainage hole.

12 Keep the plant in medium light—no sun—for a few days.

 CARE

Cut back that **poinsettia** you've been nursing along since December. After you prune its stems to 4 to 6 inches tall, repot it into a larger container (if you'd like to try bringing it back into flower in the fall) or plant it in the ground (if you'd like a large, exotic green plant in the garden over summer—it will be killed by frost). Fertilize the **poinsettia** and move it outdoors after nighttime temperatures remain above 60 degrees Fahrenheit. It will thrive in a spot that receives morning sun. Wear rubber gloves so the white sap from the **poinsettia** won't get on your skin. It can be an irritant.

 WATERING

With warmer weather, most houseplants need water more frequently than in winter. Be especially alert to the watering needs of those plants that don't like their soil to dry out at all—**African violet, Boston fern, grape ivy, lipstick plant, Norfolk Island pine, parlor palm, peace lily, polka-dot plant, prayer plant**, and **spider plant**.

Most plants are watered from the top. That is, you pour the water over the top of the soil so it runs through to the bottom. But a few plants—**African violet, cyclamen**, and **gloxinia**—may be watered from the bottom instead, since they don't like water on their foliage (**African violet**) or they grow from a corm that shouldn't stay wet (**cyclamen** and **gloxinia**). To water from the bottom:

- Fill the saucer with water.
- Come back in a few minutes. If the water has disappeared, add more.
- In half an hour, feel the surface of the soil to see whether it feels damp.
- If the soil feels damp, pour any excess water from the saucer.
- If the soil is still dry, add more water to the saucer. But don't let any remain more than half an hour.

In my experience, bottom watering sounds better than it actually works. Many times, the moisture never reaches the soil's surface. If that happens to you, return to watering from the top, but be careful not to overwater or to get water on the leaves. Or you can try self-watering pots or wick-watering systems, which automatically water from the bottom.

 # FERTILIZING

Fertilize houseplants once a month with a balanced fertilizer (5-5-5, 14-14-14, etc.). Or for flowering plants, consider using a houseplant fertilizer made for blooming plants. If you don't enjoy fertilizing, consider a timed-release product, such as Osmocote®, which automatically feeds your plants. You can apply it now and not have to use it again this year.

 # GROOMING

When cutting off a brown or yellow leaf, cut it all the way back to the stem or the base of the plant. Don't let dead or dying foliage remain where it falls on top of the soil. Because it can attract insects and diseases, it should be removed.

 # PROBLEMS

A white crust on the top edge of houseplant pots (or on the sides of clay pots) indicate fertilizer salts. And that means you may have been overfertilizing. Since stems or leaves touching the concentrated salts will be harmed, move the plants into new containers and use less fertilizer in the future. (The general rule is to fertilize only from March to October and not more than once a month at regular strength.) Soak crusted containers in soapy water, and then scrub them clean if you'd like to use them again for other plants.

Check for insects or other problems whenever you water; problems are more easily nipped in the bud when they're caught early.

You may notice tiny insects on the new growth of your houseplants, or you may notice the effects of these aphids: leaves that become pale and distorted or stunted. See how many you can wash off with a spray of water directed at the affected leaves. After the plant's foliage dries, spray with insecticidal soap. Repeat at twice-weekly intervals, if necessary.

MAY

PLANNING

Do you tend to avoid all but a few "tough" houseplants because you travel quite a bit and aren't home to give them the water they need? One solution is self-watering planters. These are great for anyone who over- or underwaters. But if you want indoor plants that don't require much attention in the moisture department, look into the **cactus** family. These plants can often get by without watering for several weeks at a time. And their appearance is much more varied than most people imagine. The only drawback to **cactuses** is that they almost always need at least some sun. But if you can provide that, keep an eye out for interesting **cactuses** and succulents as you shop in local nurseries, garden centers, home stores, and grocery stores.

PLANTING

All during May, continue repotting houseplants that need it. How do you know if a plant needs to move to a larger pot? Signs include:

- The plant has stopped growing or blooming.
- The plant needs watering frequently.
- Roots are growing through the drainage hole.

- Roots completely cover the surface of the rootball, growing around and around.

Clivia and **amaryllis** are two plants that prefer to be potbound, so don't routinely repot them. When you do finally have to repot **clivia**, it will usually take a year before it blooms again.

What can you do about plants that have grown too large and heavy to be repotted? It helps to remove the top inch or two of soil and replace it with fresh new soil annually. This is called *topdressing*.

As you move plants outdoors or repot them this month, it's also a good time to expand your plant collection by taking cuttings. It's easy:

1 Fill a 2¹/₂- to 3-inch pot with moistened commercial potting mix.

2 Using pruning shears or a sharp knife, cut off a 3- to 5-inch stem.

3 Pinch off all but the top two leaves.

4 Dip the end of the cutting into a rooting hormone, such as Rootone®.

5 Use a pencil to poke a hole in the soil, and then stick the cutting in it.

6 Firm the soil around the cutting.

7 Water.

8 Cover the pot with a plastic bag and seal.

9 Place the pot in a place that receives medium light but not sun.

10 When new growth appears, open the top of the plastic bag permanently and water enough to keep the soil moist.

11 Remove the plastic bag within two weeks.

Houseplants that are easily propagated by cuttings include **African violet, angelwing begonia, aluminum plant, arrowhead plant, Chinese evergreen, croton** (*Codiaeum variegatum pictum*), **dieffenbachia, English ivy, flowering maple, grape ivy, heart-leaf philodendron, lipstick plant, peperomia, polka-dot plant, pothos, prayer plant, purple passion plant, rubber plant** (*Ficus elastica*), **snake plant, Swedish ivy, wandering Jew,** and **weeping fig** (*Ficus benjamina*).

CARE

Many indoor gardeners like to let their houseplants vacation outdoors in the summertime. It's a matter of personal preference, but if you'd like to move your plants outside, wait till temperatures are consistently 60 degrees, even at night. Gradually get plants used to outdoor conditions—wind, rain, and much brighter light.

- Move the plants to a shady spot first, on the porch if you have one.
- Then move them to a still-shady spot that's not quite as protected from wind.
- Finally, move the plants to where they will stay for the summer.

Remember that even shady spots outdoors are likely equal to medium or bright light indoors. An hour or two of filtered morning sun is fine for plants that like high light levels, but those that normally grow in medium or low light should be kept in shade.

Amaryllis and **poinsettia** plants may also be moved outdoors now, if you'd like. **Poinsettias** should be cut back and repotted (see page 128). Don't do anything to **amaryllis**, which prefer to stay in the same pot for three or four years. Both will appreciate a few hours of morning sun.

Make sure plants that stay indoors are not in the direct path of cold air from an air conditioner.

 WATERING

Houseplants that are outdoors need watering much more frequently than when they were indoors—especially those in 6-inch pots and smaller. Get in the habit of feeling the soil of your outdoor houseplants at least every other day. Or invest in a moisture meter and stick it into the soil of smaller plants every other day and big plants at least twice a week. Water when indicated.

Just because you're spending more time outdoors, don't neglect the plants still inside the house. Have a regular schedule to check whether the soil is dry or still slightly moist, and then water if the plant needs it. (See page 117.)

 FERTILIZING

Which method of fertilizing houseplants works best outdoors depends on your method of watering. If you use a watering can, mixing up a liquid or water-soluble fertilizer is simple and gives you the opportunity to do some foliar feeding—wetting the leaves, as well as the soil, of those plants that look a bit rundown. But if you use a hose or set up drip irrigation, it may be easier to use a timed-release fertilizer such as Osmocote®. Either the three- or six-month type is fine for all plants. Choose a balanced formula, such as 14-14-14.

 GROOMING

When plants are outdoors, sometimes watering or rain causes soil to splash up on the undersides of leaves. To prevent this, cover the soil with a very thin mulch—aquarium gravel, decorative stones, pea gravel, or Spanish moss.

PROBLEMS

Among the insects that suck the juices from a houseplant, scale is the easiest to recognize but sometimes the hardest to notice—until there are a number of them; then you'll see them either on the stems or undersides of leaves. They get their name because of their hard scale-like covering. They can attack just about any houseplants, but those most likely to be affected by scale are **bromeliads, cactuses, dieffenbachia, ferns, ficus, schefflera,** and some **palms**.

To control scale:

- Scrub as many of the insects off as you can with a soft old toothbrush dipped in warm soapy water.
- If the infestation is severe and the plant is large, consider spraying with a light horticultural oil (sometimes called *sun oil*).
- Check with the Extension Service for advice on chemical control.

JUNE

PLANNING

What houseplants intrigue you the most? Maybe it would be fun to develop a collection of that type of plant—a number of different **African violets** with variegated leaves or double flowers, for instance. Or several different varieties (and variegations) of **Chinese evergreen**, or ten **cactuses** of various shapes and sizes, and so forth. If you have a particular plant that you really like, spend some time this month seeing whether you can find others that are slightly different.

PLANTING

Most **cactuses** don't need repotting more often than every three or four years. But if you have a **cactus** that has definitely outgrown its container, summer is a good time to repot it. Because this is a sticky job, you may want to recruit a friend or family member to help you.

1 Use a special potting soil for **cactuses**, or make your own by adding 1 part sand to 2 parts commercial potting soil.

2 Water the plant and moisten the potting soil the day before transplanting.

3 Buy thorn-proof gloves. (These are also good when you're working around **roses**.)

4 Fill a clay pot about half full of potting mix.

6 For a large **cactus**, get three or four full-sized pages of newspaper and fold them into a strap. For a small **cactus**, use a pair of tongs.

7 Tighten the newspaper strap around the **cactus**, and use it to move the plant from the old container to the new. Or use the tongs.

8 Place the **cactus** at the same depth it grew before.

9 Fill in around the plant with soil.

10 Water thoroughly.

11 Place the plant in bright light, but no sun, for two weeks, then move it to a sunny location.

Continue repotting any houseplants that need it. (See page 128.)

If you see brown or green spots in a regular pattern on the back of your **fern** fronds, don't panic. They're just spores, and you can use them to grow more **ferns**, if you like. It's not a quick process, but it isn't difficult.

1 Cut off a frond covered with spores. Place it in an envelope or on a piece of paper (spore-side down).

2 Collect the spores when they fall off the frond.

3 Fill a large pot or small flat with moist potting mix and sprinkle the spores over the mix.

4 Mist with water.

5 Cover the surface with a piece of glass or enclose the container in a plastic bag.

6 Place the container in a warm spot that receives bright light, but no sun. Outdoors is fine this time of year.

7 Keep an eye on the container, and mist again if needed to keep the soil moist.

8 In a few months, you'll see something that looks like moss. This is an intermediate growth stage. Keep the soil moist.

9 Move back indoors in early September if you've started the spores outdoors.

10 When little **ferns** have developed two or three fronds, transplant them to individual pots.

CARE

During dry spells, occasionally hose down outdoor houseplants with a light mist to keep their leaves clean. Do this in

Houseplants indoors and out that are actively growing should be fertilized about every four to five weeks if you use a water-soluble or liquid plant food.

the morning so the foliage will dry before dark. Consider giving plants inside the house a shower every few months. Clean plants grow better.

WATERING

The hotter the weather, the more important it is to make sure that houseplants aren't allowed to become bone dry. Have a routine of walking around the house or yard to check them several times a week. The list on pages 119 to 121 tells which plants like to dry out somewhat between waterings and which need their soil to be slightly moist at all times.

If **bromeliads** are outdoors, you may need to pour water in their cups daily or every other day.

FERTILIZING

Houseplants indoors and out that are actively growing should be fertilized about every four to five weeks if you use a water-soluble or liquid plant food. Although those in the yard or on an outside porch are being watered more

frequently than those indoors—and therefore losing more nutrients—the extra light and fresh air outdoors compensate for the difference. Don't overfertilize. Not only will it cause too-quick growth that isn't good for the plants, it also causes them to outgrow the spots you have for them in the house.

Plants in low-light situations—**peace lilies** in bathrooms without windows, for instance—may not need fertilizing each month because they probably aren't growing much. Every other month may be sufficient. Don't try to force growth by fertilizing too much. Without good light, the new growth will be spindly and not attractive.

GROOMING

A **poinsettia** grows quite large outdoors (the ones you buy at Christmas have been treated with a growth retardant), so you may want or need to cut it back some this month or next. Wear rubber gloves so the white sap doesn't irritate your skin.

PROBLEMS

Keep an eye on houseplants that are summering outdoors. They may be knocked over by wind, thunderstorms, or dogs. Their leaves may be nibbled by cats or insects. If you're in the habit of checking them every day or two, though, the damage will usually be negligible because you catch and correct the problem in time. Sometimes, if wildlife is troublesome, moving a plant to a different location—or up off the ground—can help. Other times you need to build a temporary barrier of chicken wire or hardware cloth.

JULY
Houseplants

PLANNING

Before you go on vacation, think about what will happen to your houseplants while you're gone. If your absence is a week or less and all your plants are indoors, you may not need to do a thing beyond watering all the plants thoroughly and keeping the air conditioning on (the temperature should be no higher than 80 degrees Fahrenheit). Or you may be able to ask a knowledgeable gardener to water while you're gone. Otherwise, these are your alternatives:

1 Move all plants at least 5 feet away from a window. Water them till the excess runs out the drainage hole. When the saucer is empty, fill it again.

2 If you have a tub or sink reasonably close to a window, line the bottom of it with four layers of newspapers. First, remove the sink plug and the saucers. Then water the plants so the newspaper is soaked through. Turn on the faucet so that it drips once every thirty to sixty seconds.

3 Another bathtub technique if your bathroom has at least medium light is to line the bottom of the tub with several sheets of newspaper. Get as many bricks as you have plants (large containers may require two bricks), and place the bricks on the newspaper. Plug up the opening and run enough water into the tub to barely cover the bricks. Remove the saucers from your pots and set the pots on top of the bricks.

4 If you have only a few small plants, poke a hole in the lid of a clean margarine tub. Fill the tub with water. Using a pencil or knitting needle, poke a piece of yarn or a wick made from pantyhose into the drainage hole and up several inches into the soil. Then poke the other end through the hole in the lid and let the rest dangle in the water. Water the plant so the wick becomes moistened; then it transfers the water from the tub to the pot.

5 Water the plant well, and remove any flowers or yellowing leaves. Place the plant inside a clear plastic bag (for big ones, use dry-cleaner bags). Use slim stakes to keep the plastic away from the leaves. Blow into the bag and seal the top with a twister tie. Place the plant in medium light but not where the sun will shine on it.

6 Ask at a nursery about a capillary mat system. These water very gently but effectively.

PLANTING

Repot houseplants anytime this month. See page 128 for directions. You may also want to take cuttings (page 130) or divide overgrown plants (page 126). July is a good time to do any of this because temperatures are warm and the plants are actively growing and will respond well.

If you took cuttings of **English, grape,** or **Swedish ivy; heart-leaf philodendron; pothos**; or **wandering Jew**, why not combine several cuttings in a hanging basket? Very likely you have a few of those green plastic baskets left over from previous years' purchases of **petunias** and other trailing annuals for the garden. Hanging baskets of house-

End of wick pushed with tweezers through hole. Must be in contact with potting soil.

Hole cut in lid. Pour water through here.

Water

Plastic margarine tub

Wick cut from pair of pantyhose

Wick Waterer

plants are just as nice as those of annual flowers. You could place them on a screened porch or deck during the rest of the summer and then take them indoors in fall. By September, you'll find that those tiny rooted cuttings have grown into full plants.

Another way to handling vining houseplants is to plant them in a good-sized container and let them grow up a support. Or you can take cuttings of trailing houseplants and root them in a hanging basket (see directions on page 130). That way they'll be right where you want them to grow. Cuttings root fast outdoors in the heat of July. Just keep them away from sun.

CARE

If a houseplant is staked or is growing on a support, regularly tie or attach the plant to the support. This is especially important if the plant is growing outdoors, where wind can cause damage. If a plant is often blown over because it's top-heavy, cover the bottom of a larger, heavier container (terra cotta is good) with gravel. Place the plant—pot and all—inside the bigger container and fill in between the two pots with Spanish moss.

WATERING

Water, water, water. That's the song that outdoor houseplants are singing. Be sure you don't let them dry out. Because of the long hours of daylight, indoor plants also use quite a bit of moisture this time of year. Check them regularly, and provide what they need.

Houseplants don't generally appreciate hard water. But what's a gardener to do if that's what there is? In summer the solution may be to collect rainwater and use that to water your houseplants. They will really appreciate it.

FERTILIZING

If you forget to fertilize once or twice in summer, it's no big deal. Plants don't seem to mind a bit. But if you want to be sure of feeding regularly—or of not overdoing it—mark a monthly fertilizing date on your calendar. If you decide upon something that's easy to remember, such as the first of each month, or the last day of each month, you may not even need a reminder.

GROOMING

Houseplants should be growing well this time of year. But that growth may not be always in the direction you want or it may not be symmetrical. To encourage bushier growth, pinch the tip of a stem back to a leaf.

PROBLEMS

If a houseplant collapses or portions of the stem turn brown, the culprit is usually rot. **African violets, begonias, cactuses**, and **gloxinias** are susceptible to rot, but it can happen to any plant—or to a portion of a plant (such as a segment of **holiday cactus**). It's usually caused by overwatering or by old houseplant soil that has become compacted (so it contains no air, an essential element for roots). If the whole plant has collapsed, you'll have to get rid of it. But if it's just a portion, trim off the rotted part and repot the healthy section of the plant in a new container filled with fresh potting soil. Then water less frequently.

AUGUST

Houseplants

PLANNING

By next month, plants that have spent the summer in the yard will return to the house. Before they do, you may want to think about which will need to be repotted first and what cuttings you may want to take. Prepare for these by picking up extra houseplant pots and a bag or two of your favorite potting mix the next time you're at the nursery or home store. And while you're shopping, look around to see what's new (to you, at least). You may find that moisture meter that you've been wanting to try, a small trellis to insert in the pot of a climbing plant, or different types of self-watering containers to experiment with.

If you like **weeping figs** and have been planning to buy one, this is a good month to do so. **Weeping figs** need high light levels, so moving one into your home during a month with plenty of sun gives it an opportunity to gradually get used to the shorter days that are on the horizon during fall and winter.

PLANTING

All houseplants that have outgrown their containers may be repotted this month. See page 128 for general repotting instructions, page 132 for **cactuses**, and page 124 for **orchids**. Because repotting can be a little messy, it's best to repot plants when it can be done outdoors—in the shade, of course—rather than in deep winter, when it must be done inside. After repotting, give extra attention to watering—let the soil stay slightly moist except for **cactuses**—and keep repotted plants in bright light but away from sun until they've begun growing again.

A simple way to propagate trailing or vining houseplants (**arrowhead plant, English ivy, heart-leaf philodendron, pothos**, etc.) is by layering.

- Fill a pot with dampened potting soil, and place it next to the plant you want to start a new plant from.
- Choose a stem, and pin it to the soil of the empty pot so that they are in direct contact.
- Keep the soil moist.
- When the portion of the plant in the new pot begins to grow, use hand clippers to remove the rooted portion from the mother plant.

CARE

What's the humidity like inside your house this time of year? If your central air conditioning is on twenty-four hours a day, it may not be quite high enough for plants that crave high humidity, such as **Boston fern, bromeliads, croton, English ivy**, and **nerve plant** (*Fittonia verschaffeltii*). If leaf tips of houseplants brown regularly and flower buds turn brown instead of opening, the air may be too dry. Try grouping a number of plants together, or consider the other suggestions on page 118.

Do you have a stack of empty houseplant containers left over after repotting this summer? Why not clean them now? Then they'll be ready for reuse whenever you need them.

- Soak pots in a tub of water for several hours (overnight for heavily crusted containers). If pots have a lot of fertilizer salts accumulation, add vinegar to the water.
- Scrub the pots with a stiff brush, using soap and water. Rinse well.
- Refill the tub with a mixture of 1 part liquid bleach and 9 parts water.
- Soak pots for thirty minutes.
- Rinse thoroughly and let dry.

WATERING

If you're planning to take an extended vacation this month, read the tips for July about how to keep your indoor houseplants watered while you're gone.

Because repotting can be a little messy, it's best to repot plants when it can be done outdoors—in the shade, of course—rather than in deep winter, when it must be done inside.

Typical high temperatures in August cause the soil houseplants are growing in to dry out sooner. But don't jump to conclusions and automatically water potted plants outdoors. Keep in mind that scattered showers and thunderstorms are ubiquitous throughout the month. Rain may fall on your yard but not at the official weather station for your county. The only way to know for sure if a plant needs watering is to feel or test the soil, or use a moisture meter.

Remember that the soil of some plants, such as **cactuses**, needs to dry out between waterings. If afternoon thundershowers are occurring every couple of days, **cactuses** in pots outdoors may be staying too moist. Consider moving them to a porch or other spot out of the weather for a week or ten days so their soil can dry out again.

 FERTILIZING

If you use a liquid or water-soluble fertilizer, feed all your houseplants again this month. If you applied a timed-release plant food in late spring or early summer, you don't need to use it again unless you applied it twelve weeks ago and it was supposed to work for only three months.

Tend to outdoor houseplants before working elsewhere in the yard. Sometimes insects or diseases from vegetable or flower gardens can get on your hands or clothes unnoticed. You don't want to pass these along to your houseplants.

Easiest houseplants to grow: If you'd like to introduce someone to the pleasures of houseplants but you're not sure how much attention the plants will get, these are the most fool-proof choices: **arrowhead plant, cast iron plant, Chinese evergreen, heart-leaf philodendron, spider plant**, and **snake plant**.

Timed-release formulas remain effective for different periods—frequently six months, sometimes as long as nine months. But you have to read the label to be certain. You may want to mark the end date (or the application date and length of effectiveness) in your garden notebook or on your calendar.

GROOMING

Make grooming your houseplants—indoors and outdoors—a monthly ritual. Plants look better when fading leaves are removed, old flowers are snipped off, and foliage is kept clean. They'll remain healthier, too.

PROBLEMS

Ants may be a problem in houseplants outdoors, mostly because you don't want to bring them back into the house next month. First, spray the plant twice with insecticidal soap, three days apart. Be sure you spray under the leaves. This will help get rid of any insects that are attracting the ants. Then remove the saucer and pour water through the soil repeatedly. You may have to do this several times before all the ants leave for a drier home.

SEPTEMBER

 ## PLANNING

Near the beginning of September, prepare spots indoors for plants that will be brought back inside about the middle to the end of the month. Do you need new containers for repotting? Attractive cachepots to hide ho-hum pots? It's always a good idea to keep a bag of houseplant potting soil on hand in case you want to make cuttings during the winter or repot a plant that grows faster than expected.

In the past, have you put **Christmas** or **Thanksgiving cactuses** outdoors in spring and found that they'd begun developing buds by the time they'd been brought into the house in fall? Or that after they'd been left outdoors until late September or early October, they tended to bloom long before Christmas? The blooms on these **holiday cactuses** are triggered by two things: One is thirteen hours of darkness each night. (See **October**.) The other is temperatures below 58 degrees Fahrenheit. So if you'd prefer that your **holiday cactus** doesn't bloom quite so early, bring it in from the yard before nighttime temperatures begin to fall below 60 degrees Fahrenheit.

 ## PLANTING

September is a good month to take cuttings because it's nice to have a number of small houseplants on hand in the fall. They can be donated for sale at church fairs and carnivals. You may want to take one to a friend who's under the weather or give it as a gesture of welcome to a new neighbor. See page 130 for tips on rooting cuttings.

Since it's easier to repot plants outdoors than indoors, September is probably your last opportunity until spring. Check all your houseplants—those growing outdoors as well as inside the house—to see whether root growth has covered a plant's ball of soil. If so, it's a good candidate for repotting. (Page 128 has repotting instructions.)

If you took cuttings last month and rooted them in water, place the cuttings in individual pots as soon as a moderate root system has developed. Many cuttings will live in water for quite some time, developing extensive roots. But the longer those roots live in water, the harder it will be for them to adjust to growing in soil.

 ## CARE

Most of us tend to wait till the last possible moment before bringing houseplants back inside the house in fall. But such procrastination makes it harder for your houseplants to adapt to life indoors once again. When leaves turn yellow and fall off, the plants are telling you they're not very happy. So how do you treat plants so that they adjust seamlessly to the move?

1 The ideal time to move plants is when outdoor and indoor temperatures are about the same. When nighttime temperatures begin to slip to the 60-degree Fahrenheit range, take the plants indoors.

2 Clean them up first. (See **Grooming**.)

3 Make sure you don't bring any insects indoors, even worms. (See **Problems**.)

4 Don't move the plants directly to the spots where they'll be spending the winter. Instead, move them to very bright light (but not where they'll be touched by sun).

5 If possible, group plants together and use pebble trays to increase humidity.

Many cuttings will live in water for quite some time, developing extensive roots. But the longer those roots live in water, the harder it will be for them to adjust to growing in soil.

6 In two weeks, move medium- or low-light plants away from bright light into medium light.

7 After the plants have spent two or three weeks in medium light, move them to their final destinations.

8 Plants that have been gradually acclimated to indoor conditions adjust more readily and don't lose quantities of leaves or develop other problems.

Have you kept last year's **poinsettia** in hopes of bringing it back into bloom this year? The key is to give the plant fourteen hours of *complete* darkness and ten hours of light each day, beginning the third week of September and continuing until the first week of November. The options for providing the dark include:

- Place the plant in a dark closet each night, bringing it out again the next day.
- Cover the plant with a black cloth at 5 p.m. each day and remove it at 7:00 the next morning.
- Put the plant in an unused bedroom where it will get normal light-dark cycles. Just be sure that a dusk-to-dawn light outdoors doesn't shine into the windows.
- Keep the soil moist. Also, during the day, keep the plant in bright light. A little morning sun is okay.

WATERING

Continue to water plants as they need it. (Preferences are included in the chart on pages 119 to 121.) At the first of the month, begin to cut back slightly on watering **Christmas** or **Thanksgiving cactuses**. Don't stop watering. Just let them go a day or two longer between waterings than before. This helps encourage blooms.

FERTILIZING

If plants haven't been fertilized in the past four to six weeks, feed them now with a liquid or soluble fertilizer added to water. A timed-released fertilizer applied in late spring may be coming to the end of its effectiveness. If so, switch over to a product added to the water monthly. There are two reasons: Most houseplant fertilization stops in October, when the majority of plants begin a rest period. Also, the majority of timed-release fertilizers don't work in cool temperatures.

GROOMING

Be sure all houseplants are well groomed before they go back indoors. Remove all yellowed or damaged leaves and faded flowers. Clean all foliage, top and bottom. Clean splattered dirt off the pots, too. If containers can't be scrubbed clean, consider new pots or hide the pots in a plastic-lined basket or a decorative container.

 PROBLEMS

When you bring houseplants back inside your house this month, don't let any insects hitchhike indoors. How do you prevent it?

- Mix up a tub or bucket of 5 parts warm water and 1 part insecticidal soap. Remove plants from their pots, place them in the mixture, and let the plants stand for an hour. Some gardeners mix up a mild solution of all-purpose insecticide and pour this over the leaves and through the soil of their houseplants before they take them indoors. Check with the Extension Service for advice on which pesticide to use and how.
- Even after doing this, you may want to keep outdoor plants isolated for about a month from those that spent the summer inside. Sometimes a stray insect manages to get in anyway, or insect eggs hatch. The problem will be easier to deal with when you can keep the infestation confined to one or two plants.

OCTOBER

 PLANNING

As days begin to grow shorter and you're indoors more, houseplants seem more important. Begin thinking about where you might like to put a new plant or two, and start looking at the selections when you visit your favorite garden center, grocery store, or home center. Always read the label and match the conditions the plant needs with those in your home.

 PLANTING

Continue repotting plants that need it. If the temperature outside is above 60 degrees Fahrenheit, it's fine to do the transplanting outdoors. Otherwise, repot inside so the plants won't be exposed to cold.

Does your **spider plant** have lots of "babies"? (These are known as *plantlets*.) It's easy to root them this month:

- Fill a 2- to 3-inch pot with moistened potting mix.
- Place the pot next to the **spider plant**.
- Pin the plantlet to the soil using a V-shaped piece of thin, flexible wire.
- Keep the soil moist.
- Remove the pin and cut the plantlet from the mother plant after it has rooted.

Or you can remove the plantlet from the parent plant in the beginning and place it in its own pot so that it's in constant contact with the moist soil.

Keep potting up plants that you rooted in the past six weeks. These will make nice gifts or provide you with more plants to place around the house. Once rooted cuttings have been placed in pots of soil, put them somewhere you can give them extra attention for the next three or four weeks. They may need a little more water, humidity, or light as they're adjusting to their new homes.

 CARE

All houseplants should be back indoors now. If you're growing a few annuals—**coleus** or **impatiens**—as houseplants, see the chapter on **Annuals** for tips on their care.

Now's the time to begin looking ahead to Christmas—**Christmas cactus** blooms, that is. (The plant with the smooth ends on the segments is the true **Christmas cactus**. The one with the hook- or crab-like ends is **Thanksgiving cactus**. They're treated the same, so they're usually referred to as **holiday cactus**.)

To get your **holiday cactus** to bloom:

1 Cut back on watering the plants. That doesn't mean not watering them; just water less than usual. Let the soil dry out completely between waterings. (If leaves begin to shrivel, water.)

2 Place the plants where temperatures are between 45 and 58 degrees Fahrenheit at night until buds form. Do not expose the plants to freezing temperatures.

3 Or, if you don't have a place where temperatures are within the 45 to 58 degree Fahrenheit range, move the plants to a spot where they can have thirteen hours of complete darkness and eleven hours of bright light each day. (Watch out for lamps and for street lights shining through windows.) The second part of that regimen is essential. Sometimes gardeners just place a **holiday cactus** in a dark closet and leave it there. But the plant needs light, as well as a period of darkness.

4 As soon as buds form, move the plants into bright light (no sun—if the foliage turns reddish, it's getting too much light).

5 Keep the soil moist and fertilize every other week until blooming is complete.

Keep an eye on houseplants that summered outdoors to see whether they are affected by lower humidity levels (flowers dropping off prematurely, leaf tips drying up, leaves curling or becoming deformed). If so, increase humidity levels where possible. (See page 118.) Remember that misting doesn't do much more than temporarily raise the amount of moisture in the air. It's not a long-term solution.

 # WATERING

Most houseplants require less soil moisture from now through winter. Since the plant won't need watering as often, you may need to develop a new watering schedule. For most plants, it's best to err on the side of watering just a bit too *infrequently* than to water too often, especially in cooler weather. Review the watering needs of your plants in the chart on pages 119 to 121, and then water accordingly. Don't let water accumulate in saucers, in the bottoms of cachepots, or in decorative foil wrapping around gift plants; this leads to root rot.

To get older **cactuses** to bloom in spring, stop watering the plants at the end of October and water as little as possible until March. At the same time, it's also a good idea to place **cactuses** in the chilliest spot in your house (but where it's above freezing). The combination will cause flowering in spring, as long as the **cactus** is old enough to bloom.

 # FERTILIZING

Fertilize all houseplants—except **holiday cactus**—one last time near the beginning of October. Then you won't need to feed most of them again until March. As temperatures cool down and light levels become less bright, many houseplants go dormant or rest through the winter. During that time, they aren't growing and therefore don't need fertilizer. If you feed plants when they don't need it, you've wasted your money and time, but more important, the excess fertilizer will build up in the soil.

The exceptions to the rule are flowering plants and plants that continue to grow during winter. These generally need fertilizing about every four to six weeks.

 # GROOMING

Yellowing and fallen leaves sometimes accompany houseplants' readjustment to the indoor environment after being in the yard all summer. Pick these up daily, as they may harbor or attract insects.

Make it a weekly ritual to remove past-prime flowers from **African violets** and other blooming plants. This will encourage continuing bloom.

 # PROBLEMS

Because tobacco mosaic virus can be transmitted from smokers' hands to plants, always wash your hands thoroughly with soap and water before touching or working with houseplants, if you smoke. Better yet, wear gloves. Once an indoor plant has developed a virus, it usually has to be destroyed.

NOVEMBER

PLANNING

Watch out when you buy houseplants this time of year. Many of them will be harmed if they're exposed to cold. That means carefully covering them up so they aren't exposed to low temperatures between the store and your vehicle or when going between your car and the house. It also means going directly home if you've bought a plant on a day that temperatures are below 50 degrees Fahrenheit. Sitting in a cold car can also harm a plant.

If the children are no longer at home or maybe you're going away for part of the holidays, you may not want to put up a Christmas tree. Consider a **Norfolk Island pine** as a stand-in. It can be decorated in December and then provide a strong green accent in any room in the house the rest of the year.

PLANTING

Grow a **sweet potato vine** indoors since November is definitely the month for eating **sweet potatoes**. Just buy an extra one as you shop for your Thanksgiving meal. You'll need a tall glass or jar, some toothpicks, water, and a fresh **sweet potato**—preferably one that's home-grown or from a farmers' market (the ones at the supermarket have sometimes been treated with growth retardant).

1 Fill the glass with water.

2 Stick toothpicks around the middle of the **sweet potato**.

3 Position the **sweet potato** so that the bottom half is in the water.

4 Place the **sweet potato** on a sunny windowsill.

5 Add water several times a week so that half the **sweet potato** is always beneath water.

Roots will develop from the bottom, and green stems and leaves from the top of the tuber.

What do you do when a tall plant such as **dracaena** gets too big or has dropped so many lower leaves that most of those remaining are near the top of a tall stalk? You can air layer the top portion of the plant so that it will develop roots and can be moved to a new pot.

1 Using a sharp knife, cut one-third of the way into the stem. Use a pin or small sliver of wood to hold the cut piece open.

2 Brush a rooting hormone onto the cut portion of the stem.

3 Moisten long-fibered sphagnum moss and place it inside the plastic so it covers the wound.

4 Loosely wrap a piece of plastic (cut from a dry-cleaner bag—or use plastic wrap from the kitchen) around the wound and tape it at the bottom. Leave the top open.

5 Close the top of the plastic (with duct tape or a twister tie).

6 Don't let the moss dry out. If necessary, loosen the top of the plastic so you can water.

7 When you see a mass of roots in the plastic, cut the plant's stem below the roots.

8 Remove the plastic and the moss.

9 Plant in a new pot.

10 Keep in a warm spot with bright light for several weeks before moving the plant to its final location.

CARE

As soon as **Christmas** or **Thanksgiving cactuses** have formed buds and **poinsettias** have begun to develop colored bracts (leaves), they can be moved into the locations where you want them to grow. Bright light is recommended for both plants (**poinsettia** can take a few hours of sun, but not **holiday cactus**). Keep the soil barely moist. **Poinsettias** prefer warmth during the day and don't like drafts.

As soon as Christmas or Thanksgiving cactuses have formed buds and poinsettias have begun to develop colored bracts (leaves), they can be moved into the locations where you want them to grow.

How cool do you keep your house? Some homeowners like it warm all winter, and others turn the thermostat way back (either all the time or when they're away from home). Although many plants can adjust to lower temperatures, just as people do, some really need warmth.

Plants that can tolerate temperatures of 50 to 60 degrees Fahrenheit in the daytime and 45 to 55 degrees at night include:

- **Cast iron plant**
- **Cactuses** (only while resting in winter)
- **Cyclamen**
- **English ivy**
- **Norfolk Island pine**
- **Miniature rose**
- **Wandering Jew**

Plants that grow well in medium temperatures: 60 to 65 degrees Fahrenheit during the day and 55 to 60 degrees at night:

- **Aluminum plant**
- **Asparagus fern**
- **Bromeliads**
- **Flowering maple**
- **Peperomia**
- **Piggyback plant** (*Tolmiea menziesii*)
- **Purple passion plant**
- **Schefflera**
- **Snake plant**

Plants for warm temperatures (70 to 80 degrees Fahrenheit in daytime and 65 to 70 degrees at night):

- **Arrowhead plant**
- **African violets**
- **Bromeliads**
- **Chinese evergreen**
- **Cactuses**
- **Croton**
- **Dracaena**
- **Ficus**
- **Gloxinia**
- **Grape ivy**
- **Peace lily**
- **Philodendron**
- **Poinsettia**
- **Prayer plant**
- **Snake plant**

 # WATERING

Water all indoor plants as they need it—either when the soil dries slightly all the way through or when the soil's surface begins to dry (see the needs of particular plants on pages 119 to 121). One exception this time of year is **holiday cactus**, which should be kept on the dry side until buds form. After **Christmas** and **Thanksgiving cactuses** have developed buds or flowers, keep the soil moist. Another exception is regular **cactus**, which should be watered minimally—if at all—until March.

FERTILIZING

Only plants in bud or bloom need fertilizing in November—**orchids, bromeliads, African violets, holiday cactus, amaryllis, poinsettia**.

GROOMING

Want to clean a small plant without giving it a shower? Fill a bucket with tepid water, turn the plant upside down (with your hand over the soil), and dunk the leaves in the water.

Keeping Plants Clean

PROBLEMS

Once the furnace goes on, the humidity level in homes generally decreases. And many plants do best in medium or high humidity. You can increase the humidity around your plants (see page 118), but another way to tackle the problem is to grow plants that don't mind low humidity. These include **aloe, bird of paradise** (*Strelitzia regina*), most **cactuses, cast iron plant, clivia, heart-leaf philodendron, jade plant** (*Crassula argentea*), **pothos**, and **snake plant**.

DECEMBER

PLANNING

If you're going to be away from home during the holidays, plan to have someone water your plants if you'll be away for ten days or longer, or use the vacation-watering techniques on page 134. It's not a good idea to turn the heat off while you're gone. That may make the temperature too low for many tropical houseplants (see **November** for temperatures that various plants prefer). You may also want to move plants to the room that stays the warmest in your house. Then if the power should go out because of an ice storm, the plants may still be okay.

PLANTING

If you pot up cuttings this month or repot houseplants that have outgrown their containers, do it in a warm room and don't let the roots stay exposed very long.

CARE

This is the month of the **poinsettia**—and many other flowering plants. Here's how to choose and care for a **poinsettia**:

1 Choose plants with stiff stems and no signs of wilting. Look for dark-green leaves all the way to the base. (Lower leaves of **poinsettias** that have been in decorative sleeves too long often turn yellow and fall off.) The tiny yellow buttonlike flowers in the middle of the bracts should be closed or barely open. If they've fallen off, the plant is past its prime.

2 If outdoor temperatures are below 50 degrees Fahrenheit, make sure the plant is protected (by being wrapped in paper or placed in a large shopping bag) before you take it from the store to your car and from the car into your house. If weather is cold, take the **poinsettia** straight home; don't leave it in the car while you spend a couple of hours at the mall.

3 Remove any decorative wrapping when you get home. It isn't good for the plant. See the next page.

4 **Poinsettias** like room temperatures between 68 and 75 degrees Fahrenheit and bright indirect sunlight for at least six hours daily.

5 Avoid placing a **poinsettia** on top of the TV set, in front of heating vents, near an outside door, or in front of a fireplace.

6 Water frequently enough to keep the soil slightly moist to the touch, but not soggy. Don't fertilize your **poinsettia** until January.

These are the conditions needed by other common holiday plants:

Azalea—chilly temperatures, bright light, moist soil.

Calamondin orange (x *Citrofortunella microcarpa*)—at least four hours of sun, average to cool temperatures. Let soil dry between waterings. Watch out for mealybugs and spider mites.

Holiday cactus—see page 140.

Cyclamen—chilly temperatures; bright light. Don't let the soil dry out.

Jerusalem cherry (*Solanum pseudo-capsicum*)—half a day of sun, chilly temperatures, moist soil. Watch out for whiteflies.

Kalanchoe—half day of sun, warm to average temperatures. Let the soil dry out before watering again.

Ornamental pepper—sun, moist soil, warm temperatures in the daytime, about 60 degrees Fahrenheit at night.

 # FERTILIZING

Fertilize **orchids, African violets**, and other blooming plants once this month. Most other houseplants don't need feeding until early spring.

 # WATERING

Watch out for foil wraps around **poinsettias** and other holiday plants. Water can collect in the bottom of the foil, keeping the plant's roots wet all the time and without needed oxygen. This leads to rot, which generally kills the plant. If you must keep the foil wrapped around the plant, punch some holes in the bottom and set the plant in a saucer to catch excess water, which can then be emptied.

The same is true for cachepots and other decorative containers in which indoor plants are placed. If you tend to overwater, avoid these. Grow your houseplants only in pots that have drainage holes.

Keep the potting mix of *Paphiopedilum* **orchids** slightly moist.

 # GROOMING

Another reason to remove decorative foil wraps around plants is that they tend to hide the bottom leaves of the plant until they turn yellow and fall off from lack of light and air circulation. When you bring a wrapped plant home, pull the foil down below the rim of the container so that all the leaves are visible.

 # PROBLEMS

If your plants are growing on windowsills, foliage can be damaged if it touches cold glass when temperatures are far below freezing.

- When low temperatures are forecast, move the plants off the windowsill in the evening and put them back the next day after temperatures have climbed a little higher.

- Place a piece of cardboard between the glass and the plants at night.

- Tape Bubble Wrap® to the window so it provides some protection from the cold while letting through the light.

- When temperatures are very low, never close draperies or curtains over windowsills that hold houseplants.

If you're trying—but not succeeding—at bringing *Cattleya, Paphiopedilum,* or *Phalaenopsis* **orchids** back into bloom, give them temperatures that are ten degrees cooler at night than in the daytime.

CHAPTER FIVE

Lawns

A lush green lawn is one of the most versatile elements in your landscape. It's useful, it's beautiful, and it serves as the perfect complement to everything in your yard—trees, shrubs, flowers, vines—while letting them be the center of attention.

It's true that a thick carpet of deep-green grass is going to take at least a small to moderate amount of effort. Don't think of it as work, though. Instead, consider it *exercise*. After all, mowing the lawn about once a week from March until November uses up calories—and doesn't require a gym membership. And once a thick stand of grass has been achieved, it doesn't take much to keep it that way.

Ah, but how do you transform your current plot of anemic grass and robust weeds into that elusive soft carpet of grass that you'd love to own? Success lies in choosing the right type of grass for your part of the region, as well as for the conditions in your yard, then establishing and caring for it "by the calendar"—doing certain tasks only in certain months.

Many garden activities can be accomplished on a very flexible schedule. But when you're dealing with grass, the time of the year matters. When you fertilize, when you sow grass seed or plant sod, the best time to control crabgrass—there's a right and wrong time to do each of them. And the wrong timing can cause failure. But don't worry. In the following pages, we tell you exactly which month to take all the steps that will make your lawn a cut above.

First, take a moment to assess your lawn:

1 How much of your lawn is in sun most of the day or in shade most of the day? Knowing this will help you choose the right type of grass and know how to care for it.

2 What kind of soil and drainage do you have? As you've learned by now, clay will hold more moisture than fast-draining soils. It may mean that you won't have to water your grass as often. But water-holding clay can also be responsible for drainage problems. Note any wet-weather damp spots and any "streams" that cut through the lawn in heavy rains. It's going to be hard to grow grass in either situation, so you may need to correct these problems in order to have a decent-looking lawn.

3 Do you know what type of grass is growing in your yard right now? If you're not the original owner, you may not. The type of grass you have determines how you care for it—and when. So check with your county's Extension Service office (see the lists on pages 344 to 353) to see if they will agree to identify the type or types of grass growing in your lawn. Many people are surprised to discover that they have several different grasses mixed together in their lawn.

4 Do you need outdoor play areas (for children's swing sets, slides, or a spot for impromptu football games)? Do you do a lot of entertaining outside? As you'll learn in the next section, some types of grass can stand up to heavy traffic; some can't. For those areas that are going to receive hard wear, seed or sod the grasses that can take lots of wear.

5 How do you feel about your lawn? Does it have bare spots or brown patches? At certain seasons, does it seem to be filled with weeds? Does that bother you? Do you see your lawn as passable–neither a dream

Lawns

lawn or a yard you're ashamed of? Each homeowner has different standards for judging a lawn. You're the only one who can decide how perfect you want your lawn to look–and how much time you're willing to spend to get it that way.

The first step in getting to the root of a good lawn—one that will meet your needs, be attractive, and be as little trouble as possible—is choosing the right grass. You probably want to know: What's the best grass for the Kentucky or Tennessee homeowner? There are many answers to that question.

Like every other plant in your yard, grass serves a purpose. It may provide the soft cushioning beneath a child's play set. It can serve as the backdrop for frequent summer cookouts in the backyard. It may set the scene for flower beds. It can prevent the soil from washing away on a hill.

Once you know what you want your grass to do—even if it's just "look good"—you're ready to start deciding which type of grass will accomplish what you have in mind. Look at the chart on pages 150 to 151. It explains the good and bad points of various grasses grown in Tennessee and Kentucky. If you want a grass to serve as living carpet underneath a swing set,

check the ones that rate high in traffic tolerance. Those who do lots of warm-weather entertaining may want a grass that looks fabulous in summertime and not worry that **bermuda** and **zoysia** go brown in the winter. But someone who grows plenty of perennials may want to avoid **bermuda** since it creeps into flower beds and is hard to eradicate.

Lawn grasses that perform well in this area are divided into two categories: cool-season and warm-season. A *cool-season grass* is one that grows best in the relative coolness of the spring and fall, grows slowly in the heat of summer, and stays green year-round. A *warm-season grass* grows most actively in the heat of summer and goes brown (dormant) in winter. Some warm-season grasses aren't cold-hardy.

There's no such thing as a perfect lawn grass for our region. We're in what lawn experts call "the transition zone" for grass. That means our summers are often too warm for the cool-season grasses of the North to be successful, but our winters are too cold for many of the warm-season grasses of the Deep South to do well. So we usually compromise by choosing a grass that we hope will provide most of the qualities we're looking for. The majority of

Tennessee and Kentucky lawns are sown in one type of **fescue** or another, but you'll want to check the discussion of pros and cons on page 150 before deciding. This will help you find the grass that meets your needs and expectations.

WHEN TO PLANT

Seed in fall. If you've been around lawns much, you know about sowing seed to start or patch up a lawn. The ideal time to do that for cool-season grasses such as **tall fescue** and **Kentucky bluegrass** is early fall. There are several reasons for this:

- Cool-season grasses grow best in the moderate temperatures of fall.
- The grass then has eight months to grow deep roots to help it cope with the heat of summer (the roughest time of year for a cool-season grass).

Even if you keep a spring planting watered well over summer, it still won't do as well as a lawn planted or renovated in September. See pages 166 and 167 for complete directions on planting a cool-season lawn and page 154 for tips on patching a poor-looking lawn.

Lawns

Because it may be a temporary fix and since it won't require much water, patching can be done in spring or fall.

The rule for renovating is that if more than half of your lawn consists of weeds or bare spots, it's best to kill it all and start over. If at least half of the lawn is green and weed-free, you may be able to obtain desirable results just by killing the weeds, overseeding, fertilizing, and, in general, rehabilitating your lawn (or the worst-looking portions of it).

Sod in late spring or early summer. Because warm-season grasses take off once temperatures begin climbing, wait till the weather is consistently warm in your area before establishing **bermuda** or **zoysia**. (Usually that's at least May.) The latest you should establish one of these grasses is two months before your county's average first-frost date.

These grasses aren't available as seed (they don't produce enough seed to sell). Instead they come in strips of grass and soil called *sod*. They look like short carpet runners. You'll also find that occasionally **bermuda** or **zoysia** are available as plugs or sprigs. These are less expensive than

sod but take much longer to become established. They are installed at the same time of year as sod—May-July. See pages 158 and 159 for everything you need to know to install sprigs and plugs, and see page 158 for directions on laying sod.

FERTILIZER

Everyone knows what lawn care is all about—mowing, watering, weeding, fertilizing. The first three are common sense, but we've included lots of tips in the pages ahead. Most homeowners, though, aren't as conversant with fertilizer—what to choose, how to use it, and when to use it.

A good lawn fertilizer contains quite a bit of nitrogen, a nutrient that promotes growth and good color. It's what grass needs most. The nitrogen content is shown in the first number of the three shown in large letters on the bag—22-4-4, for instance. Some fertilizers release their nitrogen content quickly, which causes quick green-up but doesn't feed the grass over a longer period. Others may release the nitrogen over an extended period. Usually, the quick-release formulas are

less expensive than the slow-release ones. A good compromise—for the grass, as well as your pocketbook—is to choose a formula that includes some quick-release nitrogen for fast results and some slow-release that will keep feeding.

The most common lawn fertilizers are synthetic, but organic fertilizers are available, too. Their big advantages are that they slowly release the nutrients to the grass and you can't accidentally burn the grass when applying them. Generally, organic lawn fertilizers contain less nitrogen per bag than synthetic products; therefore, more must be applied to get the same results.

Many experts recommend against using weed-and-feed products, combinations of fertilizer and herbicide. Often the treatment for the weeds isn't needed at the recommended time for fertilizing. Besides, a homeowner must apply at the correct amount for the herbicide and not the amount of fertilizer needed. The most serious problem, though, is that when too much is spread on grass near shrubs and trees, the herbicide can harm or kill them.

Lawns

WHEN TO FERTILIZE YOUR LAWN

COOL-SEASON GRASSES
(fescues, Kentucky bluegrass)

Application Date	Total pounds of nitrogen per 1,000 square feet*
March 15	1/4 to 1/2
April 15	1/4 to 1/2
September 1	1/2 to 1
October 15	1/2 to 1
November 15	1/2 to 1

*Tall fescues usually require the higher amount; chewings and red fescues, less. If your lawn is mostly shady and sown primarily with fine and chewings fescues, you may want to fertilize *only* in September, October, and November.

WARM-SEASON GRASSES
(bermuda, centipede, and zoysia)

Application Date	Total pounds of nitrogen per 1,000 square feet
April 15	1
June 1	1
July 15	1
September 1	1

The dates to fertilize seem clear enough, but you may be wondering what "total pounds of nitrogen per 1,000 square feet" means? How does that translate into the amount of fertilizer you should spread on your lawn? Here's another chart to help.

Type of fertilizer	Percent nitrogen	Pounds fertilizer*
15-5-5	15	6 1/2
20-10-10	20	5
24-8-8	24	4
27-3-3	27	4
Milorganite**	6	17

*Total pounds of fertilizer to supply 1 pound of nitrogen
**processed sewage sludge

No lawn is an even 1,000 square feet, of course. Measure to be sure of your lawn's size. Multiply the length in feet times the number of feet wide to get the square footage of your lawn.

For those of you with small lawns, a pound of fertilizer is approximately 2 cups.

High vs. low maintenance. Why fertilize at all? It just makes the grass grow faster so you have to mow more, right? Just as food provides people the nutrients they require to keep them healthy and strong, fertilizer gives grass good color and helps it resist insects, diseases, and weeds.

The recommendations for fertilization amounts and times are for "full fertilization" or *high maintenance*. If your lawn has been neglected or if you're a "lawn ranger" who wants to have the best-looking lawn in the neighborhood, follow these suggestions carefully.

But if your lawn is a nice green color, contains only a few weeds, and is growing well, you may prefer a *low-maintenance* regimen. In that case you may want to try fertilizing only twice a year instead of four times. Note on the chart, though, that some grasses just need more fertilizer than others. **Fescue** in good condition can typically get by with less.

There's a lot of talk in gardening circles about getting rid of lawns or making them smaller, but there's something about a thick green carpet of grass that appeals to many of us. Sure a lawn takes regular attention, but I can't imagine walking barefoot on a ground cover or setting up a sprinkler in a flower bed on a hot day for the kids to run through. Lawns amply repay the hours spent mowing them, and I think they're in no danger of disappearing anytime soon.

Lawns

Grass	Bermuda	Centipede	Fine fescue*	Kentucky bluegrass	Tall fescue	Zoysia
Type	Warm-season	Warm-season	Cool-season	Cool-season	Cool-season	Warm-season
Zone	6-8	7b, 8	5, 6	5, 6	6-8	6-8
Method Of planting	Sod, sprigs, or seed	Sprigs, sod	Seed	Seed	Seed, sod	Sprigs, plugs
Heat tolerance	Good	Good	Poor	Poor	Fair	Good
Cold tolerance	Fair	Poor	Good	Good	Good	Good
Drought tolerance	Good	Fair	Fair	Fair	Fair	Good
Shade tolerance	Poor	Fair	Good	Fair	Good	Fair
Traffic (wear) tolerance	Good	Poor	Varies	Fair	Fair	Good
Mowing Height (Inches)	1/2 to 1 1/2	1 to 2	1 1/2 to 2 1/2	1/2 to 2 1/2	2 to 3	1/2 to 1 1/2

*Fine fescue = chewings, hard, and creeping red fescues

Advantages and Disadvantages of the Most-Used Lawn Grasses

Bermuda

Pros: A beautiful grass that makes your lawn look like a green carpet. It stands up to heat, survives drought well, and tolerates heavy traffic across the lawn. Good spreader.

Cons: Subject to a number of insects. Not at all good in shade. Goes brown as soon as cold weather arrives in fall and doesn't green up until warm weather returns the next spring. Requires lots of attention—watering, fertilizing, mowing, thatch removal. Becomes a real pest when it spreads into flower beds. Not always cold-hardy.

Fine fescues (chewings, hard, and creeping red fescue)

Pros: Fine leaf texture. These are low-maintenance grasses well-suited for shade and poor soil.

Cons: Tend to die out in high temperatures, making them of limited use in the warmer parts of the region.

Kentucky bluegrass

Pros: Hardy and adaptable in the cooler sections of the area. Nice color and texture. Withstands foot traffic.

Cons: Not heat-tolerant. Subject to diseases and insects. Needs heavy watering and fertilization.

Lawns

Tall fescue

Pros: Low-maintenance. Relatively inexpensive. Seed readily available. Cold-tolerant. Tolerates partial shade.

Cons: Older varieties such as Kentucky 31 clump instead of spread. Coarse texture. Goes dormant during drought and when temperatures get over 90 degrees Fahrenheit.

Zoysia

Pros: Beautiful appearance. Slow growing. Heat- and drought-tolerant. Resists weeds and most insects.

Cons: Goes brown quickly in cold weather. Some species and cultivars aren't as cold-hardy as others and may be killed in cold winters. Must be dethatched regularly.

Other Grasses Homeowners Sometimes Consider

Centipede

Pros: In the warmest areas of the region, it's a low-maintenance grass that resists insects and diseases. Tolerates poor soil and grows well in acid soil. Grows slowly so less mowing is needed.

Cons: Not very cold-tolerant (is killed by prolonged exposure to temperatures of 5 degrees or lower). Shallow-rooted so not good for areas of high traffic. Needs frequent watering. Turns brown in cold winters.

Ryegrass (annual and perennial)

Pros: Popular for overseeding lawns during winter, so they'll look green. Germinates quickly. Because it can't tolerate heat and humidity, it dies out about the time warm-season grasses are coming into their own. Tolerant of partial shade.

Cons: Lack of heat-tolerance means that it's not recommended as a permanent grass in this area. May need mowing in winter. Repeated use may restrict spread of your permanent warm-season grass.

St. Augustine

Pros: Relatively shade-tolerant (the best among the warm-season grasses). An aggressive grower that crowds out weeds. Doesn't mind hot weather. Excellent for lawns that have high foot traffic. Not subject to many diseases.

Cons: Lack of tolerance to low temperatures means that it is not recommended for for this region. Turns brown in cold weather. Subject to chinch bugs. Needs frequent watering and thatch removal.

JANUARY

PLANNING

Vroom-vroom. Is this the year you buy a new lawn mower? Start the year off right by spending some time talking to dealers, collecting brochures, comparing features and prices, and figuring out the right model for your yard. Chat with friends to find out what they like, or don't like, about the mowers they own. And ask the man who runs your favorite lawn-mower repair shop for his opinion; he sees all brands and models.

Reel time. No, not fishing—reel mowers. They're wonderful for **zoysia** and great for touch-up mowing in tight places. Since they're making a comeback, maybe you want to look at a few of these as you're shopping, too.

PLANTING

Take a break from planting in January. If your cool-season lawn needs patching, wait until at least March. As the name implies, warm-season lawns are sprigged, sodded or renovated after weather has become warm—generally May or later.

CARE

Leaves. If you or a next-door neighbor have quite a few trees, you'll find stray leaves blowing onto your lawn all winter. On a nice day during the January thaw, get your exercise close to home by raking leaves instead of heading for the gym and working out. Or haul out the lawn mower—if it wasn't winterized—and *if the lawn is dry enough*, mow over the leaves until they're finely chopped. Let the shredded leaves remain on the lawn as topdressing. This helps reduce problems with thatch (a layer of undecayed material between the soil and the grass that lessens water penetration into the soil).

Watch where you walk. If possible, avoid walking on the lawn when it's wet—that compacts the soil.

WATERING

The first month of the year provides a vacation from watering. Grass, like all plants, needs moisture only when it's actively growing.

FERTILIZING

If you have cool-season grass—**fescue** or **Kentucky bluegrass**—you get a two-month break from fertilizing—no lawn feeding is required before March. Owners of lawns planted with warm-season grasses—**bermuda** or **zoysia**, for instance—won't need to fertilize until the grass greens up.

MOWING

It's not likely that you'll need to mow this month, but occasionally, during a milder than usual winter, overseeded **rye** or **tall fescue** has grown too tall by January. (See the plant chart on page 150 for recommended mowing heights.) If so, it's a good idea to mow. Otherwise, the grass will fall over.

PROBLEMS

Soil test time. Although getting your soil tested isn't a problem, it can prevent problems later by identifying any needed improvements for soil health. If the soil beneath your lawn hasn't been tested in the past five years, have it tested now. The local office of the Agricultural Extension Service has directions for taking a soil test and instructions for sending it off. It's important to get this done before applying fertilizer so you'll know how much and what kind. Also, if your lawn needs it, liming should be done before spring since it takes some time for the lime to become effective. But lime and nitrogen fertilizer should *not* be applied together.

FEBRUARY

 PLANNING

Think ahead. Before you know it, lawn-mowing time will be here. Is your mower ready for the eight or nine months of work ahead? February is a good time to get your mower into the shop for a tune-up—especially to have the blade sharpened. Avoid the inevitable crowds by getting your mower in now. If you'd like to do the job yourself, here's what's involved for a walk-behind mower:

- Change the spark plug.
- Clean the fans.
- Change the engine oil. Check the manufacturer's directions for the right type of oil to use.
- Install a new air filter.
- Sharpen the blade.
- Remove all those caked-on grass clippings from beneath the mower's deck.
- Check to see whether the wheels need lubricating.

Testing time. Did you get the soil test recommended in January? If so, read it over and call your county's Extension Service office if you have any questions. If you have procrastinated, take samples of your soil and get them in to be tested now. It could save you quite a bit of money when you learn that you may not need to apply all the nutrients you usually do.

 PLANTING

Although February usually brings a few warm days, it's still not quite time to patch bare spots in the grass or to completely renovate the lawn. Be patient. Soon warmer weather will arrive.

 CARE

Liming. If your lawn's soil test indicates a need for lime (that is, the pH is below 6.0), use a drop or gravity spreader for the most even application. Many gardeners believe that pelleted lime is less messy to work with than ground limestone.

 WATERING

What's your equipment like? It's not likely that you'll need to water your lawn in February, but you may want to think back to the last dry spell, when you dragged the sprinklers out. Did you vow to buy some new ones? Or maybe investigate professionally installed in-ground irrigation? This is a good time to make a start on that. And while you're shopping, you may want to look at new hoses or convenient holders for the hoses you have. Good equipment makes lawn work go faster.

 FERTILIZING

Not yet. Although warm spells may make you wonder whether it's time to get the fertilizer/crabgrass preventer out on the grass, you still have a few more weeks.

 MOWING

A combination of fall fertilization and mild spells throughout winter can make cool-season grasses grow. If your grass is one-third taller than the recommended mowing height (see the chart on page 150), use that as an excuse to get out of the house on a sunny, relatively warm afternoon and do a little mowing.

 PROBLEMS

Wild onions and wild garlic. If these weeds are in your lawn, they're highly visible this time of year. This is a good time to get rid of them. Wait till rain has moistened the soil, and then pull or dig them out by hand.

MARCH

PLANNING

Cool-season grasses. March is the beginning of the active lawn-care season in many parts of the region. But that doesn't mean you don't have some planning to do for later in the year.

- **Spring vs. fall renovation.** If your lawn isn't in good shape—lots of weeds, bare spots here and there— you may be getting all geared up to tackle this renovation on the first warm, sunny weekend. Wait. Spring is *not* the time to renovate cool-season lawns in this part of the country. Fall is the ideal time if you really want to ensure success. Summer's heat stresses cool-season grasses, and a lawn that's had only a couple of months to get established before high temperatures arrive isn't going to fare well. But when renovation takes place in September, the grass has a long time to establish deep roots that will let it sail through the next summer with ease.

- **Deliberate procrastination.** Mark your lawn renovation project on the calendar for Labor Day weekend. Your cool-season grass will perform much better when seeded then.

Warm-season grasses. If you've been dreaming of transforming your plot of **Kentucky 31 fescue** into a carpet of zoysia or **bermuda**, maybe this is the year to do it. You have at least two months before you need to tackle the project, and that's plenty of time to do research.

- **Which cultivar?** First, decide which cultivar of **bermuda** or **zoysia** is right for your location. Some are hardier than others, and some newer kinds need less fertilization or watering. Learn all you can, and balance the advantages against the disadvantages.
- **Planting method.** Will you establish the grass by sprigs, sod, or plugs? Don't decide based on cost alone. Sprigs especially take a long time to become established. In the meantime, you may not be happy with how your lawn looks.
- **Who will do the work?** If you think this is a job for a lawn professional, start looking for the right person. Get references and check them so you'll be confident this person will do a good job.

PLANTING

Patch bare spots. Although you should not start a cool-season lawn in spring, there's no reason you can't repair small sections of your lawn this month or next.

1 Remove all grass and weeds from the area.

2 Square off the edges.

3 Dig the soil to a depth of 6 inches, removing any roots, rocks, and debris.

4 Mix compost or other organic matter (rotted leaves, fine bark) with the soil.

5 Rake the area and then water.

6 Sow grass seed at the rate recommended on the bag or box.

7 Using the back of the rake, the back of a hoe, or your hand or foot, make sure the seed comes into contact with the soil.

8 Cover with a light layer of straw.

CARE

Aeration and dethatching. If your lawn has accumulated a layer of thatch, it should be removed so that water and fertilizer can easily get to the roots of the grass. It may also need to be aerified if the soil has become compacted. You may dethatch and aerate cool-season lawns this month, if you like. But September is the usual choice. The best time to dethatch or aerate warm-season lawns is late spring. See page 167 for directions.

Liming. Spread lime over the lawn early in the month, following soil-test recommendations.

If your lawn has accumulated a layer of thatch, it should be removed so that water and fertilizer can easily get to the roots of the grass. It may also need to be aerified if the soil has become compacted.

WATERING

Keep seeds moist. Usually March is a rainy month in Kentucky and Tennessee. But if rainfall is lacking, you may have to water any seeds you sowed to repair bare spots in cool-season lawns. Don't let the seeds dry out; otherwise, they won't germinate. Once the seeds have sprouted, continue to water about every other day—if there's no rain—so the young grass doesn't wilt.

FERTILIZING

Feed cool-season lawns. About the middle of the month, fertilize **Kentucky bluegrass** and **tall fescue** with one-half pound of nitrogen per 1,000 square feet of lawn. See the chart on page 149 to determine how much of various fertilizers is needed to supply 1 pound of nitrogen. Shady lawns that consist mostly of **fine fescues** may be fertilized lightly now or not at all until fall. (See page 165 about growing grass in the shade.)

MOWING

Ready, set, mow. Set the mower blade to its lowest position. Normally, mowing cool-season grasses high is the best thing you can do for them. But not the first two mowings of the season. That's

when you want to cut close—in order to remove winter damage and to stimulate new growth.

New grass. Newly seeded grass seems so fragile that you may hesitate to mow it. But mowing is good for it. Wait till the soil is dry, though. Cut an inch off newly sown **Kentucky bluegrass** when it reaches 3 1/2 inches tall and **tall fescue** when it reaches 4 inches high.

PROBLEMS

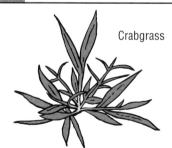

Crabgrass

Prevent crabgrass. Crabgrass, which in hot summers seems to grow as fast as kudzu, is more easily prevented than killed once it appears. Any garden center or home store will have lawn fertilizers that contain a pre-emergent crabgrass killer.

- **Application time.** These have to be applied *before* the seeds of this annual weed germinate in the spring. That can happen from mid-March into early April, depending on the weather and the area of the region. Many gardeners apply a pre-emergent crabgrass control when **forsythia** bushes bloom in their neighborhood. Or you can ask the Extension Service what the best time for your area is.
- *No* **seeds will germinate.** It's important for you to know, however, that these products work by preventing crabgrass seeds from germinating. In most cases, you cannot apply this product and then sow grass seed—it won't germinate either.
- **Once or twice?** In the warmer parts of the region, you may have to apply a pre-emergent herbicide once in March and again in late spring.

APRIL

 ## PLANNING

While you may be tempted to install **bermuda** sod or sprig **zoysia** during April, it's best to wait until the weather's at least 60 degrees Fahrenheit, day and night. Most years, that means at least May. Have you measured your lawn, or the portion of it you're going to plant, to determine the amount of sod, plugs, or sprigs you need? Do that this month; then you can arrange delivery for later.

 ## PLANTING

Not too late to patch. Continue patching bare spots in cool-season lawns. (See directions on page 154.)

Overseeding. If your cool-season lawn looks awful, and you dread the idea of living with it until September, you could overseed it now. It's not an ideal solution—and you may have to water weekly from now through August. But it will give you a green lawn. To overseed:

1 Set the mower blade at its lowest setting and mow the grass.

2 Rake up the clippings.

3 Mow again. Rake again. This exposes more of the soil, so the grass seed can come into contact with it.

4 Rough up the soil with a hard metal garden rake.

5 Sow one and a half to two times more seed than recommended on the label for new lawns. The reason you need more is that some of it won't germinate because it won't come into contact with the soil.

6 Rake lightly to help the seed get next to the soil.

7 If possible, sprinkle a 1/4-inch layer of sand, topsoil, or compost on top.

8 Water daily to keep the soil moist till most of the seeds germinate.

 ## CARE

Keep debris picked up. As you walk in the yard, make it a habit to pick up leaves, small branches, and trash that may have blown onto the lawn. Not only does it look better, but it makes mowing go more quickly.

Dethatch or aerate warm-season lawns after the grass has completely greened up and has been mowed several times. Depending on where you live, that may be late this month or in May. See page 167 for directions.

 ## WATERING

April showers? If Mother Nature doesn't supply plenty of rainfall this month, you may need to water. It's especially important for newly seeded areas and lawns that have been renovated in the past year.

 ## FERTILIZING

Feed all lawns this month. About April 15, spread 1/2 pound of nitrogen per 1,000 square feet **fescue** and **Kentucky bluegrass** lawns. Use 1/4 pound of nitrogen for **fine fescues** and 1 pound of nitrogen for **bermuda** and **zoysia**. See the chart on page 149 to figure out how much you'll need for the type of fertilizer you've chosen.

 ## MOWING

Bermuda and zoysia. If warm-season grasses have greened up completely this month, mow them with the blade at its lowest setting to remove any winter damage and to encourage new growth.

Fescue and bluegrass. After the second mowing of the season, raise the height of the mower blade.

Mowing makes a difference. Mowing is the most frequent lawn activity—and it's also the most important. When you mow a lawn, you're doing more than cutting the grass. If done properly, mowing can prevent and kill weeds, conserve water, and lessen the need for fertilizer.

- **When to cut.** Instead of mowing the lawn every Saturday morning, cut the grass when it has grown one-third taller than the recommended mowing height. (See the chart on page 150 for the correct mowing height of your grass.) If you're trying to keep your lawn at a recommended 2 inches tall, remove 1 inch when the grass has grown to 3 inches tall. That's called the *one-third rule* of lawn mowing. It encourages a deep root system and helps avoid stress on your grass.
- **Don't "scalp" your lawn.** While warm-season grasses need to be mowed short, cool-season lawns should *not*. Many people cut their cool-season grasses very short because they think it will take longer for it to grow back. Just the opposite is true. The advantages of mowing **fescue** and **Kentucky bluegrass** at the high end of the suggested height range are many: Taller grass helps keep moisture in the soil and moderates soil temperature. And because, generally, root growth mirrors top growth, taller grass means deeper roots. Deeper roots withstand drought, heat, and cold. And here's the

best part: Taller grass crowds out weeds naturally. Try it, and find out for yourself.

- **Leave the clippings on the lawn—most of the time.** Those clippings provide valuable nutrients to your soil. Why toss away free fertilizer? But there are times when it's *not* a good idea to leave the clippings where they fall. And that's when—after a long rainy spell or you've been out of town—the grass has grown quite tall before you got around to mowing it. Then the excess clippings will lie on the lawn in big clumps. That doesn't look good, and it isn't good for your lawn. So for those times only, collect the clippings. Add them to the compost pile, or spread them in a single layer to dry and use them as mulch.

Timely Tip

Pet damage. Does your pet—or a neighbor's—always wet on the same place in the lawn, causing the grass to turn yellow or brown? You have several solutions:

1 Put up a barrier so the animal can't reach the spot. Sometimes a large overturned flower pot will cause pets to move on to another location.

2 Use a product sold to repel cats and dogs. (It will have to be resprayed periodically, especially after rain.)

3 Water the area frequently to dilute the urine.

4 Replace the damaged grass, water and fertilize it, and start again with Steps 1 to 3, if needed.

 PROBLEMS

Moss. There are products you can buy to kill moss that's taken over lawn areas. But the problem will return unless you correct the cause. Here are some of the reasons the moss may be there: too-acidic soil (correct the pH by liming), damp soil (improve drainage), too much shade (if possible, prune nearby trees or shrubs to allow more light to reach the area), and poor soil (mix soil with one-third organic matter, such as fine bark or compost).

MAY

PLANNING

How much of your lawn is weeds? If the answer is half or more, you need to start over. For warm-season lawns, that can be done beginning this month. (See the **Planting** section below.) For cool-season lawns, wait till September. With four months to plan, you can investigate some of the new varieties of **tall fescue**. Maybe one will be the improvement you've been looking for.

PLANTING

Instant results. Sodding is the fastest—and most expensive—way to install a new lawn. Often it's the only way for warm-season grasses. But increasingly in our region, **fescue** sod is also widely available.

When to sod. For warm-season grasses, wait till the soil has warmed up to 70 degrees Fahrenheit in spring, and don't install it any closer than two months before your estimated fall frost. May and June are the best months for **bermuda, centipede**, and **zoysia**, although it also can be done in July if temperatures don't climb out of the low-80 degrees Fahrenheit range and you water copiously. Early September is best for **fescue**, but it can be installed in March if you water regularly the first year when rainfall isn't ample.

Installing Sod

1 Estimate the amount of sod you need. First, measure the area you plan to plant and convert those figures into square feet (100 feet by 50 feet equals 5,000 square feet). Most sod is sold by the square yard (9 square feet). Divide the square footage of the lawn area by 9 to arrive at the amount of sod you need. (For 5,000 square feet, that will be at least 556 square yards. Some experts recommend ordering 5 to 10 percent more, to be certain you have an adequate amount.)

2 Have your soil tested.

3 Prepare the soil by removing all existing grass, roots, and rocks.

4 Apply fertilizer as recommended by the soil test. Till fertilizer and a 1-inch layer of compost, well-rotted manure, or fine wood chips into the top 6 to 8 inches of the soil.

5 Rake the soil so it's level.

6 When the sod is delivered, place it in the shade and water it.

7 Begin laying sod near a straight edge such as a walkway.

8 Fit the strips together so that there are no gaps between them.

9 Use a sharp knife to cut any strips that must be divided.

10 Roll the lawn to make sure the sod comes into firm contact with the soil.

11 Water well.

12 Keep the sodded area moist for two weeks. Then gradually cut back on watering, but watch the edges—they're the first to dry out.

Sprigs. Bermuda, centipede, and **zoysia** grasses are also available as sprigs—pieces of grass stems. To sprig follow Steps 1-6 for installing sod. The

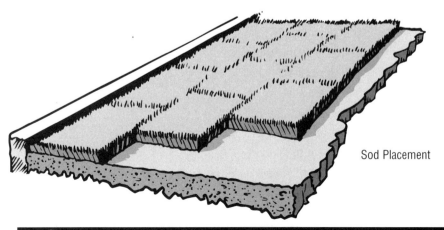

Sod Placement

quickest way to plant sprigs is to broadcast them over moist soil (1 bushel of sprigs per 200 square feet). Cover them with soil, roll the surface, and water. Keep them moist for at least two weeks or until most have begun to grow. Then water regularly.

CARE

Remove sticks and trash from the lawn the day before you mow. Or maybe you can have the children take over this weekly job.

If your warm-season lawn has at least 1/2 inch of thatch, you should remove it now. See page 167 for directions.

WATERING

Keep up with the rainfall. When was the last time it rained? How much rain did your yard receive? There's the "official" rainfall for your county, and then there's how much fell on your yard. They often aren't the same. The only way to know exactly how much rain your yard received is to put up a rain gauge. Once you have one, you'll wonder how you ever managed to garden without it. Also, it's always a good idea to note rainfall amounts and dates in your garden notebook. That will remind you when you need to water your lawn.

FERTILIZING

Take the month off. Cool-season grasses won't need feeding again until fall. Warm season grasses such as **bermuda** and **zoysia** should be fertilized again in June.

MOWING

How often? In spring, when rainfall is usually abundant and temperatures moderate, grass grows fast—especially if you've fertilized it. Sometimes it may need mowing twice a week instead of the usual once. The decision to mow should be made by the height of the grass, not by the day of the week. This time of year it's not always easy to follow the one-third rule; nevertheless, you should try to mow when the grass gets one-third taller than the recommended mowing height and then remove only one-third of the grass blade. If you use that as your general guide most of the time, your lawn will improve.

PROBLEMS

Watch for insect or disease damage, especially brown patches, dead grass, and anything that looks out of the ordinary. Cut a plug of the damaged grass—taking some soil and roots with

it—and also a plug of healthy grass. Take them to a good garden center or the Extension Service for diagnosis and advice.

White Grub

White grub control. The grubs of Japanese beetles and June bugs are close to the surface of the soil twice a year—in May and in September. That's the time to get rid of as many as you can by treating the lawn. Check with your local Extension Service office for specific advice. If you've had severe problems with Japanese beetles in the past, you may want to consider spreading milky spore, an organic control that continues to work in the soil for up to fifteen years. It's most effective if you get your neighbors to treat their yards, too. Getting rid of the grubs helps prevent lawn damage and also reduces the number of beetles that will hatch and affect your garden all summer.

Dandelions. If you see only a few growing in your lawn, you may want to dig them out by hand. Be sure to get all of the long taproot. If you aren't able to get to this as soon as the plants have bloomed, pick off all the flowers—that will prevent seeds being formed and scattering about.

JUNE

PLANNING

Grass trials. Did you know that the Extension Service tests many different species and cultivars of grass? Often these are new ones that promise improvements over other grasses. Check with your local Extension agent to find out where grass trials are being held. These can be quite interesting to visit if you're not pleased with the grass you're currently growing.

PLANTING

Plugging away. Sod and sprigs (see pages 158 to 159) aren't the only ways to establish a new warm-season lawn. **Zoysia** is also available as plugs, which are small pieces of sod (including soil and roots). They establish a lawn more quickly than sprigs, but slower than sod. Plant them in June or May, preferably, but they can also be planted in early July. Plugs can be placed anywhere from 6 to 12 inches apart, but the closer they are, the faster they will grow together.

Plug Spacing	Number of Plugs needed per 1,000 square feet
6 inches	4,000
8 inches	2,250
12 inches	1,000

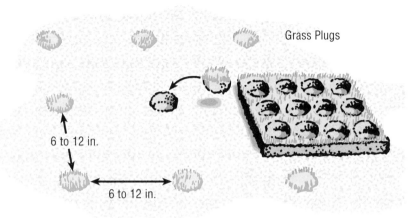

Grass Plugs

6 to 12 in.

6 to 12 in.

How to Plant Grass Plugs

1 Follow steps 1-5 on page 158.

2 Using a plugger or trowel, dig holes in a checkerboard pattern 6, 8, or 12 inches apart.

3 Lightly water the plugs when they arrive, and keep in the shade those not being used.

4 Place plugs in the holes so that the bottom of the grass blades is level with the ground.

5 Firm the soil around the plugs.

6 If you're planting just a few plugs, step on the newly planted plugs to make sure they come into contact with the soil. If you're planting an entire lawn, it's best to roll them instead.

7 Water.

8 Keep the area constantly moist for twelve to fourteen days, and then water regularly.

CARE

Edging. If you like to edge your lawn, make sure your edging tool is sharp. The job will go faster, and the lawn will look neater.

WATERING

The *amount* of water your lawn needs depends upon:

- Recent rainfall—or the lack thereof.
- The type of soil in your yard (clay holds more moisture than sandy or rocky soil).
- The type of grass you're growing (some grasses need watering more frequently than others).
- Whether the grass is in the sun or in the shade.
- Whether the area is sloped or level.
- The temperature and humidity.

How to Tell Whether Your Lawn Needs Water

- The grass isn't as green as usual or has a grayish cast.
- When you walk on it, your footprints remain.
- The grass blades fold up vertically.

Avoid frequent, shallow watering. How *often* you water isn't as important as *how* you water. In order to develop deep roots (which help grass withstand heat, cold, and drought), grass should be watered slowly and enough to wet the soil 6 to 8 inches deep. Watering lightly but more frequently both causes grass to develop shallow root systems and encourages weeds.

Measure the amount. To figure out how long you need to leave your sprinkler on to wet the soil to the desired depth, set out tuna or cat-food tins (or aluminum pie plates) at intervals around the area to be watered. Let the sprinkler run for thirty minutes. Then measure how much water is in the containers. That will tell you how long you have to run the sprinkler to give your grass the needed 1 to 1½ inches of water each time.

Water-Saving Tips

- Get rid of weeds, which compete with grass for the available moisture.
- Increase the mowing height. Taller grass shades the soil and conserves water.
- Water early—before 8 a.m.—to avoid excess evaporation.
- Dethatch the lawn (see page 167) if the thatch layer is ½ inch thick or greater.
- Go easy on fertilizing, which causes grass to grow and use more water.

FERTILIZING

Warm-season lawns. On June 1, spread 1 pound of nitrogen over **bermuda** and **zoysia** lawns. See the chart on page 149 to determine how many pounds of various fertilizers it takes to equal 1 pound of nitrogen. Apply the fertilizer when the lawn is dry. The best time is just before rain is forecast. Otherwise, you need to water the fertilizer into the soil after you've applied it. *Don't* fertilize **centipede** this month; overfertilization can lead to the decline of the grass.

Cool-season lawns. Do *not* fertilize cool-season lawns during the summer. High temperatures can burn fertilized grass, and fertilizer stimulates the growth of weeds and crabgrass.

MOWING

Let the grass be your guide. If temperatures have been high and rainfall low, your grass may not be growing much. But if June sees plenty of rain and moderate temperatures, your grass could be growing rapidly and need more frequent cutting.

PROBLEMS

Too much clover. Excess amounts of white clover on your lawn tell you that the soil lacks nitrogen. Fertilizing warm-season grasses this month and cool-season grasses in the fall will help.

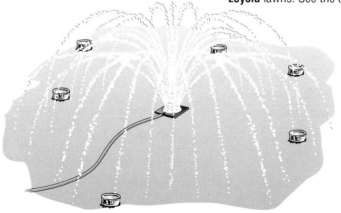

Measuring 1-Inch of Water

JULY

PLANNING

Are you ready for a change? September will be here before you know it. And with it comes a wonderful opportunity to tear out that weedy grass in your yard and start over. You may find that since the last time you renovated a cool-season lawn, there are many more cultivars of **tall fescue** crowding store shelves. All are improvements over the old **Kentucky 31**. Some are improvements over the later **Rebel** and **Rebel II**. During July, why not talk with a knowledgeable Extension Service agent about what these cultivars might offer.

PLANTING

Warm-season lawns. If you get it done before the end of the July, you can still install or renovate a new **bermuda** or **zoysia** lawn by sodding, sprigging, or plugging. (See directions on pages 158 and 159) This isn't an ideal month since it can be very hot and dry. But it can work if you do *all* the following:

- Keep the sod moist as you work.
- Don't let the new grass dry out even momentarily for two weeks.

- Provide 1 to 1½ inches of water to the lawn weekly until the end of September (provided rainfall doesn't do it for you).

CARE

Traffic patterns. Sometimes bare spots in the lawn are caused by people or pets cutting across the grass instead of going around. Evaluate why this is happening. You may decide to set up a barrier to prevent the traffic. Or it may be that the informal walkway makes sense and therefore the grass should be removed and a path created.

WATERING

New grass. Water newly sodded, sprigged, or plugged lawns enough that they stay constantly moist for the first two weeks, paying attention to the corners of sod strips, which dry out easily. After that, you can gradually cut back to daily watering, then every other day, and so forth. But keep a careful eye out for the first sign that the new grass isn't getting enough water. You have a big investment in this lawn now, and you want to protect it.

Established lawns. When rain hasn't fallen in seven to ten days, or less than an inch of rain has fallen, water the lawn deeply (until the soil is wet 6 to 8 inches down).

FERTILIZING

Feed bermuda and zoysia. The third fertilizer application of the growing season should be made about the middle of July. Use 1 pound of nitrogen per 1,000 square feet. (See the chart on page 149.) Water well.

Cool-season lawns. Take a break from fertilizing during the hot weather. **Kentucky bluegrass** and **fescue** are fed only in the spring and the fall.

MOWING

How often? Cool-season grasses usually slow their growth this month. You may have to mow them only every other week. Warm-season grasses, especially those that have been fertilized recently, will continue going strong, so they'll likely need weekly cutting.

PROBLEMS

Dandelion

Too many weeds. Few of us like to spray herbicides, but ignoring some aggressive weeds may allow them to take over. If you water and fertilize your lawn, weeds cost you money because they use moisture and nutrients intended for your grass.

Options in the Fight Against Weeds

• Prevent them in the first place. Thick, healthy turf crowds out weeds. Cutting your grass on the tall side of the recommended mowing height helps create shade that prevents weed seeds from germinating and prevents sun-loving weeds from getting enough light to thrive.

• Prevent them from going to seed. *Always* remove the seedheads even if you don't have time to get rid of the entire weed till later.

• Dig weeds out by hand. Annual weeds are usually easier to eradicate this way than perennial weeds—especially those that spread by underground stolons. It's important to remove all the root; otherwise, the plant will grow back.

• Use pre-emergent weed control in early spring. These are chemicals that prevent seeds from germinating. They work well to stop weeds that come up from seeds—usually annuals—but have no effect on weeds that are already in place. Ask at a garden center about an organic pre-emergent weed control made from corn gluten. Spread early in the season, it can reduce weeds and crabgrass considerably.

Herbicides come in a variety of types. There are even organic weedkillers, although most kill only the top of the plant, not the root. For lawns, two types of weedkiller are most commonly used:

• **Selective weedkiller** can be sprayed over the lawn and will kill weeds but not harm grass. Some of these weedkillers persist in the soil for a time, so don't use them when you'll be renovating the lawn later.

• **Nonselective weedkiller** kills everything it touches—weeds *and* grass. It can be used when getting rid of

Water runoff. If you find that when you water your lawn, you're also watering the street, the driveway, and the front walk, you may just need to position your sprinkler more carefully. But sometimes the soil can't absorb the water at the rate it's receiving it and the water just runs off. If you find this is happening, turn the sprinkler off for fifteen minutes, then on for half an hour—or whatever combination of times works over a period of a couple of hours to avoid runoff and wet the soil deeply.

grass and weeds in preparation for replanting because it doesn't remain in the soil.

If you plan to spray weedkillers, ask the Extension Service for current recommendations. When using weedkillers:

• Always read and follow the label.

• Water the lawn the day before (the weedkiller will be more effective).

To avoid burning the grass, **don't use a weedkiller if the temperature is over (or predicted to go over) 85 degrees Fahrenheit** or during times of drought.

AUGUST

PLANNING

Does the lawn pass muster? Look over your lawn and evaluate its deficiencies. Are there chronic bare spots underneath tall **pines**? Are mushrooms or moss growing in and around the grass in shady areas? Does the lawn have more weeds than grass? August is the time to plan what you're going to do next month—maybe renovate bare spots, start over with a new cultivar of **fescue**. Or you may give up on grass where it simply isn't suitable because of shade or competition from tree roots and plant an evergreen ground cover instead.

Soil test. Here we go again about testing your soil. If you followed our advice and took care of it earlier in the year, great. You already know what your soil needs in order to grow good grass. But if you haven't had a soil test done within five years (less if soil conditions have changed during that time because you added a great deal of organic matter, topsoil, etc.), do it during August. Then you'll be ready for September—to tackle your cool-season lawn renovation or just fertilize, if that's all you have to do.

1 Ask the local Extension Service office for a box and form to use when sending in soil to be tested.

2 With a trowel, take ten or twelve samples of soil from various parts of your yard and mix them together thoroughly in a bucket.

3 Take a small sample of the mixture, place it in a plastic bag, and put it in the box. Be sure to mark on the form that you want recommendations for your lawn.

PLANTING

No planting this month. It's too hot, and August is often dry. Neither provides good conditions for establishing new grass.

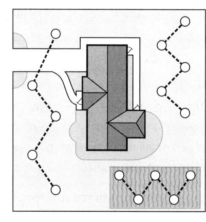

Soil Sampling

CARE

Dull blades. It's time to sharpen your lawn mower's blade once again. Dull blades tear grass instead of cutting it cleanly. That allows disease organisms a place to enter the blades of grass.

WATERING

Should you water? During drought or periods of high temperatures and no rain, cool-season grasses such as **tall fescue** protect themselves by going dormant. They don't look great when they turn brown, but unless the drought is severe, they revive and green up when rainfall returns. The problem is that if you occasionally water—thinking you're doing the lawn a favor—you will bring the grass out of dormancy and have to keep watering it.

Choose your spots. An alternative to watering the entire lawn during prolonged dry spells is to select some areas that you will water and let the rest go. Maybe you want to keep the front lawn looking nice. Or the area visitors see when they first come to your house.

FERTILIZING

Take a break. Sit down with a good gardening book and a glass of fresh-squeezed lemonade. Neither cool- nor warm-season grasses should be fertilized this month.

Mow high in hot weather. Mow the lawn anytime the grass is one-third taller than the suggested mowing height. In hot weather, mowing high can keep the soil cooler and conserve moisture.

 # MOWING

Mow high in hot weather. Mow the lawn anytime the grass is one-third taller than the suggested mowing height. In hot weather, mowing high can keep the soil cooler and conserve moisture. Check the recommended mowing heights on page 149, and mow at the higher number for your type grass throughout August.

Arrange vacation mowing. If you're going to be out of town for ten days or more, ask someone in the neighborhood to mow your grass if needed while you're gone. It'll be one less thing you have to catch up on when you return. An unmowed lawn advertises to burglars that no one's home. Besides, regular mowing, as you know, is good for the grass.

 # PROBLEMS

Grass and shade. The two are less than perfect partners. But if you follow these few tips, you can grow grass in moderately shady spots.

1 Choose a shade-tolerant grass. See the list on page 150.

2 Have your soil tested, and then adjust the pH if needed.

3 Mow shaded grass higher. Grass growing in the shade needs extra leaf surface for photosynthesis, so mow it higher than grass growing in full sun.

4 Fertilize less. Feed about one-half as much as you feed the portion of the lawn growing in the sun.

5 Overseed shady-area cool-season grasses each fall—or in spring and fall, if needed.

6 Trim nearby trees or remove the lowest branches to allow more light.

Timely Tip

Do you have an occasional scalped spot on your lawn, even though you try to mow high? Sometimes this is due to uneven terrain, and sometimes it's caused by the lawn mower sinking into thatch, an undecayed layer of organic material that builds up at the base of grass blades. When this layer gets to be 1/2 inch deep or thicker, you should dethatch the lawn. See page 167 for directions to correct thatch. Add sand, topsoil, or compost to low areas in September.

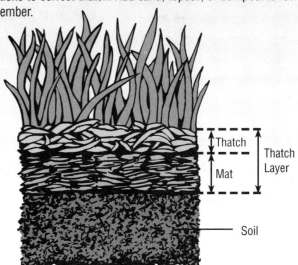

Crabgrass. If crabgrass has popped up in the lawn, small amounts probably aren't worth spraying with a herbicide now since it will be killed by frost. But one precaution you can take to minimize problems next year is to dispose of grass clippings instead of leaving them on the lawn, as usual. That will get rid of the crabgrass seeds, instead of allowing them to sprout and cause problems in the future.

SEPTEMBER

PLANNING

Tired from watering all summer? Maybe you're growing the wrong grass. Check the list on page 150 to find the most drought-resistant grasses and decide if one's for you. Since the best choices for drought tolerance in our region are warm-season grasses, you'll need to decide whether the disadvantages of **zoysia** or **bermuda**—cost of establishment, going brown in winter, and occasionally, iffy cold-hardiness—outweigh their ability to withstand hot, dry weather.

PLANTING

Fescues and **Kentucky bluegrass** may be seeded anytime in September, but the sooner it's done, the longer the lawn has to become established before cold weather arrives.

Choose Your Grass Seed

- Consult the chart on page 150 for characteristics of common cool-season grasses.
- Choose between cultivars, based on a discussion with an Extension Service agent or a knowledgeable person at your favorite garden center.
- Consider a blend—several cultivars of the same species of grass; a combination of three **tall fescue** cultivars, for instance, can be advantageous because you'll get the best quality of each grass.
- **Avoid mixtures**—combinations of two or more different *types* of grass. Often they're formulated for shade and contain grasses—**creeping fescue**, for example—that, while quite tolerant of shady conditions, are problematic in the warmer parts of the region because they don't perform well in hot, humid weather. The big problem with mixtures is that the various grasses in them don't necessarily need the same conditions, mowing height, and care. So it's hard to provide what they require to thrive. Also, if one is more aggressive than another, it's likely to crowd out the more timidly growing species.

Overseeding. If your cool-season grass is just thin, you may want to overseed it. If you don't like the brown look that warm-season lawns sport all winter, you can overseed **bermuda** and **zoysia** with **annual** or **perennial rye** so it will look green. Do it two to four weeks before the average first frost date for your area. That could mean mid-to-late September for some sections of the region. See directions for overseeding on page 156.

How to Seed a New Lawn

1 Have your soil tested if you haven't yet. If you did it earlier in the year, follow the recommendations you received.

2 Remove the grass and weeds that now constitute your lawn. You can remove them by hand or spray Roundup® over the grass two weeks before you plan to reseed. Avoid spraying Roundup® on windy days, and be very careful that the chemical does not touch such desirable plants as shrubs or ground covers.

3 Add organic matter to your soil if it's clay or if you've had problems in the past with grass not growing well. Spread up to an inch of fine bark (such as Nature's Helper™), compost, well-rotted manure, sawdust, or topsoil over the lawn.

4 Till the soil 6 to 8 inches deep.

5 Remove rocks and debris. Rake the area smooth. Fill the sections that aren't level with topsoil.

6 Spread fertilizer over the soil, and lightly rake it in.

7 Sow the seed you've selected. Determine how much you'll need, according to the amount recommended on the label for your size lawn. (Overseeding is just as bad for

Avoid mixtures—combinations of two or more different types of grass. The big problem with mixtures is that the various grasses in them don't necessarily need the same conditions, mowing height, and care.

your lawn as not seeding enough, so don't overdo it.) Then divide the recommended amount into two equal batches. Using a hand, drop, or rotary spreader, apply half the seed in one direction. Then sow the second batch at right angles to the first. This ensures even coverage.

8 Roll the lawn (lawn rollers can be found at rental supply companies) to make sure the soil and seed come into firm contact with one another.

9 Mulch with a light covering of straw. You should still be able to see the ground through the straw; if you can't, it's too thick.

10 Water thoroughly.

11 Keep the soil constantly moist until the seed germinates. (Don't water so much that you create puddles.) This may mean watering several times a day for up to two weeks. It is essential that the seed not be allowed to dry out anytime after the first watering.

CARE

Early September is the ideal time to correct a couple of problems in cool-season lawns—getting rid of excess thatch and aerifying the soil (that is, allowing air to reach the soil and the grass's roots).

What is thatch? It's a layer of dead organic matter—usually grass stems, roots, and so forth—that builds up between the soil and the grass blade. A little thatch is always present, and it's not necessarily a bad thing since it helps protect the grass's roots. It also keeps the soil from compacting. But if this layer of thatch builds up thicker than 1/2 inch, it can prevent water and nutrients from reaching the roots. It also provides an excellent home for insects. Because overfertilizing is one cause of thatch buildup, the problem is most prevalent with warm-season grasses that are heavy feeders—**bermuda** and **zoysia** among them.

Homeowners will find dethatching machines at tool rental stores. These remove the decayed layer, which is then raked up and tossed onto the compost pile. (Condo owners and others with tiny plots of grass may find a thatching rake just as convenient.)

Aeration is the process of creating spaces in the soil so that air and nutrients can get to the roots. It's often recommended for compacted soils, but is just as frequently part of the dethatching process. Aeration machines are available for rental, but manual models (about the size of a small spade, with three prongs where the shovel would go) make sense for those with small lawns.

WATERING

Haul out the sprinklers? If rainfall has been nil for the past two weeks, you may need to water. If you're not sure, glance over the list on page 161 for signs that the lawn needs watering.

FERTILIZING

Feed all lawns on September 1. The recommended amount is 1 pound of nitrogen per 1,000 square feet of lawn. (How that translates into pounds of commercial fertilizer is explained on page 149.) This is the *last* fertilizer application of the year for warm-season grasses.

MOWING

Continue mowing all types lawns this month, just as you have since March.

PROBLEMS

White grubs. These grubs, most the larvae of Japanese and June beetles, are close to the surface of the lawn in September. That means it's a good time to spread an insecticide or organic control. See page 159, and ask your Extension Service agent for advice about products.

OCTOBER

PLANNING

Poor drainage. It's a problem that plagues many Kentucky and Tennessee homeowners because of all the clay soil. If water stands in portions of your yard or grass won't grow because the soil stays too wet, this is a good time of year to begin investigating remedies.

PLANTING

Cool-season grasses. If you missed establishing a **fescue** or **Kentucky bluegrass** lawn in September, is there still time to get it done in October? Maybe. It depends on when the first frost arrives and whether temperatures remain cool after that. Obviously, you'll get more reliable results the first part of the month—cool-season grasses germinate best if the soil temperature is 58 degrees Fahrenheit or above. But if you've just completed a new house the middle or end of the month, plant grass anyway—anything that takes hold is better than bare ground. See pages 166 and 167 for tips on starting a new lawn from seed.

Warm-season grasses. Because **zoysia** and **bermuda** perform their best when temperatures are high, October—when they start going dormant—is *not* a month to lay sod or to plug or sprig these grasses.

Overseeding with rye. This month is a good time to overseed warm-season grasses with **annual** or **perennial rye** so they will be green, not brown, all winter. See page 156 for tips on overseeding.

- **When:** Try to do it two to four weeks before the first-frost date for your area. But since **rye** germinates very quickly, you can usually oversow the seed up to and just beyond the first fall frost.
- **How much:** Use about 10 pounds of **rye** seed for each 1,000 square feet of lawn.
- **Fertilizer:** Don't use a high-nitrogen fertilizer when overseeding warm-season grasses. That can bring the **bermuda** or **zoysia** out of dormancy just as cold weather begins.
- **Water:** The seed will need to be kept constantly moist—through either watering or rainfall—until germination.

The downside of having a green lawn all winter is the need for occasional mowing, especially in fall and spring. Mow when the **rye** gets to be about 3 inches tall and cut it to about 2 to 2½ inches high.

CARE

Leaves. October is the month for leaf removal. A few leaves won't hurt an established lawn—particularly if they aren't left for longer than a week. But a complete blanket of leaves will mat down—especially if it gets wet—and smother the grass underneath. Remove leaves from *new* lawns about three times a week. Rake or blow them off established lawns weekly throughout the fall.

Acorns. If you have **oak** trees, you get a good crop of acorns dropping onto your lawn every fall. Usually the squirrels that live in the **oaks** take care of most of them for you. But some years the raining down of acorns is so heavy that even the squirrels can't keep up. Try to remove as many as you can by hand. (Or see whether you can hire a kid for this.) Acorns really mess up your lawn mower if they're left in place.

WATERING

Four groups of homeowners should keep watering in mind this month:

- Those with new lawns.

• Those who are overseeding or have just overseeded warm-season lawns.

• Those who have overseeded cool-season lawns.

• Those who live where rainfall hasn't added up to 1 inch for the past week or ten days.

Play close attention to watering new cool-season lawns that were sown last month. Until cold weather arrives, they should receive 1 to 1½ inches of water weekly, through either rainfall or your efforts.

FERTILIZING

Cool-season lawns. About the middle of the month, spread 1 pound of nitrogen on **tall fescue** and **Kentucky bluegrass** lawns. (See the conversion chart on page 149 for the correct amount of the fertilizer you've bought.) Either spread fertilizer just before rain arrives or water it well after application.

Warm-season grasses. No more feeding is required this year. Fertilizing **zoysia** and **bermuda** too late in the fall can reduce the grass's winter hardiness and encourage weed growth.

Liming. Fall is an excellent time to lime your lawn if a soil test shows that lime is needed.

MOWING

When to stop? Keep mowing the grass as long as it's growing. When **zoysia** and **bermuda** lose their green, that's the signal to stop mowing them. But **fescue** and **Kentucky bluegrass** like cooler weather. If there's been ample rainfall and especially if they've been fertilized this fall, they'll be growing nicely until a hard frost comes along.

PROBLEMS

Grub control. In warmer parts of the area, you can still spread white grub controls the first part of the month.

Weeds. As long as pesky weeds are still green, it's not too late to dig them out by hand, especially if the ground is wet from rain (which makes pulling them much easier). If you plan to eradicate the last of the lawn's weeds with a herbicide, be sure to read the back of the label to see in what temperature range it is effective. Most don't work if temperatures are too low or high.

Henbit. Keep an eye out for this pretty little weed since it germinates and grows in the fall. Henbit has rounded, toothed leaves and violet flowers. It remains in the lawn over winter and is often most noticeable in the spring.

Two Methods of Control

• As soon as you see henbit this month, begin pulling it out. It has shallow roots, so it's easy to control by hand. But if left in the lawn, it tends to take over areas that have thin stands of grass.

• If you've had henbit in your yard before, spread a pre-emergent control first thing this month, before it appears again. This weed comes back from seeds, so a pre-emergent product will prevent the seeds from germinating—and break the cycle of henbit showing up in your lawn in ever-larger quantities each year.

NOVEMBER

 PLANNING

Keep a record. Next year's great-looking lawn begins now. Take time to write down:

- When you fertilized the lawn this year and what type and brand of fertilizer you used.
- If and when you spread lime.
- Any soil improvement that you undertook.
- Any seeding or reseeding you did and what kind and brand of seed you used.
- Weed or insect problems you encountered and what you did about them—and whether you were successful.
- Places where the grass was thin. Especially note where wimpy stands of grass continue even though you've tried to correct the problem.

The lawn-care season is winding down, so now is a good time to bring your garden notebook up to date. Add those notes above to those you jotted down throughout the season about prolonged dry—or wet—spells and periods of unseasonable temperatures. You'll have a good picture of the past grass-growing season. And often you can understand from those notes why the lawn did better than ever or didn't live up to expecta-

tions. Use that hindsight to make changes so you can have a better lawn next year.

Too much shade? Year by year as trees grow, they cast more and more shade. With shrubs, trees, flowers, and vines, we can compensate by choosing selections that prefer (or at least will tolerate) shade. But grass is a sun-loving plant. Some grasses tolerate shade better than others (see the list of grasses on page 150). But there may come a time when you're frustrated to find that even one of those grasses isn't growing well, although you followed the recommendations on page 150. That's when you have a choice to make:

- Trim the trees. Remove lower limbs so that they're no closer than 10 to 20 feet from the ground (10 feet for smaller trees, 20 for tall ones). Have a professional arborist thin some of your trees so that more light will reach the lawn. Late fall and winter, when deciduous trees are dormant, is the best time to prune them or have them pruned. Never top a tree or allow someone to top your tree, even if you're trying to get grass to grow. Topping is bad for trees. (See page 262.)

- Form an island in the lawn around groups of tall trees, and replace the grass beneath them with mulch.
- Plant a ground cover. You'll find a list of suitable ground covers on pages 292 and 293, and an entire chapter, beginning on page 288, devoted to their selection and care. Many evergreen ground covers love medium to heavy shade as much as grass dislikes it.

 PLANTING

There's no planting in November. Homeowners get a minimum of four months' vacation from grass planting. Who says that winter doesn't offer anything to look forward to?

 CARE

Falling leaves. Don't let them mat down on the lawn. A heavy covering of thick, wet leaves can smother the grass. Remove them from established lawns once a week and dump them onto the compost pile. Check newly seeded areas twice weekly so you can rake or blow leaves away before they cause any damage.

When you think you've gotten to the end of the leaf season, leave ¹/₂ to 1 inch of leaves on the lawn and mow over them several times—a mulching mower works best; it chips them up into tiny pieces. This creates a topdressing of organic matter that will filter down to soil level. It helps prevent thatch by adding microorganisms to the soil and also increases the soil's content of organic matter.

WATERING

About once a week during November—if temperatures remain moderate and rainfall is less than usual—check lawns that were newly seeded in September to make sure portions aren't drying out. If you see sections that seem to need moisture, water.

FERTILIZING

Fertilize cool-season grasses about the middle of the month. Warm-season lawns are not fertilized this month.

MOWING

Continue mowing cool-season grasses and overseeded **rye** as long as they keep growing. Some experts suggest that for your last mowing of the season, you should leave the grass slightly taller than usual. That will help protect the grass from cold, they say, and encourage deeper root systems. Other knowledgeable observers recommend mowing shorter than usual the last mowing. They point out that in our part of the country, cool-season grasses often continue to grow all winter during warm spells. If you leave **tall fescue** at 3¹/₂ inches high in November, it could be 4 inches or taller in February. (That's especially true for lawns that are heavily fertilized.) Grass that's too tall can fall over on itself, which isn't good. It also forces you to start mowing earlier next spring or, sometimes, to have to mow during the January thaw. The choice is yours. But whichever method you decide to adopt, in our climate it's hard to figure out just when you'll be mowing for the last time during fall. It all depends on the weather. Some years we may be still mowing in December.

PROBLEMS

What's that brown spot in my lawn? Actually, it can be caused by a number of different problems, from a female dog wetting in the same spot over and over to drought stress to hot coals from a late-season barbecue being accidentally dropped on the lawn. It may have been caused by an insect or a disease. This time of year it can be difficult to identify the culprit. But make a note now that you've noticed the problem and keep an eye on it next spring to see whether it gets worse. That's when you'll want to call the Extension Service for advice.

DECEMBER

 ## PLANNING

Winterize your lawn mower in December. Think ahead to that first warm weekend in March when you pull the cord on your lawn mower. Is there any worse sound than a weak putt-putt-putt—then silence? Ensure that your mower will be ready to start cutting grass when the lawn needs it next spring by winterizing your mower the first part of this month—or as soon as you've finished mowing for the season.

1 Let the engine run until all the fuel is gone. Gas left in the tank can cause a buildup in the carburetor that can prevent the engine from starting.

2 Drain the old oil and replace with fresh oil. Dispose of the old oil at a recycling station.

3 Clean the deck beneath the mower and make sure the engine's cooling fans aren't clogged with grass.

4 Clean the air filter according to directions in the owner's manual and oil the spark plug, as recommended by your mower's manufacturer.

 ## PLANTING

Grass planting—whether sowing seeds, putting down sod, planting sprigs and plugs—is over for the year.

 ## CARE

Last leaf removal. Some years, the leaf season seems to drag on and on. If this is one of those years, keep up with raking or blowing them off the lawn. Where leaves overwinter on lawns, they can kill the grass. It's cheaper and easier to remove them now than to have to plant new grass next spring.

Don't bag those leaves and put them out for the trash collection. If you pile up fall leaves and let them rot, they will break down into leaf mold, an excellent soil amendment for any lawn project you'll be tackling in the future. Or mow over any remaining leaves and let the small particles sink down into the soil. In both cases, they will serve to improve the soil for your grass—and they're completely free and natural.

 ## WATERING

It's not usually necessary to water your lawn during winter.

Drain hoses and take them indoors for the winter so they aren't subject to freezing. As you wind up the hoses, check over the connections to see whether you need to do any repairs over winter. Also put portable sprinklers into the garage, basement, or storage building this month, if you haven't already, cleaning and drying them before storing them out of the weather till spring.

 ## FERTILIZING

Because of the cold weather and because grass goes dormant in this area during winter, grass doesn't need feeding in December. The usual months for fertilizing a cool-season lawn—**fescue** or **Kentucky bluegrass**—are March, April, September, October, and November. We fertilize warm-season lawns—**bermuda** and **zoysia**, primarily—in April, June, July, and September.

 ## MOWING

Should the grass still be growing for some reason and it has reached more than one-third higher than the recommended height for that particular grass (see the chart on page 150), cut it. But most homeowners won't need to crank up the lawn mower for a few months.

 ## PROBLEMS

Jot down in your garden notebook any problems you see so that you can take care of them in the spring.

CHAPTER SIX

Perennials & Ornamental Grasses

For many people, perennials represent the fun part of gardening. They're a wonderful way to express creativity and individuality. That's because perennials—which live from year to year—are such a varied group of plants. Ferns, daylilies, peonies, and chrysanthemums are all perennials.

There are thousands and thousands of perennials in the world. Many haven't been domesticated, and others need a much colder or warmer climate than that found in Tennessee and Kentucky. But gardeners still have so many perennials to choose from that no one person could grow them all. Still, such a wide choice means that we can all find a number of perennials that we like.

Select perennials based not just on your favorite flower colors, but also on:

- their blooming time
- how long the plant stays in bloom
- height, spread, and plant habit
- what the plant will add to the garden once its flowers have faded (interesting leaves, showy seedpods?)
- growing conditions, such as sun or shade, and soil preferences
- winter hardiness

Planning is more important with perennials than it is with annuals or bulbs. When you put in annual bedding plants in spring, you expect them to bloom until fall. But a perennial may flower for two weeks in May, half of July, or all fall. Many gardeners plan perennial plantings so that something is blooming constantly from early spring till late fall. That means learning the blooming times of many different species and also coordinating flower colors so the plants that bloom at the same time complement each other.

Colors are generally divided into two categories—cool (green, blue, violet) and warm (orange, red, yellow). Warm or hot colors are more exciting and make the garden look closer to the person viewing it. Cool colors are more peaceful and tend to recede—to appear to be farther away from the viewer. Light colors tend to illuminate dark areas (and white or light-colored flowers tend to stand out at dusk).

Often gardeners keep blocks of cool and warm colors separate, but if you do plant them together (and there's no reason not to), put the warm colors in the foreground so the cool flowers don't get "lost." Also, avoid planting so many types of variegation that they clash.

A blue perennial is a most desirable plant, but it's difficult to find a true blue. All too often when you think you're getting blue, it turns out to be violet or purple. In your search for a real blue, you can't go by catalog or book photographs because film rarely captures blues correctly. Read plant descriptions and talk to experienced gardeners in your area to find the blue cultivars of various perennials. They're out there, but they're not always easy to locate.

Since perennials are in flower for a relatively short time each year, how they look the rest of the growing season makes a big difference in the appearance of your border or flower bed. Give thought to a plant's form and texture. **Ferns** and **hostas**, for instance, are both mostly green, but each group of plants adds something different to the mix. Some perennials are big and bold; others are tiny and delicate.

Just as with bulbs, perennials are not planted singly; they're grown in groups—usually of three or six. These then spread into blocks or patches of color, which make quite an impact in the perennial border. You may want to repeat a certain group of flowers at intervals throughout the bed or yard.

Most gardeners add bulbs, annuals, ornamental grasses, and even shrubs to perennial borders. Evergreens and grasses provide structure, and other flowers prolong the blooming period. So don't be afraid to experiment.

Most of all, a perennial garden is personal; it should contain plants that *you* like. It should look the way you want and not follow the latest garden trend.

Because perennials live where they're planted for many years, it's important to prepare the soil well before planting. In spring or fall, till the soil 8 or 10 inches deep, and mix in ample quantities of fine pine bark, compost, aged mushroom compost, rotted leaves, or other organic material.

It may seem odd, but the addition of organic matter to clay soil improves drainage, and when thin, poor soils are amended with organic matter, they hold moisture better.

Actually, most perennials want moisture-retentive soil when they're growing, but need good drainage, too. Fast drainage is most important during winter. **The leading cause of perennials' failure to return in the spring is death due to too much water around their roots the winter before.**

Some perennials, such as **hosta**, require little maintenance. Others need to be divided every few years. Just about all must be deadheaded (have spent blooms removed) and pinched back occasionally, and a few must be staked. Whether you cut back the plants right after they've been killed by frost or wait until early spring is up to you—cutting back early looks neater, but often small wildlife will enjoy the seeds if they're left in the garden.

ORNAMENTAL GRASSES

Although they've really come into their own in the past ten or fifteen years—primarily through the work of two landscape architects and a nurseryman in the Washington, D.C. area—ornamental grasses aren't anything new. In fact, the Victorians loved to use them.

How they fell out of fashion is a mystery since ornamental grasses are easy to grow, require little care, add drama to the summer garden, and interest to the yard in the fall and winter. Some grasses thrive in hot, dry places; live comfortably next to a pond or even in standing water. They can cover slopes, be part of a meadow garden, and serve as effective screens to block unsightly views. Ornamental grasses may also serve as specimen plantings or accents, or be massed. They attract a variety of wildlife to the garden, and nicest of all, they add sound and movement to your garden as the wind gently blows them about.

Most ornamental grasses are perennial, but there are a few annuals. If you want a grass that returns year after year, be sure that the one you choose is perennial.

Before buying an ornamental grass, know its eventual height and spread. Some grasses can get quite large, so they'll need plenty of room.

Not all grasses have the same form. They may be mounded or weeping, upright, upright and spreading, arching, upright and arching, and tufted (with spiky foliage rising from a clump). They also have varying colors—white and yellow variegation, for instance—as well as summer or fall plumes in a range of shades from red, pink, and silver to gold, bronze, tan, and gray.

Fortunately, few grasses are fussy about the soil they're planted in. They usually adapt to whatever is in your yard, although like all plants, they prefer enriched soil. Other requirements are few. Grasses rarely need fertilizer, and once they've gotten established, they don't usually have to be watered. The main chore with ornamental grasses is cutting them back each spring before new growth begins. That makes them true low-maintenance plants.

Perennials and ornamental grasses add a special, distinctive touch to yards from the first blooms of **Lenten rose** in late winter or early spring to the frosted fronds of grasses waving in the fall breezes. They're a pleasure to grow, and they provide the homeowner with an ever-changing landscape.

Perennials

Common Name (*Botanical Name*)	Height (Inches)	Width (Inches)	Flower Color	Season	Light
Anemone (*Anemone* x *hybrida*)	24 to 60	24 to 36	White, rose, pink	Late summer; fall	Partial shade, partial sun
Artemisia 'Powis Castle' (*Artemisia* 'Powis Castle')	24 to 36	36	Grown for foliage	Summer to fall	Sun, partial sun
Baptisia (*Baptisia* species and hybrids)	36 to 48	48 to 60	Blue, white	Spring	Sun (blue-flowered cultivars); Partial shade (white types)
Black-eyed susan (*Rudbeckia* species and hybrids)	8 to 36	18	Gold, yellow	Summer to fall	Sun, partial sun
Bleeding heart (*Dicentra spectabilis*)	8 to 24	12 to 18	Pink, red, white	Late spring; (some cultivars: summer to early fall)	Partial shade, shade
Boltonia (*Boltonia asteroides*)	48 to 72	48	White, pink, violet	Late summer, early fall	Sun
Butterfly weed (*Asclepias tuberosa*)	18 to 36	12 to 24	Orange, red, white, pink, yellow	Summer	Sun
Candytuft (*Iberis sempervirens*)	4 to 12	6 to 18	White	Spring	Sun, partial sun
Cardinal flower (*Lobelia cardinalis*)	18 to 48	24	Red, pink	Late summer	Partial shade, partial sun
Chrysanthemum (*Dendranthema* x *grandiflorum*)	10 to 48	10 to 30	Yellow, pink, red, white, orange, lavender	Fall	Sun
Columbine (*Aquilegia* species and hybrids)	9 to 36	12	Red, white, pink, blue, purple	Spring	Partial shade, partial sun
Coreopsis (*Coreopsis grandiflora*)	12 to 36	6 to 18	Yellow, gold	Late spring, early summer	Sun
Daylily (*Hemerocallis* species and hybrids)	6 to 72	18 to 36	All but true blue and white	Late spring through end of June; some cultivars rebloom later in summer and in fall.	Sun, partial sun
Dianthus or Pinks (*Dianthus* species and hybrids)	2 to 24	12 to 24	Pink, red, white	Late spring to early summer	Sun, partial sun
Ferns (Many genera, species, and hybrids)	12 to 72	12 to 48	Grown for foliage	Spring through fall. Some are evergreen and stay green through winter.	Shade to partial shade. A few can take full sun.
Foxglove (*Digitalis* species and hybrids)	24 to 60	18	Lavender, pink, yellow, purple, bicolors	Spring and summer	Partial shade, partial sun

Perennials & Ornamental Grasses

Common Name (Botanical Name)	Height (Inches)	Width (Inches)	Flower Color	Season	Light
Gaillardia (*Gaillardia grandiflora*)	6 to 24	12 to 24	Red, yellow	Summer to fall	Sun
Gaura (*Gaura lindheimeri*)	24 to 48	18 to 36	White, aging to pink	Late spring to fall	Sun
Goldenrod (*Solidago* species and hybrids)	12 to 60	12 to 36	Yellow, gold	Late summer, fall	Sun, partial sun
Hardy begonia (*Begonia grandis*)	10 to 18	24	Pink, white	Summer to fall	Shade, partial shade
Heuchera (*Heuchera* species and hybrids)	12 to 24	12 to 18	Pink, red, white. (Grown mostly for foliage.)	Spring	Partial shade, shade
Hosta (*Hosta* species and hybrids)	6 to 36	12 to 60	Lavender, pink, white. (Grown primarily for foliage.)	Late spring through fall	Partial shade, shade
Joe-pye weed (*Eupatorium purpureum*)	36 to 84	24 to 48	Pink, purple, white	Late summer to fall	Sun, partial sun
Lenten rose (*Helleborus orientalis*)	14 to 18	12 to 24	White, lime, rose, maroon	Late winter, early spring	Partial shade, shade
Peony (*Paeonia lactiflora*)	12 to 30	12 to 30	Pink, white, red, yellow, purple	May	Sun, partial sun
Perennial hibiscus (*Hibiscus* species and hybrids)	18 to 74	36	Red, pink, white	Summer	Sun
Phlox (*Phlox* species and hybrids)	18 to 60	12 to 36	Pink, red, white, magenta, lavender	Summer	Partial sun, sun
Purple coneflower (*Echinacea purpurea*)	24 to 48	12 to 24	Pink, white	Summer into fall	Sun, partial sun
Red valerian (*Centranthus ruber*)	12 to 36	24 to 36	Pink, red, white	Late spring	Sun, partial sun
Russian sage (*Perovskia* species and hybrids)	36 to 48	36 to 48	Blue, lavender	Mid to late summer	Sun
Salvia (*Salvia* species and hybrids)	12 to 24	12 to 36	Blue, purple, white, pink, red	Late spring into fall	Sun, partial sun
Sedum 'Autumn Joy' (*Sedum* x *telephium* 'Autumn Joy')	18 to 24	18 to 24	Pink or reddish	Late summer into fall	Sun, partial sun
Shasta daisy (*Leucanthemum* x *superbum*)	12 to 36	18 to 24	White and yellow	Late spring and into summer	Sun, partial sun
Stokes' aster (*Stokesia laevis*)	10 to 24	8 to 18	Blue, white, lavender, purple	Summer	Sun
Sundrops (*Oenothera fruticosa*)	12 to 24	12 to 24	Yellow	Late spring to early summer	Sun

Common Name (*Botanical Name*)	Height (Inches)	Width (Inches)	Flower Color	Season	Light
Verbena (*Verbena* species and hybrids)	6 to 36	36	Purple, pink, lavender, white	Spring to fall	Sun
Yarrow (*Achillea* species and hybrids)	6 to 48	12 to 48	Yellow, white, pink	Summer to fall	Sun, partial sun

Ornamental Grasses

Common Name (*Botanical Name*)	Height (Inches)	Width (Inches)	Growth Habit	Landscape Uses	Culture
Carex (*Carex* species and hybrids)	4 to 36	6 to 36	Arching	Woodlands, ground cover, wet spots, accent	Grow in moist, fertile soil in light shade.
Feather reed grass (*Calamagrostis* x *acutiflora*)	18 to 96	24 to 48	Upright	Fall color, massing	Full sun in almost any soil. Doesn't mind clay.
Fountain grass (*Pennisetum* species and hybrids)	12 to 60	24 to 60	Arching	Accent, on slopes, perennial borders	Sun, partial sun. Mix average to poor soil with organic matter before planting.
Japanese blood grass (*Imperata cylindrica* 'Rubra')	12 to 18	12	Upright	Edging, fall color, containers	Partial sun, sun. Grows in any soil except those that don't drain well.
Liriope (*Liriope* species and hybrids)	8 to 18	12 to 18	Arching	Edging, ground cover, in rock gardens, at bases of trees, as a border	Shade, partial shade. Tolerant of most soils.
Miscanthus (*Miscanthus sinensis*)	36 to 144	24 to 72	Arching and upright	Screen, fall color, accent	Sun, partial sun. Grows in just about any soil. Some cultivars grow in wet sites, others tolerate drought.
Mondo grass (*Ophiopogon japonicus*)	6 to 8	12	Arching	Ground cover, rock garden, edging	Shade, partial shade. Moist, well-drained soil. Zone 7.
Pampas grass (*Cortaderia selloana*)	20 feet	15 to 20 feet	Arching	Dramatic accent, screening, windbreak	Sun. Tolerates a wide range of conditions. Zone 7.
Switch grass (*Panicum virgatum*)	36 to 96	24 to 36	Upright	Background, at edge of pond, on hillsides	Sun, partial sun. Tolerates both wet and dry sites.

JANUARY

Perennials & Ornamental Grasses

 PLANNING

This month anything and everything is possible in the garden. Now's the time to pull out those magazine clippings you've saved, pore over the catalogs that have arrived and probably continue to arrive, and search the Internet for design ideas and tips. As you drool over the photographs, read carefully and decide whether these plans and plants are right for your yard. Do they require too much sun? Are they too formal to look right around a casual lakefront cabin?

A perennial border on a budget. As you winnow your choices, you may want to make a three-year plan—unless you have an unlimited budget. This year plant one bed, next year the second bed, and the final year the third bed. Or plant one-third of a bed with perennials the first year, filling the rest with annuals and spring-flowering bulbs. Next year's additions to the bed should make it two-thirds perennials and one-third annuals. The third year you will have a bed full of perennials—and the perennials planted the first year can probably be divided the third or fourth years to create even more plants.

Besides planning for the plants you want to grow this year, plan the beds they will go in. Do you like island beds or traditional borders? It's best to start small and expand as you go. The important thing is not to make a perennial bed too deep from front to back. Be sure you can easily reach into the bed from a path or the lawn. This enables you to groom and care for your perennials without walking on the bed's soil and compacting it.

Gather all the equipment you need to start seeds later this month or next month—potting soil, flats or other containers, plastic or other clear covering for the tops of the containers, and maybe some fluorescent lights. And don't forget to buy the seeds!

 PLANTING

A number of perennials are easily grown from seed. But perennial seed may not be easy to find, so you're generally limited to what's available from catalogs or seed racks in local stores.

Some perennials that are started from seed now—**coreopsis, purple coneflower**, and **black-eyed Susan**, for instance—will bloom this year, although maybe slightly later than they will in future years. But a number of perennials take two years to reach blooming size. If

you start the seed now and plant them in the garden after all chance of frost has passed, they will grow well, but won't bloom until next year.

See page 32 (**January, Annuals** chapter) for full directions on how to start flowers from seed.

CARE

Occasionally check perennial borders or beds to make sure that no perennials or ornamental grasses that you planted or divided and replanted in the fall have been heaved out of the ground by alternate freezing and thawing of the soil. When you find them, scoop out the soil with your hand and firmly replace the plant in the ground. Then replace the mulch around the plant. If the mulch has gotten thin, add more so that it's about 3 inches deep.

That old Christmas tree may still be around early in the month, awaiting pickup by the trash collector. Remove the boughs and place them carefully over any fall-planted perennials, as well as other plants that are not always hardy in your area. Or trim the limbs off the tree and keep them handy by the perennial border to use as instant protection when an extra-cold snap is predicted.

Indoors, keep an oscillating fan running in the room where you have started seeds. Good air circulation helps prevent fungal problems.

 WATERING

No watering is needed outdoors since the ground is likely to be frozen and no plants are growing.

Indoors, the soil around seedlings started earlier in the month should be kept moist but not soggy.

 FERTILIZING

When seedlings have developed two sets of true leaves, fertilize them with a house-plant fertilizer or 20-20-20 water-soluble fertilizer diluted to half strength. (This may happen in January or February, depending on when you started the seeds and what type they are.)

Outdoors, no fertilizing is necessary since plants aren't growing.

 GROOMING

January isn't a month when grasses or perennials are ordinarily pruned, but if you're in the yard on a mild day and want to cut back any that you left standing in the fall, that's fine. Do prune back any plants damaged by wind or knocked over by snow.

Timely Tips

Perennials for deep shade. Many perennials grow well in light or dappled shade, but deep shade—such as beneath evergreen trees whose branches start lower than 10 feet off the ground—is often difficult. These perennials (and one grasslike plant) generally grow well in such situations:

- Many **ferns**
- **Hardy begonia**
- **Hosta**
- **Lenten rose**
- **Liriope**
- **Lungwort** *Pulmonaria*
- **Trillium**

Perennial plant winners:

Every year the members of the Perennial Plant Association (www.perennialplant.org) vote for what they consider an outstanding perennial plant that is low-maintenance, suitable for many climates, easily propagated (by seed or vegetatively), and interesting in more than one season. These are some of the winners:

1990 *Phlox stolonifera*
1991 *Heuchera micrantha* 'Palace Purple'
1992 *Coreopsis verticillata* 'Moonbeam'
1993 *Veronica* 'Sunny Border Blue'
1994 *Astilbe* 'Sprite'
1995 *Perovskia atriplicifolia*
1996 *Penstemon digitalis* 'Husker Red'
1997 *Salvia* 'Mainacht' ('May Night')
1998 *Echinacea purpurea* 'Magnus'
1999 *Rudbeckia fulgida* 'Goldsturm'
2000 *Scabiosa columbaria* 'Butterfly Blue'
2001 *Calamagrostis* x *acutiflora* 'Karl Foerster'
2002 *Phlox* 'David'
2003 *Leucanthemum* 'Becky'

 PROBLEMS

Occasionally, such problems as damping off occur in seed starting. If young plants suddenly fall over, it's usually damping off. See page 135 for what to do.

FEBRUARY

 ## PLANNING

If you're planning a new perennial bed this year, have its soil tested right away. That way you'll know which plants do well in your soil's pH, whether you need to apply lime, and how much and what type of fertilizer is recommended.

When you're choosing perennials and ornamental grasses, check their USDA hardiness zone rating to be sure they'll make it through the winter in your part of the region. But sometimes when you're dealing with mail order and a plant or group of plants that's unfamiliar to you, you might also check the hardiness zone in a garden reference book. A catalog may say that a certain plant is rated for Zones 5 to 9, but it still might not stand up to the summer heat and humidity common in our part of the country.

If you plan to buy perennials or grasses by mail, place your orders soon. Popular plants, especially new introductions, often sell out quickly. Getting your order in early doesn't mean you will receive plants right away; you can have them delivered near the frost-free date for your area or just ask that the plants be sent at the proper planting time.

There are advantages to buying perennials and grasses from a local nursery:

- You can see the quality of the plants and make sure they're disease- and insect-free.
- You can get larger plants than are available by mail order.
- The price is generally lower.

The main advantage of mail order is locating rare or unusual plants that aren't yet available locally. It may also be more convenient to order at night in your own home instead of going to a nursery—although many gardeners enjoy visiting garden centers to see what's available.

Lenten roses may be blooming in some areas this month. It's delightful to have such fascinating flowers to enjoy in late winter. If you don't have any, consider buying and planting some. If you have a grouping but it's not in a spot you walk by every day in winter, start another bed. The flowers are quite variable—in color and markings—so try to choose them when they're in bloom. Since **Lenten roses** spread and also reseed, see if a neighbor has plants of this wonderful evergreen perennial to share in spring.

 ## PLANTING

Decide when to plant perennial seeds. First check the packet label to see how many days the plant needs from the time the seed is sown until it can be planted outdoors. Then take your area's average last frost date and count back the number of weeks the plants need to germinate and grow. That gives you the approximate date for sowing seeds. If you don't know the last frost date for your area, call your local Extension Service office (pages 344 to 353) and ask.

Although you don't want to plant perennials or ornamental grasses outdoors in February, you can prepare a new flower bed on a mild weekend, provided the soil isn't wet. Till the soil 8 to 10 (or even 12) inches deep. Then spread 2 to 4 inches of organic matter on top of the soil—fine bark, compost, rotted leaves, or aged mushroom compost—and till it in.

In the warmer parts of the region, ornamental grasses may be divided and replanted in February. See page 182 for directions.

If you plan to buy perennials or grasses by mail, place your orders soon. Popular plants, especially new introductions, often sell out quickly.

CARE

In our part of the country, winters are fairly variable. The ground freezes for a day or two, then temperatures climb and the weather is relatively warm. All this freezing and thawing of the soil sometimes causes shallow-rooted plants (those that were planted last fall, for instance) to end up with their roots above ground instead of below, where they belong. If they're left out of the ground, the roots may freeze; they're also likely to dry out. So replant any perennial or ornamental grass that's been heaved out of the ground, and mulch it with 3 to 3 1/2 inches of organic mulch (shredded leaves or pine straw) for protection.

If you potted up young perennials or grasses last fall and left them in a cold frame, be sure to check the temperature inside the cold frame on sunny days this month. The frame may need venting to make sure temperatures inside don't climb too high.

WATERING

Daily check flats of seeds that were sown earlier and also containers of young seedlings to see whether they need watering. You must perform a balancing act when it comes to watering seedlings—you can't let them dry out, but you don't want to drown them, either. Both extremes are bad. Achieving that balance sounds harder than it is. It comes easily with a little experience.

FERTILIZING

When seedlings have two sets of true leaves, begin fertilizing the young plants every other week with a water-soluble fertilizer diluted to half strength.

GROOMING

If the weather's nice for being outdoors near the end of the month, those living in Zone 8 and the warmer parts of Zone 7 can cut back all ornamental grasses and grasslike plants (the latter includes **liriope** and **mondo grass**). How far you cut them back depends on the size and type of plant. **Liriope, mondo grass**, and **carex** may all be pruned to an inch or two tall. Try to cut back big grasses to 6 inches high, although the clump may be so thick that isn't always possible.

 PROBLEMS

See **January** to learn more about damping-off disease in seedlings.

If February is rainy, try to walk by your perennial beds after a day or two of rain. Look at the soil: Is it soggy? Is there standing water in places? Poor drainage during winter months kills perennial plants faster than anything else. Plan to improve the drainage in the spring.

MARCH

PLANNING

Are you a relatively new gardener? If so, this may be the time to think about the tools you need to grow and care for perennials. You'll mostly use a spade or shovel, a trowel, a hose (regular or soaker type), pruning shears, garden scissors, and a pair of sturdy gardening gloves. A rake and hoe may also come in handy, but wait to buy them until you know they're needed.

If you plan to build raised beds, purchase the materials sometime this month—wood or other framing, nails, and high-quality topsoil. (See page 92 for instructions.)

Check your supply of fertilizer, mulch, and soil amendments, and make a list of what's needed on the next trip to the home store or garden center.

PLANTING

Before they've started growing, divide those ornamental grasses that need it—early in the month for Zones 7 and 8, late in the month for Zone 6. Cut the foliage back so that only one-fourth is left. Dig up the plant with a shovel, and then use an ax or a saw to divide the roots into three or four equal sections. Leaving as

much soil as you can on the roots, replant quickly so the roots don't dry out.

For dividing perennials, wait till your frost-free date has arrived and the plants have grown to about 4 inches tall. That may mean the end of March for the warmest regions and April (or early May) in cooler areas.

1 The day before you plan to divide a plant, water the soil.

2 Dig up the plant.

3 Wash the soil from the roots so you can see what you're doing.

4 For clumping perennials and those that develop a mass of crowns, use two spading forks, back to back, to break the roots into smaller sections.

5 For perennials that grow from rhizomes, see page 74 in the **Bulbs** chapter for instructions.

6 Use a sharp knife to divide in half plants that grow from fibrous roots.

7 As quickly as possible, replant divisions in new spots or in pots.

8 Water with a transplanting solution.

When young seedlings started indoors have developed several sets of new leaves, transplant them to individual containers. See the **Annuals** chapter, page 36, for directions.

About the end of the month, those in Zone 8 can begin hardening off seedlings that were planted in January. Take them outdoors and expose them—gradually over a period of seven to ten days—to sun, wind, and cooler temperatures. (For more information, see page 38.) Wait to start this until you're sure no more frosts are expected.

CARE

Remove twigs and debris from beds in which perennials and grasses are planted. If at all possible, avoid walking in the beds when they're wet, since that compacts the soil.

If you have mulch over the crowns or tops of plants (put there to protect young plants or those that are marginally hardy), remove it. Gardeners in Zone 8 should begin doing this the first to the middle of the month; Zones 7 and 6, the middle to the end of the month. But leave mulch *around* the plants.

Don't set the temperature too high in the room where you're starting seeds. Warmth aids germination, but once the seeds have sprouted, the stockiest plants are produced when the thermostat is lowered to 60 to 65 degrees Fahrenheit (you may partially or fully close the heating vent in that room for the same result).

We never know what to expect from spring weather. Warm spells in February may cause too-early blooms in March or April, before frosts have truly ended. If you find that sometimes happens in your yard, listen to the weather forecast nightly and keep near the back door an old blanket, mattress pad, spun-bond fabric such as Reemay®, or some other protection so you can gently cover plants and flowers threatened by cold. Remove the covering the next day once temperatures have risen above freezing. Don't cover sensitive plants with plastic; plants get much too hot when the sun shines through it.

Strong light is essential for young plants started from seed. If the plants seem to be reaching for the sun, consider placing them under grow lights instead of on windowsills.

 # WATERING

Indoors, don't let young seedlings dry out. Touch the soil to see whether the surface has dried out, and then water if it has.

March is typically a rainy month in our region, so watering outdoors isn't usually called for. But if there's no rain, check plants that have begun to grow in the perennial border and water them if the soil appears to be dry.

 # FERTILIZING

Fertilize perennials lightly as soon as you notice new growth. In Zones 7 and 8, that's likely to be this month. Ornamental grasses rarely need fertilizing after their first year in your yard. With perennials, you have a choice of fertilizer types—granulated 10-10-10 or 6-12-12, pelleted slow-release fertilizer, water-soluble fertilizer, or organic products such as cottonseed meal. Granulated and water-soluble types produce quick results, but the effects aren't lasting. With slow-release and organic fertilizers, the plants are fed over a longer period.

The main thing to know about fertilizing perennials is that if you prepared the soil well, the plants need little fertilizer. Too much can lead to lanky growth that easily falls over and needs staking. Many perennial gardeners use as fertilizer a yearly or twice-yearly application of 2 inches of sifted compost around each plant. For most perennials, that's all that's needed.

 # GROOMING

The first week of the month, cut back all ornamental grasses. See **February**. When grasses have been in place several years and have grown large, pruning them becomes increasingly difficult. If you have trouble cutting through the thick base, consider using electric hedge clippers or a small chain saw.

If perennials weren't cut back in the fall, do so now—before they begin growing.

Shear **creeping phlox** (often called **thrift**) after blooming to keep the plants compact and to encourage new growth.

 # PROBLEMS

Watch out for weeds. They're probably trying to pop up again. Be sure to pull up henbit (a weed with rounded leaves and purplish flowers that grows from fall to spring). There's a temptation to ignore it because it's rather attractive and it disappears once hot weather has arrived. But the problem is that if left in place, it drops its seeds and comes back to haunt you next fall and winter.

APRIL

Perennials Ornamental Grasses

 PLANNING

If you've had perennials and ornamental grasses in your yard for some time, check back through your garden journal or notebook to see how they've performed for the past several years. The best rule of thumb on perennials is to give a plant three years to prove itself. If at the end of that time it hasn't performed as well as you expected, dig it up and give it to someone else or move it to another spot in the garden if you suspect that it doesn't have just the right conditions it needs where it is now. With all the wonderful perennials out there, there's no point giving room to a problem plant. Instead move on to something that will thrive. This advice especially applies to those plants that have been attacked by insects or disease two of the past three years—they're more trouble than they're worth. If you love the particular species of plant, check to see whether less pest- or disease-prone cultivars are available.

Take your list of desirable plants with you when you head out to nurseries and home stores this time of year. While everyone buys a few plants on impulse, remember that they have to fit into your overall design. Read labels carefully when deciding between plants—especially note the height. Various cultivars of the same perennial may vary quite a bit in height and spread.

 PLANTING

Begin planting ornamental grasses and perennials about the time of your area's average last frost. (Your local Extension office can tell you the date, if you don't know it.) Plant container-grown perennials at the same depth they grew before unless label instructions direct otherwise. (See **Annuals** chapter, page 38, for more information.) Be sure to give the plants plenty of room to grow—spacing them close may look better now, but it means dividing plants or grasses much sooner than you would otherwise have to.

Should you receive a bare-root perennial from a mail-order catalog, dig a hole at least 6 inches deep and 6 to 8 inches wide in a prepared bed. Mound the soil in the middle of the hole, and place the roots over the top so that they drape down the sides. Holding the plant in place, fill the hole with soil so that the crown of the plant is at the level of the surrounding ground. Water with a transplant solution, and add more soil if necessary.

In cooler areas, ornamental grasses may still be divided if they haven't yet begun to grow.

When it comes to dividing perennials, some gardeners go by the rule of dividing spring-blooming plants in the fall and summer- or fall-flowering ones in the spring. But much depends on the weather and how busy you are. You may also divide spring-blooming perennials after they finish blooming, provided you keep them watered throughout the summer as needed. See **March** for directions on dividing perennials.

Don't dig up and transplant or try to divide perennials that have deep tap roots, such as **butterfly weed**. They don't transplant well.

 CARE

Protect tender plants from frost. (See page 183.)

If you have **oak** trees, you'll often see squirrels rummaging around in flower beds to dig up acorns. Check the beds several times a week to make sure the squirrels didn't dig up any plants, too. They don't usually harm the plants, but exposed roots can dry out, causing the plant to die.

Renew all mulches so they're 3 inches thick. Don't pile the mulch right up to the stem of perennial flowers. Instead, start it an inch or two away.

The best rule of thumb on perennials is to give a plant three years to prove itself. If at the end of that time it hasn't performed as well as you expected, dig it up and give it to someone else or move it to another spot in the garden if you suspect that it doesn't have just the right conditions it needs where it is now.

Put stakes or supports in place for **peonies** and **foxgloves**. Tall **foxgloves** can get knocked over in April or May showers and thunderstorms, and **peonies** often end up trailing their blooms in the mud when it rains as they're flowering. It's best to get the supports in place early in the season so the plants grow up through them and eventually their foliage hides the metal or wood. Check garden centers and catalogs for the various types of supports available for perennials; you're not limited to wood stakes.

 WATERING

Newly planted perennials may need watering several times a week if there's little rain. Be sure the soil around them doesn't dry out. The roots of young plants aren't well developed, so they require more water than those of established plants.

Ornamental grasses are mostly drought tolerant, but they, too, need regular watering during dry spells that occur the first year after planting.

 FERTILIZING

Fertilize perennials lightly as they begin growing. Grasses don't need fertilizer except at planting time. A couple of inches of compost or Milorganite® (processed sewage sludge) are often better for the plants and soil than granular fertilizer.

 GROOMING

In areas with colder climates, perennials that have not yet begun growing should be pruned back now. Even if new growth has started at the base of the plant, carefully cut off any dead flower stalks from last year. This improves the garden's appearance.

If you didn't prune ornamental grasses last month, do so right away. It's a more difficult job once the plants have begun to grow because you can't just lop off all the old leaves; you have to be careful not to damage the new growth. But a mixture of brown and green stalks detracts from the grass's appearance.

Remove faded flowers from early-blooming wildflowers such as **May apple** and **bleeding heart**.

Timely Tip

How do you know whether a perennial needs dividing? If it isn't blooming as well as it used to and the plants are crowded, it should be divided. This shows you the importance of spacing correctly when you plant so the plants don't become crowded too quickly. Some perennials, such as **hostas** and **peonies**, rarely need dividing, but **chrysanthemums** should be divided at least every other year. Most other perennials should be divided every three to five years.

 PROBLEMS

If it's been a wet spring, slugs may become troublesome around **hostas**. See page 303 for tips on controlling them.

Ignore ants on **peonies**. They're attracted by a sweet sticky substance and do no harm.

If **mums** that had been in the garden for more than a year didn't return this year, the reason is usually that they weren't divided and replanted regularly. On the other hand, when **mums** planted the previous fall don't come back, you can usually blame cold weather.

MAY

 PLANNING

Are you noting in your garden journal the times when your perennials bloomed? It's helpful for future reference to write down the date blooming started and also how long it lasted.

Most plants are up and growing now. Look over your garden: Do you need a few plants of a certain color? Are there bare spots? Is there at least one group of perennials in bloom all the time from spring through fall frost? That's a good goal, though sometimes it takes a few years to achieve. Late-spring and early-summer bloomers are the most common, so you may need to think more about adding plants that flower in the hottest part of summer (**perennial hibiscus** and **yarrow**, for example) or those that flower in late summer or fall (everything from *Chelone* to **Joe-pye weed**). See the list on pages 175 to 177.

When possible, choose perennials with interesting leaves. They add interest to the flower bed or border even when they're not in bloom.

 PLANTING

Continue planting perennials and ornamental grasses in all parts of the region. See page 182 for more information.

After woodland wildflowers finish blooming, divide them if needed. (See page 182.)

You may also divide other perennials, especially in Zone 6, but it's best to wait till early next spring to divide ornamental grasses. If the perennials you plan to divide have gotten taller than 4 or 5 inches, cut them back by one-third before you start.

Want to increase your stock of perennials? Division (discussed in **March**) isn't the only way. Some perennials root easily from tip or stem cuttings. For **asters, catmint, dianthus, penstemon,** and **salvia**, take tip cuttings:

1 Using sharp pruners, cut a 3- to 4-inch piece from the tip of a healthy, actively growing stem.

2 Remove the lower leaves.

3 Fill a pot or flat with moistened potting soil, and poke holes in it with a pencil.

4 Wet the stem ends of cuttings, and dip them in a rooting hormone.

5 Insert the cuttings into the holes, and firm the soil around them.

6 Water.

7 Cover the pot with a plastic bag, and place it in a warm spot that has bright light but doesn't receive sun.

Perennials with pithy or hollow stems are more easily propagated by stem cuttings. These include *Campanula*, *Chelone obliqua*, **chrysanthemum, gooseneck loosestrife, obedient plant, phlox, rose campion, veronica**, and **yarrow. Catmint** may also be propagated by this method.

1 When new shoots are about 3 or 4 inches tall, use hand pruners or a sharp knife to cut stems close to the ground (so some of the woody part of the stem is included).

2 Wash any soil off the cutting.

3 Follow steps 2 through 7 of taking tip cuttings.

After cuttings start to grow, let them develop adequate new roots so they can live on their own, then pull the cuttings away from each other and replant them individually.

Fill in bare spots in the perennial border with annuals, if necessary. Be patient; your young plants will soon begin growing together.

 CARE

Are all perennial beds covered with about 3 inches of mulch? Be sure the mulch isn't piled up against the plants themselves, but starts 1 to 2 inches away from the stems.

All newly planted, divided, or transplanted perennials and ornamental grasses should be watered enough that their soil doesn't dry out—once or twice a week if there's no rain.

Stake or support **peonies** if you haven't already. Earlier is better because it is easier when plants are small. But unsupported **peony** flowers—especially doubles—often end up falling over and getting muddy if it rains when they're in bloom.

 # WATERING

All newly planted, divided, or transplanted perennials and ornamental grasses should be watered enough that their soil doesn't dry out—once or twice a week if there's no rain.

Established perennials generally don't need much watering unless rain fails to fall for two or three weeks. There are exceptions, though: plants that prefer moist soil (**foxgloves, hardy begonia**, and most **ferns**, for instance); don't let them dry out.

Established ornamental grasses rarely need watering except in a drought.

Keep cuttings moist until they begin growing, then water enough to keep the soil from drying. Plants in containers need water more often than those planted in the yard, so feel the soil frequently and water them before they dry out completely.

 # FERTILIZING

Fertilize established perennials only if you haven't done so earlier in the spring. You may want to lightly apply organic fertilizer around newly planted divisions. Milorganite® is a good choice. Rotted manure is all right, if you have some on hand.

Use a water-soluble fertilizer twice monthly on cuttings once they begin to grow. Apply timed-release fertilizer to plants in containers. A fertilizer formulated for flowering plants is best.

 # GROOMING

Thin **asters** and **garden phlox** by removing some plants from the stand. This enables the remaining plants to receive more sun and helps avoid mildew problems.

Remove faded flowers from perennials and wildflowers that have already bloomed.

Pinch back all or some of your **bee balm, shasta daisies, obedient plant, phlox**, and **spiderwort**. This helps control the height and also—if you pinch some plants and not others—produces flowers over a longer period.

Pinch all stems of **mums** monthly between now and the middle of July. This ensures a more compact plant that blooms in the fall, not in the summer.

 # PROBLEMS

Aphids often appear on new growth this time of year. Try washing them off with a steady stream of water. Or spray them with insecticidal soap.

Slugs may still be a problem around **hostas**. See page 303 for control techniques. Ask at a garden center about an organic slug control. It may make your life much easier.

Some spring wildflowers begin to look awful about this time. Don't worry; unless there was a drought and you didn't water, this is normal—many native plants go dormant in the summer. If possible, keep them watered during dry spells until the end of June; this is especially true during the first two years they're in your yard. But if one day you look and there's bare ground where a spring wildflower was, it's usually all right. Be careful, though, about planting something else in that area since you don't want to damage the native plant's roots.

JUNE

PLANNING

Damp spots in your yard don't mean you have to forego perennials. Just plan to plant those that don't mind constantly moist or even wet soil. Your choices include sun lovers **cardinal flower, perennial hibiscus** (*Hibiscus moscheutos*), **Japanese iris, Joe-pye weed**, and **yellow flag iris**. For shade, try **maidenhair fern, carex, ligularia**, and **rodgersia**.

What if you have the opposite conditions—hot and dry? Consider *Artemisia* 'Powis Castle', **butterfly weed, coreopsis, dianthus, gaillardia, goldenrod**, and **sundrops**.

Keep your garden journal current by noting what you've planted (including variety and color) and where new perennials and grasses were placed, as well as blooming times and durations as well as weather details.

PLANTING

Continue to plant container-grown perennials, especially in the cooler parts of the region. See page 182 for planting advice. If temperatures are high, try to wait for a day that's more moderate. If none is in the forecast, plant on an overcast day or at dusk.

It's all right to divide or transplant perennials in the first half of the month, if necessary. Cut them back by about one-half first. Keep the new plantings well watered. To increase your chance for success, rig up a way to keep the plants shaded for a week afterward.

As plants begin to grow well, some crowding may occur in a flower border that's several years old. Remove some of the excess plants when the weather is moderate. Give them to friends, put them in pots (to be shared later or planted in a new bed in the fall) or transplant them to another part of the garden right away, cutting the tops of the plants back by half.

Continue to propagate perennials by taking stem or tip cuttings (see page 186) or by layering (page 190).

CARE

Check stakes and supports to be sure they're firmly in the ground, and make sure plants stay attached to them.

As we head into hot weather, look over the mulches in your perennial borders and around ornamental grasses; add more mulch if necessary to keep it 3 inches deep.

WATERING

Regularly water perennials growing in containers since the soil in pots dries out quickly in hot weather.

Keep new plantings of perennials and ornamental grasses watered so they don't wilt.

When an inch of rain hasn't fallen in the last week or so, check to see whether the soil around perennials is beginning to dry out. Water as needed. Perennials and ornamental grasses planted this year may need watering much more often than established plants.

Gardeners usually think of **daylilies** as plants that need very little watering. And it's true. Still, like other plants, they bloom better if watered when rainfall has been lacking. But the one time you definitely want to water **daylilies** is after rebloomers finish flowering. Water weekly if rainfall isn't regular so the reblooming buds form.

FERTILIZING

Fertilize new perennials and ornamental grasses when planting or shortly afterward.

The biggest job in the perennial garden during the summer is deadheading— cutting back each perennial flower after it dies. This keeps the garden looking neat, prevents seed formation, and causes some plants to rebloom.

If slow-release fertilizer wasn't applied to containers, fertilize twice monthly with a water-soluble plant food.

There's no need now to fertilize perennials planted in the garden—spring is the best time for that. Ornamental grasses rarely need fertilizing beyond their first year.

GROOMING

If you have a thick stand of **goldenrod**, it will grow and bloom better—and have fewer disease problems—if you cut some of the plants back to the soil level.

The biggest job in the perennial garden during the summer is deadheading— cutting back each perennial flower after it dies. This keeps the garden looking neat, prevents seed formation, and causes some plants to rebloom. On plants with a small number of individual flowers and soft stems, deadheading is often done by hand. But when it comes to stands of plants—**coreopsis** and **perennial geraniums** for example—sometimes it's easier to shear off the old blossoms. Use hand pruners to deadhead plants with sturdy stems so you don't tear the stem or cause other damage.

If you'd like to increase your collection of **coreopsis**, cut or pinch the mature seedheads off and scatter them on top of the soil wherever you'd like the new plants. They grow easily.

Pinch back **mums** once this month so the plants don't grow too large and to encourage them to develop a compact shape.

Prune back spring-flowering perennials and wildflowers that look ratty. Cut or pinch off any yellow or brown foliage.

Enjoy some of your perennial flowers indoors. In the morning, take a bucket of tepid water with you into the garden and put flowers in it as soon as you've cut them. Let them soak in the water for an hour or two, if possible, then recut their stems underwater just before arranging the blooms.

PROBLEMS

Once humidity levels ratchet up, carefully watch perennials that are susceptible to mildew—**asters, bee balm**, and **phlox**. Prevent powdery mildew from appearing by regularly using a fungicide (always reapply after a rain). If using an organic fungicide, read the label and observe temperature restrictions— some may burn plants when the weather is hot.

Other tricks to prevent the spread of mildew are increasing air circulation among the plants and picking off infested leaves the minute the first few show the tell-tale white blush. Avoid using sprinklers or other overhead watering techniques around plants susceptible to mildew.

If the infestation gets too bad, cut the plants back and consider planting more mildew-resistant cultivars next year. If you can't bring yourself to replace mildew-prone plants, you may want to transplant them to the back of the border so their condition won't be as noticeable.

Japanese beetles can be a problem this month. Pick them off by hand and drop them in a jar of soapy water, or consult the Extension Service for the latest recommendations for controlling these pests.

Keep an eye out for spider mites, which make foliage look bronzed. They often appear to be dust on the undersides of the leaves. Spider mites aren't usually a problem in rainy weather or when the soil is kept moist. Try to control them with insecticidal soap, but if you prefer to use a chemical method, get a miticide; regular insecticides don't kill mites, which technically are not insects.

JULY

PLANNING

Keep notes of those periods when no perennials are in bloom so you can fill in the gaps in the fall or next year.

Visit good gardeners and public gardens to see how others' plants cope with the heat and humidity. Jot down the names of the plants that look good, and then look them up in this book or in the *Kentucky Gardener's Guide* or *Tennessee Gardener's Guide: Third Edition* to see whether they'll perform well in your yard's conditions, too.

Beds and borders aren't the only places to grow perennials and ornamental grasses. If you need more places for these delightful plants, consider placing them in a shrub border or a rock garden, or beside a water garden or pond. Shade-lovers are right at home in a woodland garden.

PLANTING

Although it's possible to move plants around the garden in hot weather and to plant container-grown grasses and perennials, relentlessly high temperatures stress the plants. On the other hand, it may be better to go ahead and plant the perennial or ornamental grass you have received from a friend or neigh-

bor—or that perennial in a 4-inch pot that you just haven't gotten around to planting yet. To make the best of a less-than-ideal situation, cut the plant back by one-third to one-half and try to plant on the day after a soaking rain, on an overcast day, or in early evening. Water and mulch well to keep much-needed moisture in the soil. If possible, also shade the plants for several days after planting.

Another option for taking advantage of free plants from friends or reduced-price bargains at garden centers is to pot large containers of mixed perennials and small ornamental grasses. Plants that do nicely in containers include **carex, hosta**, *Hakonechloa macra*, short cultivars of **perennial hibiscus, sedum**, *Heuchera*, **creeping thyme** (see the **Herbs and Vegetables** chapter), *Vinca minor* and *V. major*, **miniature daylilies** that bloom repeatedly during the summer, small cultivars of *Gaillardia*, and **blue salvia**.

Dianthus is easily propagated by layering. Move back the mulch, and place a mixture of rich topsoil and sand on the ground next to the plant to be propagated. Choose a stem that has no flowers or buds on it and—leaving it attached to the plant—strip off the bottom foliage (keep four or five pairs of leaves at the top of the stem). Use a sharp knife to cut a very small incision in

the bottom of the stem. Place the cut stem on the sand-soil mixture and pin it down with a piece of wire. Water well and keep the area moist until rooting occurs. When new roots have developed, cut the rooted stem from the main plant and plant it where you want it to grow.

Divide and replant **bearded iris** near the end of the month. (See the **Bulbs** chapter, page 74.)

CARE

Keep plants mulched with organic matter. This prevents weed seeds from germinating, keeps the soil a moderate temperature, and conserves moisture. As mulch eventually breaks down or rots, it also improves the soil's organic content.

Stake or provide support for perennials that have begun to sprawl.

WATERING

If temperatures are high and rainfall is absent, keep a close eye on perennials and ornamental grasses that were planted or transplanted in the past year. Don't let them dry out.

Beds and borders aren't the only places to grow perennials and ornamental grasses. If you need more places for these delightful plants, consider placing them in a shrub border or a rock garden, or beside a water garden or pond.

If you have soaker hoses, this is the time to bring them out and weave them among your perennial plantings—especially if you're going to be away for a few days and no rain is forecast. Soaker hoses and drip irrigation can be hooked up to mechanical timers attached to an outdoor water faucet to water your plants automatically. Or you can turn the hoses on and off by hand. Just remember to leave them on long enough that they deliver enough water to soak the soil at least 8 inches deep. Measure the depth to which the soil was wet after the first time you use the hose on a new bed and note how long it took to produce the desired results. Then you know how long to leave the hose on in the future.

 ## FERTILIZING

No fertilizing is necessary in July except for perennials growing in containers. Feed container-grown plants with a slow-release fertilizer or use a water-soluble fertilizer every ten days or so.

 ## GROOMING

Pinch **chrysanthemums** back one last time this month—early to mid-month for those in the colder sections of the region and before the end of the month in Zone

8. Mature **mums** that aren't pinched usually bloom in the summer—and that's a waste of flower power. Many plants bloom in the summer, but far fewer do so in the fall. Remove the tips of the stems one last time so **mum** plants won't get leggy and the blooms will appear when they should—September and beyond.

Deadhead all perennials, including **daylilies** and especially **phlox**, after they have flowered. On plants such as 'Moonbeam' **coreopsis**, you may want to use hedge shears to lop off the multitude of small flowers. Old blossoms left on the plants will form seeds. This takes energy away from the plant and also usually prevents any more blooms this year.

Cut off yellowing leaves or foliage damaged by disease or insects, especially leaf miners (which leave what look like trails in the leaves).

PROBLEMS

Even though it's hot, keep up with any necessary weeding. Ten minutes early each morning should do it. Think of it as your fitness routine. Don't allow weeds to go to seed. If you aren't able to dig up the weeds right away, pinch off the seedheads and put them in a paper bag.

Close the bag and toss it in the trash.

Keep after spider mites, thrips, and Japanese beetles. Ask the Extension Service for recommendations if your control efforts haven't worked and any of these pests have gotten out of hand.

Should the month be relatively rainy, watch out for slugs and snails. You'll likely need to set out organic or homemade bait. (See page 303.)

AUGUST

 ## PLANNING

Like January, August is the perfect month to plan. At this point in the year, you've planted, transplanted, pruned, maybe battled insects or a disease problem—and best of all, you've reaped what you sowed, beautiful flowers brightening your yard over a long period. So plop down in a hammock if you have one (and everyone should!) or in a lounge chair on a screened porch or deck, and read back through your garden journal, adding information from this season that you didn't have time to write down earlier. Catch up on that stack of gardening magazines that remained unread during the height of the active growing season. And most of all, just dream about what you'd really like in a perennial border or bed. From these daydreams often come wonderful, practical ideas.

If you're going to be away from home during August, arrange for someone to take care of necessary watering and deadheading, as well as keep an eye out for pests. Maybe you and a gardening friend or neighbor can exchange duty when each other is away.

 ## PLANTING

Since it's so close to September, when temperatures will moderate, it's best to postpone planting till next month. But you may still divide and replant **bearded irises** the first part of August (see the **Bulbs** chapter, page 74). And if you still have any seed-started plants growing in containers that didn't get large enough to go into a regular bed, plant them in a "nursery bed" of rich soil, where they can be given special attention and care.

In Zone 6, **peonies** may be divided. (See page 182.)

 ## CARE

After thunderstorms, check for perennials that may have been knocked over. Gently move them back to a standing position and stake them if necessary.

If rain often washes off mulch used to cover flower beds on slopes, switch to pine straw (pine needles), which stays in place. (It's also useful for windy spots.)

 ## WATERING

Watering during dry spells contributes greatly to the quality and number of flowers. Watering often makes the difference between whether a plant lives or dies. When rainfall is less than an inch per week, check perennials and ornamental grasses planted this year to see whether they're low on moisture. Also keep an eye on perennials that need moist soil—**ferns**, for example. Don't let them dry out. Many mature perennials and all established ornamental grasses usually survive short dry spells without help.

When you water perennials and grasses—or any other plant for that matter—water deeply and then don't water again until the soil has dried somewhat. Frequent, shallow waterings contribute to plants' developing shallow roots, which are more susceptible to drought damage.

This is the month when weather forecasts almost always include "scattered afternoon thunderstorms." If rainfall has been sparse, you may hope that you live in an area that gets visited by one. By the very nature of scattered thunderstorms, some areas can get quite a bit of rain and others, none. So unless you live close to the airport or other place in your county where the official rainfall is measured, you need a rain gauge. Put it up in an open, unobstructed spot. It will tell you how much rainfall your yard received on a certain day and in a week, and you can base your watering decisions on that, instead of guessing.

 # FERTILIZING

Neither perennials nor ornamental grasses need fertilizing in August. The only exceptions are those plants growing in containers. If they're still blooming or growing, they will appreciate an application of water-soluble fertilizer about once every ten days.

 # GROOMING

Don't let **phlox** drop its seed around; remove old flowers promptly. When **phlox** reseeds, the flowers on the new plants don't have the same color as the original—usually they're magenta. And if those are left in place and continue to reseed, soon the original planting is crowded out altogether.

Cut back tired-looking plants. Don't let them spoil the look of your garden.

Pinch or cut off faded flowers from all perennials. This is the basic chore in caring for perennials this time of the year. Flower beds look better when plants are quickly deadheaded, and it's best for the plants, too. It prevents unwanted reseeding and allows the plant to devote its energy to top and root growth and, sometimes, to producing new flowers.

Don't let plants crowd one another. Prune them back so they fill the space they're supposed to.

Remove dead or yellowing leaves.

 # PROBLEMS

Caterpillars are a conundrum for the ecologically minded gardener. On one hand, they can quickly destroy those plants for which you paid hard-earned money and then carefully tended. On the other, many caterpillars are butterfly larvae—and you may be trying to attract butterflies to your garden. One solution is to pick caterpillars by hand and move them onto plants in the woods or a natural area. If the infestation is severe, Bt (*Bacillus thuringiensis*) kills all types of caterpillars and what gardeners often refer to as "worms" (but which are really members of the caterpillar family).

If **asters** turn yellow and become stunted, they're suffering from a disease called aster yellows. The recommended control is to pull the plants up and destroy them. Then don't plant in that spot for the next two years.

Keep after any weeds that pop up. Perennial weeds that spread by underground runners are a particular problem since they're hard to eradicate by hand. Try to get every piece of root when you're pulling it up. Then be persistent. Sometimes it helps to lay a thick layer of newspaper over the ground where the weed is. (Cover with mulch for a more aesthetically pleasing look.) That can help prevent it from coming up again. Otherwise, your choice is a herbicide, such as Roundup®. The organic herbicides on the market don't have much effect on perennial weeds— though it surely won't be too long before one is developed.

If *Boltonia asteroides* flops over, the problem may be too-rich soil, too much fertilizer, or too much shade. If given full sun, shelter from winds, and average soil, **boltonia** shouldn't need staking or support. Another way to keep it from getting too tall and rangy is cutting it back by one-fourth to one-third in early July.

SEPTEMBER

PLANNING

What perennials besides **chrysanthemums** come into their own in fall? **Asters, boltonia, Joe-pye weed**, and **sedum** are a few for sun. And don't overlook **goldenrod** just because of roadside examples. Many interesting **goldenrod** cultivars are available that provide shorter plants and bigger blooms. For shade, consider **cardinal flower, Japanese anemone, toadlily** (*Tricyrtis hirta*), **bugbane** (*Cimicifuga racemosa*) for Zones 6 and 7a, and **turtlehead** (*Chelone* species and hybrids).

If you spent more time watering this past summer than you wanted, consider grouping together plants with similar watering needs. Keep those that require moist soil in one spot and those that tolerate dry soil in another section. This simplifies watering—and is easy to do when you renovate beds or prepare new ones.

PLANTING

Peonies don't need dividing often and shouldn't be divided until they really need it because they don't perform well for a year or more afterward. But when it becomes necessary, the first half of September is the time to get the job done. See page 182. Replant no more than 2 inches deep, leaving three to five eyes or buds per division.

This is also the month for dividing or transplanting spring- or summer-flowering perennials that need it—except **hostas**, which should be divided only in the spring. Another exception is ornamental grasses, which are divided only in early spring. See **March** for instructions on division. Water thoroughly, and mulch with 3 inches of organic material such as cocoa hulls, pine needles, Nature's Helper™, or shredded leaves. See **October** for advice on preparing new beds, which can be done anytime in the fall, including this month.

Unusual perennials are often available by mail order this time of year. Check the fall catalog of your favorite supplier—or call and ask. If you're buying perennials locally, make sure they aren't extremely rootbound. See page 38 in the **Annuals** chapter for planting tips. Ornamental grasses are planted in the spring and early summer, not the fall.

This is a good time to transplant to the garden perennials that grew in containers over the summer. They are more likely to survive in the ground than in pots, especially in Zone 6 and in unusually cold winters elsewhere in the region.

Plant container-grown **chrysanthemums** anytime this month. Use them to fill in spots where other flowers have faded. To help the **mums** survive winter, avoid planting them where they're exposed to winds or where the drainage is poor.

CARE

If mulch is looking a bit weary in prominent spots or in beds of fall-flowering perennials and around ornamental grasses just coming into their own, add a thin layer of fresh mulch.

Stakes and supports don't matter as much as the season winds down, unless they're being used for perennials, such as **mums**, that flower in the fall. Make sure the plant is completely supported as it grows and that, as far as possible, the supports or stakes are unobtrusive.

WATERING

If September is a dry month, continue watering those plants that need it, giving first preference to perennials and ornamental grasses planted this year. Those divided, transplanted, or planted this month may need twice-a-week watering for a few weeks if there's no rain or if rainfall is light.

If you spent more time watering this past summer than you wanted, consider grouping together plants with similar watering needs.

Each day, water containerized plants until the excess flows from the drainage holes.

Water newly planted **mums** or **asters** so that their soil is moist but not soggy. This increases their chances of surviving the winter.

In the southern sections of the region, continue watering reblooming **daylilies** during dry spells if they haven't yet flowered.

Check emitters in drip irrigation systems to find any that have gotten clogged. Clean and replace them.

FERTILIZING

Don't fertilize **mums**. This includes those you just bought and those that have been growing in the garden for a year or more. Late fertilizing encourages tender new growth, which is likely to get killed by frost. You want the plants to be developing deep, strong roots to carry them through the winter instead of new growth.

No fertilizing—either of perennials or ornamental grasses—is necessary from now until next March. When planting new perennials this month or dividing and transplanting older ones, mix plenty of organic matter with the soil in the bed; that provides all the nutrients the plants need until next spring.

GROOMING

Continue pinching or pruning off all dead flowers. At this point in the year, you don't want perennial plants devoting energy to seed production—which is what happens if you leave dying blooms on the plants. Instead, remove the old blossoms and let the plant put its energy toward root growth.

Cut back any plants that have already bloomed and look bad.

Pinching Off
Dead Perennial
Flowers

PROBLEMS

Heavily sprinkling black pepper on the ground around newly planted perennials may deter squirrels and chipmunks, which can otherwise do quite a bit of damage by digging.

If Japanese beetles were a particular problem in your garden this year, contact the Extension Service office in your county (see pages 344 to 353) for advice. Some gardeners spread a recommended insecticide on the lawn this time of year to kill the grubs before they burrow lower into the soil in anticipation of colder weather. You can also apply milky spore, an organic control that gradually kills the grubs and prevents reinfestation for up to fifteen years.

OCTOBER

 ## PLANNING

Do you have enough perennial beds or would you like to be able to plant even more flowers? Do some planning this month by walking around the yard to remind yourself what you already have and to find possible spots for new plantings. You might plan to plant small pockets of perennials here and there or in and among shrubs and in flower beds usually filled with annuals.

Reading back through your garden notebook for the past couple of years, you may find that one or two species have been troublesome. Maybe now's the time to get rid of them and make room for more desirable and less time-consuming plants.

While the larger types of ornamental grasses make wonderful specimen plants, grasses can fill an entire border by themselves if one only plants grasses. An ornamental grass bed is intriguing in all seasons except for a few weeks in very early spring, when the grasses have to be trimmed back. If you decide to try one, put it where you can see it (and maybe even hear it, as the winds blow through the grasses) in the winter.

 ## PLANTING

The cooler days of October present an excellent opportunity to prepare new beds for ornamental grasses and perennials. There are four ways to prepare areas not previously used for growing plants. Choose the one that works best for you.

1 Kill grass and weeds by smothering them. First, mow as close as you can. Then cover the area with a thick layer of newspaper, topped by a thick layer of mulch. An alternative to the newspaper is black plastic, which works very quickly to kill existing vegetation in hot, sunny spots. You may want to cover the black plastic with an organic mulch, so it won't look so bad. When you're ready to plant, remove the plastic and till the mulch and newspapers into the soil. Add one-fourth to one-third the volume of the soil in organic matter (aged mushroom compost, rotted leaves, compost, fine pine bark, etc.).

2 Mow the area closely. Till the soil and then water. Wait seven to ten days and then till up any weeds or grass that have sprouted. You may need to do this three more times, at ten-day intervals, to ensure that most weed seeds have germinated. (This method doesn't work well if the area contains weeds that spread by underground runners.) Then amend the soil with organic matter (see No. 1) and plant or leave fallow till spring.

3 Rent a sod cutter and remove existing sod (this can also be done by hand, with a shovel, in small areas). Move the strips of sod wherever you need new grass. Water the area to encourage weed seeds to sprout. Kill them by method No. 1, by digging them out, or by spraying them with a nonspecific weed killer such as Roundup®, which doesn't persist in the soil and thus allows replanting in two weeks. After the first removal of weeds, water again and remove the weeds two weeks later. Then till ample organic matter into the soil (see step 1).

4. Mow the existing vegetation very short. Spray the area with Roundup®—being careful that the weedkiller doesn't touch desirable plants or grass. Wait two weeks and see whether new weeds sprout. If so, apply Roundup® a second time. Then at planting time, improve the soil as outlined in No. 1 above.

Fall's first frost comes to many parts of the region this month. Be prepared to cover those plants that need protection to keep them blooming a while longer.

Once the bed is prepared, it's a good idea to cover it with layers of newspapers (held down by rocks) or with a 3-inch layer of mulch (shredded leaves would be good and they're readily available this month). This helps prevent any weeds or seeds from taking hold before spring planting.

 CARE

Fall's first frost comes to many parts of the region this month. Be prepared to cover those plants that need protection to keep them blooming a while longer. Also plan—after the first killing frost—to take down supports and stakes, clean them off, and store them out of the weather so they'll last longer. Some supports may need a coat of green spray paint after a year or two of use. This is a good time to take care of that so they'll be ready to put into action when needed next spring.

 WATERING

If October isn't rainy, keep perennials and ornamental grasses watered going into cold weather. Winter hardiness is improved if plants haven't been under stress before frost occurs.

Water any container-grown grass or perennial daily if rainfall doesn't do the job for you.

 FERTILIZING

Gardeners don't need to spend much money on fertilizer for ornamental grasses and perennials since most aren't heavy feeders. The first year, they're fertilized at planting time; the second and following years, when perennials begin growing, they may be top-dressed with organic matter such as rotted manure or Milorganite®. No perennials or ornamental grasses are fertilized in autumn. Put the fertilizer back on the shelf (in a cool, dry place) until spring.

 GROOMING

Deadhead **asters, mums, boltonia**, and other fall flowers that have finished blooming. Cut these back or not, as you prefer, after they've been nipped by frost. The ones that have seeds attract birds (especially goldfinches) to the garden. But in spots highly visible from the street or your front windows, large areas of dead perennials look messy.

 PROBLEMS

Is your large ornamental grass standing straight and tall, or does it appear to need staking? Floppy growth on ornamental grasses is due to too much fertilizer (established grasses don't need fertilizing) or too little light. If more sun is needed, replant them early next spring.

Why did your 'Stella d'Oro' or 'Happy Returns' **daylily** stop or slow its repeat blooming halfway through the summer? **Daylilies** that repeatedly bloom throughout the season need dividing much more often than **daylilies** that bloom only once a year. If they're allowed to build up a big clump, the flowering slows or stops. Another help is to foliar feed (spray the entire plant, leaves and all) with a water-soluble fertilizer (20-20-20, fish emulsion, or liquid seaweed) in midspring and again in early summer.

197

NOVEMBER

PLANNING

If you don't grow **Lenten roses**, start searching the catalogs or ask your favorite nursery to order some for you next spring. They're evergreen, grow in shade (even deep shade), and bloom in late winter (sometimes as early as January, depending on the weather and where you live). Not many other plants flower that time of year, so **Lenten roses** are a delight. As you consider where to put them, think of a spot that you walk by daily in the winter so you can enjoy the blooms. The plant reseeds, so a neighbor who's growing **Lenten roses** may be willing to share. Or perhaps you can work out a trade for one of your perennials.

PLANTING

Do no more planting in Zone 6 or Zone 7a. Experienced gardeners in Zones 8 and 7b can get by with late planting, transplanting, or division, but you should try it only with a plant you don't mind losing. If you plant early and mulch heavily, and the winter is mild, everything *may* be all right. But perennials must have time to grow the roots they need to live through the winter—and there's no telling about the weather—so late planting is risky at best.

As long as the weather's nice and the ground isn't frozen, you may continue to prepare beds for next year. See **October**.

CARE

Containers of perennials have to be protected from cold throughout the region, but especially where temperatures may fall into the teens or even to 0 degrees Fahrenheit. You may want to move large pots to protected places during the day and then take them in out of the weather if temperatures fall below 20 degrees Fahrenheit. Some people wrap the pot in insulation. All perennials or grasses in small pots (8 inch or smaller) should be stored in an unheated garage, basement, or crawlspace where temperatures remain chilly but above freezing.

As long as the weather is still mild, garden cleanup is an ideal chore in November. Temperatures are cool enough that you don't sweat and may sometimes be mild enough that you're pleased to be outside getting some exercise. Remove debris and excess leaves from woodland beds. The mulch around perennials should never be thicker than 3 inches; if leaves are left where they fall year after year, perennials may soon get buried and fail to return in the spring.

Blow some leaves out of the beds if there are too many, and add them to the compost pile or shred them and use them as mulch elsewhere in the garden.

Clean all tools, and oil those that need it. If you don't have a regular place to hang your tools so you can grab them whenever they're needed, this is a good time to create one.

If you don't reuse potting soil from year to year, dump it from containers into the compost pile or an area in the yard that needs some soil. (Old potting soil may also be used to provide winter protection around **roses**.) Clean the pots; wash them with soapy water mixed with 1 part bleach to 9 parts water, then rinse them thoroughly and let them dry. Store the pots in your garage or basement, covered with plastic so they won't get dirty. If you have too many pots—especially those black-plastic gallon-sized ones—think of who might be able to use them. A gardening program at a local school? A community garden? A Master Gardener who's conducting a greenhouse program?

Mulch perennial beds well after a hard freeze or two.

WATERING

Since you don't need to water perennials or ornamental grasses until at least spring, take up soaker hoses and drip irrigation systems and drain them. Store them in a cool, dry spot over the winter. They will have to be replaced more frequently if they are left out in freezing weather.

As long as the soil isn't frozen, occasionally water your container plants if they don't receive any rainfall—but water just enough to prevent the soil from completely drying out.

 # FERTILIZING

Here's something to be thankful for: There's no fertilizing this month or next month—not until sometime in March. Your perennials and ornamental grasses are resting, and you can, too.

 # GROOMING

Do they go or do they stay? With ornamental grasses, there's no question. They are never pruned back until very early spring because they add so much winter interest to our yards. The answer isn't as clear-cut for perennials. Once upon a time, every perennial was pruned back to ground level as soon as it was killed by frost. But now we've learned that natural is fine. So sometimes we cut back plants in the fall and other times we wait till late winter or early spring. There's no right or wrong way, but here are a few guidelines:

- If any perennials were attacked by insects or disease this year, cut them back now and remove them from the garden. *Don't* add them to the compost pile. Both actions will help prevent problems next year.
- Finish deadheading perennials in prominent locations, but leave some seeds for the birds.

- Don't cut back **chrysanthemums**, but do mulch **mums** that were newly planted this fall.
- Don't prune **evergreen ferns** or tender perennials.
- Leave standing anything that has an interesting look.

 # PROBLEMS

On a mild day, make one last trek through woodland gardens and perennial borders and beds to pull stray weeds. This is easier if done after a rain. Henbit, with its lavender flowers, is an attractive weed, and you may be tempted to leave it. Don't. It continues to reseed and spread and can take over an area of garden or lawn in just a couple of winters.

DECEMBER

 PLANNING

As a refuge from the hectic pace of the holidays, set aside a "garden corner" in your favorite room. Have a comfortable chair, a good lamp, a study table beside the chair, and a large basket to hold a supply of garden reading. As catalogs arrive in the mail, drop them in the basket with magazines you've saved, your garden notebook, and your favorite garden books. Then read and think and make notes to your heart's content. The prettiest gardens always sprout in your imagination in the dead of winter.

Check over the year's notes in your garden journal to see whether you have any ideas to move forward to next year—maybe plans you wanted to accomplish or plants you decided to try after seeing them elsewhere. If you've noted some plants that have passed their third year in your yard without ever performing satisfactorily—or that always attract insects or diseases—maybe next year is the time to replace them with better plants.

 PLANTING

No grasses or perennials are planted this month, although expert gardeners may start seeds that need stratifying. This means the seeds need some weeks or months of exposure to cold temperatures before they germinate. Some that need stratification include *Amsonia*, **monkshood** (*Aconitum* species), and **turtlehead** (*Chelone* species). Check catalogs and seed packets to determine which others should be stratified. Plant seeds according to the directions on page 180; label and enclose them in a plastic tag sealed with a twister tie. Place them in a cold frame or other protected location where the temperature stays below 40 degrees Fahrenheit for the next six to eight weeks. Seeds will begin to germinate in the spring and can be planted in the garden when they reach bedding-plant size.

 CARE

Mulch perennial beds if you haven't already.

Continue your garden cleanup if you didn't finish last month.

If you don't have a bird feeder in the yard, why not put one up? You'll enjoy the antics of the birds, and many eat insects, as well as seeds. Place a feeder near a shrub or large clump of ornamental grass to provide the birds with some nearby cover. Birds like to feel that they have a hiding place from danger, if needed.

 WATERING

Have hoses been drained and moved out of the weather? They'll last much longer if they aren't left exposed to the cold and the elements. If you haven't stored your hoses already, you might as well get to that now since you don't have to water for the next few months.

 FERTILIZING

There's no fertilizing in December.

 GROOMING

If the birds have stripped all the seeds or berries from any perennial, you may cut it back, if you like.

 PROBLEMS

Winter drainage is crucial for all perennials except those that can take wet conditions (see the partial list on page 188). Keep an eye out for areas of poor drainage as you walk through the yard on nice days. You may not be able to do anything now, but if you know where the problem spots are, you can take steps to improve drainage in the spring.

CHAPTER SEVEN

Roses

Everyone loves roses, but many people are convinced that growing roses is too much trouble. Not so! Raising roses may not be quite as simple as growing marigolds, but they're not nearly as troublesome as their reputation suggests.

In fact, you may spend less time on some of the newer roses than you do on **marigolds**, since the roses are planted once and return year after year—with gorgeous blooms.

So what does it take to grow great roses without their care taking all your spare time? The basics are just common sense: choosing and buying wisely, planting carefully, providing ample water when needed, fertilizing, taking care of pests, protecting the bushes over winter, and pruning at the right time in early spring.

There's nothing difficult there, right? So why are roses considered so time consuming? Because people don't always follow those rules—starting with buying a "bargain bush" or one that's known to break out in blackspot every June. When rose society members start describing their planting mixtures and how often and how much they spray—most of us shy away. It sounds too technical and like too much work. Besides, we may feel uncomfortable around all those chemicals.

But we can all learn a great deal from members of rose societies—they

know so much more than the rest of us ever will and are so generous in sharing their hard-won knowledge. But their goals in growing roses and yours may differ quite a bit. They want perfection. After all, their roses will be entered in shows and people will be visiting their gardens throughout the season. Most homeowners just want nice-looking roses. If there's a yellow leaf here or there, or a bloom or two is a bit ragged from Japanese beetles, we don't mind too much.

In a way, growing roses is comparable to lawn care. If you devote a great deal of time and energy to your grass—or your roses—you'll produce a lawn or rose garden that everyone will envy. But you can have nice-looking grass or rosebushes—which give you much pleasure—by doing the right things at the right time.

PICKING THE PLANTING SPOT

The "right thing" starts with choosing the site. Roses need sun—at least six hours a day of direct sunlight. More is better. If you have a choice of a spot

that receives mostly morning sun or mostly afternoon sun, choose the one with morning sun. It will enable leaves wet from dew or rain to dry off quicker in the day and so avoid possible fungal diseases.

Excellent drainage is a must wherever roses are planted. Although roses need plenty of moisture, they die if planted where their roots stay wet. If you don't have any sunny spots with good drainage, build a raised bed 24 inches deep.

CHOOSING ROSEBUSHES

Most of us choose a rose because we like how it looks. There's nothing wrong with wanting to grow roses that we love—but all roses aren't equal. Some roses perform better than others. They grow better, they have bigger blooms and more of them, they're less disease-prone, and they're not as likely to be killed during a cold winter.

That's not to say that you are going to have to settle for ugly roses—if there is such a thing as an ugly rose. Instead, if your aim is relatively care-free rose growing, you're going to have to find out which roses are the absolute best and grow them instead of choosing casually from a catalog picture or picking out a potted rose at the garden center without knowing anything about it.

So how do you discover which roses are going to perform best? There are several ways. On its Website (www.ars.org), the American Rose Society (P.O. Box 30000, Shreveport, LA, 71130) has a list of those rated 8.0 and above. These are the ones that you want to grow. The organization also publishes an annual booklet called *Handbook for Selecting Roses*, which is a handy size to carry with you when you go rose shopping. Instead of listing just the top-rated roses, it lists and ranks most of the roses sold at garden centers. (Exceptions are roses introduced in the past year or two, which are too new to be ranked.)

There are a number of rose societies in Kentucky and Tennessee that are associated with the American Rose Society, and most of them have lists of the top roses recommended by their members. These are the ones that have done best in the yards of Memphis, Louisville, Nashville, Lexington, and Chattanooga. Contact information is available on the ARS Website for the clubs that are part of the Tenarky District (Tennessee, Kentucky, and Arkansas). Also included

are links to the societies' Websites, which contain lots of helpful information on choosing and growing roses. If you're not able to locate this information, write the ARS or call the Extension Service office in your county (pages 344 to 353) and ask who to contact about the nearest rose society.

Each society has at least one and often more consulting rosarians. These are experienced rose growers who are available to give free advice on selecting roses and just about anything else you'll need to know to make roses happy in your yard.

One other list of excellent roses is those that have won the All-America Rose Selections awards (see www.rose.org). These roses have been tested in many different parts of the country and while there may be an occasional less-than-stellar performer in our hot, humid climate, you can usually buy AARS winners with confidence. This is especially true of those that have won in the past ten years. They are particularly disease-resistant, which is important for the home rose grower.

You can often evaluate rose performances in person at public gardens around the region. Your nearest botanical garden is likely to have a lovely rose garden. Visit several times a year, and take along your garden notebook to write down the names of your favorites. (If you're new to the area and

don't know about nearby public gardens, the AARS Website contains a list of gardens that test or grow the AARS winners. These gardens usually have many other roses, as well.)

KNOW THE TYPE OF ROSE

Roses are classified by growth habit. Knowing this won't make much difference in your success with roses, but it will improve the appearance of your landscape because knowing what type of rose you're buying makes a difference in where you put it. Here are a few of the classifications:

Hybrid teas are strong upright growers with single flowers (often large) borne on long stems. **Hybrid tea roses** are just right for arrangements.

Floribundas have smaller flowers than **hybrid teas,** but more of them. The flowers grow in clusters instead of on single stems, so they aren't as attractive as cut flowers but look wonderful in the yard. Often the bush is smaller than a **hybrid tea.**

Grandifloras combine characteristics of **hybrid teas** and **floribundas,** with bushes taller than **hybrid teas,** blooms that flower in clusters but look more like **hybrid tea** blooms, and long stems.

Climbers and ramblers have long arching canes that can be trained to

Roses

Timely Tip

When to Plant and Prune Roses*

City	Pruning date	Planting date for bare-root roses
Tennessee:		
Chattanooga	March 20-31	February 15-March 7
Knoxville and Nashville	End of March	Mid-March to mid-April
Memphis	February 15-March 1	February and March
Murfreesboro	April 15	April 15
Kentucky:		
Louisville	Mid-March to early April	Late March, early April
Perryville (central Kentucky)	April 15	Fall pruning possible

*If your city isn't listed, follow the dates of a city that has a climate similar to yours.

grow on fences and trellises. They have to be tied to their supports. **Ramblers** tend to grow larger than **climbers** and have smaller flowers (often in dense clusters).

Miniatures aren't necessarily tiny. They may grow as tall as 4 feet, so if you want something 19 inches, check the average height (in Kentucky and Tennessee, most will grow at least a bit taller). The blooms, however, are small. They're dainty delights.

Old garden roses and **David Austin roses** have a romantic, old-fashioned look. Be sure you know the eventual height and spread of the bush, as some can grow quite large. Also on true **old garden roses**, learn whether they bloom more than once a year;

many don't. Often, roses in these groups are highly fragrant. Some are disease-resistant, but despite what you may read—not all are.

Shrub roses, especially newer types, are often referred to as **landscape roses**. They come in a wide range of sizes, forms, and looks—of both bush and flower. But all are summer- and winter-hardy, vigorous, and usually disease-resistant, and they can get by with less care than other types of roses.

Buying Roses

Once you've selected the roses you want to grow, you'll need to find a local nursery or garden center that carries

them, or a reliable rose nursery from which you can order. Too many people think nothing of paying $50 for a dozen roses on Valentine's Day but balk at spending $15 to $20 for a quality rosebush that will produce hundreds of blooms for many years.

There are no bargains in roses. You get what you pay for. If you buy a bare-root specimen in a tiny pot at the grocery store or a roadside stand, you've started down the road to failure. Instead, avoid problems and weak growth by purchasing strong, high-quality roses from a reputable dealer. (Early in the year, these will be bare-root roses—just canes and roots. After the frost-free date, local nurseries will have container-grown rosebushes.

Roses

These are increasingly popular because they don't take any special preparation for planting.)

PLANTING AND PRUNING

Planting bare-root and container-grown roses is covered on pages 210 and 214. The main thing is to dig the holes big enough and improve poor soil—especially clay—with plenty of organic matter. Space roses this far apart:

Hybrid teas . . . . 3 to 4 feet
Floribundas . . . . 2½ to 3 feet
Grandifloras . . . . 4 feet
Miniatures . . . . 1 to 3 feet
(depending on eventual size)
Old garden roses and
Shrub roses . . . . 4 to 6 feet
See label or other description for mature width (spacing can be 6 or more feet in our climate).

Except for **ramblers, climbers,** and **old garden roses** that bloom only once, roses are pruned annually in early spring, before new growth starts. This will take only a few minutes per bush. Since the majority of roses bloom on "new wood"—canes that grow in the current year—pruning stimulates this new growth and encourages the formation of more flowers. It also thins out excess growth on the inside of the plant, which allows in sun and air.

INSECTS AND DISEASES

Bugs seem just as fond of roses as people do. Aphids, thrips, spider mites, Japanese beetles, rose chafers (which are also beetles), stem borers, and rose midges occasionally appear and do damage. Small infestations may often be controlled organically. Many serious rose growers spray insecticides weekly to prevent insect damage. The problem with this approach is that the chemicals also kill the bad insects' natural enemies such as ladybugs, lacewings, and trichogramma wasps.

The two most commonly encountered rose diseases are blackspot (which produces little black spots on the leaves, causing the foliage to eventually fall off) and powdery mildew, which leaves a white coating on the leaves.

The little-known truth about rose growing is that many disease and insect problems can be avoided or controlled by taking a few simple steps:

1 Select disease-resistant roses. Catalog and book descriptions will note "blackspot-resistant," "mildew-resistant," or "disease-resistant." Casual rose growers should never buy a rose that isn't described this way. Who wants to be outside on summer days spraying fungicide?

2 Grow roses only in the sun. Also, plant them in soil that's rich in organic matter and water and fertilize them regularly. Plants that are stressed are more likely to succumb to insects and diseases.

3 Don't plant roses too close together. Give them space so air can circulate well. This reduces the risk of disease.

4 Water roses first thing in the morning and avoid getting water on the canes or leaves. Wet leaves are more likely to develop diseases.

5 Practice good hygiene around your roses. Remove all infected leaves and other parts from the bush and the ground beneath and toss those into the trash. At the end of the growing season, rake up the mulch beneath roses and remove it from the garden so insects, eggs, and disease spores won't overwinter in the old mulch.

6 Don't overfertilize. Too much nitrogen fertilizer causes fast green growth much loved by aphids.

7 Look over plants several times a week so you can catch small problems before they become big ones.

Many gardeners successfully grow the "queen of flowers" without pampering. You can be among them. We *are* promising you a rose garden, the kind you've dreamed about. And we're showing you that having that rose garden is much easier than you ever thought. Not convinced? Read on.

Roses

Name	Type	Flowers	Comments
'Abraham Darby'®	English	Pink	Has the look of an antique rose, but blooms over and over all season.
'America'	Climber	Salmon pink	Beautiful blooms with a spicy fragrance. Blooms repeatedly.
'Betty Prior'	Floribunda	Medium pink	Single flowers that will remind you of dogwood blossoms. Fragrant. Vigorous.
'Bonica'	Shrub rose	Light pink	Double flowers.
'Carefree'™ series	Shrub rose	Pink, yellow	Single flowers, easygoing performance.
'Don Juan'	Climber	Dark red	Dark green foliage is disease-resistant.
'Europeana'	Floribunda	Red	Sprays of flowers all season long. Disease-resistant foliage.
'Flower Carpet'™ series	Landscape	White, pink, yellow	Pest-resistant. Tough enough to be used as a flowering ground cover shrub.
'Gold Medal'	Hybrid tea	Golden yellow	Vigorous grower. Flowers not bothered by rain.
'Graham Thomas'®	English	Deep yellow	Bush grows up to 8 feet tall. Cupped blooms with an old-fashioned feel.
'Gruss an Aachen'	Shrub rose	Pink to white	Bush grows only 4 feet tall. Foliage is disease-resistant. Double flowers have a lush look.
'Iceberg'	Floribunda	White	The whole bush turns white when 'Iceberg' blooms. Very few thorns.
'Knockout'	Landscape	Red	Single flowers on a very disease-resistant plant.
'Louis Phillippe'	Old garden rose	Red	Disease-resistant. Flowers all summer
'Magic Carousel'	Miniature	Pink-yellow- white	Unusual color. Vigorous plant.
'Meidiland'™ series	Shrub rose	Red, pink, white, yellow	Good for a low-maintenance landscape. Needs very little care.
'Mister Lincoln'	Hybrid tea	Red	Tall vigorous bush. Lots of blooms. May mildew. Gorgeous combined with 'Iceberg'.
'New Dawn'	Climber	Light pink	Large fragrant flowers. Repeat bloom. Vigorous grower.
'Peace'	Hybrid tea	Pink/yellow	Introduced to mark the end of World War II and a favorite ever since. Highly rated.
'Queen Elizabeth'	Grandiflora	Medium pink	One of the best grandiflora roses. Lots of flowers on long, strong stems.
'Sexy Rexy'	Floribunda	Pink	Prolific bloomer. Hardy.
'Souvenir de la Malmaison'	Old garden rose	Light pink	Dates to 1843. Flowers look as though they belong in a painting by one of the Old Masters. Doesn't like rain.
'Starina'®	Miniature	Reddish-orange	One of the highest-rated miniatures.
'Sunsprite'	Floribunda	Lemon yellow	One of the best yellow roses. Color doesn't fade in the sun. Disease-resistant. Blooms best in May and autumn.
'The Fairy'	Polyantha	Light pink	Rounded bush form covered with tiny blooms. A group makes a nice edging.
'Tropicana'	Hybrid tea	Luminous orange	Fruity fragrance.

JANUARY

PLANNING

Anyone who wants to grow roses should start the year off right and take one important action this month—purchase a pair of thorn-proof gloves. These are available at garden centers, at home stores, and by mail order. They'll make your life much rosier.

If you plan to add new roses to your garden this year, January's the time to decide what they will be and to get them ordered, if you haven't already. Send off for catalogs as soon as possible. (If you're new to roses, see the American Rose Society's Website (www.ars.org) or ask someone at your local rose society to recommend mail-order suppliers.). You'll glean quite a bit of information from catalogs, even if you plan to buy locally. The advantage of mail order is that you can usually find a much larger and more varied supply. But locally you'll be able to look over the bushes and see exactly what you're getting.

As you consider which roses you want to grow and where you'll put them, reread the information on pages 201 to 202 about selecting top-rated roses. Print out the list from the ARS Website and buy a copy of the handbook. It's smart to plant roses that other gardeners have found to be fairly trouble-free.

Have your soil tested, if you haven't done this in several years or if you're planning a new rose bed. Write on the form that you send to the state lab that you're growing roses so the recommendations will be tailored to roses and not just flowers. The best pH range for growing roses is between 6.0 and 6.8. Above and below that range, roses can't absorb nutrients efficiently and leaves will turn yellow.

As you think about rose purchases, be aware that roses are sold according to grade—from 1 to 2. A No. 1 rose has at least three canes that are a minimum of $5/16$ inch in diameter. (An exception is **polyantha roses**, such as 'The Fairy', which must have four canes that size.) No. 1 is the top grade and what beginners should buy. A No. 1½ rose needs to have only two canes of the requisite size. It should be less expensive but will take longer to grow into a strong bush. Avoid roses that are graded No. 2. They require too much effort and success is iffy.

How's your supply of tools? Maybe you've been thinking about buying a new pair of pruners, a backpack sprayer, or other equipment. Put this shopping on your to-do list and start looking around to find the tools that have the qualities you want and need. Pruners and many other hand tools are now being ergonomically designed and require less brute strength than older tools. If you

haven't looked over the tool selection in the past few years, you may be pleasantly surprised.

You will be warmly welcomed at a meeting of your local rose society this month—or anytime. It's a great place to learn the local ins and outs of rose growing.

PLANTING

Because of the weather, no rose planting is done in January in this part of the country.

You may, however, transplant roses from one part of the yard to another if you need to. See page 214.

On a mild day, you may also till up the soil to prepare a rose bed. (See page 210 for information on amending the soil.)

CARE

Are your hand pruners and loppers clean and sharp? They should be for pruning and grooming roses. When blades are dull, they can crush canes. January is a good month to examine your pruning tools and take them to be sharpened—or sharpen and oil them yourself.

If we're going to get any particularly bad winter weather, it often occurs in January or February. As we head into a new year, take time to check the winter protection around your roses and see that it's still okay. Rain, snow, and wind can often scatter leaves, mulch, or soil that was mounded over roses to protect them from cold. It's always a good idea to have an extra supply on hand to replenish whatever may have been washed away.

Apply a lime sulfur spray to roses and to the surrounding soil if you didn't last month. This helps kill overwintering diseases and insect eggs. Read the label carefully and follow instructions regarding weather and temperatures.

 # WATERING

Outdoors, watering isn't necessary this month. But if you have purchased a potted **miniature rose** and are growing it on a windowsill, it may need frequent watering. Keep the soil moist, but don't let the plant stand in water.

If potted roses are overwintering in the basement or garage, water them lightly once this month.

 # FERTILIZING

Outdoors, give the fertilizer a rest this month. Roses are fertilized only when they're growing. Indoors, fertilize **miniature roses** that are actively blooming once a month with a balanced water-soluble fertilizer, such as 20-20-20.

 # PRUNING

Pruning season begins next month in the warmest parts of the region and in March and April in the cooler sections. There are two exceptions to the no-January-pruning rule:

1 If canes that grew very long last year weren't trimmed in the fall and are being blown about in the wind, rubbing other canes, cut them back to about 4 feet long.

2 If the bush has sustained damage from a storm, a falling branch, construction, or other cause, prune out the dead or damaged parts as soon as possible—as long as temperatures are above freezing.

 # PROBLEMS

Spider mites are often a problem on **miniature roses** grown indoors. See page 217. When spider mites are present, leaves will appear dull and then mottled. They may seem to be dusty underneath. Eventually the foliage will curl up and fall off. It helps to raise the humidity level around the plants and each week to spray water on the foliage (both the tops and the undersides of the leaves).

FEBRUARY

PLANNING

As you continue to think about adding new roses to your yard, consider **miniature climbers.** They're delightful growing up mailbox posts. 'Jeanne LaJoie' is a pink one that has an ARS Rose in Review rating of 9.3, which translates to "one of the best roses ever."

Roses don't have to be grown in beds by themselves; they combine nicely with other plants in the landscape, as long as you're careful not to crowd them. Here are some suggestions to get you started:

- Gray-leaved *Artemisia* 'Powis Castle', **dusty miller**, and **santolina** make a nice border around a bed of pink roses. So does *Liriope* 'Silver Dragon'.
- Perennials with spiky blooms also complement roses—**blue sage (perennial salvia), lavender**, and **red valerian** (although be careful about color clashes with the latter).
- Ornamental grasses—especially those with reddish leaves (including *Pennisetum* 'Rubrum') or themes with flower spikes that turn reddish in autumn.
- Low-growing **miniature** and **shrub roses**, as well as **polyanthas,** make nice borders along driveways and walks, and they also look good massed to form a solid block of color.

- When landscaping with **climbers,** choose a dark flower to contrast against a light background and select a **climber** with light-colored blooms that will show up against a dark background.
- Avoid ground covers around roses because they interfere with work around the bushes.
- For the same reason, think twice before planting bulbs or annuals in and among roses. Will you have to step on **daffodils** in order to prune or have to dodge **daylilies** when you need to fertilize?
- Choose plants that have the same cultural requirements as roses—full sun and plenty of moisture.
- Avoid placing near roses any plants that develop mildew (**bee balm, zinnia**, or old-fashioned **crapemyrtles,** for instance).

PLANTING

Planting of bare-root roses starts in March in the warmest parts of the region. Containerized roses are planted in late spring and early summer.

CARE

Check on winter protection and renew if necessary. (See **January**.) This helps to moderate temperatures and prevent

roses from leafing out in warm spells only to get killed by the cold snaps that follow. Leave the bud union (the swelling where the stem joins the roots) covered until all chance of frost is past.

In all but the warmest parts of the region, you may spray lime sulfur or dormant oil on rosebushes to kill overwintering pests, if you didn't get to this earlier.

WATERING

Because of low temperatures and the fact that roses have not yet begun to grow, outdoor watering isn't needed.

Indoors, don't let container-grown **mini roses** dry out. Keep the soil moist but not soggy. Feel the soil's surface every few days, and water when it has become slightly dry.

FERTILIZING

Some rose growers like to fertilize right after pruning. Others prefer to spread the season's first fertilizer two weeks after pruning. And there are those who wait to fertilize when new growth appears. If you live in Zone 8 this is a decision you'll be making this month.

Indoors, continue to feed **miniature roses** in containers monthly with a water-soluble fertilizer made for flowering plants.

When you prune, immediately seal the cut tips of the cane with nontoxic glue (white glue, such as Elmer's), shellac, or a rose-pruning sealant or wax.

PRUNING

In most parts of our region, rose growers prune all roses except **climbers** and **old garden roses** when **forsythia** blooms. That's typically about the middle of this month in Zone 8. Because of widely variable temperatures this month, some growers in Zone 8 wait to prune about March 1.

Gardeners in other, colder parts of the region prune roses at different times, due to variations in weather. But use the flowering of **forsythia** as your guide.

Make sure your cutting tools are sharp. Use hand pruners for canes up to ³/₄ inch in diameter, loppers for stems ups to 1³/₄ inches around, and saws for anything larger. The folding Japanese-type saws can be handy when you're working in tight quarters and for **climbers**.

General Pruning Rules

- Remove diseased or damaged canes or stems, canes that are rubbing against one another, and canes that are growing toward the middle of the bush instead of toward the outside.
- On grafted roses, dig up suckers that grow from ground level. Also, remove all growth that comes from on or below the bud union. This growth will

not be the same rose as the variety you bought, and since it's overly vigorous, it will take over, giving you inferior red roses.

- Make all cuts at a 45-degree angle so water will run off the tips of the canes, decreasing the chance of decay. Cut ¹/₄ inch above an outward-facing bud.
- If a cane is discolored, cut back until you reach green wood.
- Remove canes that are the diameter of a pencil or less.
- Clean up all debris and remove it from the rose garden.

Pruning Roses

Specific Pruning Advice

Hybrid teas: You want to end up with three to six healthy canes that are from 12 to 18 inches tall.

Floribundas and polyanthas: You should leave six to eight healthy canes (remove the oldest ones) about 20 to 28 inches high.

Grandifloras: After pruning, there should be four to five large healthy canes about 36 inches high.

Climbers, ramblers, old garden roses: These are pruned **after** blooming since they often bloom on the previous year's wood (unlike the roses listed above, which produce flowers on canes that grow this year). See page 216 for directions.

Miniatures: If you have just a few **miniatures,** prune them like **hybrid teas** to 10-16 inches high. If you have many, just clip them back with hedge trimmers.

PROBLEMS

Borers can be a real problem with roses, even going so far as to kill most of the canes. Since they enter the bush through the soft ends of canes that have been pruned, there is a simple way to prevent borers from causing damage. When you prune, immediately seal the cut tips of the cane with nontoxic glue (white glue, such as Elmer's), shellac, or a rose-pruning sealant or wax.

MARCH

PLANNING

If you're planning on buying **climbing roses**, read the descriptions carefully. Some are more vigorous than others and will need stronger supports. All supports must be anchored firmly at the base. Also be aware that **climbing roses** produce more blooms if they're trained horizontally—on a fence or wall—than if they grow straight up.

PLANTING

March marks the beginning of rose planting time in the warmest parts of the region. Bare-root roses are planted in Zone 8 beginning about the middle of the month. See the list of cities and dates on page 203 to find when bare-root roses are generally planted in your area. Your local rose society or your county's Extension agent may provide even more specific guidance, based on this particular year's weather.

What if a mail-order rose arrives in the middle of a cold snap or as you're headed out of town? You have several options:

- If the weather is predicted to improve within a few days or you're only gone for the weekend, keep the bush in the box and place it in a cool, dark spot. If the roots appear to be dry, sprinkle them lightly with water.

- The roses can be heeled in outside—placed at a 45-degree angle in a trench about a foot deep. This should be in a shady protected spot.
- If it appears you won't be able to plant for several weeks, get 3- to 5-gallon black pots from a nursery (they will have been used for trees) and plant the roses in the containers. Place them outdoors in the daytime and bring them in at night if temperatures are expected to fall below freezing.

Before planting a bare-root rose, always soak the roots overnight in a mixture of water and transplanting solution, water and fish emulsion, or water in which thin weeping willow branches are also soaked. Any of these will help improve rooting. Soak for 12 hours or less—no longer.

How to Plant a Bare-root Rose

1 First, prune any broken roots from the plant. The canes don't need pruning unless they were damaged in some way.

2 Dig a hole 24 inches deep and 24 inches wide.

3 Mix the soil removed from the hole with organic matter—compost, fine pine bark, old mushroom compost—in a ratio of 2 parts soil to 1 part organic matter.

4 Use the soil mixture to build a firm cone or pyramid in the center of the hole.

5 Place the rose on top of the cone with the roots draped down the sides. The bud union should be 1 inch above the level of the surrounding ground or, for the coldest parts of the state, at ground level.

6 Carefully pour the soil mixture into the hole around the roots, packing it around the roots.

7 Pour into the hole some of the water in which the roots soaked.

8 After the water soaks in, add more soil till the hole is filled.

9 Pour the remainder of the soaking water into the hole. (If you are planting many roses at once, there won't be enough of the water in which roses

Bare Root Rose on Soil Cone

were soaked. In that case, substitute water mixed with transplant solution.)

10 Cover the bud union with a mound of soil or mulch until the chance of frost has passed.

CARE

Once you have pruned and planted, renew mulch on the ground around your rosebushes so that it's about 3 inches deep. Pine straw is an excellent mulch in the rose garden. Cocoa shells are, too, but are expensive.

Even though there may be a warm spell this time of year, don't begin pulling back the winter-protection mulch from over the bud union until closer to the average last frost date for your county. (You want to avoid damage by a hard freeze.)

WATERING

Water roses deeply after planting and after fertilizing. March tends to be a wet month, so little other watering should be necessary. But if growth has started and rainfall doesn't arrive, water enough to wet the soil about 12 inches deep.

Regularly water **miniature roses** being grown indoors as houseplants. They tend to dry out quickly.

FERTILIZING

See **February** for a discussion of whether to start seasonal fertilizing at pruning time or afterward. Fertilizers made especially for roses are a good choice. There are a number of them, including an organic mixture, Mill's Magic Rose Mix®, which is made in Tennessee. Other organic choices are alfalfa meal and fish emulsion (the latter is usually mixed with water and applied later in the season to supplement the alfalfa meal). Roses respond well to both. Some growers also like to sprinkle a handful of Epsom salts around the base of roses first thing in the spring. It helps produce very green leaves.

General Rules for Fertilizing Roses:

• Follow the directions on the label for the correct amount to use. Smaller bushes (miniatures and those 12 inches tall) should receive a smaller "serving."

• Sprinkle the fertilizer around the rose in a spiral beginning near the base and continuing out beyond the roots.

• Always water thoroughly after applying dry fertilizer.

• Roses are generally fertilized each time a flush of blooms fades (every four to six weeks) until late summer, when most fertilizing stops to allow growth to slow in preparation for cold weather.

PRUNING

See page 203 for the recommended date to prune roses in your area. But remember: **Climbers** and **old-fashioned roses** are *not* pruned until after they bloom.

Read the instructions on page 209 before picking up your loppers—and always wear long sleeves and pants, plus thorn-resistant gloves, which help prevent damage to your hands and arms.

PROBLEMS

Watch out for weeds. Warmer weather encourages growth of weeds, as well as roses. Try to remove them as you notice them—if the bed is mulched, they should pull out easily. If the problem is **bermudagrass** or perennial weeds that spread by underground runners, consult the Extension Service for recommendations.

APRIL

PLANNING

Stick with your landscape plan for roses, and don't be seduced by boxed roses being sold inexpensively at grocery and discount stores. These roses are not of high quality.

Many roses grow nicely in containers—**miniatures, polyanthas,** and some smaller **shrub roses**, for instance. If this idea intrigues you, start shopping for large pots as you make the rounds of garden centers and nurseries this month. A 5- to 8-gallon container will hold a full-size rose, although larger containers are better. A **miniature** should go in at least a 3-gallon pot. It will quickly outgrow anything smaller and need repotting.

If yellow roses are favorites and you have an entire bed of them, consider bordering it with **creeping thyme. Woolly thyme** and **sedum** are nice edging plants with pink roses.

PLANTING

Homeowners in the cooler parts of Zone 6 plant bare-root roses about the middle of the month. See the chart on page 203 for other cities. It's important to plant bare-root roses early so they can develop a good root system before hot summer weather arrives. That doesn't mean that if you've missed the March 15-April 1 planting date for Memphis, for instance, you have to forego roses this year. Instead, buy container roses.

In most parts of Tennessee, you can buy container roses this month—but don't plant them in the ground yet. They were probably potted up in February and March and haven't yet developed enough roots to be removed from their pots. If the soil ball falls apart when you're removing it from the container, it can harm the roots and the plant may not live. There's no rush. Wait until you see some roots growing through the drainage hole. In Kentucky, buy potted roses in May or June.

CARE

If you've been growing **miniature roses** indoors, begin to gradually acclimate them to the outdoors about two to three weeks before the last frost date. First, place them outside all day in a shaded, protected place and bring them indoors at night. Then gradually move them into more and more sun, but still bring the pots back in if frost threatens. After two weeks, prune the roses to 8 inches tall and plant them in the ground, just as you would any other container-grown rose. (See page 210.)

As soon as the chance of frost has passed, remove mulch mounded over the bud union and rake it into the rose bed.

Mulch the rose bed with 3 inches of organic matter if you haven't yet. This helps the soil retain moisture.

WATERING

Once roses have started growing, they will need 1 to 1½ inches of water per week in cooler weather and up to 3 inches when the weather's hot. Drip irrigation, soaker hoses, or in-ground irrigation—which keep the moisture at the base of the plant and don't splash it up on the foliage—are best for roses. If possible, water early in the day so that any plant part that got wet will dry out quickly.

FERTILIZING

Begin fertilizing roses after new foliage appears, if you haven't earlier. Use the recommended amount of a granular rose fertilizer and water it in. Or spread pellets of a slow-release fertilizer such as Osmocote®, which will fertilize the bushes all summer with one application.

The effects of water-soluble fertilizer aren't long lasting, so if you choose to use it on **miniature roses**, you will have to reapply it about twice a month.

PRUNING

In Zones 7 and 8, roses still may be pruned the first two weeks of the month if they aren't pruned earlier. If you prune later, that will delay blooming considerably. If you live in one of those areas and didn't prune roses in time, do a light pruning instead: Remove all dead wood and crossing or rubbing branches, as well as suckers and growth at or below the bud union. Prune all canes back lightly (no shorter than 24 inches on regular bushes, 18 on minis), and then, during the growing season, cut longer stems than usual as you remove roses to stimulate new growth.

In Zone 6, wait until April 15 to prune most roses (all except **climbers, ramblers**, and **species** or **old garden roses** that flower only once a year).

PROBLEMS

Once foliage has begun to appear on bushes, roses must be protected from insects and diseases. Some rose growers spray a fungicide and insecticide every seven to ten days as a preventive. Other people like to use a fertilizer that contains a systemic insecticide. Unfortunately, it doesn't protect against blackspot and mildew, diseases that are serious problems in our hot, humid climate.

It's easier to "go organic" with rose fertilizing and insect control than it is with blackspot and mildew. Part of the problem is that fungal diseases can only be prevented—they can't be cured. By the time they've put in an appearance, it's too late to do much but pick off the affected leaves and destroy them. The other difficulty is that organic controls of rose diseases haven't always proven effective. (And some, such as sulfur, can't be used during our typical high summer temperatures.) If you'd like to try it, one homemade fungicide is 1½ tablespoons baking soda and 1 tablespoon light horticultural oil mixed with 1 gallon of water. Spray onto rosebushes every seven to ten days.

Rose growers who use commercial fungicides recommend alternating two or three different fungicides, instead of using only one.

Don't spray chemicals on **rugosa roses**; they can harm the leaves.

And if your roses get blackspot or mildew anyway? See page 217.

Aphids are attracted to tender new growth of roses. If not controlled, these pear-shaped insects suck the juices from the leaves and buds or blooms. Wash off as many as possible with a spray of water from a hose. If that doesn't get them all, use insecticidal soap. Cut off and destroy any damaged plant parts. If they're present in the garden, ladybugs and syrphid fly larvae will consume aphids.

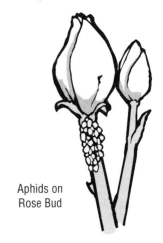

Aphids on Rose Bud

MAY

PLANNING

Don't forget to note in your garden journal the dates that each rose first bloomed this year. It's also good to record pruning times, what new fertilizer or other product you tried, the date of the last frost, and of course, all the details about any new roses you added to the garden this year. Over a couple of years, this information will give you a good picture of rose growing in your part of the state. It will also help if something goes wrong and you need to ask a consulting rosarian for advice.

Want to honor Mom in a special way? Instead of buying her a dozen roses, why not invest in several rosebushes that have flowers in her favorite color? Container roses are an especially good choice. Deliver them with big bows tied to the pots and with a promise to dig the holes and plant the bushes for her. Then get them in the ground the weekend after Mother's Day. Rather than having a dozen roses that last for maybe a week, she'll have dozens each month from now until November.

PLANTING

It's too late in the year to plant bare-root roses, but you should find a good selection of container-grown roses at local nurseries and garden centers. Before you plant, make sure the roots have grown enough that they fill the root ball. If the root ball falls apart during planting, the rose may not survive.

1 Twenty-four hours before planting, water the rose until the excess drains freely from the bottom of the container.

2 Choose a spot for the rose that receives at least six hours of daily sunshine and has well-drained soil.

3 Dig a hole 2 feet wide and 2 feet deep.

4 Mix the soil removed from the hole with organic matter—aged mushroom compost, fine pine bark, rotted leaves, and so forth. Use 2 parts soil to 1 part organic matter.

5 Wearing thorn-proof gloves and long sleeves, place the container on its side and grasp it just below the bud union to remove it from the pot. If it doesn't release easily, use a knife or tin shears to make three or four cuts from the rim to the base of the container.

6 If roots are growing around and around the root ball, loosen them.

7 Place the rose in the hole so that the bud union is 1 inch above ground level or, in the coldest parts of the state, exactly at ground level. You don't want to plant too deeply.

8 Refill the hole about halfway with the amended soil mixture. Water with a transplanting solution.

9 Fill the hole to the top and water again, using a transplanting solution.

10 Mulch around the rose with 3 inches of organic matter, starting 3 inches away from the base of the bush.

CARE

Check **climbing roses** every ten days or so, and tie their canes to their supports.

WATERING

Now that new roses are growing well, see that the soil is kept moist 12 to 16 inches deep. Measure after watering to see how long it takes to accomplish this.

Fertilize rosebushes with a granular rose food after the first flush of blooms has faded. Apply the amount recommended on the label, starting in a spiral near the base of the plant and working outward to just beyond the ends of the canes.

If you have just a few rosebushes, consider buying a bubbler to place on the end of your hose. Then you can put the hose at the base of the plant and the bubbler prevents water from getting on the foliage. It also allows the water to slowly penetrate the soil. If you can't find a bubbler attachment, look for a watering wand. These have many small holes in the head and let you direct the water to the root system but not so that it splashes up on the leaves.

 ## FERTILIZING

Fertilize rosebushes with a granular rose food after the first flush of blooms has faded. Apply the amount recommended on the label, starting in a spiral near the base of the plant and working outward to just beyond the ends of the canes. Then water well. If you applied a timed-release fertilizer to rosebushes last month, you may want to use a water-soluble fertilizer after flowers fade. If you have several rosebushes, put the fertilizer mixture in a hose-end sprayer and spray it over the entire plant. (If you have only one or two roses, put the fertilizer mixture in a watering can and pour it over the bushes.)

 ## PRUNING

When flowers wilt and turn brown, cut them off. Not only can decaying blossoms attract insects, but the bush won't start growing a great crop of new blooms until the old ones are removed.

Each time you cut a rose from the plant—whether to take it indoors or to remove it from the plant because it has faded—you're actually pruning. And how you do it makes a difference in how the bush grows and blooms. The correct procedure is simple:

- Make the cut ¼ inch above a cluster of five leaves that's facing the outside of the bush. This causes a dormant bud to break or begin growing outward. You want the new stem to go toward the outer portion of the bush so as not to crowd the interior, which can create favorable conditions for fungal diseases.

Cutting a Rose

- Always make the cut at a 45-degree angle.
- Using white glue or shellac, seal any cuts that are ¼ inch in diameter or larger.

After they finish flowering, prune **climbers, ramblers,** and old types of roses that bloom only annually. See page 209.

 ## PROBLEMS

Continue weekly spraying to prevent blackspot, mildew, and other fungal diseases. See **April.**

Japanese beetles may become a problem by the end of the month. They are very fond of roses—some roses seem to attract them more than others, but it varies from location to location. Pick them off by hand, and drop them in a jar of soapy water daily or spray with a contact insecticide (ask for advice at your favorite garden center). Spraying Neem (which is organic) over the bushes works well in some locations, but others find that it must be applied before the beetles have discovered the roses and then reapplied after every rain.

JUNE

PLANNING

Take time to smell the roses this month. Cut a bouquet, and take it to cheer someone up or to say thank you. Then go to the library and check out a book about the history and lore of roses. It's fascinating.

PLANTING

If local nurseries still have container roses available, it's fine to continue to plant these, but they may require more watering during the summer.

Why not grow some roses in containers so that you can move them around to where you'd like a little extra color—along a deck when you're having a cookout or on the front porch when you have friends coming for a luncheon. Be sure that you choose a large-enough pot. If it doesn't have drainage holes in the bottom, drill at least four.

Since roses are thirsty plants and containers dry out more quickly than in-ground plantings, be sure you mix a water-holding polymer such as Moisture Mizer™ into the soil before you plant. It holds the moisture in the soil and lets you wait twice as long between waterings than if you didn't use it. (And although they're not cheap, polymers

continue to work for about five years, which gives you a lower yearly cost.)

CARE

As **climbing roses** grow, they have to be tied to their supports. Don't tie it so tight that you damage the canes. Arrange the canes so they are positioned as horizontally as possible—they bloom better that way.

WATERING

As temperatures climb in June, monitor the soil around your roses to see that it doesn't get too dry. Roses need a great deal of water and perform much better when they get it. Water early in the day, and be sure to keep the water off the foliage of the plants if at all possible.

FERTILIZING

Fertilize roses each time they finish blooming and you've removed the dead blooms. The exception is for those **old-fashioned roses** that flower just once yearly. They are fertilized in the spring and then once or twice more, lightly, between June and frost with a balanced granular fertilizer, such as 10-10-10, or with an organic fertilizer such as

Rosetone® or Mill's Magic Rose Mix. Or you can fertilize them once with a timed-release fertilizer. That will help them grow strong stems, which will produce next year's blooms.

PRUNING

Remove flowers when they fade. See page 215. Don't delay too long because this slows down the next round of blooms.

Would you like larger flowers on your **grandiflora** or **floribunda roses**? Pinch off the center bud in a flower cluster, and the two side buds will put on quite a show.

Old garden roses that bloom once a year (in May or June, depending on where you live) are pruned more like shrubs than like **hybrid tea roses**. Remove any dead or diseased wood, as well as suckers, whenever you see them. After they flower, cut the main canes back lightly, if needed to shape the bush. Once the rose is four or five years old, begin cutting one-fourth of the oldest canes back to the ground every year.

Ramblers are vigorous growers that bloom once a season on canes that grew the year before. They are pruned after they've finished flowering. Some rose growers cut **ramblers** back almost to the

As temperatures climb in June, monitor the soil around your roses to see that it doesn't get too dry. Roses need a great deal of water and perform much better when they get it. Water early in the day, and keep the water off the foliage.

ground after they flower. (If you do this, be sure to water and fertilize them well afterward.) But you may also cut out dead and diseased wood, canes smaller than a pencil in diameter, and one-third of the old canes.

Climbing roses that produce just a single flush of blooms each year are pruned lightly after blooming to remove unproductive and too-small canes. Prune repeat-blooming **climbing roses** by removing the flowers back to a five-leaf cluster.

Don't start pruning **climbers** or **ramblers**—except to remove damage—until they're four years old.

Older **climbing roses** and **ramblers** have thick canes that may require the use of a pruning saw, rather than hand pruners or loppers. Folding saws are handy, but it's important to be aware that they cut as you pull the blade toward you, not when you push it away.

You may continue to prune **miniature roses** by shearing them, or you can take the time to prune them as you would other roses—by cutting off the individual blooms back to above an outward-facing five-leaf cluster. At least once a year, it's good to give **mini roses** a "correct" pruning.

 PROBLEMS

Spider mites may attack rose foliage in hot, dry weather. The leaves will appear speckled or spotted. Try spraying with insecticidal soap or light horticultural oil. Ladybugs, lacewings, and predatory insects also control mites. If the infestation is heavy and you feel you need to turn to a chemical control, choose a miticide. A regular insecticide doesn't control spider mites.

If you use a rose fertilizer that contains a systemic insecticide, reapply it as often as recommended on the label. If you forget, your plants will go unprotected. Keep up any regular spraying program that you've started. This is especially important with fungicides. (See page 127.)

If little black round spots appear on the leaves of roses, that's the aptly named disease blackspot. If you leave it alone, the affected leaves will fall off and new leaves will grow. But the problem with ignoring blackspot is that growing new leaves weakens a rose and those diseased leaves down in the mulch hold spores that can continue to affect the plant—next year, as well as this. The best plan of action is to remove diseased leaves and destroy them. Also remove

Timely Tip

The second round of roses may be smaller than the first—both in quantity and the size of the blooms—especially if hot weather has arrived in earnest. That's natural in our part of the country. Flowers may also not last as long on the bush in 90-degree Fahrenheit temperatures as they do in the relatively cool temperatures of late spring and fall. And their coloration may be slightly different in hot weather than in spring. Don't feel discouraged. If you water regularly, fertilize every four to six weeks, and control most pests, your roses will continue to flower nicely at regular intervals throughout summer. Then if you've been faithful with the TLC, the same size and quantity of roses will grace your bushes in the fall.

any from the ground. Then begin spraying a fungicide to prevent any more blackspot. (Fungicides also protect against powdery mildew.)

JULY
Roses

 ## PLANNING

Are you happy with how your roses have performed so far this year? Take time to sit on the screened porch in sight of the rosebushes and record your impressions in your garden notebook—the good, the not-so-good, and what you'd like to do differently next year. If you have any unsolved rose problems, now's the time to track down one of your area's consulting rosarians (see page 202). These are local experts who give free advice about rose selection and growing.

Before you head out on vacation, check the Website of All-America Rose Selections (www.rose.org) for a list of more than one hundred thirty accredited public rose gardens around the country. They're well worth visiting because they contain such a wide variety of roses, including the latest award winners. You can see for yourself how tall and wide various roses get—how the flowers really look (not just in a photo)—and you get to sniff the fragrance for yourself, which is much better than reading about it.

If you like fragrant roses, they're becoming more common, thank goodness. But rose scents vary greatly—from spicy to sort of lemony to musk. Once you learn your favorites, begin to look for more roses whose fragrance is described that way in catalogs and books.

 ## PLANTING

Container roses can actually be planted all summer, but you'll need to water them more often than roses that were planted in the spring. **Miniature roses** adjust well to summer planting. When planted in the ground, they grow taller than they generally do in containers.

 ## CARE

Keep mulch at an even 3 inches deep in rose beds. If pine straw has settled to less than that, buy a bale or two at the nursery and spread some more around. Don't let mulch be pushed up against the base of a rosebush. Instead, move the mulch back so that it starts in a circle 3 or 4 inches away from the bush. When mulch touches rose canes, it can keep them wet, leading to fungal problems.

Once a month, check **climbing roses** to see whether new growth needs to be tied to supports or if any canes tied up earlier have come loose. When winds and thunderstorms knock **climbing roses** down, it's quite a job to get them back up again, so it's best to see that it doesn't happen.

 ## WATERING

Container roses may need watering every other day or even daily by this time. Make sure you don't let them dry out.

Water deeply each time you water roses. Shallow watering helps plants develop shallow roots, which require more frequent watering—and so on, in a vicious cycle. There are a couple of ways to determine how deeply the soil is wet: Dig down into the soil with a trowel—carefully so as not to disturb the rose's roots. You may also stick a thin stake (one of those green bamboo stakes, for example) down in the soil; when you pull it back up, measure how deeply it's wet.

If there's no rain at all and temperatures are high, roses may need watering twice a week.

 ## FERTILIZING

Just as regular as clockwork, roses bloom every four to six weeks, and after they finish, gardeners fertilize them to

Don't let mulch be pushed up against the base of a rosebush. Instead, move the mulch back so that it starts in a circle 3 or 4 inches away from the bush. When mulch touches rose canes, it can keep them wet, leading to fungal problems.

help them form the next set of flowers. Use a granular rose fertilizer or alfalfa meal, usually about a cup per bush. Water well. If you applied a timed-release fertilizer in the spring, you may want to supplement it now with a water-soluble fertilizer made for flowering plants (Super Bloom™, for instance).

Fertilize roses in containers about twice a month if using a granular rose food or weekly if using a liquid mixed with water. Because so much watering is necessary, nutrients drain out of the soil and must be replaced.

 # PRUNING

As you remove dead and dying blossoms at the end of a bloom cycle, you're pruning to encourage new growth and new flowers. Some growers like to cut back farther than just the first five-leaf cluster. On taller, older plants, they may go back to the second or third five-leaf cluster that's facing the outside of the bush and make a cut ¼ inch above it.

 # PROBLEMS

"But that's not the rose I bought!" It happens fairly frequently—a homeowner buys a lovely pink or yellow or white rose and enjoys it for a year. But when it blooms the next season, or the one after that, instead of lush flowers in the original color, the bush now produces puny red single blooms. What happened? Most hybrid roses sold today are grafted—the top part of the bush is one rose and the roots are from another. Traditional rose root stock is very vigorous, which is good, but what happens is that sometimes it's too eager to grow. It puts out shoots at ground level and below the bud union (where the two roses are grafted together). If these aren't promptly pruned off, they will grow aggressively, eventually smothering out the less-vigorous hybrid rose.

What can you do about it?

1 Keep all growth at or below the bud union cut off. This includes suckers that come up from the ground at the base of the bush (these often have to be dug up, instead of just cut off).

2 Buy roses that are called "own root." This means that they aren't grafted. All **miniatures** are grown on their own roots and are hardier as a result. You'll pay more for own-root roses, but many growers think they're worth it.

Some years the Japanese beetles are worse than others. If this is a bad year and you haven't been able to keep after them, you may want to try cutting all the roses and buds off the bush, then spraying the beetles with a contact insecticide. That may lessen the number of beetles you have to contend with for a little while anyway. In years when the beetles are just regular pests, pick them off by hand and drop them in a jar of soapy water, spray them with Neem, or use an insecticide recommended by the Extension Service. Don't use traps—they attract more beetles to the yard.

AUGUST

PLANNING

Is August vacation time in your household? What will happen to the roses if there's little rainfall? Or who will watch out for pests? The solution to the watering is fairly easy. Wind soaker hoses in and among the bushes and connect them to a mechanical timer attached to a faucet. (Water once or twice before you leave to find out how long you need to leave the hoses on.) Then alert a neighbor to what you've done and ask him or her to turn the timer off if rainfall occurs. As for the pest patrol, you may want to trade favors with a fellow rose fancier— I'll keep an eye on your garden while you're away if you'll do the same for me.

Rose fragrance is often at its peak early in the day. Why not walk through your roses tomorrow morning and enjoy the enticing scents?

PLANTING

Potted roses may still be planted the first week of the month, but not afterward. They need time to become established before cold weather arrives. Place the rosebush in the hole so that the bud union is 1 inch above soil level or at soil level (the latter for Zone 6 gardeners— see the maps on pages 18 to 19). Then mulch with 3 inches of organic material—pine straw, cocoa hulls, shredded pine bark, and so forth. Even if you don't usually give your roses winter protection, it's important for roses planted as late as August. (See page 228.)

CARE

Check **climbers** and **ramblers** to see whether canes need to be tied to fences or other supports. They'll bloom better if you can arrange the canes in a fan shape or horizontally.

Remove and destroy any yellowed or diseased leaves that have fallen off the bush and into the mulch. Practicing good sanitation can help prevent insect and disease damage.

If this is your rose bed's first year and you didn't have the soil tested before you started, why not take samples of your soil now and send them off to be tested? The Extension Service will tell you how. Then you'll learn the pH of your soil (which makes a difference in how well roses grow) and get specific fertilizer recommendations for next year. If your soil is too acid, your results will recommend an application of lime, which can be done this fall.

WATERING

Know how much rain has fallen on your rose garden by putting up a rain gauge. Often the difference is striking between the amount of rain that fell at the airport or other official measuring station for your county and what fell in your yard. This is especially true in August, when the weather forecast so often includes scattered thundershowers. Roses need an inch or more of water per week, but you don't want to water any more than you have to.

Containers, on the other hand, need daily watering or at least every second day. If you have to be away, you can set up drip watering that's made for container gardens.

FERTILIZING

In parts of the region with colder winters (Zone 6), stop fertilizing the first part of the month. In Zone 7, stop spreading granular fertilizer before the middle of the month, and in Zone 8, before the end of the month. You want roses to slow down their growth going into winter so they won't be harmed by the first cold snap. If you plan to enter a rose show in September, use a water-soluble fertilizer once this month to help the bush produce larger blooms. (Do this no later than the middle of the month in the colder areas.)

Fertilize roses in containers with a water-soluble plant food for blooming plants twice this month at half the recommended amount.

PRUNING

Promptly prune any dead or dying (brown) wood back to where the cane is green. Seal the cut ends of the stems with white glue, shellac, or clear fingernail polish to prevent borers and other insects from getting into the canes.

Make sure your pruners are still sharp. Dull pruner blades can do quite a bit of damage to rose canes.

Prune off roses as they begin to fade, cutting at a 45-degree angle ¼ inch above an outward-facing cluster of five leaves. This can be the next five-leaf cluster down or several below that. Just make sure the leaves are on the outer part of the bush, not facing the inside. You may have to stand on a ladder to do this for repeat-blooming **climbing roses**.

PROBLEMS

Powdery mildew—a white film on leaves—often shows up on rosebushes in August, especially if fungicide spraying has been spotty because you've been on vacation or frequent afternoon thundershowers keep washing it off. While mildew can be prevented, it can't be cured. Remove affected leaves from the

bush and from the ground beneath. Then fertilize and water the bush to help it grow new leaves. After that, renew a regular weekly schedule of spraying. (See page 213 for a discussion of fungal problems on roses and some options.)

SEPTEMBER

Roses

PLANNING

Many local rose societies have fall rose shows. Why not check with the group nearest you to see if one is scheduled? (You can find out how to contact area rose societies on the website of the American Rose Society, www.ars.org.) A rose show is a wonderful place to learn a great deal about roses—and to fall in love with some new flowers. Society members are always present to give advice and answer questions, too, which can be a big help to novices and even those more experienced who still are looking for answers.

Is there any class of rose you are interested in that you haven't yet grown? Maybe you think **mini roses** are cute, but you've never tried them. Or you're fascinated by the lush, romantic blooms of the **English roses**. This is a good time to start reading on the subject so you'll know whether they're right for you. Some of the **English roses** do better in the South than others. You may want to ask for advice from a consulting rosarian in your area. The same is true of **old gar-**

den roses, which have once again become highly popular. Some are better in our climate than others—and some fit into small home landscapes better than others. Ascertain whether the **old garden rose** you're considering blooms more than once a season. It may not matter to you, but growers have gotten so used to repeat-blooming roses that many feel "cheated" if a rose flowers just one time.

PLANTING

Rose planting season in our region is officially over. If you've moved to the area from elsewhere, you may be used to planting bare-root roses in the fall. But that isn't recommended here; winter weather is simply too variable.

If you have a sunroom or greenhouse, you can plant a **miniature rose** in a good-sized pot and grow it indoors. They need at least eight hours of sun, though, which isn't always easy to provide in winter.

CARE

Sometime in September, perform your two monthly tasks—check and replenish mulch if necessary, and see whether **climbers** or **ramblers** need to be tied to supports.

WATERING

September can be a fairly dry month. That means you may need to water several times this month. Since rosebushes welcome the cooler temperatures of autumn by blooming freely, don't neglect them—give them the moisture they need to produce those beautiful blooms. Avoid evaporation by not watering in the middle of the day. Morning is the best time to water; second best is at least four hours before dark.

Don't let roses growing in containers dry out. Even though temperatures may be cooling down some, the soil in containers is light, so it still dries out quickly.

Just as there's no more planting of roses from now until late winter or early spring, gardeners should stop fertilizing roses before September to help the bushes harden off for winter.

 # FERTILIZING

Just as there's no more planting of roses from now until late winter or early spring, gardeners should stop fertilizing roses before September to help the bushes harden off for winter.

 # PRUNING

Wait until next spring to do extensive pruning. But continue to cut off fading flowers and remove any diseased, dead, or damaged stems or canes. After pruning, seal canes with white glue or shellac. Dig out suckers that have grown up from the roots, and cut off any new stems that are coming from or below the bud union.

 # PROBLEMS

Don't let down your guard when it comes to controlling insects and diseases. It wouldn't matter so much if the problems ended when the roses went dormant, but if they're not stopped now, they can linger over winter and affect your roses next year, too.

Rose scale is much like other types of scale—hard-shelled little insects that are often found on stems and that weaken the plant by sucking the sap. Sometimes scale can be scraped off with a fingernail. Other times you'll need to spray with a light horticultural oil.

Thrips may still be a problem this month on rosebuds. They cause flowers to become distorted and not open. Always remove and destroy the affected blooms. Thrips, like whiteflies, can be controlled with yellow sticky traps. Spiders and lacewings are predators of thrips and so should be encouraged. If an insecticide becomes necessary, check with the Extension Service for a recommendation.

Get rid of weeds before they drop and scatter their seeds. If you have applied a 3-inch mulch, most can be pulled out by hand after a soil-soaking rain.

Timely Tips

If a rose has the same problem repeatedly over a period of two years, seriously consider digging up the rose and getting rid of it. Replace it next spring with a rose that's more disease resistant.

Never plant a new rose where another rose was removed. The new rose simply won't grow well, because of a toxic substance exuded by the roots of the first bush.

If you need to resort to a herbicide to kill **bermudagrass** or perennial weeds that spread by underground runners, be careful to shield the roses so that not even the fumes get near the bushes. Never spray a herbicide (or any other product) when the wind is blowing. In some cases, you may want to apply a herbicide to a weed with a paintbrush instead of spraying it. A herbicide will be more effective if the weeds have been rained on or watered twenty-four hours before you plan to apply the product.

OCTOBER

PLANNING

Has this year's experience with roses got you dreaming about more roses for next year?

- Start collecting catalogs of rose suppliers now. Many rose nurseries accept orders in the fall for delivery at the right planting time in spring. Local nurseries that sell a lot of roses may also let you order ahead. Talk to several and see what their policies are. Also find out how they decide which roses to order for delivery in late winter or early spring.
- Check the All-America Rose Selections Website (www.rose.org) to learn about next year's award-winning roses. AARS roses are grown for at least two years in various test gardens around the United States and Canada, where they're given ordinary care and graded on their performance. While not every rose that wins an AARS award is ideal for the growing conditions in the South, most are disease-resistant bushes that have much to recommend them. They're a good place to start your search for new roses.

- Also ask friends who love roses about their favorites. Many older roses are tried and true, and will give you no trouble whatsoever.
- The selection of top-rated yellow roses is smaller than for other colors, but there are some excellent choices. If you haven't bought the *American Rose Society's Handbook for Selecting Roses*, jot a reminder in your garden notebook to get a copy of the latest edition after the first of the year.

Remember all those times this past growing season that you had to drag a hose around the yard to water your roses? Wouldn't you rather avoid that next year? Now's the time to investigate your watering options (see pages 11 and 12).

PLANTING

October isn't a good month for planting roses. Bare-root roses are planted beginning in late winter or early spring and continuing through mid-spring (depending on which part of the region you live in), and container roses are best planted from late spring through early summer.

CARE

Pick or rake up fallen rose foliage and remove it from the garden. Insects and diseases can overwinter in old leaves that are left on the ground.

In the coldest parts of the area, consider what you're going to do with container-grown roses over the winter. Your choices include:

1 Leave them outdoors, in a protected spot, mounding an organic mulch over the pot and canes. (There should be about 12 inches over the bud union.). You may use anything from shredded leaves (although they blow off rather easily) to aged mushroom compost.

2 Dig a hole big enough for the pot, place the container in the hole, replace the soil around it, and then build up a 12-inch mound of mulch over and around the bush.

As long as there are leaves on a rosebush, it's important to continue protecting them from fungal diseases such as blackspot and mildew. This may be with a commercial fungicide or a homemade concoction.

3 Let the rose stay outside until after the first frost or two (as long as temperatures don't fall into the low-20 degrees Fahrenheit). Then move the containers into an unheated garage or basement for the winter. Many gardeners choose this option for tree roses, which are hard to protect over winter.

 # WATERING

As temperatures cool down more, the need for moisture lessens somewhat. Since rainfall can be abundant this month, you may not have to water. But if there's no rain in a particular week, check the moisture level in the soil around roses.

 # FERTILIZING

Put the rose fertilizer on the shelf until spring. (Make sure it's somewhere that stays dry.) Like other plants, roses are fertilized when they're growing. Since this is a month when roses are usually still blooming (often despite a light frost or two) but not growing, fertilizer isn't needed or recommended.

 # PRUNING

If you live in USDA hardiness Zone 6 (see the maps on pages 18 and 19), stop cutting off dead roses the first week of the month. This tells the rosebush to stop growing, which is essential for its winter survival. Many of the old flowers will form rose hips (seedpods), which is fine.

In some parts of the country, roses are pruned in the fall. But in Kentucky and Tennessee, the only pruning required is to cut too-tall canes back in late November or early December in preparation for applying winter protection. (See page 227.)

 # PROBLEMS

Most insects are no longer a problem by October. But should you spy some, identify them and then take appropriate action.

As long as there are leaves on a rosebush, it's important to continue protecting them from fungal diseases such as blackspot and mildew. This may be with a commercial fungicide or a homemade concoction (like that on page 213). You may not need to spray it every seven days, as you did during the height of the growing season, but don't wait longer than ten days.

NOVEMBER

Roses

Roses

PLANNING

As activities in the rose garden slow down and you begin to bring your garden notebook up to date, begin planning what you'd like to do next year. Gather lists of roses that are favorites with other area gardeners (your local rose society has these, and some may also be found on the American Rose Society's Website at www.ars.org).

Always choose roses first by hardiness for your area and for their disease resistance. Some other criteria that may influence your selection include the type of bush (**hybrid tea, miniature, English rose**), whether the rose is fragrant (and what type of fragrance it has), and the colors of the flowers. Roses aren't necessarily just red, cream, or orange.

- A bicolor rose has one color on the front of the petals and another color on the back. Multicolor roses have more than one color on the front or the back.
- A blend has two colors on the fronts of the petals.
- Striped roses have bands of color on the petals.

As you're planting next year's rose garden, consider the myriad options among the types of blossoms, since a variety of shapes is as important to the landscaping effect as the colors you choose.

- Single roses have five to twelve petals in a single row.
- Semidouble rose flowers have eight to twenty petals in two (or sometimes three) rows.
- A double rose has seventeen to twenty-five petals.
- What's called a full rose has twenty-six to forty petals, and a very full rose has more than that (up to a hundred petals).

The number of petals, combined with what's called *substance* (the thickness of the petals), contributes to the fullness of the flower.

Rose flowers may also be distinguished by interior shape—cupped, pompom, quartered, saucer, and so forth. Rose growers often favor one type bloom over another, although it's fun to try a few of each if you have room for new bushes.

Hankering for a romantic **climbing rose** to clamber up each side of a lovely trellis? Although you'll want to buy locally, start looking through catalogs and at magazine pictures for good examples of what you like and what you think fits best with your overall landscape. Consider also the material from which the trellis or arbor is made. Wood is appealing because it's natural, but consider the difficulty of painting it when needed (since the rose canes will be covering most of the structure all year).

PLANTING

Roses aren't planted until late winter or early spring (see page 203 for planting dates in various parts of the area). But if you need to transplant a rose, that can be done after it has gone fully dormant (usually December). See page 228.

CARE

Rake up old mulch, and remove it from the garden. It sometimes can harbor overwintering insects and their eggs or disease spores. Replace the mulch with 3 or 4 inches of new mulch—shredded leaves, Nature's Helper™, cocoa hulls, pine straw, or whatever your favorite mulch is. Spread the mulch in an even layer over the bed.

When nighttime temperatures are consistently in the upper 20 degrees Fahrenheit, move container roses and tree roses to an unheated garage or basement, or protect them outdoors. See **October**.

Because our area's winter weather can vary so greatly, there are as many opinions about providing cold-weather protection for roses as there are rose growers. Basically, some roses are hardier than others. **Miniatures,** roses grown on their own roots (not grafted), and **shrub roses** tend to be the hardiest. In Zone 7 and Zone 8 (see the USDA Hardiness Zone maps on pages 18 and 19), you may be able to get by during a typical winter without providing winter protection for most of your roses. But then will come an extra-frosty winter that kills some bushes. In Zone 6, winter protection is needed around all grafted roses (those that have a bud union). Usually this is applied beginning around Thanksgiving and into the first two weeks of December in Zone 6 and anytime during December in Zones 7 and 8. See page 228 for details.

 ## WATERING

Except for container roses, which will still need to be watered if they're outdoors, little watering is necessary unless there's no rain and the ground hasn't frozen.

 ## FERTILIZING

There's no need to fertilize roses in November. Wait until planting or pruning time in late winter or early spring. But winter is a good time to investigate the various fertilizers available for roses. Every serious rose grower has a favorite commercial option or homemade mix. Organic rose fertilizers are gaining in popularity because they improve the soil and because they give a slow natural boost to growth rather than a big spurt.

 ## PRUNING

If roses have grown tall this year, cut the canes back to about 4 feet high so they won't whip around in the wind and cause damage. Do this just before you apply winter protection (see **Care**), which is usually after two or three substantial freezes—the end of November to the first of December in the colder parts of the region, from December and into January for the warmer areas (and in milder winters).

 ## PROBLEMS

Check over the rose garden weekly to make sure that all is well. Pay special attention to drainage if you have clay soil. Roses don't like "wet feet" any time of year but especially not in winter.

DECEMBER

Roses

 ## PLANNING

Have you made your holiday gift list with an eye toward making your rose-growing easier and more fun? Every gardener can use a sturdy professional pair of hand pruners and a good sprayer. What about asking for a truckload of mushroom compost or manure that can age in an out-of-the way spot until spring? Or maybe you'd like to build a few raised beds for roses next year. Why not request some stacking stones or landscape timbers?

 ## PLANTING

Once a rosebush is fully dormant, it may be transplanted to another location this month or next—choose a time when the soil isn't too wet or isn't frozen and the temperature is above freezing. First, cut the canes back to 3 to 4 feet high. Dig the new hole ahead of time, and quickly move the rose into the new hole. After replanting, mound the soil 8 to 12 inches over the plant.

 ## CARE

Protecting a rose over winter is an inexact science. Rose growers in warmer areas debate whether they should do it, and those in colder sections debate timing. A typical scenario is to prune rose canes back to 3 feet (in colder climates) or 4 feet (in warmer climates); then mound 8 to 12 inches of organic matter or soil (the lesser amount in Zone 7 and the greater in Zone 6) over the plants, especially over the bud union. For some unknown reason, lighter mulches such as shredded leaves don't work nearly as well for some gardeners as do the heavier mulches—regular soil, potting soil that's been emptied from containers, and mushroom compost. In colder climates, most gardeners prefer to encircle rosebushes with a cylinder of chicken wire and fill it with whatever organic matter they choose. This keeps the protective mulch in place.

 ## WATERING

Lightly water roses that are in the basement or garage once this month.

 ## FERTILIZING

No fertilizing is needed this month.

 ## PRUNING

Roses are typically cut back a little when winter protection is applied. See **Care**. Even if you decide not to mulch your roses heavily for the rest of the winter, cut back extra-long canes that may blow about in the wind and cause damage to one another or loosen the roots from the soil.

 ## PROBLEMS

As a preventive, you may want to spray rosebushes this month with a dormant oil spray to kill overwintering insects and their eggs. Follow the temperature requirements on the label, and make sure no rain is forecast for twenty-four hours. Instead of using dormant oil, some rose growers prefer to spray lime sulfur, which should be directed to the soil around the roses, as well as onto the plants. Both products are organic.

CHAPTER EIGHT

Shrubs

No other group of plants can make such a difference in your landscape as shrubs. That's why if you're planning a new landscape or renovating a tired one, you should invest a good portion of the budget in shrubs.

You plant them once and give them some TLC for the first three years they're in your yard. Then they continue to beautify your landscape with little or no further care on your part.

Shrubs are the most useful plants in your landscape because they offer so much versatility—from the practical (hedges and barriers) to seasonal beauty (springtime flowers and fall berries to feed the birds).

Before you buy new shrubs, you should determine what you want these plants to accomplish in your yard and assess the conditions of the places you want the plants to go. Sometimes homeowners don't think about *why* they're buying a shrub. Maybe it's pretty and they just like the way it looks. And that's reason enough. But often we choose shrubs to accomplish a purpose, and when we do, we need to select the ones that will best fill the need.

HEDGES, SCREENS, AND BARRIERS

Do you need a hedge, screen, or barrier? If so, ask yourself:

- Do I prefer a formal hedge? You'll probably have to trim it four or five times a year, so you'll need to find a shrub that can tolerate frequent shearing.
- What about an informal hedge? It won't need trimming as often, but sometimes homeowners think a shrub's natural growth habit doesn't look neat enough. If you're a neatnik, go for formal.
- What height hedge do I need? All too often, homeowners choose the tallest-growing shrubs for their hedges. If the plants must screen off an ugly area or be a high barrier, that's fine. But if you just want to delineate an area, maybe a low or medium hedge is a better choice. It will need far less pruning.
- What about width? Find out how wide the shrub you're considering grows. Width provides extra privacy, but it can also mean more pruning.
- Do I need an impenetrable barrier? Then do you want a shrub with thorns (**barberry,** for instance) or prickles (such as **holly**), or would you rather have a shrub that grows thick?

SEASONAL COLOR

Kentucky and Tennessee homeowners have a wide choice of flowering shrubs. Here's what to think about when selecting one:

- What season will the shrub bloom? Spring is the most common time for flowering shrubs in this region, but consider also shrubs that bloom in summer (**clethra** and **hydrangea**, for instance) and other times of the year. What a treat it is to look out the window on a chilly February day to see **witch hazel** in full bloom.
- What color are the flowers? Will this color complement whatever else is in bloom in your yard at the same time?

But in a search for seasonal color, don't overlook shrubs with variegated or colored leaves. Many may be evergreen (**euonymous** in green and gold, **barberry** in red, *Osmanthus heterophyllus* 'Variegatus' in green and white). Also look for deciduous shrubs that have excellent fall color (**burning bush**, for example).

Shrubs

Other general decisions about shrubs include:

- Do you want an evergreen shrub or one that's deciduous (loses its leaves in fall)? Evergreens provide structure and form to the yard in winter. But deciduous shrubs may have foliage that turns brilliant colors in the fall before it falls off—and that's a nice addition to the landscape, too. Most gardeners choose a mixture of deciduous and evergreens for variety.
- Are you trying to attract wildlife or have a naturalistic landscape? Look for native plants and those that have berries. (Berries, usually red, but sometimes yellow, orange, or black, add color to the landscape in fall and winter.)

Once you have some idea of the purpose a new shrub will fill in your yard, then you have to match the conditions with a shrub that needs and wants the same thing. It doesn't do you much good to decide you want **evergreen azaleas** if you have full sun or alkaline soil in your yard. Or to put a **rhododendron** in a spot that stays damp.

Light

It's easy if the spot you want to plant a shrub is in full sun or all shade. But most locations are in shade part of the time and in sun the rest of the day. It's up to you to determine how much time the area spends in sun and in shade. And that will dictate which shrubs will grow there.

Drainage

Drainage is a big consideration in our area, where so much of the soil is hard clay, which doesn't drain well. If your home is new or you're new to gardening and aren't sure about your yard's drainage, dig a hole 2 feet deep and 1 foot wide. Fill the hole with water. If all the water drains out within twenty-four hours, drainage should be good. If some is left, you should amend the soil with one-third organic matter (fine bark, compost, rotted sawdust, or leaves) to improve drainage. Or plant in raised beds. If you notice that an area stays wet just about all the time—or at least, for several days after a rain—don't plant a shrub there, or else use one of those listed on page 366.

Space

The one thing that hardly anyone pays much attention to when buying a shrub is what its eventual height and width are going to be. The new shrub is a little thing, after all, sitting there in a one-gallon pot. It looks so lost if you plant it very far away from another shrub or the house. So we make the biggest mistake we can in planting a shrub—putting it where it will quickly outgrow its location. And that's a mistake we pay for over and over—in having to do frequent pruning or eventually having to remove it (always more labor-intensive and expensive than planting).

A warning: Don't put your trust in the word "dwarf." In the plant world, dwarf doesn't mean small. It means only that the dwarf version of a shrub grows smaller than the original. But it can still grow 12 feet tall or higher!

If there's only one thing you take away with you from this book, it should be to know what the mature size of the shrub is and to match it to the available space.

Planting

Most shrubs nowadays are sold in containers. Some are sold balled and burlapped (that is, the rootball is covered with burlap). And a few are sold bare-root (usually by mail order).

How to plant a bare-root shrub:

1 Dig a hole as deep as the length from the bottom of the roots to where they join the top of the plant (the crown) and slightly wider than the spread of the roots.

2 Using the soil removed from the hole, build a cone in the center of the hole, with its top an inch or two lower than the level of the ground.

Shrubs

3 Prune away any dead or damaged roots or stems.

4 Place the shrub on top of the cone of soil, with its roots spread out down the sides of the cone. The crown of the plant should be at about soil level.

5 If your soil is hard clay, mix the rest of what was removed from the hole with one-third compost, Nature's Helper™, or old mushroom compost.

6 Have one person hold the shrub in place while a second person fills the hole with the soil mixture, firming it around the roots. Make sure the crown of the plant doesn't sink below the level of the surrounding ground.

7 Water well.

8 Cover the area around the shrub with 2 to 3 inches of mulch, such as shredded leaves, but don't let it touch the trunk of the plant.

For planting a balled-and-burlapped or container-grown shrub, see page 240.

Pruning

If you choose the right size shrub for the place where it is to go, many shrubs will seldom need pruning unless they've sustained some damage or they need to be shaped. But beyond controlling size, shrubs are also pruned to encourage dense growth (as for a screen or hedge) and to promote an abundance of flowers (**butterfly bush** is a good example of this).

To control the size of a deciduous or broadleaf evergreen shrub, use hand pruners or loppers to thin the plant. This opens it to air and sunlight, while maintaining the natural shape.

1 Remove excessive twiggy growth.

2 Cut off crowded branches and stems that cross or rub one another.

3 Use loppers to cut one-fourth of the largest stems back to the branch from which they grew.

When removing occasional wayward growth from a shrub, always cut back to just above a bud (one that's facing the outside of the plant, if possible).

Rejuvenating a Shrub by Pruning

• The best method: Each year for three years, cut one-third of the shrub's stems back to ground level. This is the ideal way to prune **forsythia** so that it retains its natural shape but doesn't get huge.

• If a shrub has gotten quite overgrown, you may want immediate results. In that case, cut the plant back to within 6 inches of the ground.

Some old plants may not grow back from this traumatic experience. But if the choice is severe renovation or removal, it's usually worth a try. A shrub cut back like this won't be very attractive for at least a year.

Severe Heading Back of a Shrub

There are times of the year that are ideal for pruning some shrubs and not others, and times that are all wrong for some and not others. For example, flowering shrubs need to pruned at a time of year that doesn't remove their flowers. The best times will be noted in the monthly pruning sections.

Shrubs are the foundation of any landscape. Whatever size you decide upon, whatever characteristics you want in a shrub, you're sure to find a number of choices. Shrubs of just about any size, shape, flower and foliage color, and cultural requirements can be found at any good nursery. It's fun to spend a Saturday morning visiting several nurseries to look over what's available and to fine-tune your list. Happy hunting!

Shrubs

Common Name (*Botanical Name*)	Height (Feet)	Width (Feet)	Deciduous or Evergreen	Flowers or Berries	Culture
Aucuba (*Aucuba japonica*)	6 to 15	5 to 10	Evergreen	Berries	Shade, partial shade. Plant in moist, well-drained soil to which you've added organic matter.
Beautyberry (*Callicarpa* species and hybrids)	3 to 10	4 to 8	Deciduous	Berries	Sun to partial shade. Prefers average soil.
Boxwood (*Buxus* species and hybrids)	2 to 20	3 to 25	Evergreen	Berries (inconspicuous)	Sun to partial shade. Avoid clay soil or amend it heavily with organic matter.
Buckeye (*Aesculus* species and hybrids)	8 to 20	8 to 25	Deciduous	Flowers (red or white)	Any light exposure is fine. Moist, well-drained acid soil is ideal.
Burning bush (*Euonymus alatus*)	6 to 20	10 to 20	Deciduous	Berries	Any light exposure is okay. Grows well in any soil except one that stays wet.
Butterfly bush (*Buddleia davidii*)	6 to 15	7 to 10	Deciduous	Flowers (pink, white, purple, blue, and yellow)	Sun. Plant in any type of soil that drains well.
Camellia (*Camellia* species and hybrids)	10 to 15	5 to 10	Evergreen	Flowers (pink, white, red, bicolors)	Partial shade. Prefers acidic soil that's been mixed with fine pine bark. Zones 7 and 8.
Carolina allspice (*Calycanthus floridus*)	6 to 10	6 to 12	Deciduous	Flowers (maroon)	Sun to partial shade. Grows in just about any type of soil.
Crapemyrtle (*Lagerstroemia* species and hybrids)	2 to 30	2 to 25	Deciduous	Flowers (pink, red, lavender, white)	Sun. Place in moist, well-drained soil.

Shrubs

Common Name (*Botanical Name*)	Height (Feet)	Width (Feet)	Deciduous or Evergreen	Flowers or Berries	Culture
Deciduous azalea (*Rhododendron* species and hybrids)	3 to 20	4 to 15	Deciduous	Flowers (cream, yellow, yellow, orange, lavender, red)	Deciduous azaleas require more sun than evergreen azaleas. Half a day is excellent. Give the shrubs moist, acidic soil that's been enriched with organic matter.
Deciduous holly (*Ilex* species and hybrids)	2 to 18	4 to 10	Deciduous	Berries	Sun. Fairly adaptable as to soil, but most prefer it to be well drained. Need a male holly to pollinate the female hollies in order for berries to develop.
Evergreen azalea (*Rhododendron* species and hybrids)	1 to 10	3 to 10	Evergreen	Flowers (pink, red, orange, white, lavender)	Evergreen azaleas bloom and grow best in partial shade not deep shade. Moist, acid, well-drained soil is recommended. Enrich soil with organic matter.
Evergreen holly (*Ilex* species and hybrids)	1 to 8	4 to 15	Evergreen	Berries	Sun, partial sun.
False cypress (*Chamaecyparis* species and hybrids)	4 to 20	6 to 18	Evergreen	Some species have yellow needles	Sun. Moist, well-drained soil.
Florida anise (*Illicium floridanum*)	6 to 10	7 to 12	Evergreen	Flowers (maroon, white)	Partial shade. Keep soil moist.
Flowering quince (*Chaenomeles* species and hybrids)	2 to 10	3 to 10	Deciduous	Flowers (red, pink, white, or orange)	Sun. As long as soil is acid, it tolerates most types of soil.
Forsythia or **yellow bells** (*Forsythia* species and hybrids)	2 to 10	4 to 15	Deciduous	Flowers (yellow)	Sun, partial sun. Not picky about soil.

233

Shrubs

Common Name (Botanical Name)	Height (Feet)	Width (Feet)	Deciduous or Evergreen	Flowers or Berries	Culture
Fothergilla (*Fothergilla* species and hybrids)	2 to 10	2 to 9	Deciduous	Flowers (white)	Sun, partial sun. Doesn't like wet or alkaline soils. Enrich poor to average soil with organic matter before planting.
Glossy abelia (*Abelia* x *grandiflora*)	1½ to 9	3 to 5	Semievergreen	Flowers (white, pink)	Sun, partial sun. Moist, well-drained soil.
Hydrangea (*Hydrangea* species and hybrids)	3 to 10	3 to 10	Deciduous	Flowers (Blue, pink, white, red)	Place where the shrub gets morning sun and afternoon shade, if possible. Provide moist, well-drained soil.
Kerria (*Kerria japonica*)	3 to 8	6 to 10	Deciduous	Flowers (yellow, gold)	Shade, partial shade. Tolerates any soil.
Leucothoe (*Leucothoe* species and hybrids)	2 to 6	3 to 7	Evergreen	Flowers (white)	Shade to partial sun. Avoid windy, rocky sites. Moist, well-drained soil is preferred.
Loropetalum (*Loropetalum chinense*)	6 to 12	5 to 10	Semievergreen to evergreen	Flowers (red, pink, white)	Partial sun to full sun. Acid soil is a must. Zones 7 and 8.
Mountain laurel (*Kalmia latifolia*)	2 to 10	4 to 8	Evergreen	Flowers (pink, red, coral)	Partial sun. Amend acid, well-drained soil with organic matter.
Nandina (*Nandina domestica*)	1 to 8	2 to 4	Evergreen	Berries and flowers (white)	Any type of sun. Shade is preferred for taller, upright-growing cultivars; sun for small, rounded types. Rich, moist, well-drained soil.
Redvein enkianthus (*Enkianthus campanulatus*)	6 to 10	4 to 12	Deciduous	Flowers (cream, pink, red, white, orange)	Sun, partial sun. Moist, well-drained acid soil.

Shrubs

Common Name (*Botanical Name*)	Height (Feet)	Width (Feet)	Deciduous or Evergreen	Flowers or Berries	Culture
Rhododendron (*Rhododendron* species and hybrids)	1 to 15	1½ to 12	Evergreen	Flowers (lavender, pink, red, white, yellow)	Partial sun, partial shade. Excellent drainage and acid soil are essential. Amend soil with organic matter.
Rose-of-Sharon (*Hibiscus syriacus*)	8 to 12	6 to 10	Deciduous	Flowers (pink, red, white, lavender)	Sun, partial shade. Not picky about soil.
Smoke bush (*Cotinus coggygria*)	8 to 25	10 to 20	Deciduous	Flowers (yellow) or fade to pink or purple (smoke) cluster.	Sun. Tolerates any soil that's well-drained.
Spirea (*Spirea* species and hybrids)	1½ to 9	4 to 8	Deciduous	Flowers (white, pink)	Sun, partial sun. Adapts to all soils except those that don't drain well.
Summersweet (*Clethra alnifolia*)	4 to 10	4 to 8	Deciduous	Flowers (white, pink)	Partial sun, partial shade. Likes acid soil and can be placed in wet spots.
Viburnum (*Viburnum* species and hybrids)	2 to 30	4 to 15	Deciduous or evergreen, depending on species	Flowers (white, pink) and berries	Sun, partial sun. Slightly acidic, well-drained soil.
Virginia sweetspire (*Itea virginica*)	3 to 5	3 to 6	Deciduous	Flowers (white)	Sun to partial shade. Likes wet soil.
Weigela (*Weigela florida*)	6 to 9	6 to 11	Deciduous	Flowers (pink, red, white, yellow)	Sun, partial sun. Grows in average soil.
Witch hazel (*Hamamelis* species and hybrids)	6 to 30	10 to 25	Deciduous	Flowers (yellow, red, orange, rust)	Sun, partial sun. Good choice for clay; likes to stay moist.

JANUARY

PLANNING

On a cold winter evening, plop down beside the fireplace with a warm cup of hot chocolate and read through entries in your garden notebook or journal about the shrubs in your yard. Have you made notes about shrubs that you saw in others' yards or in public gardens that you wanted to try? Maybe this is the year to see how they fit into your landscape. Check catalogs and ask at your favorite nursery.

Or maybe you've noted the same problem several years in a row. Save yourself from facing the same difficulty again this year by calling the Extension Service office and asking for advice.

As you pore over those garden catalogs that are so enticing this time of year, look for these important words: *disease-resistant* and *insect-resistant.* Homeowners often insist they want a low-maintenance landscape. Well, one key to having that is to avoid plants that are highly attractive to insects or that are subject to certain diseases. Why buy trouble?

PLANTING

Yes, it's possible to plant deciduous shrubs this month—provided the ground isn't frozen. Leave the shrub in the basement, garage, or other protected spot while you dig the hole, following the instructions on page 240. Carefully firm the soil around the rootball so that no holes or pockets remain that will allow in cold air, which can harm roots. Mulch with 3 inches of organic material, such as shredded leaves.

CARE

If temperatures are predicted to fall into the low 20 degrees Fahrenheit or below, you may want to move shrubs in containers into the garage overnight for protection. They shouldn't be placed in a heated area (this could cause them to break dormancy, which could be fatal when they were moved back outside). But place them near windows if you expect to keep them in the garage or basement for a day or two, during a prolonged cold spell.

Some **camellias** will bloom during warm spells this month. Listen to the weather forecast each morning and evening so you can cut the blooms and bring them indoors to vases when cold is predicted. If the predicted cold is just overnight and the next day is expected to warm up above freezing, you may be able to protect the flowers by covering the bush with a heavy quilt or blanket. (Don't use plastic; when the sun shines on it the next day, it burns the leaves of the **camellia**.) Temperatures in the 20s don't harm **camellia** buds that haven't opened—just the opened flowers.

When the ground freezes, evergreen shrubs can't take up water from the soil to replace that lost through respiration. Then, when morning sun hits the frozen leaves, they "burn"—dry out and turn brown. (This can also happen when shrubs are buffeted by drying winds.) Some gardeners spray susceptible evergreen shrubs with an antidessicant spray, such as Wilt-Pruf®, to prevent this. Not everyone agrees that this helps, but you may want to treat a few shrubs that have had this problem in the past and leave one or two untreated to see what you think.

In winter, how do you know whether a branch is dead or alive? The fingernail test will tell you: Scrape a tiny bit of the surface with your fingernail. If you see green underneath, that's live wood. If it's brown and dull, it's dead.

 # WATERING

Shrubs planted in the yard rarely need watering this time of year. But those in containers might. Make sure the soil isn't frozen. If you leave shrubs in containers in the garage for a few days, they probably will need watering.

 # FERTILIZING

Because shrubs aren't growing, they don't need fertilizer this month. But if you're thinking of planting new shrubs this year or if some of your shrubs haven't been doing as well as you'd expected, consider having a soil test done to find out how much fertilizer you should use and what type.

 # PRUNING

It's still a bit early to prune most shrubs. But anytime a shrub has dead or damaged branches, it's wise to take care of them. Using hand pruners, loppers, or a pruning saw (depending on your prefer-

 ## Timely Tip

The best time to cut a **camellia** bloom to bring it indoors is when the bud is just beginning to show color. It should last in a vase for up to a week, especially if kept in a cool room. Don't toss away the foliage when the flower fades. It will look nice for several weeks longer and can be used as greenery in another arrangement.

Check **pussy willow** stems. If they're plump, cut some and bring them indoors to a vase of water. They're guaranteed to raise your spirits and encourage you to believe that spring is really on its way.

ence and the size of the stem), cut dead branches back to the main branch or to the ground. Prune damaged branches to live wood and just above a bud. In winter, how do you know whether a branch is dead or alive? The fingernail test will tell you: Scrape a tiny bit of the surface with your fingernail. If you see green underneath, that's live wood. If it's brown and dull, it's dead.

PROBLEMS

Keep an eye out for deer or rodent damage, if that's been a problem for you in the past. On warmish days, you can spray repellents or pepper sprays on your shrubs to keep animals from doing too much damage. But tall fences are the only sure cure for really hungry deer. If trunks are being damaged by wildlife, loosely circle the shrub with a cylinder of chicken wire. Deer-Off® is the most weather-resistant of the repellents, so you don't have to reapply it as often.

FEBRUARY
Shrubs

PLANNING

Look at your yard, paying particular attention to your shrubs. What do you see? Are the shrubs in your landscape providing color this time of year, or do they mostly fade into the background? If you'd like a more lively winter landscape, consider these shrubs. Their colorful or interesting bark, stems, twigs, or buds are visually appealing in a season when everything else seems to be brown.

• **Crapemyrtle**—many have beautiful bark
• **Deciduous holly**—berries that persist into winter
• **Harry Lauder's walking stick** (*Corylus avellana* 'Contorta')—twisted stems, leaves, and twigs
• **Kerria**—bright green stems
• **Witch hazel**—red, orange, or yellow flowers in winter

PLANTING

In the warmest sections of the area, bare-root shrubs can be planted near the end of the month, if the ground isn't frozen. Before planting, soak bare-root shrubs overnight in a bucket or tub of tepid water into which you've added several stems from a **weeping willow**, if possible. (The **willow** contains a chemical that encour-

ages root formation.) Do this in your garage or basement, where the soaking shrubs will be out of the weather. Follow the planting tips on page 240.

Container-grown deciduous shrubs may be planted this month if the ground isn't frozen. It's best to wait to plant evergreens. Due to with their small root systems, they may not be able to take up enough water from the soil during prolonged freezes.

If a few warm days have you itching to get out and garden, it's fine to prepare holes wherever you know you'll be planting new shrubs in spring. It's important to cover any holes, though, with a board, so no one can fall in by accident.

CARE

In most parts of our region, snow does not last too long on plants because temperatures warm up in a day or two and melt it. But occasionally we get a heavy snow that hangs around a few days. These can sometimes bow over shrubs. Most deciduous shrubs are flexible enough to shrug these off, but the leaves and needles of evergreens can catch and hold the snow. If you think the weight of the snow may cause damage, try to brush the snow off **yews** or, on other shrubs, lift the branches up from

beneath using a broom. Don't try to do anything if shrubs are covered with ice; you're more likely to cause harm than to help.

Are your tools in good shape for another growing season? Sharpen dull blades of loppers and pruners with a metal file, and coat them lightly with oil. Or spray a lubricant onto moving parts to keep them working smoothly and to prevent rust. If one of the blades of your favorite pair of hand pruners was damaged last year, you may be able to find a replacement. Look for an e-mail address on the company's Website.

WATERING

If precipitation has been less than usual, container-grown shrubs may need watering whenever the soil isn't frozen. Poke a stick into the soil to see whether it comes out wet. If it does, watering is not necessary. If the stick is dry, water until the excess runs out the drainage hole. Also water shrubs planted last fall or this winter, if rainfall has been lacking and the ground is not frozen.

FERTILIZING

The purpose of fertilizer is to aid plant growth, so when plants aren't growing, they don't need it and can't use it. Since shrubs aren't growing in February, there's no need to fertilize any of your shrubs this month.

 # PRUNING

Take care of any storm damage soon after it occurs. Broken stems and branches provide places for insects to enter plants and can become home to diseases.

Toward the end of the month, if the weather is mild, you may want to start pruning overgrown deciduous shrubs that produce berries or that flower in summer. These include **beautyberry, burning bush**, **deciduous holly, rose-of-Sharon**, and **summersweet**. Prune **butterfly bush** and **smooth hydrangea** (*Hydrangea arborescens*) to about a foot tall. Wait to prune other **hydrangeas**. Do *not* prune any spring-flowering shrubs now. Wait until they've finished blooming. See page 231 for a discussion of pruning techniques.

Branches of flowering shrubs may be forced into bloom in the house a month or two before they would bloom outdoors. Some good choices are **bridalwreath spirea** (*Spirea prunifolia*), **forsythia, flowering quince, kerria**, and **spicebush** (*Lindera benzoin*). Here's how to do it:

1 Cut 12- to 18-inch stems with the biggest buds on them. Do this on a day when the temperature is above freezing.

2 Slit and scrape the ends of the branches about 3 inches up. (Some gardeners hit the ends of the stems with a hammer to slit them.)

3 Place the branches in a container of warm water for twenty-four hours.

4 Pour out the water from the container and fill it with cool water mixed with floral preservative (from a florist or craft supply store).

5 Place the container in a relatively dark spot, such as a basement, where the temperature is kept between 60 and 65 degrees Fahrenheit.

6 When the buds show color, move the container into average household temperatures and where the branches can get light but no sun (a north-facing windowsill or back a bit from an east window).

7 Add water to the vase as necessary, or replace the water if it isn't clean. Add more floral preservative.

8 When flowers begin to open, move the vase into full sun.

PROBLEMS

Try to keep deicing salt away from the roots of shrubs; it can damage them. If large or valuable shrubs are right next to the front walkway or your driveway, consider using the more environmentally friendly magnesium chloride or calcium acetate.

If scale or lace bugs have been a problem on shrubs over the past year, a warm February day is a good time to apply a coat of horticultural oil, sometimes called *dormant oil*. This organic treatment smothers the scales and other insects. Make sure temperatures will remain above 45 degrees Fahrenheit for twenty-four hours after application and that no precipitation is in the forecast.

239

MARCH

 PLANNING

March rains may remind us that this could be a good time to talk with a landscape architect or designer about how to solve drainage problems. If you have just a few wet spots in your yard, consider planting shrubs that don't mind heavy, wet soil:

- **Carolina allspice** (*Calycanthus floridus*)
- **Inkberry** (*Ilex glabra*)
- **Redosier dogwood** (*Cornus sericea*)
- **Summersweet** (*Clethra alnifolia*)
- **Swamp azalea** (*Rhododendron viscosum*)
- **Tartarian dogwood** (*Cornus alba*)
- **Winterberry** (*Ilex verticillata*)

 PLANTING

Although shrubs may be planted in our region many months of the year, March and April are ideal times because the weather is warming up, growth is starting, and rainfall is usually ample. If it's been a rainy month, test first to see whether the soil is dry enough to work with (see page 38). To plant a container-grown or balled-and-burlapped shrub, water the shrub well, then:

1 Move the shrub by the rootball, never by the stem.

2 Dig a hole two to three times as wide as the rootball and about the same depth. (Measure a balled-and-burlapped rootball before digging so that you don't have to keep moving it in and out of the hole if you missed the mark.)

3 Mix the soil that's removed from the hole with fine bark, compost, peat moss, or another organic material. Add one-fourth to one-third organic matter to the soil, depending on how bad your soil is. (You can skip this step if you're planting in an area where the soil has been amended or where it's naturally of high quality.)

4 Remove the shrub from its container. If the roots are tightly wound around the rootball, loosen them. Place the shrub in the hole. For a balled-and-burlapped plant, loosen the top of the covering, toss away the twine, and place the shrub in the hole.

5 Check to be sure that the shrub is growing at the same level it did before.

6 Remove the covering from around the roots of a balled-and-burlapped shrub and slide the wrapping out of the hole. Discard the wrapping.

7 Fill the hole halfway with the soil mixture.

8 Water, using a transplanting solution (available at garden centers).

9 Add the rest of the soil.

10 Water again, using a transplanting solution.

11 Using the extra soil, make a rim or saucer around the hole and fill that with water.

12 Mulch around the planting area, but not in the saucer, which will hold water for the shrub during its important first year in your yard.

Hole Height and Width

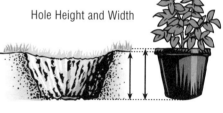

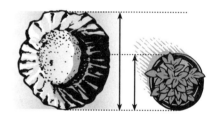

 **CARE**

Early spring, before garden tasks become so numerous in the yard, is an excellent time to check the mulch around the shrubs in your yard and add more to bring the level up to 3 inches. Don't form conical "mountains" of mulch, and do be sure to keep the mulch a few inches away from the shrubs' stems to avoid

It's important to water those shrubs that have been planted in your yard during the past three years. This helps get them off to a good start. If rainfall is less than an inch per week, water slowly and deeply at ground level.

disease problems. If you have a large yard and a great deal of mulching to do, consider ordering pine straw, fine bark, or whatever mulch material you prefer and have it delivered. You won't have to schlep bags back and forth from the driveway to the back of the property, and you'll always have mulch on hand.

Weeding goes easier when done after a rainfall.

WATERING

Mature shrubs often don't require much supplemental watering (see page 246 for a list of those that may need watering during dry spells). But it's important to water those shrubs that have been planted in your yard during the past three years. This helps get them off to a good start. Follow the usual rule: If rainfall is less than an inch per week, water slowly and deeply at ground level, recognizing that (unless the shrub was just planted), all the roots aren't concentrated right around the trunk; they're spread out.

FERTILIZING

Some gardeners don't like to use chemical fertilizer around shrubs and instead prefer nature's way—letting organic material slowly break down and provide

a mild source of nutrients for the plants. Those gardeners can rake off the mulch around a shrub and apply 2 inches of composted cow manure or aged mushroom compost around the base of the shrub. Water, and then replace the mulch in a week or so. Cottonseed meal is also an excellent organic fertilizer for shrubs. Follow the directions on the container.

March, April, and May are the best months in which to fertilize shrubs in this area. You may apply granular fertilizer (10-10-10, for instance) according to package directions as soon as the shrub has begun to leaf. Or you can divide the total amount by three and spread one-third at the end of March, one-third at the end of April, and one-third at the end of May. That gives your shrubs a gentle and gradual boost. Spread the fertilizer in a circle outward from the main trunk. To avoid burning, keep the fertilizer off the leaves or stems (wash it off quickly should it accidentally fall onto the shrub). Water the shrub after fertilizing. If you prefer to use a timed-release fertilizer, wait until April when the weather has warmed up a bit.

Azaleas and **rhododendrons** prefer an acid fertilizer. Fertilize **butterfly bush** after pruning it. (See **Pruning**, in the next column.)

 PRUNING

If you didn't cut your **butterfly bush** back to about a foot tall last month, do so now. Because **butterfly bush** blooms on new wood—that is, stems that it grows this year—pruning it severely causes increased new growth and therefore an abundance of flowers.

Remove one-third of the old stems of **bottlebrush buckeye, beautyberry, bush cinquefoil**, and **Carolina allspice**. Cut them back to ground level. On *Hypericum* and **summersweet**, cut only one-fourth of the canes annually.

Early in the month is a good time to renovate old **boxwoods**. (See page 231.)

PROBLEMS

If you keep a mulch around shrubs, weeds are usually not numerous and are fairly easy to eradicate by hand. Should you have problems with perennial weeds or bermudagrass getting into shrub areas and be tempted to use a weedkiller, be very careful to follow a few rules so the product doesn't harm the shrub:

- Spray on a day when there's no wind.

- Use some sort of a shield (a piece of cardboard, for instance) to keep the chemical from touching the shrub's foliage or stems.

APRIL

PLANNING

One of the delights of **evergreen azaleas** is the wide range of flower colors. But beware if you're mixing lots of different **azaleas** in close proximity in your yard, especially over a period of several years. If you buy two different cultivars of **azaleas**—both with red flowers—they often won't be the same hue. And the same is true of the various shades of red, orange, and pink—which, unfortunately, don't combine harmoniously. What seemed like red at the nursery may appear to be more orangish or pinkish when you get it home and put it next to the red **azaleas** you already own. One solution is to always buy **azaleas** when they're in bloom. Buy one plant, take it home, and see whether its flowers harmonize with the **azaleas** you already own. Then go back and buy as many as you want. Another way to solve this common problem is to always save the labels of all the plants you buy, especially shrubs and trees. Keep them in a manila envelope with your garden notebook so that you can find them quickly. Then you'll be able to tell the nursery owner what you have in your yard now.

Your yard should look wonderful this month, so get out the camera. It's fascinating to look back at yearly garden photos a few years later. You may be surprised at how things have grown and gradually changed. Photos can also show us, sometimes more clearly than when we're on the spot, where a new shrub or other landscape element is needed. Or that an old shrub has reached the end of its usefulness and should be removed.

April is probably the month in which homeowners buy most shrubs. It's the time when warm weather calls to us and we feel the need to get out and plant. So we end up at the garden center, bowled over by the plants. We can't wait to get them home. If you buy a few flats of annuals that you don't need, it won't matter much; you can always find a spot for them. But a shrub purchased on impulse is a different story. How does it fit into your landscaping plan? Do you have the right conditions for it in your yard? Instead of buying it on the spot, write down the name of the shrub that impresses you, come home, and look it up in the *Tennessee Gardener's Guide: Third Edition* or the *Kentucky Gardener's Guide*. Then maybe you'll discover it's exactly the plant you need in your yard. If it isn't, that's valuable knowledge, too. And you've been saved from making an expensive mistake.

PLANTING

This is an excellent month to plant shrubs—deciduous, evergreen, flowering—whatever your yard needs most.

See **March** for shrub planting instructions. One important key is to make sure that the shrub isn't planted any lower than it grew before. Before planting, see whether the soil is dry enough to work. Pick up a ball of soil and squeeze it in your hand. If it forms a hard ball, the soil is too wet. If it forms a ball that then falls apart, it should be fine.

CARE

The easiest way to damage your shrubs is with a string trimmer. Next is with a lawn mower. Why take a chance on harming a good shrub? Remove weeds and grass in a wide circle around shrubs, fill it in with 3 inches of organic mulch, and then it won't be necessary to mow or trim close to shrubs.

WATERING

Keep any eye on newly planted shrubs. Because they haven't developed extensive root systems yet, they need water more frequently than established shrubs—maybe as often as twice a week in the first month they're in your yard, even if rainfall is about an inch a week. Water slowly enough that there's no runoff and the ground gets soaked 6 to 10 inches deep. If you have a border of shrubs or new foundation shrubs, con-

This is an excellent month to plant shrubs—deciduous, evergreen, flowering—whatever your yard needs most. One important key is to make sure that the shrub isn't planted any lower than it grew before.

sider using a soaker hose or putting drip irrigation at the base of the plants. It will water efficiently without your spending a great deal of time doing it by hand.

FERTILIZING

If you didn't fertilize shrubs last month, do it now. If you applied one-third of the recommended amount of granular fertilizer at the end of March, do the same at the end of this month, too. See page 241.

PRUNING

If the winter was colder than normal, wait until **crapemyrtle** begins to leaf before pruning what you think are dead stems. It's very difficult beforehand to know which portions were killed and which are alive.

If they need it, prune deciduous **magnolias**, such as **star magnolia** (*Magnolia*

stellata), by thinning (see page 231) within a month after they have finished flowering. Not all shrubs need pruning every year—many need minimal pruning—but for spring-flowering shrubs, the best time to prune them is right after they finish blooming. Actually, what you want to do is prune spring bloomers within a month after they stop flowering, but sometimes you get busy and forget. So it's usually easier to remember to do it when flowers first fade. Why not wait two months or do it in the fall? Because shrubs that bloom in spring begin forming next year's flower buds beginning in late spring and continuing all summer. When you prune late, you'll be removing the flowers that you would have enjoyed the following year.

If a hedge has become overgrown or straggly, it may be rejuvenated by cutting it down to about 6 inches high. Or you can cut one-third of the stems back to the ground each year.

PROBLEMS

Aphids are tiny insects that are very fond of tender new growth on plants. They like to suck the juices out of it. Since aphids congregate on new leaves and stems, you may notice them. Or you may see that new growth isn't as green and fresh-looking as it should be. Try washing aphids off shrubs with a spray of water from the hose (aim under leaves, too). Don't use such force that you tear the leaves. Once the water has dried, spray with insecticidal soap. Lady bugs also eat large quantities of aphids.

Tiny yellow speckles on **evergreen azalea** leaves may indicate that lace bugs are present. Ask the Extension Service or a good garden center for advice on controlling lace bugs.

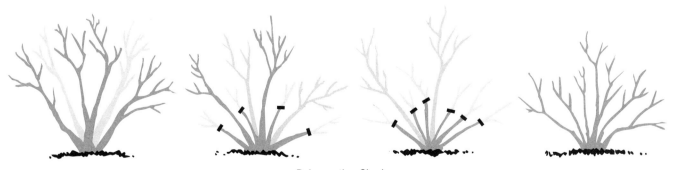

Rejuvenating Shrubs

MAY

 PLANNING

Want to attract more butterflies to your garden? Shrubs can help. There's still time to plant shrubs that are favored by these "winged jewels." Some that you'll want to consider are:

- **Azalea**
- **Blue mist shrub** (*Caryopteris incana*)
- **Butterfly bush**
- **Button bush** (*Cephalanthus occidentalis*)
- **Daphne** (*Daphne* species and hybrids)
- **Glossy abelia**
- **Lilac** (*Syringa* species and hybrids)
- **Mock orange** (*Philadelphus* species and hybrids)
- **Privet** (*Ligustrum sinense*)
- **Snowball** (*Styrax* species and hybrids)
- **Summersweet**
- **Virginia sweetspire**

Think about moving beyond purple or lilac flowers when you buy your next **butterfly bush**. You can now find **butterfly bushes** with red, pink, white, or yellow blooms.

 PLANTING

May is a good month to transplant shrubs that are growing in containers around your yard or on the deck or patio. Once these have been in their containers for two or more years, they're either ready for a larger container or they need fresh soil. Because packaged potting soil is too lightweight for outdoor shrubs, you should make your own mix. One mix recipe to consider is 2 parts top soil, 1 part Nature's Helper™, 1 part commercially composted cow manure (from a 40-pound bag), and ¼ part sand. Add a water-holding polymer, such as Moisture Mizer™, according to package directions. (Never use more than called for on the label.) That will help hold moisture in the soil so you don't have to water quite as often. Then mix in a timed-release fertilizer, such as Osmocote®. Place a piece of screening (or a coffee filter) over the drainage hole, pour in the moistened soil mix, then place the shrub in the container. Water and then fill the container to within an inch of the rim with soil. Water again.

It's fine to plant all types of container-grown shrubs in the yard this month. Tips for planting are on page 240.

 CARE

When was the last time you checked the mulch beneath your shrubs? Since this is their first line of protection from heat, drought, and weeds, take time this month to make sure the mulch is about 3 inches deep everywhere.

 WATERING

Shrubs growing in containers will need watering much more often than those planted in the ground. Every time you water pots or hanging baskets of annuals, check the soil of shrubs on decks and porches to see whether they are dry, too. The larger the container, the longer it takes for the soil to dry. Plastic will hold moisture longer than clay or terra cotta. But once temperatures start to climb, all container-grown plants need frequent watering. Shrubs are especially vulnerable because if they're allowed to dry out, they probably won't recover.

When using a sprinkler to water the lawn, try to make sure the water doesn't get onto shrubs. Wet shrubs can lead to powdery mildew or fungal diseases.

May is a good month to transplant shrubs that are growing in containers around your yard or on the deck or patio. Once these have been in their containers for two or more years, they're either ready for a larger container or they need fresh soil.

FERTILIZING

If you haven't fertilized shrubs at all this spring, feed them now with a shrub fertilizer applied according to directions.

Those who fed their shrubs one-third of the recommended amount of granular 10-10-10 fertilizer the last weeks of March and April should finish the regimen by applying the last third at the end of the month. Spread the fertilizer in a spiral outward from the main trunk. To avoid burning, keep the fertilizer off the leaves or stems (wash it off quickly should it accidentally fall onto the shrub). Water the shrub after fertilizing.

With container-grown shrubs, homeowners have several choices when it comes to fertilizer. As noted in the **Planting** section for this month, a timed-release fertilizer that feeds all season is one option. You may also use a granular fertilizer this month, as you do with shrubs that are planted in the ground. Or you may use a water-soluble fertilizer every other week from now through the middle of July.

PRUNING

Often all the pruning that **evergreen azaleas** need is some shaping of errant growth. But if a plant has gotten very

straggly or overgrown, an **azalea** may be pruned severely by cutting it back to 6 to 12 inches high.

This month is last call for pruning **bridal-wreath spirea, deutzia, flowering quince, forsythia**, and **mock orange**, as well as **azalea**. If you prune these spring-flowering shrubs later than the end of May, you'll be lessening or eliminating next year's flowers.

How to prune an overgrown **forsythia**? It's easy. Each year for three years, cut one-third of the stems back to the ground. That preserves the shrub's attractive shape but makes it a more manageable size.

Snap off faded blooms of **rhododendrons** and **mountain laurel**.

Each time a hedge has 2 to 3 inches of new growth, use hedge trimmers to shear the top and sides back to just about the place where you trimmed it the last time. Start at the bottom and work up so that the base is wider than the sides. If a hedge needs to be rejuvenated, see page 243.

PROBLEMS

If spring was wet, you may notice what appear to be hard green, brown, or white "growths" on your **azaleas**. These are

galls. Remove them by hand and dispose of them away from the garden.

What's causing the yellow leaves on your **boxwood**? There may be several causes—from dogs wetting on the same spot over and over to the soil having the wrong pH for **boxwoods**. Sometimes it takes some detective work to come up with the answer by the process of elimination. If you see little trails in the leaves, though, the cause is leaf miners. Check with the Extension Service for recommended products that will help take care of the problem. Often a systemic insecticide is applied to the soil.

A whitish coating on **crapemyrtle** leaves is powdery mildew. This usually affects only older shrubs since most of the newer cultivars (the ones with Indian names) are mildew-resistant. Increasing air circulation in and around the shrub helps prevent mildew. For severe cases of mildew, ask a nursery for advice about fungicides. One organic remedy that helps prevent new outbreaks of mildew fairly well, in my experience, is 1 tablespoon baking soda and 1 tablespoon light horticultural oil (sun oil) mixed with 1 gallon of tepid water and sprayed on plants.

JUNE

 PLANNING

Are you thinking about your summer vacation? Why not plan to visit a garden or two wherever you go? Not only is it enjoyable to see public gardens of all sizes, but you can usually pick up quite a bit of helpful information and even learn of new plants that should grow well in your garden. Trial gardens and arboreta associated with universities are especially good for visiting because they are seen as teaching tools. Plants are well labeled and often include new cultivars that you may not have seen. Take your camera along and capture some of your favorites on film.

The beginning of the month isn't too late to plant new shrubs. What about some that flower in summer?

- **Buckeye (red** and **bottlebrush)**
- **Butterfly bush**
- **Crapemyrtle**
- **Hydrangeas**
- **Rose-of-Sharon**
- **Summersweet**

 PLANTING

Although shrubs that come from the nursery in containers may be planted just about any month of the year (provided the ground isn't frozen in winter and you're prepared to water quite a bit in summer), it's best *not* to plant when temperatures are in the mid-80 degrees Fahrenheit and above. June should offer some milder days for shrub planting, though. If it's been a while since you planted shrubs or you're new to gardening, see page 240 for directions.

 CARE

You probably know that the color of some **bigleaf hydrangea** flowers depends on the pH (acidity or alkalinity) of the soil in which the shrub grows. Low pH, which indicates acidity (6.5 and lower), produces blue flowers. High pH, which indicates alkalinity (7.0 and above), produces pink flowers. The problem usually comes when your soil's pH is in the middle and the flowers don't have a distinct blue or pink cast. You can change that by adding dolomitic lime to the soil to make it more alkaline or aluminum sulfate (soil sulfur is another choice) to make it more acid. Ask at a nursery about this technique. There are also several **hydrangeas** that produce flowers that stay pink, no matter what your soil is like.

 WATERING

As temperatures rise, shrubs are more likely to need occasional watering if rainfall doesn't measure an inch per week. Many mature shrubs can go several weeks without receiving moisture, but some can't—and these are the ones that should be watered first if there are no water restrictions. Which are most vulnerable to lack of moisture?

- Shrubs planted in the past year (check them twice weekly)
- Shallow-rooted shrubs (such as **azalea**, **clethra**, and **hydrangea**)
- Shrubs that are developing fall berries or flowers for next spring
- Plants that need constantly moist soil

These are the mature shrubs most likely to need supplemental watering during summer dry spells: **aucuba, beautyberry, butterfly bush, camellia, evergreen azalea, fothergilla, redvein enkianthus, hydrangea, leucothoe, rhododendron, summersweet**, and **witch hazel**.

To check the level of moisture in the soil, insert a thin stake or stick into the ground and measure to see at what point it comes out moist. Water if if the soil is dry in the top 4 to 6 inches. You can use the same method to measure whether shrubs in containers need watering. This

Many mature shrubs can go several weeks without receiving moisture, but some can't—and these are the ones that should be watered first if there are no water restrictions.

is a good idea if you're not sure how much moisture a stray thunderstorm provided. Daily check shrubs growing in containers to make sure they haven't dried out.

FERTILIZING

The only shrubs that need fertilizer during June are those in containers. If they weren't fed with a granular or timed-release fertilizer in the spring, mix a liquid or soluble fertilizer with water and apply it sometime this month.

PRUNING

Trim hedges when shrubs have 2 to 3 inches of new growth. If you have a short hedge that consists of broadleaf evergreens (**holly** or **boxwood**, for example), you may find that you get better results with hand pruners than with an electric trimmer since the pruners won't cut the leaves in half.

Shear needled evergreens—**arborvitae, false cypress, juniper** and **yew**—early in the month if you're maintaining a formal shape. It's fine to use an electric trimmer to do this.

Pinch candles (new growth) of **mugo pine** in half to encourage denser growth.

PROBLEMS

If **bermudagrass** grows over into shrub beds, try pulling it out by hand. If you spend ten minutes early in the morning weeding, it won't be a burden. If the problem has gotten out of hand, consider spraying a nonselective herbicide such as Roundup® (remember that broadleaf weedkillers won't affect grass). If so, protect your shrubs with cardboard (or even plastic dry-cleaner bags, if you make sure that no sun is shining on the shrub) before you apply. Remove them as soon as the chemical has dried. Or dip a clean paintbrush into the herbicide and "paint" the **bermudagrass** with it. Don't use herbicides under the following conditions:

- On hot days (check the label for temperature restrictions)
- When it's windy
- When rain is forecast within twenty-four hours

Herbicides are most effective if the weeds were watered twenty-four hours before the product was applied.

Japanese beetles may be troublesome to some shrubs from now until August. Pick them off by hand, and drop them in a jar of soapy water to drown. Neem, an organic product, sometimes helps, espe-

cially if you begin spraying susceptible shrubs before the beetles arrive. For other recommendations, check with the Extension Service. A long-term control is to spread milky spore on your lawn, which keeps the Japanese beetle grubs from developing. (See page 159.)

Dry weather tends to bring out spider mites. They suck the juices from foliage and flowers so that leaves look spotty or bronzed and flowers are distorted. If you notice an infestation (spider mites look like dust or webbing on the undersides of leaves), hose the shrub thoroughly. Once it has dried, spray with insecticidal soap (or mix 5 drops of dishwashing liquid with a quart of water and use that). Do not apply an insecticide. Spider mites technically aren't insects, so insecticides don't control them. If you want to use a chemical control, ask at a garden center about a miticide. Light summer oil (sometimes called "sun oil") is another solution for infested broadleaf evergreens, but can't be used when temperatures are approaching the 90-degree Fahrenheit range.

JULY
Shrubs

PLANNING

While you're still up in the air on a land-scaping project—Do I need more shrubs here or there? And what kind should they be?—you don't have to do without the strong green impact that shrubs can provide. Consider planting dwarf shrubs in large containers as a temporary measure and plan to plant them later in the garden when you've decided just where they should go. Large terra cotta pots are excellent for this. So are the recently introduced pots that appear to have been made from natural materials but are actually very lightweight. These have the advantage of being easy to move from one place to another. Unlike high-quality terra cotta, these pots, made of various space-age materials, may also be left outside all winter, in freezing temperatures, without harm. Dwarf evergreen shrubs are the most natural choice since they look good all year. Good locations for potted shrubs include by the front door and on either side of the entrance to the garage. They also look attractive on porches, patios, and decks.

PLANTING

Although shrubs aren't generally planted in summertime, you may as long as temperatures are not above the low 80 degrees Fahrenheit and you're willing to water regularly—maybe every other day—for as long as the weather's hot. Your local garden center has container-grown shrubs outdoors now, so they're already used to the weather. You may even find some on sale. But think twice before buying them if you have a vacation planned.

CARE

In the heat of summer, mulch is more important than ever. It retains moisture in the soil and generally prevents annual weeds from germinating. Another advantage is that any weeds that do pop up in the mulch are easily pulled out. Pine straw (pine needles sold in a bale) and fine pine bark are good organic mulches that provide excellent protection to your shrubs, summer and winter, while slowly breaking down and improving the soil.

WATERING

Keep an eye on your rain gauge so you'll know how much moisture your shrubs have received in the past week. (If you don't have a rain gauge, you owe it to yourself to buy one. They're invaluable.) Whenever rainfall is less than an inch a week, shrubs that need a constant supply of moisture (see page 246) and those that have been planted within the past year may need watering. The shrubs planted in rocky soil will need watering sooner than those that are growing in soil that holds moisture. That's why it pays to check your shrubs to see whether their soil is dry 4 to 6 inches down. There's no point in watering unless you have to.

Water at the base of shrubs to prevent potential disease problems. While it's fine to water lawns with a sprinkler, that's not the best choice for shrubs. Trickle irrigation or soaker hoses should be your first choice. If you have only a few shrubs that regularly need watering, you may prefer to use a hose.

If a shrub has dropped leaves that were infected with a fungus, pick these up and dispose of them in the trash. If left beneath the shrub, the spores causing the problem will stay in the area and may affect the plant again later.

FERTILIZING

Put the fertilizer bag or box back on the shelf. Your shrubs won't need to be fed this month. The one exception might be shrubs growing in containers. Because they're watered so frequently in hot weather, they may need nutrients replenished. Most gardeners use a water-soluble fertilizer. A balanced formula—14-14-14 or 20-20-20—is recommended.

PRUNING

Cut off faded flowers from **butterfly bush**. This encourages the shrub to produce even more blooms. As you remove the flowers, cut the stem at a 45-degree angle just above a bud to encourage new growth.

Shear hedges when they have grown 2 to 3 inches. Start with the bottom and work up, trying to keep the bottom wider than the sides. Why? So the sun will be able to shine on the bottom portion of the hedge; without sun, it declines.

PROBLEMS

If this is a bad year for Japanese beetles, July will continue to be a problem month. Keep them picked off by hand or spray with a contact insecticide recommended by the Extension Service or a garden center.

Caterpillars may appear on various shrubs. Unless they're doing considerable damage or the shrub is very young or not in good shape, you may want to let the caterpillars alone. They are, after all, one of the life stages of moths and butterflies. Some gardeners like to move troublesome caterpillars to other plants where their damage won't be as obvious or won't make a difference. If you have woods on your property, maybe you can "transplant" some there. But if they're harming your plants, use Bt (*Bacillus thuringensis*), an organic control for all types of caterpillars (including those we sometimes call "worms").

If a shrub has dropped leaves that were infected with a fungus (they probably are covered with spots), pick these up and dispose of them in the trash. If left beneath the shrub, the spores causing the problem will stay in the area and may affect the plant again later.

If a **rhododendron** dies this month, especially after buds have turned brown and branches have drooped, you may think it's due to lack of water. And that's certainly possible, if you didn't pay attention to the shrub's watering needs. But more likely it's rhododendron dieback, when plants are infected by the fungus *Phytophthora cactorum*. There's no cure, but preventive steps include providing excellent drainage, not planting **rhododendrons** where others have already died from the disease, planting far enough apart so the shrubs have good air circulation, and using a sprinkler to water. Ask at a nursery about **rhododendrons** that resist dieback, and get advice from the Extension Service on control of the disease if it hasn't advanced too far.

AUGUST

PLANNING

In summer, when the family is in the yard a great deal, we notice how much privacy we have when we're entertaining or even outside by ourselves. While we may like our neighbors a lot, we don't want to feel as though we're living in a goldfish bowl—and they don't either. Privacy can be very welcome. It doesn't have to be provided by a tall fence between the two pieces of property. Instead, consider a naturalistic hedge or some sort of shrub screen that gives inhabitants in both houses something green and pleasant to look at while offering some solitude. Choices include:

- **Cherry laurel** (*Prunus laurocerasus*)
- **Chinese holly** (*Ilex cornuta*)
- **Euonymous** (*Euonymus fortunei*—shrub form)
- **False cypress**
- **Inkberry** (*Ilex glabra*)
- **Pyracantha**
- **Rosebay rhododendron**
- **Silverberry** (*Elaeagnus commutata*)
- **Yaupon holly** (*Ilex vomitoria*—Zones 7 and 8 only)

PLANTING

If you've waited this long to plant shrubs, it's probably best to wait another month or so, when temperatures are lower and regular rainfall more likely. But if someone gives you a shrub or you see one you just have to own, go on and plant it if temperatures are staying in the low 80 degrees Fahrenheit. But resign yourself to doing quite a bit of watering.

CARE

Keep an eye on the shrubs in your yard even though it may be unpleasantly hot outside. A walk through the garden or checking them as you water will alert you to possible signs of struggle from newly planted shrubs. If that's the case, make plans to move them later in the year.

WATERING

Watering may be your primary activity during August. It depends on how high the temperatures climb, how much rain falls and how often, the kinds of shrubs you have, and the type of soil in the yard. Because there are so many variables, it isn't possible to say specifically that you should water every week. That may be too little—or not enough. To be sure your shrubs should be watered, test the soil to see whether it's drying out. When the weather's hot and rain has been making itself scarce, you need to check more frequently. Once most shrubs are established, they can weather a dry spell. But others need help from the homeowner to get the moisture they need when they aren't getting it the normal way. See the list of plants (on page 246) that are more likely to need watering first. Shrubs are vulnerable and may suffer from lack of water for the first three years they're in your yard. After that, they're considered established and are more capable of making it without help, except during droughts. But if you want your new shrubs to be a long-term asset, give them the moisture they need for two or three years, or longer.

The best time to water is early in the morning. Since you may not want to be up dragging hoses about before work, consider connecting your drip irrigation or soaker hoses to a mechanical timer. It will turn the water on at a preset time (even 4 a.m., if you desire) and turn it off an hour or two later. Your shrubs will receive the moisture they require without any effort on your part.

If you have only a few shrubs and you water by hand, *slowly* and *deeply* are the bywords.

Because there are so many variables, it isn't possible to say specifically that you should water every week. That may be too little—or not enough. To be sure your shrubs should be watered, test the soil to see whether it's drying out.

 # FERTILIZING

There's no need to fertilize any shrubs this month.

 # PRUNING

If branches with all-green leaves appear on variegated shrubs, promptly cut them back to the main branch. If you don't, the whole shrub may revert to green, instead of having the variegation that was the reason you probably bought it.

Shear hedges one last time this month. Using hedge trimmers, cut new growth back to just above where you made your last cuts.

Cut off fading **crapemyrtle** blooms. Also cut off those on **butterfly bushes** and other summer-flowering shrubs.

Whenever a shrub sustains damage or a stem or branch dies, prune the dead or damaged wood out of the plant. Otherwise, insects or disease could get a foothold. But wait until winter or next year to do any other pruning. August isn't a good month for general pruning.

 # PROBLEMS

Azalea lace bugs may again put in an appearance in August. They suck sap from the leaves, leaving them looking dry. They may also leave shiny blackish deposits under the leaves. Lace bugs are most likely to proliferate when **azaleas** are in sun. Spray with insecticidal soap twice a week for two weeks. Or ask a knowledgeable nursery professional about a chemical control and for the names of **azaleas** that resist lace bugs.

By mid-month, we should finally have relief from Japanese beetles. They will have laid eggs and disappeared from sight for another year. Unfortunately, they will become grubs in the soil from now until they emerge late next spring. See the Lawn chapter (page 159) for advice on long-term control of Japanese beetles, if their levels have become intolerable.

Japanese
Beetle

Bagworms are almost invisible on needled evergreen shrubs until one day when you notice there are many of them. The best solution is to wait till dusk, when the "worms" will have returned to the bags, and then pick them off by hand. Drop them in soapy water and dispose of them. You'll probably have to do this several times a week over a period of several weeks in order to get rid of them all. It's very easy to overlook a few each time. Then check over the shrub once a month or so after that to make sure you're taken care of them all.

If you can't keep up with weeds this month—or you're faced with more than you can handle as you return from vacation—at least pull the seedheads off them. You'll have to contend with far fewer weeds in the future if you prevent weeds from self-sowing their seeds everywhere.

SEPTEMBER

PLANNING

As we head into fall, you may be looking forward to the glorious fall color of deciduous trees—either in your yard or along the highways. But have you considered planting shrubs that have excellent fall color? They really make a yard "shine" in autumn. Berried bushes also add color—mostly red—and food for migrating birds. Ask a nursery professional about those listed here. Not all species or cultivars of each will have colorful foliage, but a professional can recommend the best.

Colorful foliage:

- **Bottlebrush buckeye**
- **Burning bush**
- **Carolina allspice**
- **Crapemyrtle**
- **Deciduous azalea**
- **Fothergilla**
- **Loropetalum** (Zones 7 and 8)
- **Redvein enkianthus**
- **Smoke tree**
- **Spirea**
- **Summersweet**
- **Viburnum**
- **Virginia sweetspire**
- **Witch hazel**

Berries:

- **Barberry**
- **Beautyberry**
- **Chinese holly**
- **Cotoneaster**
- **Deciduous hollies**
- **Nandina** (tall cultivars)
- **Oregon grape holly** (*Mahonia* species)
- **Pyracantha**
- **Viburnum**

When was the last time you had your soil tested, and why does it matter? It's a good idea to have your soil tested every few years because conditions change. What does a soil test tell you? The pH of your soil, for one thing. This really matters for some shrubs. They need either acid or alkaline soil and won't perform well (and may die) if it isn't available. A soil test will also tell you what type of fertilizer to use around your shrubs. Knowing this can save you money; there's no point in buying the wrong fertilizer or in spreading it each year when it may not be needed.

PLANTING

Once the weather has begun to cool from summer's torrid levels, you can begin to plant shrubs, if you like. Garden centers often get a new crop of shrubs for fall planting. If you've been looking for something special, you may find it now. Or you may just enjoy seeing what's available. Seek out a knowledgeable person at your favorite nursery and ask for advice. Describe the conditions in your yard and the type of shrub you have in mind and see what's new. Refer to page 240 for shrub planting tips. Although fall is considered the ideal planting time for shrubs in our part of the country, I like to plant evergreen shrubs early in fall—September and October—and deciduous shrubs later, if I don't have time to get to them earlier. The whole idea behind fall planting is that mild temperatures and reasonable rainfall combine to get shrubs off to a good start before they have to face the heat of summer. Even though the tops of the shrubs aren't growing, the roots will be, and that helps them to get established. Once every eight or ten years, we have an unusually cold winter and just about any evergreen shrub planted in the previous mid- to late fall won't make it—especially broadleaf evergreens and those that are less hardy in a particular part of the region. The choice is yours. Shrub selection in autumn is excellent, and planting now isn't such sweaty work for a homeowner. But you may not want to install an entire new landscape unless the plants are guaranteed.

CARE

If you spray weeds with a herbicide, take care to keep the product from coming into direct contact with any part of a shrub—trunk, branches, leaves, or flowers. Avoid spraying when there's even the slightest whiff of wind or on a day when temperatures are high (see the label for temperature restrictions). All this is a good recommendation for keeping an organic mulch around all shrubs. Weeds will be far fewer, and most that appear can be easily pulled out through the mulch.

WATERING

In the first part of the month, dwarf shrubs in containers may need daily watering. But as temperatures cool down later in September, the shrubs may be able to skip a day of watering, especially if there's been a bit of rain. Why not get the moisture meter you use for houseplants and stick that in the soil? It will give you a quick answer to the question, Do I water or do I wait?

FERTILIZING

No fertilizing this month. Fertilizer stimulates new growth, and tender new growth is likely to be killed by cold weather. In fall, you want a shrub to slow its growth so that it's ready to go dormant by the time freezing temperatures arrive.

PRUNING

Prune only dead or injured wood.

PROBLEMS

Less heat and humidity may inspire you to get out and get some exercise in the yard—better known as weeding. The tops of weeds may be killed back by frost in a month or more, but perennial weeds will pop up again next year. Even annual weeds leave behind seeds that sprout in spring and continue to plague us. Ten minutes a day should take care of all the weeds once and for all.

Problems with insects are usually fewer in the fall than in late spring and in summer. But keep an eye out for potential problems. If you're in the yard and see something a bit odd on one of your shrubs, stop for a closer look.

String trimmers and shrubs don't go together. Keep them as far apart as possible. In a flash, a string trimmer can damage the tender stem of a shrub. And that opening can be the entrance to the shrub for disease and insects.

OCTOBER

PLANNING

Have you admired espaliered shrubs and thought about having one in your yard? These shrubs trained against walls or fences to look like vines take quite a bit of pruning and training, but no special skills. Good choices for espalier are **cotoneaster, flowering quince, forsythia**, and **pyracantha**.

PLANTING

October is a perfect month for transplanting shrubs.

1 Wet the soil deeply at least twenty-four hours before you plant to move a shrub.

2 Dig a new hole where the shrub will be planted. Estimate the size, keeping in mind that it's better to be too wide than not wide enough. Roots must be given room to spread out.

3 Use a spading fork to gently probe the soil, starting 4 feet out from the trunk. The object is to locate as many roots as possible, especially the major roots.

4 Dig under and around the main trunk of the shrub, at least 2 feet around.

5 Find and loosen vital roots by rocking and lifting.

6 When a shovel can fit all the way underneath the shrub, tip the rootball to one side so you can get a tarp or piece of strong burlap beneath it. Do the same to the other side.

7 Use the tarp or burlap to help lift the shrub out of the hole. This may take several people, depending on the size of the shrub. If you have to break off chunks of soil because the whole thing is too heavy, that's all right. But take care to preserve as many roots as possible. They're the secret to success.

8 Gently ease the shrub from its burlap covering into its new hole, making sure that it's at the same level it grew before, never any deeper.

9 Arrange the roots so they aren't crowded.

10 Fill the hole about halfway with soil.

11 Water with a transplanting solution.

12 Add the rest of the soil.

13 Water again with a transplanting solution.

14 Cover with 3 inches of organic mulch—shredded leaves, pine straw, or fine bark.

15 Water regularly until the ground freezes.

You may also plant shrubs from the nursery at this time, either those sold in containers or balled-and-burlapped (see page 240). If you're planting broadleaf evergreen shrubs, as well as deciduous shrubs, get the evergreens planted first during the month, then tackle the deciduous shrubs.

CARE

Have you been growing **figs, gardenias,** or **lemon** or **orange** "trees" in containers on the patio or in the yard? Move them back indoors before the first frost. Some may have grown to such a hefty size that they require the efforts of two people as movers.

WATERING

Little supplemental watering may be necessary if rainfall is abundant. But sometimes October is dry, so be alert for shrubs that have to be watered. See the list on page 246 for those most likely to need watering. Water any shrubs planted this month or last at least weekly until frost, if rainfall doesn't add up to about an inch per week.

Shrubs survive the cold better if they go into winter well watered. This is especially true of evergreens. So don't avoid watering thirsty shrubs now, thinking it isn't necessary at the end of the season. If rainfall is below normal, it very well may be needed. Check the soil to be sure.

FERTILIZING

Delay fertilizing until next spring.

PRUNING

Prune out storm damage, but otherwise, wait until late winter or early spring to do any needed pruning.

Deciduous **hollies** develop such an enormous crop of berries that it may take your breath away. Often they completely line the branches. Cut a few branches covered with berries, bring them indoors, and place them in a vase. They'll last a very long time. When cutting the berried branches, prune back to a main branch, to the ground, or to just above a bud on the branch. Use sharp pruners and cut at a 45-degree angle.

PROBLEMS

If you live in an area where deer are a problem, they may begin showing up this month to see what's on the winter menu. If you don't want it to be your shrubs, you'll have to take action. Many "remedies" against deer work for a time—bars of Irish Spring™ soap, commercially bottled urine of wolves or other predators, human urine, human hair scattered around, hot pepper sprays, etc. Repellents such as Deer-Off® are among the most effective controls. Spray your shrubs now if you decide to go this route. Electric fences offer more protection if the problem is severe, but a

10-foot fence around your property is the only guarantee to keep deer away if they're really hungry.

If there were bagworms on your needled evergreen shrubs this summer, check again early this month to make sure you got them all.

Don't let down your guard against insects until after frost. True, there are generally fewer pests in fall, but that doesn't mean they completely disappear. On evergreen shrubs, take action if the insect is making a visible difference. On deciduous shrubs, the leaves will be falling soon anyway.

NOVEMBER

Shrubs

PLANNING

As you look at your yard, are you pleased with the shrubs you have and how they fit into your landscape? One of the biggest trends in landscaping is four-season color—having something in the yard that's blooming or colorful at every season of the year. If you acted on the suggestions made in February, your yard will be more interesting this winter than ever before. Looking ahead to spring, do you have enough flowering shrubs? It's such a delight to welcome spring with a riot of flowers, and when those flowers are provided by shrubs, they're easy care—plant them and reap the rewards for years to come. Here are a few spring-flowering shrubs to consider:

- **Evergreen azalea**
- **Deutzia** (*Deutzia gracilis*)
- **Flowering quince**
- **Forsythia**
- **Fothergilla**
- **Kerria**
- **Leucothoe**
- **Rhododendron**
- **Spirea**
- **Viburnum**

PLANTING

Continue planting shrubs when temperatures are above freezing. At this point, you may want to plant only deciduous shrubs. But many people plant evergreens, too. If the weather is chilly, prepare the hole first, then move the shrub to the planting area so its roots won't be exposed to cold for any longer than necessary. Always water a shrub twelve to twenty-four hours before it's to be planted. See page 240 for more details.

CARE

If a needled evergreen is planted in a woodland site, leaves from deciduous trees often get caught in the needles. Usually the wind blows these away, but sometimes a few remain and can kill the needles by blocking the sun. This may also happen at the base of small **evergreen azaleas**. As you're walking in the yard on a pretty November day, take a few moments to remove stray leaves that are still on shrubs.

Leaves make excellent free mulch around shrubs. When shrubs are in naturalized areas beneath tall trees, gardeners often just let the autumn leaves remain where they fall. If there are so many leaves that they form a thick barrier that could prevent rain from penetrating to the soil below, rake or blow some off. You can then shred some of the leaves and return them to shrub beds that need additional mulch. Break up leaves by placing them in a single layer and running over them with the lawn mower several times.

Renew mulch around all shrubs so that it's about 3 inches thick. Think of it as your shrubs' security blanket. It will protect their roots from extreme cold and from constant freezing and thawing as the weather goes from cold to warmer and back again. Mulch, as you know, also holds moisture in the soil, so shrubs don't dry out.

Before you add more mulch, remove shrub leaves from the area if they have fallen off because of insect or disease damage. This will help keep disease and insects from overwintering at the base of shrubs and affecting the shrubs again next year.

Move shrubs growing in large containers on decks, patios, and elsewhere in the yard to protected locations. A spot where they can still get some sun is ideal, but they shouldn't be exposed to high winds. If they're placed closer to the house (on a porch, for instance), they won't be as vulnerable to below-freezing temperatures.

Consider taking samples of soil in shrub beds and around the foundation of your house and sending them off to the Extension Service's state testing lab if you haven't done this before, or not in the past few years. Knowing the pH of the soil helps you choose the right plants to go in a particular place since some prefer acid soil and others need more neutral or alkaline conditions.

 # WATERING

Shrubs in pots will need watering in November and all winter if they're on a porch or if rainfall is slight.

Keep on eye on the watering needs of newly planted and transplanted shrubs. Don't let their soil dry out as long as the ground isn't frozen.

 # FERTILIZING

Wait until spring, just as new growth starts, to fertilize all shrubs in your yard.

But some gardeners like to provide shrubs with a thin layer of well-rotted manure this month. It slowly breaks down and gently feeds shrubs.

PRUNING

Forego pruning this month unless it's to repair dead, damaged, or diseased growth. It's also all right to cut **holly** branches, whether deciduous or evergreen. Do this when temperatures are above freezing. But avoid other shrub pruning until late winter.

 ## Timely Tip

It's fine to put low-voltage outdoor Christmas lights on shrubs this month. They don't generate enough heat to do any harm.

PROBLEMS

If deer pose a problem for landscapes in your county, check with your local Extension Service office to see whether it has a list of deer-resistant shrubs. These lists abound in books and on the Internet, but what works best in one locale doesn't always transfer to another place. It seems that deer in different areas have varied tastes. Talk with neighbors and members of local garden clubs and plant societies to find out what shrubs deer have passed by in others' yards.

Covering vulnerable newly planted shrubs with plastic netting isn't a cure-all—the deer can nibble through the holes—but it does sometimes slow down damage since the deer don't like to get tangled up in the netting.

DECEMBER

PLANNING

Have you been faithful this year in keeping up your garden journal or notebook? It's not too late to go back and supplement your notes. Information that's handy to have in the future includes the name, size, and price of any new shrubs you bought; the date they were planted; any performance notes about them (when they began blooming and how long they bloomed, for instance); and any problems that cropped up during the year. You may also want to keep a running wish list in your garden notebook of plants you may have read about in a magazine or seen in someone else's yard and you'd love to try. Writing them down makes it less likely that you'll forget them, and keeping the names all on one page helps you prioritize which ones you'd like to try first, such as those that will mix well with shrubs and trees already in the landscape.

PLANTING

When the ground isn't frozen and temperatures are above freezing, you may continue to plant shrubs this month, especially deciduous shrubs. But be sure that you firm the soil around the rootball and don't leave any air pockets for cold to get in. Also, spread a 3-inch mulch as soon as you finish planting. Never let mulch touch the trunk of a shrub. It creates conditions that can lead to insect or animal damage or disease.

CARE

Be prepared to bring shrubs growing outdoors in large containers into a garage or basement overnight if temperatures 20 degrees Fahrenheit and below are forecast.

WATERING

Keep an occasional eye on shrubs planted this fall if rainfall is less than normal. But usually winter is a rainy season in our region, so homeowners don't have to think much about watering this month or in the next few months.

The only exception is container shrubs that are in locations—such as on a porch—where rainfall doesn't reach them. Because of much cooler temperatures, they won't need water nearly as much as when it's warmer, but they shouldn't be allowed to dry out completely.

FERTILIZING

Don't fertilize any shrubs until spring.

PRUNING

Except for removing dead, diseased, or damaged wood, put off shrub pruning until at least late winter. Don't prune spring-flowering shrubs until *after* they've bloomed. You may, however, cut **holly, nandina**, and **pyracantha** stems to provide berries for holiday decorations. Cut the entire stem back to where it joins a branch, back to the ground, or just above a bud. Use sharp pruners or loppers when making your cuts—they won't cause damage the way dull blades can.

PROBLEMS

Few problems crop up in December. You may want to walk around the yard occasionally to keep any eye on your shrubs. Pay close attention to drainage if you have hard clay soil. If water is standing in a particular spot, that may need correcting if it affects shrubs or other plants.

CHAPTER NINE

Trees

Trees bring a sense of beauty, serenity, strength, and permanency to our landscapes. It's hard to imagine a yard—or a world—without towering oaks, flowering dogwoods, and hollies that produce red berries just when they're needed for holiday decorating.

Everyone has a favorite tree. Maybe it's a **saucer magnolia** that serves as a harbinger of spring or a tall **pine** that you sat under as a kid, listening to the breeze blow musically through the branches. It could be a **sweet gum**, with its fiery fall foliage, or the **tulip poplar**, the official state tree of Kentucky and Tennessee.

But trees provide so much more. They're a practical part of the landscape, too. They give protection from the sun and may help control erosion, reduce noise, deflect winds, purify the air, and cut your home cooling costs. In landscape design, trees are used to frame a view, provide privacy, and mark boundaries.

What the homeowner needs to know about trees can be summed up in two words: selection and care. A tree is a long-term investment. Many can easily live for several generations, so you want to make sure you select the right tree for your yard and that you take care of it properly so it lives up to its potential.

CHOOSING A TREE

Because so many different trees grow well in our region, we have a wide choice. Some of the selection criteria should include aesthetic and climate considerations, as well as matching the conditions in your yard—light, soil, drainage—with those needed by various kinds of trees.

HARDINESS

The first question to ask about a tree you're considering planting in your yard is: Does it grow well here? You might think this question isn't necessary, but occasionally you'll find trees being sold in your area that aren't going to grow well there. And when you buy by mail order, you have to determine this for yourself. Start by checking the list on page 263. Those trees should grow anywhere in the region. If you're looking at a catalog, see what USDA Zones are listed for the tree. (You can find your zone on pages 18 to 19.) Be cautious when your zone is listed at the end of a list (Zones 4 to 7, for example). That may indicate this

Tree Layout Diagram

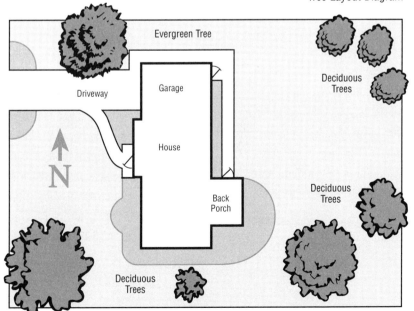

tree doesn't like heat and humidity. If you're still not sure, call your local Extension Service office and ask whether the tree is recommended.

EVERGREEN OR DECIDUOUS

An evergreen tree stays green all year, providing winter color in the yard. Deciduous trees, which lose their leaves in fall, may help cool the house in summer and allow the warming sun to reach it in winter.

MULTISEASONAL INTEREST

The big buzz in landscaping is having plants that have attractive qualities—flowers; berries; attractive stems, shape, or bark—in more than one season. **Dogwoods**, which have flowers, berries, and brilliant red fall foliage, are a good example. (See the list on page 280 for some others.)

POTENTIAL PROBLEMS

Ask whether a tree produces fruits or pods. Some gardeners live to regret planting **sweet gum** trees because the balls fall onto the lawn and get tangled up in the mower. The same is true of **southern magnolia**. **Crabapples** may litter the lawn in summer and **persimmons** in fall. Some of these drawbacks can be mitigated by siting the trees where the fruits or pods fall onto a mulched bed instead of into a driveway. But for everyone who loves these trees, there are others who wish they had never planted them. Know your tolerance level before you buy.

CONDITIONS IN YOUR YARD

If you've read through the book to this point, you may be tired of hearing this, but the key to success with any plant is selecting one that likes the conditions of the location you choose. If the spot where you want to plant is shady and has wet soil, but you plant a tree that requires full sun and fast-draining soil, it isn't going to look good or live very long. Get to know your yard—the soil type, the pH, the amount of light that falls on various sections, and even the wind (what direction it comes from, whether it's likely to be excessive at times, and if there's good air circulation). Then learn the same things about the trees you're considering—and be a matchmaker.

SIZE

Size is generally the most overlooked question in choosing a tree: How big is this tree going to get? That **tulip poplar** "twig" given away on Arbor Day is going to grow rapidly to 80 or 100 feet high. A **redbud** will probably stay under 35 feet, but it will be about as wide as it is tall. It's vital to find this out before you select a tree because the eventual height and spread tell you where you can plant—how close to the house, power lines, the front walk, the driveway, the street, a fence, and the neighbor's yard. A young tree may cost relatively little, but it will be quite expensive to have it removed if it grows into the power lines, causes the paint to mildew on your house, or showers so many leaves on the roof that your gutters get clogged.

TREE CARE

The basics of taking care of a tree are much the same as for any other plant. Trees may sometimes need watering, fertilizing, and treatment for insects or diseases. In addition, there are times when a tree will need protection (from lawn mowers, string trimmers, deer, and deicing salt, as well as during construction on your property). Training

Trees

and pruning a tree can help it develop a desirable shape and keep it healthy.

WATERING

Whether your trees need watering, how often, and how much depends upon several factors. These include:

- Rainfall amounts (the ideal is an inch of water per week).
- Temperature (the lower the temperature, the less likely you'll need to water).
- The type of soil in your yard (clay holds more moisture than rocky or sandy soils).
- The species of tree (some are more drought-tolerant than others).
- The age and size of the tree (a newly planted tree will need watering more frequently than one that's been in your yard for five years, and in general, the larger the tree, the more moisture it requires).
- Mulch (2 to 3 inches, especially around the base of young trees—which have compact root systems easily covered with mulch—helps the soil retain moisture).

It takes one to three years for a newly planted tree to become established. During that time—especially the first six months—you should watch the tree carefully to see whether it needs watering, particularly during the hottest days of summer and in dry spells.

How do you tell if a tree needs watering? You should test the soil by inserting a thin stick to see at what level it becomes damp. Other signs are:

- Leaves look dull instead of shiny or bright.
- Leaves look grayish instead of bright green.
- Leaves drop off.
- Wilting. (When this happens, it may be too late to revive the tree.)

Important Watering Rules of Thumb

1 In the absence of rainfall, a recently planted tree will need about a gallon of water per week for each inch of its height—6 gallons for a 6-foot-tall tree, 4 gallons for a 4-footer, etc.

2 Most tree roots are located in the upper 12 inches of soil, but those roots extend as much as two to three times beyond the ends of the branches. That's the area where water needs to be applied.

What are the best ways to apply this water?

- Soaker hose (coil it in spirals starting near the trunk to distribute the water evenly).
- Sprinkler (for large trees whose leaves are high enough not to get wet during the process). Place empty tuna or cat-food tins about to measure when an inch of water has been applied.
- Drip or trickle irrigation (handy if a number of trees are growing close together).
- A shallow basin in the soil around newly planted trees (helps hold rainfall or water from a hose or watering can).

FERTILIZING

Tree fertilization is a subject on which the experts disagree. Some believe that trees should be fertilized each year to keep them healthy and growing. Others think that if a tree puts on 9 to 12 inches of new growth annually (6 to 8 inches for a mature tree), it doesn't need fertilizing. Most homeowners fertilize young trees but tend not to bother when it comes to older, long-established trees. A good compromise is yearly fertilizing for young trees that you want to grow faster and then feeding mature trees once every three to four years.

261

Trees

You may already be feeding your trees and not even recognize it. If trees are growing in the lawn area or their roots have extended under the lawn, and you fertilize the grass several times yearly, those trees are being fertilized some, too.

What time of year to feed trees is also a matter of discussion. Some experts recommend spreading fertilizer beneath trees once between the period when the leaves fall off in autumn until just before they begin to grow again in spring. Others say the best time to fertilize is in early to mid-spring.

PRUNING

Pruning a tree should be for the purpose of enhancing its natural shape and to prevent damage to the tree. How and when to prune are fully covered in this chapter, but it's important to remember that working in very tall trees is a job best left to experienced and insured professionals.

Never top a tree or allow someone to top your trees. It destroys the trees' shape and it causes ugly new growth (called *water sprouts*) that will need

pruning again before long. If a tree has grown too tall or if it's casting too much shade, talk with a qualified arborist about thinning or reducing the crown of the tree.

Use hand pruners on stems up to $3/4$ inch in diameter. Loppers are the tools of choice for stems of $1 3/4$ inches or less in diameter. (Look for ratcheted or geared loppers if you do a lot of pruning; they require less effort.) Pruning saws are effective for limbs up to 4 to 5 inches across. A good-quality folding saw can be especially handy to carry with you as you walk about the yard, but should be confined to smaller branches.

Pruning isn't a complicated process. It's mostly a matter of knowing why, when, and how. And that's what we'll be explaining in the pages to come. Think of it as one small portion of caring for your trees so they live up to their full potential.

The small things you do now will help ensure that the trees in your yard will be around to beautify and cool future generations.

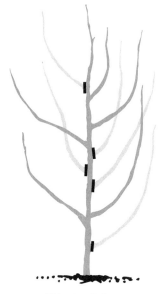

Thinning Before

Thinning After

Trees

Common Name (*Botanical Name*)	Height (Feet)	Width (Feet)	Deciduous or Evergreen	Culture
Bald cypress (*Taxodium distichum*)	50 to 85	18 to 65	Deciduous	Sun or partial sun. Prefers moist soil but will tolerate virtually any soil except alkaline.
Canadian hemlock (*Tsuga canadensis*)	8 to 90	25 to 35	Evergreen	Partial shade or shade. Needs moist, well-drained soil.
Carolina silverbell (*Halesia tetraptera*)	30 to 45	20 to 35	Deciduous	Partial shade, partial sun. Likes moist, acidic, well-drained soil.
Chaste tree (*Vitex agnus-castus*)	8 to 25	15 to 20	Deciduous	Sun. Tolerant of many types of soil.
Dogwood (*Cornus* species and hybrids)	20 to 30	20 to 25	Deciduous	Partial shade, partial sun. Prefers soil that's acidic, moist, and well-drained.
Flowering cherry (*Prunus* species and hybrids)	6 to 40	8 to 30	Deciduous	Sun. Mix clay soil with ample organic matter when planting. Needs good drainage.
Fringe tree (*Chionanthus virginicus*)	12 to 30	10 to 25	Deciduous	Sun, partial sun. Adaptable as to location, but prefers moist, well-drained soil if available.
Ginkgo (*Ginkgo biloba*)	25 to 50	15 to 40	Deciduous	Sun. Well-drained soil preferred; may be acidic or alkaline.
Golden rain tree (*Koelreuteria paniculata*)	30 to 40	25 to 35	Deciduous	Sun. Adapts to almost any type of soil.
Holly (*Ilex* species and hybrids)	15 to 40	8 to 30	Evergreen	Sun, partial sun. Moist, well-drained, acidic soil.
Japanese cryptomeria (*Cryptomeria japonica*)	6 to 60	6 to 30	Evergreen	Sun, partial sun. Likes rich, moist, acid soil that drains well. Shelter from strong winds.
Japanese maple (*Acer palmatum*)	6 to 40	8 to 30	Deciduous	Partial shade, partial sun. Plant in moist, well-drained soil.
Japanese zelkova (*Zelkova serrata*)	50 to 90	30 to 60	Deciduous	Sun. Tolerant of most soils.
Lacebark elm (*Ulmus parvifolia*)	40 to 50	30 to 50	Deciduous	Sun. Will adapt to any well-drained soil.
Oak (*Quercus* species and hybrids)	40 to 80	25 to 60	Deciduous	Sun, partial sun. Moist, well-drained acidic soil. Plant in late winter when the tree is dormant.
Ornamental pear or callery pear (*Pyrus calleryana*)	30 to 50	15 to 35	Deciduous	Sun. Tolerates wide range of soils. Avoid 'Bradford' because the trees often split due to weak limbs.
Paperbark maple (*Acer griseum*)	25 to 30	12 to 30	Deciduous	Sun, partial sun. Tolerates a variety of soil types.
Redbud (*Cercis canadensis*)	20 to 35	25 to 35	Deciduous	Sun, partial sun. Adapts to virtually any site except one with standing water.
Red maple (*Acer rubrum*)	40 to 70	40 to 45	Deciduous	Sun. Adaptable as to soil, but can be planted in those difficult wet spots.
River birch (*Betula nigra*)	40 to 70	40 to 60	Deciduous	Sun, partial sun. Likes moist soil, but will grow in drier soil, too. Soil must be acidic.
Saucer magnolia (*Magnolia soulangiana*)	10 to 30	15 to 20	Deciduous	Sun, partial sun. Prefers a spot with moist, well-drained soil.
Serviceberry or Juneberry (*Amelanchier* species and hybrids)	15 to 30	20 to 30	Deciduous	Any light level, but prefers partial shade. Tolerant of many types of soil.
Sourwood (*Oxydendrum arboreum*)	25 to 50	15 to 20	Deciduous	Sun, partial sun. Likes acidic soil.
Southern magnolia (*Magnolia grandiflora*)	20 to 80	20 to 50	Evergreen	Sun, partial sun. Adaptable, but prefers moist, well-drained, acidic soil.
Sweet gum (*Liquidambar styraciflua*)	60 to 75	30 to 45	Deciduous	Sun. Needs acidic soil. Can tolerate wet sites.
Yellowwood (*Cladrastis kentukea*)	30 to 60	40 to 50	Deciduous	Sun. Adaptable to any type of soil.

PLANNING

January presents a golden opportunity to look over your landscaping plan and see what might be on the agenda in the coming year as far as trees are concerned:

Will you need to have an old, diseased tree removed? Or maybe one that was planted in the wrong place by a previous owner? Many people are reluctant to have trees taken down. But if one is damaged or if it's in a spot where it presents yearly problems (dumping tons of leaves on your roof, for instance), it's often best to remove it. Winter's a good time to have that taken care of. Call an experienced tree professional for an estimate. And instead of feeling sad, make a list of possible replacement trees. Enjoy doing some research on those, then decide what tree you'd like to plant in place of the one that's removed.

Are trees casting too much shade, so that plants nearby aren't growing well? Begin "limbing up" young trees in the fourth year they're in your yard. That is, remove a few of the tree's lower limbs each winter so that more light comes through. Tall, stately trees can be limbed up so their lowest limbs are 15 to 20 feet high. But don't do it all at once—just a few at a time. And *don't* limb up trees whose shape it destroys—**Japanese maples, dogwoods**, and **southern magnolias**. Another solution to the "too much shade" problem is to thin a tree. (See page 262.)

PLANTING

Small deciduous trees are sometimes sold bare root (that is, without any soil around the roots). These inexpensive trees were fairly common in the past, but are now generally available only by mail order. Bare-root trees should be planted when they're dormant (not growing). That typically means December-February, although in colder parts of the region, the planting time could extend into the first of March.

Here's how to plant a bare-root tree:

1 Choose a day when the temperature is above freezing and the ground isn't frozen.

2 Dig a hole as deep as and slightly wider than the spread of the roots.

3 Using the soil removed from the hole, build a cone in the center of the hole, with the top of the cone of soil 1 to 2 inches lower than the level of the ground.

4 Cut off any dead or damaged roots or stems from the tree.

5 Place the young tree on top of the cone of soil, with its roots spread down the sides of the cone. Make sure the tree is at the same level it grew before (never any deeper).

6 Have a helper hold the tree in place while you fill the hole about halfway with soil removed from the hole, firming it around the roots.

7 Water, using a transplant solution.

8 Fill the rest of the hole with soil, making sure you leave no air pockets.

9 Some gardeners like to form a saucer-shaped rim in the soil on top of the ground to hold water.

10 Water again, using a transplant solution.

11 Cover the area around the tree with 2 to 3 inches of mulch, such as shredded leaves, but don't let it touch the trunk of the tree.

12 Do *not* routinely stake a tree. That's no longer recommended.

You may also transplant trees from one part of your yard to another. See page 286.

CARE

If you had a tree professionally installed last year and it was staked, the apparatus should be removed within 12 months. Often they can be removed sooner. Until then, be sure that the guying material (which fastens around the tree) is not cutting into the bark and that the wooden stakes have not come out of the soil.

 # WATERING

Because the ground can be frozen in January and it may be a wet month, watering is not usually necessary. But should the weather be warmer and drier than usual, you may need to water trees that were planted in the fall. Give them a gallon of water for each inch of the tree's height.

Dwarf trees growing in a large pot on the deck or patio may need routine watering during the winter, if rainfall is less than usual, or if the tree is in a protected place where it doesn't receive rain. Test the soil to be sure if it's dry beneath the surface. Don't water when the soil is frozen.

 # FERTILIZING

Fertilize young trees once yearly. It may be anytime between late November and the end of February, or it can be done in March or April. See page 269 for directions.

 # PRUNING

Winter is the time to prune deciduous trees that need it—as long as they are *not* ones that flower in winter or spring. In Tennessee and Kentucky, February is better than January for extensive pruning because the trees start growing not too long afterward and therefore recover more quickly. But if you need to prune in January—especially to take care of damage—that's fine. Just do it on a day when temperatures are above 25 degrees Fahrenheit.

Limb Removal

A typical pruning job this month would be removing a tree limb that's diseased, damaged, or growing out of bounds. It's a simple, three-step process. Don't try to just cut off a heavy limb close to the trunk—that often causes the bark to tear from the tree, which can lead to insect or disease damage. This is the better way:

1 Measure a spot on the branch that's about a foot from the trunk. Using a saw, make a cut underneath the branch and about one-third of the way through it.

2 Move about 3 inches beyond the first cut and, from the top, saw off the branch.

3 Cut off the rest of the limb, making the cut just outside the branch collar—the swollen area at the base of the branch. (See the drawing.) Don't cut into the collar—it contains substances that keep the area from decaying.

PROBLEMS

Walk around the yard occasionally, paying attention to your trees so you can catch any problems that might pop up.

FEBRUARY

 PLANNING

If winter has been colder and snowier than usual, about the first of February you may be longing for trees to turn green. It's not necessary to wait until spring if you have evergreens. They're always green.

Needled evergreen trees you may want to consider include:

- **Canadian hemlock**
- Many *Chamaecyparis* species and hybrids that grow 20 feet high and taller
- **Japanese cedar** (*Cryptomeria japonica*)
- **Norway spruce** (*Picea abies*)

Broadleaf evergreens that are useful in Tennessee and Kentucky yards:

- **American** and hybrid **hollies**
- **Southern magnolia**
- **Sweet bay magnolia** (*Magnolia virginiana*)
- **Carolina cherry laurel** (*Prunus caroliniana*)

Also consider whether a few dwarf fruit trees might fit into your landscape plan, especially near the vegetable garden. It's wonderful to have fresh fruit from your own trees, but remember that these are high-maintenance. They need yearly pruning and regular spraying.

 PLANTING

Continue to plant small bare-root trees or transplant small or medium-size established trees. See pages 268 and 286 for instructions.

Toward the end of the month you may also want to begin planting container-grown or balled-and-burlapped trees purchased at a local nursery. (Page 268 has tree-planting tips.)

 CARE

Check the mulch around newly planted trees to make sure it hasn't been blown off by wind or washed away by rains. An organic mulch about 3 inches thick is ideal year-round.

You may be concerned about evergreen trees in ice storms, but there's little you can—or should—do. Let the ice melt naturally off the leaves and needles, and take care of any damage later. If smaller evergreens (especially **Canadian hemlocks**) are uprooted by a heavy load of ice or snow, reset them as soon as you're able to get out in the yard. Give them support, if needed, to stand upright, mulch and then water regularly and fertilize during the next year. Often these trees recover without a hitch.

If branches are weighted down with snow and the forecast is for continuing precipitation or low temperatures, you may sweep the snow off the branches, but be very careful that you don't cause more problems. Instead of sweeping from the top in an outward motion, clear excess snow from beneath, with the upward motion of a broom.

 WATERING

Little watering should be needed due to low temperatures and the usual amount of rainfall that occurs in our region over the winter. But when precipitation is lacking and the ground isn't frozen, keep an eye on the moisture needs of trees planted in the past six to eight months. See page 261 for advice on how to determine whether trees need watering and how much and how often to apply it.

Don't allow containerized trees to dry out completely. Check their soil weekly and water if dry as long as it isn't frozen.

 FERTILIZING

If you're of the school that believes trees should be fertilized during the dormant season, feed trees this month, if you did not do so in the past few months. But if you prefer spring fertilizing, wait until

If branches are weighted down with snow and the forecast is for continuing precipitation or low temperatures, sweep the snow off the branches. Clear excess snow from beneath, with the upward motion of a broom.

March to fertilize all trees. Page 269 has more information.

PRUNING

Safety first is the best motto when dealing with large trees. When you have tree limbs that grow up into or very near power lines, never trim them yourself. *Always* call the electric company or an arborist (tree specialist).

Other potential hazards that may call for hiring a professional include:

- Trees that have started to lean to one side.
- Cracks in the tree's trunk or in major limbs.

Many trees need minor pruning each year, and February is an excellent time to tackle these little tasks:

1 Thin, broken, diseased, or insect-riddled stems or branches. (If left on the tree, these can become a target for insects or diseases.) Thinning—the practice of cutting a limb back to where it joins a main branch or the trunk—helps the tree maintain its natural shape while opening it up to health-giving sunlight and air.

2 If you notice suckers—thin upright growth at the base of the tree—dig them up. They drain energy from the tree.

3 For the same reason, also remove water sprouts—thin flexible shoots that grow upright from branches.

4 Remove one of each pair of crossing or rubbing branches. These are easy to see this time of year. Rubbing causes wounds, which harm the tree.

5 Should you need to remove a large limb, see page 265.

6 On young trees, remove branches that join the trunk at very narrow angles. These are likely to break off in the future.

7 Don't cover the wounds with any sort of paint, dressing, or homemade concoction. They don't help, and they may even slow healing.

Although February is an excellent month to prune most trees, there are certain trees that should not be pruned in winter because they "bleed"—that is, their sap runs freely when they're pruned in cold weather. Bleeding won't kill a tree, but it's unsightly. Wait until summer to prune **dogwood, elm, maple, river birch, walnut**, and **yellowwood** trees.

Wait to prune spring-flowering trees until after they've bloomed.

Timely Tip

Toward the end of February is an excellent time to bring small branches of flowering trees indoors. These will burst into bloom, providing blooms several weeks ahead of when they'll appear outdoors. This is called *forcing*, and directions are given in the **Shrubs** chapter (page 239). Trees that easily bloom indoors are **apple, cherry**, and **dogwood**.

PROBLEMS

Spraying trees, especially broadleaf evergreens and small deciduous ones, with dormant oil this month can kill overwintering insects, insect eggs, scale, mites, and other pests. This is an organic treatment that helps prevent many problems during the growing season. Find just the right day on which to spray—no precipitation forecast for forty-eight hours and temperatures that are above freezing and will stay there for the next twenty-four hours. Read the label carefully before application.

This month, reapply deer and rodent repellents (Deer-Off® and Ro-Pel®, for example) to trees that have proven tasty to those pests. See page 269 about spraying **hemlocks**.

MARCH

PLANNING

Everyone has a favorite tree, and it's natural to include that tree in our yards. But it's not a good idea to overdo it—plant too many of one kind of tree to the exclusion of others. Or to have mostly just one kind of tree throughout a neighborhood. The problem is that when a disease or insect comes along that decimates the kind of tree you have planted—**American elms**, flowering **dogwoods** in the mountains, **pines** where bark beetles are active—you have a much greater loss than if you had only one or two of the affected trees. In this region, we are fortunate to be able to grow a wide variety of trees. Look around a nursery and ask questions to find some excellent trees that you may not be familiar with. Choose the criteria you want—small flowering tree or tall shade tree—and ask what's available. You may find that you like the new tree even better than those you're more familiar with. You may have discovered a new favorite by using this method.

PLANTING

Although fall is also a fine time to plant trees, most homeowners prefer to plant in spring. That's when we get in the mood and when garden centers are overflowing with choices. Most trees will be growing in containers; a few will be balled and burlapped (which means they were growing in a field and have been recently dug up). Trees in containers are generally the simplest to plant and have less adjusting to do. But large trees may not be available except as balled and burlapped. With proper care, each type should perform equally well in your yard. Here's how to plant:

1 Water the tree's roots well twenty-four hours before you plan to plant.

2 Dig a hole that's just as deep as the rootball and three times as wide.

3 Make sure the bottom of the hole is firm and the sides are slanted at a 45-degree angle. This encourages the roots to grow out into the soil.

4 Cut off any broken branches or stems.

5 Remove the tree from the container and look at the roots. If they're growing around and around the soil, loosen them. If you see a broken or dead root, prune it off.

6 Remove the twine that secures the burlap on a balled-and-burlapped tree.

7 Place the tree in the hole at the same depth it grew before.

8 Carefully remove the burlap or other coverings.

9 Fill the hole half full with the soil removed by digging.

10 Water with a transplanting solution.

11 Fill the hole with more soil.

12 Make sure the tree isn't any deeper than it grew before. Nothing will kill a tree faster than planting it too deep.

13 Water again, using a transplanting solution.

14 Many gardeners like to form a saucer in the soil around a newly planted tree to catch rainfall.

15 Mulch with 3 inches of organic material, such as pine needles or fine bark.

Planting a Tree

16 Don't stake the tree unless it's in an exceptionally windy area or very tall.

17 Water regularly for six to twelve months after planting. That helps the tree become established in your yard.

CARE

Check mulch around all trees this month. It should be an even 3 inches deep—no pyramidal mounds—and come no closer to the trunk than 6 inches.

WATERING

March is often a wet month, but if it isn't, check newly planted trees every few days to make sure they're not drying out. If you have clay soil, see that the soil around a new tree isn't soggy; that means you're overwatering. When there's been no rain in a week and the ground isn't frozen, be sure the soil is moist 6 to 8 inches down.

FERTILIZING

Young trees are the most likely candidates for fertilizer.

• Choose a high-nitrogen fertilizer such as 16-4-8. If available, a slow-release fertilizer is best.

• Apply the amount recommended on the label—unless the tree is growing in the lawn and you also fertilize your grass. In that case, use one-third to one-half the recommended amount.

• Apply the fertilizer in a circle beginning about 12 inches from the trunk of a small tree and 18 inches from a large one and continuing beyond the ends of the branches. (The roots extend about two times the width of the tree's crown.)

• Water in or fertilize just before a rainfall.

Don't fertilize newly planted trees. The rule of thumb is to wait a year before feeding them.

PRUNING

See **February**. Early March isn't too late to remove water sprouts, suckers, and crossing or rubbing branches. Try to get all this done, though, before trees leaf out. But there's one exception to the rule—whenever you spot damage, take care of it then, before insects or disease can gain a foothold.

Prune **chamaecyparis, hollies, Japanese cedar, hemlock,** and **southern magnolia** the first part of March, if necessary to maintain their shape. Use the thinning technique of removing stems back to a larger branch or to the trunk. Don't just shear the trees—that causes regrowth to occur too quickly.

March isn't a good month to prune any trees that flower in spring or that "bleed" when pruned (see the list on page 267).

PROBLEMS

Tent caterpillars may become active and visible this month. You'll notice the white fuzzy webs in the crotches of trees. If you can reach the "tents," the best way to get rid of these pests is to wait till dusk and pull them down by hand (wear gloves). Drop the nest in a bucket of soapy water. When the tents and caterpillars are still small, you may also control them by spraying with Bt (*Bacillus thuringiensis*) in early evening. Make certain that you wet the tent thoroughly with the Bt mixture.

If you have fruit trees, pick up a spraying schedule from the Extension Service and follow it throughout the year.

Spray **hemlocks** with horticultural oil if you haven't done so earlier. Choose a day when temperatures will remain above 45 degrees Fahrenheit for twenty-four hours and no precipitation is forecast.

APRIL

PLANNING

Flowering trees bring so much beauty to our yards in early to mid-spring. But then what? Does the flowering stop in your yard? It doesn't have to. Consider planting some trees that bloom in late spring or early summer. These include:

- **Chinese fringe tree** (*Chionanthus retusus*), which has white flowers
- Yellow-blooming **Chinese flame tree** (*Koelreuteria paniculata*)
- **Golden raintree**
- **Yellowwood**

Both **Chinese flame tree** and **golden raintree** are highly recommended for urban areas.

PLANTING

Tree planting continues in April. See page 268 for planting advice. If you're planting a balled-and-burlapped tree, always remove the wrapping around the rootball (even if you're told that it's natural burlap and will rot). These can prevent the roots from growing out into the soil. Also toss away the twine or wire that fastens the covering to the trunk. Large trees (often installed by the nursery) are sometimes sold in wire baskets that hold the rootball together. These are left in place since they are designed with plenty of room for roots to make their way through the cage.

CARE

Rarely is it necessary for homeowners to stake a tree. Leaving it unstaked helps the tree develop a stronger root system. But should you be planting a tall tree, it

Tree Planting with Stakes

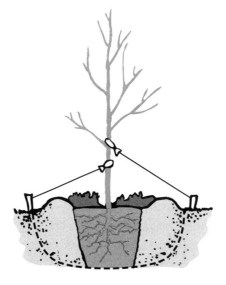

might be necessary since the root system may not be large enough in the beginning to keep the tree upright in strong winds. When planted on a steep hill, trees may also need to be staked. But avoid staking trees when possible. If staking is necessary, cover the guy wires with rubber hosing, flexible plastic, or soft cloth where they will touch the tree.

Attach the hosing to the lowest part of the limbs, allowing some room for the trunk to be able to sway slightly. Stakes should never be left in place more than a year. It's better to remove them even sooner—when the roots have taken hold and can support the tree on their own.

If there's been a lot of rain this month, mulch may have washed close to the trunks. Take a moment to rake it back so it isn't touching the trunk, which can lead to disease damage.

Be very careful when using string trimmers near trees. They can quickly cause trunk damage that is an open invitation to insects. Dogwood borers, which often kill trees, get into a tree through a wounded trunk. It's better to encircle lawn trees with mulch so it's not necessary to trim near trees.

WATERING

Frequently check trees that have been planted recently to make sure their soil doesn't dry out. Drying will be faster in fast-draining soils than in clay, but all young trees may need watering a couple of times weekly the first few weeks they're in your yard, if rainfall is less than normal or it doesn't rain weekly. During dry spells, pay attention to the watering needs of trees that have been planted in

If you're planting a balled-and-burlapped tree, always remove the wrapping around the rootball (even if you're told that it's natural burlap and will rot). These can prevent the roots from growing out into the soil.

the past year or two. Most mature trees, except those that need moist soil (see the list on page 263), don't require extra watering except during drought.

 FERTILIZING

Fertilize **hollies, southern magnolias**, and other young evergreen trees if you didn't in February. Use 1 pound of 10-6-4 or a similar high-nitrogen fertilizer per inch of trunk diameter. Spread it in a spiral outward—starting about 12 inches from the trunk and continuing beyond the tips of the branches. Water.

What about pounding fertilizer spikes into the ground? If you like them, fine. But it's much easier to spread granular or pellet fertilizer by hand than it is to pound spikes into the ground. Besides, the spikes don't evenly distribute the fertilizer.

Also fertilize trees planted in large tubs. It's best to use a slow-release fertilizer for container-grown trees since it provides a constant replacement for the nutrients in the soil that may be washed away through frequent watering.

 PRUNING

Once trees have leafed out, stop pruning unless it's to remove dead, diseased, or damaged limbs.

 PROBLEMS

Leaf miners leave what look like tunnels in the leaves of **hollies**. These are easier to control when you can spray (with pyrethrin) the small black flies or gnats as they fly around before laying eggs. But if you don't catch leaf miners at that stage, consult the local Extension Service for control advice.

Once temperatures have warmed up, put away the dormant oil and apply a light horticultural oil to fight scale and mites on **holly**. They suck the juices from the leaves.

In a wet spring, sometimes **dogwood** flowers and foliage may be covered with small disfiguring spots. This is called leaf anthracnose (not to be confused with the much more serious dogwood anthracnose). It doesn't do any lasting harm; it just looks ugly. Spraying with a fungicide is an option if you've had the problem several springs in a row. It won't cure the

disease, but can help keep it from returning. Check with the Extension Service for advice. You may also want to consider whether your **dogwood** is in too much shade; if it is, prune some larger surrounding trees to let in some sunshine.

Brown spots on **crabapple** leaves are signs of cedar-apple rust. Since the spores are produced by **eastern red cedar** trees, it's important to never plant **crabapples** anywhere near **red cedars**. If this is a recurring problem in your yard and you're determined to grow a **crabapple**, consider planting a resistant variety. A nurseryman should be able to recommend a number of them. The list includes 'Adams', 'Adirondack', 'Centurion', 'Donald Wyman', 'Indian Summer', 'Molten Lava', 'Red Jewel', 'Sargent', 'Sugar Tyme', and 'White Cascade'.

Caterpillars and what we often call "worms" (but are really caterpillars) may be a problem on flowering forms of fruit trees—**flowering cherry, peach, plum**. Spray with Bt if the damage is severe.

MAY

PLANNING

Are you keeping notes about your trees as the spring progresses? Dates of bloom, problems, names of new trees you've planted, a wish list of trees you'd like to add to the yard in coming years? That's what a garden notebook is for; it gives you an informal record of what happened in the garden in the past and what you hope might happen in the future. You can keep a large manila envelope with your notebook or journal to hold photographs (ones you've taken or those you've torn from a newspaper or magazine). You also should put labels of new plants into the envelope; they come in handy in the future.

In keeping with the idea of having something blooming in your yard during every season, have you thought about summer-flowering trees? Admittedly, there aren't as many of them as there are trees that bloom in spring, but they're all the more welcome—and admired—for that reason. Some to consider:

- **Chaste tree**
- **Franklin tree** (*Franklinia alatamaha*)
- **Japanese pagoda tree** (*Sophora japonica*)
- **Sourwood**
- **Southern magnolia**
- **Stewartia** (*Stewartia ovata* and *S. pseudocamellia*)
- **Sweet bay magnolia**

PLANTING

Because trees prefer to be planted when weather is moderate, now is a good time to plant container-grown or balled-and-burlapped trees—before the heat of summer is upon us. See page 268 for advice. If you plant during May, remember that you'll need to water frequently throughout the next few months. If you'd rather not do that or if you're planning to be away, it may be better to wait until fall to plant.

CARE

Too much mulch around trees can be as bad as too little. The ideal amount is 3 inches. Organic mulch should *not* be used as a decoration—placed in mounds around trees. That will cause the tree's roots to grow up to the surface, leaving them more vulnerable to drought and cold. Plastic mulch isn't acceptable around trees. It does prevent weed growth, but doesn't let needed air and moisture through to the roots.

WATERING

With newly planted trees, the rule is this: Keep the soil moist but not wet. Because the root system of a young tree is still small and can absorb only so much moisture at a time, it's best to water frequently—enough to thoroughly wet the rootball each time.

The rule is different for established trees (those that have been planted for more than a year). For bigger trees, apply larger amounts of water, but do it less frequently. That helps them develop deep root systems. For more information, see page 261 of the introduction.

Check the soil around dwarf trees growing in tubs or large containers. When the soil is dry 4 inches down, water. Container plants need watering more often than trees planted in the ground, so if you have deck or patio trees in pots, get in the habit of regularly feeling the soil to determine whether it needs watering.

FERTILIZING

Fertilize fast-growing trees or young trees planted a year ago, if you haven't done so earlier in the season. See page 269.

Too much mulch around trees can be as bad as too little. The ideal amount is 3 inches. Organic mulch should not be used as a decoration—placed in mounds around trees. That will cause the tree's roots to grow up to the surface, leaving them more vulnerable to drought and cold.

When you plant a tree (see page 268), don't fertilize it; it won't need food for about a year.

You may use a liquid or water-soluble fertilizer on potted trees, but a slow-release fertilizer or a granular fertilizer is effective for a longer time.

 PRUNING

Little pruning is needed this month except to remove damaged or diseased wood.

PROBLEMS

Why didn't my tree flower? It's a common question, and there are a variety of answers.

1 **Not enough sun.** Although some flowering trees are considered shade-tolerant, most require about half a day of sunlight to produce a good crop of blooms.

2 **Too much fertilizer.** This may be a problem when trees are planted in lawns fertilized five times a year. Large amounts of fertilizer produce lots of leaf and shoot growth, but can diminish development of flower buds. Also, early fall fertilization can cause a tree not to go dormant before cold weather arrives—and therefore kill new growth.

3 **Pruning at the wrong time or incorrect pruning.** Prune spring-flowering trees right after they've finished blooming. For summer-flowering trees, you may do the same, or wait until late winter.

4 **Diseases and insects.** Note the symptoms or cut off an infected part and talk with a knowledgeable person at your favorite nursery about how to control the problem.

5 **Freeze damage.** Late-spring frosts may kill flower buds.

Dogwood borers can be quite a problem in this area. If **dogwoods** have broken places in their bark, they may be susceptible to borers. Ask the Extension Service for a pesticide recommendation. And prevent future problems by keeping lawn mowers, string trimmers, and other sharp implements away from the trunks of **dogwood** trees.

It's easy to overlook a few bagworms on **arborvitae, hemlocks, Leyland cypress**, and **spruce** trees. They're perfectly camouflaged. But once there are dozens, even hundreds of them, you notice. The most effective way to get rid of bagworms is to wait until dusk and pick them off by hand. Pick as many as you see, and then go back a few nights later. You'll probably find a few more that you missed in out-of-the-way spots. Continue this for a week or two, and you should get them all. But look over the affected plant occasionally in the next month or two to make sure the bagworms are all gone.

JUNE

PLANNING

The best thing any homeowner can do at the beginning of summer is to go buy a large, comfortable hammock and suspend it between two big trees. When the temperature and humidity climb toward the stratosphere or you're tired from watering or spreading pine straw, it's refreshing to be able to collapse into a hammock, grab a glass of lemonade, and enjoy the shade for a while. All too often gardeners don't make time to truly appreciate the landscape that they've designed and nurtured. There's always one more little task, one or two weeds to pull, the hose to move from one side of the yard to another. . . the list can seem endless.

But why should only the neighbors enjoy the beauty your hard work has produced? Don't just "stop and smell the roses," but take time to enjoy the shade of your trees, the acrobatics of the squirrels jumping from branch to branch, the cardinals darting here and there among the limbs. Children instinctively know how to do this. They can sit and watch a line of ants for hours. But we adults often lose the ability to "do nothing" as we grow older. Make a vow that this is the summer you slow down and notice what's going on in the natural world that surrounds you.

While you're in that hammock, maybe you'll be thinking of your summer vacation. No matter where you plan to go these days, there's likely to be an excellent public garden nearby. It's amazing how many useful ideas you can pick up in a botanical garden or the garden around a historical house—design ideas you'd like to copy, plants that you aren't familiar with but would like to try, interesting color combinations. Be sure to take your camera and a notepad so you can bring your discoveries back home.

PLANTING

Theoretically, container-grown trees can be planted almost any month of the year. But realistically, hot weather isn't the best time to plant a young tree. It will be put under stress immediately, and you will need to water frequently to protect your investment.

If you must plant this month, do it on an overcast day when the temperature should go no higher than 80 degrees Fahrenheit. When choosing a spot for your tree, always look up (how close are power lines?) and to the sides (don't plant closer than 15 to 20 feet from a building, no matter how small the tree may be). See page 268 for planting instructions.

CARE

Put up netting on peach and other fruit trees if birds are usually a problem.

Remove the stakes from any tree planted more than a year ago. With trees planted fewer than twelve months ago, check the guy wires every month or so to make sure they aren't cutting into the trunk. And see whether wooden stakes need to be pounded back into the ground.

WATERING

When there's been no significant rainfall within a week, water trees that you've planted in the past year. Those set out in the past six months may need watering twice or more a week, depending on the type of soil, the temperature, the type of tree, its size, and whether the tree is growing in full sun or partial shade. Except in droughts, large trees can usually manage to get through a few dry spells, but younger trees haven't yet established an extensive root system; they need extra moisture when rainfall isn't adequate.

Except in droughts, large trees can usually manage to get through a few dry spells, but younger trees haven't yet established an extensive root system; they need extra moisture when rainfall isn't adequate.

FERTILIZING

No fertilizing is recommended this month except that you may use a water-soluble fertilizer on trees growing in planters if they weren't fertilized in the spring.

PRUNING

Using hedge shears, shear needled evergreen trees this month to shape them. Have you ever noticed the ends of the stems turning pinkish brown after shearing? There's a simple way to avoid this: Prune when the tree is wet from rain, dew, or being sprayed with a hose. (Naturally, you won't use electric hedge trimmers around a wet tree or wet ground, but it's okay for gas-powered trimmers.)

Another way to prune needled evergreens is to use hand pruners to cut back the "candles" (new growth) on the top and sides of the tree. If you cut off about half the new growth this month, the result is a more compact shape. Always make these cuts at a 45-degree angle.

Never cut needled evergreen back severely because most won't produce new growth. One exception is **yews**.

If you put off pruning trees that "bleed" (exude sap) when they're pruned in cold weather, summer is the time to tackle them. These include **elm, dogwood, golden chain tree, maple, walnut, river birch**, and **yellowwood**. See the pruning discussion on page 262.

PROBLEMS

A white coating on **dogwood** leaves is powdery mildew. Check with the Extension Service about a control since this can reduce the tree's growth. 'Cherokee Brave' is a flowering **dogwood** cultivar that is resistant to powdery mildew. **Kousa dogwoods** are also generally resistant, as are *Cornus kousa* x *florida* hybrids 'Aurora,' 'Constellation', and 'Stellar Pink'.

Japanese beetles may become a problem this month on some trees, particularly on the flowering forms of fruit trees (**flowering cherry**, etc.). On small trees and with light infestations, you can hand pick the beetles off and drop them into a can of soapy water. If the problem is severe, consider a contact insecticide. Ask the Extension Service or a garden center to recommend one. Whatever you do, don't put up traps to attract the beetles. That frequently makes the problem worse.

Hemlocks should be sprayed twice a year with horticultural oil—regular oil in cool weather and light oil in summer—to control hemlock woolly adelgids. The first spraying comes this month. The second one can take place from October through March.

JULY

PLANNING

How well do you know the trees in your yard? Unless you planted the trees yourself, the answer may be "not well at all." As you've seen so far in this chapter, you can do a better job caring for your trees if you know their names and their likes and dislikes. If there are just a few trees you aren't familiar with, a neighbor may know what they are or you can cut a stem with leaves from each and take it to a nursery where you've bought plants. Also take any fruits, seeds, or flowers. They should be able to identify the trees for you. If you have many "unknown" trees, get a tree identification book at the local library or a bookstore.

It's too late to do anything about the trees that you already have in your yard, but a handy hint for the next time you plant or the next time you landscape a yard is to group together plants—especially trees and shrubs—that have similar watering needs. If most of the trees or shrubs that need moist soil, for instance, are near one another, you can snake soaker hoses or drip irrigation among them.

How have your trees performed so far this year? Are you happy with their performance? Unhappy? Or haven't you given it much thought? Stop occasionally to evaluate your landscape and all the plants in it. Then make a few notes in your garden journal about changes you'd like to make or questions you want to have answered.

PLANTING

Because it's typically hot in July, it's not the best month to plant trees. But if you will be at home for the rest of the summer (so you can water frequently), you may plant container-grown trees, although it's not generally recommended. Do the planting on a cloudy day, maybe one that's misting rain. Early evening is the best time if temperatures are high. You'll find tree-planting advice on page 268.

CARE

If someone besides you cares for your lawn, be sure that caretaker keeps equipment—especially string trimmers—away from the trunks of any trees. Young trees are especially susceptible to damage, but older trees can be harmed, too. The wound that's created is an open invitation to insects and borers. A 3-foot-wide circle of mulch around your trees will help keep lawn equipment at bay.

If any construction is taking place on your property this month, or any month, see that the workers know to keep heavy equipment away from the root zones of trees in the yard. You don't want it brushing up against the bark, either. Shallow trenches dug nearby can also harm a tree. Consult a tree-care professional, and rope off trees with a 10-foot safety zone to be sure they aren't harmed during construction. You may not see immediate signs of damage; it may take a tree as long as five years to die of construction damage. But once a large tree is lost, it can be replaced only by one that's much smaller, a loss to your landscape.

WATERING

If you're spending a great deal of time watering, maybe you need to think about drip irrigation or soaker hoses. For large trees that you feel the need to water during long dry spells, investigate a water spike, which puts water down into the soil where the roots are.

Remember that you can do a few things to keep the soil moist besides frequently watering: mulch with 3 inches of organic material, keep weeds removed, and water slowly and deeply.

If you notice suckers—thin upright sprouts—at the base of any tree, dig them up. They steal nutrients and water from the tree and attract insects. The same is true of water sprouts—flexible upright growth on limbs. Cut these back to their base.

 FERTILIZING

There's no need to fertilize trees this month.

 PRUNING

You may remove diseased, dead, or broken limbs or stems anytime you see them.

Trees that bleed when cut back in winter should instead be pruned in hot weather. See page 275 for a list of the trees that may be pruned this month, if they need it.

If you notice suckers—thin upright sprouts—at the base of any tree, dig them up. They steal nutrients and water from the tree and often attract insects. The same is true of water sprouts—flexible upright growth on limbs. Cut these back to their base.

 PROBLEMS

Summertime and weeds just naturally go together. We all know that weeds aren't good for our plants, but when it's hot, we often let their removal slide. It's easier if you set aside ten minutes first thing in the morning for pulling weeds. You'll be surprised how satisfied you feel getting rid of those weeds that have been around for weeks.

Use extreme caution with weedkillers this time of year. Most have an upper temperature limit for use. And sometimes in hot weather the chemical can vaporize, harming a nearby desirable plant. If you use a weedkiller near a tree, do not let the product get on the trunk. Cover the trunk with plastic for ten minutes or so to give you time to spray and the herbicide time to dry. Or hold a large piece of cardboard or poster board between the area being sprayed and the tree. Another method is to dip a paint brush into the chemical and paint it on the weed. Or if you're spraying just a few weeds, cut the bottom and top from a gallon milk jug, place it over the weed and then spray down into the jug.

Check again for bagworms on needled evergreens. Do this at dusk, when the worms will be inside the "bags" they have built for a home. Pick them off by hand (sometimes more mature bags will have to be cut off with hand pruners), then crush them individually under foot.

If you have **Canadian hemlocks** in your yard, see **Problems** under the **June** entry.

AUGUST

Trees

PLANNING

August is a month when shade comes into its own. Is anything more welcome in the yard than cooling shade? Just gazing at a shady area makes the temperature more bearable. Actually sitting beneath a shade tree is one of the pleasures of summer. Look ahead to tree planting time in a couple of months, and consider adding a shade tree or two to the yard if you have mostly sunny areas. Here are some suggestions if you don't have a favorite shade tree:

- **American beech** (*Fagus grandiflora*)
- **Ginkgo**
- **Lacebark elm**
- **Linden tree** (*Tilia tomentosa*)
- **Oak**
- **Red maple**
- **River birch**
- **Tulip poplar**
- **Yellowwood**

This is the month when one of our most spectacular and dependable native trees becomes more visible. If you spy a flash of red as you drive by some woods, that's **sourwood**. If you don't have one in your yard, you owe it to yourself to consider planting one some fall, if you have room. **Sourwood** adds beauty to the yard in three seasons. Don't try to dig one from the woods, though; they do not transplant well from the wild. Instead, buy one grown in a container.

PLANTING

Unless you must plant a tree this month, it's best to wait a little longer when fall temperatures are more moderate. Trees planted in August—especially when temperatures are high—will be more stressed, which doesn't help them get off to a good start. Also, they will need frequent watering, which could be a problem if you're planning to take a vacation in the next few weeks.

CARE

Have thunderstorms washed away mulch, particularly on slopes? Replace it with pine straw, which stays in place. Don't pile mulch up against tree trunks. That may keep the trunk moist, which creates conditions for disease.

Don't leave fallen **peaches** or **plums** on the ground to attract yellowjackets.

WATERING

Young trees are more likely than established trees to need watering in hot weather. See page 261 for signs of a thirsty tree. If you're able to water only so much—either because of local government restrictions or the size of your water bill—decide which trees will get preference. At the top of the list, put trees with sentimental value, those that were quite expensive, those that are hard to replace, and newly planted trees, which may not make it without watering.

Water dwarf trees in tubs daily to be sure they don't dry out.

FERTILIZING

Fertilizing is not necessary this month. Fertilizer can cause plants to put on a spurt of growth—which you don't want between now and cold weather. Lots of tender new growth is likely to be killed by frost.

PRUNING

See **July**. Prune trees that bleed if cut in cold weather, cut back water sprouts on limbs, and dig suckers from the base of trees.

Take care of storm damage right away. A broken limb is often the entryway for insects or diseases. Some trees have weak wood and are frequently damaged by storms—**silver maple** and **weeping**

Fertilizing is not necessary this month. Fertilizer can cause plants to put on a spurt of growth—which you don't want between now and cold weather.

willow are two. 'Bradford' **pear** often splits in two because it has weak crotch angles (where the limbs join the trunk is at too narrow an angle). Be alert for damage on these trees, and correct it.

 PROBLEMS

If **tulip poplar** leaves yellow and begin to fall off this month, the problem is often lack of moisture.

Have you noticed a white or grayish powdery coating on the leaves of **tulip poplar** or **oak** late this month? That's powdery mildew. Although it doesn't look great, it has little effect on the trees. But it is important to rake and remove from the area all leaves that fall off (now and in fall) so that the problem doesn't perpetuate itself.

Before the end of the month, Japanese beetles will disappear. They haven't flown off. They are actually going to spend the winter as grubs under your lawn. The only long-term control for these voracious pests is to apply milky spore to your lawn and to encourage your neighbors to do the same.

Spider mites are often a problem in hot, dry weather on a variety of small trees. If leaves look bronzed, the problem is probably spider mites. You can be certain by holding a piece of white paper beneath an affected leaf and tapping it over the paper. Specks will fall from the bottom of the leaf onto the paper, and generally they'll move. Several applications of Neem or an insecticidal soap may help. If not, check with a nursery about a miticide. General insecticides don't affect spider mites since these pests are not technically insects (they are arachnids).

If insects are causing serious damage to a large tree, there isn't much you can do about it. Home spraying equipment will reach only so far. But if the tree is valuable (and large trees usually are), you may want to talk with a professional arborist. Tree-care professionals have equipment and methods not available to homeowners.

If you didn't spray **hemlocks** with a light horticultural oil in June or July, do it this month. A twice-yearly spraying helps keeps woolly adelgids at bay.

White Grub

SEPTEMBER

PLANNING

Once Labor Day is past, September has the feeling of a new beginning. Younger children have gone back to school; older ones have left for college. Some mornings there's a nip in the air. Maybe this is a good time to look over your landscape plan and see whether you need any more trees. Take this opportunity between the end of summer and the beginning of cold weather to do some research on the right trees for various areas in your yard. After you'd decided whether you need an evergreen, deciduous, or flowering tree, learn about the various characteristics of trees you think might fit well in your yard—growth habit, shape, and mature size.

A few isolated trees may have already begun putting on their fall finery, but the big show is yet to come. Do you have plenty of trees in your yard that produce colorful fall foliage? If not, now's the time to consider some more. These are good choices:

- **Black gum**
- **Dogwood**
- **Fringe tree**
- **Ginkgo**
- **Japanese maple**
- **Ornamental pear**
- **Red maple**
- **Sassafras**
- **Serviceberry**
- **Sourwood**
- **Stewartia**
- **Sweet gum**

PLANTING

Want to try growing flowering **dogwoods** from seeds? You won't end up with a 6-foot tree in a year, but the trees you grow will be free, which is nice.

1 Watch flowering **dogwoods** this month, and gather a handful of berries as soon as they turn red (and before the birds and squirrels can grab them).

2 Peel off the fleshy red covering to get to the hard seed inside.

3 Place the seeds in a zipper-style plastic bag and put them in the refrigerator for three to four months. (Mark the date on the bag with a permanent marker so you'll know when the time is up.)

4 Then plant them ¹/₂-inch deep in a flat or container of moistened potting soil.

5 Keep the container somewhere that temperatures remain at least 70 degrees Fahrenheit.

6 Once germination has taken place (two to four weeks), move the seedlings into bright light.

7 Twice a month, fertilize with a houseplant fertilizer diluted to half strength.

8 When the seedlings are 2 inches tall, transplant them to individual 4-inch pots.

9 Continue to give the plants bright light, but fairly cool temperatures.

10 Water as needed so the soil doesn't dry completely.

11 As soon as the chance of frost has passed, plant the little trees in the yard, marking them carefully so they won't get stepped on or mowed down.

You may plant container-grown evergreen and deciduous trees this month, if you'd like. (See page 268.) Wait until October to plant balled-and-burlapped trees.

When you plant trees, do not amend the soil with peat or bark as you do with most other plants. University tests have shown that a tree has fewer problems getting used to its new home in your yard if it's planted only in the soil that's already there. That's a win-win situation since using the soil in the yard is cheaper and less time consuming for the gardener.

If you plan to move a small tree from one section of your yard to another this winter, now's the time to prune the tree's roots.

- First, determine the size of rootball the tree will need to survive after it's moved. Measure the diameter of the trunk 6 inches above the ground. This is the trunk caliper. Add 12 inches of rootball for each inch of caliper. That means that if the trunk is 2 inches in diameter, move the tree with a rootball that's at least 24 inches across.
- Insert a spade into the soil 8 to 12 inches deep in a circle whose diameter you determined in the first step.
- See **December** for information on completing the transplanting.

CARE

Harvest apples as soon as they ripen. Pick up and discard fruit that falls on the ground.

Remove stakes that have been in place for a year. Allowing trees to remain staked for longer than a year can harm them.

WATERING

Keep the soil of newly planted trees moist but not wet. Remember that they may need to be watered frequently if rainfall isn't adequate because their root systems are still small for the size of the tree.

Always water trees slowly so the water sinks deep into the soil. You want to soak the soil at least 8 inches deep.

FERTILIZING

September isn't a month when many plants are fertilized; we're heading into cold weather and want plants to slow their growth in preparation. Trees are no exception. Never fertilize them this month. There are two times of the year that trees may be fertilized: One is from the time deciduous trees lose their leaves until just before the leaves begin to grow again the next spring. The second is in spring as trees are leafing out.

If at all possible, avoid spreading fertilizer over the root area of trees when you fertilize your lawn this month.

PRUNING

Prune to remove dead, diseased, or damaged branches or stems. Otherwise, wait till winter.

It's especially important to *avoid* pruning spring-flowering trees now. If you do so, you'll cut off some or all of the flower buds that would bloom next year.

 PROBLEMS

Check for fall webworm nests. If you find some, remove them from trees with a gloved hand and destroy.

You may think you can forget about weeds since they'll just be killed by frost next month or in November. But only the tops of perennial weeds are killed. If they're not dug up or eradicated by a weedkiller this year, they'll return next year.

As you walk about your yard this month, keep an eye out for possible problems. Signs include:

- Leaves falling off prematurely.
- Dying or discolored leaves.
- Stem die-back.

If you spot any of those signs, look closer to see whether you can determine the problem. Look for tell-tale signs of insects or diseases. See whether the soil seems very dry or excess water is standing in a puddle. If you're not sure, ask the Extension Service or a knowledgeable employee at a good nursery for advice.

OCTOBER

PLANNING

When you're considering a new tree for the yard, do you wonder whether to buy a large tree and have it planted by the nursery or to buy a small tree that you can easily handle?

- Factors that favor getting a large tree: You've moved into a new house and this tree will be in a prominent place in the landscape. In effect, it will become a focal point while smaller plants grow. (A larger tree gives a more finished look to a landscape.)
- Factors that favor purchasing a small tree: It's cheaper and will require less watering. Because a smaller tree adjusts to being planted better than a big one, the two trees may be the same size in just a few years.

As the outdoor gardening season begins to wind down, take time to update your garden journal or notebook. Note autumn rainfall—or its absence—the date of the first frost, and particularly the dates on which the leaves of various trees began changing color and when they started falling. It's fascinating to look back at these notes in coming years and see how the rituals of fall vary by several weeks from year to year. It's also interesting to see how sometimes the leaves all seem to fall within a short period, while in other years, you spend two months raking.

PLANTING

See the **September** entry for tips on starting **dogwood** trees from seed. Children usually enjoy helping with this.

October is a good month to plant evergreen and deciduous trees, both those grown in containers and those balled and burlapped. The size of the planting hole is very important for the survival of a newly planted tree. It should be at least three times as wide as the rootball, but not any deeper. See page 268 for more tree-planting tips.

Never pick up or carry a tree by its trunk. Instead, handle it by its container or rootball.

Handle root systems of balled-and-burlapped trees carefully to make certain they're not damaged while being transported home, moved to the planting site, or placed in the hole. If the rootball falls apart, the tree may die. This is especially true of a needled evergreen. Also take pains not to damage the bark since wounds leave openings for insects or diseases to enter.

Remove all tags and labels before you plant the tree. Do keep them, though, so you know the name of the tree and what type of care it needs. A good place to store these is in an envelope kept with your garden notebook.

When you choose a spot to plant a tree, be sure that it's not within 15 feet of a sidewalk. The roots of some trees can crack the sidewalk.

It's rarely necessary to wrap the trunk of a tree when it's planted. Wrapping may cause an increase in disease, insect, and water damage to the trunk.

CARE

October is leaf time in our region. So many of those wonderful trees you appreciated during the spring and fall are going to drop their leaves now. Don't think of their clean-up as a chore. Rather, think of it as the trees' providing soil amendments and mulch.

- Remove leaves at least weekly. If they get too thick, they'll smother the grass and, in mulched areas, can prevent rainfall from penetrating.
- Pile leaves onto the compost pile. If you don't have a compost pile, this is an ideal time to start one. (See page 356.)
- Save some leaves (usually the last ones of the season) to shred into mulch. Spread the leaves an inch thick in a circle on the driveway. Mow over them until they're in small pieces. If you have a shredder, use that instead.
- Be careful to rake up and remove from the yard all leaves of trees that

suffered disease damage during the year—leaf spots, mildew, etc—or those that were nfested with insects. Getting them away from the susceptible tree helps prevent future problems.

WATERING

October can be a rainy month in Kentucky and Tennessee. But if rain has not totaled an inch per week, you may need to water trees planted this year. Check the soil to see whether it's dry. Newly planted trees may have to be watered twice a week, or even more often, during dry spells. You'll want to protect the investment you made in that young tree by watering it sufficiently, but not so much that it drowns.

FERTILIZING

There's no fertilizing this month. If you haven't had your soil tested in four or five years, you might want to do that this month. That will provide fertilizer recommendations for your trees—what type to use, how much is needed, and when to fertilize.

PRUNING

Fall is the worst time of the year for pruning trees. Put up the loppers and pruning saw unless you're taking care of diseased, damaged, or dying limbs or branches. These should always be dealt with as they occur. But save other pruning until late winter.

PROBLEMS

An application of horticultural oil to **Canadian hemlocks** this month can help control woolly adelgids. If you don't get to it this month, do it on a nice day between now and the end of March.

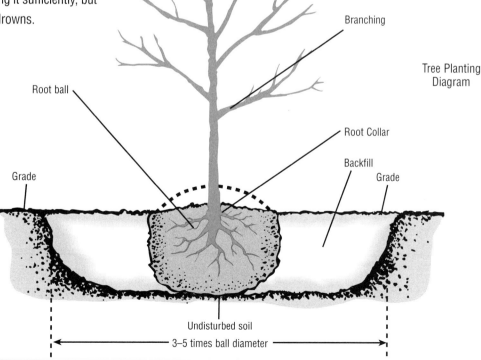

Branching

Tree Planting Diagram

Root ball

Root Collar

Backfill

Grade

Grade

Undisturbed soil

3–5 times ball diameter

NOVEMBER

PLANNING

This time of year, you may sometimes find trees on sale at garden centers, home stores, and nurseries. If you are still looking for a few trees to add to your landscape, this can be a nice opportunity since November isn't too late to plant trees in this area, especially deciduous trees (those that lose their leaves). But check the trees carefully to determine if they're on sale simply because the store doesn't want to have to care for them over the winter or they've become a bit shop-worn. Do they appear to have been well cared for? Are the roots girdling the rootball (completely covering it in an almost impenetrable mass)? Since a tree is a long-term investment, purchase the best quality available.

November may see the beginning of the frequent rains that are a feature of our winters. The clay soil so many of us contend with can cause drainage problems. But some trees don't mind poorly drained areas. Consider these:

- **Bald cypress**
- **Black gum**
- **Green ash** (*Fraxinus pennsylvanica*)
- **Hawthorn** (*Crataegus viridis* 'Winter King')
- **Red maple**

- **River birch**
- **Sweet bay magnolia**
- **Sweet gum**
- **Willow oak** (*Quercus phellos*)

If you have woods on your property, it's tempting to think of transplanting flowering **dogwoods** from there so they'll be closer to your house. It usually isn't a good idea unless the tree is very small (say, 3 feet tall or less), and that size means the tree probably won't bloom for many years. Since the tree is of unknown parentage, you have no idea how many blooms it will produce or what kind. Another difficulty is that in a wooded area, **dogwood** roots are hard to separate from those of other trees and shrubs. If you're determined, see the **Planting** section for **December**. But you're probably better off buying a small **dogwood** in bloom in spring. Then you have instant color and know what you're getting.

PLANTING

As long as the ground isn't frozen or likely to freeze in the next few days, you may plant trees. For almost-certain success, stick with deciduous trees grown in containers. Before digging, test the soil to be certain it isn't too wet to work with. Pick up some soil in your hand and form it into a ball. If it holds together at first, then breaks apart, the soil is moist enough for planting. If it doesn't form a ball at all, it needs watering before you plant. If the ball stays together, the soil is too wet to work; wait a few days before digging that hole.

Be very careful to plant a tree at the same depth it grew before. Trees that are planted too deeply or that are placed in too-deep holes and gradually sink lower than they grew previously are not likely to survive.

CARE

The leaves of broadleaf evergreen trees such as **hollies** lose moisture during winter through transpiration. They usually replace this moisture by taking it up from the soil. But if the ground is frozen and the tree can't draw water from the soil, the result can be "burned" foliage, which is unsightly. There are several ways to overcome this. One is to make sure your evergreens are deeply watered going into winter. Another is to plant broadleaf evergreens so that the morning sun does not shine on them (when the leaves are likely still to be frozen). Some gardeners also like to spray susceptible trees and shrubs with an antidesiccant such as Wilt-Pruf™. It helps reduce the amount of moisture lost. The drawback is that the coating doesn't last all winter and may have washed off by the time the trees really need it, unless applied a second time. Follow label directions.

Check the ties on staked trees to make sure that the wire isn't biting into the trunk and that the tree is able to move some. If stakes have been in place a year, remove them immediately.

Also remove trunk wrappings.

Check mulch around all trees to make sure it's 3 inches deep. A less-thick mulch isn't going to be much protection, and one that's much too deep can cut off water and oxygen flow to the roots. Don't let the mulch touch the trunk.

 # WATERING

It probably won't be necessary to water any trees this month except those growing in containers. But if rainfall is deficient, keep an eye on trees planted since September and water as necessary to make sure the soil they're growing in doesn't dry out.

 # FERTILIZING

If you prefer to fertilize trees in winter, rather than spring, you may fertilize deciduous trees this month. Wait until they've lost their leaves. The theory of fertilizing from late fall through very early spring is that the fertilizer has a longer time to penetrate the soil and will be in the roots and available for growth in the spring. See page 269 for fertilizing directions.

 # PRUNING

Little pruning is done in November. But take care of any stems or branches that may be dying, diseased, or broken.

 # PROBLEMS

Dogwood anthracnose is quite a problem here and can kill or weaken an affected tree. It mostly affects those flowering **dogwoods** growing in full shade and is more prevalent at higher elevations. It's not always simple to tell the difference between a mild case of dogwood anthracnose and other fungal problems, but one good clue this

Timely Tip

Trees that prefer acidic soil:

- **Canadian hemlock**
- **Carolina silverbell**
- **Franklin tree**
- **Fringe tree**
- **Holly**
- **Magnolia**
- **Pin oak** (*Quercus palustris*)
- **Sourwood**
- **Spruce**
- **Stewartia**
- **Yellowwood**
- **Willow oak**

time to year is that the leaves don't fall off as they should. Consider planting **dogwoods** in a sunnier site and growing a resistant variety such as 'Appalachian Spring'. But if you think the disease is present, consult the Extension Service for the latest research recommendations.

Spray a coating of horticultural oil on **hollies** and other trees affected with scale. Carefully follow the label directions concerning application during the correct temperature and weather conditions.

DECEMBER

PLANNING

If you've decided to buy a live Christmas tree this year and plant it in the landscape after the holidays, it's a good idea to dig the hole ahead of time because the weather may not be suitable for hole digging when you need to plant the tree. See page 282 for recommendations on the best size and type of planting hole for trees. After the hole has been prepared, fill it with leaves or mulch and cover it with a board or piece of plywood so no one accidentally trips into it.

If you've moved to property where the trees were allowed to become overgrown, you may be contemplating quite a bit of pruning in the next few months. If this involves large trees, consult an arborist. Few homeowners are equipped to work in tall trees. The International Society of Arboriculture (www.isa-arbor.com) can provide a list of certified arborists (those who have passed a test on their knowledge) in your area.

Take a few minutes after the holidays to bring your garden notebook up to date.

PLANTING

As long as the ground isn't frozen, homeowners may plant container-grown deciduous trees this month.

Beginning in December and continuing through March, you may also transplant trees from one part of your property to another. For transplanting to be successful, a large number of roots must be moved with the tree. This means a fairly large and heavy rootball is necessary—so two people are generally required.

1 You should have prepared trees for moving by root pruning three to six months ahead of time. See **September**.

2 Water the tree thoroughly two days before you expect to transplant it.

3 Dig a circle around the tree that's 4 to 6 inches outside the root pruning. This allows you to gather the new roots the tree formed after some of the old roots were severed. The depth of the rootball should be about one-half to two-thirds of the width.

4 Don't let the rootball fall apart.

5 Roll the rootball onto a piece of burlap that's been placed beside the tree.

6 Fasten the burlap around the rootball.

7 Dig a hole. See page 282.

8 Plant the tree in its new hole.

9 Water thoroughly, and mulch with 3 inches of organic material.

CARE

If you cut needled evergreens this month to make into wreaths or to use as greenery around the house during the holidays, you don't want the material to dry out and lose its needles. The best way to prevent this is to place the greenery in a bathtub and completely immerse it in water for twenty-four hours. Let it dry, and then arrange it. Keep fresh greenery away from heat sources such as fireplaces and candles.

You may also want to spray outdoor wreaths with hair spray or an antidesiccant to help them last longer.

A cut Christmas tree will last longer if you pick one that's fresh and then keep the end of the trunk immersed in water from then on. Here are some tips:

1 Test for freshness by holding a branch between your thumb and fingers and pulling lightly toward you. If few needles fall off, the tree is fresh. If the end of a branch bends easily, that's also a sign of freshness. It's natural to have some yellowing, browning, or falling of interior needles, but this shouldn't be excessive. And if you pick up a tree a few inches and plunk it back down on the ground, needles shouldn't fall from the outside of the tree.

If you cut needled evergreens this month to make into wreaths or to use as greenery around the house during the holidays, you don't want the material to dry out and lose its needles. The best way to prevent this is to place the greenery in a bathtub and completely immerse it in water for twenty-four hours.

2 Most tree lots now cut the trunk of the tree for you. This allows for fast water uptake. You need to get the tree home and into water quickly.

3 If you're not ready to take your cut tree indoors, place it in a bucket of water and keep it on a porch or in the garage—where it's cool but sheltered from wind and sun.

4 You may want to cut about an inch off the bottom of the trunk before bringing the tree indoors.

5 A tree will absorb about a gallon of water the first twenty-four hours. Be sure to keep the stand full. From then on, add water daily as needed.

6 Keep cut trees away from fireplaces and other sources of heat.

WATERING

Newly planted trees may occasionally require water if there's been little rain and the ground isn't frozen. But check the soil first to see whether it's dry. You don't want to overwater, especially in clay soil.

FERTILIZING

You may fertilize trees in winter or spring. If you prefer winter feeding, fertilize now. See page 269.

Timely Tip

A living Christmas tree—one that's planted outdoors after the holidays—is a nice tradition.

1 Choose a species that grows well in your area. Unfortunately, our hot, humid summers limit our selection to **eastern red cedar, Leyland cypress, Norway spruce, pine**, and—in Zone 6 only—**Colorado blue spruce**.

2 Examine and feel the rootball before you buy. It should be wide and heavy and not broken.

3 Move the tree carefully to protect the rootball.

4 Have a tub or container large enough to hold the rootball.

5 Water the rootball if it feels dry to the touch when you get it home.

6 Place the tree in a basement or garage when temperatures are cool but don't drop to freezing. This allows the tree to gradually get used to indoor temperatures.

7 After three or four days, move the tree into the house. It shouldn't stay in a heated room for more than five days.

8 Use only tiny lights.

9 Don't let the rootball stand in water, but keep it barely moist.

10 Move the tree back to the garage or basement for several days. Don't let the soil dry out.

11 Plant outdoors when the ground is not frozen. Dig the hole before you take the tree outside.

PRUNING

When cutting stems of **hollies** and other evergreens for holiday decorations, cut back to the main branch or at a 45-degree angle just above a bud.

PROBLEMS

Problems should be few this month, but keep an eye out when you're in the yard.

CHAPTER TEN

Vines & Ground Covers

"Attractive and useful" is how gardeners should think of the role vines and ground covers can play in the landscape. Instead of being the "stars," of your yard, they're more like character actors.

They're essential, they're long-lasting, but they don't necessarily grab a lot of attention. Still, they can be real problem-solvers in a number of situations, and for most homeowners, that's better than glitz any day.

VINES

Put a vine to work in your yard by letting it:

- Hide an ugly fence.
- Cover a boring blank wall or the side of a garden shed.
- Climb a trellis that's used to separate or differentiate sections of the landscape.
- Bring beauty to a small spot. Most vines don't take up much space at their base, but their climbing and spreading top portions can make quite an impact. Some will even grow in containers.
- Create shade, trained over an arbor.
- Add height to the garden.
- Attract birds.

- Serve as a screen.
- Produce flowers, berries, fruits, or fall color.

As you can see, vines are versatile. You can use them for many purposes. Some are annual, others are perennial; of those vines that are perennial (long-lasting), some are evergreen, and some are deciduous. One type isn't necessarily better or more useful than another; it all depends on what you need the vine for. An evergreen vine might be better covering a fence between you and your neighbor, if the purpose is privacy. If the vine is just a way to improve the looks of an old fence, it may not matter if the vine keeps its leaves in the winter or not. You might think that perennial is better than annual, since you don't have to replant perennial vines, but they may have to be pruned yearly. And annual vines are cheap, grow easily from seed, and give fast, temporary cover wherever you need it. The chart on page 291 tells which vines are evergreen, which are deciduous, and which are annuals.

The chart also lists how a vine climbs. That's another factor in matching the right vine with its function. These growth habits dictate the type of structure or support on which a vine should be trained.

1 Clinging vines develop rootlets, called *holdfasts*, that cling tightly to a support such as a wall or a bare hillside. (But if you ever have to take this vine down, the holdfasts are very difficult to remove completely.)

2 Twining vines wrap themselves around a vertical post, chain-link fence, arbor, or lattice. Don't plant a twining vine on a tree—it can strangle it.

3 Vines that attach themselves by tendrils reach out to grab something. It may be a string, netting, chain link, lattice, or even a shrub.

4 Climbers, such as **rambler roses**, aren't true vines. They don't attach themselves to a structure. Instead, the gardener ties the plant's long stems to a rail fence, lattice, or trellis.

Vines & Ground Covers

The final consideration in choosing a vine is aggressiveness. We are all too familiar with aggressive vines—**kudzu** covering entire hillsides, trees and all, in summer and **wisteria** climbing to the uppermost portions of tall trees in spring. (**Wisteria** looks wonderful—as long as it isn't in *your* yard.)

Several fairly aggressive vines appear on the list because those plants can be useful in certain situations. If you have a large area to cover quickly, they get the job done. But in the future, you may have to prune them back a couple of times each year.

For most purposes in the home landscape, though, it's best to be patient and not go for the fastest growing vine. Instead, choose one whose eventual size matches the spot where it will grow.

GROUND COVERS

The same holds true for ground covers. Some spread faster and farther than others. If you have an empty slope to fill, you want a plant that will cover it as quickly as possible. **Ivy, bugleweed**, or **creeping juniper** are possibilities. Slopes drain quickly, so choose ground cover that can tolerate dry spells once it's established.

But if you need a plant for a small space, choose one that's more mild-mannered—such as **candytuft**, **liriope**, or **foamflower** (see the **Perennials** and **Ornamental Grasses** chapters).

Because gardeners in Tennessee and Kentucky can grow so many evergreen ground covers—which look good all year round—we consequently plant few deciduous ones. The main exception is **spotted dead nettle**, which is often planted to complement perennials.

Why plant a ground cover? You might use it to:

- Prevent erosion.
- Reduce the amount of grass that must be mowed weekly in season.
- Cover exposed tree roots.
- Replace grass in areas that are too shady.
- Serve as a barrier around trees to keep mowers and string trimmers from damaging trunks.
- Edge a walkway.
- Hang over tops of walls.
- Unify the landscape.

As with all plants, choose the ground cover that best fits the conditions where it will grow—amount of sun or shade, soil type, drainage, and moisture. The *Tennessee Gardener's Guide: Third Edition* and the *Kentucky Gardener's Guide* provide all that information and suggest the best ground covers for your area.

A soil test is a good investment before you choose ground covers. It tells you the pH of the soil, which nutrients are present, and which are lacking. Call your county's Extension Service office (see pages 344 and 253) for directions on how to take and submit a soil sample. It's an inexpensive process that saves you time and money in the long run.

Since a ground cover will be in the same place for many years, you should improve the soil before planting. Thoroughly mix in one-third to one-half fine pine bark, such as Nature's Helper™, compost, rotted mushroom compost, or leaf mold (composted leaves). If you're digging a number of holes, it's often a good idea to spread 3 or 4 inches of pine straw over the bed after you prepare the soil and before you plant. That keeps the soil in tip-top shape until you're able to get all the plants in the ground.

Vines & Ground Covers

Planting ground covers is much like planting annuals or perennials—remove them from their containers, place them at the same depth they grew before, add some soil, water, and then mulch.

But the technique is a bit different when planting ground covers on a slope. First you dig the holes, next you spread an organic mulch, and then you cover the mulch with netting—either burlap netting (which will eventually decompose) or plastic bird netting.

Cut holes in the netting to insert the plant. Place the plant at the same depth it grew before. Refill the hole with soil, leaving a saucer or lip of soil in the front to catch and hold water. Then tuck the netting around the plant. That will prevent the mulch—and plants—from washing away in heavy rains. Staggering the holes, instead of digging them in straight lines, also helps prevent run-off and erosion.

One of the most puzzling parts of planting ground covers is trying to decide how many plants you need. Mostly, it depends on spacing. The farther apart you plant them, the longer it takes them to cover an area. On the other hand, if you plant too closely, the ground cover quickly becomes overgrown. Whichever spacing you decide upon, below is the formula I use when I'm setting out one hundred plants.

Once you know how many you need, you're on your way to a more attractive and carefree landscape.

Formula for Setting Out One Hundred Plants

Planting Distance Apart (in inches)	Area Covered (in square feet)
6	25
12	100
18	225
24	400
30	625
36	900
48	1,600
60	2,500

Vines & Ground Covers

Vines

Common Name (*Botanical Name*)	Type	Height (Feet)	Foliage Type	Flower Color	Light Level	How Climbs
Black-eyed Susan vine (*Thunbergia alata*)	Annual	6 to 8	NA	Orange, yellow, white	Sun	Twining
Carolina jessamine (*Gelsemium sempervirens*)	Perennial	20	Evergreen or semievergreen	Yellow	Sun, partial sun	Twining
Clematis (*Clematis* species and hybrids)	Perennial	5 to 30	Deciduous	White, pink, red, purple, blue-violet	Sun	Twisting
Climbing hydrangea (*Hydrangea anomala petiolaris*)	Perennial	50 to 60	Deciduous	White, cream	Shade, partial shade, partial sun	Clinging
Climbing rose (*Rosa* species and hybrids)	Perennial	8 to 30	Deciduous	White, red, pink, yellow, orange, bicolors	Sun	Climbing
Crossvine (*Bignonia capreolata*)	Perennial	20 to 40	Evergreen to semievergreen	Orange, yellow, reddish-purple	Sun, partial sun	Clinging
Cypress vine (*Ipomoea quamoclit*)	Annual	10 to 20	NA	Red, white	Sun	Twining
Fiveleaf akebia (*Akebia quinata*)	Perennial	20 to 40	Deciduous	Lavender, pink, white	Sun, partial sun	Twining
Goldflame honeysuckle (*Lonicera* x *heckrotti*)	Perennial	10 to 15	Deciduous	Coral, maroon, pink	Sun, partial sun	Twining
Hardy kiwi or **actinidia vine** (*Actinidia kolomikta*)	Perennial	15 to 30	Deciduous	White	Sun, partial sun	Twining
Hyacinth bean (*Dolichos lablab*)	Annual	10 to 20	NA	Purple	Sun	Twining
Mandevilla (*Mandevilla* x *amoena*)	Annual (but may be overwintered indoors)	10 to 20	Evergreen (if overwintered)	Pink, red	Sun, partial sun	Twining

Vines & Ground Covers

Vines

Common Name (*Botanical Name*)	Type	Height (Feet)	Foliage Type	Flower Color	Light Level	How Climbs
Moonflower (*Ipomoea alba*)	Annual	10 to 12	NA	White	Sun	Twining
Morning Glory (*Ipomoea tricolor*)	Annual	10 to 12	NA	Blue, pink, red, white	Sun	Twining
Passionflower (*Passiflora* species)	Perennial	15 to 25	Deciduous	Lavender, white	Sun, partial sun	Tendrils
Sweet potato vine (*Ipomoea batatas*)	Annual	10 to 12	NA	Grown for colorful foliage	Sun	Climbing
Trumpet creeper (*Campsis* species and hybrids)	Perennial	30	Deciduous	Orange, red, yellow	Sun, partial sun	Twining
Trumpet honeysuckle (*Lonicera sempervirens*)	Perennial	10 to 25	Deciduous	Yellow, orange-red, red	Sun, partial sun	Twining
Wisteria (*Wisteria* species and hybrids)	Perennial	40 to 50	Deciduous	Lavender, pink, white	Sun	Twining

Ground Covers

Common Name (*Botanical Name*)	Type	Light Level	Height (Inches)	Flower Color	Comments
Bugleweed (*Ajuga reptans*)	Evergreen	Any	2 to 6	Blue, pink, white	Colorful, easy to grow. Not for small spaces because it spreads aggressively.
Creeping juniper (*Juniperus* species and hybrids)	Evergreen	Sun	4 to 36	None	For filling in large spaces and banks. Needs excellent drainage.
Creeping phlox or thrift (*Phlox subulata*)	Evergreen	Sun to partial shade	4 to 6	Pink, blue, white	Watch out for the ones with magenta flowers. They can clash with azaleas and other spring bloomers.

Vines & Ground Covers

JANUARY · FEBRUARY · MARCH · APRIL · MAY · JUNE · JULY · AUGUST · SEPTEMBER · OCTOBER · NOVEMBER · DECEMBER

Ground Covers

Common Name (*Botanical Name*)	Type	Light Level	Height (Inches)	Flower Color	Comments
Creeping thyme (*Thymus praecox*)	Evergreen to semi-evergreen	Sun, partial sun	2 to 4	Lavender, pink, red, white	Nice between stepping stones. Emits a nice fragrance when stepped on. Can be mowed.
English ivy (*Hedera helix*)	Evergreen	Any	3 to 8	None	Slow to become established, but may become aggressive. Give it plenty of room.
Foamflower (*Tiarella* species and hybrids)	Evergreen	Shade, partial shade	6 to 18	White, pink	A pretty ground cover that thrives in woodland sites.
Pachysandra (*Pachysandra* species and hybrids)	Evergreen	Shade, partial shade	6 to 12	White, pink	Easy to grow. Nice choice for partial shade. Has interesting texture.
Spotted dead nettle (*Lamium maculatum*)	Deciduous	Shade, partial shade	6 to 12	White, pink, violet	Heart-shaped, variegated leaves really brighten shaded areas.
Sweet box (*Sarcococca hookerana humilis*)	Evergreen	Shade, partial shade	8 to 18	White	Sweet box has shiny leaves and black berries in fall for the birds.
Vinca (*Vinca minor*)	Evergreen	Shade, partial shade	4 to 6	Blue, white, purplish	Easy to grow and always looks neat.
Wild ginger (*Asarum* species and hybrids)	Either, depending on species	Shade, partial shade	4 to 9	Reddish-brown	Has glossy heart-shaped leaves. Look for cultivars with silver veining in the foliage. Good woodland plant.
Wintercreeper (*Euonymous fortunei*)	Evergreen	Any	12 to 24	White	Often grown as a vine. There are many cultivars with variegated foliage. Some produce pink berries.

JANUARY
Vines & Ground Covers

PLANNING

A new year always gives us something to look forward to. In the garden, it may be a new plant or that decorative trellis you've been admiring for some time. As garden catalogs arrive in the mail and gardening magazines proliferate on newsstands, January is a great time to get caught up on your reading—and dreaming. It's fun to list the exciting plants you see (oh, how enticing those color pictures are!) and the equipment you need (toss away those cheap pruners and buy a really good pair). You may even want to make a "dream to-do list" of those projects you'd love to accomplish, if you had the time or the funds—maybe hire a landscaper or have someone build a low stacked-stone wall around the patio. Wouldn't that look great with **creeping thyme** or **vinca** growing over the top? You'll find that when you make these lists and tuck them into the back of your garden note-book, the ideas often stick in your mind and eventually they—or something similar—really do get done.

Be creative when it comes to ground covers. All the good plants for this purpose aren't necessarily called *ground covers*. You'll find some in the shrub section of the local nursery (**cotoneaster**, for instance), among fruits (**strawberry** and **native low-bush blueberry**), with the perennials (**candytuft, ferns, daylilies**, and **lily-of-the-valley**), even **roses** (a number of new easy-care **roses** fit into the ground cover category).

If you enjoy growing plants from seed, some of the most colorful flowering vines are quite easy to start from seed. Since they're fast to germinate and grow, you shouldn't start them this early, but do look for seed packets this month and next so you can plant in late February or early March. Readily available vine seeds that grow well in this region include:

- **Black-eyed Susan vine** (*Thunbergia alata*)
- **Cardinal climber** (*Ipomoea x sloteri*)
- **Cup-and-saucer vine** (*Cobaea scandens*)
- **Cypress vine**
- **Gourds**
- **Hyacinth bean**
- **Moonflower**
- **Morning glory**
- **Purple bell vine** (*Rhodochiton atrosanguineus*)
- **Spanish flag** (*Mina lobatas*)
- **Sweet autumn clematis** (*Clematis terniflora*)
- **Sweet pea** (*Lathyrus odoratus*)

Vines look attractive growing up some buildings, but it's usually best to keep them off houses built of wood because the moisture can cause the wood to mildew or rot. Then, too, there's the problem of what to do when it comes time to paint. One solution is to grow the vine on a trellis 6 to 12 inches away from the building. Build these supports of sturdy, long-lasting materials and hinge them so the vine can be easily moved when painting or other building maintenance is required. This idea works well for older brick buildings, too, since vines can loosen mortar.

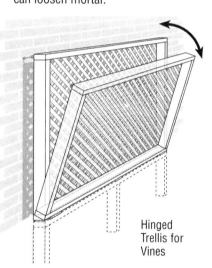

Hinged Trellis for Vines

PLANTING

Vines and ground covers aren't usually planted until early March, but provided the ground isn't frozen, it is possible to transplant a dormant deciduous vine this month if you prepared for it some months ago. (See page 298.) Check the soil to see that the moisture content is right for digging: Squeeze a handful of the soil into a ball. If it crumbles instead of forming a ball, the soil is too dry and should be watered—both the vine to be moved and the new hole and its soil. If the soil forms a tight ball, it's too wet to dig. Wait a few days. But if the soil forms a ball for a few seconds and then crumbles, it has the right amount of moisture.

 ## CARE

If you planted a ground-cover bed in the fall, walk by it occasionally this month and next to make sure that alternate freezing and thawing of the soil hasn't heaved any of the plants out of the ground. If you notice one that has, gently replant it so the roots won't dry out or be harmed by cold.

On a day when you'd like to get a breath of fresh air, check perennial vines to make sure they're attached to their supports. Take some soft twine or vinyl-coated twister ties with you so you'll be prepared to tie up any that have come loose.

 ## WATERING

It shouldn't be necessary to water outdoors. But any vines being grown indoors should be watered as houseplants—let the soil surface dry and then water thoroughly until water drains out the bottom of the pot. Vines receiving high light or warm temperatures need water more frequently than those in low light or a cool room.

 ## FERTILIZING

Outdoors, there's no need to fertilize ground covers or vines. But you may want to feed tropical vines that overwinter indoors in large containers—**allamanda, bougainvillea, mandevilla**. If they're in a sunroom or other spot with high light levels, you can feed them with a houseplant fertilizer—especially **bougainvillea**, which may be blooming this month. But if the plants are in low light—just holding on until they can go back outside at the beginning of hot weather—skip the fertilizer; they won't be able to use it until they're actively growing again.

 ## PRUNING

If you got busy and didn't take down the frost-killed foliage of annual vines in fall, do that on a pleasant January weekend. The garden will look neater and be ready for spring.

 ## PROBLEMS

Where deer and rodents are big problems, reapply repellents this month. Some home remedies (spreading human hair about, hanging cakes of Irish Spring® soap, etc.) work for a short time, but most are not long-term solutions. One advantage of commercial products such as Deer-Off® is that they don't have to be reapplied after every rain. The only real solution for deer is an 8-foot fence, but until you get desperate enough to build one, you may want to try alternating several remedies instead of depending on just one.

FEBRUARY

PLANNING

Do you have any spots in your lawn where grass simply won't grow? If the lack of grass growth is due to excessive shade, maybe this is the year you give up on the grass and plant a shade-loving ground cover instead. Once it gets established, it requires much less maintenance than trying to grow grass in a spot that's no longer suitable for it. See the list on pages 292 and 293 for ground covers that grow well in shade.

There are fewer vines than ground covers that prefer shade, but if you have a mostly shady yard, you don't have to go without vines completely. These will tolerate at least some shade:

- **Climbing hydrangea**
- **False climbing hydrangea**
  (*Schizophragma hydrangeoides*)
- **Fiveleaf akebia**
- **Hardy kiwi**
- **Wood vamp** (*Decumaria barbara*),
Zone 7

Catch up on your garden reading on February's cold evenings. Learn about new flowering vines and ground-cover plants, as well as interesting ways to integrate them into your landscape. Pick up some gardening magazines at the bookstore or stop by the public library to see what books they have that will bring you closer to your goal of a good-looking low-maintenance yard.

During winter months—when there's little going on in the garden—attend a gardening class, visit a flower show, or take a plant-related workshop. Enjoy yourself, and find an idea you can look forward to putting to use.

PLANTING

No planting takes place outdoors this month, but if you'd like to try growing some annual vines from seed indoors, count back six to eight weeks from your area's average last frost date (if you don't know when that is, ask the Extension Service in your county). If that six- to eight-week date falls sometime in February, you can sow seeds of **cup-and-saucer vine** (*Cobaea scandens*), **hyacinth bean**, and **purple bell vine** (*Rhodochiton atrosanguineus*). See the **Annuals** chapter, page 42, for directions.

CARE

Check perennial vines each month. If they've come loose from their supports, reattach them. Pull down remnants of last year's annual vines if you didn't do it earlier.

Are 3 inches of mulch in place at the base of the vines in your yard? If not, replenish the mulch on a nice day this month. There may still be cold weather ahead, and mulch protects the roots.

Sometime this month, look over the sites in which ground-cover plants were set out during the past year. If you see that a little plant has been heaved up out of the soil, gently replant it. If it hasn't been exposed too long, it should be fine.

WATERING

Vines and ground covers usually manage to get through the winter without any supplemental moisture.

Take care of tropical vines that are overwintering indoors by watering them regularly, as soon as the surface of the soil dries out.

FERTILIZING

Fertilizer isn't needed by vines or ground covers in the yard, but may be welcomed by tropical vines being grown in a sunroom. If the vines are being kept alive in low light and look a bit anemic, don't fertilize yet. But if they're in sun or very bright light and growing or blooming apply a houseplant fertilizer once every four weeks.

Rejuvenate a severely overgrown vine by cutting it back to 12 inches high, or cut it back to one or two young stems at the base, leaving several vigorous side shoots.

PRUNING

Vines that bloom on the current year's stems should be pruned in early spring, just before new growth starts. In some years and in the warmest parts of the region, that may mean late February. In others, pruning is done in March. Plants that need pruning in early spring include:

Some **clematis** hybrids (see **Timely Tip** for a more complete discussion of **clematis** pruning)

- **Climbing hydrangea**
- **Crossvine**
- **Fiveleaf akebia** (cut to ground)
- **Hardy kiwi**
- **Trumpet creeper**
- **Wintercreeper** (if grown as a vine instead of ground cover)
- **Wisteria** (see page 302)

Wait to prune these vines: **Carolina jessamine, climbing rose, goldflame honeysuckle, mandevilla,** and **trumpet honeysuckle.** They're pruned after they finish flowering.

How to prune vines:

Annually prune established vines—but only as needed and with a light touch.

- Trim back damaged shoots and those that have grown out of bounds.
- To thin crowded vines, cut some side stems back to the main stem.

Timely Tip

When to prune clematis? Whenever you buy **clematis**, save its tag; it will come in handy when you're trying to figure out when you need to prune. Or observe when and how the vine blooms:

1 If the **clematis** blooms on old wood (stem growth from last year) in late spring, little pruning is needed except to keep the vine in shape. Examples include *C. armandii, C. montana, C. macropetala, C. indivisa,* and *C. alpina.*

2 If a **clematis** vine blooms twice—in early summer on old growth and in late summer on new growth—then undertake mostly light pruning, or you may remove flowers inadvertently. Remove weak or dead stems this month. Prune back flower shoots after blooms fade. **Clematis** in this group are 'Nelly Moser', 'Barbara Jackman', 'Belle of Woking', 'Hagley Hybrid', and double-flowered varieties.

3 **Clematis** that bloom on new wood are pruned hard in early spring. This month or in early March, cut back to one pair of buds 12 inches from ground level. This group includes *C.* x *jackmanii, C. flammula, C. integrifolia, C. orientalis,* and *C. viticella.*

- If a vine is lanky, cause it to branch out by cutting a few inches off the ends of the stems. Pinching the stems of any vine encourages it to branch and fill out.
- In late winter or early spring, cut back to 12 inches high those vines that flower on the current season's growth.
- Rejuvenate a severely overgrown vine by cutting it back to 12 inches high, or cut it back to one or two young stems at the base, leaving several vigorous side shoots. Pinch the tips of the new stems lightly when

they're 6 inches long so the new growth will be full.

PROBLEMS

If spider mites were a recurring problem on vines last summer, or **euonymous** and **vinca** plants have scale, spray them with dormant oil on a day that's about 45 degrees Fahrenheit with no precipitation in the forecast for the next two days. The scale won't disappear right away; it usually takes up to a month to wash or slough off.

MARCH

Vines & Ground Covers

 PLANNING

When you're going to turn an area of the lawn into a ground-cover bed, kill the grass beforehand. If you use a nonselective herbicide such as Roundup®, you can begin planting within two weeks. Or you may cover the area with thick layers of newspapers, weighted down so no light gets through, until the grass dies. A third option is to dig up the grass and place it elsewhere in your yard where it's needed. (But get all the roots, or you'll be battling grass in the ground cover for a long time to come.)

Still thinking about trying a few unusual ground covers? Although they aren't evergreen and last only a few years, **strawberries** do make a nice short-term ground cover, especially to edge an area. You might consider planting them while you're deciding what to do with that section of the yard. The easiest to grow are the **alpine strawberries** (*Fragaria vesca*). The leaves are small and attractive, and so are the berries. You'll get just about enough berries for your breakfast cereal. If you'd prefer to try regular **strawberries**, consider June-bearing types such as 'Apollo', 'Sure Crop', 'Chandler', and 'Earliglow'.

 PLANTING

If your area's last-frost date is sometime in April, you may start seeds of these quick-growing annual vines indoors. (See page 32 for details.) They all require about four weeks from sowing seed to setting the plant out in the yard. (Seeds of these vines may also be planted outdoors in May or June; see page 42.)

- **Black-eyed Susan vine** (*Thunbergia alata*)
- **Cardinal climber** (*Ipomoea* x *sloteri*)
- **Cypress vine**
- **Gourds**
- **Moonflower**
- **Morning glory**
- **Spanish flag** (*Mina lobatas*)

Plant bare-root vines this month. These are planted much like bare-root **roses**:

1 Test the soil to see whether it's too wet to dig. Squeeze a handful of soil into a ball. If the soil stays in the ball and doesn't crumble after a few seconds, wait a few more days for the soil to dry.

2 Dig a hole that's as deep as the roots and twice as wide as their spread.

3 Build a mound of soil in the center of the hole. Its top should be even with the surrounding ground.

4 Place the vine on top of the soil, spreading the roots down the sides of the mound.

5 Mix the soil removed from the hole with fine bark or compost and a pelleted slow-release fertilizer (such as Osmocote®).

6 Fill the hole half full with the soil mixture.

7 Water, using a transplant solution.

8 Completely fill the hole with soil, firming it around the roots.

9 Water thoroughly, using a transplant solution.

10 Mulch with 3 inches of organic material, such as pine straw or finely shredded bark.

In warmer areas, it's fine to plant container-grown vines toward the end of the month, as long as the vines have been growing outdoors and were not protected at night. This means they've been hardened off and most likely won't be harmed by a bit of cold weather after you get them home. If vines or ground-cover plants were in a greenhouse, or moved indoors after dark, wait until near the last frost date before planting.

Plant **strawberries** this month or next, if using them as a temporary ground cover.

CARE

Check mulch around vines and especially in and among ground-cover plantings where the plants haven't grown together yet. If the mulch isn't 3 inches thick, add more. Pine needles (available at garden centers in bales) make an excellent mulch for ground covers and for vines. Other good mulches include shredded leaves, old grass clippings, rotted sawdust, and fine bark.

Direct new growth of young vines onto the trellis or support, if needed.

Tie up last fall's growth of climbers.

Remove excess debris from ground-cover beds—leaves that are covering the plants, small tree branches, etc.

WATERING

Keep the soil moist but not wet around newly planted vines or ground-cover plants.

If the usual March rains don't fall this month, keep an eye on ground covers planted last fall. Their root systems still won't be fully developed, so the plants could need watering in dry weather. A sprinkler is the simplest way to water ground covers. See page 302.

FERTILIZING

Only *young* vines and ground covers—those that you want to grow larger—really need fertilizing. Apply a slow-release fertilizer according to label directions this month or next.

PRUNING

About mid-March, clip off all winter-killed and damaged stems and leaves from ground covers and discard. During winters when **English ivy** is hit hard, you may want to cut it back a few inches beyond the damage to stimulate new growth.

Remove dying or damaged stems on all vines in the yard. If you didn't do so last month, cut back to 12 inches tall perennial vines that flower on the current year's wood. This includes **clematis** species and hybrids that produce blooms only on this year's growth. (See page 297.)

Cut back overgrown vines. Also prune **passionflower**. See February's **Pruning** section for more information.

Give established **Japanese wisteria** the first of its three annual prunings. Prune all new growth from the previous year back to two buds. See page 302 for more about **wisteria**.

Indoors, groom tropical vines growing in pots—remove yellowing or browning leaves and pick off flowers as they fade.

PROBLEMS

Since weeds are the biggest problem with ground covers, you may want to investigate pre-emergent weed controls. These products (such as Preen for Ground Covers®) are sprinkled over the soil to prevent seeds of annual weeds (and sometimes grasses) from germinating. If you decide to go this route, read the label carefully to see which plants the product may be safely used around and which weeds they help control.

Ground covers that grow next to lawns may invade the grass. Many, such as **bugleweed**, may be easily mowed down. Others may be kept in bounds by edging the beds this month and again in summer. (Use an edging tool, or stick a sharp spade into the soil where the ground cover and grass meet.) If the problem becomes severe, you may want to have heavy edging 12 inches deep, installed as a barrier between the grass and ground cover.

PLANNING

If you have a shady yard and acidic, clay soil, you're likely to have one or two spots where moss is growing. You may have tried to get rid of it, but found that it returned. (For permanent control, you have to correct the conditions that caused the moss). But an alternative is to join the if-you-can't-beat-'em school of thought and cultivate moss as ground cover. When you visit garden centers this time of year, you'll likely find several different types of moss. It has turned out to be quite a trendy plant!

Take a moment to jot down in your garden journal or notebook the names of any ground covers and vines you're planting, the date on which you plant them, and the store where you bought them (this can come in handy when you want to buy the same variety next year and can't seem to find it anywhere).

PLANTING

All vines and ground covers may be planted this month. Choose plants that like the light and soil requirements of the planting area (see pages 291 to 293). To plant a container-grown vine or ground cover:

1 Dig a hole that's as deep as the root-ball and twice as wide.

2 Remove the plant from its pot. If roots are growing around and around the root ball, loosen them so they will grow out into the soil.

3 Place the plant in the hole at the same level it grew before.

4 Mix the soil removed from the hole with fine bark or compost and a slow-release fertilizer.

5 Add the soil mixture to the hole until it's about half full.

6 Water, using a transplant solution.

7 Finish filling the hole with soil, firming it around the roots.

8 Water thoroughly, using a transplant solution.

9 Mulch with 2 to 3 inches of organic material.

Directions on planting a bare-root vine are on page 298. Advice on planting ground cover on a hill is on page 290.

More About Planting Clematis

- **Clematis** prefers to be planted with its leaves in the sun and its roots in the shade. You can accomplish this with mulch or a stone over the root area. Or you can plant it where a nearby shrub or building will cast a shadow on the root zone. Or plant it behind the trellis and let it grow forward.

- Instead of planting a **clematis** vine at the same depth it grew previously, plant it 2 to 3 inches deep. It will send out new roots, which help it survive clematis wilt. (See **Problems**.)

- **Clematis** prefers alkaline soil (pH above 7.0), but will grow in neutral to slightly acidic soils. In very acidic soils, you must apply lime several months before planting. (If you don't know the pH of your soil, have the soil tested. Kits are available at garden centers, and the Extension Service offers more extensive testing.) If your soil is acidic, you might place some cold fireplace ashes around your **clematis** vine once or twice during the winter.

CARE

Clean up ground-cover beds if you didn't do that last month. Remove excess leaves and tree debris, and cut back cold-damaged stems and leaves.

Harden off annual vines that were started indoors in February or March so they can be set outside after the chance of frost is past. See the chapter on **Annuals**, page 38, for more details.

Tie vines lightly to their supports so the tie won't cut into the vine's stem as it grows.

Check monthly during the growing season to make sure that vines are attached securely to the structure on which they're growing.

 # WATERING

After vines and ground covers have been growing in your yard for a year or so, they won't need much supplemental watering unless there's no rainfall for two weeks. Plants that have been set out this year will generally need water whenever rainfall has not totaled an inch per week.

Soaker hoses and drip irrigation are excellent methods of watering vines because they deposit the water at the root zone, where it's needed, and keep it off the foliage.

 # FERTILIZING

An alternative to using a slow-release fertilizer on ground-cover beds is to mix a water-soluble plant food (14-14-14 or 20-20-20) in a hose-end sprayer and spray all the plants thoroughly once or twice a month from now until mid-August.

Never, ever fertilize wisteria, even if you're trying to get it to bloom. Instead of encouraging flowers, fertilizer produces excessive leaf and stem growth on **wisteria**— and fewer flowers.

 # PRUNING

Although March is a better month to prune vines than April, it's not too late to trim back dead leaves or stems and thin crowded vines. (See page 297.) If you haven't cut back a vine that flowers on this year's growth, you may still do so. (See page 297 for a list of these vines.) The vine may flower later than it did last year. On the upside, a vine that blooms on the current season's wood and is pruned to 12 inches high the first to middle of April will bloom much more bountifully than if it isn't pruned at all.

Carolina jessamine is pruned this month or next—after it has finished flowering.

To encourage new growth, cut back **creeping phlox (thrift)** after the flowers fade.

 # PROBLEMS

Aphids are tiny pear-shaped insects that suck the juices from plants, and they're especially attracted to plants' new growth, which is why you tend to see them this time of year. They're particularly fond of **clematis**, but may show up on just about any vine or ground cover. Wash as many as possible off with a strong blast from the hose. When the leaves dry, spray with insecticidal soap.

MAY

PLANNING

Talk with good gardeners you know—neighbors, family, friends, Master Gardeners. These people have faced the same gardening problems that you have and often have answers from their own experience. Besides, it's fun to talk gardening with fellow plant enthusiasts.

PLANTING

You may continue to plant vines and ground covers in May. Planting directions are on page 300.

Once the weather has warmed up and stays that way, seeds of these annual vines may be planted outdoors where they are to grow: **black-eyed Susan vine, cardinal climber, cypress vine, gourds, moonflower, morning glory**, and **Spanish flag**. See the chapter on **Annuals**, page 42, for advice on sowing seeds outdoors.

Check to see whether tropical vines that wintered indoors have outgrown their containers and need repotting. If so, replant them in a larger pot, mixing in slow-release fertilizer and a water-holding polymer such as Moisture Mizer™.

CARE

As soon as nighttime temperatures remain above 60 degrees Fahrenheit, move **mandevilla, bougainvillea, allamanda**, and other potted tropical vines back outdoors for the summer. Don't place them in full sun immediately. Instead, put them first on a porch or shady area, then gradually move them into more and more light.

WATERING

A sprinkler is the easiest way to water a ground-cover bed. The first time you use one, set up tuna or cat-food tins in various areas of the ground cover and keep track of how long it takes the sprinkler to deliver an inch of water. The next time you turn the sprinkler on, you can set it on a timer or just note the time that you need to come back and turn it off.

Don't let any plants that you set out this spring dry out. If rainfall is less than usual, check plants every few days as the weather gets warmer and water as necessary to keep the soil moist.

Few established vines or ground covers need watering unless there's a drought. But look for signs that a plant needs more moisture—dull foliage and leaves that turn yellow or fall off prematurely.

Tropical vines grown in pots like lots of water. Check their soil daily to make sure it doesn't dry out more than an inch or two deep.

FERTILIZING

If you didn't fertilize the vine that you planted this spring or if you haven't yet feriilized those vines planted in the past year, do so now. Use a slow-release or a granular fertilizer for vines and shrubs.

Very vigorous vines *never* need fertilizer: **fiveleaf akebia, trumpet creeper**, and **wisteria**.

Young ground-cover plants are more likely than young vines to need fertilizer. Apply a slow-release fertilizer to the soil or spray a water-soluble fertilizer on the foliage, as well as the ground. Avoid using a granular fertilizer on ground covers—it can burn the leaves.

PRUNING

Pinch the stems of perennial vines so they will grow fuller and not just straight up.

After **wisteria** blooms, cut back leaf-less shoots and shorten long twining side branches. Remove any growth that's coming from below the graft union (a swollen area near the base) of a grafted vine.

As soon as nighttime temperatures remain above 60 degrees Fahrenheit, move potted tropical vines back outdoors for the summer. Don't place them in full sun immediately. Instead, put them first on a porch or shady area, then gradually move them into more and more light.

Prune **Carolina jessamine** if needed. Cut back some of the stems near the bottom of the vine to encourage them to fill out.

Prune and shape **goldflame** and **trumpet honeysuckle** after they stop blooming.

PROBLEMS

If **euonymous** has scales (they look like tiny bumps on stems, branches, or leaves), spray with a light horticultural oil. It may be necessary to repeat the application in a few weeks.

Slugs and snails become a problem in ground-cover plantings when spring weather has been wet. You'll see slime trails and large, ragged holes in the leaves. You can control them by:

• Picking the snails off by hand (after dark, with a flashlight).

• Putting out eaten grapefruit or orange halves (for the slugs to crawl under and you to gather up the next day and destroy).

• Placing saucers of water mixed with 1 teaspoon of yeast around the area (the slugs crawl in and drown). Beer also works, but is more expensive.

• Applying slug bait. Until recently, many gardeners avoided this because it was toxic. But an organic product, Sluggo™, which is just iron phosphate, is nontoxic to pets and wildlife. Ask at

a garden center about this or a similar product.

If a newly planted **clematis** droops, the cause is usually clematis wilt. It tends to strike during a vine's first two years. Prune off all the wilted stem—even if you don't reach good wood until you're below ground—and put the affected material in the trash. Quite often, the vine grows back from those underground roots it formed when you planted it deeply. If it doesn't, do not plant another **clematis** in the same spot.

Why didn't my wisteria bloom?
Wisteria is a beautiful vine, but not easy to grow. There are many reasons it may not have ever flowered. These include:

1 The flower buds (usually formed in summer) were inadvertently pruned.

2 The plant was overfertilized, especially with too much nitrogen (the first of the three numbers on the label of the fertilizer container). This usually causes lush leaf growth at the expense of flowers. In reasonably good soil, **wisteria** needs no fertilization.

3 The flower buds are killed by low temperatures or late frosts.

4 The vine isn't mature enough. Vines grown from seeds take many years to reach blooming stage. Grafted vines flower sooner.

If none of those causes are accurate with your **wisteria**, the usual remedy is to root prune the vine. Wait until after flowering, then with a spade cut vertically into the ground in a circle out from the plant but within the root zone.

How to train a young vine. Now that vines planted this spring are beginning to grow and to climb, May is a good time to think about how to care for them.

1 Cut back the vine by one-third to one-half when planting it. This encourages faster growth and branching.

2 Help young vines reach their supports, if needed.

3 Regularly attach stems of climbers to their supports. The easiest fasteners are soft cloth, twine, and plastic-covered wire. Screw hooks and special masonry fasteners may be used on wood and brick.

4 Pinch the tips of shoots to encourage the vine to fill out.

JUNE

PLANNING

Take a moment to evaluate your progress so far. Which vines and ground covers have performed as well as—or even better than—you hoped? If you've had to contend with insects or other problems this year, make a note in your garden journal—the name of the plant, the problem, what you did about it, and the approximate date. That can be a help in the future.

Beginning in June and continuing throughout the summer, take time to visit botanical and other public gardens. Not only can you observe plants when they're blooming, but you can easily tell which ones can take the heat and which can't. In our part of the country, that's a valuable piece of information.

PLANTING

It's okay to plant container-grown vines and ground-cover plants in June. Try to choose a day when temperatures are still in the range of 70 degrees Fahrenheit. Then plant at dusk or on a cloudy day. The two most important steps when planting during the summer are watering thoroughly and mulching with 2 to 3 inches of organic matter.

During the first part of June, it's still fine to sow seeds of annual vines outdoors: **black-eyed Susan vine, cardinal climber, climbing snapdragon** (*Asarina scandens*), **cypress vine, hyacinth bean, moonflower, morning glory**, and **sweet potato vine**.

If you'd like to increase your stock of ground-cover plants, it's easy:

- Some ground covers, such as **bugleweed, English ivy**, and **winter-creeper**, form roots along the stems. Cut off the tips of plants that have rooted and replant them where you need them. They'll need to be watered frequently until they settle in.
- Layering is a method of propagating that works on most perennial ground covers—also vines—that have woody stems. In early summer or late spring, bend a stem over to the ground (if it isn't already growing horizontally). Make a 1/4-inch cut or scrape a spot in the bottom surface of the stem. Cover the stem with rich soil, and weigh down the cutting. When new growth is apparent, cut the rooted cutting from the parent plant.

- **Pachysandra, ivy**, and **clematis** may be rooted from cuttings. Using a sharp knife or pruners and cutting at a 45-degree angle, take 4- to 6-inch cuttings. Remove the bottom leaves, dip the base of the stem in a rooting hormone, and insert it in a flat or pot of moistened peat moss, peat, and sand, or just commercial potting soil. This time of year it isn't necessary to cover the pots with plastic. Just keep the soil moist until the cuttings begin to grow.

CARE

Keep an eye on annual vines as they begin to grow, and guide them to the trellis. One way to do this is to place a string or small bamboo stake from the vine to the support when you plant. Otherwise, just do it by hand.

How thick is the mulch around vines or ground covers in the yard? The ideal depth is 3 inches. That's enough to protect plants from temperature extremes, conserve moisture, and help prevent weeds, but not so deep it will keep needed oxygen and water from reaching roots. As we head into the hottest part of the gardening year, take a moment to check on all your mulched plants and add to them if they've gotten a bit thin. Don't let mulch touch the stems of plants or cover the crowns of ground covers; that can cause rot.

WATERING

Even as hot weather is upon us, most established vines and ground covers won't need watering unless several weeks go by without rain. But it's important to watch any plant that has been in the landscape for a year or less—especially those vines and ground covers planted this spring—to make sure they don't dry out. Water when the top 4 inches of soil is dry, and water long enough to wet the soil 6 to 8 inches deep.

Vines in containers may need watering daily this month if they are on a covered porch or if rainfall isn't frequent. Water until the excess pours from the drainage hole.

You may be getting tired of watering young ground covers on slopes. A good way to water them effortlessly—as well as eliminate wasteful runoff—is to place soaker hoses among the plants.

FERTILIZING

If vines growing in containers were not fertilized with a slow-release plant food last month, you may apply one in the first half of the month. Otherwise, feed twice a month with a water-soluble fertilizer made for blooming plants.

Established vines and ground covers rarely need fertilizer; they usually manage just fine with the nutrients naturally in the soil. Homeowners tend to overfertilize, and that has unintended results—excessive leaf growth at the expense of flowers.

However, **clematis** vines that bloom in summer and were not fed with a slow-release fertilizer in the spring would probably appreciate an application of water-soluble fertilizer this month.

PRUNING

If one of a vine's holdfasts or aerial roots comes loose from its support, it will not reconnect. So if that has happened, cut it off above a bud that's below the stem that has become unattached.

Clematis species and hybrids that have just finished blooming need little pruning. (See page 297.) Remove dying or diseased leaves or stems, and thin as needed to keep in shape.

Very vigorous vines—**fiveleaf akebia, trumpet creeper**, and **wisteria**, for instance—may need to be cut back several times during the growing season to

keep them in bounds. Don't let them get away from you.

Pinch back the tips of annual vines to make the plant bushier.

Prune **rambler roses** after they finish blooming. Remove a portion of the older canes back to the base.

Deadhead **climbing roses**, and cut lateral canes back to three buds.

PROBLEMS

If foliage looks bronzy, the cause is probably spider mites. Water the plant, hosing down the leaves. When the foliage is dry, spray with insecticidal soap. If the problem is chronic, check with the Extension Service about a recommended miticide. Common insecticides won't do the job.

JULY

Vines & Ground Covers

 ## PLANNING

Is July a vacation month in your household? Since you know it's going to be hot and you have no way of telling how much rain will fall, plan to water all your vines and ground covers a day or so before you leave (unless they're already wet from rain). That should hold them for absences of up to two weeks. If you expect to be away longer than that, ask a knowledgeable neighbor to step in when rainfall has been less than an inch per week to water any plantings made this spring.

Everyone loves flowers, but rarely do we think of flowers in connection with ground covers. Yet there are several blooming ground covers, in case you're planning ahead for fall planting. They include:

- **Bishop's weed**
- **Bugleweed**
- **Creeping phlox**
- **Dianthus (pinks)**
- **Green-and-gold** (*Chrysogonum virginianum*)
- **Lily-of-the-valley**
- **Liriope**
- **Spotted dead nettle**
- **Thyme**
- **Vinca**

 ## PLANTING

Container-grown vines and ground covers can be planted just about any time of the year if the ground isn't frozen. But unless there's a reason to plant in the heat of July, you may want to wait until September or October. Still, if someone gives you a potted vine or some ground-cover plants, go ahead and plant them—preferably on an overcast day. See page 300 for tips.

Check ground covers that were rooted last month to see whether they need to be moved into larger pots (for planting in September). Or if they have rooted well already, they can be planted in the garden if the soil is moist and the temperature is 80 degrees Fahrenheit or below.

 ## CARE

Check mulch on hillside ground-cover plantings. If it has washed off, replace with pine straw.

Make sure that vines are attached securely to supports. Thunderstorms can sometimes shake them mightily.

Each time **climbing roses** and other vines that must be tied by hand put on 8 inches of growth, tie them loosely to their posts or fences. One way of doing this is a double tie. Make a loop around the trellis, and tie it as though you were going to tie a shoe. But pass the two ends around the vine and pull the vine near the trellis (not up against it). Tie a secure knot in the second loop so there's enough space for the vine to grow without the twine cutting into it.

 ## WATERING

Spring-planted ground covers and vines may need watering this month if rainfall doesn't provide an inch of moisture per week. Check the soil to be sure.

Tropical vines like plenty of water, and that goes double for those planted in large terra-cotta containers.

If you're growing moss or ferns as ground covers, remember that both need moist soil and should be checked regularly to make sure they don't dry out. If moss begins to turn a bit brown, it will perk back up when you water or when rain falls.

Don't let fast-growing annual vines wilt from lack of water. Check the soil to see whether it's dry 4 inches down. If so, water slowly and thoroughly.

Everyone loves flowers, but rarely do we think of flowers in connection with ground covers. But there are several blooming ground covers, in case you're planning ahead for fall planting.

FERTILIZING

Fertilize vines in containers every other week with a water-soluble plant food for flowering plants.

If you're trying hard to get a ground cover to grow faster, spray it once or twice a month with a water-soluble fertilizer (14-14-14 or 20-20-20)—provided you can keep the planting watered regularly.

No other vines or ground covers need fertilizing until next spring.

PRUNING

Clip off errant stems and suckers at the base of vines.

Always remove dying, diseased, or broken stems when you see them. They can attract insects or disease if left on the vine.

Mow or use the string trimmer on ground covers that are straying into the lawn. Consider installing edging to prevent ground covers from escaping.

On **wisteria**, remove leafless shoots and shorten the lateral branches by half.

PROBLEMS

Yes, it's July, but any weeds that have popped up through the mulch still must be removed from ground-cover beds. Do it as early in the morning as you can, and take it in short spurts. Drink plenty of water, and tell yourself how much better your little ground-cover plants are going to grow now that they don't have competition from weeds.

If you can't get to weeds right away, remove the tops so they don't form seeds. Once weeds have gone to seed, the problem will be greatly increased in the future.

Japanese beetles are attracted to some vines. If they become a problem, try:

- Spraying with Neem (an organic insecticide derived from neem trees).

- Picking the glossy green beetles off by hand and putting them in a jar of soapy water.

If the infestation is extreme, ask at a garden center for a recommendation of an insecticide that kills the beetles on contact.

Don't hang Japanese beetle traps. They tend to attract more beetles to your property than they catch.

If **bugleweed** has blackened leaves and looks dead in the center, give it a tug. If it pulls out of the ground readily, the problem is probably crown rot. Remove the affected plants, and correct the drainage. If you plan to replant **bugleweed** in the same area, you may need to treat the soil with a fungicide. Ask the Extension Service for advice.

If you resort to a herbicide to rid ground cover of weeds and grasses that have grown up in it, you *must* be careful when and how you apply it. Most herbicides have temperature recommendations on the label. Observe these stringently; otherwise, your plants may be harmed. Also, if most weedkillers get onto the ground cover plants, they will harm them. Here's a technique used by many gardeners who use Roundup® to kill weeds and grass growing close to desirable plants: Dip a paint brush into the liquid and "paint" the weed.

AUGUST

PLANNING

Most of us aren't very patient—we want instant results in the garden. So it's hard to wait while ground-cover plants grow into a mat. But there are several ways to achieve faster coverage:

1 Buy large plants instead of small ones.

2 Plant closer together.

3 Fertilize once or twice monthly from April until the first of August, using a water-soluble plant food.

4 Water regularly.

Think ahead about vine placement and removal, if you decide you don't like the current location. This is especially true with vines that attach themselves to a wall or structure with holdfasts. These are very difficult to pull off, and they leave a real mess behind.

Remember that it's much harder to remove an overgrown vine—especially one that's been trained up onto a house or now covers a wall—than it is to plant it.

It's not one of those things you think about until it happens—but the next time you decide where to place a flowering vine, you may want to consider the bees they attract—and keep the vine away from the swimming pool area.

Maybe you're still on the fence about planting a vine; watching kudzu devour the countryside will do that to you. But not all vines are that aggressive. Do a little research and choose one that's mild-mannered—**clematis** or **Carolina jessamine**, for instance. Then have some fun looking through magazines, books, catalogs, and the Internet, or visiting local stores, to find a trellis or other attractive structure on which it can grow.

PLANTING

Yes, it's possible to plant container-grown plants this month, but it isn't generally recommended. Why not wait till the middle of next month, when temperatures have moderated?

However, should temperatures be mild and rainfall abundant, it's all right to plant ground covers or vines rooted earlier in the summer—provided you can keep them watered if necessary. If you want to set them out now and will be going on

vacation, put drip irrigation or soaker hoses on a mechanical timer to turn the water on and off at predetermined times so the plants won't dry out.

If you have to water vines in containers more than once a day, the plant may be rootbound and need repotting. (Remember that **bougainvillea** blooms better when it's slightly potbound.) To repot:

1 Choose a container that's no more than one size larger (or 2 inches greater in diameter, measured at the top rim).

2 Moisten a commercial potting soil, and mix it with a water-holding polymer if the soil doesn't already contain one.

3 If the vine's roots are growing round and round the ball of soil, loosen them before planting.

4 Set the plant in the new pot at the same depth it grew before.

5 Fill the container with soil.

6 Water well.

7 Place out of the sun but in bright light for two days before moving back into full sun.

Think ahead about vine placement and removal, if you decide you don't like the current location. Remember that it's much harder to remove an overgrown vine—especially one that's been trained up onto a house or now covers a wall—than it is to plant it.

 CARE

Keep **roses** and other climbers tied to their supports. As you do, check to make sure that canes or stems tied up earlier aren't rubbing against their ties or that the ties aren't cutting into the stems or canes.

Pick off dead, diseased, or insect-damaged leaves from ground covers and vines. If diseased vine leaves have fallen to the ground, gather them up and remove them from the garden. Don't put them on the compost pile.

 WATERING

Vines and ground covers that are less than a year old may need water when the weather is dry. Check their soil. If it's dry 4 inches down, water slowly until the soil is wet 6 to 8 inches deep.

Daily watering is probably necessary for container-grown vines this time of the year, especially those under overhangs and that don't get wet in the usual afternoon thunderstorms so often a feature of August.

 FERTILIZING

Avoid fertilizing vines this month unless they're growing in containers. Perennial vines planted in the ground are fertilized twice—when they're planted and the next spring. That's usually all that's required. Plants in containers are fertilized more often because their nutrients are washed from the soil by frequent waterings.

 PRUNING

Deadhead flowering vines as needed.

If a thunderstorm damages a vine, prune the affected part as soon as possible. Cut back to healthy wood. Do the same with diseased stems, and remove insect-damaged leaves if you have time. Your mama always told you that cleanliness was next to godliness, and that sure holds true in the garden. Keep up the good grooming, and your plants often will have fewer insects and diseases.

 PROBLEMS

If you're seeing spots—leaf spots, that is—the cause is a fungus. Some aren't the least bit serious—they don't cause defoliation—and can usually be controlled by removing the affected leaves. But if stems start to turn black or the infestation is severe, you may need to spray a fungicide. Ask for a recommendation from the Extension Service or at your favorite garden center. If regular fungicide applications become necessary, consider replacing the plant with something more carefree.

Spider mites and aphids may still be troublesome this month. So may snails or slugs, if the weather has been wet. See pages 217 and 39 for control advice.

Deformed flowers or blooms that fail to open are usually caused by thrips. Spray with insecticidal soap or an insecticide recommended by the Extension Service. Another method of control is sticky yellow traps, available at garden centers.

SEPTEMBER

PLANNING

It won't be long before fall color fills the forests and landscapes of our region. You know about planting trees and shrubs that produce colorful fall foliage, but did you realize that some vines also have vibrant (usually red) leaves that can really liven up your property? You might want to consider these:

- **Boston ivy** (*Parthenocissus tricuspidata*)
- **Climbing hydrangea**
- **Crimson glory vine** (*Vitis coignetiae*)
- **Virginia creeper** (*Parthenocissus quinquefolia*)

PLANTING

Now that more moderate weather has returned or is on its way, plant perennial vines and ground covers grown in containers and those you rooted yourself during the summer. See pages 298 and 300 for planting tips. The only difference is that for fall planting, don't mix fertilizer with the soil. The most important thing you can do to get your ground cover or vine off to a good start is to improve the soil where you plan to plant. Few soils in Tennessee or Kentucky are excellent. Some are rocky; many are clay. All can be greatly improved by the addition of organic matter—anything from rotted mushroom compost and composted sawdust to Nature's Helper™ (fine pine bark) and shredded leaves. If you take time to do the ground work before you plant, your chores will be much fewer later on because the plants will have the foundation they need.

During the first part of the month, you may still plant cuttings of rooted **ivy** and **wintercreeper** where you need some new ground-cover plants. (See page 304.) Keep the soil moist around them until they've developed enough additional roots that they can go slightly longer between waterings.

CARE

The time to take potted tropical vines—including **allamanda, bougainvillea**, and **mandevilla**—indoors for overwintering is when nighttime temperatures threaten to fall below 55 degrees Fahrenheit. There will be less acclimation for the plant if it is moved when outdoor and indoor temperatures are about the same. Besides, tropical vines don't like cold temperatures.

- Unfasten the vine from its support if it's growing on one that's outside the container.
- Spray the plant—being careful to wet the undersides of the leaves and the stem—with insecticidal soap to ensure that no insects hitchhike into the house on the vine.
- Trim back the longest shoots to the main stem or above a bud.
- Move the container to the sunniest spot in the house.
- Be careful not to overwater; once the vine is indoors, the soil won't dry out as quickly.

It's simple to save seeds of many of the annual vines you grew this year since most are not hybrids. They will provide a free supply for the future.

Seeds should be ready within a few weeks after the flowers fade and the petals drop off. **Nasturtium vine** seeds are ready when the mature fruit that holds them is dry. When the capsule that holds **morning glory** seeds is dry, you may harvest the seeds. Allow **purple hyacinth bean** pods to dry on the vine. For others, notice the changes and determine when you think the seed is dry.

- Save seeds only from vigorous, disease-free plants.
- Spread the seeds evenly on a screen so they aren't touching. Let them dry indoors for ten to fourteen days.

- Separate the seeds from any plant chaff you managed to collect.
- Place the seeds in a plastic bag or glass jar, and seal tightly. Label the container with the name of the plant and the date.
- Store them in the freezer or a cool place.

WATERING

lewly planted vines and ground covers, s well as ground covers planted earlier n the year, may need water if rainfall s below normal. Check the soil around ew plants a couple of times a week nd around spring-planted ground overs once a week whenever rainfall s less than an inch. Although temperaures are beginning to fall, watering is till important.

Timely Tip

When you're in the yard a great deal, are you bothered by a lack of privacy? Vines make excellent screens to ensure privacy. Fast-growing annual vines can provide quick coverage while an evergreen vine is taking hold. Some good choices are:

- Annual vines that are good for screening: **cup-and-saucer vine, cypress vine, morning glory, moonflower, purple hyacinth bean**, and **sweet potato vine**.
- Perennial vines that grow rapidly and make good screens: **fiveleaf akebia, trumpet vine**, and **Virginia creeper**.
- Evergreen vines for screening: **Carolina jessamine** (may be semi-evergreen in some areas), **cross vine, English ivy**, and **wintercreeper**.

 FERTILIZING

No fertilizing is necessary on any vines or ground covers until spring.

If you have a source of well-rotted manure, spread it about 1 inch thick in a circle around the base of a **clematis** vine. (Don't touch the vine itself.) This provides slow-release nutrients to the plant.

Did your most recent soil test show that your soil is quite acidic? To bring it into a more neutral zone, you can apply lime now. This is a good idea if you'd like to plant **clematis** next spring. The effects of the lime take several months to be felt.

 PRUNING

There's no pruning this month except to snip off faded flowers from vines and to remove dying, damaged, or diseased leaves and stems from ground covers and vines.

PROBLEMS

Thrips and spider mites may still be active. See page 217 for control recommendations.

If you notice scale on **ivy** or an evergreen vine, spray with a light horticultural oil.

OCTOBER

 ## PLANNING

Vines can grow up walls and on fences, and can climb strings. But if you're going to build or buy a trellis or arbor, it's important to match the support to the vine that's going to be growing on it. Because annual vines are relatively light, if you make a mistake when placing them, they're gone by fall; you can try them somewhere else next year. But big vines require sturdier support, and **wisteria** needs the strongest of all.

 ## PLANTING

Cut off a few rooted pieces of gold-and-green or green-and-cream-leaved variety of **English ivy**. Place these in a 6-inch pot of moistened commercial potting soil, and take them indoors. **Ivy** works well as a trailing houseplant if you can keep the humidity high near it. Or bend a wire coat hanger into a circle and insert that into the pot, then let the **ivy** grow decoratively up onto that.

Plant evergreen ground covers the first part of the month, if you like. Do not fertilize them. See page 315 for more information. Vines are not usually readily available this time of year, but if you find a **Carolina jessamine**, go ahead and plant it before the middle of the month. It will reward you by blooming very early next spring.

 ## CARE

Remove seedpods on annual vines, and save the seeds to plant next year. See **September** to learn more.

Dig up the roots of the **sweet potato vine** after a frost has killed the leaves. Remove the leaves, and discard any tubers that were damaged when digging. Let the vine dry in a warm dry place for twenty-four hours. Put the plant in a flat or box of peat moss, and store it in a cool, dark location. Replant next spring.

Don't let leaves smother ground covers. Once leaves start falling heavily, blow them off evergreen ground covers at least weekly. An alternative is to do what many gardeners do to keep leaves out of their ponds: Place netting over the ground cover and let the leaves fall into

that. Then pull the net and leaves off, empty the leaves onto the compost pile, and replace the net.

Mulch matters to plants year-round, but the two most important times of the year to make sure your plants are protected by a blanket of mulch are going into summer and getting ready for winter. Three inches of an organic material such as pine needles, cocoa hulls, rotted sawdust, or fine pine bark can protect roots from both temperature extremes. It also holds moisture in the soil for use during dry spells, and it helps eliminate a lot of weeding that would otherwise be necessary. Check all your vines and ground-cover plants this month to see that their mulch is 3 inches thick. If it isn't, add more. To prevent damage from moisture, keep the mulch away from the stems of vines and from the crowns of ground-cover plants.

 ## WATERING

Evergreen vines and ground-cover plants should go into winter well watered. This helps prevent the "burning" of leaves that you sometimes see during cold weather.

Newly planted ground-cover plants and vines need frequent watering until frost, if rainfall is lacking. Don't let them dry out, but in clay soil, avoid watering so much that the plants stand in water or the soil is soggy.

Put tropical vines that you are wintering inside the house on a regular schedule—watering them once a week or, if they're in big pots, twice a month. Use a moisture meter (see the **Houseplants** chapter) to measure the soil's moisture which will indicate the right time to water.

Timely Tip

Harvesting Gourds

- Leave **ornamental gourds** on the vines until they mature. This is usually when the stems turn brown and the tendrils are completely dry.
- Remove the gourds from the vines.
- Wash them with soapy water to which a little liquid bleach has been added.
- Place the gourds on a screen or wire mesh that's several feet up in the air.
- Rotate the gourds as they dry, so they won't develop any soft spots.
- The time it takes for a gourd to dry varies according the type of gourd, its size, and the thickness of the shell. A gourd is ready when it feels light and you can hear the seeds rattle inside.

 FERTILIZING

Neither vines nor ground covers should be fertilized again until spring.

 PRUNING

Wait until late winter to prune. Any pruning done now could cause the plant to be damaged by cold.

 PROBLEMS

Don't let weeds go to seed. Snap or cut off the seedheads if you don't have time to pull up the weed. Or use a spot weedkiller. Don't think that because weeds will soon be killed by frost, that will be the end of them—perennial weeds will return next year and those seeds will remain in the soil to germinate. While weeds aren't really welcome anywhere in the yard, they're a special problem in ground-cover beds. They make older beds look messy, and they steal moisture, space, and nutrients from young plants. Don't let them get the upper hand.

NOVEMBER

 ## PLANNING

As annual vines are cleared from the garden, it's a good time to assess your need for new trellises or arbors and whether any repairs need to be made to current structures before the growing season resumes next spring.

These days, landscape designers and gardeners are paying more attention to how the garden looks during every season, not just in spring and summer. Often they choose plants based on the effect they create in the winter garden with either their attention-grabbing shape or their bark. If you'd like a vine with an interesting winter silhouette, consider:

- **Climbing hydrangea**
- **False climbing hydrangea**
- **Grape**
- **Hardy kiwi**
- **Trumpet vine**
- **Wisteria**

 ## PLANTING

Planting season is over for the year. But if you have a containerized vine or ground-cover plants that you just didn't get planted earlier in the year and the choice has come down to planting it now or possibly losing it, go ahead and plant, following the directions on page 298 or 300. When you plant late in the fall, be sure to firm the soil carefully around the roots so that no air holes remain to permit the entrance of cold that can harm or kill roots. It is also important to mulch with 3 inches of organic material such as pine needles, shredded leaves, or fine bark.

 ## CARE

Pull down frost-killed annual vines, and toss the debris on the compost pile.

Increase humidity around tropical vines being overwintered indoors and rooted **ivy** cuttings that were taken inside the house. See the **Houseplants** chapter, page 118.

Leaf removal is the main gardening chore in November. Don't let falling leaves smother ground covers, especially evergreens, that are planted beneath trees. A thick, wet mat of leaves can do just that. Use a leaf blower weekly. If the plants need some winter protection, wait until all the leaves have fallen and then shred as many as needed (in a shredder or by spreading them on the driveway and running the lawn mower over them several times until they're in small pieces). Sprinkle the shredded leaves back around the ground covers. But don't let even this light material cover the crowns of the plants. If the ground cover is mulched well already, compost the leaves. Rotted leaves make an excellent soil conditioner and mulch.

 ## WATERING

Little watering should be needed this month, except for vines and **ivy** growing indoors in pots. Let their soil dry slightly between waterings.

Leaf removal is the main gardening chore in November. Don't let falling leaves smother ground covers, especially evergreens, that are planted beneath trees. A thick, wet mat of leaves can do just that. Use a leaf blower weekly.

Should November be a dry month and you're out in the yard, water evergreen ground covers and vines one last time. They generally have a better appearance over winter if they go into cold weather well watered.

 FERTILIZING

There's no fertilizing this month. Ground covers and vines are fertilized again in the spring. Occasionally, home and hardware stores put fertilizer on sale this month to make way for holiday decorations. This may be a good time to stock up on pelleted slow-release fertilizer if you have a cool, dry place in which to store it. Such fertilizers are relatively expensive, but desirable, and if you can get a bargain, take advantage of it.

 PRUNING

November is a good month to take care of any necessary vine removal. If the vine is old and heavy, start cutting at the top and move downward, being careful that none falls on you.

If an overly vigorous vine has grown into trees and you don't want it there—or you liked it once but have now changed your mind—cut the vine at the base using loppers or a pruning saw. In the spring, the vine may fall out of the tree on its own or you may need to carefully cut out the dead portion, starting at the top. If you want to kill the vine, wait until it leafs out and then brush it with a herbicide or dig up all its roots.

 PROBLEMS

Deter rabbits by putting chicken wire around desirable ground-cover plants, but arrange it so they can't nibble through the wire. Repellents may also keep rabbits at bay. This is the time of year to apply a deer repellent if Bambi is a real problem on your property during the winter. If you're not ready to put up a fence to keep deer out, try stretching 10-foot-high black netting as a temporary barrier and see whether that helps.

Timely Tip

Homeowners who want to attract birds and small wildlife to their yards often plant berried bushes and trees. A few vines also produce berries or other showy fruit that attract wildlife:

- **American bittersweet** (*Celastrus scandens*)
- **Hyacinth bean**
- **Pepper vine** (*Ampelopsis arborea*), Zone 7 only, may become a weed
- **Sweet autumn clematis**
- **Trumpet honeysuckle**
- **Virginia creeper**

DECEMBER

 ## PLANNING

Update your garden journal or notebook after the holidays have passed—or earlier if you need a break from the hectic pace. Have you written down all the ground covers and vines that you planted this year? If not, give each its own page so that in the future if you need to know anything about that plant—the date it was planted, what variety it is, the insects or other problems that it has encountered—it's all available in one spot.

Take time to do some daydreaming this last month of the year. Place on your nightstand a stack of gardening magazines (maybe those you didn't get to read when they arrived because you were too busy gardening), catalogs, and a gardening book or two. You'll be amazed how this bedtime reading relieves some of the stress of the season. Or stack garden literature by your favorite chair and take a few minutes here and there to dip into them and do some planning. You may even decide to add to your gift list a plant or two you've been admiring.

 ## PLANTING

Unless a perennial vine is being transplanted from elsewhere on your property (see the **Shrubs** chapter, page 254, for directions on how to do this), there's generally no planting this month. Put up the shovel and wait for spring.

 ## CARE

This is the last call for leaf removal. Fallen leaves are often left in place around shrubby ground covers such as **junipers** and **cotoneaster**; they can make an excellent mulch. But they shouldn't be too thick (no more than 3 inches if they're light leaves, about 2 inches if they're heavy leaves, such as **oak**). Also, they shouldn't be allowed to crowd up against the plant or be caught in and among the shrub's leaves or needles. It's best to shred leaves, when possible, for use as a general-purpose mulch.

If you haven't already, drain hoses, including soaker hoses, and store them in the basement or garage. If they're protected over winter, they'll last much longer than if they're left out in the cold weather. Leave one short hose where you can get to it if it's needed for a quick, small watering job.

 ## WATERING

The ground will probably be frozen at various times during the month, so watering won't be required.

 ## FERTILIZING

Take a holiday from fertilizing. Vines and ground covers won't need fertilizer again until spring.

 ## PROBLEMS

Whenever the weather and your schedule allow, walk through the yard looking for any problems. Carry a small notebook and pencil in your coat pocket, and jot down anything that you notice. Most problems can be dealt with later but wildlife damage early in the season signals that more is likely to come, so you may want to investigate what you can do to protect your valuable plants. Talk with someone at your favorite nursery or call the Extension Service (pages 344 to 353) for advice.

CHAPTER ELEVEN

Water Gardens

Imagine it's the hottest day of summer. You've just brought the bills in from the mailbox, and even that tiny exertion has you sweating. But as you sit on the patio to rest a moment, all of a sudden you feel cooler and more peaceful.

The temperature didn't change but your perception of it did, thanks to your nearby water garden—the gurgle of the waterfall, the ribbit-ribbit of a frog who's made the pond his new home, the fleeting glance of a goldfish lazily searching for insect larvae.

It's hard to tear yourself away, and after a few minutes, you decide you don't really have anything more important to do.

Welcome to the rewards of owning a water garden. It's a pleasure anyone can experience, even if you have a small yard or you've never gardened before. It's as easy as 1-2-3. First you plan, then you build, and finally you plant.

PLANNING THE LOCATION

Where in your yard is the perfect spot for a water garden? You'll want to take into consideration the following:

- How much light the area receives. Is it in sun most of the day, or shade?
- Can you see this place from inside the house?
- Is there a tree nearby?
- Is it away from septic tank field lines?
- Is there enough room for the size pond you'd like to build?

Yes to sun. The ideal location for a water garden is a spot that receives at least six, preferably more, hours of sunlight a day, since the most spectacular water plants are sun lovers. But because shallow ponds can overheat in summer (not good for plants and fish), the ideal location is one that is in shade several hours during the afternoon.

No to trees. Avoid sites beneath trees. Sure, they look cool and inviting, but digging through tree roots isn't any fun (for you or the tree), and constantly having to clean fallen leaves from the pond gets tiresome quickly.

Power to the pond. If you plan for your decorative pool to have a fountain, filter, pump, waterfall, or lights, make sure your chosen spot is near an electrical outlet. You'll also want a water faucet near enough to run a hose from.

Steep slopes. Get some professional advice before choosing a site that isn't fairly level. Constant runoff into your pond creates a number of problems.

Decide what the pond will look like:

- **Formal vs. informal?** Most water gardens today are informal, to go with our lifestyles and our houses, but if you live in a Williamsburg-style home or a Victorian, you may want to consider a formal look. Rounded and wavy shapes are informal. Squares, oblongs, and straight lines are formal. Mountain stone is informal. Brick is formal.
- Take a hose or a thick rope and form a shape on the ground in various places around the yard to get an idea of what will work.

Water Gardens

JANUARY · FEBRUARY · MARCH · APRIL · MAY · JUNE · JULY · AUGUST · SEPTEMBER · OCTOBER · NOVEMBER · DECEMBER

• **How wide? How deep?** Unlike the advice in every other type of gardening, *don't* start small with water gardens. If you have the room, go for the size you can afford (or have the arm power to dig). The depth should be at least 18 to 24 inches. That's ideal for plants and fish and a comfortable depth for the person who has to wade out into the pool to plant.

CONSTRUCTION MATERIALS

Sure, it's possible to dig a hole in the ground and pour some water in. But the water may drain out, and even if it doesn't, it's likely to stay muddy—which isn't attractive. So you want to line that hole you're going to dig. You have a trio of basic choices:

1 **Preformed rigid units of various sizes and shapes.** Good for smaller ponds and a formal look, they offer less flexibility in shape. Go for Fiberglass that's 1/4-inch thick; the cheaper ones aren't as durable.

2 **Flexible liners.** These are PVC or rubber and are the most versatile choices. Buy the kind made especially for water gardens. You'll find that 32-millimeter, 2-ply PVC is more durable than thinner grades. Rubber liners last the longest and are easiest to install.

3 **Concrete.** It cracks easily and is costly. If you must have a concrete-lined pond, hire a professional to do the job.

How big a liner? To determine the correct size of flexible liner, measure the length and add twice the depth to that figure. Then measure the width and add twice the depth. Finally, add one foot to both figures to allow for overlap. So if your pond is 7 feet long, 5 feet wide, and 2 feet deep, you want a 12-foot by 10-foot liner.

Goodbye grass. Whichever type of pond you decide to build, the first step is to remove the grass where you plan for the pool to go—plus an extra 12 or 13 inches all around to allow for edging.

Hello sand, shovel, and level. The equipment you need for installation is low-tech: a shovel to dig with (or hire someone with a backhoe for larger ponds), a measuring stick, and a carpenter's level. Sand lines the bottom of the hole. If you're installing a flexible liner, you'll also need a 2 by 4 and some old carpet or other material to lay under the liner.

Installing a preformed pool:

1 Place the unit where you want it to go, and pound stakes at 1-foot intervals around it, following the contours.

2 Dig a hole that's about 2 inches deeper than the form, to accommodate a layer of sand.

3 Lift the form into the hole to be sure it fits all the way around. Check to be sure the bottom of the hole is level, and remove all stones and other sharp objects.

4 Pour sand into the hole, tamp it down firmly, and level again.

5 Lift the liner into place and check at several spots to be sure the edges are level. (Remove the form and adjust the hole if needed.)

6 With a hose, run 4 inches of water into the pool and begin using the soil removed from the hole to backfill around the sides. Continue adding 4 more inches of water and 4 inches of soil—checking occasionally to be sure the pool remains level—until you're finished.

7 Install edging of your choice.

Installing a flexible liner:

1 Invite a friend to help you. One person can install a liner alone, but it's easier if two or three work together.

2 Mark off the shape you want.

3 Dig the hole, frequently laying a 2 by 4 across the top edge with a level on it to be sure you're staying even. Remove all sharp objects from the hole so they won't damage your liner.

4 Pour 1 inch of sand in the bottom, tamp down, and level.

5 Cover the bottom and sides of the pool with discarded carpeting or layers of newspaper. This provides cushioning and makes your liner last longer.

6 On the day you're going to install your liner, open it up completely and spread it on the ground in the sun several hours beforehand, so it will be easier to work with.

7 Place the liner in the hole, smoothing it and making folds and pleats as necessary to get it to fit the contours of the hole.

8 Fill the hole to within 1 inch of the rim with water.

9 Trim off the excess liner, leaving about a foot all around. Anchor it.

10 Edge the pond.

11 Test and treat the water. (Test kits are available at water-garden retailers and at pet stores.)

12 Install plants.

WAITING

If you're going to put fish in your pond, wait at least a week—two is good—after testing and treating the water before adding the fish.

Portable water garden. Just because you live in a condo, you don't have to forego the pleasures of a water garden. Consider building a little water garden in a container. It's simple, fast, and fun. See page 332 for directions.

Whether you choose to create a simple water garden in a large tub or build a good-sized pond to fill with plants and fish, you'll find that a water garden brings beauty and serenity to your yard. It relaxes and refreshes you. Doesn't that sound like what you want for your yard? Maybe that's a clue that you should start thinking about where a water garden would look good on your property.

Water Garden

Water Gardens

Common Name (*Botanical Name*)	Type of Plant	Hardiness*	Comments
Anacharis (*Egeria densa*)	Oxygenating	Hardy	Native plant with tiny white flowers. Trim back in July to keep in bounds.
Arrow arum (*Pelrandra virginica*)	Bog or marginal	Hardy	Arrow-shaped leaves with arum-like flowers in summer.
Butterfly fern (*Salvinia rountundifolia*)	Floater	Hardy	Good for small ponds. Excellent for partial shade.
Cardinal flower (*Lobelia cardinalis*)	Bog or marginal	Hardy	Lovely red flowers. Place in 2 inches of water.
Cattail (*Typha* species)	Bog or marginal	Hardy	Look for dwarf varieties for small ponds. May be aggressive. Common cattails are best for big ponds but dwarfs are available. The brown cylindrical spikes are excellent for dried arrangements.
Fairy moss (*Azolla caroliniana*)	Floater	Tropical	Lacy fronds turn red in fall. May be invasive.
Four-leaf water clover (*Marsilea mucronata*)	Floater	Hardy	Patterned leaves resemble large four-leaf clovers. Will grow in partial shade. May be aggressive.
Golden club (*Orontium aquaticum*)	Bog or marginal	Hardy	Native plant. White flower spikes tipped with yellow.
Hardy water canna (*Thalia dealbata*)	Bog or marginal	Hardy	5 feet tall. Bluish-purple blooms.
Iris (*Iris* species)	Bog or marginal	Hardy	Excellent choices include Japanese iris (*I. ensata*), Louisiana iris, yellow flag (*I. pseudacorus*), and blue flag (*I. versicolor* and *I. virginica*).
Lizard's tail (*Saururus cernuus*)	Bog or marginal	Hardy	Heart-shaped leaves and long arching white flower spikes. May be aggressive.
Lotus (*Nelumbo* species)	Floating	Hardy	Need lots of sun and heat. Blooms last 3 days and are followed by interesting pods.
Papyrus (*Cyperus* species)	Bog or marginal	Tropical	The leaves form an intriguing umbrella shape. Wonderful for shade. Dwarfs are available.

Water Gardens

Common Name (Botanical Name)	Type of Plant	Hardiness*	Comments
Pickerel rush (*Pontederia cordata*)	Bog or marginal	Hardy	Native plant. Purplish or blue flower produced over a long period.
Sweet flag (*Acorus* species)	Bog or marginal	Hardy	Iris-like foliage; may be variegated. Some are fragrant.
Taro (*Colocasia* species)	Bog or marginal	Tropical	Enormous leaves; some are variegated, others are purplish-black. Taros give a pond a very exotic look. Some will tolerate partially shady locations.
Water lettuce (*Pistia stratiotes*)	Floater	Tropical	Helps keep water clean. May be invasive; remove excess plants and compost them.
Water lily (*Nymphaea* species)	Floater	Hardy & tropical types	If your pond is large enough, try to have at least 2 topical water lilies: one night-blooming and one day-blooming.
Water milfoil (*Myriophyllum* species)	Oxygenating	Hardy	The feathery foliage is good for filtering pond water.
Wild celery (*Vallisneria americana*)	Oxygenating	Hardy	Tall, ribbonlike foliage.

*Hardy = lives through the winter outdoors when sunk to the bottom of the pond.
*Tropical = killed by frost.

JANUARY
Water Gardens

 PLANNING

Investigate. This is the time of year to learn more about water gardening. Check out books at the library and local bookstores, as well as on the Internet, for more information about fish, waterfalls, or whatever your special enthusiasm is.

Send off for catalogs from water-garden suppliers. They're often filled with good advice, as well as photos of beautiful plants.

Discover what appeals to you. If you're new to water gardening, start thinking about the type of pond you want. Take some virtual tours of water gardens on the Web to get ideas that will translate well to your yard. It's also a good idea to visit a local water-garden retailer in the off-season because the personnel will have more time to talk with you and answer your questions.

Keep records. If you have a garden notebook, sit down beside the fireplace, put your feet up, and read back over your entries for last year. That will remind you

what went well last season and what didn't—what you'd like to duplicate this year and what you want to avoid. If you haven't started a garden notebook, now's the time to do it.

Get organized. Set aside a spot to keep all your water-gardening books, catalogs, magazine articles, and printouts from Web sites. It's easier to find what you're looking for when you follow the advice that Mom always gave you: a place for everything and everything in its place.

 PLANTING

January's typically cold weather lets you off the hook for planting this month—unless you'd like to try an indoor water garden. (See page 343 for directions.)

CARE

Is it time for a little cleanup? Take a close look at the area adjacent to the pond. After fall frosts, many gardeners don't cut back the perennial plants standing beside the water garden since birds enjoy seeds left on them. But on a relatively warm day this month, you may

want to do a bit of cleanup if your water garden is highly visible from the street or the house—especially if wind or snow knocked over tall plants around or in the pond, or if the seeds have been consumed. It will look much better.

Frozen water. Weather in January can vary greatly in our region. One day, temperatures may reach a balmy 70 degrees Fahrenheit, and a week later, a cold snap has frozen the water on the pond. If you have a pond that's at least 24 inches deep, your fish should be fine for a week or a bit more even though the surface of the water is a solid sheet of ice. But if the condition lasts ten days, you'll want to make a hole in the ice to release trapped methane gas. The *wrong* way to do this is with a hammer (which creates shock waves that can kill the fish). The *right* way is to pour boiling water at a spot along the edge to melt the ice so the gas will escape. You can buy pool heaters that will keep a small section of the surface thawed. A submersible pump with a bubbler will do the job, too.

Power outage? If you keep a pump on all winter, check it anytime the power goes out for more than a few hours in cold weather. Sometimes when the power goes out, the discharge pipe becomes covered with ice.

Pick some cattails. Looking for material for dried arrangements inside the house? See what's still available around the edges of the pool. **Cattails** are excellent as long as the brown spikes haven't started to break up.

 # FERTILIZING

You don't have to be concerned about fertilizing outdoors for several months, as plants are dormant. But if you have a containerized indoor water garden in a sunroom, insert a fertilizer tablet made for water gardens into the soil of any plants actively growing and blooming.

Timely Tip

Types of water-garden plants. Although you may be attracted to water gardening by exotic **water lilies** and **lotuses**, not all plants that go in a water-garden float. In fact you wouldn't want all floaters—that would look dull. Besides, you'll want to include some lesser-known submerged plants to help keep the water clean. Here's what's available:

- **Bog or marginal plants:** These are moisture-loving plants that grow in shallow water along the edges of a garden pond. They add beauty and help protect the pond from strong winds.
- **Floaters:** As the name implies, some portion of the plant floats on the surface of the water. They often have spectacular flowers and help shade the water.
- **Oxygenating plants:** Also called submerged plants, these absorb nutrients through their leaves. Their appearance is usually unassuming, but never overlook their importance. Every water garden needs one bunch of oxygenating plants per 1 to 2 square feet of water surface to help keep the water clear.

Plants in all of these categories are either tropical (killed by hard frosts) or hardy (returning year after year). See the plant list on pages 320 and 321 for more specific information.

 # GROOMING

Remove dead or damaged leaves on plants in indoor water gardens.

PROBLEMS

The off-season is the best time to find solutions for problems that affected your water garden last summer—including algae, predators, insects, run-off, plants

not blooming as much as much as you'd hoped. During January, talk with an expert or a fellow water-gardening enthusiast, read a book, or call your local Extension Service office.

FEBRUARY

PLANNING

Follow the rules. Does your community have any building or zoning laws or regulations that might affect your water garden? It's important to check before you dig. Are there any small children in your neighborhood who might be attracted by your pond? Always keep safety in mind.

Learn more. Continue making plans for your new water garden or for adding existing features to the water garden you already have. Go to garden shows to pick up new ideas and discuss the subject with other water-garden enthusiasts.

Stock up. Now's a good time to order any supplies you'll need this season—from a flexible liner for a new pond to plenty of pots in case you're buying new plants or have to divide and repot existing plants.

Containers. If you already have a water garden and it's just not enough, consider a container water garden. They can be as big or tiny, decorative or plain as you like. You can even hook up a fountain in a potted water garden. Think how delightful that will sound when it's placed on your porch, patio, or deck. Everything you need, except plants, is available now if you'd like to get a headstart on spring.

Drawn to scale. The next time you're at an office-supply store, pick up a small pack of graph paper and use it to sketch out your ideas for that water garden you want to build.

PLANTING

If you've been growing tropical water plants indoors as houseplants this winter, you may find that they begin sending up new shoots sometime this month. That's a signal to repot them into large containers if they've been in their current pots for more than a year. Large, heavy plants may need to be divided before they're repotted to keep them in correct proportion to the size of the water garden. (See instructions on pages 326 and 327.)

CARE

Time to feed the fish? On warmer days as you're out in the yard, you may see some movement from the fish that live in your water garden. Does that mean you should feed them? No, they don't need food yet. The rule on feeding fish is to do it only when water temperature (*not* air temperature) is above 50 degrees Fahrenheit and seems likely to remain there.

Skim off debris. On a nice day, remove fallen leaves or twigs that have accumulated on the pond's surface or bottom, to reduce algae growth. (Small pools aren't able to cope with excess debris as readily as larger ones are.) There are two ways of doing this—with a skimmer net or a little vacuum built for the purpose. After you've finished, make a note to put up a net over your water garden next fall to catch falling debris.

How are the tropicals doing? Occasionally check the tropical plants that you're overwintering indoors to make sure the tubers are covered with water. If the water level is getting low, add more distilled water to the container. Keep the temperature about 55 degrees Fahrenheit. If it's warmer, they may sprout, and if it gets too chilly, they may suffer harm.

Equipment check. Pull out those direction booklets and see what maintenance needs to be done to your mechanical devices and filters. It's best to get this done before warm weather arrives, to avoid the usual rush.

On a nice day, remove fallen leaves or twigs that have accumulated on the pond's surface or bottom, to reduce algae growth.

 # FERTILIZING

Did you know that you don't use regular fertilizer in water gardens? Special fish-safe water garden fertilizer tablets, often called "tabs," look like giant bluish green pills. Get ready for the growing season ahead; order a supply now.

 # GROOMING

Anytime the weather's nice this month or next, cut back perennials growing along the sides or margins of the pond. Leave anywhere from a few inches to a foot of the plants showing above the pond's surface. This will allow early-flowering bulbs planted in the area to be more readily seen and admired.

 ## Timely Tip

Shady solutions. Water gardens and sun go hand in hand, and it's always a good idea to place your water garden where it gets maximum exposure to the sun. But trees have a habit of growing, and sometimes that means shade encroaching on your pond. Thinning trees and removing some of their lower limbs may help. But you may also want to try shade-tolerant plants (those that will bloom with only three to four hours of direct sunlight). Here are some that are recommended:

Hardy Water Lilies: 'Comanche', 'Indiana', 'Attraction', 'James Brydon', 'Texas Dawn', 'Virginia', and 'Charlene Strawn'.

Tropical Water Lilies: 'Panama Pacific', 'Tina', 'August Koch', 'Director Moore', and 'Shirley Bryne'.

Bog or Marginal Plants: Arrow arum, cardinal flower, golden club, Louisiana iris, lizard's tail, pickerel rush, taro, umbrella palm, variegated sweet flag, and **yellow flag.** (You'll find more information on these in the plant list on pages 320 and 321.)

Others: Floaters such as **fairy moss** and **water lettuce**, and the lily-like aquatic plant known as **four-leaf water clover** are good for water gardens in partially shady spots. You'll find more details in the plant list.

PROBLEMS

Don't panic when you see the first algae growth of the season. It's perfectly normal and signals that spring is on its way. But a green pond doesn't look great, so you may want to do the following:

- Remove as much decaying matter as possible.
- Scoop up string-like algae with an algae net.
- Use a special pond dye to cut the amount of sunshine that reaches beneath the water's surface. That will slow algae growth.

MARCH

PLANNING

Looking forward to hot weather. Do some research about tropical plants you want to grow in your water garden. Most tropicals shouldn't be added to your pond until water temperature is much warmer. But it's fun to make lists of your favorite tropicals this time of year, knowing that it won't be too much longer before you can place them in the water garden. Then you'll know that summer has really arrived.

Digging time. In the meantime, whether the month comes in like a lamb and goes out like lion, or vice versa, you can finally stop dreaming and start acting on some of your plans. Are you ready to dig that new pond? You can—as long as the weather isn't too cold. The introduction to this chapter provides directions to guide you through the process.

Water lilies need *still water*. If you're planning a fountain or waterfall, keep **water lilies** away from the agitated water they produce. They won't live in turbulent water.

PLANTING

Is the water warm enough? Buy a water thermometer, if you don't own one, so you can measure the pond's tempera-

ture. It's important to know for certain whether the water's warm enough for plants or if you should wait a while longer. You can't go by what the weather gurus report as the air temperature. When your handy thermometer tells you that the water is at least 60 degrees Fahrenheit, you may plant *hardy* **water lilies** and *hardy* marginal plants. (For *tropicals*, wait till the water warms up to 70 degrees Fahrenheit.)

It's fine to put underwater plants in the water garden late this month. Plant oxygenating or submerged plants in 1-gallon containers filled with sand or pea gravel, then lower them to the bottom of your pond.

Division time. When water plants, particularly **lilies** and **lotus**, have been in the same pots for several years, they often become potbound and bloom less. Here are two quick ways to tell if your plants need repotting:

- If you see lots of shoots coming from the rhizomes. These are potential new plants that will crowd the main plant in the container.
- The rhizomes grow over the edge of the pot, as if they're looking for somewhere to root. They need more space to expand.

March through May are the best times of year to divide and repot your plants. The procedure is simple:

1 Buy containers and make sure you have enough soil. (Clay loam is best. Don't use general potting soil. It washes away.). You can find special pots for water-garden plants, but you may also use tubs and black plastic pots that you already have on hand—provided they *don't* have holes in the bottom. The best containers for **water lilies** and **lotuses** are wider than they are deep (10 inches wide for small plants and about 16 inches for larger ones; 6 or 7 inches deep is fine for both widths). Many people like the fabric pots sold specifically for water gardening.

2 Do your dividing in the shade, not out in the sun, to avoid having the plants dry out.

If any of the extra containers you're repotting into have been used, wash them well. Fill each about half-full with soil.

3 Remove the plants from their pots (you may have to cut the container) and hose the soil off the rhizomes.

4 With a sharp knife, cut the rhizomes into 4- to 6-inch sections, each having an eye that looks like a potato eye.

5 Wrap the cut rhizomes in wet newspaper or paper towels while you're working with the others.

6. Replant, adding 10-20-10 fertilizer tablets to the pot, according to directions. (If you're new to water gardening and you've been helping a friend divide plants in return for some of the extras, see the full planting directions given in April.)

CARE

There's plenty to do this month:

• Feed the fish when water temperature reaches about 50 to 55 degrees Fahrenheit. Start with a low-protein food, and feed from three to six times weekly, depending on how hungry your fish seem and how they're growing. Scoop out any food that remains in the water after five minutes.

• Buy a water-testing kit, if you don't own one, and check your pond's pH (it should range from 6.8 to 7.4) monthly from now through November.

• Add water if the weather has been unusually dry and the pond's level is down several inches. Use a dechlorinator to remove chlorine from municipal water and test again to see whether the additional water has upset the pond's balance. Treat as necessary.

• Watch out for fertilizer runoff from your lawn. It can be harmful to fish and also cause algae growth.

 ## FERTILIZING

Insert fertilizer tablets made especially for water gardens in containers as you pot or repot hardy **lilies** and marginal plants. For plants that are staying in last season's containers, begin fertilizing again when water temperatures begin to rise above 55 degrees Fahrenheit.

Rule of thumb. Beginning in spring and continuing until one month before your first expected fall frost, fertilize **lilies** and **lotuses** once a month when the air temperature is 75 degrees Fahrenheit or less and *twice* a month when temperatures climb higher. Feed marginal or bog plants every five to seven weeks. Use fertilizer specially made for water gardens; too much nitrogen from regular fertilizer, in the main part of the pond, unbalances the water.

 ## GROOMING

About the first of March, cut back all ornamental grasses around the pond. It's important to get to this before new growth starts. Put the trimmings on the compost pile, or use them as mulch in informal woodland pathways. If you don't cut back grasses before new growth starts, new and old growth intertwine—and look messy.

 ## PROBLEMS

Use Mosquito Dunks® or other biological controls (one per 100 square feet of water surface) to prevent mosquito larvae from hatching in your water garden. Start your preventive measures now and continue until frost, even in container water gardens.

APRIL

Water Gardens

PLANNING

Rocky road ahead. You've chosen a site for your water garden, but after you start digging, you find a big boulder or two. You may want to switch sites, but you can also dig the pond around the rocks, using them as part of your design.

PLANTING

Most gardeners in our region will pot *hardy* water plants this month (as soon as water temperature is 50 to 55 degrees Fahrenheit) and *tropical* ones next month, after temperatures are reliably warm. The time to add **water lettuce** and **water hyacinth** to your water garden is after all chance of frost has passed. In much of the area, that will occur by the end of April. For those in the colder sections, it could be next month.

How to plant hardy water lilies:

1 Have all your supplies on hand before you begin: pea gravel, clay loam soil (dug from your yard), water-garden fertilizer tablets, and containers. You can buy a soil substitute at water-garden stores, but it is expensive. Because hardy **lilies** grow horizontally, their pots should be 14 to 16 inches wide and 7 to 9 inches deep. You may also need some bricks to

place beneath the pots on the bottom of the pond.

2 Prune damaged roots or dead leaves.

3 Fill the container about half full of soil, and add two water-garden fertilizer tablets. Add more soil so the container is about three-fourths full.

4 Position the rhizome so the cut end rests against the inside of the container and the growing tip is held out of the soil at a 45-degree angle, facing the opposite side of the container. Add more soil to within 2 inches of the container's rim, making sure the growing point is *not* covered.

5 Carefully add 1 inch of pea gravel. This keeps the soil from washing out of the pots and helps prevent fish damage.

6 Water the container gently.

7 Lower the pot into the pond so the growing tip is covered by 3 inches of water.

8 Over the next few weeks, gradually lower the pot so that it's beneath 12 to 18 inches of water. (You can put **water lilies** into deep water right away, but many gardeners believe they grow faster early in the season if they're gradually lowered to the correct depth.)

How to plant lotus:

1 When you buy a **lotus**, get a recommendation on a container size from the seller. Small ones may fit in 3-gallon pots, but others may require a pot ten times that size. **Lotuses** won't bloom well unless they have enough room.

2 You also need clay loam soil, fertilizer tablets, and a stone that will fit into the pot with the **lotus**.

3 Fill the pot halfway with soil and place several fertilizer tablets in the soil. (Use more fertilizer for bigger containers.) Add more soil to within a few inches of the pot's rim.

4 Handle the tuber very carefully since it's brittle. Place the tuber on top of the soil with the cut edge against the inside of the container. Put the stone on top of the tuber to hold it in place.

5 Add more soil, but don't cover the growing tip.

6 Carefully place 1/2-inch of gravel over the soil—but not over the growing tip.

7 Place the pot on the edge of the pond so that it's initially covered with only a few inches of water. Then gradually lower the container as the plant grows.

Even though fish eat mosquito larvae, it's a good idea to regularly use a natural control made for water gardens. These need to be renewed every thirty days.

CARE

Increase fish feeding. Once water temperatures rise reliably above 60 degrees Fahrenheit, switch to a high-protein fish food and use it one to three times a day the first week. Remember to feed only an amount that the fish will consume in five minutes. Scoop out any food that the fish don't gobble up. Never feed *catfish food* to goldfish or koi. It's not good for them.

Prevent mosquitoes. Even though fish eat mosquito larvae, it's a good idea to regularly use a natural control made for water gardens. These need to be renewed every thirty days. Since it's a monthly chore, you may want to mark it on your calendar so you don't forget.

Leaves fall in spring, as well as in autumn. Some trees keep their dried leaves all winter and then drop them in spring. So your pond may be picking up a few leaves about now. If you have many such trees, you may want to spread netting over the water's surface for a week or so. But most people take care of the debris by skimming it out two or three times a week.

FERTILIZING

Begin fertilizing hardy **water lilies** and marginal or bog plants using special compressed fertilizer tablets made for water gardens. Larger plants need several tabs inserted in each pot. See package directions for the number of tablets required for the size containers you have.

GROOMING

Thin out your supply of oxygenating plants such as **anacharis**. Too many will clog the pond and prevent growth of flowering plants. Toss the excess on the compost pile.

PROBLEMS

Aphids. These tiny sucking insects are especially attracted to the fast new growth that your plants are beginning to produce. Try hosing them off or dunking the affected leaves in the pond's water. Dragonflies and ladybugs are excellent controls if this is a continuing problem for you. If you have fish in your water

Timely Tips

Potting tall plants. Before you pile soil into the pot, put a rock in the bottom of the containers of tall plants to help prevent their being blown over by strong winds. Wide pots also help keep tall plants from toppling over.

Buy lotus locally. Lotus tubers are easily damaged in transit because they're brittle. You may want to look for a local supplier instead of ordering them by mail.

garden, don't use any chemical controls since they may be toxic to koi or goldfish. Check with a water-garden dealer or your local Extension Service office for recommendations; there are natural products made especially for water gardens that may help.

MAY

PLANNING

To save money, you might be thinking of planting just hardy water-garden plants since they come back year after year and tropicals won't. But you may want to reconsider.

- Tropical **water lilies** are more spectacular than hardy ones, and they come in a wider array of dazzling colors.
- In the fall, tropicals continue flowering a month or a month and a half longer than hardy **water lilies** do.
- Tropical and hardy **water lilies** bloom at different times of day. Hardy **lilies** begin to bloom when the sun strikes them in the morning and finish about mid-afternoon. If you leave for work at 7 a.m. and don't get back till 6 p.m., you may miss the show, except on weekends. But tropical **water lilies** are divided into two types: day bloomers and night bloomers. Day-blooming tropical **water lilies** flower until about 6 p.m., about the time the night-blooming tropicals are just beginning to unfurl their flowers. Then the flowers of the night bloomers stay open until late the next morning.

PLANTING

Once all chance of frost has passed and air and water temperature stay about 70 degrees Fahrenheit, you may plant tropical **water lilies**.

How to plant tropical water lilies:

1 Have everything ready before you start: clay loam soil, fertilizer tablets, pea gravel, and plenty of containers. Pots for tropical lilies should be about 10 to 12 inches in diameter. You may also need some bricks to place under the pots so they'll be at the proper depth.

2 Make sure the water temperature is 70 degrees Fahrenheit. Colder water will stunt the plant.

Fill containers about half full of soil, add two fertilizer tablets and more soil, stopping about 2 inches from the rim.

3 Place the tuber of a tropical **lily** on top of the soil in the middle of the container with its roots spread out. Gently push the roots into the soil and make sure the growing tip or eye is *not* covered by the soil.

4 Gently add an inch of pea gravel to prevent the soil from washing away and so fish won't muddy the water by poking around.

5 Water the container gently but thoroughly.

6 There are two theories about placing plants in water gardens. One school says to immediately lower them to the correct depth (12 inches of water over the growing tip for tropical **water lilies**). But some water-garden experts think it's better to first place the plants in more shallow water—with about 6 inches of water over the growing tip—then gradually lower it to a foot deep as the plant grows. You may want to see which works best for you.

CARE

To feed or not to feed? If your fish don't seem hungry when you toss food into the pond, the reason may be that they're eating plenty of insects and larvae. Cut back on feeding frequency and amount.

FERTILIZING

Insert fertilizer tablets into the containers of any new plants before placing the pots in the pond. Also fertilize hardy **water lilies** and **lotuses** that were planted last month and are already growing.

If fish munch up all your young submerged plants, you can buy plant protectors to place over the plants. These allow the plants to become established.

 # GROOMING

Neatness counts. Keep the water garden tidy by removing damaged foliage and debris knocked into the water by storms. If the pond looks messy, you may have too many plants. Invite a friend over and share your excess.

 # PROBLEMS

Hungry koi. If fish munch up all your young submerged plants, you can buy plant protectors to place over the plants. These allow the plants to become established.

Fish predators. One morning you may wake up and find that you no longer have fish in your water garden—or you may find that the number of your fish is gradually diminishing. Blame wildlife predators such as raccoons, blue herons, turtles, and occasionally, a neighborhood cat. What can you do?

Timely Tips

Beware of gift plants. Accept all **water lilies** that a buddy is dividing and giving you, of course. But sometimes the plants that gardeners most readily share—because they have an abundance of them—are aggressive plants that grow quickly. Watch out for some of these. They can take over even a medium-sized water garden, or the area next to it, before you realize what's happening. These include:

- **Horsetail** (*Equisetum hyemale*)
- **Duckweed** (*Lemna minor*)
- **Bamboo**
- **Chameleon plant** (*Houttuynia cordata* 'Chamaeleon')
- **Water hyacinth** (*Eichhornia crassipes*)

Attracting butterflies. These wonderful plants attract butterflies to your water garden: **cardinal flower** (*Lobelia cardinalis*), **water mint** (*Mentha aquatica*), and **water snowball** (*Gymnocoronis spilanthoides*). **Cardinal flower** and **water mint** also attract hummingbirds.

- Place a plastic net over the pond for several weeks.
- Although their effects aren't long lasting, try noisemakers, scarecrows, and other devices sold to keep wildlife at bay.
- Remove large turtles to another home.
- Stack cinderblocks in several places in the pond to provide hiding places for the fish.
- If the problem is persistent, you could consider redigging the edges of the water garden. Ponds with edges that go straight down are less likely to have problems than those with shallow "shelves" built into the sides.
- Let the dog stay outside in the yard at night.

JUNE

PLANNING

Still time to get going. Sure, it's summer and it may be hot outdoors, but there's plenty of time to get things done if you weren't able to accomplish them earlier in the season. Still waiting to fulfill your dream of constructing a water garden? Do it now. If you weren't able to get **water lilies** divided in the spring, and all of a sudden you notice they're not blooming as much as they once did, it's still possible to divide and replant them now, or anytime during the summer. You'll miss out on a few weeks of flowering as plants recover, but you should be able to skip dividing next year, which will give you something to look forward to.

Relax. Sit down and enjoy yourself by the water garden. That's what you built it for. Consider adding some lights so you can enjoy the pond in the evening, as well as during the day.

PLANTING

Make a portable water garden. Containers make water gardens possible on patios, decks, porches, and terraces—anywhere you'd like the refreshing feel of water.

The choice of containers is almost limitless—plastic, pottery, ceramic, earthenware, wood—whatever can be made waterproof. (Avoid copper and lead, unless you line them with a flexible liner.)

1 Buy a brush-on sealant made for water gardens, and brush it generously over your chosen container. When the sealant has dried, set the container in the driveway and fill it with water. Observe it for twenty-four hours to see whether it leaks.

2 Fill minor leaks with a silicone caulk made for use around water gardens.

3 Line wooden containers with a sheet of heavy-duty flexible plastic, attaching it to the edges of the container with staples, nails, or silicone sealer.

4 Move to the desired location— somewhere that you'll be able to see and enjoy it frequently and an area that receives a minimum of five hours of sun daily. Fill about two-thirds full with water. Treat with a dechlorinator if you're going to have fish.

5 Add plants that have been potted up. Some may need to be positioned on top of bricks so they grow at the right level. Many miniature water-garden plants are available. Don't limit your selection just to floating plants. You may want to choose a **dwarf papyrus** or **dwarf cattail** to go with your **water lily**. And always add one bunch of oxygenating plants to the tub or container to help keep the water clean.

6 Wait two weeks before introducing fish (no more than one goldfish per 10 gallons of water).

7 All that's necessary from then on is to replace evaporated water, feed any fish occasionally, remove dead leaves and faded flowers, and fertilize plants once a month in moderate weather and twice a month when temperatures are high.

8 When cold weather arrives, the container garden can be sunk into the ground or taken indoors. Or you may want to just dismantle it and start again next year. (Another alternative is given in the **October** section.)

Trim back plants to keep one-third of the water garden's surface open. Having no more than two-thirds of the water covered allows built-up gases to escape from the water and beneficial oxygen to get into it.

CARE

Watch the water level. When the water in your pond is an inch below normal, very slowly add more. A flexible liner that's exposed to sunlight because it's not covered with water has a shorter life.

Avoid overcrowding. Trim back plants to keep one-third of the water garden's surface open. Having no more than two-thirds of the water covered allows built-up gases to escape from the water and beneficial oxygen to get into it.

Monthly tasks: It's time to test your water and renew your organic mosquito larvae control. Feed fish sparingly.

Pump time. When temperatures climb toward—or beyond—90 degrees Fahrenheit, it's a good idea to increase water aeration to increase oxygen in the water and help remove other gases.

FERTILIZING

Feed more frequently. When air temperature is 75 degrees Fahrenheit or below, fertilize **water lilies** once a month using special water-garden fertilizer tablets. Once temperatures head higher than 75 degrees, many experts recommend that you feed twice a month. Fertilize **lotuses** twice a month throughout the growing season.

Timely Tip

Water lilies indoors. Did you know that you could use **water lilies** as cut flowers? They're real dazzlers at parties. Charles Thomas, founder of Lilypons Water Gardens in Maryland, passed this trick along to me. The procedure is simple:

- On the first day a flower opens, cut the stem about 12 inches under the water, using sharp pruning shears.
- Carry the **lily** by the stem, holding it right side up, into the house.
- Light a white candle and allow a drop of wax to drip at the base of each petal. This holds the flower open.
- Place in a vase so that the water does *not* touch the flowers.
- **Water lilies** often last three, sometimes four, days as cut flowers indoors.
- Always keep them away from the sun.

GROOMING

Good grooming. Remove any damaged, browning, or yellowish leaves whenever they appear. Also deadhead regularly—cutting off dying or spent flowers close to the crown. But if you want to have those interesting brown **lotus** pods to use later in dried arrangements, do *not* remove spent **lotus** flowers.

PROBLEMS

Why isn't my water lily blooming as much as it did last year? Possibilities include:

- It's potbound and needs to be divided.
- It isn't getting enough sunlight.
- The pond has too many plants competing against each other.
- You haven't removed old flowers or dying leaves.
- It needs fertilizer.

JULY

PLANNING

When the temperature and the humidity levels are both headed for the stratosphere, no one wants to work in the garden. So don't. Relax beside your water garden and read a book—about water gardening, what else? It's a great way to plan ahead for next year.

Heading away on vacation? Have a neighbor keep an eye on your pond. July can be a dry month, so if you're going to be away as long as two weeks, you may want to fill the pond to the brim before you leave. Larger cities may have pond-maintenance services that can take care of your water garden if you're away longer than that.

PLANTING

Never too late? You can continue adding new water-garden plants to your pond, if you want to. You may also divide **water lilies** that need it. (Sorry, you'll have to wait until next year to separate overgrown **lotuses**. They should be divided only in spring.)

Plants for container water gardens. These water plants do well in tubs:

- **Dwarf lotuses**
- Hardy **water lilies**: 'Comanche', 'Berit Strawn', and 'Indiana'.
- Tropical **water lilies**: 'Albert Greenberg', 'Golden West', 'Green Smoke', 'Panama Pacific', 'Tina', and 'Yellow Dazzler'.
- Others: **dwarf cattail, dwarf papyrus, knot grass, umbrella palm**, and **variegated rush**.

CARE

Controlling algae. Green water is the bane of every water gardener's experience. Algae is normal early in the season before plants begin to grow and take care of the problem. A green mosslike covering on the sides of the pond and on the undersides of **water lily** leaves is normal, and even beneficial to tadpoles.

In summer, though, the problem usually requires some action. It's generally caused by:

- Overfertilization or incorrect amount of fertilizer.
- Overfeeding fish and leaving the unconsumed food in the water to rot.
- Not enough plants.
- Too many plants.
- Too many fish.

Do you see the cause of your problem listed here? After you've made corrections and determined that you have an adequate number of oxygenating plants in the water garden, wait two weeks and see what happens. Whatever you do, don't think you'll get rid of the problem by changing the water. You have to develop a balanced ecosystem. If you still have a severe algae problem, consider adding a pump and filter.

Oh, those skeeters! Studies have shown that bug zappers attract and kill more of the "good guys" and aren't very effective against mosquitoes, the very pest that causes most homeowners to buy a zapper in the first place. Pond owners can help prevent mosquitoes by monthly use of a special formulation of Bt (*Bacillus thuringiensis*) in their ponds. It prevents mosquito larvae from hatching.

The bog garden. If rainfall is less than normal, you may need to water the marginal plants planted along the shallow edges of the water garden. Check them weekly throughout the growing season to make sure they never dry out. Since these are plants that need wet soil, they suffer if they don't have enough moisture.

If rainfall is less than normal, you may need to water the marginal plants planted along the shallow edges of the water garden. Check them weekly throughout the growing season to make sure they never dry out.

 # FERTILIZING

Feeding your water-garden plants should be routine by this time in the growing season. Twice a month, add more fertilizer tablets to the containers of **water lilies** and **lotuses**. Once every five to seven weeks, do the same for marginal or bog plants. *Never* feed oxygenating plants.

 # GROOMING

Continue to deadhead all plants as you notice faded flowers. Also remove damaged foliage.

 # PROBLEMS

Pest patrol. Pick off caterpillars and Japanese beetles by hand. If you see tunnels on **water lily** leaves, these are made by an insect called the false leaf-mining midge. The easiest control is to cut off the affected leaf and put it out with the trash. Wash aphids off foliage with a blast of water from the hose. Round holes in the leaves are usually caused by the larvae of leaf cutter moths. Check the undersides of holey leaves for the egg cases, and remove and destroy them. The pond looks better if you cut off the affected leaf, too. Bt is a recommended control if those measures don't work. If you have fish in your water garden, always consult an expert—a retailer who specializes in water gardens or an agent from the Extension Service office—before using any insecticides in your pond. Even some products that are considered mild or organic may be toxic to fish. Water-garden suppliers stock organic controls that are safe to use around fish.

Timely Tips

How many plants are too many? The rule of thumb is that one-third of the surface of the water garden should be clear of plants. When your plants have expanded beyond that, remove some and give them to friends or neighbors.

Excess fish. Too many fish cause the water in your pond to become unbalanced and turn green. While it's fun to watch the colorful fish who make their home in your water garden, harden your heart and give some of the extras to friends who are just getting started in water gardening. Or use them to stock a second pond. Because they're exotics and may upset the natural balance of things, koi or goldfish should *not* be released into rivers or streams.

Fishy rule of thumb. The maximum for any water garden is 1 inch of fish per 5 gallons of water. For koi, you may want to stock about half that amount.

AUGUST

 PLANNING

When is a water garden not a water garden? When it's a water feature. That means the look and sound of running water but no plants. It's an ideal way to enjoy the pleasures of water gardening without many of the cares. It's a nice solution for those who are away from home a great deal. Here's how to make one:

1 Buy a concrete planter with a drain hole in the bottom. Coat the inside with water sealer.

2 Buy a small submersible pump that will fit nicely into the size pot you've selected. Select the type nozzle you prefer: spray, jet, bubble.

3 Remove the plug from the end of the pump's cord and then place the pump in the planter. Run the cord through the hole in the bottom of the container.

4 Leave enough of the cord inside the container to give the pump any needed height and then plug the hole (and hold the cord in place) with a cork.

5 Seal around the cork and hole (inside and outside the container) with silicone, to prevent leaks.

6 Let the silicone dry for twenty-four hours.

7 In the meantime, replace the plug you removed from the cord with a new one.

8 Place the planter where you want it to go, and place gravel in the bottom to raise the pump and adjust the height of the nozzle.

9 Fill the pot with water, and plug in the pump.

10 Enjoy the beguiling sound of cascading water whenever you want.

PLANTING

Are there areas beside your water garden that always remain wet? These spots are good candidates for planting marginal or bog plants such as **old-fashioned flags** and **cardinal flower**. August isn't too late to plant these moisture-loving perennials. In fact, you may find that nurseries have them on sale. Armed with a list (see pages 320 and 321), check the perennial collection at regular nurseries, as well as water-garden retailers. It's fun to experiment with marginal plants to see what you like best and which combinations of plants look best around your water garden.

 CARE

Fish feeding. Occasionally switch to another type food to give your fish a change of taste. Feed less when temperatures climb above 85 degrees Fahrenheit to avoid stressing the fish any further. You may find that koi enjoy some of the excess produce from your garden. They're known to like fruits and veggies. Cut the produce into small pieces, and remove any that's uneaten after five minutes.

Dunk time. No, not doughnuts (although that may be appealing as you sit on the deck first thing in the morning and listen to the tinkling sound of your water garden). These dunks control mosquito larvae in your pond. Use 1 per 100 square feet of water surface.

Evaporation. Top off the pond when it gets 1/2 to 1 inch low. Those with larger, more elaborate water gardens may want to investigate automatic refill valves.

You may find that koi enjoy some of the excess produce from your garden. They're known to like fruits and veggies. Cut the produce into small pieces, and remove any that's uneaten after five minutes.

Green strings. If you see long strings of green algae in your water, remove them with a stick or rake.

FERTILIZING

Once more. Do you have enough fertilizer tablets to last through the month? Water gardeners should continue fertilizing their plants at the regular rate during August. But you should *stop* fertilizing about a month before fall's first frost. If you don't know the date of your average first frost, call your local Extension Service office and ask.

GROOMING

Seeing spots. Trim off plant foliage that's covered with black spots. That's an indication of a fungus, and it's best to get it out of the water garden.

PROBLEMS

Deer and other critters. As a last resort if deer, possums, raccoons, and other wildlife have made your water garden their regular dinner table, you may want to consider surrounding the pond with an unobtrusive low-voltage electric fence. This isn't a good idea around young children and pets, but sometimes it can be a temporary measure—sending the critters off elsewhere, after which you can turn it off.

Tadpoles. If, all of a sudden, your pond seems overrun by little black tadpoles, don't get concerned. They don't mean you're going to be overwhelmed by frogs. Instead they result from the eggs of toads, which lay eggs in the pond, but live on dry land once they mature.

Snails. It's true that snails do eat algae, but only from surfaces and not as much as fish do. They also eat plants and host parasites that may affect your fish. They reproduce rapidly, so remove them by hand or in a fine net whenever you see them.

Timely Tips

Go visiting. Take the opportunity to visit other water gardens for inspiration and ideas. These may be part of a garden tour in your own or a nearby community; they may be friends' gardens or they can be part of public gardens in your area. It's fun to see what others have done, what plants they're using, and how they have cleverly handled little problems that have plagued you, too. Take a camera and notebook with you to record your observations. You'll enjoy looking back over them in the dead of winter.

Light up the night. You can hook your water-garden lighting—either spotlights shining on the pool or underwater lights—on a timer so they come on the same time each evening and go off automatically as a preset time. Then you don't have to remember to turn the lights off every night.

SEPTEMBER

PLANNING

Update your garden notebook. As the water-gardening season begins to wind down a bit, look back over what has happened in your pond the past few months, and write it down, if you haven't already. What worked even better than you had hoped? What problems did you encounter—and how did you solve them? What was the weather like this particular year—wetter, drier, hotter, cooler than usual—and how did that affect your water garden? Keep at least one page for plans that you'd like to accomplish next year or the year after. You may want to write down the names of particularly attractive **water lilies** that you would love to own or tuck a brochure about a new fountain into the book. It takes only a few moments to update a garden notebook during the season, but you'll find yourself using the information over and over in coming years.

PLANTING

Don't say no. If a water-gardening friend has too many **water lilies** and other plants and offers you a few hardy ones, accept them, even though it's late in the season. Keep them cool and damp, and pot them as quickly as possible. Especially if this happens early in the month, the plants will very likely have time to become established before cold weather arrives. Don't expect any bloom, though, until next year.

CARE

Cut back on fish food. When water temperature falls to 60 degrees Fahrenheit—possibly later this month—give fish less food than you may have been providing in summer and feed them less frequently (no more than once a day). Water-garden suppliers have special fish food that provides what fish need going into winter.

Water quality. Even though we're headed into the down season for water gardens, you should still test the pond's water monthly, particularly if you have fish. A balanced pond that has only a little algae, no nitrates, no ammonia, and the correct pH (6.8 to 7.8) is a healthy pond. It's also a more beautiful one because the fish and underwater plants are easily seen and admired.

Cleaning out the pond. It's a chore that doesn't have to be done very often—maybe every four or five years—and it's one that you can postpone even longer by paying attention to keeping leaves and other debris from settling into the bottom of your pond. But eventually sludge will build up and have to be removed. Too much can be toxic to fish and encourages algae, the bane of the water garden.

1 Remove as much of the water as possible, and place the fish in a temporary tank. Consider covering containers so the fish can't jump out.

2 Remove plants from the pond and place them in the shade. Don't let them dry out.

3 Pump the rest of the water from the water garden.

4 Remove all the solids at the bottom of the pond. Do *not* scrub the sides of the pond or use any cleaning chemicals.

5 Return any saved water to the pond.

6 Place fish and plants back in the pond.

7 Slowly add fresh water to fill the pond, adding a dechlorinator and any other products you normally use to remove chemicals in your water supply.

Even though we're headed into the down season for water gardens, you should still test the pond's water monthly, particularly if you have fish. A balanced pond that has only a little algae, no nitrates, no ammonia, and the correct pH (6.8 to 7.8) is a healthy pond.

 FERTILIZING

Time to stop. Hardy **water lilies** and marginal or bog plants need to gradually slow down their growth and get ready for winter. To help them do that, stop fertilizing at least a month before your first frost date. Some gardeners like to end feeding about six weeks before they expect a fall frost. If plants are actively growing when frost arrives, they are likely to be harmed by the sudden cold.

 GROOMING

Even though the season is beginning to wind down, keep up good grooming practices. Remove dead or diseased leaves regularly.

 PROBLEMS

Double-duty leaf netting. By the end of the month, have leaf netting in place. It's much easier to prevent leaves from getting into your water garden than it is to remove them once they're there. But netting can also prevent damage—to fish and plants—by wild animals, ducks, and herons.

Locating a leak. One day the pond is full, and the next day the water level is down considerably. If the situation continues, suspect a leak. Sometimes these are obvious—there's a wet spot beside the pool. But other cases require detective work.

• Shut off any pumps. If the water level stops falling, you've located the leak—in the waterfall or plumbing system. Closely inspect all connections. Look for backups caused by plant material or other obstructions.
• If the water level continues to fall after you've turned off the pump, the leak is probably in the liner or edge. Drop a few drops of food-safe vegetable dye (available at grocery stores) in the water along the sides to see whether you can find where colored water is escaping the pond.
• Once the water reaches below the leak, it stops and that makes it harder to find the leak. You can add some

Timely Tips

Fish and fountains. If you have fish in your water garden, avoid any fountains or statues made of lead. Lead can be toxic to fish.

Not so narrow. Many water gardeners add a stream to their already built ponds. It's a fairly simple and inexpensive procedure. If you do it, consider making the stream slightly wider than you'd planned. The reason? Once you've lined both sides of the stream, it may appear more narrow than you expected.

more water (treating for chlorine and other water chemicals) and then run the dye test just described. Or you can move rocks here and there and check in the folds of the liner for the leak.
• Patching material is available to fix liner leaks.

OCTOBER

PLANNING

Fall's grasses. This is the time of year when ornamental grasses come into their own. But they really should be part of every water gardener's plans from the beginning. The upright, spiky effect they provide is a delightful complement to the pond and helps soften the lines between water and land. Determine whether the soil in the planting area around your water garden is naturally moist, dry, or average. Then turn to the chapter in this book on perennials and ornamental grasses to find some selections that will work for your situation. You'll find grasses that are short, tall, like wet feet, tolerate dryness, need lots of sun, and can get along in shade just fine. They all add another element of sound to the water garden as the wind rustles through them. One of their best qualities is that they add interest to the water-garden area all winter. Make a note to pick up a few grasses for planting around the garden next spring.

PLANTING

Transplants. While marginal or bog plants like plenty of moisture in the summertime, not all like to have wet feet in the winter. Two that should be removed from the water garden and planted in the yard for winter are **cardinal flower** and **Japanese iris**. Mulch them with 3 inches of shredded leaves.

Cannas. Just as **cannas** grown in soil sometimes don't make it through a very cold winter, the same is true for **cannas** grown in water. The solution in both cases is the same. Dig up the rhizomes after the foliage has been killed by frost and store in slightly moist sand or peat moss in a basement or other area where the temperature stays about 50 degrees Fahrenheit. Don't put them back into the water garden next year until air and water temperatures are reliably above 70 degrees Fahrenheit.

CARE

Net time. If you didn't get netting put up over your water garden last month to catch falling leaves, do it now. The netting you buy should have small- to medium-sized holes. Large openings leave too much space for debris to fall through. Too many leaves in the pond will upset the balance. If you've had problems with cats, raccoons, and other animals preying on your fish, the problem can sometimes get worse in cold weather because the fish are more sluggish. In that case, you may want to leave the netting over the pond all winter to foil the intruders.

Fish food. When the water temperature is between 52 and 60 degrees Fahrenheit, continue to feed the fish, but don't feed them as much as usual or more often than once a day. A reminder for the colder parts of the state and during those years when cold weather seems to arrive early: Stop feeding fish when the water temperature falls below 50 degrees Fahrenheit, and resume next spring when the temperature in the pond again climbs above 50 degrees.

Winterize hardy plants. As hardy **water lilies** fade, cut back dead and dying leaves, and sink the plants to the bottom of the pond. Do the same with marginal plants. Some of these may survive if left along the edges of the water garden. But since we don't know what winter's going to bring, it's best to put them in deep water where their roots won't freeze.

Taking care of container gardens. After a hard freeze kills the foliage of water plants growing in containers, here's what you need to do:

• Empty all the water from the pot.

If you didn't get netting put up over your water garden last month to catch falling leaves, do it now. The netting you buy should have small- to medium-sized holes. Large openings leave too much space for debris to fall through.

• Store any cold-sensitive containers— ceramic, pottery, terra cotta— indoors so they aren't affected by the weather.
• Consider discarding inexpensive plants such as bunches of **anacharis**.

If you'd like to try keeping **water lilies**, there are two methods: Dig a hole in an area of the yard that has moist soil. Place the pots of plants in it and nestle some soil around the containers—it doesn't have to come up to their top rims. Just before the next predicted hard freeze, cover the pots with shredded leaves. A second technique is to place the plants—still in their pots—in a plastic tub that's kept in an unheated garage or basement. Check weekly to make sure the soil is slightly moist.

Timely Tips

They keep on blooming. It seems an anomaly given the name *tropical water lilies*, but these plants keep blooming after several frosts in fall— and quite a while after hardy **lilies** finish flowering. It's not at all unusual to have tropical **water lilies** still flowering at Thanksgiving. If that happens to you one year, why not cut a blossom and display it in a vase on your dining table? It's one more thing to be thankful for.

 ## FERTILIZING

Feeding time ends. Plants don't need any more fertilizer until next spring.

 ## GROOMING

Keep tropical plants looking neat by removing faded flowers and damaged leaves.

 ## PROBLEMS

Fish in container gardens. If you have a fish or two living in a small potted water garden, what do you do with it during the winter? One solution is to take the fish indoors into an aquarium that's kept between 45 and 60 degrees Fahrenheit. Use an air pump to supply oxygen. You can also overwinter fish in the basement in any clean container. Count on 1 gallon of water per inch of fish. Feed occasionally. About once a month, remove one-fifth of the water and replace it with fresh water.

NOVEMBER

PLANNING

Wait till next year. Are you ready to add some more features to your basic water garden? Possibilities include waterfalls, streams, bridges, stepping stones, fountains, spotlights, and underwater lighting. Now's the time to do your homework to find out what equipment is needed, the range of costs, and whether this is a do-it-yourself project or you need professional help.

PLANTING

Tropical plants. They won't survive outdoors over winter, so what do you do with them?

- Toss them out, and buy new ones next year.
- Bring them indoors as houseplants. But they'll need at least six hours of sun (or grow lights) and temperatures of 70 degrees Fahrenheit or above. Place the plants in tubs or trays that have no holes so they may be kept full of water to keep the plants wet. **Umbrella palm** makes an interesting houseplant in medium light.

- After the foliage has been killed, remove the tuber from the pot and place it in a tub of slightly moist sand or peat moss. Place it in an area where the temperature stays about 55 degrees Fahrenheit.

CARE

Playing catch-up. If for some reason you didn't get hardy plants cleaned up and moved to the bottom of the water garden, do it right away.

The perennial border. Decide whether to leave the plants growing near the water garden or to cut them back. Trimming them definitely makes the pond area look neater. But many birds and small wildlife are attracted to the seeds that remain on plants that are not cut back.

Pumps. It's possible to keep pumps and filters working all winter in our climate (ask an expert at a water-garden retailer for details). But most people disconnect them. Overwinter the pump in a bucket of water in a heated basement so the seals don't dry out. Next spring, clean the filter before placing the pump back in the water garden.

FERTILIZING

Take a break. Unless you've created an indoor water garden under lights or in a sunroom, it's not necessary to fertilize any more until spring and warm weather arrive.

GROOMING

There is not much need to groom plants at this time of year.

PROBLEMS

Biological filters don't work in cold weather, but water-garden shops carry products that contain bacteria that works when temperatures hover around freezing. They also help decompose any leaves that fell through your net.

December

Water Gardens

 PLANNING

Deicing. Is this the year you buy a deicer for your pond? In the warmer parts of the region, ponds don't freeze over for very long. But when we experience an extra-cold winter, we usually wish we'd invested in a deicer. They keep a small section of the water surface open so that oxygen can enter and gases harmful to the fish can escape. Floating on the surface of the pond, the device has a thermostat that turns on the heat when water temperature goes below 40 degrees Fahrenheit. It's an excellent investment for keeping hardy plants alive in shallow water gardens.

Wish list. Does everyone know what water-garden-related gifts you'd like for the holidays? A lighting kit? A new fountain? A large boulder for a focal point, or a load of mountain stone? A great stocking stuffer is a good book on watering gardening. It will keep you going through the cold days of winter until it's time to plant the pond again.

 PLANTING

Indoor water gardens. Place tropical plants in tubs or decorative containers (Chinese fish bowls are attractive) filled with water, place them in a room where the temperature remains at 70 degrees Fahrenheit or warmer and the plants can be in the sun five or six hours. What a winter delight! (See page 342 for detailed directions.)

 CARE

Just checking. One of the best things you can do to make sure your water garden stays in tip-top shape is to go out and look at it—daily in summer, two or three times a week in cold weather. When you're on the spot, you'll quickly notice any problems that have cropped up since your last visit and you'll probably be in time to come up with a solution before it's too late.

 FERTILIZING

Plants in indoor water gardens need light fertilization, but outdoors, no more feeding is necessary until spring.

 GROOMING

Take a winter vacation from grooming.

Timely Tip

In colder parts of the region, where ponds are more likely to freeze over at least part of the winter, one of the dangers is that the ice will exert pressure on a pond's rigid liner. One way to avoid this is by placing a piece of Styrofoam 12 inches wide and 2 inches thick into the water to absorb some of the stress. An alternative is a large ball such as a soccer or basketball. You may have to place them beneath netting to prevent them from blowing away.

PROBLEMS

Shallow ponds. One of the problems of water gardens that are fewer than 18 inches deep is that they may be too shallow to keep plants from freezing during winter. One practical, although not elegant, solution is to cover the pool with boards—leaving several inches of space between the boards and the water—and place bags of leaves or bales of straw on top.

UT Extension Service Offices

Anderson County
100 N. Main Street, Room 213
Clinton
(865) 457-6246

Bedford County
1 Public Square
Suite 11
Shelbyville
(931) 684-5971

Benton County
119 B. Cole Avenue
Camden
(731) 584-4601

Bledsoe County
108 Courthouse Street
Pikeville
(423) 447-2451

Blount County
219 Court Street
Maryville
(865) 982-6430; 982-5250; 982-2226

Bradley County
95 Church Street, SE
Cleveland
(423) 476-4552

Campbell County
Hatmaker Hall Bldg.
Main Street
Jacksboro
(423) 562-9474

Cannon County
614 Lehman Street
Woodbury
(615) 563-2554

Carroll County
625 High Street
Suite 107
Huntingdon
(731) 986-1976

Carter County
824 E. Elk Avenue
Elizabethton
(423) 542-1818

Cheatham County
162 County Services Drive, Suite 110
Ashland City
(615) 792-4420; 792-2013; 792-2055

Chester County
159 E. Main Street
Henderson
(731) 989-2103

Claiborne County
Courthouse Annex
1732 Main Street, Suite 4
Tazewell
(423) 626-3742

Clay County
Clay County Community Center
145 Cordell Hull Dr.
Celina
(931) 243-2311

Cocke County
360 East Main Street
Room 110
Newport
(423) 623-7531

Coffee County
1331 McArthur Drive
Manchester
(931) 723-5141; 723-5142

Crockett County
20 S. Johnson Street
Alamo
(731) 696-2412

Cumberland County
1398 Livingston Road
Crossville
(931) 484-6743

Davidson County
800 Second Avenue N.
Suite 3
Nashville
(615) 862-5995

Decatur County
71 West Main Street
Decaturville
(731) 852-2831

Dekalb County
1010 W. Broad Street
Room 100
Smithville
(615) 597-4945

Dickson County
204 Henslee Drive
Dickson
(615) 446-2788; 446-3290

Dyer County
151 Everett Avenue
Dyersburg
(731) 286-7821

Fayette County
302B Midland Street
Somerville, TN
(901) 465-5233

Fentress County
207 Smith Street N.
Jamestown
(931) 879-9117

Franklin County
406 Joyce Lane
Winchester
(931) 967-2741

Gibson County
1252 Manufacturers Row
Trenton
(731) 855-7656

Giles County
132 S. Second Street
Pulaski
(931) 363-3523; 363-3524; 424-7004

Grainger County
Hwy 11-W, Old Health Department
Rutledge
(865) 828-3411

Greene County
204 North Cutler Street, Suite 105
Greeneville
(423) 798-1710

Grundy County
Highway 56 & Phipps Street
Coalmont
(931) 592-3971

Hamblen County
511 W. 2nd North Street
Room 204
Morristown
(423) 586-6111

Hamilton County
6183 Adamson Circle
Bonny Oaks Industrial Park
Chattanooga
(423) 855-6113

Hancock County
Post Office Building, 2nd Floor
Main Street
Sneedville
(423) 733-2526

Hardeman County
200 Market Street
Bolivar
(731) 658-2421

Hardin County
601 Main Street
Savannah
(731) 925-3441

Hawkins County
850 W. Main Street, Suite 1
Rogersville
(423) 272-7241

Haywood County
100 S. Wilson Street
Brownsville
(731) 772-2861

Henderson County
County Office Bldg.
35 E. Wilson
Lexington
(731) 968-5266

Henry County
101 S. Market Street
Paris
(731) 642-2941

Hickman County
114 Huddleston Street
Centerville
(931) 729-2404

Houston County
Main Street
Courthouse
Erin
(931) 289-3242

Humphreys County
101 S. Church Street
Waverly
(931) 296-2543; 296-6512

Jackson County
757 Grundy Quarles Hwy. S.
Suite D
Gainesboro
(931) 268-9437

Jefferson County
1111 Lake Drive
Dandridge
(865) 397-2969; 397-3969

Johnson County
222 W. Main Street
Mountain City
(423) 727-8161

Knox County
400 W. Main Ave.
Suite 560
Knoxville
(865) 215-2340

Lake County
229 Church Street
Tiptonville
(731) 253-6528

Lauderdale County
217 N. Main Street
Ripley
(731) 635-9551

Lawrence County
2385 Buffalo Road
Lawrenceburg
(931) 762-5506

Lewis County
Courthouse
110 Park Ave.
Hohenwald
(931) 796-3091; 796-6004

Lincoln County
208 E. Davidson Drive
Fayetteville
(931) 433-1582; 438-1556

Loudon County
County Office Building
100 River Road
Loudon
(865) 458-5612; 458-5613

Macon County
113 E. Locust Street
Lafayette
(615) 666-3341

UT Extension Service Offices

Madison County
309 N. Parkway
Jackson
(731) 668-8543

Marion County
302 Betsy Pack Drive
Jasper
(423) 942-2656

Marshall County
230 College Street
Suite 130
Lewisburg
(931) 359-1929

Maury County
#10 Public Square
Hunter-Matthews Building,
Second Floor
Columbia
(931) 388-9557

McMinn County
107 W. College Street
Athens
(423) 745-2852

McNairy County
703 Industrial Park Road
Selmer
(731) 645-3598

Meigs County
City-County Bldg.
River Road
Decatur
(423) 334-5781

Monroe County
105 College Street
Madisonville
(423) 442-2433

Montgomery County
1030A Cumberland Heights Road
Clarksville
(931) 648-5725

Moore County
241 Main Street, Suite 214
Lynchburg
(931) 759-7163

Morgan County
Courthouse
Room 207
Wartburg
(423) 346-3000; 346-3609

Obion County
302 South 3rd Street
Union City
(731) 885-3742

Overton County
317 E. University Street
Courthouse Annex, Suite 131
Livingston
(931) 823-2735

Perry County
124 Main Street
Linden
(931) 589-2331

Pickett County
Community Center
Byrdstown
(931) 864-3310

Polk County
6042 Highway 411
Benton
(423) 338-4503; 338-4504

Putnam County
900 S. Walnut
Room 4
Cookeville
(931) 526-4561; 526-8377

Rhea County
125 Court Street
Unit 3
Dayton
(423) 775-7807

Roane County
200 E. Race Street
Kingston
(865) 376-5558

Robertson County
514 Hill Street
Springfield
(615) 384-7936; 384-0207

Rutherford County
1026 Golf Lane
Ag. Center
Murfreesboro
(615) 898-7710

Scott County
2845 Baker Highway
Scott County Office Bldg.
Huntsville
(423) 663-4777

Sequatchie County
303 Church Street
Dunlap
(423) 949-2611

Sevier County
125 Court Avenue
Room 102
Sevierville
(865) 453-3695

Shelby County
5565 Shelby Oaks Dr.
Memphis
(901) 544-0243

Smith County
125 Gordonsville Hwy.
Suite 300
Carthage
(615) 735-2900; 735-3077

Stewart County
Courthouse
Dover
(931) 232-5682

Sullivan County
3258 Highway 126
Suite 104
Blountville
(423) 279-2723

Sumner County
155-A E. Main Street
Gallatin
(615) 451-6050

Tipton County
111 W. Washington Ave.
Covington
(901) 476-0231

Trousdale County
214 Broadway
Hartsville
(615) 374-2421; 374-2410

Unicoi County
100 Main Avenue
Suite 107
Erwin
(423) 743-9584

Union County
Courthouse
Suite 99
Maynardville
(865) 992-8038

Van Buren County
Burritt College Bldg.
Spencer
(931) 946-2435

Warren County
201 Locust Street
Suite 10
McMinnville
(931) 473-8484

Washington County
206 W. Main Street
Jonesborough
(423) 753-1680

Wayne County
525B U.S. Hwy. 64 East
Waynesboro
(931) 722-3229 or 722-3673

Weakley County
Courthouse
Dresden
(731) 364-3164

White County
117 S. Main Street
Sparta
(931) 836-3348

Williamson County
4215 Long Lane
Suite 200
Franklin
(615) 790-5721

Wilson County
925 E. Baddour Pkwy.
Suite 100
Lebanon
(615) 444-9584; 443-6193

UK Extension Service Offices

Adair County
409 Fairground Street
Columbia
Phone: (270) 384-2317
E-mail: cesadair@uky.edu

Allen County
Courthouse
Scottsville
Phone: (270) 237-3146
E-mail: cesallen@uky.edu

Anderson County
1026 County Park Road
Lawrenceburg
Phone: (502) 839-7271
E-mail: cesander@uky.edu

Ballard County
110 Broadway
La Center
Phone: (270) 665-9118
E-mail: cesballa@uky.edu

Barren County
936 Happy Valley Road
Glasgow
Phone: (270) 651-3818
Email: cesbarre@uky.edu

Bath County
53 Miller Drive
Owingsville
Phone: (606) 674-6121
E-mail: cesbath@uky.edu

Bell County
101 Courthouse Square
Pineville
Phone: (606) 337-2376
E-mail: cesbell@uky.edu

Boone County
6028 Camp Ernst Road
Burlington
Phone: (859) 586-6101
E-mail: cesboone@uky.edu

Bourbon County
603 Millersburg Road
Paris
Phone: (859) 987-1895
E-mail: cesbourb@uky.edu

Boyd County
2420 Center Street
Catlettsburg
Phone: (606) 739-5184
E-mail: cesboyd@uky.edu

Boyle County
127 By-Pass North
Danville
Phone: (859) 236-4484
E-mail: cesboyle@uky.edu

Bracken County
1120 Brooksville-Germantown Road
Brooksville
Phone: (606) 735-2141
E-mail: cesbrack@uky.edu

Breathitt County
1155 Main Street
Jackson
Phone: (606) 666-8812
E-mail: cesbreat@uky.edu

Breckinridge County
Intersection of Hwy 60 & Hwy 261S
Hardinsburg
Phone: (270) 756-2182
E-mail: cesbreck@uky.edu

Bullitt County
384 Halls Lane
Shepherdsville
Phone: (502) 543-2257
E-mail: cesbulli@uky.edu

Butler County Office
113 E.G.L. Smith Street
Morgantown
Phone: (270) 526-3767
E-mail: cesbutle@uky.edu

Caldwell County
1025 U. S. Hwy. 62W
Princeton
Phone: (270) 365-2787
E-mail: cescaldw@uky.edu

Calloway County
310 South Fourth Street
Murray
Phone: (270) 753-1452
E-mail: cescallo@uky.edu

Campbell County
3500 Alexandria Pike
Highland Heights
Phone: (859) 572-2600
E-mail: cescampb@uky.edu

Carlisle County
Bardwell
Phone: (270) 628-5458
E-mail: cescarli@uky.edu

Carroll County
Courthouse, 440 Main Street, Suite 6
Carrollton
Phone: (502) 732-7030
E-mail: cescarro@uky.edu

Carter County
300 W. Main Street. Room 121
Grayson
Phone: (606) 474-6686
E-mail: cescarte@uky.edu

Casey County
1517 S. Wallace Wilkinson Blvd.
Liberty
Phone: (606) 787-7384
E-mail: cescasey@uky.edu

Christian County
2850 Pembroke Road
Hopkinsville
Phone: (270) 886-6328
E-mail: ceschris@uky.edu

Clark County
1400 Fortune Drive
Winchester
Phone: (859) 744-4682
E-mail: cesclark@uky.edu

Clay County
69 Jameson Road
Manchester
Phone: (606) 598-2789
E-mail: cesclay@uky.edu

Clinton County
Courthouse
Albany
Phone: (606) 387-5404
E-mail: cesclint@uky.edu

Crittenden County
Courthouse, Suite 101
107 South Main Street
Marion
Phone: (270) 965-5236
E-mail: cescritt@uky.edu

Cumberland County
212 N. Main Street
Burksville
Phone: (270) 864-2681
E-mail: cescumbe@uky.edu

Daviess County
4800A New Hartford Road
Owensboro
Phone: (270) 685-8480
E-mail: cesdavie@uky.edu

Edmonson County
227 Mammoth Cave Road
Brownsville
Phone: (270) 597-3628
E-mail: cesedmon@uky.edu

Elliott County
Sandy Hook
Phone: (606) 738-6400
E-mail: cesellio@uky.edu

Estill County
149 Richmond Road
Irvine
Phone: (606) 723-4557
E-mail: cesestil@uky.edu

Fayette County
1140 Red Mile Place
Lexington
Phone: (859) 257-5582
E-mail: cesfayet@uky.edu

Fleming County
Elizaville Road
Flemingsburg
Phone: (606) 845-4641
E-mail: cesflemi@uky.edu

Floyd County
921 South Lake Drive
Prestonsburg
Phone: (606) 886-2668
E-mail: cesfloyd@uky.edu

Franklin County
101 Lakeview Court
Frankfort
Phone: (502) 695-9035
E-mail: cesfrank@uky.edu

Fulton County
2006 South Seventh St
Hickman
Phone: (270) 236-2351
E-mail: cesfulto@uky.edu

Gallatin County
US 42 West
Warsaw
Phone: (859) 567-5481
E-mail: cesgalla@uky.edu

Garrard County
1302 Stanford St.
Lancaster
Phone: (859) 792-3026
E-mail: cesgarra@uky.edu

Grant County
224 S. Main St.
Williamstown
Phone: (859) 824-3355
E-mail: cesgrant@uky.edu

Graves County
251 Housman St.
Mayfield
Phone: (270) 247-2334
E-mail: cesgrave@uky.edu

Grayson County
123 Commerce Drive
Leitchfield
Phone: (270) 259-3492
E-mail: cesgrays@uky.edu

Green County
106 S Public Square
Greensburg
Phone: (270) 932-5311
E-mail: cesgreen@uky.edu

UK Extension Service Offices

Greenup County
226 W. Main St.
Greenup
Phone: (606) 473-9881
E-mail: cesgrnup@uky.edu

Hancock County
1605 US Highway 60 West
Hawesville
Phone: (270) 927-6618
E-mail: ceshanco@uky.edu

Hardin County
201 Peterson Drive
Elizabethtown
Phone: (270) 765-4121
E-mail: ceshardi@uky.edu

Harlan County
519 South Main St.
Harlan
Phone: (606) 573-4464
E-mail: cesharla@uky.edu

Harrison County
668 New Lair Road
Cynthiana
Phone: (859) 234-5510
E-mail: cesharri@uky.edu

Hart County
821 North Main Street
Munfordville
Phone: (270) 524-2451
E-mail: ceshart@uky.edu

Henderson County
3341 Hwy 351 East
Henderson
Phone: (270) 826-8387
E-mail: ceshende@uky.edu

Henry County
Highway 421
New Castle
Phone: (502) 845-2811
E-mail: ceshenry@uky.edu

Hickman County
116 S. Jefferson, Courthouse Square
Clinton
Phone: (270) 653-2231
E-mail: ceshickm@uky.edu

Hopkins County
75 Cornwall Road
Madisonville
Phone: (270) 821-3650
E-mail: ceshopki@uky.edu

Jackson County
McKee
Phone: (606) 287-7693
E-mail: cesjacks@uky.edu

Jefferson County
8012 Vinecrest Ave., Suite 1
Louisville
Phone: (502) 425-4482
E-mail: cesjeffe@uky.edu

Jessamine County
205 South First St.
Nicholasville
Phone: (859) 885-4811
E-mail: cesjessa@uky.edu

Johnson County
Courthouse, Room 323
Paintsville
Phone: (606) 789-8108
E-mail: cesjohns@uky.edu

Kenton County
10990 Marshall Road
Covington
Phone: (859) 356-3155
E-mail: ceskento@uky.edu

Knott County
Masonic Lodge Building, Main Street
Hindman
Phone: (606) 785-5329
E-mail: cesknott@uky.edu

Knox County
215 Treuhaft Boulevard, Suite 7
Barbourville
Phone: (606) 546-3447
E-mail: cesknox@uky.edu

LaRue County
807 Old Elizabethtown Road
Hodgenville
Phone: (270) 358-3401
E-mail: ceslarue@uky.edu

Laurel County
200 County Extension Rd.
London
Phone: (606) 864-4167
E-mail: ceslaure@uky.edu

Lawrence County
Courthouse Square
310 East Main St.
Louisa
Phone: (606) 638-9495
E-mail: ceslawre@uky.edu

Lee County
Courthouse
Beattyville
Phone: (606) 464-2759
E-mail: ceslee@uky.edu

UK Extension Service Offices

Leslie County
22045 Main Street
Hyden
Phone: (606) 672-2154
E-mail: ceslesli@uky.edu

Letcher County Office
2 Main Street
Whitesburg
Phone: (606) 633-2362
E-mail: cesletch@uky.edu

Lewis County
806 East Second Street
Vanceburg
Phone: (606) 796-2732
E-mail: ceslewis@uky.edu

Lincoln County
104 Metker Trail
Stanford
Phone: (606) 365-2459
E-mail: ceslinco@uky.edu

Livingston County
Wilson Avenue
Smithland
Phone: (270) 928-2168
E-mail: ceslivin@uky.edu

Logan County
121 S Spring Street
Russellville
Phone: (270) 726-6323
E-mail: ceslogan@uky.edu

Lyon County Office
231 W Main Street
Eddyville
Phone: (270) 388-2341
E-mail: ceslyon@uky.edu

McCracken County
2705 Olivet Church Road
Paducah
Phone: (270) 554-9520
E-mail: cesmccra@uky.edu

McCreary County
McCreary Campus, Somerset
Community College
Whitley City
Phone: (606) 376-2524
E-mail: cesmccre@uky.edu

McLean County
Farm Bureau Building, 670 Main St.
Calhoun
Phone: (270) 273-3690
E-mail: cesmclea@uky.edu

Madison County
230 Duncannon Lane
Richmond
Phone: (859) 623-4072
E-mail: cesmadis@uky.edu

Magoffin County
333 W. Maple Street
Saylersville
Phone: (606) 349-3216
E-mail: cesmagof@uky.edu

Marion County
135 E. Water Street
Lebanon
Phone: (270) 692-2421
E-mail: cesmario@uky.edu

Marshall County
1933 MayField Highway
Benton
Phone: (270) 527-3285
E-mail: cesmarsh@uky.edu

Martin County
1338 Main Street
Inez
Phone: (606) 298-7742
E-mail: cesmarti@uky.edu

Mason County
800 U.S. Highway 68
Maysville
Phone: (606) 564-6808
E-mail: cesmason@uky.edu

Meade County
1041 Old Ekron Road
Brandenburg
Phone: (270) 422-4958
E-mail: cesmeade@uky.edu

Menifee County
Bryant Realty Building
Frenchburg
Phone: (606) 768-3866
E-mail: cesmenif@uky.edu

Mercer County
215 Morris Drive
Harrodsburg
Phone: (859) 734-4378
E-mail: cesmerce@uky.edu

Metcalfe County
422 East Street
Edmonton
Phone: (270) 432-3561
E-mail: cesmetca@uky.edu

Monroe County
Old PCA Building, 1194 Columbia Ave.
Tompkinsville
Phone: (270) 487-5504
E-mail: cesmonro@uky.edu

UK Extension Service Offices

JANUARY · FEBRUARY · MARCH · APRIL · MAY · JUNE · JULY · AUGUST · SEPTEMBER · OCTOBER · NOVEMBER · DECEMBER

Montgomery County
106 East Locust Street
Mt. Sterling
Phone: (859) 498-8741
E-mail: cesmontg@uky.edu

Morgan County
110 Court Street
West Liberty
Phone: (606) 743-3292
E-mail: cesmorga@uky.edu

Muhlenberg County
3690 State Route 1380
Central City
Phone: (270) 338-3124
E-mail: cesmuhle@uky.edu

Nelson County
317 S. Third Street
Bardstown
Phone: (502) 348-9204
E-mail: cesnelso@uky.edu

Nicholas County
368 East Main Street
Carlisle
Phone: (859) 289-2312
E-mail: cesnicho@uky.edu

Ohio County
1337 Clay Street
Hartford
Phone: (270) 298-7441
E-mail: cesohio@uky.edu

Oldham County
1815 North Highway 393
La Grange
Phone: (502) 222-9453
E-mail: cesoldha@uky.edu

Owen County
265 Ellis Highway
Owenton
Phone: (502) 484-5703
E-mail: cesowen@uky.edu

Owsley County
218 Church Street
Booneville
Phone: (606) 593-5109
E-mail: cesowsle@uky.edu

Pendleton County
45 David Pribble Drive
Falmouth
Phone: (859) 654-3395
E-mail: cespendl@uky.edu

Perry County
933 Perry Park Rd.
Hazard
Phone: (606) 436-2044
E-mail: cesperry@uky.edu

Pike County
148 Trivette Drive
Pikeville
Phone: (606) 432-2534
E-mail: cespike@uky.edu

Powell County
169 Maple Street
Stanton
Phone: (606) 663-6404
E-mail: cespowel@uky.edu

Pulaski County
28 Parkway Drive
Somerset
Phone: (606) 679-6361
E-mail: cespulas@uky.edu

Robertson County
Walnut Street
Mount Olivet
Phone: (606) 724-5796
E-mail: cesrober@uky.edu

Rockcastle County
1050 West Main Street
Mount Vernon
Phone: (606) 256-2403
E-mail: cesrockc@uky.edu

Rowan County
627 East Main St.
Morehead
Phone: (606) 784-5457
E-mail: cesrowan@uky.edu

Russell County
2340-B South Highway 127
Russell Springs
Phone: (270) 866-4477
E-mail: cesrusse@uky.edu

Scott County
1130 Cincinnati Road
Georgetown
Phone: (502) 863-0984
E-mail: cesscott@uky.edu

Shelby County
1201 Mt. Eden Rd., Suite 200
Shelbyville
Phone: (502) 633-4593
E-mail: cesshelb@uky.edu

Simpson County
300 N Main (Old Post Office)
Franklin
Phone: (270) 586-4484
E-mail: cessimps@uky.edu

Spencer County
66 Spears Drive
Taylorsville
Phone: (502) 477-2217
E-mail: cesspenc@uky.edu

Taylor County
1143 South Columbia Ave
Campbellsville
Phone: (270) 465-4511
E-mail: cestaylo@uky.edu

Todd County
Courthouse
Elkton
Phone: (270) 265-5659
E-mail: cestodd@uky.edu

Trigg County
Farm Bureau Building
Cadiz
Phone: (270) 522-3269
E-mail: cestrigg@uky.edu

Trimble County
43 High Country Lane
Bedford
Phone: (502) 255-7188
E-mail: cestrimb@uky.edu

Union County
1938 US Highway 60 West
Morganfield
Phone: (270) 389-1400
E-mail: cesunion@uky.edu

Warren County
3132 Nashville Rd.
Bowling Green
Phone: (270) 842-1681
E-mail: ceswarre@uky.edu

Washington County
211 Progress Ave.
Springfield
Phone: (859) 336-7741
E-mail: ceswashi@uky.edu

Wayne County
Farm Bureau Building,
1820 N. Main St., Suite B
Monticello
Phone: (606) 348-8453
E-mail: ceswayne@uky.edu

Webster County
19 Stegal Street
Dixon
Phone: (270) 639-9011
E-mail: ceswebst@uky.edu

Whitley County
428 Main Street
Williamsburg
Phone: (606) 549-1430
E-mail: ceswhitl@uky.edu

Wolfe County
Courthouse
Campton
Phone: (606) 668-3712
E-mail: ceswolfe@uky.edu

Woodford County
184 Beasley Road
Versailles
Phone: (859) 873-4601
E-mail: ceswoodf@uky.edu

It's easy to add the pleasure of fluttering butterflies to your yard. But it takes a bit more than just planting the flowers that attract them. Butterflies require various conditions for different stages of their life cycles. They crave sunshine, shelter from the wind, flowers to provide nectar, a garden free from pesticides, and certain plants on which to lay eggs.

Colorful flowers are popular with butterflies—orange, yellow, red, pink, or purple. Butterflies like blossoms with short tubular flowers (as on **yarrow**, for instance) and those that have petals wide enough for a butterfly to land upon (**coreopsis** and most daisy-type flowers). Butterflies also like strongly scented blooms.

To entice butterflies to make their home in your yard, try to have something blooming from spring until fall, when butterflies are active. A mass of flowers is more likely to attract them than a few flowers here and there.

But don't forget that beautiful butterflies start life as lowly caterpillars. Butterflies lay eggs on host plants (which may be specific to the species of butterfly—Monarchs, for instance, like members of the **milkweed** family). Then the eggs hatch into caterpillars, which munch on the plant's leaves. This is probably the toughest time for the gardener, but it's necessary if you want to make a welcoming home for these winged jewels. Eventually the caterpillar will spin a chrysalis, from which a butterfly will emerge.

It's an age-old process and one worth encouraging in your yard, given the environmental stresses on butterflies. It's also educational for your kids or grandkids.

Here's a sampling of butterfly-enticing plants (nectar plants) to help lure these gossamer-winged creatures to your yard.

Plants That Attract Butterflies

Common Name (*Botanical Name*)	Bloom Time
ANNUALS	
Cosmos (*Cosmos bipinnatus*)	Summer
Heliotrope (*Helitropium arborescens*)	Late spring to summer
Impatiens (*Impatiens walleriana*)	Spring to frost
Lantana (*Lantana* hybrids)	Summer
Marigold (*Tagetes* hybrids)	Spring to frost
Mexican sunflower (*Tithonia rotundifolia*)	Summer
Pentas (*Pentas lanceolata*)	Summer
Petunia (*Petunia* x *hybrida*)	Spring to frost

Common Name (*Botanical Name*)	Bloom Time
Sunflower (*Helianthus annuus*)	Summer to frost
Sweet alyssum (*Lobularia maritima*)	Spring to fall
Zinnia (*Zinnia* species and hybrids)	Summer to frost
PERENNIALS	
Aster (*Aster* species and hybrids)	Fall
Black-eyed Susan (*Rudbeckia* species and hybrids)	Summer
Boltonia (*Boltonia asteroides*)	Midsummer to fall
Butterfly weed (*Asclepias tuberosa*)	Summer
Daylily (*Hemerocallis* hybrids)	Summer

Plants That Attract Butterflies

Common Name (Botanical Name)	Bloom Time
Coreopsis (*Coreopsis grandiflora*)	Late spring, early summer
Goldenrod (*Solidago* species and hybrids)	Fall
Hibiscus (*Hibiscus* hybrids)	Mid- to late summer
Japanese anemone (*Anemone* hybrids)	Fall
Joe-pye weed (*Eupatorium purpureum*)	Late summer to fall
Lavender (*Lavandula* species and hybrids)	Early summer
Purple coneflower (*Echinacea purpurea*)	Summer
Phlox (*Phlox* species and hybrids)	Summer
Red valerian (*Centranthus ruber*)	Late spring to frost
Sedum (*Sedum* species and hybrids)	Summer to fall
Shasta daisy (*Leucanthemum* x *superbum*)	Summer
Stokes aster (*Stokesia laevis*)	Late spring, early summer
Yarrow (*Achillea* species and hybrids)	Summer

SHRUBS

Common Name (Botanical Name)	Bloom Time
Butterfly bush (*Buddleia davidii*)	Summer
Crapemyrtle (*Lagerstroemia indica*)	Summer to early fall
Deciduous azalea (*Rhododendron* species and hybrids)	Spring into summer
Evergreen azalea (*Rhododendron* species and hybrids)	Spring
Glossy abelia (*Abelia* x *grandiflora*)	Summer
Privet (*Ligustrum* species and hybrids)	Summer to fall
Summersweet (*Clethra alnifolia*)	Mid- to late summer

TREES

Common Name (Botanical Name)	Bloom Time
Chaste tree (*Vitex agnus-castus*)	Summer
Kousa dogwood (*Cornus kousa*)	Spring

VINES

Common Name (Botanical Name)	Bloom Time
Carolina jessamine (*Gelsemium sempervirens*)	Spring
Moonflower vine (*Ipomoea alba*)	Summer
Morning glory (*Ipomoea* species)	Summer
Passionflower vine (*Passiflora*)	Summer to fall

Composting

Think of composting as recycling for the yard. You take material that you would otherwise put out for garbage collection—grass clippings, leaves, twigs—and turn them into a free mulch or soil amendment. This saves money. At the same time, you're lessening the burden on landfills that are already crammed full. So compost is good for the homeowner and good for the environment.

Composting isn't at all difficult. You don't even need any equipment; you can make compost in a black plastic garbage bag.

Materials that are good for compost:

- Frost-killed flowers, vegetables, and vines
- Grass clippings (although it's best to leave them on the lawn unless the grass was so tall when cut that the clippings are in thick layers)
- Leaves
- Excess or damaged produce from the garden
- Kitchen scraps—egg shells, vegetable and fruit peelings, coffee grounds, tea leaves
- Paper (use only small amounts and shred it first)
- Sawdust
- Small sticks and twigs
- Wood shavings
- Straw
- Pine needles
- Rotted manure

Avoid these in the compost pile:

- Animal droppings (can harbor disease)
- Bones (don't readily break down; can attract animals)
- Meat scraps (attract animals)
- Glossy magazines (pages may contain metals)
- Weeds that have seedpods (the seeds often germinate when you spread the compost)
- Diseased or insect-infested leaves or plants (the pathogens may survive composting and be passed on)
- Bermuda grass (may not be killed)
- Grass clippings from a lawn that's been treated with a herbicide
- Wood ashes (see page 357).

Types of containers:

1 Small-mesh wire fencing can be fastened together to make a compost bin. If you're using only leaves, concrete reinforcing wire (sold for tomato cages) also works.

2 Drill six to nine rows of $1/4$- to $1/2$-inch holes into a 55-gallon trash can. Place the barrel on top of bricks or concrete blocks.

3 Build a three-bin structure from rot-resistant wood. Leave space between the slats for air circulation.

4 Buy a rotating compost bin or other commercial container.

5 You don't even need a bin in some cases. If you have some fallow land, or an area of the vegetable garden that's not being used, just pile the compost materials right on the ground. Or make rows of compost between the vegetables.

6 The ideal size for a compost pile is 4 to 5 feet high and 3 to 4 feet wide. One that's too small won't "heat up" (develop the high temperature to facilitate decomposition).

7 Place a compost bin where it will be convenient to use, but avoid putting it in the "back forty" where you don't have to look at it, but your neighbors do. A partially shady spot is ideal. (Too much sun dries out the materials and calls for extra watering.)

There are two conventional ways of making compost. One is simple and slow. The other requires more attention, but is faster.

Cold compost—or "forget it while it rots." Pile everything in a bin and forget it. Eventually it will rot. Many homeowners do this with fall leaves. In about a year, the leaves will have rotted and created leaf mold, which is an excellent soil amendment and mulch. There are two disadvantages of this type of composting: The pile doesn't heat up enough to kill any weeds or disease organisms, and it's very slow.

The fastest decomposition depends on maintaining certain combinations of materials and activities.

1 Oxygen is needed for efficient and odor-free decomposition.

2 Moisture helps breaks down the organic matter.

3 Temperature makes a difference because colder air temperatures slow down rotting, while warmer temperatures encourage it.

Leaves are often thought of as the ideal compost material, but they are mostly carbon. The best microbial activity takes place with a mixture of high-nitrogen and high-carbon ingredients.

The ratio should be 2 to 3 parts carbon to 1 part nitrogen. The easy way to remember this is to think "brown" for carbon (leaves, twigs, sawdust, straw, cornstalks) and "green" for nitrogen (grass, vegetable peelings, moist kitchen waste, green leaves or stems pinched or pruned from plants).

Composting

Building the Pile

An effective compost pile can be constructed in various ways. Here's one that works well:

1 Shred, cut, or break materials into small pieces so they will decompose faster.

2 Place the coarsest materials on the bottom of the pile.

3 Water.

4 Put down an 8- to 10-inch pile of organic material (both brown and green).

5 Water.

6 Add 1 inch of soil.

7 Water.

8 Sprinkle with 2 to 3 inches of manure or 1/3 cup of ammonium sulfate per 25 square feet of surface. (Or use 1 cup of 10-10-10 fertilizer for each 25 square feet of surface area.)

9 Repeat layers, watering after each addition. If you prefer, you can place brown and green materials into separate layers instead of mixing them. Just keep the ratio at 3 parts carbon or brown to 1 part green or nitrogen.

10 Make an indentation in the top layer to hold water.

11 Turn the pile with a spading fork once a month.

12 Water the pile after turning if it's very dry.

13 Bury kitchen wastes and fresh vegetables down in the pile to avoid attracting small wildlife.

How do you know when the compost is ready to use? When it has shrunk considerably and you can no longer recognize the ingredients that went into it.

What About Lime?

Lime and wood ashes are generally not recommended for addition to the compost pile. They do hurry along decomposition, but they also speed up loss of nitrogen from the pile.

But if you don't add lime, won't the compost be too acid, especially if it contains lots of oak leaves? No; finished compost is almost always in the slightly acid to neutral range (pH of 6.5 to 7.0).

Why Didn't My Compost Pile Heat Up?

- Too small
- Not enough green (nitrogen) materials
- Lack of oxygen (wasn't turned)
- Too much moisture. (Cover newly constructed compost piles with a waterproof tarp if heavy rains or a long period of rain is forecast soon afterward.)
- Not enough moisture. (The pile should be damp but not soggy.)

If you don't have space for a traditional compost bin, try composting in a barrel or in a plastic garbage bag.

Garbage-can compost:

1 Drill holes in a plastic can or metal barrel as described on the previous page.

2 Fill the container about two-thirds full with organic matter.

3 Add 1/4 cup ammonium sulfate or other high-nitrogen fertilizer.

4 Sprinkle with water until the materials are moist.

5 Replace the lid.

6 Twice a week, put the can or barrel on its side and roll it around to aerate the contents.

7 Remove the lid after turning the container. Replace it if heavy rainfall is expected.

The compost should be ready in several months.

Plastic-bag compost:

1 Place one 30- to 40-gallon bag inside another.

2 Layer green and brown organic materials in the bag, sprinkling lime between the layers (use 1 cup lime, total).

3 Add 1 tablespoon of high-nitrogen fertilizer.

4 Add 1 quart of water.

5 Close the bag and seal tightly.

6 Place in a relatively warm place (outdoors in summer, heated garage in winter) for six months to a year.

The reason lime is used in the bag-composting method (although not in regular composting) is that it helps control excess acidity caused by lack of oxygen inside the bag.

Drought Defense

One of the hardest things about gardening is that homeowners can't control everything. The weather, for instance. If gardeners controlled the weather, there would be an exact inch of rain weekly, gently falling between midnight and 6 a.m. Unfortunately, it doesn't work that way.

So there are times that we must manage to keep the yard looking nice with less than optimum moisture.

If that means an August without rain, homeowners usually drag out the hoses, sprinklers, and watering cans. But if lack of rainfall drags on and becomes an official drought, there may be watering restrictions in your community. What then?

Several strategies help make every drop count; they range from when and how to water to which plants should be watered and which can be skipped.

First, read the discussion about watering on pages 11 and 12, then consider these points:

What Needs Watering?

- All plants are most vulnerable to water stress in the first three to six months after planting. When possible, regularly water plants for the first six months (preferably the first year) that they're in your yard. These plants should get precedence in times of dry weather.
- Because annuals, vegetables, and perennials have smaller root systems than shrubs and trees, they need watering more frequently. In times of official water restrictions, you may have to let some of them go.
- Containers, raised beds, and berm plantings dry out faster than regular in-ground plantings.
- Plants with shallow roots and those that prefer moist soil (**ferns, azaleas**, and **rhododendrons**, for example).
- Shrubs or other trees that are near the house and under roof eaves may not get as much rainfall as plants in the yard, and in the summer, they may have to cope with reflected heat from house walls.

Some Rules of Water Conservation

- Mulch—3 inches of organic mulch can make a big difference when conserving moisture. See pages 360 and 361. Don't overdo it—4 inches is the maximum. Why organic mulches? Although plastic mulches *do* keep water in the soil, they also prevent water from penetrating the soil.
- Get rid of weeds. They compete with your good plants for water.
- Soil that's rich in organic matter generally dries out more slowly than unamended soil.
- If a container plant is potbound and must be watered daily, repot it, mixing a water-holding polymer in the soil (or choose a potting mix that contains water-holding crystals).
- Avoid run-off. If excess water falls on the street or other hard surfaces, adjust the sprinkler pattern. If water puddles up and runs into the lawn or other area when you're watering shrubs, trees, or flowers, stop watering and finish the job later in the day. Sometimes clay soil simply can't absorb the water as quickly as it's being applied.
- Always use a nozzle with a shut-off valve on your garden hose. A hose without a nozzle can gush out 10 gallons of water per minute—while you're walking back to turn the faucet off.
- Fix leaky hose connections. They waste a lot of water.
- Listen to the local weather report. If scattered thundershowers are forecast, wait to see whether they fall on your yard before you water.

Make a Limited Amount of Water Go Farther

- Water less often, but water longer. Frequent waterings lead to shallow roots, which, in turn, dry out faster during droughts or dry spells.
- Except for lawns, it's best to keep watering at root level, where it does the most good. (Use drip irrigation or soaker hoses, where possible.)
- Know how much water is being applied. A few hours after watering, dig into the soil to see how deep it is wet. This tells you how long it took to apply a certain amount of water and should guide you in how long to water the next time.
- Reduce evaporation by watering from 2 to 6 a.m. Set hoses, sprinklers, and irrigation systems on mechanical timers that can be moved from one faucet to another.

Special Tips for Lawns

- Don't fertilize. That causes new growth, and new growth requires additional water.
- Mow high. (See page 165.)
- Leave the clippings on the lawn.
- Keep your mower blades sharp so they cut cleanly. (Ragged edges cause additional transpiration or water loss.)
- A lawn that looks parched isn't necessarily a signal that the grass is dying. Cool-season grasses typically go dormant when they don't receive enough water. After rainfall returns, they usually green up again. Except in prolonged drought, when you fear losing your lawn altogether, you may need to decide whether to water or

Drought Defense

not. Watering just occasionally does more harm than good. Watering indicates to the grass that the dry spell is over and it can green up and begin actively growing. Then you'll need to keep watering.

- Impulse sprinklers apply water more efficiently than oscillating ones.

Plants That Can Tolerate Limited Watering

If dry spells are frequent in your area, consider some drought-tolerant plants. The problem is that they don't really help in the current dry spell—all new transplants need water for at least three to six months. But once they're established—which usually takes two to three years, except for annuals—these plants can survive some drought.

ANNUALS

- **Celosia** (*Celosia argentea plumosa*)
- **Cornflower** (*Centaurea cyanus*)
- **Cosmos** (*Cosmos bipinnatus*)
- **Globe amaranth** (*Gomphrena globosa*)
- **Madagascar periwinkle** (*Vinca rosea*)
- **Melampodium** (*Melampodium paludosum*)
- **Moss rose** (*Portulaca grandiflora*)
- **Strawflower** (*Helichrysum bracteatum*)
- **Sunflower** (*Helianthus annuus*)

GROUND COVERS

- **Creeping juniper** (*Juniperus horizontalis*)
- **Creeping phlox** (*Phlox subulata*)
- **English ivy** (*Hedera helix*)
- **Liriope** (*Liriope* species and hybrids)
- **Mondograss** (*Ophiopogon japonicus*)
- **Vinca** (*Vinca minor*)
- **Wintercreeper** (*Euonymus fortunei*)

PERENNIALS

- **Artemisia** (*Artemisia* 'Powis Castle')
- **Black-eyed Susan** (*Rudbeckia* species and hybrids)
- **Boltonia** (*Boltonia asteroides*)
- **Butterfly weed** (*Asclepias tuberosa*)
- **Coreopsis** (*Coreopsis grandiflora*)
- **Daylily** (*Hemerocallis* species and hybrids)
- **Gaillardia** (*Gaillardia grandiflora*)
- **Gaura** (*Gaura lindheimeri*)
- **Goldenrod** (*Solidago* species and hybrids)
- **Purple coneflower** (*Echinacea purpurea*)
- **Verbena** (*Verbena* species and hybrids)

SHRUBS

- **Aucuba** (*Aucuba japonica*)
- **Barberry** (*Berberis* species and hybrids)
- **Beautyberry** (*Callicarpa americana*)
- **Boxwood** (*Buxus* species and hybrids)
- **Butterfly bush** (*Buddlea davidii*)
- **Cotoneaster** (*Cotoneaster* species and hybrids)
- **Crapemyrtle** (*Lagerstroemia indica*)
- **Flowering quince** (*Chaenomeles speciosa*)
- **Forsythia** (*Forsythia intermedia*)
- **Glossy abelia** (*Abelia grandiflora*)
- **Juniper** (*Juniperus* species and hybrids)
- **Mahonia** (*Mahonia* species and hybrids)
- **Nandina** (*Nandina domestica*)
- **Pyracantha** (*Pyracantha coccinea*)
- **Spirea** (*Spirea* species and hybrids)

TREES

- **Bald cypress** (*Taxodium distichum*)
- **Black gum** (*Nyssa sylvatica*)
- **Carolina silverbell** (*Halesia carolina*)
- **Chaste tree** (*Vitex agnus-castus*)
- **Crabapple** (*Malus* species and hybrids)
- **Dawn redwood** (*Metasequoia glyptostroboides*)
- **Deodar cedar** (*Cedrus deodara*)
- **Fringe tree** (*Chionanthus virginicus*)
- **Ginkgo** (*Ginkgo biloba*)
- **Golden rain tree** (*Koelreuteria paniculata*)
- **Green ash** (*Fraxinus pennsylvanica*)
- **Holly** (*Ilex* species and hybrids)
- **Japanese pagoda tree** (*Sophora japonica*)
- **Japanese zelkova** (*Zelkova serrata*)
- **Lacebark elm** (*Ulmus parvifolia*)
- **Leyland cypress** (*Cupressocyparis leylandii*)
- **Linden** (*Robinia tomentosa*)
- **Oak** (*Quercus* species)
- **Ornamental cherry** (*Prunus* species and hybrids)
- **Redbud** (*Cercis canadensis*)
- **Red maple** (*Acer rubrum*)
- **Saucer magnolia** (*Magnolia* x *soulangiana*)
- **Sourwood** (*Oxydendrum arboreum*)
- **Southern magnolia** (*Magnolia grandiflora*)
- **Sweet gum** (*Liquidambar styraciflua*)
- **Tulip poplar** (*Liriodendron tulipifera*)

VINES

- **Carolina jessamine** (*Gelsemium sempervirens*)
- **Fiveleaf akebia** (*Akebia quinata*)
- **Trumpet honeysuckle** (*Lonicera sempervirens*)
- **Trumpet vine** (*Campis radicans*)
- **Wisteria** (*Wisteria* species)

Mulch

As many times as mulch is mentioned in this book, you might wonder if the publisher or author owns a mulch factory! No, we don't, but we highly recommend mulching as the single most important thing you can do in the yard to lessen your workload and make plants grow better. If you want to spend less time worrying about weeds or watering and more time on the golf course or with a fishing pole in your hands, mulch can help—in a big way.

Mulch—a covering placed on top of the soil—has numerous benefits:

- Suppresses weeds
- Controls water run-off
- Conserves moisture in the soil
- Maintains an even soil temperature (not too cold in winter or too hot in summer)
- Prevents erosion
- Helps keeps plant roots from being heaved out of the ground by alternate freezing and thawing in winter
- Prevents lawn mowers and string trimmers from getting too close to shrubs or tree trunks and causing damage
- Keeps vegetables and flowers from getting dirty
- May eventually break down and improve the soil

So what is this miracle material? The most common mulch "ingredients" are natural—grass clippings, pine needles, decayed sawdust, pine bark, shredded leaves, straw, even newspaper and pea gravel. There are also several man-made mulch materials—landscape fabric and black plastic among them.

Choosing the right mulch for your yard depends on several factors:

- **Cost.** If you already have pine needles or shredded leaves, those are ideal for mulching because they don't cost anything.
- **Appearance.** Several thicknesses of newspaper won't look very good in the perennial border but may be acceptable in the vegetable garden.
- **Performance.** Black plastic, for instance, warms the soil, which can be helpful in the spring vegetable garden. But it prevents air and water from getting to plant roots, and may make the soil too hot in summer. Landscape fabrics may perform well around shrubs, but be a bad choice for a ground-cover bed because they don't allow roots to spread underground and new plants to come up.
- **Durability.** The faster a mulch breaks down, the more frequently you'll have to replace it. On the other hand, the quicker an organic mulch breaks down, the more it improves the soil. Grass clippings and compost may diminish by half or more in just a few months. Coarser mulches, such as shredded pine bark, last longer.

To help you decide, this is what you need to know about the most common natural mulching materials:

- **Bark chips or granules:** Look good, perform well, easy to spread, readily available at retail outlets.
- **Buckwheat hulls:** Nice appearance, slow to break down, not easy to find, may be expensive.
- **Cocoa hulls:** Strong chocolate fragrance when first spread, neat appearance, may wash or blow away, may stick to your shoes.
- **Compost:** Appearance varies (looks neat if screened), free, mild fertilizing effect, may contain weed seeds.
- **Evergreen boughs:** Used mostly in winter when a limb has been removed or branches are cut from Christmas trees, good over bulb plantings, can be a fire hazard if left in place after the needles have browned.
- **Grass clippings:** Free—but should not be used when fresh and may contain herbicide residues, decompose quickly.
- **Hay:** Easily obtained in rural areas, easy to apply; save for the vegetable garden.
- **Leaves:** Free, adds nutrients to the soil, should be shredded or composted before use as mulch; otherwise, a layer of thick whole leaves may prevent water and air from reaching the soil.
- **Newspapers:** Free and easy to obtain, poor appearance, time consuming. To use: Wet the soil, wet the paper thoroughly, and anchor the edges so the papers won't blow away (pages with color pictures are fine, but don't use magazines).
- **Pea gravel, stones, lava rock:** Rarely looks natural, surface dries out quickly, laborious to remove, may be costly for large areas.

Mulch

• **Pine needles (also called** *pine straw*): Nice natural appearance—especially in wooded areas, easy to obtain, hard to judge how thickly to apply since pine straw is so light and airy.

• **Sawdust:** Best to let age before using, may be free or inexpensive, surface may crust over and prevent water penetration.

• **Straw:** See **hay**, above. Weed seeds may be a big problem, best for the vegetable garden.

How much mulch should you apply?

The recommended depth is 2 to 3 inches. (With pine straw, apply a couple of inches more because it will quickly compress.) The maximum is 4 inches. This is not a case of "if a little is good, a lot is much better." You want water to be able to get through the mulch to the soil—and roots—below.

Never, ever form a thick mound or pyramid of mulch around a tree or other plant. If you do pile mulch against a tree or shrub, here's what you face:

1 The trunk stays moist, which can lead to disease or rot.

2 The mulch is too thick and won't allow moisture or oxygen to penetrate through to roots.

3 Small animals may make their home in the mound—especially in winter—and then cause damage to the tree or shrub—or to other desirable plants.

When's the best time to mulch?

• After you've weeded. If you apply a mulch on top of weeds or grass, they will just pop through.

• When you plant. That provides protection from the beginning.

• In the vegetable garden, let the temperature be your guide. You don't want to mulch too soon in spring; instead, you need to allow the soil to heat up. But you want to cool the soil in the heat of summer.

• When a mulch has decreased to 2 inches thick. Check mulches twice a year—spring and fall or summer and early winter—and add to them as needed.

Mulching Tips

• Water the soil before applying mulch, and then wet down the mulch.

• Leave a mulch-free area around the base of each plant. Start mulching 1 to 2 inches away from the base of an annual and 6 to 8 inches from a tree trunk.

• Don't mulch areas that stay wet.

• There are advantages to mixing mulches. Apply a fine layer of compost to the soil, then top it with a coarser mulch. Top landscape fabric with cocoa hulls or pine straw. Spread newspapers in a new bed to kill weeds, then cover them with a better-looking mulch on top.

• When planting ground covers or small bedding plants, it is often more efficient to prepare the bed and mulch it completely, digging holes through the mulch for the plants.

Integrated Pest Management

You may have noticed that no chemical insecticide recommendations have been given in this book. There are a trio of reasons for that.

1 Increasingly, homeowners are turning to organic remedies.

2 Recommendations change, and it's best to get the latest advice from the Extension Service.

3 Spraying with an insecticide the moment you see a pest isn't always the best action. Often you also kill the beneficial insects and organisms that may have taken care of the problem naturally.

But there's a method you should know of, one that isn't all organic or all chemical. **Integrated pest management** (IPM) is the practice of using a combination of methods to keep pests from damaging or ruining good plants while minimizing environmental risks.

Here is how IPM works:

1 Walk through the garden at least once a week and check on plants, noting any problems.

2 Identify the pest or problem. You may need help from the Extension Service or a good nursery to do this. Not all insects cause damage.

3 Assess the damage. Is it small enough that you can live with it or is it likely to increase unless you do something?

4 If possible, learn something about the life stages of the insect. It's easy to kill some pests at one stage of their lives and very difficult at others. If spraying isn't going to help, there's little point in doing it.

5 Choose a control method, starting with the least toxic method likely to do the job.

6 Implement your chosen strategy.

7 Evaluate its effectiveness.

Control Methods

Cultural control includes techniques such as crop rotation in the vegetable garden. Insects that attack a certain plant can become established in the soil if the plant is in the same spot year after year. Also important is keeping plants growing vigorously by choosing healthy specimens, planting them in good soil, and seeing that they receive the correct amounts of light and water. Insects are more likely to attack stressed plants than healthy ones.

Mechanical control can mean picking off egg masses or bugs by hand. But sometimes you may want to put up barriers—row covers, for example, which exclude insects while letting air, light, and moisture through. Traps are available for apple maggots in trees. Yellow sticky traps catch whiteflies. Paper collars are often placed around the stems of young vegetable and flower seedlings to prevent cutworm damage. You might also try washing some insects, such as aphids, off the plant with a strong stream of water from a hose.

Sanitary control means removing damaged vegetables and fruits so they don't attract insects. Keep the garden free of debris—boards, brush piles, etc.—that can provide breeding and hiding places for slugs and insects. Pinch off heavy infestations of a plant and remove them from the garden.

Biological control relies on beneficial insects or organisms to attack the pest and kill it. Lady bugs feed on aphids, for instance. Many beneficial insects are now sold by mail order.

Chemical control includes synthetic herbicides, insecticides, miticides, and fungicides, as well as inorganic, botanical, and microbial pesticides, soaps, and horticultural oils. Botanical and biological controls persist in the garden for only a short time, which is good for the environment, but might not offer a long-enough period of protection for plants.

These are all used by organic gardeners. You may want to try them first:

- Sulfur, copper, and lime sulfur are natural fungicides.
- Rotenone, pyrethrum, and neem are insecticides derived from plants.
- Bt (*Bacillus thuringiensis*) is a microorganism that controls all types of caterpillars and "worms."
- Horticultural oil suffocates insects and eggs.
- Insecticidal soap kills soft-bodied insects by drying them out.

Whether you use an organic or chemical control, it's important to follow common-sense safety rules:

- Read the label, especially any cautions. These include time and temperature restrictions (such as advising you to spray when bees have left the garden for the day or when temperatures are below a certain level).
- Wear protective clothing, as recommended on the label.
- Mix the product according to directions. Using too much not only costs you more, but can harm the plant.

- Never spray on a windy day.
- Keep products away from bodies of water or drains.
- Store in a cool dry place where children or animals can't accidentally reach the products.
- Buy only as much as you can use in a year. Many products lose their effectiveness rapidly.

Preventing Disease in the Garden

The sports maxim "Sometimes the best offense is a good defense" is as true in the garden as it is on the playing field. Homeowners can do many things to avoid having to deal with diseases:

1 Choose disease-resistant plant varieties. Old-fashioned types of **crapemyrtle** are likely to mildew, but the newer ones (with the Indian tribe names) aren't. Choose **tomatoes** that have VFN after the variety name. These are resistant to verticillium and fusarium wilts, as well as nematodes.

2 Buy disease-free plants. Look them over carefully before you take them home. Check the undersides of the leaves, too. Check bulbs carefully, too. If they feel soft, have an odd odor, have black or brown portions, or are covered with a white fuzzy film, leave the bulb behind.

3 Control insects. Many spread diseases.

4 Get rid of diseased plant parts, including those that are mildewed. If a small plant such as a flower is diseased, pull up the entire plant and remove it from the garden so the disease won't spread.

5 Remove and dispose of diseased plant debris. When leaves fall off rosebushes because of blackspot, for instance, pick up all the affected leaves and dispose of them so the disease organisms don't remain near the susceptible plant. Other plants that may need this care include **apple** and other fruit trees, fruit vines (such as **raspberries**), **tomatoes**, and **hollyhock**. Don't add diseased leaves to a compost pile.

6 Rotate vegetable crops. Certain plants are members of the same family and are susceptible to the same diseases. See pages 94 and 95 in the **Vegetable** chapter for more information.

7 Don't wet the leaves of plants that are likely to develop mildew—**zinnia, bee balm**, etc. Instead of using a sprinkler or overhead watering, use drip irrigation, soaker hoses, or other methods that keep the water at the base of the plant. If you must use overhead watering, try to do it early in the day so the foliage has time to dry by evening.

8 Space plants so they have good air circulation.

9 Don't smoke or chew tobacco in the garden. And if you're a smoker, wash your hands thoroughly with soap and water before touching plants. This can help prevent tobacco mosaic disease.

10 Fertilize adequately but don't overfertilize. A plant that's growing well is more likely to resist disease, but one that's coping with excess fertilizer may be weakened.

11 Plant disease-free seeds.

12 Sanitize garden tools when they've been used on diseased plants. Disinfect tools easily by dipping them in a mixture of 3 cups liquid bleach to 1 gallon of water or a mixture of 2 parts Lysol® (the old-fashioned, awful-smelling kind) to 8 parts water. You can also use Pine Sol® full strength. After using bleach or Pine Sol®, however, rinse the tools carefully, and then dry and oil them to prevent rust since these two products are corrosive.

Plants for Acid or Alkaline Soils

Most plants prefer to grow in a soil that's slightly acid to neutral (pH of 6.5 to 7), but what do you do if your soil isn't in that range? Soils in Tennessee and Kentucky tend to be acid (some much more so than others), but people who live near or on the site of old rock quarries have to contend with alkaline soil. Soil pH can be changed (see page 11) although it's an ongoing process to keep it that way. Many people, especially those with large properties, try to stick with plants that prefer the pH of the soil in their yard. These two lists serve as starting points so you can discover the plants that perform well in one or the other:

Plants for Acidic Soil (as low as 5.5 pH)

Common Name (*Botanical Name*)	Sun or Shade
PERENNIALS	
Asters (*Aster* species and hybrids)	Sun, part sun
Baptisia (*Baptisia* species and hybrids)	Sun, part sun
Black-eyed Susan (*Rudbeckia* species and hybrids)	Sun, part sun
Boltonia (*Boltonia asteroides*)	Sun
Chrysanthemum (*Dendranthema* x *grandiflorum*)	Sun
Columbine (*Aquilegia* species and hybrids)	Part shade to sun
Coreopsis (*Coreopsis* species and hybrids)	Sun
Lily (*Lilium* species and hybrids)	Sun, part sun
Lily-of-the-valley (*Convallaria majalis*)	Shade, part shade
Virginia bluebells (*Mertensia virginica*)	Shade, part shade
SHRUBS	
Azaleas, deciduous (*Rhododendron* species)	Part sun, part shade
Azaleas, evergreen (*Rhododendron* species)	Part shade, shade
Camellia (*Camellia japonica*)	Part shade
Crapemyrtle (*Lagerstroemeria* species and hybrids)	Sun

Common Name (*Botanical Name*)	Sun or Shade
Forsythia (*Forsythia* species and hybrids)	Sun, part sun
Holly (*Ilex* species and hybrids)	Sun, part sun
Juniper (*Juniperus* species and hybrids)	Sun
Leucothoe (*Leucothoe* species and hybrids)	Shade, part shade
Magnolias (*Magnolia* species and hybrids)	Sun, part sun
Mountain laurel (*Kalmia latifolia*)	Part sun
Rhododendron (*Rhododendron* species and hybrids)	Part sun, part shade
Spruce (*Picea* species and hybrids)	Sun
Summersweet (*Clethra alnifolia*)	Part sun, sun
Yew (*Taxus* species and hybrids)	Part sun, sun
TREES	
Canadian hemlock (*Tsuga canadensis*)	Part sun, part shade
Fringe tree (*Chionanthus virginicus*)	Sun, part sun
Holly (*Ilex* species and hybrids)	Sun to part shade
Magnolia (*Magnolia* species and hybrids)	Sun, part sun

Plants for Acid or Alkaline Soils

JANUARY · FEBRUARY · MARCH · APRIL · MAY · JUNE · JULY · AUGUST · SEPTEMBER · OCTOBER · NOVEMBER · DECEMBER

Common Name (*Botanical Name*)	Sun or Shade	Common Name (*Botanical Name*)	Sun or Shade
Oaks (*Quercus* species and hybrids)	Sun, part sun	**Spruces** (*Picea* species and hybrids)	Sun

Plants for Alkaline Soil (up to 8.0 pH)

Common Name (*Botanical Name*)	Sun or Shade	Common Name (*Botanical Name*)	Sun or Shade
ANNUALS		**Primrose** (*Primula* species and hybrids)	Part shade, part sun
Cosmos (*Cosmos bipinnatus*)	Sun	**Red valerian** (*Centranthus ruber*)	Sun, part sun
Phlox (*Phlox drummondi*)	Sun	**Verbena** (*Verbena* species and hybrids)	Sun
BULBS		**SHRUBS**	
Bearded iris (*Iris germanica*)	Sun, part sun	**Mock orange** (*Philadelphus coronarius*)	Sun, part sun
Canna (*Canna* species and hybrids)	Sun	**TREES**	
Crocus (*Crocus* species and hybrids)	Sun	**Black locust** (*Robinia pseudoacacia*)	Sun
Snowdrops (*Galanthus* species and hybrids)	Sun, part sun	**Golden chain tree** (*Laburnum* x *watereri*)	Sun
PERENNIALS		**Thornless honey locust** (*Gleditsia triacanthos* var. *inermis*)	Sun
Baby's breath (*Gypsophila paniculata*)	Sun, part sun	**VINES**	
Dianthus (*Dianthus* species and hybrids)	Sun, part sun	**Clematis** (*Clematis* species and hybrids)	Sun
Globe thistle (*Echinops ritro*)	Sun	**Dutchman's pipes** (*Aristolochia macrophylla*)	Sun to shade
Hibiscus (*Hibiscus moscheutos*)	Sun	**English ivy** (*Hedera helix*)	Shade to sun
Hollyhock (*Alcea rosea*)	Sun	**Trumpet honeysuckle** (*Lonicera sempervirens*)	Sun, part sun
Lenten rose (*Helleborus orientalis*)	Part shade, shade	**Wisteria** (*Wisteria* species and hybrids)	Sun
Peony (*Paeonia lactiflora*)	Sun, part sun		

Plants for Wet Soils

JANUARY · FEBRUARY · MARCH · APRIL · MAY · JUNE · JULY · AUGUST · SEPTEMBER · OCTOBER · NOVEMBER · DECEMBER

Many homeowners have clay soil, which doesn't drain well. This can be discouraging when plant descriptions say, over and over, "prefers moist, well-drained soil." While drainage problems can often be remedied, sometimes the simplest solution is to grow plants that don't mind "wet feet" (having their roots moist all the time). Here are some of the best.

Common Name (Botanical Name)	Sun or Shade
PERENNIALS AND ORNAMENTAL GRASSES	
Astilbe (*Astilbe* species and hybrids)	Shade
Cardinal flower (*Lobelia cardinalis*)	Any
Carex (*Carex* species and hybrids [grass])	Shade
Goat's beard (*Aruncus dioicus*)	Part sun, part shade
Japanese iris (*Iris ensata*)	Sun, part sun
Japanese blood grass (*Imperata cylindrica* 'Rubra')	Sun, part sun
Joe-pye weed (*Eupatorium purpureum*)	Sun, part sun
Louisiana iris (*Iris* species and hybrids)	Sun
Maidenhair fern (*Adiantum pedatum*)	Shade
Marsh marigold (*Caltha palustris*)	Sun
Rose mallow (*Hibiscus moscheutos*)	Sun
Siberian iris (*Iris siberica*)	Sun, part sun
Sweet flag (*Acorus calamus* [grass])	Sun, part sun
Turtlehead (*Chelone glabra*)	Sun, part sun
SHRUBS	
Carolina allspice (*Calycanthus floridus*)	Sun to part shade

Common Name (Botanical Name)	Sun or Shade
Inkberry (*Ilex glabra*)	Any
Redosier dogwood (*Cornus stolonifera*)	Any
Summersweet (*Clethra alnifolia*)	Part shade to full sun
Swamp azalea (*Rhododendron viscosum*)	Sun to part shade
Tartarian dogwood (*Cornus alba*)	Sun to part shade
Virginia sweetspire (*Itea virginica*)	Part shade, shade
Winterberry (*Ilex verticillata*)	Sun
Witch hazel (*Hamamelis* species and hybrids)	Sun, part sun
TREES	
American persimmon (*Diospyros virginiana*)	Sun
Bald cypress (*Taxodium distichum*)	Sun, part sun
Black gum (*Nyssa sylvatica*)	Sun, part sun
Red maple (*Acer rubrum*)	Sun, part sun
River birch (*Betula nigra*)	Sun
Sweet gum (*Liquidambar styraciflua*)	Sun
Water oak (*Quercus nigra*)	Sun
Willow oak (*Quercus phellos*)	Sun

Landscaping for Wildlife

While many people enjoy inviting butterflies into their garden, other gardeners decide to go a step further and plant their yards as wildlife habitats, which attract an array of small wildlife. These may be birds, beneficial insects, and small animals, in addition to butterflies. With so much wildlife habitat being destroyed, it makes a gardener feel good to play a small part in improving the environment and protecting natural resources.

The effort to turn your property into a wildlife habitat starts with appropriate trees, shrubs, and nectar-producing flowers, and then moves on to adding feeders, nesting boxes, and water to make your landscape appealing.

Your yard may already contain many of the recommended elements. They fall basically into four categories that wildlife need for survival: food, water, cover (somewhere to hide), and a place in which to raise their offspring (such as nesting spots).

Food plants include those that produce berries, nectar (for hummingbirds and butterflies), nuts, and seeds.

Providing fresh, unfrozen water for drinking and bathing is just as vital as furnishing food because it may be harder for wildlife to find—especially in winter. Once you start supplying water, keep it up year-round, and you'll be amazed at the little creatures it attracts. Your winter water supply may be in an upturned garbage can lid fitted with a water heater; you may want to put out a birdbath or, most enjoyable of all, make your dream of a small pond a reality. Change standing water every few days so it stays fresh and clean.

Have you ever put up a bird feeder and no birds came to it? Often the reason for the lack of visitors is that it's in the center of the yard, with no vegetation nearby. But when the feeder is placed near a shrub or trees, which a bird can land on first—and go into for protection if a cat or other predator threatens—quite a crowd gathers. Cover is essential to small wildlife, to provide protection from harsh weather and from enemies.

Generally, if you create a wooded, natural landscape, there will be plenty of nesting areas for birds and small wildlife. They'll use evergreen and deciduous trees, shrubs, mulch piles, holes in dying trees, woodpiles, and—for frogs, toads, and dragonflies—a pond or wetland. You may also want to get plans for nesting boxes for bluebirds and purple martins.

The National Wildlife Federation (www.nwf.org), which certifies backyard wildlife habitats that meet certain criteria, suggests that your first step be to assess your yard to see what you're already growing that provides habitat for small animals and birds.

Naturally, you should choose plants that match your soil type, amount of sunlight, and climate. Most backyard habitat gardens depend heavily on shrubs and trees to provide many of the needs of their small visitors; then they supplement those plantings with perennial flowers. Because various kinds of birds and animals will visit your yard at different times during the year, it's a good idea to think about plants that can meet needs in several seasons. **Cotoneaster, holly**, and **juniper**, for example, will provide winter food, as well as cover. **Oaks** will provide acorns for squirrels, as well as nesting sites for birds.

Here are more hints on creating a wildlife habitat:

- Forego chemical insecticides and herbicides. Remove pests by hand, wash them away with the hose, prevent damage with barriers, and use beneficial insects such as ladybugs, praying mantises, and lacewings.
- Choose native plants.
- Practice diversity; grow a variety of plants instead of just a few types.
- Don't put up just any attractive purchased birdhouse, but make sure you build or buy birdhouses that will *exclude* starlings, sparrows, crows, and other birds that may be nuisances. The size of the entrance hole is critical, but box size and the height it's placed above the ground, the amount of sunlight it receives, and the direction the hole faces make a difference, too.
- Unless it's a safety hazard, don't remove a dying tree. Many birds and small animals find a hole in a dying tree to be an ideal home or place to raise their young.
- Create a "basking site" for butterflies, toads, frogs, and turtles. It should be a warm, sunny spot where cold-blooded creatures can raise their body temperature. This doesn't have to be elaborate; a basking spot may be as simple as a few smooth, light-colored rocks placed in a sunny place.
- Keep cats indoors.
- Use several different types of feeders—and seed—to attract various kinds of birds.
- If you use a hummingbird feeder, fill it with 1 part sugar to 4 parts water, then empty and clean it every third day—rinsing well with clear water afterward.
- Woodpeckers like suet, so do nuthatches and chickadees. Chopped fruit (including raisins, apples, bananas, and citrus) attracts mockingbirds, nuthatches, robins, woodpeckers and titmice.
- If there's a spot in your yard that stays wet or damp most of the time, don't try to drain it. Instead, grow plants that don't mind overly moist soil. (See page 366.) On the plus side, damp areas can be an advantage in attracting wildlife, since many birds and small animals are drawn to a wetland.

Glossary

Alkaline soil: soil with a pH greater than 7.0. It lacks acidity, often because it has limestone in it.

All-purpose fertilizer: powdered, liquid, or granular fertilizer with a balanced proportion of the three key nutrients—nitrogen (N), phosphorus (P), and potassium (K). It is suitable for maintenance nutrition for most plants.

Annual: a plant that lives its entire life in one season. It is genetically determined to germinate, grow, flower, set seed, and die the same year.

Balled and burlapped: describes a tree or shrub grown in the field whose soilball was wrapped with protective burlap and twine when the plant was dug up to be sold or transplanted.

Bare root: describes plants that have been packaged without any soil around their roots. (Often young shrubs and trees purchased through the mail arrive with their exposed roots covered with moist peat or sphagnum moss, sawdust, or similar material, and wrapped in plastic.)

Barrier plant: a plant that has intimidating thorns or spines and is sited purposely to block foot traffic or other access to the home or yard.

Beneficial insects: insects or their larvae that prey on pest organisms and their eggs. They may be flying insects, such as ladybugs, parasitic wasps, praying mantids, and soldier bugs, or soil dwellers such as predatory nematodes, spiders, and ants.

Berm: a narrow raised ring of soil around a tree, used to hold water so it will be directed to the root zone.

Bract: a modified leaf structure on a plant stem near its flower that resembles a petal. Often it is more colorful and visible than the actual flower, as in dogwood.

Bud union: the place where the top of a plant was grafted to the rootstock; usually refers to roses.

Canopy: the overhead branching area of a tree, usually referring to its extent including foliage.

Cold hardiness: the ability of a perennial plant to survive the winter cold in a particular area.

Composite: a flower that is actually composed of many tiny flowers. Typically, they are flat clusters of tiny, tight florets, sometimes surrounded by wider-petaled florets. Composite flowers are highly attractive to bees and beneficial insects.

Compost: organic matter that has undergone progressive decomposition by microbial and macrobial activity until it is reduced to a spongy, fluffy texture. Added to soil of any type, it improves the soil's ability to hold air and water and to drain.

Corm: the swollen energy-storing structure, analogous to a bulb, under the soil at the base of the stem of plants such as crocus and gladiolus.

Crown: the base of a plant at, or just beneath, the surface of the soil where the roots meet the stems.

Cultivar: a CULTIvated VARiety. It is a naturally occurring form of a plant that has been identified as special or superior and is purposely selected for propagation and production.

Deadhead: a pruning technique that removes faded flower heads from plants to improve their appearance, abort seed production, and stimulate further flowering.

Deciduous plants: unlike evergreens, these trees and shrubs lose their leaves in the fall.

Desiccation: drying out of foliage tissues, usually due to drought or wind.

Division: the practice of splitting apart perennial plants to create several smaller-rooted segments. The practice is useful for controlling the plant's size and for acquiring more plants; it is also essential to the health and continued flowering of certain ones.

Dormancy: the period, usually the winter, when perennial plants temporarily cease active growth and rest. Dormant is the verb form, as used in this sentence: *Some plants, like spring-blooming bulbs, go dormant in the summer.*

Glossary

Established: the point at which a newly planted tree, shrub, or flower begins to produce new growth, either foliage or stems. This is an indication that the roots have recovered from transplant shock and have begun to grow and spread.

Evergreen: perennial plants that do not lose their foliage annually with the onset of winter. Needled or broadleaf foliage will persist and continues to function on a plant through one or more winters, aging and dropping unobtrusively in cycles of three or four years or more.

Foliar: of or about foliage—usually refers to the practice of spraying foliage, as in fertilizing or treating with insecticide; leaf tissues absorb liquid directly for fast results, and the soil is not affected.

Floret: a tiny flower, usually one of many forming a cluster, that comprises a single blossom.

Germinate: to sprout. Germination is a fertile seed's first stage of development.

Graft (union): the point on the stem of a woody plant with sturdier roots where a stem from a highly ornamental plant is inserted so that it will join with it. Roses are commonly grafted.

Hands: the female flowers on a banana tree; they turn into bananas.

Hardscape: the permanent, structural, nonplant part of a landscape, such as walls, sheds, pools, patios, arbors, and walkways.

Herbaceous: plants having fleshy or soft stems that die back with frost; the opposite of woody.

Hybrid: a plant that is the result of intentional or natural cross-pollination between two or more plants of the same species or genus.

Low water demand: describes plants that tolerate dry soil for varying periods of time. Typically, they have succulent, hairy, or silvery-gray foliage and tuberous roots or taproots.

Mulch: a layer of material over bare soil to protect it from erosion and compaction by rain, and to discourage weeds. It may be inorganic (gravel, fabric) or organic (wood chips, bark, pine needles, chopped leaves).

Naturalize: (*a*) to plant seeds, bulbs, or plants in a random, informal pattern as they would appear in their natural habitat; (*b*) to adapt to and spread throughout adopted habitats (a tendency of some nonnative plants).

Nectar: the sweet fluid produced by glands on flowers that attract pollinators such as hummingbirds and honeybees for whom it is a source of energy.

Organic material, organic matter: any material or debris that is derived from plants. It is carbon-based material capable of undergoing decomposition and decay.

Peat moss: organic matter from peat sedges (United States) or sphagnum mosses (Canada), often used to improve soil texture. The acidity of sphagnum peat moss makes it ideal for boosting or maintaining soil acidity while also improving its drainage.

Perennial: a flowering plant that lives over two or more seasons. Many die back with frost, but their roots survive the winter and generate new shoots in the spring.

pH: a measurement of the relative acidity (low pH) or alkalinity (high pH) of soil or water based on a scale of 1 to 14, 7 being neutral. Individual plants require soil to be within a certain range so that nutrients can dissolve in moisture and be available to them.

Pinch: to remove tender stems and/or leaves by pressing them between thumb and forefinger. This pruning technique encourages branching, compactness, and flowering in plants, or it removes aphids clustered at growing tips.

Pollen: the yellow, powdery grains in the center of a flower. A plant's male sex cells, they are transferred to the female plant parts by means of wind or animal pollinators to fertilize them and create seeds.

Glossary

Raceme: an arrangement of single stalked flowers along an elongated, unbranched axis.

Rhizome: a swollen energy-storing stem structure, similar to a bulb, that lies horizontally in the soil, with roots emerging from its lower surface and growth shoots from a growing point at or near its tip, as in bearded iris.

Rootbound (or potbound): the condition of a plant that has been confined in a container too long, its roots having been forced to wrap around themselves and even swell out of the container. Successful transplanting or repotting requires untangling and trimming away of some of the matted roots.

Root flare: the transition at the base of a tree trunk where the bark tissue begins to differentiate and roots begin to form just before entering the soil. This area should not be covered with soil when planting a tree.

Self-seeding: the tendency of some plants to sow their seeds freely around the yard. It creates many seedlings the following season that may or may not be welcome.

Semievergreen: tending to be evergreen in a mild climate but deciduous in a rigorous one.

Shearing: the pruning technique whereby plant stems and branches are cut uniformly with long-bladed pruning shears (hedge shears) or powered hedge trimmers. It is used when creating and maintaining hedges and topiary.

Slow-acting fertilizer: fertilizer that is water insoluble and therefore releases its nutrients gradually as a function of soil temperature, moisture, and related microbial activity. Typically granular, it may be organic or synthetic.

Succulent growth: the sometimes undesirable production of fleshy, water-storing leaves or stems that results from over-fertilization.

Sucker: a new growing shoot. Underground plant roots produce suckers to form new stems and spread by means of these suckering roots to form large plantings, or colonies. Some plants produce root suckers or branch suckers as a result of pruning or wounding.

Tuber: a type of underground storage structure in a plant stem, analogous to a bulb. It generates roots below and stems above ground (example: dahlia).

Variegated: having various colors or color patterns. The term usually refers to plant foliage that is streaked, edged, blotched, or mottled with a contrasting color, often green with yellow, cream, or white.

White grubs: fat, off-white, wormlike larvae of Japanese beetles. They reside in the soil and feed on plant (especially grass) roots until summer when they emerge as beetles to feed on plant foliage.

Wings: (*a*) the corky tissue that forms edges along the twigs of some woody plants such as winged euonymus; (*b*) the flat, dried extension of tissue on some seeds, such as maple, that catch the wind and help them disseminate.

Bibliography

Ajilvsgi, Geyata. *Butterfly Gardening for the South.* Dallas: Taylor Publishing, 1990.

Armitage, Allan M. *Armitage's Manual of Annuals, Biennials, and Half-Hardy Perennials.* Portland, OR: Timber Press, 2001.

Armitage, Allan M. *Herbaceous Perennial Plants.* Champaign: Stipes Publishing, 1997.

Brooklyn Botanic Garden. *The Potted Garden.* Ed. Scott D. Appell. Brooklyn: Brooklyn Botanic Garden, 2001.

Brooklyn Botanic Garden. *Summer-Blooming Bulbs.* Ed. Beth Hanson. Brooklyn: Brooklyn Botanic Garden, 2001.

Chambers, David, Lucinda Mays, with Laura C. Martin. *The American Garden Guides: Vegetable Gardening.* New York: Pantheon Books, 1994.

Cullina, William. *Native Trees, Shrubs, and Vines.* Boston: Houghton Mifflin, 2002.

Cutler, Karan Davis, *Burpee's The Complete Vegetable & Herb Gardener.* New York: Macmillan, 1997.

Darke, Rick. *The Color Encyclopedia of Ornamental Grasses.* Portland, OR: Timber Press, 1999.

Dirr, Michael. *Dirr's Trees and Shrubs for Warm Climates.* Portland, OR: Timber Press, 2002.

DiSabato-Aust, Tracy. *The Well-Tended Perennial Garden.* Portland, OR: Timber Press, 1998.

Dobbs, Steve. *The Perfect Tennessee Lawn.* Nashville, TN: Cool Springs Press, 2002.

Druitt, Liz. *The Organic Rose Garden.* Dallas: Taylor Publishing, 1996.

Druse, Ken. *Making More Plants.* New York: Clarkson Potter, 2000.

Greenlee, John. *The Encyclopedia of Ornamental Grasses.* Emmaus, PA: Rodale Press, 1992.

Harper, Pamela J. *Time-Tested Plants.* Portland, OR: Timber Press, 2000.

Heath, Brent, and Becky Heath. *Daffodils for American Gardens.* Washington, DC: Elliott & Clark, 1995.

Heath, Brent, and Becky Heath. *Tulips for North American Gardens.* Albany, TX: Bright Sky Press, 2001.

Hill, Madalene, and Gwen Barcaly, with Jean Hardy. *Southern Herb Growing.* Fredericksburg, TX: Shearer Publishing, 1987.

Hodgson, Larry. *Perennials for Every Purpose.* Emmaus, PA: Rodale Press, 2000.

Lovejoy, Ann, and Leona Holdsworth Openshaw. *Ortho's All About Annuals.* Des Moines, IA: Meredith Books, 1999.

Lowe, Judy. *Tennessee Gardener's Guide, Third Edition.* Nashville, TN: Cool Springs Press, 2001.

Martin, Tovah. *Heirloom Flowers.* New York: Fireside Books, 1999.

McKeown, Denny. *Kentucky Gardener's Guide.* Nashville, TN: Cool Springs Press, 2000.

Noordhuis, Klaas, and Sam Benvie. *Bulbs and Tubers.* Buffalo, NY: Firefly Books, 1997.

Pleasant, Barbara. *The Gardener's Guide to Plant Diseases.* Pownal, VT: Storey Publishing, 1995.

Powell, Eileen. *From Seed to Bloom.* Pownal, VT: Storey Publishing, 1995.

Rice, Graham. *Discovering Annuals.* Portland, OR: Timber Press, 1999.

Rushing, Felder, and Walter Reeves. *The Tennessee Fruit and Vegetable Book.* Nashville, TN: Cool Springs Press, 2002.

Sedenko, Jerry. *The Butterfly Garden.* New York: Villard Books, 1991.

Smith & Hawken. *The Book of Outdoor Gardening.* New York: Workman, 1996.

Sternberg, Guy, and Jim Wilson. *Landscaping With Native Trees.* Shelburne, VT: Chapters Publishing, 1995.

Summit, Ginger. *Gourds in Your Garden.* Los Altos, CA: Hillway Press, 1998.

Thomas, Charles B. *Water Gardens.* Boston: Houghton Mifflin, 1997.

Thomas, R. William. *Ortho's All About Vines and Climbers.* Des Moines, IA: Meredith Books, 1999.

Toomey, Mary, and Everett Leeds. *An Illustrated Encyclopedia of Clematis.* Portland, OR: Timber Press, 2001.

Turner, Carole B. *Seed Sowing and Saving.* Pownal, VT: Storey Publishing, 1998.

Utterback, Christine, with Michael Ruggiero. *The Serious Gardener: Reliable Roses.* New York: Clarkson Potter Publishers, 1997.

Walheim, Lance. *The Natural Rose Gardener.* Tucson, AZ: Ironwood Books, 1994.

Index

abelia, glossy, 234, 244, 355, 359
Abelia grandiflora, 359
Abelia x *grandiflora*, 234, 355
Abutilon x *hybridum*, 126
Acer griseum, 263
Acer palmatum, 263
Acer rubrum, 263, 359, 366
Achillea species and hybrids, 177, 355
aconite, winter, 78
Aconitum species, 200
Acorus calamus, 366
Acorus species, 321
actinidia vine, 291
Actinidia kolomikta, 291
Adiantum pedatum, 366
Aechmea fasciata, 116
Aeschynanthus lobbianus, 121, 126
Aesculus species and hybrids, 232
African violet, 116, 118, 121, 123,
    125, 128, 129, 130, 132, 135, 141,
    143, 145
ageratum, 29, 32, 33, 49
Ageratum houstonianum, 29
Aglaonema hybrids, 119
Ajuga reptans, 292
akebia, fiveleaf, 291, 296, 297, 302,
    305, 311, 359
Akebia quinata, 291, 359
Alaska pea, 86
Alcea rosea, 365
alfalfa, 10, 108
allamanda, 295, 302, 310
allium, 55, 59
    giant, 56
Allium schoenoprasum, 91
Allium species, 59
allspice, Carolina, 232, 240, 241,
    252, 366
aloe, 126, 143
alpine strawberry, 298
aluminum plant, 116, 119, 127, 130,
    133, 143
alyssum, sweet, 31, 33, 43, 354
amaranth, globe, 29, 33, 41, 52, 359
amaryllis, 55, 62, 63, 64, 65, 67, 69,
    71, 76, 79, 80, 82, 84, 123, 125,
    130, 131, 143
Amelanchier species and hybrids, 263
American
    beech, 278
    bittersweet, 315

elm, 268
    persimmon, 366
Ampelopsis arborea, 315
Amsonia, 200
anacharis, 320, 329, 341
anemone, 175
    Japanese, 194, 355
Anemone blanda, 60
Anemone x *hybrida*, 175
Anemone hybrids, 355
Anethum graveolens, 91
angel's trumpet, 41, 42
angelwing begonia, 121, 130
anise, 94, 95
    Florida, 233
annual
    dianthus, 50
    rye, 108
    ryegrass, 151, 166, 168
anthurium, 124, 126
Antirrhinum majus, 31
apple, 56, 267, 363
    May, 185
Aquilegia species and hybrids, 175,
    364
Araucaria heterophylla, 119
arborvitae, 247, 273
Aristolochia macrophylla, 365
arrow arum, 320, 325
arrowhead plant, 115, 119, 127, 130,
    136, 137, 143
artemisia, 94, 97, 100, 102, 359
Artemisia 'Powis Castle', 175, 188,
    208, 359
Artemisia dracunculus, 91
artichoke, 95
    Jerusalem, 95
arum, 56, 59
    arrow, 320, 325
Arum italicum, 59
Aruncus dioicus, 366
Asarina scandens, 304
Asarum species and hybrids, 293
Asclepias tuberosa, 175, 354, 359
ash, green, 284, 359
Asiatic lily, 68
asparagus, 89, 90, 95, 96, 97, 98, 99,
    111, 112
    fern, 116, 119, 126, 143
Asparagus densiflorus 'Sprengeri', 119
Aspidistra elatior, 119

aster, 186, 187, 189, 193, 194, 195,
    197, 354, 364
    Stokes', 176, 355
Aster species and hybrids, 354, 364
astilbe, 366
Astilbe species and hybrids, 366
Astilbe 'Sprite', 179
aucuba, 232, 246, 359
Aucuba japonica, 232, 359
autumn crocus, 76
avocado, 122
azalea, 7, 9, 15, 68, 84, 144, 241,
    242, 244, 245, 246, 251, 358
    deciduous, 233, 252, 355, 364
    evergreen, 230, 233, 242, 243,
        245, 246, 256, 355, 364
    swamp, 240, 366
Azolla caroliniana, 320
baby lettuce, 100
baby's breath, 191, 365
bachelor buttons, 27
bald cypress, 263, 284, 359, 366
balm
    bee, 98, 187, 189, 208, 363
    lemon, 88, 91, 98, 102, 109
bamboo, 331
baptisia, 175, 364
Baptisia species and hybrids, 175, 364
barberry, 229, 252, 359
basil, 91, 92, 94, 96, 98, 102, 104,
    105, 107
bay, 94, 102, 110
    sweet, 91
bean, 93, 97, 98, 99, 100, 101, 102,
    104, 112
    bush, 86, 89, 90, 106
    hyacinth, 291, 294, 296, 304, 315
    lima, 89, 90, 95
    pole, 86, 89, 90
    purple hyacinth, 310, 311
    snap, 95
bearded iris, 55, 56, 57, 68, 71, 73,
    74, 75, 190, 191, 192, 365
beautyberry, 232, 239, 241, 246,
    252, 359
bee balm, 98, 187, 189, 208, 363
beech, American, 278
beet, 86, 89, 90, 93, 95, 97, 98, 100,
    101, 111
begonia, 34, 135
    angelwing, 121, 130

Index

hardy, 176, 179, 187
tuberous, 73
wax, 31, 32, 33, 34, 37, 45, 48, 50
Begonia grandis, 176
Begonia 'Lucerna', 121
Begonia x *semperflorens-cultorum*, 31
Belamcanda chinensis, 60
bell pepper, 85, 104
Berberis species and hybrids, 359
Bergenia, 191
bermuda, 147, 148, 150, 152, 154, 156, 158, 159, 161, 162, 166, 167, 168, 169, 172
bermudagrass, 211, 223, 247
Betula nigra, 263, 366
bigleaf hydrangea, 246
Bignonia capreolata, 291
birch, river, 263, 267, 275, 278, 284, 366
bird of paradise, 143
bishop's weed, 306
bittersweet, American, 315
blackberry lily, 57, 60, 69, 72, 74, 76, 80
black
    gum, 279, 280, 284, 359, 366
    locust, 365
    walnut, 279
black-eyed
    peas, 104
    Susan, 175, 178, 354, 359, 364
        vine, 291, 294, 298, 302, 304
bleeding heart, 175, 185
blood grass, Japanese, 177, 366
blue
    mist shrub, 244
    sage, 208
    salvia, 190
    spruce, Colorado, 287
bluebell
    Spanish, 56, 58, 60, 78
    Virginia, 364
blueberry, native low-bush, 294
bluegrass, 82, 156
    Kentucky, 147, 150, 152, 155, 156, 157, 162, 166, 168, 169, 172
boltonia, 175, 193, 194, 197, 354, 359, 364
Boltonia asteroides, 175, 354, 359, 364
borage, 96

Boston
    fern, 116, 119, 126, 128, 136
    ivy, 310
bottlebrush, 246
    buckeye, 241, 252
bougainvillea, 295, 302, 308, 310
box elder, 9
box, sweet, 293
boxwood, 232, 241, 245, 247, 359
Brachycome iberidifolia, 31
Brassica oleracea, 30
bridalwreath spirea, 239, 245
broccoli, 89, 90, 93, 94, 95, 96, 98, 99, 101, 102, 104, 106, 111
bromeliad, 116, 121, 122, 125, 126, 131, 133, 136, 143
Brussels sprouts, 89, 90, 93, 94, 95, 101, 111
buckeye, 232
    bottlebrush, 241, 246, 252
    red, 246
buckwheat, 10, 108
Buddleia davidii, 232, 355, 359
bugbane, 194
bugleweed, 289, 292, 299, 304, 306, 307
burning bush, 229, 232, 239, 252
bush
    bean, 86, 89, 90, 106
    cinquefoil, 241
    pumpkin, 90
    watermelon, 90
buttercup, 78
butterfly
    bush, 231, 232, 239, 241, 244, 246, 249, 251, 355, 359
    fern, 320
    weed, 175, 184, 188, 354, 359
button bush, 244
Buxus species and hybrids, 232, 359
cabbage, 85, 89, 90, 93, 94, 95, 96, 97, 98, 99, 100, 101, 102, 104, 106, 111
    ornamental, 30, 33, 35, 37, 48, 49, 50, 51, 52, 53
cactus, 116, 118, 123, 125, 126, 130, 131, 132, 135, 136, 137, 141, 143
    Christmas, 121, 138, 139, 140, 142, 143
    holiday, 135, 138, 140, 141, 142, 143, 144

Thanksgiving, 138, 139, 140, 142, 143
caladium, 56, 57, 60, 62, 64, 66, 68, 69, 70, 71, 72, 74, 75, 76, 77, 78, 80, 83
Caladium bicolor, 60
Calamagrostis x *acutiflora*, 177
Calamagrostis x *acutiflora* 'Karl Foerster', 179
calamondin orange, 144
calendula, 36
callery pear, 263
Callicarpa americana, 359
Callicarpa species and hybrids, 232
Caltha palustris, 366
Calycanthus floridus, 232, 240, 366
camellia, 232, 236, 237, 246, 364
Camellia japonica, 364
Camellia species and hybrids, 232
Campanula, 186
Campis radicans, 359
Campsis species and hybrids, 292
Canadian hemlock, 263, 266, 277, 283, 285, 364
candytuft, 175, 289, 294
canna, 56, 60, 62, 66, 69, 70, 71, 72, 73, 75, 76, 77, 81, 83, 340, 365
    hardy water, 320
Canna species and hybrids, 60, 365
cantaloupe, 89, 90, 95, 99, 106
Capsicum annuum, 30
caraway, 96, 98, 102
cardinal
    climber, 294, 298, 302, 304
    flower, 175, 188, 194, 320, 325, 331, 336, 340, 366
carex, 177, 181, 188, 190, 366
Carex species and hybrids, 177, 366
Carolina
    allspice, 232, 240, 241, 252, 366
    cherry laurel, 266
    jessamine, 291, 297, 301, 303, 308, 311, 312, 355, 359
    silverbell, 263, 285, 359
carrot, 86, 89, 90, 95, 96, 97, 98, 99, 100, 101, 102, 104, 106, 112
Caryopteris incana, 244
cast iron plant, 115, 126, 137, 143
Catharanthus roseus, 30
catmint, 186

Index

cattail, 320, 323
   dwarf, 332, 334
Cattleya, 124, 145
cauliflower, 89, 90, 93, 95, 96, 99, 100, 101, 104, 106, 111
cedar
   deodar, 359
   eastern red, 271, 287
   Japanese, 266, 269
   red, 271
Cedrus deodara, 359
Celastrus scandens, 315
celery, 95, 97
   wild, 321
celosia, 32, 33, 41, 359
   plumed, 41
Celosia argentea cristata, 29
Celosia argentea plumosa, 30, 359
Centaurea, 191
Centaurea cyanus, 359
centipede, 150, 151, 158, 161
Centranthus ruber, 176, 355, 365
Cephalanthus occidentalis, 244
Cercis canadensis, 263, 359
Chaenomeles species and hybrids, 233
Chaenomeles speciosa, 359
chain tree, golden, 275, 365
chamaecyparis, 269
Chamaecyparis species and hybrids, 233, 266
Chamaedorea elegans 'Bella', 119
chameleon plant, 331
chamomile, 112
chard, 95
   Swiss, 86, 96, 97, 98, 101
chaste tree, 263, 272, 355, 359
Chelone, 186
Chelone glabra, 366
Chelone obliqua, 186
Chelone species and hybrids, 194, 200
cherry, 267
   flowering, 263, 271, 275
   Jerusalem, 144
   ornamental, 359
cherry laurel, 250
   Carolina, 266
chervil, 92, 94, 95, 98, 102
chewings fescue, 149, 150
Chinese
   evergreen, 115, 119, 126, 130, 132, 137, 143

flame tree, 270
fringe tree, 270
holly, 250, 252
   sacred lily, 64, 84
Chionanthus retusus, 270
Chionanthus virginicus, 263, 359, 364
Chionodoxa species, 59
chives, 85, 91, 96, 98, 105, 108
Chlorophytum comosum, 120
Christmas cactus, 121, 138, 139, 140, 142, 143
chrysanthemum, 48, 175, 185, 186, 191, 194, 199, 364
Chrysogonum virginianum, 306
cilantro, 91, 92, 94, 95, 96
Cimicifuga racemosa, 194
cinquefoil, bush, 241
Cissus rhombifolia, 119
x *Citrofortunella microcarpa*, 144
Cladrastis kentukea, 263
clematis, 291, 297, 299, 300, 301, 303, 304, 305, 308, 311, 365
   sweet autumn, 294, 315
Clematis alpina, 297
Clematis armandii, 297
Clematis flammula, 297
Clematis indivisa, 297
Clematis integrifolia, 297
Clematis x *jackmanii*, 297
Clematis macropetala, 297
Clematis montana, 297
Clematis orientalis, 297
Clematis species and hybrids, 291, 365
Clematis terniflora, 294
Clematis viticella, 297
cleome, 29, 32, 33, 41, 43, 51
Cleome hassleriana, 29
clethra, 229, 246
Clethra alnifolia, 235, 240, 355, 364, 366
climber, 202, 203, 204, 208, 209, 211, 213, 215, 217, 220, 222
   cardinal, 294, 298, 302, 304
   miniature, 208
climbing
   hydrangea, 291, 296, 297, 310, 314
   rose, 210, 214, 216, 217, 218, 221, 226, 291, 297, 305, 306
   snapdragon, 304

hydrangea, false, 296, 314
clivia, 121, 130, 143
Clivia miniata, 121
clover
   crimson, 108
   four-leaf water, 320, 325
   sweet, 10
Cobaea scandens, 294, 296
cockscomb, 29, 33, 41, 43, 52
Codiaeum variegatum pictum, 116, 130
colchicum, 76
coleus, 29, 32, 33, 34, 42, 43, 45, 48, 140
collards, 86, 89, 90, 95, 99, 104, 108, 111, 112
Colocasia esculenta, 61
Colocasia species, 321
Colorado blue spruce, 287
columbine, 175, 364
coneflower, purple, 176, 178, 355, 359
Convallaria majalis, 61, 364
coreopsis, 175, 178, 188, 189, 191, 354, 355, 359, 364
Coreopsis grandiflora, 175, 355, 359
Coreopsis species and hybrids, 364
Coreopsis verticillata 'Moonbeam', 179
coriander, 91
Coriandrum sativum, 91
corn, 85, 86, 89, 90, 97, 98, 99, 100, 101, 103, 104
   plant, 115, 119
cornflower, 359
Cornus alba, 240, 366
Cornus kousa, 355
Cornus kousa x *florida*, 275
Cornus sericea, 240
Cornus species and hybrids, 263
Cornus stolonifera, 366
Cortaderia selloana, 177
Corylus avellana 'Contorta', 238
cosmos, 29, 32, 33, 37, 41, 43, 51, 354, 359, 365
Cosmos bipinnatus, 29, 354, 359, 365
Cotinus coggygria, 235
cotoneaster, 252, 254, 294, 316, 359, 367
Cotoneaster species and hybrids, 359
cowpea, 10
crabapple, 260, 271, 359

Index

crabgrass, 165

crapemyrtle, 43, 208, 232, 238, 243, 245, 246, 251, 252, 355, 359, 363, 364

Crassula argentea, 143

Crataegus viridis 'Winter King', 284

creeper
  trumpet, 292, 297, 302, 305
  Virginia, 310, 311, 315

creeping
  fescue, 166
  juniper, 289, 292, 359
  phlox, 15, 183, 292, 301, 306, 359
  red fescue, 150
  thyme, 190, 212, 293, 294
  zinnia, 29, 33

crested iris, 55, 56
  dwarf, 67, 68, 71

crimson
  clover, 108
  glory vine, 310

crocosmia, 55, 61, 66, 69, 76, 77, 80

Crocosmia x *crocosmiiflora*, 61

crocus, 55, 56, 58, 59, 62, 64, 66, 67, 79, 80, 82, 83, 365
  autumn, 76

Crocus species and hybrids, 59, 365

Crocus tommasinianus, 78

crossvine, 291, 297, 311

croton, 116, 130, 136, 143

crown imperial, 58, 59, 71, 78

cryptomeria, Japanese, 263

Cryptomeria japonica, 263, 266

cucumber, 85, 89, 90, 93, 97, 98, 99, 100, 101, 102, 103, 104, 106, 112

cup-and-saucer vine, 294, 296, 311

Cupressocyparis leylandii, 359

cyclamen, 123, 129, 143, 144

Cyperus species, 320

cypress
  bald, 263, 284, 359, 366
  false, 233, 247, 250
  Leyland, 273, 287, 359

cypress vine, 291, 294, 298, 302, 304, 311

daffodil, 15, 55, 56, 58, 59, 62, 64, 65, 66, 67, 68, 71, 72, 78, 80, 82, 83, 84, 208
  dwarf, 56
  miniature, 64

dahlia, 55, 56, 58, 61, 66, 69, 70, 71, 72, 74, 75, 76, 77, 79, 81, 83

Dahlia cultivars, 61

daisy
  English, 36
  Shasta, 176, 187, 355
  Swan River, 31, 32, 33

daphne, 244

Daphne species and hybrids, 244

David Austin rose, 203

dawn redwood, 359

daylily, 71, 175, 188, 191, 195, 197, 208, 294, 354, 359
  miniature, 190

dead nettle, spotted, 289, 293, 306

deciduous
  azalea, 233, 252, 355, 364
  holly, 233, 238, 239, 252

Decumaria barbara, 296

Dendranthema x *grandiflorum*, 175, 364

deodar cedar, 359

deutzia, 245, 256

Deutzia gracilis, 256

dianthus, 29, 33, 175, 186, 188, 190, 191, 306, 365
  annual, 50

Dianthus x *barbatus*, 29

Dianthus species and hybrids, 175, 365

Dicentra spectabilis, 175

dieffenbachia, 116, 119, 130, 131

Digitalis species and hybrids, 175

dill, 91, 92, 94, 95, 98, 100, 102, 105, 107

Diospyros virginiana, 366

dogwood, 9, 15, 260, 263, 264, 267, 268, 271, 273, 275, 280, 282, 284, 285
  kousa, 275, 355
  redosier, 240, 366
  tartarian, 240, 366

Dolichos lablab, 291

dracaena, 142, 143

Dracaena fragrans, 119

duckweed, 331

dusty miller, 29, 32, 33, 41, 208

Dutch iris, 55, 59, 64, 79

Dutchman's pipes, 365

dwarf
  cattail, 332, 334

crested iris, 67, 68, 71
  daffodil, 56
  lotus, 334
  papyrus, 332, 334

Easter lily, 68

eastern red cedar, 271, 287

Echinacea purpurea, 176, 355, 359

Echinacea purpurea 'Magnus', 179

Echinops, 191

Echinops ritro, 365

edible-podded peas, 89, 90, 97, 98

Egeria densa, 320

eggplant, 85, 86, 89, 90, 95, 96, 97, 98, 100, 101, 102, 103, 104, 107

Egyptian onion, 112

Eichhornia crassipes, 331

Elaeagnus commutata, 250

elephant ear, 55, 56, 57, 61, 66, 68, 70, 71, 72, 75, 77, 78, 81, 83

elm, 267, 275, 279
  American, 268
  lacebark, 263, 278, 359

English
  daisy, 36
  ivy, 119, 127, 130, 133, 134, 136, 143, 293, 299, 304, 311, 312, 359, 365
  pea, 85, 89, 90, 93, 94, 95, 96, 97, 98, 104
  rose, 222, 226

Enkianthus campanulatus, 234

Epipremnum aureum, 120

Equisetum hyemale, 331

Eranthis hyemalis, 78

euonymous, 229, 250, 297, 303

Euonymous fortunei, 293

Euonymus alatus, 232

Euonymus fortunei, 250, 359

Eupatorium purpureum, 176, 355, 366

Euphorbia marginata, 31

evergreen
  azalea, 230, 233, 242, 243, 245, 246, 256, 355, 364
  fern, 199
  holly, 233

evergreen, Chinese, 115, 119, 126, 130, 132, 137, 143

Fagus grandiflora, 278

fairy moss, 320, 325

Index

false
   climbing hydrangea, 296, 314
   cypress, 233, 247, 250
feather reed grass, 177
fennel, 91, 92, 94, 95, 96, 98, 105
fern, 9, 15, 126, 131, 132, 173, 175,
   179, 187, 192, 294, 358
   asparagus, 116, 119, 126, 143
   Boston, 116, 119, 126, 128, 136
   butterfly, 320
   evergreen, 199
   maidenhair, 188, 366
fescue, 82, 147, 149, 152, 156, 157,
   158, 162, 164, 166, 168, 169, 172
   chewings, 149, 150
   creeping, 166
   creeping red, 150
   fine, 149, 150, 155, 156
   hard, 150
   Kentucky 31, 154, 162
   Rebel, 162
   Rebel II, 162
   red, 149
   tall, 82, 147, 149, 150, 151, 152,
      155, 158, 162, 164, 166,
      169, 171
ficus, 131, 143
Ficus benjamina, 130
Ficus elastica, 120, 130
field peas, 89, 90
fig, 254
   weeping, 130, 136
fine fescue, 149, 150, 155, 156
Fittonia verschaffeltii, 136
fiveleaf akebia, 291, 296, 297, 302,
   305, 311, 359
flag
   old-fashioned, 336
   Spanish, 294, 298, 302
   sweet, 321, 366
   variegated sweet, 325
   yellow, 325
flame tree, Chinese, 270
floribunda rose, 202, 204, 209, 216
Florida anise, 233
flowering
   cherry, 263, 271, 275
   maple, 126, 130, 143
   quince, 233, 239, 245, 254,
      256, 359
   tobacco, 29, 32, 33, 43

foamflower, 289, 293
Foeniculum vulgare, 91
forsythia, 68, 155, 209, 231, 233,
   239, 245, 254, 256, 359, 364
Forsythia intermedia, 359
Forsythia species and hybrids, 233,
   364
fothergilla, 234, 246, 252, 256
Fothergilla species and hybrids, 234
fountain grass, 177
four-leaf water clover, 320, 325
four-o'clocks, 29, 33, 43, 51, 54
foxglove, 175, 185, 187
Fragaria vesca, 298
Franklin tree, 272, 285
Franklinia alatamaha, 272
Fraxinus pennsylvanica, 284, 359
French tarragon, 91, 102
fringe tree, 263, 280, 285, 359, 364
   Chinese, 270
fritillaria, 55
Fritillaria imperialis, 59
gaillardia, 176, 188, 359
Gaillardia, 190
Gaillardia grandiflora, 176, 359
Galanthus nivalis, 59
Galanthus species and hybrids, 365
garden
   phlox, 187
   rose, 88
gardenia, 254
garlic, 95, 102, 110, 112, 114
gaura, 176, 359
Gaura lindheimeri, 176, 359
Gelsemium sempervirens, 291, 355,
   359
geranium, 27, 29, 32, 33, 34, 37, 42,
   43, 45, 48, 50
   perennial, 189
   scented, 94, 102, 103, 104, 109
German iris, 68
giant allium, 56
ginger, wild, 293
ginkgo, 263, 278, 279, 280, 359
Ginkgo biloba, 263, 359
gladiolus, 55, 61, 68, 72, 73, 75,
   77, 81
Gladiolus species and hybrids, 61
glads, 66, 69, 70, 71, 72, 73, 76, 77,
   81, 83
   hardy, 75

Gleditsia triacanthos var. *inermis*, 365
globe
   amaranth, 29, 33, 41, 52, 359
   thistle, 365
glory-of-the-snow, 55, 56, 59
glossy abelia, 234, 244, 355, 359
gloxinia, 125, 129, 135, 143
goat's beard, 366
golden
   chain tree, 275, 365
   club, 320, 325
   rain tree, 263, 270, 279, 359
goldenrod, 176, 188, 189, 194,
   355, 359
goldflame honeysuckle, 291, 297, 303
Gomphrena globosa, 29, 359
gooseneck loosestrife, 186
gourd, 105, 109, 294, 298, 302
   ornamental, 313
grandiflora rose, 202, 204, 209, 216
grape, 314
   holly, Oregon, 252
   hyacinth, 55, 56, 58, 59, 78, 79
   ivy, 116, 119, 127, 128, 130, 133,
      134, 143
grapefruit, 82
grass
   feather reed, 177
   fountain, 177
   Japanese blood, 177, 366
   knot, 334
   mondo, 177, 181, 359
   pampas, 177
   switch, 177
Greek oregano, 91
green-and-gold, 306
green
   ash, 284, 359
   onion, 98
greens, 97, 100
   turnip, 89, 90, 104, 106, 108
gum
   black, 279, 280, 284, 359, 366
   sweet, 259, 260, 263, 280, 284,
      359, 366
Gymnocoronis spilanthoides, 331
Gynura aurantiaca
   'Purple Passion', 120
Gypsophila paniculata, 365
Hakonechloa macra, 190
Halesia carolina, 359

Index

Halesia tetraptera, 263
Hamamelis species and hybrids, 235, 366
hard fescue, 150
hardy
    glads, 75
    kiwi, 291, 296, 297, 314
    lily, 327, 341
    water canna, 320
    water lily, 325, 326
    begonia, 176, 179, 187
Harry Lauder's walking stick, 238
hawthorn, 284
hazel, witch, 229, 235, 238, 246, 252, 266
heart-leaf philodendron, 127, 130, 133, 134, 136, 137, 143
Hedera helix, 119, 293, 359, 365
Helianthus annuus, 31, 354, 359
Helichrysum bracteatum, 359
heliotrope, 354
Helitropium arborescens, 354
Helleborus orientalis, 176, 365
Hemerocallis hybrids, 354
Hemerocallis species and hybrids, 175, 359
hemlock, 267, 269, 273, 275, 279
    Canadian, 263, 266, 277, 283, 285, 364
Heuchera, 176
Heuchera, 190
Heuchera micrantha 'Palace Purple', 179
Heuchera species and hybrids, 176
hibiscus, 355, 365
Hibiscus hybrids, 355
Hibiscus moscheutos, 188, 365, 366
Hibiscus species and hybrids, 176
Hibiscus syriacus, 235
hickory, 279
Hippeastrum, 62
holiday cactus, 135, 138, 140, 141, 142, 143, 144
holly, 229, 247, 255, 257, 258, 263, 266, 269, 271, 279, 284, 285, 287, 359, 364, 367
    Chinese, 250, 252
    deciduous, 233, 238, 239, 252
    evergreen, 233
    Oregon grape, 252
    yaupon, 250

hollyhock, 363, 365
honey locust, thornless, 365
honeysuckle
    goldflame, 291, 297, 303
    trumpet, 292, 297, 303, 315, 359, 365
horseradish, 95
horsetail, 331
hosta, 9, 173, 174, 176, 179, 185, 187, 190, 194
Hosta species and hybrids, 176
Houttuynia cordata 'Chamaeleon', 331
hyacinth, 55, 58, 59, 64, 80, 82, 83
    bean, 291, 294, 296, 304, 315
        purple, 310, 311
    grape, 55, 56, 58, 59, 78, 79
    water, 328, 331
    wood, 55
Hyacinthoides hispanica, 60
Hyacinthus orientalis, 59
hybrid tea rose, 202, 204, 209, 216, 226
hydrangea, 229, 234, 239, 246
    bigleaf, 246
    climbing, 291, 296, 297, 310, 314
    false climbing, 296, 314
    smooth, 239
Hydrangea anomala petiolaris, 291
Hydrangea arborescens, 239
Hydrangea species and hybrids, 234
Hypericum, 241
Hypoestes phyllostachya, 120
hyssop, 92, 94, 98, 100
Iberis sempervirens, 175
Ilex cornuta, 250
Ilex glabra, 240, 250, 366
Ilex species and hybrids, 233, 263, 359, 364
Ilex verticillata, 240, 366
Ilex vomitoria, 250
Illicium floridanum, 233
impatiens, 30, 32, 33, 34, 37, 43, 48, 50, 62, 140, 354
    New Guinea, 30
Impatiens hawkeri, 30
Impatiens walleriana, 30, 354
Imperata cylindrica 'Rubra', 177, 366
inkberry, 240, 250, 366
Ipomoea alba, 292, 355
Ipomoea batatas, 292
Ipomoea quamoclit, 291

Ipomoea x *sloteri*, 294, 298
Ipomoea species, 355
Ipomoea tricolor, 292
iris, 61, 69, 72, 76, 80, 320
    bearded, 55, 56, 57, 61, 67, 68, 69, 71, 72, 73, 74, 75, 76, 80, 190, 191, 192, 320, 365
    crested, 55, 56
    Dutch, 55, 59, 64, 79
    dwarf crested, 67, 68, 71
    German, 68
    Japanese, 188, 340, 366
    Louisiana, 325, 366
    Siberian, 55, 57, 68, 69, 366
    yellow flag, 188
Iris cristata, 67
Iris ensata, 366
Iris germanica, 365
Iris x *hollandica*, 59
Iris siberica, 366
Iris species and hybrids, 61, 320, 366
Irish potato, 89, 90, 94, 95, 97, 99, 104
Itea virginica, 235, 366
ivy, 122, 289, 304, 310, 311, 312, 314
    Boston, 310
    English, 119, 127, 130, 133, 134, 136, 143, 293, 299, 304, 311, 312, 359, 365
    grape, 116, 119, 127, 128, 130, 133, 134, 143
    Swedish, 116, 120, 127, 130, 133, 134
jade plant, 143
Japanese
    anemone, 194, 355
    blood grass, 177, 366
    cedar, 266, 269
    cryptomeria, 263
    iris, 188, 340, 366
    maple, 15, 263, 264, 280
    pagoda tree, 272, 359
    wisteria, 299
    zelkova, 263, 359
Jerusalem
    artichoke, 95
    cherry, 144
jessamine, Carolina, 291, 297, 301, 303, 308, 311, 312, 355, 359
Joe-pye weed, 176, 186, 188, 194, 355, 366
jonquil, 59

Index

juneberry, 263
juniper, 14, 247, 316, 359, 364, 367
    creeping, 289, 292, 359
Juniperus horizontalis, 359
Juniperus species and hybrids, 292, 359, 364
kalanchoe, 123, 144
kale, 89, 90, 95, 99, 104, 106, 108, 111
    ornamental, 30, 33, 35, 37, 49, 50, 51, 52, 53
Kalmia latifolia, 234, 364
Kentucky
    31 fescue, 154, 162
    bluegrass, 147, 150, 152, 155, 156, 157, 162, 166, 168, 169, 172
kerria, 15, 68, 234, 238, 239, 256
Kerria japonica, 234
kiwi, hardy, 291, 296, 297, 314
knot grass, 334
Koelreuteria paniculata, 263, 270, 359
kohlrabi, 89, 90, 104, 108
kousa dogwood, 275, 355
kudzu, 289
Laburnum x *watereri*, 365
lacebark elm, 263, 278, 359
lady-slipper orchid, 116, 123
Lagerstroemia indica, 355, 359
Lagerstroemia species and hybrids, 232, 364
lamb's ear, 94, 100
Lamium maculatum, 293
landscape rose, 203
lantana, 354
Lantana hybrids, 354
Lathyrus odoratus, 294
laurel
    Carolina cherry, 266
    cherry, 250
    mountain, 234, 245, 364
Laurus nobilis, 91
Lavandula species and hybrids, 91, 355
lavender, 91, 94, 100, 102, 112, 208, 355
leaf lettuce, 89, 90, 93, 96, 98, 100, 102, 108, 112
leek, 95
Lemna minor, 331
lemon, 254
    balm, 88, 91, 98, 102, 109

verbena, 94, 99, 113
Lenten rose, 174, 176, 179, 180, 198, 365
lettuce, 85, 86, 94, 95, 97, 99, 100, 101, 102, 111
    baby, 100
    leaf, 89, 90, 93, 96, 98, 100, 102, 108, 112
    water, 321, 325, 328
Leucanthemum 'Becky', 179
Leucanthemum x *superbum*, 176, 355
Leucojum vernum, 60
leucothoe, 234, 246, 256, 364
Leucothoe species and hybrids, 234, 364
Leyland cypress, 273, 287, 359
ligularia, 188
Ligustrum sinense, 244
Ligustrum species and hybrids, 355
lilac, 244
Lilium species and hybrids, 61, 364
lily, 55, 61, 62, 66, 68, 70, 72, 74, 75, 76, 77, 78, 80, 81, 326, 327, 328, 333, 364
    Asiatic, 68
    blackberry, 57, 60, 69, 72, 74, 76, 80
    Chinese sacred, 64, 84
    Easter, 68
    hardy, 327, 341
    Oriental, 68
    peace, 115, 121, 122, 126, 128, 133, 143
    spider, 61, 74, 80
    surprise, 74
    tropical water, 325, 330
    water, 56, 321, 323, 326, 328, 329, 330, 331, 332, 333, 334, 335, 338, 339, 340, 341
lily-of-the-valley, 56, 61, 80, 294, 306, 364
lima bean, 89, 90, 95
linden, 359
linden tree, 278
Lindera benzoin, 239
lipstick plant, 121, 126, 128, 130
Liquidambar styraciflua, 263, 359, 366
Liriodendron tulipifera, 359
liriope, 177, 179, 181, 289, 306, 359
Liriope 'Silver Dragon', 208
Liriope species and hybrids, 177, 359

lizard's tail, 320, 325
Lobelia cardinalis, 175, 320, 331, 366
Lobularia maritima, 31, 354
locust
    black, 365
    thornless honey, 365
Lonicera sempervirens, 292, 359, 365
Lonicera x *heckrotti*, 291
loosetrife, gooseneck, 186
loropetalum, 234, 252
Loropetalum chinense, 234
lotus, 56, 320, 323, 326, 327, 328, 329, 330, 333, 334, 335
    dwarf, 334
Louisiana iris, 325, 366
lovage, 92, 94, 95, 98
lungwort, 179
Lycoris species, 61
Madagascar periwinkle, 30, 32, 33, 41, 43, 45, 359
magnolia, 243, 285, 364
    saucer, 259, 263, 359
    Southern, 260, 263, 264, 266, 269, 271, 272, 359
    star, 243
    sweet bay, 266, 272, 284
Magnolia grandiflora, 263, 359
Magnolia soulangiana, 263
Magnolia x *soulangiana*, 359
Magnolia species and hybrids, 364
Magnolia stellata, 243
Magnolia virginiana, 266
mahonia, 359
Mahonia species and hybrids, 252, 359
maidenhair fern, 188, 366
mallow, rose, 366
Malus species and hybrids, 359
mandevilla, 291, 295, 297, 302, 310
Mandevilla x *amoena*, 291
maple, 267, 275
    flowering, 126, 130, 143
    Japanese, 15, 263, 264, 280
    paperbark, 263
    red, 15, 263, 278, 279, 280, 284, 359, 366
    silver, 278
Maranta leuconeura, 120
marigold, 27, 30, 32, 33, 37, 41, 42, 43, 46, 51, 54, 201, 354

Index

marsh, 366
marjoram, 92, 94, 98
    sweet, 91
marsh marigold, 366
Marsilea mucronata, 320
May apple, 185
melampodium, 30, 32, 33, 41, 359
Melampodium paludosum, 30, 359
Melissa officinalis, 91
melon, 85, 86, 97, 98, 100, 102, 103,
    106, 109
Mentha aquatica, 331
Mertensia virginica, 364
mesclun, 85
Metasequoia glyptostroboides, 359
Mexican sunflower, 354
milfoil, water, 321
milkweed, 354
mimosa, 9
Mina lobatas, 294, 298
miniature
    climber, 208
    daffodil, 64
    daylily, 190
    rose, 124, 143, 203, 204, 207,
        208, 209, 211, 212, 213, 217,
        218, 219, 222, 226, 227
mint, 98, 104, 105
    water, 331
Mirabilis jalapa, 29
miscanthus, 177
Miscanthus sinensis, 177
mock orange, 244, 245, 365
modern rose, 221
mondo grass, 177, 181, 359
monkshood, 200
moonflower, 292, 294, 298, 302,
    304, 311
    vine, 355
morning glory, 33, 292, 294, 298,
    302, 304, 310, 311, 355
moss, 157
    fairy, 320, 325
moss rose, 30, 33, 41, 359
moth orchid, 116
mother of thousands, 126
mountain laurel, 234, 245, 364
mugo pine, 247
mum, 48, 185, 187, 189, 191, 194,
    195, 197, 199
Muscari species and hybrids, 59

mustard, 96, 98, 99, 104, 106, 108
Myriophyllum species, 321
naked lady, 61, 74
nandina, 234, 252, 258, 359
Nandina domestica, 234, 359
narcissus, paper-white, 62, 65, 80, 84
Narcissus species, 59
nasturtium vine, 310
native low-bush blueberry, 294
Nelumbo species, 320
Nephrolepis exaltata, 119
nerve plant, 136
New Guinea impatiens, 30
Nicotiana species and hybrids, 29
Norfolk Island pine, 119, 128,
    142, 143
Norway spruce, 266, 287
Nymphaea species, 321
Nyssa species, 279
Nyssa sylvatica, 359, 366
oak, 15, 168, 184, 263, 278, 279,
    316, 359, 365, 367
    pin, 285
    water, 366
    willow, 284, 285, 366
obedient plant, 186, 187
Ocimum basilicum, 91
Oenothera fruticosa, 176
okra, 86, 89, 90, 97, 98, 99, 100,
    102, 104
old-fashioned
    flag, 336
    rose, 211, 216
old garden rose, 88, 203, 204, 209,
    213, 216, 222
onion, 89, 90, 94, 95, 96, 97, 98, 101,
    104, 106
    Egyptian, 112
    green, 98
Ophiopogon japonicus, 177, 359
orange, 254
    calamondin, 144
orchid, 118, 121, 124, 125, 126, 136,
    143, 145
    Cattleya, 124, 145
    lady-slipper, 116, 123
    moth, 116
    Paphiopedium, 124, 145
    Phalaenopsis, 124, 145
oregano, 104, 105, 107
    Greek, 91

Oregon grape holly, 252
Oriental lily, 68
Origanum heracleoticum, 91
Origanum majorana, 91
ornamental
    cabbage, 30, 33, 35, 37, 48, 49,
        50, 51, 52, 53
    cherry, 359
    gourd, 313
    kale, 30, 33, 35, 37, 49, 50, 51,
        52, 53
    pear, 263, 280
    pepper, 30, 32, 33, 145
Ornithogalum nutans, 78
Orontium aquaticum, 320
Osmanthus heterophyllus
    'Variegatus', 229
Oxydendrum arboreum, 263, 359
pachysandra, 293, 304
Pachysandra species and hybrids, 293
Paeonia lactiflora, 176, 365
pagoda tree, Japanese, 272, 359
palm, 131
    parlor, 116, 119, 128
    umbrella, 325, 334, 342
pampas grass, 177
Panicum virgatum, 177
pansy, 27, 30, 33, 35, 36, 37, 39, 42,
    48, 49, 50, 51, 52, 53, 54
paper-white narcissus, 62, 65, 80, 84
paper-whites, 63, 64, 65, 84
paperbark maple, 263
Paphiopedilum, 124, 145
papyrus, 320
    dwarf, 332, 334
parlor palm, 116, 119, 128
parsley, 91, 92, 95, 96, 98, 105,
    107, 108, 112
parsnip, 89, 90, 95
Parthenocissus quinquefolia, 310
Parthenocissus tricuspidata, 310
Passiflora, 355
Passiflora species, 292
passionflower, 292, 299
    vine, 355
pattypan squash, 104
pea
    Alaska, 86
    sweet, 294
peace lily, 115, 121, 122, 126, 128,
    133, 143

Index

peach, 271, 278
peanut, 95
pear, 279
    callery, 263
    ornamental, 263, 280
peas, 98, 99, 100, 101, 102
    black-eyed, 104
    edible-podded, 89, 90, 97, 98
    English, 85, 89, 90, 93, 94, 95, 96, 97, 98, 104
    field, 89, 90
    southern, 89, 90, 95, 97, 98, 99, 100, 102, 104, 106, 108
    sugar snap, 85, 89, 96
Pelargonium species and hybrids, 29
Pelrandra virginica, 320
Pennisetum 'Rubrum', 208
Pennisetum species and hybrids, 177
penstemon, 186
Penstemon digitalis 'Husker Red', 179
pentas, 30, 354
Pentas lanceolata, 30, 354
peony, 176, 185, 187, 191, 192, 194, 365
peperomia, 115, 119, 127, 130, 143
Peperomia species and hybrids, 119
pepper, 86, 89, 90, 94, 95, 97, 98, 100, 101, 102, 103, 107
    bell, 85, 104
    ornamental, 30, 32, 33, 145
pepper vine, 315
perennial
    geranium, 189
    hibiscus, 176, 186, 188, 190
    ryegrass, 151, 166, 168
    salvia, 208
periwinkle, Madagascar, 30, 32, 33, 41, 43, 45, 359
Perovskia atriplicifolia, 179
Perovskia species and hybrids, 176
persimmon, 260
    American, 366
Petroselinum crispum, 91
petunia, 27, 30, 32, 33, 42, 43, 47, 134, 354
Petunia x *hybrida*, 30, 354
Phalaenopsis, 124, 145
Philadelphus coronarius, 365
Philadelphus species and hybrids, 244

philodendron, 115, 120, 143
    heart-leaf, 127, 130, 133, 134, 136, 137, 143
Philodendron species and hybrids, 120
phlox, 176, 186, 187, 189, 191, 193, 355, 365
    creeping, 15, 183, 292, 301, 306, 359
    garden, 187
Phlox 'David', 179
Phlox drummondi, 365
Phlox species and hybrids, 176, 355
Phlox stolonifera, 179
Phlox subulata, 292, 359
Phytophthora cactorum, 249
Picea abies, 266
Picea species and hybrids, 364, 365
pickerel rush, 321, 325
piggyback plant, 143
Pilea cadierei, 119
pin oak, 285
pine, 164, 259, 268, 287
    mugo, 247
    Norfolk Island, 119, 128, 142, 143
pineapple sage, 102
pinks, 29, 50, 175, 306
Pistia stratiotes, 321
Plectranthus australis, 120
plum, 271, 278
plumed celosia, 30, 41
poinsettia, 123, 125, 128, 131, 133, 139, 142, 143, 144, 145
pole bean, 86, 89, 90
polka-dot plant, 116, 120, 126, 128, 130
polyantha rose, 206, 208, 209, 212
Pontederia cordata, 321
poplar, tulip, 259, 260, 278, 279, 359
poppy, 27, 48, 53
Portulaca grandiflora, 30, 359
potato, 56, 98
    Irish, 89, 90, 94, 95, 97, 99, 104
    sweet, 86, 89, 90, 97, 98, 100, 102, 103, 111, 142
pothos, 115, 120, 127, 130, 134, 136, 143
prayer plant, 116, 120, 126, 128, 130, 143
primrose, 191, 365
Primula species and hybrids, 365

privet, 244, 355
Prunus caroliniana, 266
Prunus laurocerasus, 250
Prunus species and hybrids, 263, 359
Pulmonaria, 179
pumpkin, 85, 89, 95, 97, 98, 100, 102, 105, 109, 110
    bush, 90
    vining, 90
purple
    bell vine, 294, 296
    coneflower, 176, 178, 355, 359
    hyacinth bean, 310, 311
    passion plant, 120, 127, 130, 143
pussy willow, 237
pyracantha, 250, 252, 254, 258, 359
Pyracantha coccinea, 359
Pyrus calleryana, 263
Quercus nigra, 366
Quercus palustris, 285
Quercus phellos, 284, 366
Quercus species and hybrids, 263, 359, 365
quince, flowering, 233, 239, 245, 254, 256, 359
radish, 85, 86, 88, 89, 90, 93, 95, 96, 97, 98, 99, 100, 101, 108
rambler, 202, 203, 204, 209, 213, 215, 216, 217, 220, 222
rambler rose, 288, 305
rambling rose, 305
raspberry, 363
red
    buckeye, 246
    cedar, 271
        eastern, 271, 287
    fescue, 149
        creeping, 150
    maple, 15, 263, 278, 279, 280, 284, 359, 366
    salvia, 31, 32, 33, 41
    valerian, 176, 191, 208, 355, 365
redbud, 15, 260, 263, 359
redosier dogwood, 240, 366
redvein enkianthus, 234, 246, 252
redwood, dawn, 359
reed grass, feather, 177
Rhodochiton atrosanguineus, 294, 296
rhododendron, 15, 230, 235, 241, 245, 246, 249, 256, 358, 364
    rosebay, 250

Index

Rhododendron species and
hybrids, 233, 235, 355, 364
Rhododendron viscosum, 240, 366
rhubarb, 98
river birch, 263, 267, 275, 278,
284, 366
Robinia pseudoacacia, 365
Robinia tomentosa, 359
rodgersia, 188
Rosa species and hybrids, 291
rose, 43, 109, 132, 198, 294, 298, 309
climbing, 210, 214, 216, 217, 218,
221, 226, 291, 297, 305, 306
David Austin, 203
English, 222, 226
floribunda, 202, 204, 209, 216
garden, 88
grandiflora, 202, 204, 209, 216
hybrid tea, 202, 204, 209,
216, 226
landscape, 203
Lenten, 174, 176, 179, 180,
198, 365
miniature, 124, 143, 203, 204,
207, 208, 209, 211, 212, 213,
217, 218, 219, 222, 226, 227
modern, 221
moss, 30, 33, 41, 359
old-fashioned, 211, 216
old garden, 88, 203, 204, 209,
213, 216, 222
polyantha, 206, 208, 209, 212
rambler, 288, 305
rugosa, 213
shrub, 203, 204, 208, 212, 227
species, 213
rose campion, 186
rose mallow, 366
rose-of-Sharon, 235, 239, 246
rosebay rhododendron, 250
rosemary, 91, 100, 102, 110, 112
Rosmarinus officinalis, 91
rubber plant, 116, 120, 130
Rudbeckia fulgida 'Goldsturm', 179
Rudbeckia species and hybrids, 175,
354, 359, 364
rue, 97, 102, 103
rugosa rose, 213
rush
pickerel, 321, 325
variegated, 334

Russian sage, 176
rutabaga, 95
rye, 10, 152, 168
annual, 108
ryegrass, 151, 171
annual, 151, 166, 168
perennial, 151, 166, 168
sacred lily, Chinese, 64, 84
sage, 91, 92, 94, 97, 100, 107, 112
blue, 208
pineapple, 102
Russian, 176
Saintpaulia ionantha, 121
salvia, 176, 186
blue, 190
perennial, 208
red, 31, 32, 33, 41
Salvia 'Mainacht' ('May Night'), 179
Salvia officinalis, 91
Salvia rutilans, 102
Salvia species and hybrids, 31, 176
Salvinia rountundifolia, 320
Sansevieria trifasciata, 120
santolina, 94, 100, 102, 208
Sanvitalia procumbens, 29
Sarcococca hookerana humilis, 293
sassafras, 279, 280
Sassafras albidum, 279
Satureja hortensis, 91
saucer magnolia, 259, 263, 359
Saururus cernuus, 320
savory
summer, 91, 92, 98
winter, 102
Scabiosa, 191
Scabiosa columbaria
'Butterfly Blue', 179
scaveola, 31, 34, 37, 50
Scaveola x 'Blue Wonder', 31
scented geranium, 94, 102, 103,
104, 109
schefflera, 116, 120, 131, 143
Schefflera species and hybrids, 120
Schizophragma hydrangeoides, 296
Schlumbergera x *buckleyi*, 121
Scilla siberica, 78
sedum, 190, 194, 212, 355
'Autumn Joy', 176
Sedum species and hybrids, 355
Sedum x *telephium* 'Autumn Joy', 176
Senecio cineraria, 29

serviceberry, 263, 280
shallot, 95
Shasta daisy, 176, 187, 355
shrub rose, 203, 204, 208, 212, 227
Siberian
iris, 55, 57, 68, 69, 366
squill, 78
silver
bell, 78
maple, 278
vase, 116
silverbell, Carolina, 263, 285, 359
silverberry, 250
smoke
bush, 235
tree, 252
smooth hydrangea, 239
snake plant, 115, 116, 120, 126, 130,
137, 143
snap bean, 95
snapdragon, 31, 32, 33, 36, 39, 41,
43, 50
climbing, 304
snow-on-the-mountain, 31, 32, 33, 41
snowball, 244
water, 331
snowdrop, 58, 59, 62, 64, 65, 66, 67,
78, 365
snowflake, spring, 56, 58, 60, 78
Solanum pseudocapsicum, 144
soleil d'or, 64, 84
Solenostemon scutellarioides, 29
Solidago species and hybrids, 176,
355, 359
Sophora japonica, 272, 359
sourwood, 15, 263, 272, 278, 280,
285, 359
southern
magnolia, 260, 263, 264, 266, 269,
271, 272, 359
peas, 89, 90, 95, 97, 98, 99, 100,
102, 104, 106, 108
soybean, 108
Spanish
bluebell, 56, 58, 60, 78
flag, 294, 298, 302
Spathiphyllum wallisii, 121
species rose, 213
spicebush, 239
spider
lily, 61, 74, 80

Index

plant, 116, 120, 126, 128, 137, 140
spiderwort, 187
spinach, 86, 89, 90, 93, 94, 95, 96, 98, 99, 101, 104, 108, 112
spirea, 235, 252, 256, 359
    bridalwreath, 239, 245
Spirea prunifolia, 239
Spirea species and hybrids, 235, 359
spotted dead nettle, 289, 293, 306
spring snowflake, 56, 58, 60, 78
spruce, 273, 285, 364, 365
    Colorado blue, 287
    Norway, 266, 287
squash, 95, 96, 97, 100, 101, 103, 104, 105, 110
    pattypan, 104
    summer, 86, 89, 90, 93, 99, 100, 102, 104, 106
    winter, 86, 90, 99, 110
    yellow, 85
squill, Siberian, 78
St. Augustine, 151
star magnolia, 243
stewartia, 272, 280, 285
Stewartia ovata, 272
Stewartia pseudocamellia, 272
Stokes' aster, 176, 355
Stokesia laevis, 176, 355
strawberry, 294, 298, 299
    alpine, 298
strawflower, 359
Strelitzia regina, 143
Styrax species and hybrids, 244
sugar snap peas, 85, 89, 96
summer
    savory, 91, 92, 98
    squash, 86, 89, 90, 93, 99, 100, 102, 104, 106
summersweet, 235, 239, 240, 241, 244, 246, 252, 355, 364, 366
sundrop, 176, 188
sunflower, 31, 32, 33, 41, 42, 43, 44, 51, 52, 54, 95, 354, 359
    Mexican, 354
surprise lily, 74
swamp azalea, 240, 366
Swan River daisy, 31, 32, 33
Swedish ivy, 116, 120, 127, 130, 133, 134
sweet

alyssum, 31, 33, 43, 354
autumn clematis, 294, 315
bay, 91
    magnolia, 266, 272, 284
box, 293
clover, 10
flag, 321, 366
    variegated, 325
gum, 259, 260, 263, 280, 284, 359, 366
marjoram, 91
pea, 294
potato, 86, 89, 90, 97, 98, 100, 102, 103, 111, 142
    vine, 142, 292, 304, 311, 312
sweetspire, Virginia, 235, 244, 252, 366
Swiss chard, 86, 96, 97, 98, 101
switch grass, 177
Syngonium podophyllum, 119
Syringa species and hybrids, 244
Tagetes species and hybrids, 30, 354
tall fescue, 82, 147, 149, 150, 151, 152, 155, 158, 162, 164, 166, 169, 171
tansy, 98
taro, 321, 325
tarragon, 95, 107, 112
    French, 91, 102
tartarian dogwood, 240, 366
Taxodium distichum, 263, 359, 366
Taxus species and hybrids, 364
Thalia dealbata, 320
Thanksgiving cactus, 138, 139, 140, 142, 143
thistle, globe, 365
thornless honey locust, 365
thrift, 183, 292, 301
Thunbergia alata, 291, 294, 298
thyme, 91, 92, 94, 97, 98, 101, 107, 306
    creeping, 190, 212, 293, 294
    woolly, 212
Thymus praecox, 293
Thymus vulgaris, 91
Tiarella species and hybrids, 293
Tilia tomentosa, 278
Tithonia rotundifolia, 354
toadlily, 194
tobacco, flowering, 29, 32, 33, 43
Tolmiea menziesii, 126, 143

tomato, 73, 85, 86, 89, 90, 92, 94, 95, 96, 97, 98, 100, 101, 102, 103, 105, 106, 107, 109, 110, 112, 114, 363
Tricyrtis hirta, 194
trillium, 179
tropical water lily, 325, 330
trumpet
    creeper, 292, 297, 302, 305
    honeysuckle, 292, 297, 303, 315, 359, 365
    vine, 311, 314, 359
Tsuga canadensis, 263, 364
tuberous begonia, 73
tulip, 55, 56, 57, 58, 60, 62, 63, 64, 65, 68, 71, 72, 78, 79, 80, 81, 82, 83, 84
    poplar, 259, 260, 278, 279, 359
Tulipa species and hybrids, 60
turnip, 86, 89, 90, 95, 96, 98, 99
    greens, 89, 90, 104, 106, 108
turtlehead, 194, 200, 366
Typha species, 320
Ulmus parvifolia, 263, 359
umbrella palm, 325, 334, 342
valerian, red, 176, 191, 208, 355, 365
Vallisneria americana, 321
variegated
    rush, 334
    sweet flag, 325
verbena, 177, 359, 365
    lemon, 94, 99, 113
Verbena species and hybrids, 177, 359, 365
veronica, 186
    'Sunny Border Blue', 179
vetch, 108
viburnum, 235, 252, 256
Viburnum species and hybrids, 235
vinca, 293, 294, 297, 306, 359
Vinca major, 190
Vinca minor, 190, 293, 359
Vinca rosea, 359
vine
    actinidia, 291
    crimson glory, 310
    cypress, 291, 294, 298, 302, 304, 311
    moonflower, 355
    nasturtium, 310
    passionflower, 355
    pepper, 315

Index

purple bell, 294, 296
sweet potato, 142, 292, 304, 311, 312
trumpet, 311, 314, 359
vining
pumpkin, 90
watermelon, 90
Viola x *wittrockiana*, 30
violet, African, 116, 118, 121, 123, 125, 128, 129, 130, 132, 135, 141, 143, 145
Virginia
bluebell, 364
creeper, 310, 311, 315
sweetspire, 235, 244, 252, 366
Vitex agnus-castus, 263, 355, 359
Vitis coignetiae, 310
walking stick, Harry Lauder's, 238
walnut, 267, 275
black, 279
wandering Jew, 116, 125, 130, 133, 134, 143
water
canna, hardy, 320
clover, four-leaf, 320, 325
hyacinth, 328, 331
lettuce, 321, 325, 328
lily, 56, 321, 323, 326, 328, 329, 330, 331, 332, 333, 334, 335, 338, 339, 340, 341
hardy, 325, 326
tropical, 325
milfoil, 321

mint, 331
oak, 366
snowball, 331
watercress, 95
watermelon, 89, 95, 99, 106
bush, 90
vining, 90
wax begonia, 31, 32, 33, 34, 37, 45, 48, 50
weeping
fig, 130, 136
willow, 238, 278
weigela, 235
Weigela florida, 235
wild
celery, 321
ginger, 293
willow oak, 284, 285, 366
willow
pussy, 237
weeping, 238, 278
windflower, 56, 60
winter
aconite, 78
savory, 102
squash, 86, 90, 99, 110
winterberry, 240, 366
wintercreeper, 293, 297, 304, 310, 311, 359
wisteria, 289, 292, 297, 299, 301, 302, 303, 305, 307, 312, 314, 359, 365
Japanese, 299

Wisteria species and hybrids, 292, 359, 365
witch hazel, 229, 235, 238, 246, 252, 366
wood
hyacinth, 55
vamp, 296
woolly thyme, 212
yarrow, 177, 186, 354, 355
yaupon holly, 250
yellow
bells, 233
flag, 325
iris, 188
squash, 85
yellowwood, 15, 263, 267, 270, 275, 278, 285
yew, 238, 247, 275, 364
Zebrina pendula, 116
zelkova, Japanese, 263, 359
Zelkova serrata, 263, 359
zinnia, 27, 31, 32, 33, 37, 41, 42, 43, 44, 45, 46, 49, 51, 52, 54, 208, 354, 363
creeping, 29, 33
Zinnia elegans, 31
Zinnia species and hybrids, 354
zoysia, 147, 148, 150, 151, 152, 154, 156, 158, 159, 160, 161, 162, 166, 167, 168, 169, 172
zucchini, 85, 89, 90, 100, 102, 104

Meet Judy Lowe

Judy Lowe

Judy Lowe has had a life-long fascination with gardening starting as a child working alongside her mother, also an accomplished gardener. Later, Lowe began her garden writing career by serving as the Garden Editor at the *Chattanooga Free Press* and continued in that position after the paper became the *Chattanooga Times-Free Press*. Over the years, Lowe has shared her gardening wisdom and enthusiasm with countless numbers of readers and she currently is the Homefront Editor at *The Christian Science Monitor*.

Lowe is a past president of The Garden Writers Association, a group consisting of nearly 2,000 members of the garden writing community. Lowe's other credits and recognition include contributing articles to *Women's Day* and *Southern Living* magazines. She was the Southern Gardening Editor for www.suite101.com and appeared weekly in the gardening segment on Chattanooga television station WDEF-TV.

Lowe's many awards include five Quill and Trowel Awards from the Garden Writers Association; a Special Communication Award for Tennessee Horticulture from the Tennessee Fruit and Vegetable Growers; the Exemplary Journalism for Home Gardening Communication Award from the National Garden Bureau, and many more. Lowe's proudest gardening moment occurred when a daylily was named after her.

In addition to this book for Cool Springs Press, Lowe is also the author of *Tennessee Gardener's Guide: Third Edition*, and *Ortho's All About Pruning*.

Lowe has lived in several different regions of Tennessee, and has experienced gardening in everything from sunny sites with hard red clay to dry, shady spots with soil so rocky it ruined numerous shovels. Lowe and her husband, Carlyle, known as the couple's "official hole digger", currently live in Boston while Lowe completes her assignment at *The Christian Science Monitor*. But no matter where Lowe lives, helping gardeners is one of her life goals.